ANNUAL REVIEW OF NURSING RESEARCH

VOLUME 31, 2013

SERIES EDITOR

Christine E. Kasper, PhD, RN, FAAN
Department of Veterans Affairs
Office of Nursing Services, Washington, DC
and
Professor, School of Nursing
Uniformed Services University of the Health Sciences,
Bethesda, MD

VOLUME EDITOR

Barbara A. Smith, PhD, RN, FACSM, FAAN
Professor and Associate Dean for Research
Michigan State University
College of Nursing

Annual Review of Nursing Research

Exercise in Health and Disease

VOLUME 31, 2013

Series Editor

CHRISTINE E. KASPER, PhD, RN, FAAN

Volume Editor

BARBARA A. SMITH, PhD, RN, FACSM, FAAN

SPRINGER PUBLISHING COMPANY

NEW YORK

Springer Publishing Company, LLC
11 West 42nd Street
New York, NY 10036
www.springerpub.com

Acquisitions Editor: Margaret Zuccarini
Composition: Absolute Service, Inc.

ISBN: 978-0-8261-1972-8
E-book ISBN: 978-0-8261-1973-5
ISSN: 0739-6686
Online ISSN: 1944-4028

13 14 15/ 5 4 3 2 1

The author and the publisher of this Work have made every effort to use sources believed to be reliable to provide information that is accurate and compatible with the standards generally accepted at the time of publication. Because medical science is continually advancing, our knowledge base continues to expand. Therefore, as new information becomes available, changes in procedures become necessary. We recommend that the reader always consult current research and specific institutional policies before performing any clinical procedure. The author and publisher shall not be liable for any special, consequential, or exemplary damages resulting, in whole or in part, from the readers' use of, or reliance on, the information contained in this book. The publisher has no responsibility for the persistence or accuracy of URLs for external or third-party Internet Websites referred to in this publication and does not guarantee that any content on such Websites is, or will remain, accurate or appropriate.

Special discounts on bulk quantities of our books are available to corporations, professional associations, pharmaceutical companies, health care organizations, and other qualifying groups.

If you are interested in a custom book, including chapters from more than one of our titles, we can provide that service as well.

For details, please contact:
Special Sales Department, Springer Publishing Company, LLC
11 West 42nd Street, 15th Floor, New York, NY 10036-8002
Phone: 877-687-7476 or 212-431-4370; Fax: 212-941-7842
Email: sales@springerpub.com

Printed in the United States of America by Gasch Printing

Contents

About the Volume Editor   vii

Contributors   ix

Preface   xiii

Acknowledgments   xvii

Exercise Physiology and Impact on Human Biology

1 Animal Models of Exercise and Obesity   1
Christine E. Kasper

2 Thermoregulation: Cytokines Involved in Fever and Exercise   19
Pamela Johnson Rowsey

Exercise Across the Lifespan and Cultures

3 Overweight and Obesity in Youth With Type 1 Diabetes   47
Karl E. Minges, Robin Whittemore, and Margaret Grey

4 Physical Activity Intervention Studies and Their
Relationship to Body Composition in Healthy Women   71
*Susan Weber Buchholz, JoEllen Wilbur, Shannon Halloway,
Judith H. McDevitt and Michael E. Schoeny*

5 The Effects of Exercise During Pregnancy:
Theories, Evidence, and Interventions   143
SeonAe Yeo

6 Using Function-Focused Care to Increase Physical
Activity Among Older Adults   175
Barbara Resnick and Elizabeth Galik

7 Hispanic Women and Physical Activity:
An Integrative Review   209
Karen T. D'Alonzo and Marie K. Saimbert

Exercise in Chronic and Acute Disease States

8 Exercise Therapy in Individuals With Chronic
Kidney Disease: A Systematic Review and
Synthesis of the Research Evidence   235
*Pelagia Koufaki, Sharlene A. Greenwood,
Iain C. Macdougall, and Thomas H. Mercer*

9 Effect of Exercise on Cardiac and Metabolic
Outcomes in People Living With HIV   277
Anella Yahiaoui, Barbara A. Smith, and Joachim G. Voss

10 Interventions to Increase Physical Activity in People
With COPD: Systematic Review   297
Janet L. Larson, Carol M. Vos, and Dena Fernandez

11 Exercise and Cancer   327
M. Tish Knobf and Kerri Winters-Stone

12 ROS and RNS Signaling in Skeletal Muscle:
Critical Signals and Therapeutic Targets   367
Luke P. Michaelson, Colleen Iler, and Christopher W. Ward

Index   389

About the Volume Editor

Barbara A. Smith, PhD, RN, FACSM, FAAN, is Professor and Associate Dean for Research and PhD Program at Michigan State University School of Nursing. Her previous position was Professor and Associate Dean for Research, Director of Research, Office of Global Health and Director for Nursing Component/Senior Technical Advisor, University of Maryland, Baltimore, Institute for Human Virology, PEPFAR grant. Dr. Smith received her PhD in Exercise Physiology and as a nurse and exercise physiologist, has made significant contributions to the literature related to exercise interventions, safety and efficacy of exercise, and the use of exercise to reduce weight and modify CVD risk factors in chronically ill adults and children both nationally and internationally. She is a Fellow in the American Academy of Nursing (FAAN), a Fellow in the American College of Sports Medicine (FACSM), and is certified as an ACSM program director. Among her many accomplishments, Dr. Smith represented UMD Nursing at the WHO Nurse Collaborating Center at its Bangkok meeting, as a faculty member for a WHO Safe Motherhood survey in Malawi and in Kenya, and was invited as a delegate to the WHO and PEPFAR's Transformative Scale-Up of Medical, Nursing and Midwifery Education in Geneva in 2010. She serves on numerous foundations and editorial boards.

Contributors

Susan Weber Buchholz, PhD, APN
Associate Professor
Rush University, College of Nursing
Chicago, Illinois

Karen T. D'Alonzo, PhD, RN, APNC
Associate Professor, College of Nursing
Rutgers, The State University of
   New Jersey

Dena Fernandez, MSN, RN, ANP-C
Doctoral student
University of Michigan, School of Nursing

Elizabeth Galik, PhD, CRNP
Assistant Professor School of Nursing
School University of Maryland, Baltimore

Sharlene A. Greenwood, BSc
Lead Renal Physiotherapist
NIHR Research Fellow
King's College London

Margaret Grey, DrPH, RN, FAAN
Dean and Annie Goodrich Professor of
   Nursing
Yale University School of Nursing

Shannon Halloway, BSN, RN
Doctoral student
Rush University, College of Nursing
Chicago, Illinois

Colleen Iler
CNL student
University of Maryland School of Nursing
Baltimore, MD

Christine E. Kasper, PhD, RN, FAAN
Department of Veterans Affairs, Office of
   Nursing Services and
USUHS Graduate School of Nursing

M. Tish Knobf, PhD, RN, FAAN, AOCN
Professor
Yale University School of Nursing

Pelagia Koufaki, PhD
Research Fellow
School of Health Sciences, Division of
   Physiotherapy
Queen Margaret University, Edinburgh
   Scotland

Janet L. Larson, PhD, RN, FAAN
Professor and Division Chair
Division of Acute, Critical, and Long
   Term Care
University of Michigan, School of Nursing

Iain C. Macdougall, MD, PhD
Professor of Clinical Nephrology
Renal Unit
King's College Hospital NHS Foundation
   Trust,
Denmark Hill, London

Judith H. McDevitt, PhD, APN
Clinical Associate Professor
Rush University, College of Nursing
Chicago, IL

Thomas H. Mercer, PhD, FBASES
Professor of Clinical Exercise Physiology
and Rehabilitation
School of Health Sciences
Queen Margaret University, Edinburgh

Luke P. Michaelson, PhD, RN
Post-Doctoral Fellow
Uniformed Services University of the
Health Sciences
Bethesda, MD

Karl E. Minges, MPH
Doctoral student
Yale University School of Nursing

**Barbara Resnick, PhD, CRNP, FAAN,
FAANP**
Professor and Sonia Ziporkin Gershowitz
Endowed Chair in Gerontology
University of Maryland, Baltimore
School of Nursing

Pamela Johnson Rowsey, PhD, RN
Associate Professor, School of Nursing
The University of North Carolina at
Chapel Hill

**Marie K. Saimbert, B.S.Pharm, MSN,
MLIS, RN**
Doctoral Student, College of Nursing
Rutgers, The State University of New
Jersey

Michael E. Schoeny, PhD
Assistant Professor
Rush University, College of Nursing
Chicago, IL

**Barbara A. Smith, PhD, RN, FACSM,
FAAN**
Professor and Associate Dean for Research
and PhD Program
Michigan State University, College of Nursing

Carol M. Vos, MSN, RN
Doctoral student
University of Michigan, School of Nursing

Joachim G. Voss, PhD, RN, ACRN
Associate Professor
University of Washington, School of
Nursing

Christopher W. Ward, PhD
Professor
University of Maryland School of Nursing
Baltimore, MD

JoEllen Wilbur, PhD, APN, FAAN
Professor and Associate Dean for Research
Endowed Independence Foundation
Chair in Nursing
Rush University, College of Nursing
Chicago, IL

Kerri Winters-Stone, PhD
Research Associate Professor
School of Nursing and Knight Cancer
Institute
Oregon Health & Science University

Robin Whittemore, PhD, APRN, FAAN
Associate Professor
Yale University School of Nursing

Anella Yahiaoui, BS
Doctoral student
University of Washington, School of
  Nursing

SeonAe Yeo, PhD, RNC, FAAN
Associate Professor
University of North Carolina at
  Chapel Hill

Preface

Aerobic or resistance exercise, used on a regular basis, has many benefits and few risks. The benefits include but are not limited to improved cardiac output, enhanced skeletal muscle extraction and use of oxygen and nutrients, increased insulin sensitivity and improved metabolic function, and psychosocial enhancements. It helps prevent osteoporosis, improves lipid parameters, helps manage weight, and improves psychosocial well-being and quality of life. Many of the risks associated with exercise come from the initiation of exercise in a sedentary individual with diagnosed or undiagnosed comorbid conditions. Certain acquired or inherited cardiovascular abnormalities can put persons at elevated risk of an adverse reaction when initiating an exercise program. Prolonged vigorous exercise, even in healthy adults, can reduce immune function and render the individual more susceptible to an infection. In addition, some individuals including elite athletes use anabolic steroids to increase muscle strength and size, blood doping to increase the oxygen carrying capacity of the blood, and other high risk behaviors that may give them a performance edge but also exposes them to specific health risks.

This book provides an excellent review of the literature related to some of the latest research when aerobic and/or resistive exercise are used as an intervention to promote health, prevent a specific disease, or address an issue related to a chronic illness. It can benefit novice as well as experienced nurses, guide research, inform practice, and guide policy makers because many of the chapters describe not only the benefits of exercise but also identify many of the flaws in how the research was designed and carried out.

Besides the wealth of information shared by the authors, a careful reader will learn much from the helpful critique of many of the articles. Chapter after chapter point out issues of concern such as (a) variability in baseline measures that make it difficult to assess change; (b) lack of specificity of training for the outcome desired; (c) diminished overall training stimulus because of inappropriate progression of exercise, attrition from or adherence to the protocol; (d) inappropriate measurement; (e) inconsistency in how the results are reported; and (f) faulty conclusions in light of the data presented.

Let me specifically address the issues related directly to exercise. Early in my career, a colleague said to me: "You always hear providers say go home and get a little exercise. You never hear them say go home and take a little insulin!" They were absolutely correct. What and how much exercise your patient needs depends on why you want your patient to exercise. That is, what benefits do you want your patient to achieve? You have to be specific. For example, the current 30 min/day of moderate-to-vigorous exercise on most days of the week will help people lose weight. But to be successful, you must also reduce caloric intake. It actually requires 60–90 min of moderate to vigorous exercise most days to lose weight by exercise *alone*.

If you are interested in improving gait speed in the elderly, stationary cycling is not what is needed. A walking protocol is what helps improve gait speed along with some lower leg strengthening exercises. Abdominal strength can be improved by resistive exercises that involve all the muscles of the abdomen and lower back. If you want to become a contender for the fastest time in the 100-m dash, training for a marathon will not help but short anaerobic sprints just might. In summary, when a provider prescribes a medication for an infection, he or she specifies the drug, the dose, the route, and the timing of administration based on their knowledge of the causative agent, where the infection is in the body, and the kinetics of the medication. If exercise is not prescribed in the same way, it just will not work.

Once exercise is prescribed correctly, of course the person must "just do it"—like the Nike commercial says. It is important to work closely with the patient or the participant in your research to show up and complete the exercise. You must take into consideration the likes and dislikes of the person and help them build exercise into their life. Also, it is critical that you progress the exercise appropriately. For the appropriate biochemical changes to occur in the muscle, the muscle biochemical pathways must be challenged. Once the changes have occurred, you must "progress the activity" so that the muscle continues to be challenged, otherwise you will see a plateau in the desired effect.

In addition, it is important for investigators to consider using the "gold standard" measures for assessing the effects of your exercise intervention. Examine the literature to determine what the most reliable and valid measurements are and whether they can detect a change over the time course of your intervention. For example, the measurement of oxygen consumption while using a motor driven treadmill along with a known testing protocol is considered the "gold standard" for measuring the fitness of an individual. If your intervention is appropriately designed, this test should detect a 15% improvement over the course of a 10- to 12-week intervention.

In summary, there is a paucity of data from well-designed, randomized clinical trials (RCTs) of exercise related to promoting health and providing primary, secondary, and tertiary prevention of various diseases. We know interventional research is not easy! We hope, however, that this edition of the *Annual Review of Nursing Research* will prompt nurse investigators to "dig in" and generate the much needed interventional research using state-of-the-art biobehavioral outcome measures that will enhance the evidence base of advance practice nurses. For nurses to contribute to science and advance the discipline, we must be willing to work with our interdisciplinary colleagues with appropriate intervention and disease-specific expertise to design, conduct, and disseminate the results of rigorous RCTs of exercise interventions and their outcomes: Interventions that will likely improve the physical and psychosocial quality of life of the participants.

Barbara A. Smith, PhD, RN, FACSM, FAAN
Volume Editor

Acknowledgments

To each of the individual contributors to this volume of the Annual Review and to my parents who motivated me to be the scholar I am, to my sisters who helped me along the way and to Sue for always believing in me.

Barbara A. Smith

ANNUAL REVIEW OF NURSING RESEARCH

VOLUME 31, 2013

CHAPTER 1

Animal Models of Exercise and Obesity

Christine E. Kasper

ABSTRACT

Animal models have been invaluable in the conduct of nursing research for the past 40 years. This review will focus on specific animal models that can be used in nursing research to study the physiologic phenomena of exercise and obesity when the use of human subjects is either scientifically premature or inappropriate because of the need for sampling tissue or the conduct of longitudinal studies of aging. There exists an extensive body of literature reporting the experimental use of various animal models, in both exercise science and the study of the mechanisms of obesity. Many of these studies are focused on the molecular and genetic mechanisms of organ system adaptation and plasticity in response to exercise, obesity, or both. However, this review will narrowly focus on the models useful to nursing research in the study of exercise in the clinical context of increasing performance and mobility, atrophy and bedrest, fatigue, and aging. Animal models of obesity focus on those that best approximate clinical pathology.

INTRODUCTION

The classical research methods of organ system physiology and cell biology have traditionally and successfully used the laboratory rat along with the mouse and guinea pig for countless research studies since the early 1900s (Blood &

© 2013 Springer Publishing Company
http://dx.doi.org/10.1891/0739-6686.31.1

D'Amour, 1947; Hanson & Sholes, 1924; Parkes, 1946). The use of rodents as research subjects presents the possibility of reducing intersubject variation when using littermates or animals from the same genetically similar breeding stock while appropriately avoiding the use of humans for invasive research. Furthermore, the need to study the effects of exercise or obesity over the course of a human lifetime is impractical; whereas, animal models of aging provide a method of study, which can be achieved in months to years. To date, there exist more than 1,000 various animal models of disease. This review will focus on most commonly used in the study of exercise and obesity. Fortunately, there currently exist various extensive databases of animal models for research; and, when applicable these will be referenced for the use of the researcher. Nursing research has long used animal models in a wide range of research focused on clinical questions such as prenatal exposure to cocaine (Chae & Covington, 2009), traumatic brain injury (Kovesdi et al., 2012), the interaction of pain and cancer metastasis (G. G. Page & Ben-Eliyahu, 2002; G. G. Page, Ben-Eliyahu, Yirmiya, & Liebeskind, 1993), fever (Rowsey, Metzger, Carlson, & Gordon, 2009), the effects of transient cerebral ischemia (Briones & Therrien, 2000), aging and spatial learning (Hebda-Bauer, Morano, & Therrien, 1999), spatial disorientation following hippocampal damage (Holden & Therrien, 1993), myocardial infarction size (Smith et al., 1992), and cardiac contractility (Donaldson, Best, & Kerrick, 1978; Glenn, Kerrick, & Donaldson, 1975).

These models have used a wide variety of animals, most commonly rats, but also rabbits (Donaldson, 1985) and rhesus monkeys (Hansen et al., 2011; Reame, Peluso, & Hafez, 1977).

ORIGINS OF THE LABORATORY RAT

The modern albino laboratory rat is a descendent of the 18th century "fancy rat" (Krinke, 2006). The fancy rat originated from the sport of rat-baiting, where street rats were caught to engage in sport with terrier dogs. Over time, street rats were bred for the sport and genetic variations of color and form arose, producing the earliest albino and hooded rats.

The earliest studies refer to these rats simply as the "albino" laboratory rat, bred by each investigator for their own research (Hanson & Sholes, 1924); and, these were first used for experimental purposes in 1828 in a study on fasting (Krinke, 2006). During the next three decades, albino rats were increasingly used in experimental physiologic research becoming the first animal domesticated primarily for the purpose of research (Krinke, 2006). Since the early 1900s, various types or "strains" of rats have been developed for different research purposes, such as the Wistar, Fisher 344 (F344), Sprague-Dawley, Long-Evans, Holtzman, and Lister black hooded rats.

An extensive and detailed body of literature has been gathered on every aspect of the physiology, cell biology, brain, and anatomy of the various strains of laboratory rat (Committee on Rat Nomenclature, 1992). To date, there are in excess of 600 various inbred, outbred, hybrid, and mutant rats. Many of these are listed and described in detail by major suppliers of laboratory rat models, such as the Harlan Laboratory and The Jackson Labs (Harlan Laboratories, 2013; The Jackson Laboratory, 2013). Suppliers of research animals, such as rodents, provide detailed information about the environmental housing conditions and diets used during their birth and rearing, physiologic parameters of each model, including growth curves, common diseases, and genetics of the animal strain selected for experimental use. Therefore, the investigator is able to compare experimental conditions against well-documented parameters across the life of the animal.

COMPREHENSIVE DATABASES OF RODENT MODELS

To facilitate research and genetic studies in rats, the Rat Genome Database was established by the Medical College of Wisconsin with funding from the National Institutes of Health (NIH; Dwinell et al., 2009; Shimoyama et al., 2011). This database provides a core research resource for the use of rats, providing genetic, genomic, phenotype, models, pathways, and strain information with a focus on disease (Dwinell et al., 2009). The various disease-specific models are listed under the headings of immune and inflammatory disease, cancer, cardiovascular disease, diabetes, neurological disease, obesity/metabolic syndrome, and respiratory disease. A search of the keyword "exercise" yields 115 records for genes, quantitative trait loci (QTL), and 98 rat studies (Dwinell et al., 2009). Various ontologies are used to better specify the process of exercise. Some of these ontologies are response to activity; abnormal exercise endurance; locomotor play; asthma, exercise induced; dystonia; glucose transporter 1 (GLUT1) deficiency syndrome 2; hyperinsulinemic hypoglycemia, familial 7; myopathy with lactic acidosis, hereditary; postexercise hypotension; upper extremity deep vein thrombosis; and exercise endurance trait. These then match with references for previous research along with the genetics of each model.

A search at the Rat Genome Database using the keyword "obesity" resulted in 562 records under genes, QTL, rat strains, and references. Currently, there is one strain of rat, the obese prone rat "Crl:OP (CD)" developed by the Charles River Laboratory listed under the category of obesity. This is an outbred strain developed from a line of Crl:CD (SD) rats. This rat model becomes obese when fed high-fat diets in spite of having a normal leptin receptor. In the Phenotype

Database, data may be mined on specific strains of rats by selecting various experimental conditions, phenotypes, and measurement methods (Shimoyama et al., 2011).

A similar online database, Mouse Genome Informatics (MGI), has been created for the mouse *Mus musculus* (Bult, Eppig, Blake, Kadin, & Richardson, 2013). A search of the keyword obesity under the section International Mouse Strain Resource (IMSR) yields 40 mouse strains and the breeder. However, a search of the term exercise did not yield any mouse strains specifically modified for exercise. The mouse genome sequencing consortium published the complete mouse genome in late 2002 (National Human Genome Research Institute, 2013). Given that the complete mouse sequence is now published, it is possible to match human gene sequences of interest with those of the mouse.

Another data repository, Link Animal Models to Human Disease (LAMHDI), is a simple, comprehensive, Web-based resource to enable the researcher to search for the most appropriate animal model for their studies (National Center for Research Resources, 2013). A similar Web-based repository is the National Bio Resource Project (NBRP) for the rat in Japan (Kuramoto, 2013). This data repository collects detailed descriptions of rat strains and genetic substrains, phenotypic and genotypic characterization, cryopreservation of embryos/sperm, supply of the collected rat strains, and a publicly accessible database of all assembled data. Currently, 584 rat strains are cataloged in the NBRP. The advent of databases of this nature has made locating comprehensive research information on specific rat models readily available to the scientist. Usually, the selection of a rat strain for use in research, in general or exercise studies in particular, is based on the precedent established by prior published research studies. However, initial searches for animal models specific for exercise should begin with the American Physiologic Society's (APS) *Resource Book for the Design of Animal Exercise Protocols* (APS Animal Care and Experimentation Committee, 2006; NIH [U.S.]. Office of Laboratory Animal Welfare, 2002).

RODENT MODELS OF EXERCISE AND OBESITY

The most widely used laboratory rat is the white Wistar rat. The Wistar rat was originally developed at the Wistar Institute at the University of Pennsylvania in 1906 (Clause, 1998). At this time, at least half of all laboratory rat strains are descended from the original Wistar colony, and they continue to be one of the most popular for use in research. Currently, the Wistar, *Rattus norvegicus*, is commonly used in exercise studies because it is more active than other strains and readily adapts to exercise (APS Animal Care and Experimentation

Committee, 2006). The average adult body weight for male Wistar is 300–350 g and 180–220 g for female rats achieving adult maturity at approximately 120 days of age. Wistar rats are easily trained for treadmill or wheel running as are other rat strains such as the Sprague-Dawley and Long-Evans, which were developed from the Wistar. Sprague-Dawley rats, an outbred albino strain also commonly used in exercise studies, were developed in 1925 at the Sprague-Dawley Farms, Madison, Wisconsin as a multipurpose rat model. They are somewhat larger than the Wistar, are calm, and are easily handled (Harlan Laboratories, 2012). Both Wistar and Sprague-Dawley rats have a life span of 2–3 years (Yu, Masoro, Murata, Bertrand, & Lynd, 1982).

The use of rat models of aging provides a method to study the longitudinal effects of exercise. The National Institute of Aging of the NIH developed and maintains colonies of rats specifically bred for extended survival (Yu, Masoro, Murata, Bertrand, & Lynd, 1982). These rat models of aging are the inbred F344 and Brown Norway (BN); hybrid F344xBN F1 (F344BN; Turturro, Lewis, Hass, Lipman, & Hart, 1999). All of these strains are known to train for treadmill-based exercise (Albeck, Sano, Prewitt, & Dalton, 2006; van Praag, Shubert, Zhao, & Gage, 2005).

THE ORIGINS OF RESEARCH IN EXERCISE PERFORMANCE

The study of exercise and kinesiology has been ongoing for decades, originating in the study of human performance in the late 1960s. Most of these early studies focused on the effects of exercise in humans on body composition and skeletal muscle contractility (Holloszy, 1963; Holloszy, Skinner, Barry, & Cureton, 1964). The research of these pioneers soon expanded to focus on the physiology and metabolism of muscle contraction during exercise; and, for these studies a new mammalian model was required because these investigations needed to collect entire muscles or other large tissue samples, which was not feasible in a human population. In addition, the maximal lifespan of most rat models are approximately three years; and, the shorter lifespan of the rat made the studies of the effects of exercise and growth possible within a reasonable period.

EXERCISE PROTOCOLS USING RATS AND MICE

Rats and mice are the most commonly used animals in the study of exercise and training. Other species such as ducks, horses, rabbits, and cattle have also been used to study exercise training, albeit infrequently (DiCarlo & Bishop, 1988; Evans & Rose, 1988; Fosha-Dolezal, Avery, Wagner, & Fedde, 1988; Kiley & Fedde, 1983a, 1983b; Musch et al., 1987; Musch, Haidet, Ordway, Longhurst, &

Mitchell, 1987). The most commonly used form of exercise training in rats and mice is treadmill running. Other forms of exercise training in rodents include swimming and spontaneous wheel running; however, treadmill running is preferred because the intensity and duration of training is easily controlled. The environmental conditions of the treadmill may be easily monitored and amount of external work calculated (Brooks, Donovan, & White, 1984; Brooks & White, 1978). Metabolic rates may also be determined by monitoring oxygen uptake and carbon dioxide production, which enable the calculation of maximal aerobic power during treadmill running (Bedford, Tipton, Wilson, Oppliger, & Gisolfi, 1979; Brooks et al., 1984; Brooks & White, 1978). This model of exercise training coupled with the proper choice of rat strain allows the investigator to model the response, per se, of disease states such as obesity, heart failure, diabetes, or hypothyroidism to exercise. Many mouse strains have been developed by inbreeding, but only a few studies have examined how each mouse strain performed in response to an exercise challenge. Lerman and colleagues (2002) found that both forced and voluntary treadmill exercise performance varied markedly between mouse strains. Swiss Webster (SW) and FVB/NJ mice had a higher level of treadmill running performance and C57BL/6J has a decreased performance as compared to other mouse strains. Only the SW mouse excelled at both treadmill and wheel running.

Other rat models of exercise include spontaneous wheel running and swimming. Rats, mice, and hamsters have a natural ability to run when provided with a treadmill. Spontaneous wheel running is primarily in the study of chronic exercise (Ishihara, Roy, Ohira, Ibata, & Edgerton, 1998). An advantage of this method is that little intervention by the investigator is required and the animals do not need to be forced to run using electrical shock grids or air jets. Because wheel running is a natural form of exercise for the rat or mouse, it is not a useful model for the production of a chronic stress response in the animal. It is suggested that investigators interested in pursuing animal models of exercise refer to the APS's extensive and complete guide to the selection of training methods and animal models for the study of exercise (APS Animal Care and Experimentation Committee, 2006).

THE STUDY OF ATROPHY AND EXERCISE RECOVERY

Mobility and the capacity to carry out activities of daily living are basic issues of patient care. Given that hospitalized patients are usually subject to some level of atrophy because of loss in weight bearing or mobility, the study of the process of atrophy and the exercised recovery from various states of disability is fundamental to nursing science. This process is usually studied in human subjects.

For example, Maloni and colleagues have examined the effects and hazards of antenatal bedrest (Brandao, Mottola, Gratton, & Maloni, 2013) and others studied effectiveness of a home-based, 12-week neuromuscular electrical stimulation of the *quadriceps femoris* to decrease arthritis knee pain in older adults with osteoarthritis of the knee (Gaines, Metter, & Talbot, 2004). However, more detailed studies of the physiologic mechanisms by which skeletal muscle adapts or the metabolic system responds during illness may require the use of animal models.

There are currently multiple methods available for studying alterations in skeletal muscle structure and function resulting from changes in muscle use—be it exercise or atrophy. These changes frequently occur as a result of extended bed rest, injuries requiring immobilization, and permanent loss of function (Hutchinson, Linderman, & Basso, 2001; Natelson, Goldwater, De Roshia, & Levin, 1985; Ohira et al., 2000; Reznick, Menashe, Bar-Shai, Coleman, & Carmeli, 2003; Suetta et al., 2009). These three clinical states represent distinct forms of decreased movement and exercise. Prolonged bed rest results in skeletal muscle atrophy because of the loss of weight bearing as well as some degree of movement. Hind limbs are not restrained in this model, whereas in orthopedic injuries, limbs are either casted or restrained from movement and/or weight bearing. Loss of function is seen in paralysis or nerve damage. The study of each of these states of compromised mobility requires an animal model, which matches the movement and weight bearing of the clinical condition because the magnitude and rate of physiologic change varies directly with the degree of restraint (Booth & Lees, 2007; Kasper, Talbot, & Gaines, 2002).

MODELS OF IMMOBILIZATION AND INACTIVITY

The immobilization model requires the casting of a limb, usually the hind limb of a rodent (APS Animal Care and Experimentation Committee, 2006; Goto, Komaki, Igarashi, & Nonaka, 2000; Nonaka, Miyazawa, Sukegawa, Yonemoto, & Kato, 1997). Its purpose is to completely remove weight bearing and joint movement along with the removal of electrical and mechanical activity of the hind limb muscles (Booth & Kelso, 1973; Fitts, Metzger, Riley, & Unsworth, 1986). This model results in rapid atrophy of the muscles of the casted limb. Daily care of the animal is extensive because the casts are chewed by the rodent and require repair; and, application of the cast requires anesthesia of the animal. Although requiring time-consuming daily monitoring of cast integrity, it remains the best animal model of the mobility restrictions because of orthopedic casting. Initial studies involving human orthopedic or fixation procedures generally used casting (Booth & Seider, 1979) and pinning (Fischbach & Robbins, 1969;

Max, 1972) resulting in complete disuse and such physiological and functional effects as a decrease in muscle mass by proteasome-dependent proteolysis that is independent of protein synthesis (Krawiec, Frost, Vary, Jefferson, & Lang, 2005). Recent investigations have chosen cast over point fixation to minimize animal pain. Detailed instruction on the application and care of rodent immobilization casts is found in Appendix A of the *Resource Book for the Design of Animal Exercise Protocols* (APS Animal Care and Experimentation Committee, 2006).

Models of inactivity reflect the loss of weight bearing and decreased movement of bedrest. This model has also been used as a proxy for microgravity environments in space because it reproduces loss of weight bearing along with a 15% head-down tilt (Dehority et al., 1999; Morey-Holton & Globus, 1998), recapitulating the thoracic shift of fluid volume with loss of circulating fluid volume.

Muscle atrophy occurs when there is decrease in mobility or muscle use. Overtime, this decrease in muscle use, hypokinesia, results in a loss of muscle mass resulting from a decrease in the number of myofibrils and fibers per muscle (Faulkner, Niemeyer, Maxwell, & White, 1980). The methods of hind limb unloading used to induce immobility, and thus atrophy effects functional changes in the muscle (Kasper, McNulty, Otto, & Thomas, 1993).

Simulated weightlessness studies attempting to replicate the effects of space flight have used bed rest and water immersion studies because it is the closest equivalent that can be used in humans (Herbison & Talbot, 1985). Of the hind limb suspension models that approximate bed rest, the tail suspension model is preferred over the more restrictive harness method of Musacchia (Musacchia & Fagette, 1997) because rats are less stressed and are able to continue normal grooming and feeding behavior (Bikle & Halloran, 1999). Others have also used the hind limb suspension model to study ventricular myosin isozyme and electrocardiographic alterations after exercise and dobutamine intervention for hypokinesis/hypodynamia deconditioning (Girten et al., 1989).

There appears to be little, if any, difference in the mechanism of atrophy. Both hind limb suspension models are associated with decreased protein expression and phosphorylation of Akt (Bodine et al., 2001; Krawiec et al., 2005) and the ATP-dependent ubiquitin-proteasome pathway appears to be the dominant proteolytic pathway. Therefore, the primary considerations in selecting a model of hind limb unloading to produce atrophy should be (a) the ability to maintain the animal in the hind limb suspension mechanism, (b) the ability of the mechanism to replicate the desired conditions, and (c) the ability of the animal to maintain activities of daily living. Additional considerations include (a) physical complications of the suspension method, required monitoring, age restrictions, ability to escape from the harness or tail suspension, and effectiveness as a mechanism to induce muscle atrophy (Booth & Zwetsloot, 2010; Machida & Booth, 2004).

ANIMAL MODELS OF EXERCISE IN NURSING RESEARCH

In nursing research, the rodent models of recovery from inactivity and skeletal muscle atrophy has been extensively studied. These represent a unique nursing approach because a specific method of inducing atrophy is applied to the process to study disease-specific recovery, pain associated with recovery, or inflammatory processes associated with recovery (see Table 1.1).

TABLE 1.1

Nursing Research in the Process of Recovery From Inactivity

Principal Investigator	Paper	Model
Myoung-Ae Choe	Choe, M., Koo, B.-S., An, G. J., & Jeon, S. (2012). Effects of treadmill exercise on the recovery of dopaminergic neuron loss and muscle atrophy in the 6-OHDA lesioned Parkinson's disease rat model. *The Korean Journal of Physiology & Pharmacology, 16*(5), 305–312.	Treadmill running, brain lesion
Myoung-Ae Choe	Choe, M.-A., An, G. J., Lee, Y.-K., Im, J. H., Choi-Kwon, S., & Heitkemper, M. (2004). Effect of inactivity and undernutrition after acute ischemic stroke in a rat hind limb muscle model. *Nursing Research, 53*(5), 283–292.	Hind limb suspension
Christine E. Kasper	Kasper, C. E., White, T. P., & Maxwell, L. C. (1990). Running during recovery from hind limb suspension induces transient muscle injury. *Journal of Applied Physiology, 68*(2), 533–539.	Hind limb suspension, treadmill running
Christine E. Kasper	Kasper, C. E., & Xun, L. (1996). Cytoplasm-to-myonucleus ratios in plantaris and soleus muscle fibers following hind limb suspension. *Journal of Muscle Research and Cell Motility, 17*(5), 603–610.	Hind limb Suspension
Christine E. Kasper	Kasper, C. E., & Xun, L. (1996). Cytoplasm-to-myonucleus ratios following microgravity. *Journal of Muscle Research and Cell Motility, 17*(5), 595–602.	Spaceflight, weightlessness
Barbara A. St. Pierre	St Pierre, B. A., & Tidball, J. G. (1994). Differential response of macrophage subpopulations to soleus muscle reloading after rat hind limb suspension. *Journal of Applied Physiology, 77*(1), 290–297.	Hind limb suspension
Barbara A. St. Pierre	St Pierre, B. A., & Tidball, J. G. (1994). Macrophage activation and muscle remodeling at myotendinous junctions after modifications in muscle loading. *The American Journal of Pathology, 145*(6), 1463–1471.	Hind limb suspension

EXERCISE-INDUCED RODENT MODEL OF THERMOREGULATION

Chronic exercise training has been found to be a useful model for the study of non-specific immune changes during illness (Rowsey, Borer, & Kluger, 1993a, 1993b). Using Sprague-Dawley rats, Rowsey and colleagues (2009) demonstrated that voluntary wheel running is a reliable method for increasing core body temperature of rodents. Early work of this group demonstrated that 8 weeks of running on a wheel consistently increased daytime body temperature (Rowsey, Metzger, Carlson, & Gordon, 2003; Rowsey, Metzger, & Gordon, 2001). This was determined to be caused by chronic activation of the immune system. Further studies extended this model by demonstrating that chronic exercise wheel training using adult female Sprague-Dawley rats altered immune responses that mimic some aspects of fever. Running activity was also characterized in this model, yielding a viable model for the study of immune response and thermoregulation during chronic exercise (Rowsey et al., 2003; Rowsey et al., 2001).

ANIMAL MODELS OF OBESITY

Currently, there are hundreds of animal models of obesity. However, rodent models are the most useful for general research purposes and have human-like primary metabolic pathways, which can be genetically altered. Mice are also valuable as a model in the study of the quantitative genetics of obesity because of their short gestation, life span, and large genetic variation. These models are bred for strong heritable body fat to mass ratios. At this time, rodent genomes are screened for QTL and genes, which influence obesity in a human population (Perusse, Chagnon, Weisnagel, & Bouchard, 1999; Pomp, 1997). (See Table 1.2.)

Rat models have also been specifically developed for use in studies of obesity. Although an extensive array of animals have been bred for these studies, the most common are the Long-Evans and Zucker rats (Kurtz, Montano, Chan, & Kabra, 1989; Kurtz, Morris, & Pershadsingh, 1989). Long-Evans rats are often used in behavioral as well as obesity studies and were derived as an outbred strain of the Brown Norway or *Rattus norvegicus*; whereas Zucker rats were bread specifically for the study of hypertension and obesity. There are two varieties of the Zucker rat. The obese Zucker rat expresses a recessive trait (fa/fa) of the leptin receptor (Kurtz, Morris, et al., 1989; Takaya et al., 1996).

The polygenic models of obesity are fed a high-fat diet, which causes a diet-induced obesity (DIO). The standard outbred strains of Sprague-Dawley or Long-Evans rats are used for DIO studies. There is also a polygenic mouse model, C57BL6. It should be noted that with polygenic animals, not all respond to the diet with a significant gain in weight (Carroll, et al., 2004). A comprehensive discussion of animal models of obesity has been published by Kanasaki and Koya (2011).

TABLE 1.2
Rodent Models of Obesity

	Mutation	Abbreviation	Gene	Product
Mouse (monogenic)	Agouti	ASIP	agouti	Agouti protein (Miltenberger, Mynatt, Wilkinson, & Woychik, 1997; Perry, Whincup, & Shaper, 1994; Salton, Hahm, & Mizuno, 2000)
	Diabetes	Db	Lepr	Leptin receptor (Kanasaki & Koya, 2011)
	Fat	Fat	Cpe	Carboxypeptidase E (Tartaglia et al., 1995)
	Mahogany	Mg	Mg	Mahogany Protein (Miller et al., 1997)
	Mc4R (knockout)	Mc4R	Melanocortin 4 receptor	Receptor (Huszar et al., 1997)
	Obese	Ob	Lep	Leptin (Casper, Sullivan, & Tecott, 2008)
	Tubby	Tub	?	? (Zhang et al., 1982)
Polygenic	Strain		Method	
Rat	Sprague-Dawley		Diet Induced (Carroll, Voisey, & van Daal, 2004)	
	Long-Evans		Diet Induced (Carroll et al., 2004)	
Mouse	C57BL/6N		Nicotinamide nuclear transhydrogenase (Nnt), spontaneous deletion (Kanasaki & Koya, 2011)	
	C57BL/6J		Nicotinamide nuclear transhydrogenase (Nnt), spontaneous deletion (Kanasaki & Koya, 2011)	

HUMAN DISEASE AND ANIMAL MODELS OF OBESITY

The ultimate purpose of genetic models of obesity is to inform the biology of the disease. They do not help to illumine the interaction of how obesity can cause other health problems and diseases (Kanasaki & Koya, 2011). This relationship can be studied by using old world monkeys. Obesity models in macaques, baboons, and rhesus monkeys have provided information relevant to humans

(Eizirik, Murphy, & O'Brien, 2001; S. L. Page & Goodman, 2001). However, it should be immediately noted that the conduct of research of any kind with nonhuman primates is rapidly becoming rare, and difficult to conduct because of changing legislation and policy (Insitiue for Laboratory Animal Research, 2003). Furthermore, research with nonhuman primates requires a high level of technical expertise of the investigator and the research team.

In spite of the significant scientific and technical difficulty involved, nursing research into the mechanisms of obesity is not being studied in rodents, but in the nonhuman primate (Hansen & Bodkin, 1993; Hansen, Jen, & Schwartz, 1988; Hansen et al., 2011). Barbara C. Hansen has developed nonhuman primate models of obesity, the metabolic syndrome, diabetes and diabetic complications, and these models have been applied to studies of the underlying mechanisms of these disorders, their natural history, and their mitigation/treatment and prevention by pharmaceutical and nonpharmaceutical approaches. In addition, her research has addressed the physiological, cellular, and molecular defects underlying the development of obesity and diabetes mellitus and their prevention, as well as the long-term prevention of diabetic complications (Hansen & Bodkin, 1993; Hansen, Ortmeyer, & Bodkin, 1995).

CONCLUSION

Animal models of exercise, atrophy, and obesity provide the investigator with an alternative to the use of human subjects in research. In general, animal models permit the investigation of research questions or treatments as acute or chronic longitudinal experiments. However, the use of animal models for addressing significant clinical questions has been a standard feature of nursing research for the past 40 years. It is anticipated that their use will become increasingly common in the future nursing research.

REFERENCES

Albeck, D. S., Sano, K., Prewitt, G. E., & Dalton, L. (2006). Mild forced treadmill exercise enhances spatial learning in the aged rat. *Behavioural Brain Research, 168*(2), 345–348.

American Physiological Society Animal Care and Experimentation Committee. (2006). *Resource book for the design of animal exercise protocols.* American Physiological Society, Bethesda, MD.

Bedford, T. G., Tipton, C. M., Wilson, N. C., Oppliger, R. A., & Gisolfi, C. V. (1979). Maximum oxygen consumption of rats and its changes with various experimental procedures. *Journal of Applied Physiology: Respiratory, Environmental and Exercise Physiology, 47*(6), 1278–1283.

Bikle, D. D., & Halloran, B. P. (1999). The response of bone to unloading. *Journal of Bone amd Mineral Metabolism, 17*(4), 233–244.

Blood, F. R., & D'Amour, F. E. (1947). Suitability of the rat for routine laboratory work in physiology. *Federation Proceedings, 6*(1, Pt. 2), 77.

Bodine, S. C., Latres, E., Baumhueter, S., Lai, V. K., Nunez, L., Clarke, B. A., . . . Glass, D. J. (2001). Identification of ubiquitin ligases required for skeletal muscle atrophy. *Science, 294*(5547), 1704–1708.

Booth, F. W., & Kelso, J. R. (1973). Cytochrome oxidase of skeletal muscle: Adaptive response to chronic disuse. *Canadian Journal of Physiology and Pharmacology, 51*(9), 679–681.

Booth, F. W., & Lees, S. J. (2007). Fundamental questions about genes, inactivity, and chronic diseases. *Physiological Genomics, 28*(2), 146–157. Retrieved from http://physiolgenomics.physiology.org/content/28/2/146

Booth, F. W., & Seider, M. J. (1979). Recovery of skeletal muscle after 3 months of hindlimb immobilization in rats. *Journal of Applied Physiology, 47*, 435–439.

Booth, F. W., & Zwetsloot, K. A. (2010). Basic concepts about genes, inactivity and aging. *Scandinavian Journal of Medicine & Science in Sport, 20*(1), 1–4.

Brandao, K. L., Mottola, M. F., Gratton, R., & Maloni, J. (2013). Bone status in activity-restricted pregnant women assessed using calcaneal quantitative ultrasound. *Biological Research for Nursing, 15*(2), 205–212.

Briones, T. L., & Therrien, B. (2000). Behavioral effects of transient cerebral ischemia. *Biological Research for Nursing, 1*(4), 276–286.

Brooks, G. A., Donovan, C. M., & White, T. P. (1984). Estimation of anaerobic energy production and efficiency in rats during exercise. *Journal of Applied Physiology: Respiratory, Environmental and Exercise Physiology, 56*(2), 520–525.

Brooks, G. A., & White, T. P. (1978). Determination of metabolic and heart rate responses of rats to treadmill exercise. *Journal of Applied Physiology: Respiratory, Environmental and Exercise Physiology, 45*(6), 1009–1015.

Bult, C. J., Eppig, J. T., Blake, J. A., Kadin, J. A., & Richardson, J. E. (2013). The mouse genome database: Genotypes, phenotypes, and models of human disease. *Nucleic Acids Research, 41*(Database issue), D885–D891.

Carroll, L., Voisey, J., & van Daal, A. (2004). Mouse models of obesity. *Clinics in Dermatology, 22*(4), 345–349. http://dx.doi.org/10.1016/j.clindermatol.2004.01.004

Casper, R. C., Sullivan, E. L., & Tecott, L. (2008). Relevance of animal models to human eating disorders and obesity. *Psychopharmacology, 199*(3), 313–329.

Chae, S. M., & Covington, C. Y. (2009). Biobehavioral outcomes in adolescents and young adults prenatally exposed to cocaine: Evidence from animal models. *Biological Research for Nursing, 10*(4), 318–330.

Clause, B. T. (1998) The Wistar Institute Archives: Rats (not mice) and history. *The Mendel Newsletter,* (7), 2–7.

Committee on Rat Nomenclature. (1992). Definition, nomenclature, and conservation of rat strains. *ILAR News, 34*, S1–S26.

Dehority, W., Halloran, B. P., Bikle, D. D., Curren, T., Kostenuik, P. J., Wronski, T. J., . . . Morey-Holton, E. (1999). Bone and hormonal changes induced by skeletal unloading in the mature male rat. *American Journal of Physiology, 276*(1, Pt. 1), E62–E69.

DiCarlo, S. E., & Bishop, V. S. (1988). Exercise training attenuates baroreflex regulation of nerve activity in rabbits. *The American Journal of Physiology, 255*(4, Pt. 2), H974–H979.

Donaldson, S. K. (1985). Peeled mammalian skeletal muscle fibers. Possible stimulation of Ca2+ release via a transverse tubule-sarcoplasmic reticulum mechanism. *The Journal of General Physiology, 86*(4), 501–525.

Donaldson, S. K., Best, P. M., & Kerrick, G. L. (1978). Characterization of the effects of Mg2+ on Ca2+- and Sr2+-activated tension generation of skinned rat cardiac fibers. *The Journal of General Physiology, 71*(6), 645–655.

Dwinell, M. R., Worthey, E. A., Shimoyama, M., Bakir-Gungor, B., DePons, J., Laulederkind, S., . . . Jacob, H. J. (2009). The Rat genome database 2009: Variation, ontologies and pathways. *Nucleic Acids Research, 37*(Database issue), D744–D749.

Eizirik, E., Murphy, W. J., & O'Brien, S. J. (2001). Molecular dating and biogeography of the early placental mammal radiation. *The Journal of Heredity, 92*(2), 212–219.

Evans, D. L., & Rose, R. J. (1988). Cardiovascular and respiratory responses to submaximal exercise training in the thoroughbred horse. *Pflugers Archiv: European Journal of Physiology, 411*(3), 316–321.

Faulkner, J. A., Niemeyer, J. H., Maxwell, L. C., & White, T. P. (1980). Contractile properties of transplanted extensor digitorum longus muscle of the cat. *Journal of Applied Psychology, 238,* C120–C126.

Fischbach, G. D., & Robbins, N. (1969). Changes in contractile properties of disused soleus muscles. *Journal of Physiology (London), 201*(2), 305–320.

Fitts, R. H., Metzger, J. M., Riley, D. A., & Unsworth, B. R. (1986). Models of disuse: A comparison of hindlimb suspension and immobilization. *Journal of Applied Physiology, 60*(6), 1946–1953.

Fosha-Dolezal, S. R., Avery, T. B., Wagner, W. C., & Fedde, M. R. (1988). Changes in serum potassium concentration with exercise in Hereford calves: Effects of adrenalectomy. *Comparative biochemistry and physiology. A Comparative Physiology, 91*(1), 135–139.

Gaines, J. M., Metter, E. J., & Talbot, L. A. (2004). The effect of neuromuscular electrical stimulation on arthritis knee pain in older adults with osteoarthritis of the knee. *Applied Nursing Research, 17*(3), 201–206.

Girten, B., Smith, B. A., Bloomfield, S., Merola, A. J., Oloff, C., & Kazarian, L. (1989). Ventricular myosin isozyme and electrocardiographic alterations after exercise and dobutamine intervention for hypokinesis/hypodynamia deconditioning. *Aviation, Space, and Environmental Medicine, 60*(5), 501.

Glenn, W., Kerrick, L., & Donaldson, S. K. (1975). The comparative effects of (Ca2+) and (Mg2+) on on tension generation in the fibers of skinned frog skeletal muscle and mechanically disrupted rat ventricular cardiac muscle. *Pflugers Archiv: European Journal of Physiology, 358*(3), 195–201.

Goto, Y. I., Komaki, H., Igarashi, F., & Nonaka, I. (2000). Muscle mitochondrial changes by experimental immobility and hindlimb suspension. *Journal of Gravitational Physiology: A Journal of the International Society for Gravitational Physiology, 7*(2), P109–P110.

Hansen, B. C., & Bodkin, N. L. (1993). Primary prevention of diabetes mellitus by prevention of obesity in monkeys. *Diabetes, 42*(12), 1809–1814.

Hansen, B. C., Jen, K. L., & Schwartz, J. (1988). Changes in insulin responses and binding in adipocytes from monkeys with obesity progressing to diabetes. *International Journal of Obesity, 12*(5), 433–443.

Hansen, B. C., Ortmeyer, H. K., & Bodkin, N. L. (1995). Prevention of obesity in middle-aged monkeys: Food intake during body weight clamp. *Obesity Research, 3*(Suppl. 2), 199s–204s.

Hansen, B. C., Tigno, X. T., Benardeau, A., Meyer, M., Sebokova, E., & Mizrahi, J. (2011). Effects of aleglitazar, a balanced dual peroxisome proliferator-activated receptor alpha/gamma agonist on glycemic and lipid parameters in a primate model of the metabolic syndrome. *Cardiovascular Diabetology, 10,* 7.

Hanson, F. B., & Sholes, F. N. (1924). Seasonal differences in sex ratio,litter size and birth weight of the Albino rat under uniform laboratory conditions. *Genetics, 9*(4), 363–367.

Harlan Laboratories. (2012). Outbred rats—Sprague Dawley® Outbred Rat. In H. L.-A. R. L.-C. R. Services (Ed.).

Harlan Laboratories. (2013). *Research models.* Retrieved from http://www.harlan.com/online_literature/research_models.hl

Hebda-Bauer, E. K., Morano, M. I., & Therrien, B. (1999). Aging and corticosterone injections affect spatial learning in Fischer-344 X Brown Norway rats. *Brain Research, 827*(1–2), 93–103.

Herbison, G. J., & Talbot, J. M. (1985). Muscle atrophy during space flight: Research needs and opportunities. *Physiologist, 28*(6), 520–527.

Holden, J. E., & Therrien, B. (1993). Cue familiarity reduces spatial disorientation following hippocampal damage, *Nursing Research*, 42(6), 338–343.

Holloszy, J. O. (1963). The epidemiology of coronary heart disease: National differences and the role of physical activity. *Journal of the American Geriatrics Society*, 11, 718–725.

Holloszy, J. O., Skinner, J. S., Barry, A. J., & Cureton, T. K. (1964). Effect of physical conditioning on cardiovascular function. A ballistocardiographic study. *The American Journal of Cardiology*, 14, 761–770.

Huszar, D., Lynch, C. A., Fairchild-Huntress, V., Dunmore, J. H., Fang, Q., Berkemeier, L. R., . . . Lee, F. (1997). Targeted disruption of the melanocortin-4 receptor results in obesity in mice. *Cell*, 88(1), 131–141.

Hutchinson, K. J., Linderman, J. K., & Basso, D. M. (2001). Skeletal muscle adaptations following spinal cord contusion injury in rat and the relationship to locomotor function: A time course study. *Journal of Neurotrauma*, 18(10), 1075–1089.

Insititue for Laboratory Animal Research. (2003). *International perspectives: The future of nonhuman primate resources, Proceedings of the Workshop held April 17–19, 2002*. Washington, DC: The National Academies Press.

Ishihara, A., Roy, R. R., Ohira, Y., Ibata, Y., & Edgerton, V. R. (1998). Hypertrophy of rat plantaris muscle fibers after voluntary running with increasing loads. *Journal of Applied Physiology*, 84(6), 2183–2189.

Kanasaki, K., & Koya, D. (2011). Biology of obesity: Lessons from animal models of obesity. *Journal of Biomedicine & Biotechnology*, 2011, 197–636.

Kasper, C. E., McNulty, A. L., Otto, A. J., & Thomas, D. P. (1993). Alterations in skeletal muscle related to impaired physical mobility: An empirical model. *Research in Nursing & Health*, 16(4), 265–273.

Kasper, C. E., Talbot, L. A., & Gaines, J. M. (2002). Skeletal muscle damage and recovery. *AACN Clinical Issues*, 13(2), 237–247.

Kiley, J. P., & Fedde, M. R. (1983a). Cardiopulmonary control during exercise in the duck. *Journal of Applied Physiology: Respiratory, Environmental and Exercise Physiology*, 55(5), 1574–1581.

Kiley, J. P., & Fedde, M. R. (1983b). Exercise hyperpnea in the duck without intrapulmonary chemoreceptor involvement. *Respiration Physiology*, 53(3), 355–365.

Kovesdi, E., Kamnaksh, A., Wingo, D., Ahmed, F., Grunberg, N. E., Long, J. B., . . . Agoston, D. V. (2012). Acute minocycline treatment mitigates the symptoms of mild blast-induced traumatic brain injury. *Frontiers in Neurology*, 3, 111. http://dx.doi.org/10.3389/fneur.2012.00111

Krawiec, B. J., Frost, R. A., Vary, T. C., Jefferson, L. S., & Lang, C. H. (2005). Hindlimb casting decreases muscle mass in part by proteasome-dependent proteolysis but independent of protein synthesis. *American Journal of Physiology—Endocrinology and Metabolism*, 289(6), E969–E980.

Krinke, G. J. (2006). History, Strains and Models. In G. R. Bullock & T. Bunton (Eds.), *The Laboratory Rat (Handbook of Experimental Animals)* (pp. 3–16). New York, NY: Academic Press.

Kuramoto, T. (2013). *The National BioResource Project for the Rat in Japan*. Retrieved from http://www.anim.med.kyoto-u.ac.jp/nbr/strains/Strains_d.aspx?StrainID=904

Kurtz, T. W., Montano, M., Chan, L., & Kabra, P. (1989). Molecular evidence of genetic heterogeneity in Wistar-Kyoto rats: Implications for research with the spontaneously hypertensive rat. *Hypertension*, 13(2), 188–192.

Kurtz, T. W., Morris, R. C., & Pershadsingh, H. A. (1989). The Zucker fatty rat as a genetic model of obesity and hypertension. *Hypertension*, 13(6, Pt. 2), 896–901.

Lerman, I., Harrison, B. C., Freeman, K., Hewett, T. E., Allen, D. L., Robbins, J., & Leinwand, L. A. (2002). Genetic variability in forced and voluntary endurance exercise performance in seven inbred mouse strains. *Journal of Applied Physiology*, 92(6), 2245–2255. http://dx.doi. org/10.1152/japplphysiol.01045.2001

Machida, S., & Booth, F. W. (2004). Regrowth of skeletal muscle atrophied from inactivity. *Medicine and Science in Sports and Exercise*, 36(1), 52–59.

Max, S. R. (1972). Disuse atrophy of skeletal muscle loss of functional activity of mitochondria. *Biochemical and Biophysical Research Communication*, 46, 1394–1398.

Miller, K. A., Gunn, T. M., Carrasquillo, M. M., Lamoreux, M. L., Galbraith, D. B., & Barsh, G. S. (1997). Genetic studies of the mouse mutations mahogany and mahoganoid. *Genetics*, 146(4), 1407–1415.

Miltenberger, R. J., Mynatt, R. L., Wilkinson, J. E., & Woychik, R. P. (1997). The role of the agouti gene in the yellow obese syndrome. *The Journal of Nutrition*, 127(9), 1902S–1907S.

Morey-Holton, E. R., & Globus, R. K. (1998). Hindlimb unloading of growing rats: A model for predicting skeletal changes during space flight. *Bone*, 22(Suppl. 5), 83S–88S.

Musacchia, X. J., & Fagette, S. (1997). Weightlessness simulations for cardiovascular and muscle systems: Validity of rat models. *Journal of Gravitational Physiology*, 4(3), 49–59.

Musch, T. I., Friedman, D. B., Pitetti, K. H., Haidet, G. C., Stray-Gundersen, J., Mitchell, J. H., & Ordway, G. A. (1987). Regional distribution of blood flow of dogs during graded dynamic exercise. *Journal of Applied Physiology*, 63(6), 2269–2277.

Musch, T. I., Haidet, G. C., Ordway, G. A., Longhurst, J. C., & Mitchell, J. H. (1987). Training effects on regional blood flow response to maximal exercise in foxhounds. *Journal of Applied Physiology*, 62(4), 1724–1732.

Natelson, B. H., Goldwater, D. J., De Roshia, C., & Levin, B. E. (1985). Visceral predictors of cardio-vascular deconditioning in late middle-aged men. *Aviation, Space and Environmental Medicine*, 56(3), 199–203.

National Center for Research Resources. (2013). *LAMHDI: Laboratory Animal Models to Human Disease, 2013*. Retrieved from http://www.lamhdi.org/

National Human Genome Research Institute. (2013). *Mouse Genome Sequencing: Mus musculus*. Retrieved from http://www.genome.gov/10001859

National Institutes of Health (U.S.). Office of Laboratory Animal Welfare. (2002). *Public Health Service Policy on Humane Care and Use of Laboratory Animals*. Bethesda, MD.: Office of Laboratory Animal Welfare, National Institutes of Health.

Nonaka, I., Miyazawa, M., Sukegawa, T., Yonemoto, K., & Kato, T. (1997). Muscle fiber atrophy and degeneration induced by experimental immobility and hindlimb suspension. *International Journal of Sports Medicine*, 18(Suppl. 4), S292–S294.

Ohira, Y., Yoshinaga, T., Nonaka, I., Ohara, M., Yoshioka, T., Yamashita-Goto, K., . . . Kozzlovskaya, I. B. (2000). Histochemical responses of human soleus muscle fibers to long-term bedrest with or without countermeasures. *Japan Journal of Physiology*, 50(1), 41–47.

Page, G. G., & Ben-Eliyahu, S. (2002). Indomethacin attenuates the immunosuppressive and tumor-promoting effects of surgery. *The Journal of Pain: Official Journal of the American Pain Society*, 3(4), 301–308.

Page, G. G., Ben-Eliyahu, S., Yirmiya, R., & Liebeskind, J. C. (1993). Morphine attenuates surgery-induced enhancement of metastatic colonization in rats. *Pain*, 54(1), 21–28.

Page, S. L., & Goodman, M. (2001). Catarrhine phylogeny: Noncoding DNA evidence for a diphy-letic origin of the mangabeys and for a human-chimpanzee clade. *Molecular Phylogenetics Evolution*, 18(1), 14–25.

Parkes, A. S. (1946). Feeding and breeding of laboratory animals; rat and mouse cubes, and cube containers. *The Journal of Hygiene*, 44(6), 491–500.

Perry, I. J., Whincup, P. H., & Shaper, A. G. (1994). Environmental factors in the development of essential hypertension. *British Medical Bulletin*, 50(2), 246–259.

Perusse, L., Chagnon, Y. C., Weisnagel, J., & Bouchard, C. (1999). The human obesity gene map: The 1998 update. *Obesity Research*, 7(1), 111–129.

Pomp, D. (1997). Genetic dissection of obesity in polygenic animal models. *Behavior Genetics*, 27(4), 285–306.

Reame, N. E., Peluso, J. P., & Hafez, E. S. (1977). Effect of d-norgestrel on LH levels and ovulation in the rhesus monkey. *Contraception*, 16(5), 499–505.

Reznick, A. Z., Menashe, O., Bar-Shai, M., Coleman, R., & Carmeli, E. (2003). Expression of matrix metalloproteinases, inhibitor, and acid phosphatase in muscles of immobilized hindlimbs of rats. *Muscle Nerve*, 27(1), 51–59.

Rowsey, P. J., Borer, K. T., & Kluger, M. J. (1993a). Role of prostaglandins in exercise-induced core temperature elevation in female Sprague-Dawley rats. *The American Journal of Physiology*, 265(5, Pt. 2), R1121–R1125.

Rowsey, P. J., Borer, K. T., & Kluger, M. J. (1993b). Tumor necrosis factor is not involved in exercise-induced elevation in core temperature. *The American Journal of Physiology*, 265(6, Pt. 2), R1351–R1354.

Rowsey, P. J., Metzger, B. L., Carlson, J., & Gordon, C. J. (2003). Effects of exercise conditioning on thermoregulatory responses to repeated administration of chlorpyrifos. *Environmental Research*, 92(1), 27–34.

Rowsey, P. J., Metzger, B. L., Carlson, J., & Gordon, C. J. (2009). Long-term exercise training selectively alters serum cytokines involved in fever. *Biological Research for Nursing*, 10(4), 374–380.

Rowsey, P. J., Metzger, B. L., & Gordon, C. J. (2001). Effects of exercise conditioning on thermoregulatory response to anticholinesterase insecticide toxicity. [Research Support, U.S. Gov't, P.H.S.]. *Biological Research for Nursing*, 2(4), 267–276.

Salton, S. R., Hahm, S., & Mizuno, T. M. (2000). Of mice and MEN: What transgenic models tell us about hypothalamic control of energy balance. *Neuron*, 25(2), 265–268.

Shimoyama, M., Smith, J. R., Hayman, T., Laulederkind, S., Lowry, T., Nigam, R., . . . Jacob, H. (2011). RGD: A comparative genomics platform. *Human Genomics*, 5(2), 124–129.

Smith, B. A., Hamlin, R. L., Bartels, R. L., Evans, R. G., Kirby, T. E., MacVicar, M. G., & Weisbrode, S. E. (1992). Myocardial infarction size and scar dimensions: The influence of activity. *Heart & Lung: The Journal of Critical Care*, 21(5), 440–447.

Suetta, C., Hvid, L. G., Justesen, L., Christensen, U., Neergaard, K., Simonsen, L., . . . Aagaard, P. (2009). Effects of aging on human skeletal muscle after immobilization and retraining. *Journal of Applied Physiology*, 107(4), 1172–1180.

Takaya, K., Ogawa, Y., Isse, N., Okazaki, T., Satoh, N., Masuzaki, H., . . . Nakao, K. (1996). Molecular cloning of rat leptin receptor isoform complementary DNAs—Identification of a missense mutation in Zucker fatty (fa/fa) rats. *Biochemical and Biophysical Reseach Communications*, 225(1), 75–83.

Tartaglia, L. A., Dembski, M., Weng, X., Deng, N., Culpepper, J., Devos, R., . . . Tepper, R. I. (1995). Identification and expression cloning of a leptin receptor, OB-R. *Cell*, 83(7), 1263–1271.

The Jackson Laboratory. (2013). *Lab milestones and research highlights*. Retrieved from http://www.jax.org/milestones/index.html

Turturro A, W. W., Lewis, S., Hass, B. S., Lipman, R. D., & Hart, R. W. (1999). Growth curves and survival characteristics of the animals used in the Biomarkers of Aging Program. *Journal of Gerontology Series A: Biological Sciences*, 54(11), B492–B501.

van Praag, H., Shubert, T., Zhao, C., & Gage, F. H. (2005). Exercise enhances learning and hippocampal neurogenesis in aged mice. *The Journal of Neuroscience: The Official Journal of the Society for Neuroscience*, 25(38), 8680–8685.

Yu, B. P., Masoro, E. J., Murata, I., Bertrand, H. A., & Lynd, F. T. (1982). Life span study of SPF Fischer 344 male rats fed ad libitum or restricted diets: Longevity, growth, lean body mass and disease. *Journal of Gerontology*, 37(2), 130–141.

Zhang, Y., Proenca, R., Maffei, M., Barone, M., Leopold, L., & Friedman, J. M. (1994). Positional cloning of the mouse obese gene and its human homologue. *Nature*, 372(6505), 425–432.

CHAPTER 2

Thermoregulation

Cytokines Involved in Fever and Exercise

Pamela Johnson Rowsey

ABSTRACT

The study of fever has provided important models in understanding the cells, chemical messengers, and anatomic structures that are involved in inflammation and thermoregulation as a result of infection, stress, or trauma. After contact with a pathogen or an inflammatory stimulus, cells are activated to produce endogenous pyrogens called cytokines. Cytokine functions include a cascade of nonspecific immune responses by target leukocytes and reticuloendothelial cells inducing the synthesis of acute phase proteins by the liver, direct pyrogenic activities via the supraoptic nuclei and the hypothalamus to increase the thermoregulatory set-point (and, thus, induce fever), and a wide spectrum of additional immune effects.

The experimental data have helped us understand the redundant systems, cascades, and inhibitory feedback loops involved in these biologic processes. Acute exercise mimics the febrile state. Regular exercise, although it retains the advantage of an increase in core temperature, provides conditioning that downgrades the baseline of proinflammatory cellular products (cytokines). In this chapter, we highlight some of the current research including the foundational mechanisms that will allow us to establish the optimal exercise protocols to promote and restore health.

© 2013 Springer Publishing Company
http://dx.doi.org/10.1891/0739-6686.31.19

INTRODUCTION

The study of fever has provided important models in understanding the cells, chemical messengers, and anatomic structures that are involved in inflammation and thermoregulation as a result of infection, stress, or trauma. The experimental data have helped us understand the redundant systems, cascades, and inhibitory feedback loops involved in these biologic processes. Acute exercise mimics the febrile state. Regular exercise, although it retains the advantage of an increase in core temperature, provides conditioning that alters the baseline for proinflammatory cellular products (cytokines). In this chapter, we highlight some of the current research base including the foundational mechanisms that will allow us to establish the optimal exercise protocols to promote and restore health.

FEVER: HISTORICAL PERSPECTIVE

Fever is one of the earliest signs of infection and is a regulated elevation of body temperature greater than the normal range (36 °C–37 °C). Fever is a multiphasic response to a stimulus resulting in elevations and decline of the body core temperature as the thermoregulatory set-point is changed (Cabanac & Massonnet, 1974). The origin of the study of therapeutic fever and its relationship to disease dates back more than 2,000 years. Celsus recognized four cardinal symptoms of inflammation: heat, redness, swelling, and pain. Hippocrates, a Greek physician, had ideas about the significance of fever (Chadwick & Mann, 1950). He noted that disease was associated with four humors: blood, phlegm, black bile, and yellow bile. He thought fever was caused by an excess of yellow bile, which, like fire, was hot and dry (Atkins, 1960, 1982; Atkins, 1988).

These explanations were the basis of treatment until the mid-19th century when causal relationships between inflammation and fever were initially investigated using modern scientific methods (Cooper, 1987; Dinarello, 1988a; Kluger, 1991a). Further experimentation has identified the stimulus, mediators, and mechanisms by which fever is induced and regulated.

Two substances from different sources were initially identified. Pyrexin was extracted from inflammatory exudates, and appeared to induce the same type of fevers as gram-negative bacteria (Atkins, 1960). In 1948, granulocytic pyrogen (GP) was extracted from neutrophil and produced a fever that was different than pyrexin (Atkins, 1960).

In the 1950s, differences between pyrogens were elucidated when endotoxins were isolated from gram-negative bacteria (Atkins, 1960). Intramuscular and subcutaneous injections produced smaller fevers with a slower onset than

intravenous (iv) administration. Furthermore, altering the dose of IV administration altered the latency to onset (from 15–30 min to 8 min) and produced
the characteristic biphasic rise in temperature. It was at this time that researchers speculated that two pyrogenic substances were responsible for the different
phases: one, the injected endotoxin, and the other secreted by a blood cell. Thus,
the term endogenous pyrogen refers to the agent secreted by a cell in response to
endotoxin or other exogenous pyrogens.

Our understanding of basic mechanisms in physiology is constantly
evolving. Classical views have been reexamined and found not as credible
largely reflecting a better understanding of research design. Examples of these
reexaminations include many murine models failed to control for differences
in basic biology related to environment. Thus, mice were inadvertently sub-
jected to relative cold stress in laboratory environments. It is believed that this
may explain why findings from mouse models often failed to be replicated in
human trials (Karp, 2012). Studies regarding a vagal pathway for fever suffered
from study designs that did not control for confounding factors such as malnutrition. Thus, original findings are now subject to reinterpretations (Roth &
De Souza, 2001).

Our understanding also is enriched by new avenues of investigation: (a) transcription factors controlling the expression of cytokines such as
NF-kappaB or AP-1 (Dokladny, Lobb, Wharton, Thomas, & Moseley, 2010),
and (b) the role of heat shock response and proteins (Niven, Stelfox, &
Laupland, 2012). Figure 2.1 summarizes the current model of fever induction.
Stimuli include infectious agents or endotoxins (the lipopolysaccharide [LPS]
model), antigen/antibody reactions, and stress or trauma. Present-day research
has shown that after contact with a pathogen or an inflammatory stimulus,
cells are activated to produce endogenous pyrogens called cytokines (Cannon,
Evans, Hughes, Meredith, & Dinarello, 1986; Dinarello, 1988b; Dinarello,
Cannon, & Wolff, 1988).

Cytokines are small heat-labile proteins produced by cells in the periphery (monocytes and macrophages) and centrally in the brain (astrocytes and
microglia; Bendtzen, Baek, Berild, Dinarello, & Wolff, 1984; Cannon et al.,
1986; Dinarello, 1988b; Dinarello et al., 1988; Leon, 2002). Cytokine functions
include a cascade of nonspecific immune responses by target leukocytes and
reticuloendothelial cells inducing the synthesis of acute phase proteins by the
liver (Ahokas, Seydoux, Llanos, Mashburn, & Blatteis, 1985), direct pyrogenic
activities via the supraoptic nuclei and the hypothalamus to increase the thermoregulatory set-point, and thus induce fever and a wide spectrum of additional
immune effects. Thus, fever represents a cascade and a confluence of intracellular
mechanisms induced by cytokines (see Figure 2.1).

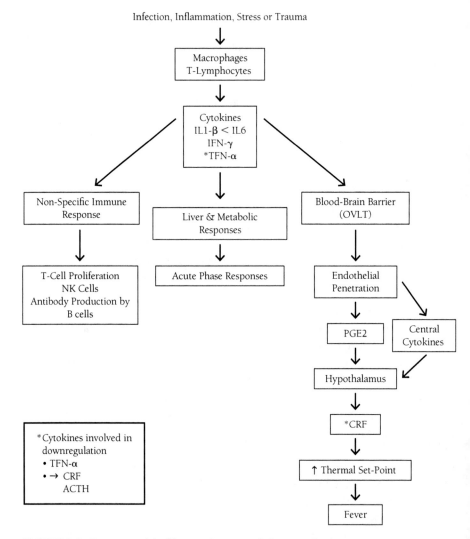

FIGURE 2.1 Current model of fever induction and downregulation.

CYTOKINES ARE ENDOGENOUS MEDIATORS OF FEVER

Currently, there are four inflammatory cytokines recognized as endogenous mediators of fever. These are interleukin-1β (IL-1β), interleukin-6 (IL-6), interferon-γ (IFN-γ), and tumor necrosis factor-α (TNF-α). Table 2.1 shows selected immune cytokines and their activities. Evidence from selected research studies on these cytokines is presented and includes demonstrations of cytokine levels during fever; identification of cytokine receptors in the blood, periphery,

TABLE 2.1

Selected Immune Cytokines and Their Activities

Cytokine	Producing Cell in Periphery	Target Cell(s) in Periphery and Activity
IL-1β	Monocytes Macrophages B Lymphocytes	Stimulate/activate T helper lymphocytes, B cells, NK cells. Induce MHC Class II production on macrophages. Induce acute phase response in liver. Induce FEVER pathway. The alternate form (IL-1α) is cell-bound.
IL-6	Monocytes Macrophages	Stimulate stem cells to differentiate into plasma cells. Activate B cells to produce antibody. Induce acute phase response in liver. Differentiation into plasma cells. Induce FEVER pathway.
IFN-γ	Th1 cells T cytotoxic cells NK cells	Dampen viral replication Induce MHC production on macrophages. Activate B cells to switch to IgG_{2a} Stimulate production of Th2 cells Stimulate proliferation of macrophages Pathogen elimination The alternate forms (IFN-α, IFN-β) also dampen viral replication and induce MHC-1 expression but not as intensely as IFN-γ.
TNFa	Macrophages, Mast cells, NK cells	Stimulate cytokine production by macrophages. Induce cell death in tumors. Induce FEVER pathway. Down-regulate FEVER pathway. The alternate form TNF-β plays a much less significant role.
IL-10	Th2 cells	Stimulate B cells to produce antibody. Down-regulate FEVER pathway.

Adapted from http://pathmicro.med.sc.edu/mobile/m.immuno-13.htm, retrieved 15 April 2013.

and brain; the body's response to cytokine or cytokine antisera administration; and early studies on fever with transgenic models. The experimental evidence is from both translational animal and human studies.

Interleukin-1

There are two types of interleukin-1 (IL-1): alpha (α) and beta (β). Both types bind to the same receptor but differ in the site of action. IL-1β is thought to be the primary secreted form of IL-1. IL-1α is thought to remain cell-associated and IL-1β is found extracellular. The synthesis of IL-1 is controlled by a complex feedback loop. IL-1 is also capable of inhibiting or promoting its own synthesis, depending on conditions and the cell types (Endres, Van der Meer, & Dinarello, 1987). Some of the biological activities of IL-1 are mediated directly and some indirectly by the induction of the synthesis of other mediators including ACTH, prostaglandin E2 (PGE2), platelet factor-4 (PF4), cerebrospinal fluid (CSF), IL-6, and IL-8.

IL-1β and Psychological Stress

The hypothesis that IL-1α and IL-1β are indeed endogenous pyrogens and responsible for rise in temperature, can be tested. In addition to exogenous pyrogens such as LPS, psychological stress has been shown to cause a rapid increase in body temperature in both animals and humans (stress-induced fever; Long, Vander, Kunkel, & Kluger, 1990). Thus, a classical stress paradigm for the rat is exposing these animals to a novel environment. This paradigm causes the rat to increase its body temperature about 1.4 °C. It is assumed that fever caused by both LPS (Verhasselt, Buelens, Williems, De Groote, Haeffner-Cavaillon, & Goldman, 1997) and psychological stress is caused by the synthesis and release of endogenous pyrogens into circulation. To test the hypothesis that IL-1α and IL-1β are such pyrogens, we can pretreat with antibodies known to block the biological actions of these cytokines.

Long, Kluger, and Vander (1988) pretreated male Sprague Dawley rats with antiserum to murine IL-1α prior to exposure to a novel environment or to LPS (Verhasselt, Buelens, Williems, De Groote, Haeffner-Cavaillon et al., 1997) injection to determine whether the antibodies could block the subsequent rise in body temperature. In an initial experiment, rats injected with antiserum to murine IL-1α attenuated the fever caused by injected IL-1α. Following 30 min of exposure to a novel environment or injection of LPS, the mean rise in body temperature of the rats injected with antiserum against IL-1α did not differ significantly from the mean rise seen in the animals that received control serum prior to stress or injection of LPS. Additional studies by Long, Vander, et al. (1990) in which animals received pretreatment with antisera to IL-1β 3.5 days prior to LPS injection showed these animals had significantly lower fevers in response to injection of LPS than animals pretreated with control serum. These data support the hypothesis that circulating IL-1α is not responsible for the increase in body temperature caused by stress or LPS (Long et al., 1988). However, IL-1β does seem to play a role in LPS- and stress-induced febrile responses (Long, Otterness, Kunkel, Vander, & Kluger, 1990).

IL-1 and PGE₂

IL-1 may directly affect brain areas involved in regulation of body temperature and evidence comes from a study by Hori et al. (1988). Microelectrophoretic

(Breder, Dinarello, & Saper, 1988) application of human ultrapure IL-l in the preoptic anterior hypothalamus of rats resulted in a decreased firing activity of warm-sensitive neurons and an increase in firing activity of cold-sensitive neurons. These responses were blocked by sodium salicylate, a cyclooxygenase inhibitor (Hori et al., 1988). The major chemical from which the cyclooxygenase pathway (eicosanoid) is derived from is the fatty acid arachidonic acid, which is present in plasma-membrane phospholipids. Blockade of IL-l actions by sodium salicylate indicates that activity of cyclooxygenase on arachidonic acid is required for IL-l to alter the activity of the preoptic anterior hypothalamic thermosensitive neurons and provides evidence for the mechanism by which prostaglandins produce an upward resetting of thermostat in fever.

IL-1 and CRF

Although only a few functional differences between the IL-1 types have been described, only IL-1β appears to be expressed constitutively in the brain (Dascombe, Rothwell, Sagay, & Stock, 1980). Katsuura, Gottschall, Dahl, and Arimura (1988) reported that IL-1β induces release of ACTH by stimulating hypothalamic release of corticotropin-releasing factor (CRF). IL-lα, on the other hand, was virtually ineffective in stimulating CRF and ACTH release. By contrast, Tsagarakis, Gillies, Rees, Besser, and Grossman (1989) reported that IL-lα stimulated CRF release from incubated hypothalamic in vitro; however, the dose of IL-lα required was 10 times greater than that for IL-1β. Rothwell (1989) also reported that prior microinjection (intracerebroventricular [icv]) of an antagonist to CRF markedly inhibited increases in core temperature, oxygen consumption, white blood cell count, and brown adipose tissue activity produced by IL-1β. These findings also suggest that the pyrogenic actions of IL-1β may be dependent on central actions of CRF to increase temperature.

In summary, IL-1β induces fever caused by stress or infection (Long, Otterness, et al., 1990) in a variety of species. Data (Long et al., 1988) confirms that circulating IL-lα is not responsible for the increase in body temperature caused by stress or LPS. IL-1β may exert its pyrogenic actions through two pathways: PGE2 and CRF inducing ACTH. Inhibition of either PGE2 or CRF significantly attenuated the pyrogenic and thermogenic responses to IL-1β (Hori et al., 1988; Katsuura et al., 1988; Rothwell, 1989; Tsagarakis et al., 1989).

Tumor Necrosis Factor

TNF is an inflammatory cytokine produced by macrophages and exists in two forms: TNF-α and TNF-β. Both forms induce similar biological effects but TNF-α is thought to be the main cytokine responsible for regulating fever. TNF is both pyrogenic and antipyretic depending on the experimental condition.

TNF has been shown to be pyrogenic in a variety of species (Dinarello et al., 1986; Kettelhut & Goldberg, 1988). Doses as small as 1 μg/kg iv produced fevers in rabbits (Dinarello et al., 1986). The fever response to TNF was blocked or attenuated by prior treatment with ibuprofen, a cyclooxygenase inhibitor. It has also been speculated that TNF induces IL-1 (Dinarello, 1988b; Dinarello et al., 1986) and works synergistically to produce fever, wasting, and negative nitrogen balance seen in disease states (Dinarello et al., 1987; Dinarello, Conti, & Mier, 1986). Finally, TNF's role as a pyrogen may occur through the cyclooxygenase pathway by directly stimulating PGE2 or by IL-6, which ultimately leads to prostaglandin production (discussed in section on IL-6). Although TNF-α may be a pyrogen involved in the development of fever, it does not appear to account for the whole febrile response.

Although TNF-α can cause fever when injected into animals (Dinarello, Cannon, et al., 1986) or people (Michie et al., 1988), there is evidence that TNF's role in fever may be as an endogenous antipyretic that modulates the rise in body temperature observed in response to injection of LPS or the stress induced by exposure to a novel environment (Long, Kunkel, Vander, & Kluger, 1990; Long, Otterness, et al., 1990; Long, Vander, et al., 1990). Long, Otterness, et al. (1990) injected iv male Sprague Dawley rats with antiserum against TNF 3.5 days prior to intraperitoneal injection of LPS. The antiserum did not block the LPS-induced fever but instead significantly enhanced the fever response. Additional studies by Long, Vander, et al. (1990), where rats received antiserum against TNF followed by ip LPS injection 2 hr later, showed that antiserum treated animals' body temperatures, 3–8 hr post-LPS injection, increased 56% higher than control-treated animals. Further evidence that endogenously produced TNF may have antipyretic properties is shown in the stress paradigm where animals increase their body temperature when exposed to a novel environment (Long, Vander, et al., 1990). Long, Vander, et al. (1990) exposed male rats to an open field or simply switched the cages of rats 3.5 days after treatment with antiserum against TNF. Animals exposed to both stress paradigms had significantly higher temperatures than control serum-treated animals. Thus, treatment with anti-TNF enhanced stress hyperthermia in rats exposed to two different stress paradigms suggesting that endogenously produced TNF is involved in limiting the magnitude of this response. Further evidence that TNF has antipyretic properties during LPS-induced fevers was shown when animals pretreated with anti-TNF had significantly larger fevers than control serum-treated animals.

In lieu of the recent evidence of TNF's antipyretic properties, it is speculated that endogenously produced TNF in the rat may participate in a negative feedback mechanism to limit the magnitude of the fever response. Further data obtained by Leon, Kozak, Peschon, and Kluger (1997) using TNF knockout mice

(mice lacking TNF receptors) support the hypothesis that TNF function as an endogenous antipyretic and has little role in fever. When injected with LPS, TNF knockout mice had higher fevers with decreased plasma levels of endogenous IL-10. These data support the hypothesis that the mechanism of TNF's ability to cause antipyresis during LPS fever is mediated by endogenous IL-10 (Leon et al., 1997; Leon, Kozak, Rudolph, & Kluger, 1999).

In summary, TNF-α works synergistically to produce fever. However, TNF-α primarily appears to modulate fevers by mechanisms yet unknown.

Interferon

Based on clinical trials with interferon, fever is a consistent side effect in both humans and animals. There are three types of interferon—alpha (α), beta (β), and gamma (γ)—and the interferon implicated in the febrile state is IFN-γ. IFN-γ is a cytokine produced by T-helper and natural killer cells. IL-1 released by activated macrophages triggers the release of IL-2 and the latter activates the T-lymphocytes into production of immune IFN-γ. Blocking of the IL-2 receptor by specific antibodies also inhibits the synthesis of IFN-γ (Ye, Ortaldo, Conlon, Winkler-Pickett, & Young, 1995). IFN-γ dampens viral replication more than the other interferons, and also enhances macrophage activity against bacterial pathogens (Schroder, Hertzog, Ravasi, & Hume, 2004).

However, the main biological activity of IFN-γ is to be immune modulatory (see Table 2.1). IFN-γ is a modulator of T-cell growth and functional differentiation. It is a growth-promoting factor for T-lymphocytes and potentiates the response of these cells to mitogens or growth factors. These functions are possible because IFN-γ acts synergistically with IL-1 and IL-2 and is required for the expression of IL-2 receptors on the cell surface of activated T-lymphocytes (Schroder et al., 2004). IFN-γ thus influences cell-mediated mechanisms of cytotoxicity.

Interleukin-6

Produced by various cells during infection, trauma, and immunological challenges, the precise physiologic role of IL-6 remains largely unknown. Recent data indicate that IL-6 may have a role in inflammatory responses (Jones, Horiuchi, Topley, Yamamoto, & Fuller, 2001). IL-6 can induce fever in animals, and is present in elevated levels in various biologic fluids from patients with arthritis, septic shock, infectious diseases, kidney transplants, and burns (Aarden, DeGroot, Schaap, & Landsdorp, 1987; De Jongh, Vissers, Booij, De Jongh, Vincken, & Meert, 2003; Nijsten et al., 1987; Wong & Clark, 1988).

Even more convincing data that centrally produced IL-6 is involved in LPS-induced fever, comes from the study by LeMay, Vander, and Kluger (1990a), who showed that after icv injection of fever-producing doses of LPS, levels of IL-6 in plasma and CSF rose significantly in male Sprague Dawley rats. LeMay et al. (1990b) also reported that IL-6 caused a significant rise in core temperature that was blocked by the cyclooxygenase inhibitor indomethacin. However, the same dose of IL-6 given iv or intraperitoneal (ip) had no effect on body temperature.

Further studies by LeMay et al. (1990a, 1990b) showed that psychological stress significantly increased the plasma concentration of IL-6 in male rats (LeMay et al., 1990a, 1990b). Although both core temperature and IL-6 levels increased in these animals exposed to open field stress, LeMay et al. (1990a) reported that the plasma levels of IL-6 are not high enough to account for the stress-induced rise in temperature. This report is based on the previous study (LeMay et al., 1990a) where plasma IL-6 levels were measured 1 and 2 hr after ip injection of IL-6. The values of IL-6 were similar to the levels found in the previous study (LeMay et al., 1990a) and in which the plasma concentrations of IL-6 did not result in a significant rise in body temperature. Works by others confirm these findings (Jablons et al., 1989; Klir, McClellan, & Kluger, 1994; Klir, Roth, Szelenyi, McClellan, & Kluger, 1993; Shalaby, Waage, Aarden, & Espevik, 1989).

IL-6 has emerged as one of the major mediators of communication among cells inside and outside the immune system (Marx, 1988a; Xin & Blatteis, 1992). IL-6 appears to be the key member of this network because of its ability to interact with many target cells (see Table 2.1; Geiger et al., 1988; Marx, 1988b).

In summary, data support the hypothesis that IL-6 is capable of causing fever, is dose dependent, and that the pathway is likely to involve the production of PGE2. In addition, IL-6 interacts with many target cells to promote nonspecific immune reponses (see Table 2.1).

CYTOKINES-INDUCED ACUTE PHASE CHANGES

As discussed, during infection, *exogenous* pyrogens such as bacterial endotoxin or LPS are thought to stimulate macrophages and monocytes to release *inflammatory* cytokines into the circulation. IL-1 and IL-6 result in hepatic acute phase actions (Atkins, 1960; Girardin, Grau, Dayer, Roux-Lombard, & Lambert, 1988; Morimoto, Murakami, Nakamori, & Watanabe, 1988).

Several acute phase changes such as fever, hypercortisolemia, and hypoferremia are thought to provide a systemic environment appropriate for the requirements of coping with significant injury or infection (Khan & Khan, 2010; Kushner & Rzewnicki, 1994). Various investigators have concluded that other changes associated with infection—neutrophilia, increased glycoprotein release, and decreased plasma iron and zinc levels, as well as symptoms such as loss of appetite, reduced activity and energy expenditure, and increased sleep time—are the result of the same mediators that are also responsible for fever

(Dinarello, 1988a; Kluger, 1991a, 1991b; Sakata, Morimoto, Long, & Murakami, 1991). These responses are called acute phase responses (APR), and they are often observed within hours following injury or infection. The assumption that the APR is physiologically useful to the host is largely based on the known functional capabilities of many of the acute phase proteins (Gabay & Kushner, 2001; Kushner & Rzewnicki, 1994).

Acute phase proteins help contain pathogens and their toxins and inactivate microbial proteases and highly reactive oxygen metabolites. However, the serum availability of these proteins varies during infection and inflammation (Dao, Bell, Feng, Jameson, & Lipton, 1988; Dinarello et al., 1988; Sobrado, Moldawer, Bistrian, Dinarello, & Blackburn, 1983; Stahl, 1987). Hepatic acute phase proteins help break down damaged tissue, help local inflammatory cells resist infection, and prepare for rebuilding and healing by scar formation (Stahl, 1987).

The two major acute phase proteins influencing inflammatory and tissue repair processes are C-reactive protein (CRP) and serum amyloid-A. Physiologically, CRP binds with phosphocholine and recognizes some foreign pathogens as well as phospholipid constituents of damaged or necrotic cells. CRP is also known to induce production of inflammatory cytokines, IL-1β, IL-6, and TNF-α, by monocytes (Gabay & Kushner, 1999). Serum amyloid-A has been shown to induce adhesion and chemotaxis in phagocytic cells and lymphocytes. Fibrinogen is another acute phase protein and is critical to tissue repair. In addition to its participation in the clotting process, fibrinogen can lead to endothelial cell adhesion, spreading, and proliferation (Gabay & Kushner, 1999).

Cytokines, Blood Brain Barrier, and Fever

Cytokines are produced peripherally by macrophages and T-lymphocytes as well as centrally by microglial and astrocyte cells. Several hypotheses exist about how peripheral cytokines can affect the central nervous system (CNS). These theories include the following: (a) peripheral cytokines act at a central site where the blood–brain barrier (BBB) is absent; (b) that they induce PGE2 production; (c) that there is a carrier-mediated transport into the brain; and (d) that they mediate induction of central cytokines (Conti, Tabarean, Andrei, & Bartfai, 2004). All of these mechanisms are likely in effect but their relative contribution is likely different, that is, the carrier-mediated transport system is easily saturated. In this review, we examine the BBB and PGE2 hypotheses in more detail.

Blood Brain Barrier

The organum vasculosum of lamina terminalis (OVLT) is part of the anteroventral third ventricle region (AV3V). It is located on the midline, in the center of the medial preoptic area. It differs from other brain tissue by having fenestrated endothelium rather than typical tight junctions between the endothelial cells. This feature indicates a lack of the BBB and thus, the permeability to proteins and peptides is similar to that seen in nonneural tissue. Blatteis, Hales, McKinney, & Fawcett (1987) discovered the existence of fever-depressing and fever-enhancing regions within the AV3V in sheep. Different portions of the AV3V were ablated and the fever response was examined. Ablation of the AV3V and of substantial amounts of the periventricular tissue surrounding it had no obvious effect on the animals' capacity to develop fever in response to a systemic pyrogen unless the base of the AV3V was included in the damage. The base of the AV3V contained a plexus of blood vessels exhibiting fenestrated endothelial cells and extensive perivascular spaces. Because the more dorsal parts of the AV3V in sheep are largely avascular, it would appear that the integrity of the vascular region is critical for the normal development of fever. In this species, this evidence prompted the hypothesis that the OVLT may be the site through which endogenous pyrogens gain entry into the brain. Additional findings of this study suggest that the integrity of the preoptic area of anterior hypothalamus (POAH) is not essential for fever production, and that endogenous pyrogen may act elsewhere in the brain besides the POAH to drive the febrile mechanisms (Blatteis et al., 1987; Fontana, Weber, & Dayer, 1984).

Cytokines and the Prostaglandin (PGE2) Pathway

The inflammatory cytokines (IL-1β, IL-6, and TNF-α) also trigger the elevation in set-point, which produces fever by inducing synthesis of PGE2 via the cyclooxygenase pathway in the endothelial cells in the CNS (Coceani, Bishai, Dinarello, & Fitzpatrick, 1983; Coceani, Bishai, Lees, & Sirko, 1987; Conti et al., 2004; Kluger, 1979, 1989, 1991b; Stitt, 1973, 1986). PGE2, a principal mediator of the cytokine-mediated APR, directly stimulates the activity of neural pathways in the POAH that activates heat production thermoeffectors and suppresses heat-dissipating thermoeffectors, leading to a regulated elevation in core temperature (fever). There are many areas in the brain that are sensitive to PGE2. Among these are the POAH and the ventromedial hypothalamus (Hori et al., 1988; Morimoto, Nakamori, Watanabe, Ono, & Mukakami, 1988).

In studies on the pathogenesis of fever, effects of bacterial LPS injected peripherally or centrally have been examined as an experimental model of fever (Dao et al., 1988; Morimoto, Murakami, et al., 1988). Coceani et al. (1987) reexamined the involvement of prostaglandins in fever production. Initial work by Coceani et al. (1983) showed that in the absence of fever, PGE2 is close to undetectable in ventricular CSF (less than 100 pg/ml) identified as the OVLT (Coceani et al., 1987). More recently, McCarthy and Daun (1993) examined the effects of cyclooxygenase inhibitors on tumor size and tumor-induced anorexia in a rat model. PGE2 inhibitors slowed tumor growth by up to 40% and lowered body temperature compared to control animals but had no effect on food intake or body weight (McCarthy & Daun, 1993). In summary, the PGE2 pathway remains firmly established as mediator of fever.

Hypothalamus and Effector Mechanisms

Inflammatory cytokines, IL-1β, IL-6, and TNF-α, mediate the increase in central PGE2 and CRF production that cause the hypothalamus to increase the temperature set-point and cause fever. In addition, hypothalamic neurons can be directly affected by inflammatory cytokines to also increase the temperature set-point (Vasilenko, Petruchuk, Gourine, & Pierau, 2000). This increase in set-point ultimately orchestrates heat effector mechanisms via the autonomic nervous system to increase heat production, that is, increase muscle tone, shivering, vasoconstriction, and tachycardia.

ENDOGENOUS CORTICOTROPIN RELEASING FACTOR AND FEVER

The production of CRF is another pathway for thermoregulatory reset leading to fever. However, because CRF causes an increase in ACTH, it is also involved in downregulation of temperature as discussed in a latter section. IL-1β and IL-6 are key mediators in the APR and stimulate hypothalamic CRF release (Busbridge & Grossman, 1991; Gabay & Kushner, 1999). IL-1β and IL-6 have been shown to directly stimulate the release of CRF from rat hypothalamus cultures, a process that was blocked by cyclooxygenase inhibitors (Busbridge, Dascombe, Tilders, van Oers, Linton, & Rothwell, 1989). In these studies, TNF-α, interferon, IL-2, and IL-8 had no effect on CRF release; and neither IL-1β nor IL-6 had a direct effect on ACTH release, suggesting that the ACTH responses to cytokines in in vivo studies may be secondary to CRF stimulation.

Blocking the biological actions of CRF within the CNS of the rat by central injection of a CRF antagonist or a neutralizing antibody to CRF significantly attenuates the hypothalamic-pituitary-adrenal (HPA) axis pyrogenic response to central injections of IL-1β and IL-6 (Rothwell, 1989; Rothwell, Busbridge, Lefeuvre, Hardwick, Gauldie, & Hopkins, 1991) and reduces the fever evoked by CRF (Figueiredo et al., 2010).

Endogenous Antipyretics

Cryogens are endogenous antipyretics and include IL-10, arginine vasopressin, α-melanocyte-stimulating hormone (α-MSH), glucocorticoids induced by CRF/ACTH pathway, and TNF-α. All of these cryogens work to limit the magnitude and duration of fever (Jenkins, Malyak, & Arend, 1994; Tatro, 2000). We have discussed the origin and role of CRF and TNF-α in previous sections. Depending on the experimental condition, TNF-α is also emerging as an antipyretic and has been used successfully in modulating LPS-induced febrile response as well as the rise in body temperature observed as a result of exposure to a novel environment. However, both TNF-α and CRF are also known to increase body temperature when injected into animals (Dinarello et al., 1986; Kettelhut & Goldberg, 1988; Morimoto, Nakamori, Morimoto, Tan, & Murakami, 1993; Rothwell, 1989; Strijbos, Hardwick, Relton, Carey, & Rothwell, 1992).

CRF exerts its anti-inflammatory or antipyretic effects via ACTH and thereby glucocorticoids. LPS-induced fever and fever induced by psychological stress (open field exposure) are modulated by endogenous glucocorticoids. When animals are pretreated with deoxycorticosterone acetate prior to LPS injection or exposure to open field, they show significantly reduced fevers. When animals are pretreated with anti-CRF prior to IL-1 injection, they also have a marked reduction in the febrile response. This provides evidence that CRF is involved in the pyrogenic pathway of IL-1 fevers, that is, limiting the febrile response.

α-MSH and arginine vasopressin are also endogenous antipyretics that modulate the febrile response in the CNS (Bell & Lipton, 1987). Both neuropeptides are released from the septum and have marked antipyretic action during fever. IL-10 is a protein product of T-helper 2 (Th2) subset cells that was originally described as a cytokine synthesis inhibitory factor. IL-10 inhibits LPS-induced synthesis and production of proinflammatory cytokines (Fiorentino, Zlotnik, Mosmann, Howard, & O'Garra, 1991; Harden, Rummel, Lusheshi, Poole, Gerstberger, & Roth, 2013), including IL-1β, IL-6, TNF, and IL-8 following in vitro activation of monocytes by bacterial LPS (Netea, Kullberg, & Van der Meer, 2000).

Pharmacologically, IL-10 functions as an antipyretic. Endogenously, IL-10 functions as an immunosuppressant by inhibiting the Th1 response through the reduction of Th1 cytokine secretion and the blockade of antigen presenting cell function. In rats, the central injection of IL-10 inhibits inflammatory febrile response to a peripheral injection of LPS (Nava et al., 1997). Similarly, pretreatment of mice with an intraperitoneal injection of IL-10 significantly attenuates inflammatory febrile responses to both a low and high dose of LPS. Injecting IL-10 into IL-10 knockout mice leads to exacerbated inflammatory fevers lasting more than 2 days (Leon et al., 1999). Enhanced plasma levels of IL-6 was found in the knockout mice at 4 hr postinjection (Leon et al., 1999), correlating with the exacerbated inflammatory fever response at the 4-hr time point whereas the second day inflammatory fever did not correlate with changes in plasma IL-6 levels. These data support the hypothesis that IL-10 has endogenous anti-inflammatory/antipyretic action during bacterial LPS-induced inflammatory fever response because of IL-10's ability to inhibit the production of endogenous IL-6 (Leon, 2002; Leon et al., 1999).

THE ADAPTIVE VALUE OF FEVER

Because the presence of fever is associated with illness, it was commonly believed that lowering fever with antipyretic drugs helps return the patient to health. However, substantial evidence suggests that fever and hypoferremia— components of the APR—are important for fighting infection (Kluger & Rothenberg, 1979). There are current programs of research that continue to investigate the hypothesis that fever is deleterious (Liu et al., 2012). However, substantial evidence suggests that moderate increases in body temperature augment various aspects of the immune response (Kluger, Ringler & Anver, 1975; Mackowiak et al., 1997; Roberts, 1991). These responses include (a) increased mobility and activity of neutrophils, (b) increased production and activity of interferon, and (c) a stimulatory effect of IL-1 on T-lymphocytes and thus an increase in T-cell proliferation. Lastly, a febrile temperature, coupled with the decrease in plasma iron concentration that occurs during infection, slows the rate of bacterial growth. This protective mechanism may be caused by the reduced capability of some species of bacteria to synthesize the necessary iron-chelating proteins at febrile temperatures, making them unable to obtain sufficient iron for growth (Kluger & Rothenberg, 1979; Mackowiak et al., 1997).

An in vitro study by Kluger and Rothenberg (1979) found that incubating bacteria in normal media at febrile temperatures or in iron-deficient media at normal temperatures did not inhibit bacterial growth. However, the combination of febrile temperatures and iron-deficient media significantly slowed bacterial growth rates, suggesting that an increase in temperature in combination with a decrease in iron may provide the host with some protection against invading pathogens (Murray & Murray, 1979).

ACUTE EXERCISE CAUSES A CHANGE IN CORE
TEMPERATURE SET-POINT

Exercise produces an elevated core temperature that persists for days after exercise ceases (Rowsey, Metzger, Carlson, & Gordon, 2009). Experimental data support that this induction of core temperature increase parallels all the hallmarks of a fever including cytokine production, acute phase protein synthesis and release, and PGE_2 and HPA axis pathway activation (Rowsey & Kluger, 1994).

The hypothesis that exercise induces fever is supported by several studies (Bosenberg, Brock-Utne, Gaffin, Wells, & Blake, 1985; Jeukendrup et al., 2000; Kenny, Proulx, Denis, & Giesbrecht, 2000) showing that moderate to intense exercise causes the release of cytokines capable of inducing fever. Human plasma, collected after 1 hr of exercise on a bicycle ergometer, was injected into rats and caused significant elevations of body temperature in these animals

(Cannon & Kluger, 1983). Monocytes isolated from the blood of these exercising subjects were already activated to produce IL-1. Cannon et al. (1986) further characterized IL-1 activity in human plasma following exercise on a cycle ergometer. This activity appeared in the plasma several hours following exercise and was neutralized with antiserum to IL-1. Taylor et al. (1987) also found that strenuous athletics activities induced an acute phase reaction as determined by a decrease in serum iron concentration and an increase in CRP.

Even more convincing evidence that exercise can result in an elevation in thermoregulatory set-point comes from studies with the poikilotherm, desert iguana, which controls body temperature by behavioral rather than thermoregulatory adjustments (Bernheim & Kluger, 1976). After treadmill exercise, the desert iguana selected a warmer thermal environment which is the equivalent of a fever in humans. Sodium salicylate, a cyclooxygenase inhibitor, impedes the production of PGE2. The administration of sodium salicylate immediately before exercise eliminated the rise in postexercise body temperature preference in the desert iguana, and actually caused a suppression of body temperature for at least three hours following exercise (Cannon & Kluger, 1985). Studies in humans replicate this animal model. Administering COX_2 inhibitors lowered core and mean body temperature during exercise and ensuing recovery (Bradford, Cotter, Thorburn, Walker, & Gerrard, 2007). These studies provide further suggestive evidence that a change in central thermoregulatory drive can occur during exercise.

The activation of the HPA axis may play an autoprotective role for the host from its own defense mechanisms. If such direct effects occur, via cytokines stimulating the HPA axis, these actions could be significant during prolonged immune stimulation such as exercise.

This author's dissertation work involved administering a monoclonal antibody to CRF to animals who were exercise trained (long-term exercise conditioning). A dose of antibody that had been shown to significantly attenuate the fever response of IL-1β was injected icv. Injection of anti-CRF had no effect on the body temperature of sedentary animals. However, when anti-CRF was given to exercising animals, the animals showed a significantly attenuated daytime body temperature 1 day postinjection. Injection of placebo had no effect on the body temperature of sedentary or exercising animals. Based on these data, it was concluded that as a result of long-term exercise conditioning, exercising animals displayed an elevation in daytime body temperature mediated through the HPA axis (increased secretion of CRF; Rowsey & Kluger, 1994).

The Role of Conditioning From Long-Term Exercise

Long-term (regular) exercise promotes a decrease in inflammatory cytokines (IL-1, IL-6, IFN-γ, and TNF-α) and an increase in IL-10 (Rowsey et al., 2009).

Regular exercise has also been shown to improve immune responses. In addition to measuring levels of cytokines in those who undergo regular exercise, tissues and cell populations are being studied to determine mechanisms by which the activity promotes a decrease in inflammation. Two such tissues are skeletal muscle (Cannon & St. Pierre, 1998) and white adipose tissue (WAT; Di Fenza & Fiorina, 2012).

Skeletal muscle secretes IL-6. Cannon and St. Pierre (1998) give an elegant exposition of the actions of cytokines, including IL-6 in acute skeletal muscle injury. In acute exercise, the secretion of IL-6 is correlated with force of the exercise and then returns to normal postexercise. However, in those who regularly exercise, baseline levels of IL-6 are lower than the level for inactive individuals (Pedersen, Akerstrom, Nielsen, & Fischer, 2007; Esposito et al., 2003).

Adipose tissue is also considered an endocrine organ. Increased adiposity initiates a plethora of disorders that involve cardiovascular, renal, metabolic, and inflammatory responses (Hall, 2000), and increased adiposity appears to be a key cause of primary hypertension (El-Atat, Aneja, Mcfarlane, & Sowers, 2003). Experimental studies have shown that cells in adipose tissue produce proteins called adipocytokines that participate in inflammatory processes (Lyon, Law, & Hsueh, 2003). Increased adiposity leads to an overproduction of these proteins, and this increased production of the inflammatory proteins appears to be directly related to cardiovascular disease (CVD) and hypertension (Lyon et al., 2003), although the pathways from inflammation to chronic disease have not been fully delineated (Trayhurn & Beattie, 2001).

According to the American Heart Association and the Centers for Disease Control and Prevention, "Virtually every step in atherogenesis is believed to involve cytokines and cells characteristic of inflammation" (Pearson et al., 2003, p. 500). WAT is a major endocrine and secretory organ that interacts with other organs to provide physiological and metabolic control, including the production of key hormones involved in energy balance (Trayhurn, 2005). WAT releases a number of proteins called adipokines or adipocytokines (Trayhurn, 2005), including adiponectin, TNF-α, IL-1β, IL-6, IL-8, IL-10, IL-18, vascular endothelial growth factor (VEGF), plasminogen activator inhibitor-1 (PAI-1), and haptaglobin (Trayhurn & Wood, 2004).

Adipocytokines are highly diverse in their physiological functions, but many are linked to the immune system. These proteins are also thought to be directly linked to pathologies associated with obesity, particularly the metabolic syndrome, which includes atherosclerosis, hyperlipidemia, and hypertension (Elenkov, Iezzoni, Daly, Harris, & Chrousos, 2005; Trayhurn, 2005). It is thought that circulating levels of inflammatory cytokines (TNF-α, IL-6, and IL-18) and acute phase proteins (CRP and haptoglobin) are chronically elevated in the obese and play a role in the development of the disorders of the meta-bolic syndrome (Bullo, Gracia-Lorda, Megias, & Salas-Salvadó, 2003; Engstrom et al., 2003; Festa et al., 2001; Yudkin, Yajnik, Mohamed-Ali, & Bulmer, 1999). That is, although most of these proteins are normal components of the immune response, in conditions of increased adiposity, they are thought to contribute to a chronic inflammatory milieu (Lyon et al., 2003; Trayhurn, 2005) that may lead to endothelial dysfunction and ultimately hypertension.

Macrophages residing in adipose tissue may be responsible for adipokine production, and visceral fat is a more aggressive producer of inflammatory cyto-kines than other fat deposits. Bruun, Helge, Richelsen, and Stallknecht (2006) placed morbidly obese subjects on a 15-week intervention program that consisted of a hypocaloric diet combined with intense exercise. The combination of diet and exercise reduced macrophage infiltration into adipose tissue. Plasma CRP and adiponectin levels significantly declined, whereas IL-6 and TNF-α levels sig-nificantly increased. These changes were paralleled by a significant improvement in metabolic status. In vitro studies have shown that adiponectin decreases pro-inflammatory TNF-α and increases anti-inflammatory cytokines such as IL-10 and IL-1 receptor antagonist (IL-1ra). These findings lead to a possible explana-tion for the weight loss reduction in overall adiposity and attenuation of chronic inflammation seen in these subjects (Brunn et al., 2006).

TNF-α was the first adipocytokine to be linked to disorders of the meta-bolic syndrome (Hotamisligil, 2000; Moller, 2000). TNF-α is overexpressed in WAT in the obese but decreases with weight loss. Antibodies to TNF-α given to obese rodents will ameliorate insulin sensitivity and protect TNF-α-deficient mice placed on a high-fat diet from obesity-induced insulin resistance (Ruan, Hacohen, Golub, Van Parijs, & Lodish, 2002).

In humans, subcutaneous WAT also produces substantial amounts of IL-6 (Bastard et al., 2002), and the amount of IL-6 is highly correlated with body mass and inversely related to insulin sensitivity (Bastard et al., 2000). Recent data sug-gest that IL-6 induces cellular insulin resistance via hepatocytes (Senn, Klover, Nowak, & Mooney, 2002). Paradoxically, IL-6-deficient mice develop maturity onset obesity that is partly reversed by IL-6 replacement given icv but not by IL-6 given ip (Wallenius et al., 2002). In other words, IL-6 in the CNS appears to exert an antiobesity effect in rodents, whereas peripheral administration of IL-6 has no effect on obesity. An intervention that would increase IL-6 accessibility to the CNS could thus be used to treat obesity and ultimately hypertension.

In addition, adipose tissue secretes several inflammatory molecules, specif-ically IL-6 and TNF-α, and adipose tissue is infiltrated with macrophages, which may be the major source of locally produced adipocytokines (Bastard et al., 2006). Although obesity is associated with a sustained inflammatory response, weight loss is associated with a reduction in macrophage infiltration in adipose tissue and reduced production of adipocytokines (Bastard et al., 2006).

Also, although many adipocytokines are proinflammatory, some have counter regulatory anti-inflammatory actions, especially in the presence of exercise (Petersen & Pedersen, 2005). For example, the anti-inflammatory effects of IL-6 are demonstrated by the fact that IL-6 stimulates the production of IL-1ra and IL-10, and IL-1ra and IL-10 in the circulation after exercise have anti-inflammatory effects. Furthermore, IL-6 is the primary inducer of hepatic acute phase proteins, which also have anti-inflammatory properties. In summary, it appears that obesity is associated with a stress-induced low-grade inflammatory response resulting from chronic activation of the immune system. This sustained inflammatory response can lead to chronic conditions like CVD (Pedersen, 2006). However, further investigation is needed to gain insights into the influence of chronic stress on obesity and on the development of a chronic inflammatory response, and to examine the influence of chronic exercise training on the stress-obesity-induced inflammatory response.

Impact of Exercise Conditioning on Cardiovascular Disease

The cytokine response to exercise differs from the response associated with CVD. The chronic low-grade inflammatory response associated with the pathogenesis of CVD appears to be primarily modulated by proinflammatory cytokines, whereas regular exercise induces an increase in cytokines with anti-inflammatory properties (Pedersen, 2000; Petersen & Pedersen, 2005).

In earlier studies, these cytokines were linked to muscle damage (Ostrowski, Rohde, Zacho, Asp, & Pedersen, 1998); but more recent studies have shown that IL-6 is produced in muscle without causing muscle damage (Pedersen, 2000). IL-6 is known to have growth factor abilities and thus may mediate exercise-induced metabolic changes by maintaining glucose homeostasis and mediating exercise-induced lipolysis (Petersen & Pedersen, 2005). Muscle-derived IL-6 may also work to inhibit the proinflammatory cytokine TNF-α, which is known to play a pathogenic role in insulin resistance and CVD. Northoff and Berg (1991) were the first to suggest a relationship between increased IL-6 levels and the APR of the liver and local inflammatory cells after exercise. They found that IL-6 levels were increased immediately after a marathon race. According to Gabay and Kushner (1999), the APR is a "complex, highly orchestrated process" that stimulates the production of hepatic acute phase proteins (CRP, plasminogen activation inhibitor-1, and serum amyloid-A) and cytokines, particularly IL-1, IL-6, IL-8, and TNF-α (Gruys, Toussaint, Niewold, & Koopmans, 2005). The APR induced by exercise has some similarities to the APR to infection (Cannon & Kluger, 1983), suggesting that exercise induces an APR. In Cannon and Kluger's (1983) study, plasma obtained from human subjects after exercise on a bicycle ergometer was injected into rats and caused the rats to have an elevated temperature. Plasma obtained prior to exercise failed to produce this response, suggesting that an endogenous pyrogen was released during exercise.

Other studies have shown that several cytokines can be detected in plasma during and after exercise (Ostrowski et al., 1998, 1999). For example, in one study, TNF-α and IL-1β levels increased twofold immediately after a marathon race (Ostrowski et al., 1998), whereas IL-6 increased100-fold (Ostrowski et al., 1999). The release in IL-6 was balanced by the release of cytokine inhibitors (IL-1ra and TNF receptors) and the anti-inflammatory cytokine IL-10. In our animal model study, after 8 weeks of running on wheels, we found that the pro-inflammatory cytokine IL-6 was suppressed in rats (Rowsey, Metzger, Carlson, & Gordon, 2006). Plasma IL-10 activity was also suppressed by exercise, whereas plasma TNF-α activity was identical in runners and sedentary animals.

Further evidence that exercise may have an inhibitory effect on the pro-inflammatory cytokine system was seen in a multidisciplinary study with obese premenopausal women. The investigators used a diet and exercise intervention to reduce the body weight of the women and looked at whether sustained reduction in body weight decreased markers of systemic inflammation. After 2 years, the women's body weight was reduced by 10% or more, and circulating levels of the inflammatory cytokines IL-6 and IL-18 and the acute phase protein CRP were also reduced (Esposito & Giugliano, 2006). Thus, this study showed that consistent daily exercise not only assists with weight reduction but also improves cardiovascular risk factors by reducing the inflammatory response associated with increased weight.

Cytokine releases during acute exercise may mirror the levels and types observed during the APR (Petersen & Pedersen, 2005; Weinstock et al., 1997). Yet, although exercise produces proinflammatory changes similar to those observed during the APR (Cannon et al., 1986; Cannon & Kluger, 1983; Evans et al., 1986; Pedersen, 2000), there is mounting evidence that individuals who are physically active on a regular basis (conditioned) show a reduction in the biomarkers generally associated with chronic inflammation. In fact, a high level of exercise or long-term exercise conditioning appears to have an anti-inflammatory influence (Flynn, McFarlin, & Markofski, 2007). Recent research also has shown that IL-6 released from muscle during exercise actually has anti-inflammatory properties because it increases the release of IL-10 and IL-1ra (Steensberg et al., 2002). This proposed biological mechanism of exercise condition is that elevation of IL-6, as a direct product of exercise, "shuts off" or dampens the inflammatory response induced by WAT. A negative a feedback mechanism is introduced through the anti-inflammatory cytokines IL-1ra and IL-10. Furthermore, there is inhibition of the inflammatory cytokine TNF-α. Finally, it may act as a counter-regulator of the obesity-induced chronic inflammatory response. This could explain the therapeutic effect of exercise conditioning on chronic CVD and provide foundational knowledge for developing individual exercise prescriptions and evaluating their efficacy.

In summary, our knowledge of cytokines with resultant inflammation and thermoregulation has provided an important framework for understanding both acute and regular exercise. Much of this important work has been done by nurse scientist (McCarthy, 2000; Rowsey, 1997; Rowsey et al., 2009; St. Pierre Schneider, 2008). Further studies are needed to understand the effect of exercise on conditions of low-grade inflammation. A more thorough comprehension of the mechanisms and molecular basis will allow us to establish the optimal exercise protocols to promote and restore health.

ACKNOWLEDGMENTS

I would like to thank Dr. Patricia Byrns who assisted me with editing numerous drafts of this manuscript. A special note of thanks to Dr. Marilyn Oermann for her encouragement to write this manuscript and her willingness to provide editorial comments.

REFERENCES

Aarden, L. A., DeGroot, E. R., Schaap, O. L., & Landsdorp, P. M. (1987). Production of hybridoma growth factor by human monocytes. *European Journal of Immunology, 17*, 1411–1416.

Ahokas, R. A., Seydoux, J., Llanos, Q. J., Mashburn, T. A., & Blatteis, C. M. (1985). Hypothalamic opioids and the acute-phase glycoprotein response in guinea pigs. *Brain Research Bulletin, 15*, 603–608.

Atkins, E. (1960). Pathogenesis of fever. *Physiological Reviews, 40*, 580–645.

Atkins, E. (1982). Fever: Its history, cause, and function. *Yale Journal of Biology and Medicine, 55*, 283–289.

Atkins, E. (1988). On new concepts on the pathogenesis of fever (editorial). *Reviews Infectious Disease, 10*, 190.

Bastard, J. P., Jardel, C., Bruckert, E., Blondy, P., Capeau, J., Laville, M., . . . Hainque, B. (2000). Elevated levels of interleukin 6 are reduced in serum and subcutaneous adipose tissue of obese woman after weight loss. *The Journal of Clinical Endocrinology and Metabolism, 85*(9), 3338–3342.

Bastard, J. P., Maachi, M., Lagathu, C., Kim, M. J., Caron, M., Vidal, H., . . . Feve, B. (2006). Recent advances in the relationship between obesity, inflammation, and insulin resistance. *European Cytokine Network, 17*(1), 4–12.

Bastard, J. P., Maachi, M., Tran Van Nhieu, J., Jardel, C., Bruckert, E., Grimaldi, A., . . . Hainque, B. (2002). Adipose tissue IL-6 content correlates with resistance to insulin activation of glucose uptake both in vivo and in vitro. *The Journal of Clinical Endocrinology and Metabolism, 87*, 2084–2089.

Bell, R. C., & Lipton, J. M. (1987). Pulsatile release of antipyretic neuropeptide alpha-MSH from septum of rabbit during fever. *American Journal of Physiology, 252*, R1152–R1157.

Bendtzen, K., Baek, L., Berild, D., Dinarello, C. A., & Wolff, S. M. (1984). Demonstration of circulating leukocytic pyrogen/interleukin-1 during fever. *New England Journal of Medicine*, *310*, 596.

Bernheim, H. A., & Kluger, M. J. (1976). Fever: Effect of drug-induced antipyresis on survival. *Science*, *193*, 237–239.

Blatteis, C. M., Hales, J. R. S., McKinney, M. J., & Fawcett, A. A. (1987). Role of the anteroventral third ventricle region in fever in sheep. *Canadian Journal of Physiology and Pharmacology*, *65*, 1255–1260.

Bosenberg, A. T., Brock-Utne, J. G., Gaffin, S. L., Wells, M. T. B., & Blake, G. T. W. (1988). Strenuous exercise causes systemic endotoxemia. *Journal of Applied Physiology*, *65*, 106–108.

Bradford, C. D., Cotter, J. D., Thorburn, M. S., Walker, R. J., & Gerrard, D. F. (2007). Exercise can be pyrogenic in humans. *American Journal of Physiology: Regulatory, Integrative and Comparative Physiology*, *292*(1), R143–R149.

Breder, C. D., Dinarello, C. A., & Saper, C. B. (1988). Interleukin-1 immunoreactive innervation of the human hypothalamus. *Science*, *240*, 321–324.

Bruun, J. M., Helge, J. W., Richelsen, B., & Stallknecht, B. (2006). Diet and exercise reduce low-grade inflammation and macrophage infiltration in adipose tissue but not in skeletal muscle in severely obese subjects. *American Journal of Physiology. Endocrinology and Metabolism*, *290*, E961–E967.

Bullo, M., Garcia-Lorda, P., Megias, I., & Salas-Salvadó, J. (2003). Systemic inflammation, adipose tissue tumor necrosis factor, and leptin expression. *Obesity Research*, *11*, 525–531.

Busbridge, N. J., Dascombe, M. J., Tilders, F. J. H., van Oers, J. W. A. M., Linton, E. A., & Rothwell, N. J. (1989). Central activation of thermogenesis and fever by interleukin-1 beta and interleukin-1 alpha involves different mechanisms. *Biochemical and Biophysical Research Communications*, *162*, 591–596.

Busbridge, N. J., & Grossman, A. B. (1991). Stress and the single cytokine: Interleukin modulation of the pituitary-adrenal axis. *Molecular and Cellular Endocrinology*, *82*(2–3), C209–C214.

Cabanac, M., & Massonnet, B. (1974). Temperature regulation during fever: Change of set-point or change of gain? A tentative answer from a behavioral study in man. *Journal of Physiology*, *238*, 561–568.

Cannon, J. G., Evans, W. J., Hughes, V. A., Meredith, C. N., & Dinarello, C. A. (1986). Physiological mechanisms contributing to increased interleukin-1 secretion. *Journal of Applied Physiology*, *61*, 1869–1874.

Cannon, J. G., & Kluger, M. J. (1983). Endogenous pyrogen activity in human plasma after exercise. *Science*, *220*, 617–619.

Cannon, J. G., & Kluger, M. J. (1985). Altered thermoregulation in the iguana dipsosaurus dorsalis following exercise. *Journal of Thermal Biology*, *10*, 41–45.

Cannon, J. G., & St. Pierre, B. A. (1998). Cytokines in exertion-induced skeletal muscle injury. *Molecular and Cellular Biochemistry*, *179*, 159–167.

Chadwick, J., & Mann, W. N. (1950). *The medical works of Hippocrates*. Oxford, England: Blackwell Scientific Publications.

Coceani, F., Bishai, I., Dinarello, C. A., & Fitzpatrick, F. A. (1983). Prostaglandin E2 and thromboxane B2 in cerebrospinal fluid of afebrile and febrile cat. *American Journal of Physiology*, *244*, R785–R793.

Coceani, F., Bishai, I., Lees, J., & Sirko, S. (1987). Effects of pyrogens on prostaglandin E2 and thromboxane A2 synthesis in brain: Implications for the pathogenesis of fever. *Advances in Prostaglandin, Thromboxane, and Leukotriene Research*, *17B*, 949–952.

Conti, B., Tabarean, I., Andrei, C., & Bartfai, T. (2004). Cytokines and fever. *Frontiers in Bioscience*, *9*, 1433–1449.

Cooper, K. E. (1987). The neurobiology of fever: Thoughts on recent development. *Annual Reviews of Neuroscience*, *10*, 297–324.

Dao, T. K., Bell, R. C., Feng, J., Jameson, D. M., & Lipton, J. M. (1988). C-reactive protein, leukocytes, and fever after central interleukin-1 and α-MSH in aged rabbits. *American Journal of Physiology*, *254*, R401–R409.

Dascombe, M. J., Rothwell, N. J., Sagay, B. O., & Stock, M. J. (1980). Pyrogenic and thermogenic effects of interleukin-1 beta in the rat. *American Journal of Physiology, 256*, E7–E11.

De Jongh, R. F., Vissers, K. C., Booij, L. H. D., De Jongh, K. L., Vincken, P., & Meert, T. F. (2003). Interleukin-6 and perioperative thermoregulation and HPA-axis activation. *Cytokine, 21*, 248–256.

Di Fenza, R., & Fiorina, P. (2012). Physical activity and inflammation. In L. Luzi (Ed.), *Cellular physiology and metabolism of physical exercise* (pp. 99–108). New York, NY: Springer Publishing.

Dinarello, C. A. (1988a). Biology of interleukin 1. *The Journal of the Federation of American Societies for Experimental Biology, 2*, 108–115.

Dinarello, C. A. (1988b). Cytokines: Interleukin-1 and Tumor Necrosis Factor (Cachetin). In: J. I. Gallin (Ed.), *Inflammation: Basic principles and clinical* (pp. 195–208). New York, NY: Raven Press.

Dinarello, C. A., Cannon, J. G., & Wolff, S. M. (1988). New concepts on the pathogenesis of fever. *Reviews of Infectious Diseases, 10*, 168–189.

Dinarello, C. A., Cannon, J. G., Wolff, S. M., Bernheim, H. A., Beutler, B., Cerami, A., . . . O'Connor, J. V. (1986). Tumor necrosis factor (cachetin) is an endogenous pyrogen and induces production of interleukin-1. *Journal of Experimental Medicine, 163*, 1433–1450.

Dinarello, C. A., Conti, P., & Mier, J. W. (1986). Effects of human interleukin-1 on natural killer cell activity: Is fever a host defense mechanism for tumor killing? *Yale Journal of Biology and Medicine, 59*, 97–106.

Dinarello, C. A., Ikejma,T., Warner, S. J. C., Orencole, S. F., Lonnemann, G., Cannon, J. G., & Libby, P. (1987). Interleukin 1 induces interleukin 1. Induction of circulating interleukin 1 in rabbits in vivo and in human mononuclear cells in vitro. *The Journal of Immunology, 139*, 1902–1910.

Dokladny, K., Lobb, R., Wharton, W., Thomas, Y. M., & Moseley, P. L. (2010). LPS-induced cytokine levels are repressed by elevated expression of HSP70 in rats: Possible role of NF-kappaB. *Cell Stress & Chaperones, 15*(2), 153–163.

El-Atat, F., Aneja, A., Mcfarlane, S., & Sowers, J. (2003). Obesity and hypertension. *Endocrinology and Metabolism Clinics of North America, 32*, 823–854.

Elenkov, I. J., Iezzoni, D. G., Daly, A., Harris, A. G., & Chrousos, G. P. (2005). Cytokine dysregulation, inflammation and well-being. *Neuroimmunomodulation, 12*(5), 255–269.

Endres, S., Van der Meer, J. W. M., & Dinarello, C. A. (1987). Interleukin-1 in the pathogenesis of fever. *European Journal of Clinical Investigation, 17*(6), 469–474.

Engstrom, G., Hedblad, B., Stavenow, L., Lind, P., Janzon, L., & Lindgärde, F. (2003). Inflammation-sensitive plasma proteins are associated with future weight gain. *Diabetes, 52*, 2097–2101.

Esposito, K., Pontillo, A., Di Palo, C., Giugliano, G., Masella, M., & Giugliano, D. (2003). Effect of weight loss and lifestyle changes on vascular inflammatory markers in obese women: A randomized trial. *Journal of the American Medical Association, 289*, 1799–1804.

Esposito, K., & Giugliano, D. (2006). Diet and inflammation: A link to metabolic and cardiovascular diseases. *European Heart Journal, 27*, 15–20.

Evans, W. J., Meredith, C. N., Cannon, J. G., Dinarello, C. A., Frontera, W. R., Hughes, V. A., . . . Knuttgen, H. G. (1986). Metabolic changes following eccentric exercise in trained and untrained men. *Journal of Applied Physiology, 61*(5), 1864–1868.

Festa, A., D'Agostino, R., Williams, K., Karter, A. J., Mayer-Davis, E. J., Tracy, R. P., & Haffner, S. M. (2001). The relation of body fat mass and distribution to markers of chronic inflammation. *International Journal of Obesity and Related Metabolic Disorders, 25*, 1407–1415.

Figueiredo, M. J., Fabricio, A. S., Machado, R. R., Melo, M. C., Soares, D. M., & Souza, G. E. (2010). Increase of core temperature induced by corticotropin-releasing factor and urocortin: A comparative study. *Regulatory Peptide, 165*(2–3), 191–199.

Fiorentino, D. F., Zlotnik, A., Mosmann, T. R., Howard, M., & O'Garra, A. (1991). IL-10 inhibits cytokine production by activated macrophages. *Journal of Immunology, 147*, 3815–3822.

Flynn, M. G., McFarlin, B. K., & Markofski, M. M. (2007). The anti-inflammatory actions of exercise training. *American Journal of Lifestyle Medicine, 1*(220), 220–235.

Fontana, A., Weber, E., & Dayer, J.-M. (1984). Synthesis of interleukin-1/endogenous pyrogen in the brain of endotoxin-treated mice: A step in fever induction? *Journal of Immunology, 133*, 1696–1698.

Gabay, C., & Kushner, I. (1999). Acute-phase proteins and other systemic responses to inflammation. *New England Journal of Medicine, 340*, 448–454.

Gabay, C., & Kushner, I. (2001). Acute phase proteins. *Encyclopedia Life Sciences*, 1–6.

Geiger, T., Andus, T., Klapproth, J., Hirano, T., Kishimoto, T., & Heinrich, P. C. (1988). Induction of rat acute-phase proteins by IL-6 in vivo. *European Journal of Immunology, 18*, 717–721.

Girardin, E., Grau, G. E., Dayer, J. M., Roux-Lombard, P., & Lambert, P. H. (1988). TNF and IL-l in the serum of children with severe infectious purpura. *New England Journal of Medicine, 319*, 397–400.

Gruys, E., Toussaint, M. J. M, Niewold, T. A., & Koopmans, S. J. (2005). Acute phase reaction and acute phase proteins. *Journal of Zhejiang University Science B, 6*(11), 1045–1056.

Hall, J. E. (2000). Pathophysiology of obesity hypertension. *Department of Physiology & Biophysics, 2*, 139–147.

Harden, L. M., Rummel, C., Luheshi, G. N., Poole, S., Gerstberger, R., & Roth, J. (2013). Interleukin-10 modulates the synthesis of infl ammatory mediators in the sensory circumventricular organs: Implications for the regulation of fever and sickness behaviors. *Journal of Neuroinfl ammation , 10 ,* 22. http://dx.doi.org/10.1186/1742-2094-10-22

Hotamisligil, G. S. (2000). Molecular mechanisms of insulin resistance and the role of the adipocyte. *International Journal of Obesity and Related Metabolic Disorders, 24*, S23–S27.

Hori, T., Shibata, M., Nakashima, T., Yamasaki, M., Asami, A., Asami, T., & Koga, H. (1988). Effects of interleukin-1 and arachidonate on the preoptic and anterior hypothalamic neurons. *Brain Research Bulletin, 20*, 75–82.

Jablons, D. M., Mulé, J. J., Mcintosh, J. K., Sehgal, P. B., May, L. T., Huang, C. M., . . . Lotze, M. T. (1989). IL-6/IFNB2 as a circulating hormone: Induction by cytokine administration in humans. *The Journal of Immunology, 142*, 1542–1547.

Jenkins, J. K., Malyak, M., & Arend, W. P. (1994). The effects of interleukin-10 on interleukin-1 receptor antagonist and interleukin-1β production in human monocytes and neutrophils. *Lymphokine Cytokine Research, 13*, 47–54.

Jeukendrup, A. E., Vet-Joop, K., Sturk, A., Stegen, J. H., Senden, J., Saris, W. H., & Wagenmakers, A. J. (2000). Relationship between gastro-intestinal complaints and endotoxaemia, cytokine release and the acute-phase reaction during and after a long-distance triathlon in highly trained men. *Clinical Sciences, 98*(1), 47–55.

Jones, S. A., Horiuchi, S., Topley, N., Yamamoto, N., & Fuller, G. M. (2001). The soluble interleukin 6 receptor: mechanisms of production and implications is disease. *Federation of American Societies for Experimental Biology Journal, 15*(1), 43–58.

Karp, C. L. (2012). Unstressing intermperate models: How cold stress undermines mouse modeling. *Journal of Experimental Medicine, 209*(6), 1069–1074.

Katsuura, G., Gottschall, P. E., Dahl, R. R., & Arimura, A. (1988). Adrenocorticotropin release induced by intracerebroventricular injection of recombinant human interleukin-1 in rats: Possible involvement of prostaglandin. *Endocrinology, 122*, 1773–1779.

Kenny, G. P., Proulx, C. E., Denis, P. M., & Giesbrecht, G. G. (2000). Moderate exercise increases the post exercise resting warm thermoregulatory response thresholds. *Aviation, Space and Environmental Medicine, 71*(9), 914–919.

Kettelhut, I. C., & Goldberg, A. L. (1988). Tumor necrosis factor can induce fever in rats without activating protein breakdown in muscle or lipolysis in adipose tissue. *Journal of Clinical Investigation, 81*, 1384–1389.

Khan, F. A., & Khan, M. F. (2010). Inflammation and acute phase response. *International Journal of Applied Biology and Pharmaceutical Technology, 1*(2), 312–321.

Klir, J. J., McClellan, J. L., & Kluger, M. J. (1994). Interleukin-1 causes the increase in anterior hypothalamic interleukin-6 during LPS-induced fever in rats. *American Journal of Physiology: Regulatory, Integrative, Comparative, Physiology, 266,* R1845–R1848.

Klir, J. J., Roth, J., Szelenyi, Z., McClellan, J. M., & Kluger, M. J. (1993). Role of hypothalamic interleukin-6 and tumor necrosis factor-α in LPS-fever in rat. *American Journal of Physiology, 265*(3, Pt. 2), R512–R517.

Kluger, M. J. (1979). *Fever: Its biology, evolution and function.* Princeton, NJ: Princeton University Press.

Kluger, M. J. (1989). Endogenous pyrogens and fever. In J. B. Mercer (Ed.), *Thermal Physiology* (pp. 35–44). Amsterdam, Netherlands: Elsevier Science Publishers Biomedical Division.

Kluger, M. J. (1991a). The adaptive value of fever. In P. Mackowiak (Ed.), *Fever: Basic mechanisms and management* (pp. 105–124). New York, NY: Raven Press.

Kluger, M. J. (1991b). Fever: Role of pyrogens and cryogens. *Physiology Review, 71,* 93–127.

Kluger, M. J., Ringler, D. H., & Anver, M. R. (1975). Fever and Survival. *Science, 188,* 166–168.

Kluger, M. J., & Rothenberg, B. A. (1979). Fever and reduced iron: Their interaction as a host defense response to bacterial infection. *Science, 203*(4378), 374–376.

Kushner, I., & Rzewnicki, D. L. (1994). The acute phase response: General aspects. *Baillieres Clinical Rheumatology, 8*(3), 513–530.

LeMay, L. G., Vander, A. J., & Kluger, M. J. (1990a). The effects of psychological stress on plasma interleukin-6 activity in rats. *Physiology & Behavior, 47,* 957–961.

LeMay, L. G., Vander, A. J., & Kluger, M. J. (1990b). Role of interleukin-6 in fever in rats. *American Journal of Physiology, 258,* R798–R803.

Leon, L. R. (2002). Invited review: Cytokine regulation of fever: Studies using gene knockout mice. *Journal of Applied Physiology, 92*(6), 2648–2655.

Leon, L. R., Kozak, W., Peschon, J., & Kluger, M. J. (1997). Exacerbated febrile responses to LPS, but not turpentine, in TNF double receptor-knockout mice. *American Journal of Physiology. Regulatory, Integrative and Comparative Physiology, 272,* R563–R569.

Leon, L. R., Kozak, W., Rudolph, K., & Kluger, M. J. (1999). An antipyretic role for interleukin-10 in LPS fever in mice. *American Journal of Physiology, 276,* R81–R89.

Liu, E., Lewis, K., Al-Saffar, H., Krall, C. M., Singh, A., Kulchitsky, V. A., . . . Steiner, A. A. (2012). Naturally occurring hypothermia is more advantageous than fever in severe forms of lipo-polysaccharide- and *Escherichia coli*-induced systemic inflammation. *American Journal of Physiology. Regulatory, Integrative and Comparative Physiology, 302,* R1372–R1383.

Long, N. C., Kluger, M. J., & Vander, A. (1988). Antiserum against mouse IL-l alpha does not block stress hyperthermia or LPS fever in rat. In S. Lomax (Ed.), *Thermoregulation: Research and clinical applications* (pp. 78–84). Odense, Denmark: Karger.

Long, N. C., Kunkel, S. L., Vander, A., & Kluger, M. J. (1990). Antiserum against tumor necrosis factor enhances lipopolysaccharide fever in rats. *American Journal of Physiology, 258,* R332–R337.

Long, N., Otterness, I., Kunkel, S. L., Vander, A. J., & Kluger, M. J. (1990). Roles of interleukin-1 and tumor necrosis factor in lipopolysaccharide fever in rats. *American Journal of Physiology, 259,* R724–R728.

Long, N. C., Vander, A. J., Kunkel, S. L., & Kluger, M. J. (1990). Antiserum against tumor necrosis factor increases stress hyperthermia in rats. *American Journal of Physiology, 258,* R591–R595.

Lyon, C. J., Law, R. E., & Hsueh, W. A. (2003). Minireview: Adiposity, inflammation, and therogenesis. *Endocrinology, 144*(6), 2195–2200.

Mackowiak, P. A., Bartlett, J. G., Borden, E. C., Goldblum, S. E., Hasday, J. D., Munford, R. S., . . . Woodward, T. E. (1997). *Clinical Infectious Diseases, 25*(1), 119–138.

Marx, J. L. (1988a). Cytokines are two-edged swords in disease. *Science, 239,* 257–258.

Marx, J. L. (1988b). Orphan interferon finds a new home (Interleukin-6). *Science, 239,* 25–26.

McCarthy, D. O. (2000). Cytokines and the anorexia of infection: Potential mechanisms and treatment. *Biological Research for Nursing, 1*(4), 287–298.

McCarthy, D. O., & Daun, J. M. (1993). The effects of cyclooxygenase inhibitors on tumor-induced anorexia in rats. *Cancer, 71*(2), 486–492.

Michie H. R., Manogue, K. R., Spriggs D. R., Revhaug A., O'Dwyer, S., Dinarello, C. A., . . . Wilmore, D. W. (1988). Detection of circulating tumor necrosis factor after endotoxin administration. *New England Journal Medicine, 318*(23), 1481–1486.

Moller, D. E. (2000). Potential role of TNF-alpha in the pathogenesis of insulin resistance and type-2 diabetes. *Trends in Endocrinology and Metabolism, 11,* 212–217.

Morimoto, A., Murakami, N., Nakamori, T., & Watanabe, T. (1988). Ventromedial hypothalamus is highly sensitive to prostaglandin E2 for producing fever in rabbits. *American Journal of Physiology, 397,* 259–268.

Morimoto, A., Nakamori, T., Morimoto, K., Tan, N., & Murakami, N. (1993). The central role of corticotrophin-releasing factor (CRF-41) in psychological stress in rats. *Journal of Physiology, 460,* 221–229.

Morimoto, A., Nakamori, T., Watanabe, T., Ono, T., & Mukakami, N. (1988). Pattern differences in experimental fevers induced by endotoxin, endogenous pyrogens, and prostaglandins. *American Journal of Physiology, 254,* R633–R640.

Murray, M. J., & Murray, A. B. (1979). Anorexia of infection as a mechanism of host defense. *American Journal of Clinical Nutrition, 32,* 593–596.

Nava, F., Calapai, G., Facciola, G., Cuzzocrea, S., Marciano, M. C., De Sarro, A., & Caputi, A. P. (1997). Effects of interleukin-10 on water intake, locomotor activity, and rectal temperature in rat treated with endotoxin. *International Journal of Immunopharmacology, 19,* 31–38.

Netea, M. G., Kullberg, B. J., & Van der Meer, J. W. (2000). Circulating cytokines as mediators of fever. *Clinical Infectious Diseases, 5,* S178–S184.

Nijsten, M. W. N., DeGroot, E. R., TenDuis, H. J., Klasen, H. J., Hack, C. E., & Aarden, L. A. (1987). Serum levels of IL-6 and acute phase responses. *Lancet, 2,* 921.

Niven, D. J., Stelfox, H. T., & Laupland, K. B. (2012). Fever in the critically ill: A review of epidemiology, immunology and management. *Journal of Intensive Care Medicine, 27*(5), 290–297.

Northoff, H., & Berg, A. (1991). Immunologic mediators as parameters of the reaction to strenuous exercise. *International Journal of Sports Medicine, 12*(Suppl. 1), S9–S15.

Ostrowski, K., Rohde, T., Zacho, M., Asp, S., & Pedersen, B. K. (1998). Evidence that Il-6 is produced in skeletal muscle during intense long-term muscle activity. *The Journal of Physiology, London, 508,* 949–953.

Ostrowski, K., Rohde, T., Zacho, M., Asp, S., & Pedersen, B. K. (1999). Pro and anti-inflammatory cytokine balance in strenuous exercise in humans. *Journal of Physiology, London, 515,* 287–291.

Pearson, T. A., Mensah, G. A., Alexander, R. W., Anderson, J. L., Cannon, R. O., III, Criqui, M., . . . Vinicor, F. (2003). Markers of inflammation and cardiovascular disease: Application to clinical and public health practice: A statement for healthcare professionals from the centers for disease control and prevention and the American Heart Association. *Circulation, 107*(3), 499–511.

Pedersen, B. K. (2000). Exercise and cytokines. *Immunology Cell Biology, 42,* 104–117.

Pedersen, B. K. (2006). The anti-inflammatory effect of exercise: Its role in diabetes and cardiovascular disease control. *Essays in Biochemistry, 42,* 105–117.

Pedersen, B., Akerstrom, T., Nielsen, A., & Fischer, C. (2007). Role of myokines in exercise and metabolism. *Journal of Applied Physiology, 103,* 1093–1098.

Petersen, A. M. W., & Pedersen, B. K. (2005). The anti-inflammatory effect of exercise. *Journal of Applied Physiology, 98*, 1154–1162.

Roberts, N. J., Jr. (1991). Impact of temperature elevation on immunologic defenses. *Reviews of Infectious Diseases, 13*(3), 462–472.

Roth, J., & De Souza, G. E. P. (2001). Fever induction pathways: Evidence from response to systemic and local cytokine formation. *Brazilian Journal of Medical and Biological Research, 34*, 301–314.

Rothwell, N. J. (1989). CRF is involved in the pyrogenic and thermogenic effects of interleukin-1 in the rat. *American Journal of Physiology, 256*, E111–E115.

Rothwell, N.J., Busbridge, N.J., Lefeuvre, R.A., Hardwick, A.J., Gauldie, J., Hopkins, S.J.(1991). Interleukin-6 is a centrally acting endogenous pyrogen in the rat. *Canadian Journal of Physiology and Pharmacology, 69*(10),1465-1469.

Rowsey, P. J. (1997). Pathophysiology of fever Part 1: The role of cytokines. *Dimensions of Critical Care Nursing, 16*(4), 202–207.

Rowsey P. J., & Kluger, M. J. (1994). Corticotropin releasing hormone is involved in exercise-induced elevation in core temperature. *Psychoneuroendocrinology, 19*(2), 179–187.

Rowsey, P. J., Metzger, B. L., Carlson, J., & Gordon, C. J. (2006). Effects of chronic exercise conditioning on thermal responses to lipopolysaccharide and turpentine abscess in female rats. *Archives of Toxicology, 80*, 81–87.

Rowsey, P. J., Metzger, B. L., Carlson, J. C., & Gordon, C. J. (2009). Long-term exercise training selectively alters serum cytokines involved in fever. *Biological Research for Nursing, 10*(4), 374–380.

Ruan, H., Hacohen, N., Golub, T. R., Van Parijs, L., & Lodish, H. F. (2002). Tumor necrosis factor-α suppresses adipocyte-specific genes and activates expression or is obligatory. *Diabetes, 51*, 1319–1336.

Sakata, Y., Morimoto, A., Long, N. C., & Murakami, N. (1991). Fever and acute-phase response induced in rabbits by intravenous and intracerebroventricular injection of interleukin-6. *Cytokine, 3*, 199–203.

Schroder, K., Hertzog, P. J., Ravasi, T., & Hume, D. A. (2004). Interferon-γ: An overview of signals, mechanisms, and functions. *Journal of Leukocyte Biology, 75*, 163–189.

Senn, J. J., Klover, P. J., Nowak, I. A., & Mooney, R. A. (2002). Interleukin-6 induces cellular insulin resistance in hepatocytes. *Diabetes, 51*, 3391–3399.

Shalaby, M. R., Waage, A., Aarden, L., & Espevik, R. (1989). Endotoxin, TNF-α and IL-1 induce IL-6 production in vivo. *Clinical Immunology and Immunopathology, 53*, 488–498.

Sobrado, J., Moldawer, L. L., Bistrian, B. R., Dinarello, C. A., & Blackburn, G. L. (1983). Effect of ibuprofen on fever and metabolic changes induced by continuous infusion of leukocytic pyrogen (interleukin 1) or endotoxin. *Infection and Immunity, 42*, 997–1005.

St. Pierre Schneider, B. (2008). Skeletal muscle biology in nursing. *Biological Research for Nursing, 10*(1), 5–6.

Stahl, W. M. (1987). Acute phase protein response to tissue injury. *Critical Care Medicine, 15*, 545–550.

Steensberg, A., Keller, C., Starkie, R. L., Osada, T., Febbraio, M. A., & Pedersen, B. K. (2002). IL-6 and TNF-alpha expression in, and release from, contracting human skeletal muscle. *The American Journal of Physiology. Endocrinology and Metabolism, 283*(6), E1272–E1278.

Stitt, J. T. (1973). Prostaglandin E1 fever induced in rabbits. *Journal of Physiology, 232*, 163–179.

Stitt, J. T. (1986). Prostaglandin E as the neural mediator of the febrile response. *Yale Journal Biological Medicine, 59*, 137–149.

Strijbos, P. J., Hardwick, A. J., Relton, J. K., Carey, F., & Rothwell, N. J. (1992). Inhibition of central actions of cytokines on fever and thermogenesis by lipocortin-1 involves CRF. *American Journal of Physiology, 263*(4, Pt.1), E632–E636.

Tatro, J. B. (2000). Endogenous antipyretics. *Clinical Infectious Disease, 31*(S5), S190–S201.

Taylor, C., Rogers, G., Goodman, C., Baynes, R. D., Bothwell, T. H., Bezwoda, W. R., Kramer, F., . . . Hattingh, J. (1987). Hematologic, iron-related, and acute phase protein responses to sustained strenous exercise. *American Journal of Applied Physiology, 62*, 464–469.

Trayhurn, P. (2005). Endocrine and signalling role of adipose tissue: New perspectives on fat. *Acta Physiologica Scandinavica, 184*, 285–293.

Trayhurn, P., & Beattie, J. H. (2001). Physiological role of adipose tissue: White adipose tissue as an endocrine and secretory organ. *The Proceedings of the Nutrition Society, 60*(3), 329–339.

Trayhurn, P., & Wood, I. S. (2004). Adipokines: Inflammation and the pleiotropic role of white adipose tissue. *The British Journal of Nutrition, 92*, 347–355.

Tsagarakis, S., Gillies, G., Rees, L. H., Besser, M., & Grossman, A. (1989). IL-1 directly stimulates the release of CRF from rat hypothalamus. *Neuroendocrinology, 49*, 98–101.

Vasilenko, V. Y., Petruchuk, T. A., Gourine, V. N., & Pierau, F. K. (2000). Interleukin-1beta reduces temperature sensitivity but elevates thermal thresholds in different populations of warm-sensitive hypothalamic neurons in rat brain slices. *Neuroscience Letters, 292*(3), 207–210.

Verhasselt, V., Buelens, C., Williems, F., De Groote, D., Haeffner-Cavaillon, H., & Goldman, M. (1997). Bacterial lipopolysaccharide stimulates the production of cytokines and the expression of costimulatory molecules by human peripheral blood dendritic cells: Evidence for a soluble CD14-dependent pathway. *The Journal of Immunology, 158*(6), 2919–2925.

Wallenius, V., Wallenius, K., Ahrén, B., Rudling, M., Carlstein, H., Dickson, S. L., . . . Jansson, J. O. (2002). Interleuki-6-deficient mice develop mature-onset obesity. *Nature Medicine, 8*(1), 75–79.

Weinstock, C., Konig, D., Harnischmacher, R., Keul, J., Berg, A., & Northoff, H. (1997). Effect of exhaustive exercise stress on the cytokine response. *Medicine and Science in Sports and Exercise, 29*, 345–354.

Wong, G. G., & Clark, S. C. (1988). Multiple actions of Interleukin-6 within a cytokine network. *Immunology Today, 9*, 137–139.

Xin, L., & Blatteis, C. M. (1992). Hypothalamic neuronal responses to IL-6 in tissue slices: Effects of indomethacin and naloxone. *Brain Research Bulletin, 29*, 27–35.

Ye, J., Ortaldo, J. R., Conlon, K., Winkler-Pickett, R., & Young, H. A. (1995). Cellular and molecular mechanisms of IFN-gamma production induced by IL-2 and IL-12 in a human NK cell line. *Journal of Leukocyte Biology, 58*(2), 225–233

Yudkin, J. S., Yajnik, C. S., Mohamed-Ali, V., & Bulmer, K. (1999). High levels of circulating pro-inflammatory cytokines and leptin in urban, but not rural, Indians. A potential explanation for increased risk of diabetes and coronary heart disease. *Diabetes Care, 22*, 363–364.

CHAPTER 3

Overweight and Obesity in Youth With Type 1 Diabetes

Karl E. Minges, Robin Whittemore, and Margaret Grey

ABSTRACT

Overweight and obesity in youth with type 1 diabetes (T1D) is now prevalent and accounts for significant health consequences, including cardiovascular complications and dual diagnosis of type 2 diabetes. Physical activity and lifestyle are modifiable and play an important role in the prevention and management of excessive weight, but it is unclear how these factors relate to overweight and obese youth with T1D. Thus, a systematic review was conducted to examine how physical activity, sedentary behavior, sleep, and diet are related to overweight/obesity in youth with T1D. Seven observational and intervention studies published between 1990 and 2013 were included in the review. Prevalence of overweight ranged from 12.5% to 33.3%. Overweight in youth with T1D was associated with infrequent napping, increased screen time, and skipping breakfast and dinner but was not related to time engaged in physical activity. Weight-related interventions indicated modest weight loss along with improved glycemic control. In light of this review, there is a need for high quality research that examines all levels of activity in youth with T1D to identify lifestyle modification targets for weight prevention and management.

INTRODUCTION

Globally, the incidence of type 1 diabetes (T1D) is increasing among youth, at an annual rate of 3%–4% per year, thus posing a significant public health problem (Bell et al., 2009; Lipman et al., 2013; Patterson et al., 2012). At the same time, the prevalence of overweight and obesity among all youth has increased precipitously over the past few decades (Wild, Roglic, Green, Sicree, & King, 2004) and has been deemed the major public health challenge facing youth in the 21st century (Jack, 2007). Surprisingly, overweight and obesity are now prevalent among youth with T1D, and a recent study demonstrated that youth with T1D are more likely to be overweight than their peers without the condition (Liu et al., 2010). Others have noted more than a twofold increase of overweight and obesity in youth with T1D since the 1990s when the Diabetes Control and Complications Trial (DCCT) availed the benefits of tight glucose control to reduce the complications of T1D (Libman, Pietropaolo, Arslanian, LaPorte, & Becker, 2003; Purnell et al., 1998). In the DCCT, a complication of intensive insulin therapy and tight glucose control was untoward weight gain, which was threefold higher in the intensive treatment group and was associated with more moderate to severe hypoglycemic events and better glucose control (American Diabetes Association, 1993; DCCT Research Group, 1988, 1993).

Because excess weight is associated with increased risk for cardiovascular disease in youth without diabetes, excess weight in youth with T1D may contribute to a higher risk of cardiometabolic complications in these youth (Purnell et al., 2013; Van Vliet et al., 2012). Indeed, youth with T1D are predisposed to such complications by having diabetes, regardless of weight status (Krishnan & Short, 2009). Furthermore, and perhaps most alarming, several case studies have been reported in which several overweight and obese youth with T1D developed type 2 diabetes (T2D) as well, or "double diabetes," whereby these youth became resistant to their exogenous insulin, insulin resistance being the hallmark of T2D (Pozzilli, Guglielmi, Caprio, & Buzzetti, 2011). Such a scenario may predispose youth to additional long-term cardiovascular complications.

Prevention of weight gain and long-term weight management can be effective measures to prevent or reduce overweight and obesity in youth with T1D, although until recently, this has not been a focus of treatment. Physical activity and lifestyle play a key role in overweight and obesity in the general population, but the contributing factors related to weight gain that are specific to youth with T1D have not been studied. Thus, the purpose of this systematic review is to explore the associations among physical activity, lifestyle (sedentary behavior, sleep, diet), and overweight/obesity in youth with T1D by synthesizing the findings for clinical application and direction of future research.

BACKGROUND

Epidemiology of Diabetes in Youth

T1D is an inflammatory autoimmune disorder that disrupts the functioning of the pancreas by destroying the insulin-producing beta cells. Most cases of T1D are diagnosed during childhood and young adulthood. Treatment of T1D involves replacement of insulin by injection and regular monitoring of blood glucose, which requires balancing of carbohydrate intake with physical activity. Although the tendency toward autoimmune disease is inheritable, multiple environmental factors are involved in presentation of the phenotype (Knip et al., 2005). On the other hand, T2D is a metabolic condition distinguished by insulin resistance and high blood glucose that presents typically during adulthood. The etiology of T2D is better understood and most likely related to lifestyle and genetic factors. Obesity is the predominant risk factor in those who are genetically susceptible (Patrick et al., 2004).

Diabetes is among the most common pediatric chronic conditions. Estimates vary widely in terms of how many youth are affected with T1D and T2D, and the incidence varies as a function of gender, seasonality, race, and geographical factors (Lipman et al., 2013; Soltesz, Patterson, Dahlquist, & Eurodiab Study Group, 2007). In the United States, the SEARCH for Diabetes in Youth Study Group reported that more than 150,000 youth had physician-diagnosed T1D and/or T2D in 2001 (SEARCH for Diabetes in Youth Study Group, 2006), and that the overall incidence was 24.3 per 100,000 person-years (SEARCH for Diabetes in Youth Study Group, 2007).

The prevalence of both T1D and T2D in youth is increasing. T1D has been rising at an average rate of 3%–4% per year in children and adolescents (Bell et al., 2009; Lipman et al., 2013; Onkamo, Vaananen, Karvonen, & Tuomilehto, 1999; Patterson et al., 2012), and although only accounting for about 6% of cases (SEARCH for Diabetes in Youth Study Group, 2006), the number of youth with T2D is also increasing, particularly among adolescents from minority populations (SEARCH for Diabetes in Youth Study Group, 2007). In fact, in one study the authors concluded that given current incidence estimates, the number of youth with T1D and T2D will increase by 23% and 49%, respectively, by 2050 (Imperatore et al., 2012). The predominant factor associated with this rise of T2D in youth is excessive weight gain (Patrick et al., 2004). As described by the "accelerator hypothesis," overweight may also partly explain the increasing incidence of T1D because of the interplay of beta-cell apoptosis and insulin resistance (Wilkin, 2001), but other environmental factors such as maternal age and birth weight may also be attributed to the rising incidence of T1D (Cardwell, Stene, Joner, Bulsara, et al., 2010; Cardwell, Stene, Joner, Davis, et al., 2010).

Recent data from the United States show that a substantial proportion of youth are overweight or obese, 16% and 12% respectively (Eaton et al., 2010). Indeed, this prevalence of overweight and obesity has maintained a nearly linear trend for decades (Han, Lawlor, & Kimm, 2010), and projections indicate that by 2050, up to 42% of the U.S. population will be obese (Hill, Rand, Nowak, & Christakis, 2010). Overweight and obese youth may develop a myriad of physical, psychological, quality of life, and psychosocial sequelae as a consequence of excess weight, and this translates to a dramatic decrease in life expectancy (Daniels, 2006; Olshansky et al., 2005). Given these adverse health outcomes and the economic impact, childhood obesity has been cited as the major public health problem for this century (Jack, 2007).

Prior to the release of the findings of the DCCT and the concomitant increase in the use of intensive insulin regimens, youth with T1D tended to be lean, mostly as a result of a loss of calories in the urine. However, corresponding to the increase of overweight and obesity in the general population, youth with T1D are also experiencing overweight and obesity (Liu et al., 2010). Trends of weight gain were found by the Pittsburgh Epidemiology of Diabetes Complications Study that showed an increase in overweight in adults with T1D, from 29% in 1986–1988 to 42% in 2004–2007, and obesity from 3% to 23% for the same period (Conway et al., 2010). There are limited epidemiologic data on youth with T1D. Recent research has demonstrated, however, that youth with T1D have a higher prevalence of overweight (22% vs. 16%) but are less likely to be obese (13% vs. 17%) than their peers without diabetes (Liu et al., 2010). Because youth with T1D, regardless of weight status, are already at greater risk of cardiovascular complications than those without T1D (Krishnan & Short, 2009; Laing et al., 2003; Soedamah-Muthu et al., 2006), the possibility of additional complications attributable to excess body weight is concerning.

Of particular concern is the emergence of double diabetes, a condition in which overweight and obese adolescents have the clinical manifestations of both T1D and T2D (Libman & Becker, 2003). This rare dual diagnosis occurs when overweight or obese youth with T1D develop insulin resistance that is characteristic of T2D. Alternatively, youth with T2D may present with autoantibodies to pancreatic beta cells, and thus develop T1D, but this scenario is less common. As the accelerator hypothesis argues, those with T1D who also have a genetic susceptibility to T2D are more likely to acquire insulin resistance, and consequently double diabetes, if they become overweight (Pozzilli et al., 2011). The manifestation of double diabetes may place overweight and obese youth at risk for high blood pressure, abnormal lipid profile, and polycystic ovary syndrome for adolescent females (Pozzilli et al., 2011). Thus, overweight or obese youth with T1D may represent an extremely at risk population. Furthermore, because insulin therapy is associated with weight gain (Purnell et al., 1998; Russell-Jones & Khan, 2007), effective physical activity and lifestyle habits must be promoted in all youth to prevent complications of overweight and obesity.

Role of Physical Activity and Lifestyle Factors in Youth

Observational and experimental studies have revealed the beneficial effects of physical activity in youth. Regular physical activity has been shown to improve health by reducing the risk of cardiovascular disease, high blood pressure, the metabolic syndrome, obesity, and depression (Warburton, Nicol, & Bredin, 2006). Importantly, even moderate participation in physical activities, such as aerobic and strength training exercise may have beneficial effects in preventing and reducing excess body weight (Janssen & Leblanc, 2010).

Pediatric organizations recommend that youth engage in moderate to vigorous physical activity for a duration of at least 60 min per day (Strong et al., 2005; World Health Organization, 2010); however, fewer than 1 in 10 U.S. youth meet this recommendation (Troiano et al., 2008). Physical activity is also recommended for youth with T1D, providing that there are no complications at the time of exercise and blood glucose levels are within target before, during, and after exercise (American Diabetes Association, 2002; Robertson, Adolfsson, Scheiner, Hanas, & Riddell, 2009). Nevertheless, epidemiologic data suggest that few youth with T1D, as low as 4.7%, meet the recommended 60 min per day of moderate to vigorous physical activity (Liese, Ma, Maahs, & Trilk, 2013; Schweiger, Klingensmith, & Snell-Bergeon, 2010). Despite the recommendations that youth with T1D participate in physical activity, youth may have fear of hypoglycemic events and may wish to delay activity until glucose levels are in the appropriate range (American Diabetes Association, 2002). This fear of hypoglycemia during exercise may lead to decreased frequency, duration, and intensity of exercise (Brazeau, Rabasa-Lhoret, Strychar, & Mircescu, 2008; Di Battista, Hart, Greco, & Gloizer, 2009; Nordfeldt & Ludvigsson, 2005).

Although the data on the role of physical activity in youth with T1D are limited, two recently published reviews have examined this topic in detail (Chimen et al., 2012; Liese et al., 2013). The authors observed that physical activity improves fitness in youth with T1D, but youth still have a low level of cardiorespiratory fitness, suggesting that aerobic power, strength, balance, and flexibility might be compromised in youth with T1D (Blair & Connelly, 1996). Regular participation in physical activities also improves lipid levels, endothelial function, and insulin resistance, but not blood pressure in youth with T1D (Chimen et al., 2012; Liese et al., 2013). Interestingly, these authors observed that although physical activity improves insulin dosage regimens in youth with T1D, the effect of physical activity on glycemic control is limited. Others have promoted the use of family-based intervention strategies to engage youth in moderate to vigorous physical activity in order to enhance fitness levels and minimize future cardiovascular risk in youth with T1D (Faulkner, 2010; Faulkner et al., 2006; Faulkner, Michaliszyn, & Hepworth, 2010).

Overweight and obesity are complex and multifactorial conditions that are associated with many risk factors. Thus, in addition to physical activity, other lifestyle behavioral factors are important to consider for youth with T1D, including sedentary behavior, sleep, and diet.

Sedentary behaviors are activities that do not increase energy expenditure substantially higher than the resting level of 1.0–1.5 metabolic equivalents (METs; Pate, O'Neill, & Lobelo, 2008) and include such activities as sitting, reading, and watching television (screen time). In a recent review and meta-analysis of sedentary behavior and health outcomes in youth, the authors found a relationship between increased sedentary behavior and unfavorable health outcomes, such as increased body mass index (BMI) and poorer psychosocial and physical health, including the metabolic syndrome (Mark & Janssen, 2008; Tremblay et al., 2011). Youth with T1D have reported a high duration of screen time per day, the typical proxy for sedentary behavior, ranging between 110 and 140 min per day of television watching, and between 40 and 255 min per day of computer use (Liese et al., 2013). In fact, in one study of youth with T1D, the average amount of accumulated screen time was 2.9 hr per day (Galler, Lindau, Ernert, Thalemann, & Raile, 2011), which exceeds the recommendation of less than 2 hr of screen time per day (American Academy of Pediatrics, 2001). Accelerometry was used in another study to assess intensity of activity in youth with T1D and it was found that 84% of recorded daily activity was in sedentary pursuits, thus potentially posing increased cardiovascular risks and poorer glucose control (Michaliszyn & Faulkner, 2010).

Lack of sleep has also been found to be associated with overweight and obesity in adults, and sleep problems, especially insomnia and sleep apnea, are prevalent in adults with T2D (Einhorn et al., 2007; Spiegel, Knutson, Leproult, Tasali, & Cauter, 2005; Vgontzas et al., 2009). Research exploring the impact of sleep in youth with T1D is beginning to emerge. Sleep restriction was associated with reduced insulin sensitivity (Donga et al., 2010); disrupted sleep was related to glucose variability (Matyka, Crawford, Wiggs, Dunger, & Stores, 2000); and, youth with T1D and those with poorer metabolic control had more bouts of sleep apnea compared to those without T1D or those whose diabetes was in good metabolic control (Villa et al., 2000). Poorer sleep behaviors were also associated with reduced quality of life, educational attainment, and psychological problems (Perfect et al., 2012). Sleep behaviors may have unique implications for overweight and obese youth with T1D because not achieving an adequate amount of sleep is associated with weight gain (Padez, Mourao, Moreira, & Rosado, 2009; Touchette et al., 2008).

Diet and nutrition are critical elements of diabetes management. Prior to the recommendations for intensive insulin therapy and better metabolic control, dietary recommendations focused on consuming sufficient calories for growth and a balanced nutrition to be distributed throughout the day. The advent of intensive therapy, with reliance on multiple daily injections or the use of an insulin pump, led to a new approach to dietary recommendations that focused on covering carbohydrates in a meal with less emphasis on balanced nutrition (Gillespie, Kulkarni, & Daly, 1998). Although this approach makes life easier for youth with T1D, because there are no restricted foods, it has opened the door to the poor dietary habits characteristic of youth in today's society. Clearly, overconsumption of calories and fat will translate to weight gain in youth (Patrick et al., 2004), which is detrimental to youth with T1D since high saturated fats adversely impacts metabolic control (Michaliszyn, Shaibi, Quinn, Fritschi, & Faulkner, 2009). Furthermore, the SEARCH for Diabetes in Youth Study group reported that most youth with T1D do not meet American Diabetes Association recommendations for total fat, vitamin E, fiber, fruits, vegetables, and grains, and fewer (6.5%) met recommendations of less than 10% of energy from saturated fat (Mayer-Davis et al., 2006).

Thus, as the incidence of T1D and weight gain are increasing, physical activity and other lifestyle behaviors need to be addressed. The purpose of this review is to identify the evidence related to physical activity, sedentary behavior, sleep, and diet, and overweight/obesity in youth with T1D. We hope to identify factors and strategies related to obesity and overweight prevention and management in youth with T1D. This work is necessary given that health behaviors are modifiable and may prevent the complications of overweight and obesity in youth with T1D, including those at risk for double diabetes.

METHODS

A systematic review using the Preferred Reporting Items for Systematic Reviews and Meta-Analyses (PRISMA) guidelines (Moher, Liberati, Tetzlaff, & Altman, 2009) was conducted by searching the following electronic bibliographic databases with the assistance of a medical librarian: Medline, EMBASE, Cochrane Library, and CINAHL. The following keywords with various logical connections were used: Obesity (overweight, body composition, BMI, waist circumference), T1D, exercise (physical activity, motor activity), and lifestyle (sleep, sedentary behavior, diet, nutrition, self-care, health behavior, health promotion). The studies included in this review were limited to full-text articles published between

1990 and February 2013. The search strategy began in 1990 because of the early evidence that intensive insulin therapy was associated with weight gain (DCCT Research Group, 1988). To identify any studies that may have been missed during the search, relevant references were also retrieved from reference lists of selected articles. The review was restricted to publications written in the English language.

The titles and abstracts of all citations identified by the literature search were reviewed. The inclusion criteria were (a) observational or intervention studies in which overweight/obesity in the context of youth with T1D was examined; (b) physical activity or lifestyle factors were reported; and (c) participants were aged ≤18 years. We focused this review on youth because childhood and adolescence is a time when diabetes self-management skills are learned and lifelong behavioral habits are formed (Bandura, 2004; Schilling, Grey, & Knafl, 2002), and overweight youth are much more likely to be overweight adults (Field, Cook, & Gillman, 2005).

Exclusion criteria were (a) studies of drug therapies or surgical interventions; (b) reviews or research that did not present original findings; (c) youth with secondary causes of obesity, such as steroid use; (d) weight not calculated using an objective measure; and (e) studies focused on celiac disease or eating disorders. We excluded studies that identified eating disorders as the outcome or explanatory variable because disordered eating is a compensatory behavior for weight control, which is not relevant given the purpose of this review, but it is not uncommon in patients with T1D (Lawrence et al., 2008).

Data extraction was facilitated by the use of a data display matrix to ascertain reliable and consistent data from the sample of studies. Study and location, sample size, participant characteristics (age, gender, race/ethnicity, diabetes duration, glycosylated hemoglobin [HbA1c]), weight status, study design, type of health behavior/outcome variables (physical activity, sedentary behavior, sleep, diet), and main findings pertinent to physical activity or lifestyle and overweight/obesity were abstracted by the first author.

RESULTS

There were 685 articles identified during the literature review and imported into Endnote software. Duplicate studies were removed via the Endnote duplicate function and any remaining duplicates were manually removed ($n = 143$). Thorough review of all 542 article titles and abstracts was conducted by two reviewers (KEM and RW); disagreement was resolved by discussion. Most studies were deemed ineligible for full-text review because of lack of an explicit focus on body weight and/or physical activity or lifestyle factors. Several manuscripts on eating disorders or celiac disease were also considered ineligible.

In total, 21 observational and intervention studies underwent complete review. After employing inclusion and exclusion criteria to the full manuscripts, 13 studies were excluded because of lack of findings related to overweight or obesity and/or physical activity or lifestyle, and one was excluded because the study focused on eating disorders. In total, seven manuscripts met inclusion criteria for our review, including the one publication from a nursing journal (Estrada, Danielson, Drum, & Lipton, 2012). No additional manuscripts were identified from reviewing the reference lists of the articles included in this review.

Study sample sizes ranged from 19 to 723 participants, and about half of the studies (4/7) had a sample size fewer than 50 participants. Two studies were conducted in the United States, and the remainder in European countries. There were five studies that employed observational methodology, and two tested an intervention. The intervention studies were also the oldest, having been conducted before the year 2000. In terms of participant characteristics, girls were the primary subjects in two studies, whereas four studies had an equal representation of boys and girls, and in one study gender was not reported (Semiz, Bilgin, Bundak, & Bircan, 2000). The age range varied from 4 to 18 years, but for those studies that reported the mean age, most focused on the preadolescent to adolescent years of 11–16 years. In only one study was a diverse sample in terms of race/ethnicity reported (Estrada et al., 2012). Diabetes duration ranged from an average of 3.7 to 7.4 years, and mean HbA1c levels ranged from to 7.5% to 13.1%, whereas the American Diabetes Association recommends levels <8.0% in this age group (Silverstein et al., 2005). The prevalence of overweight/obesity ranged from 12.5% to 33.3%, and in all but one study (Galli-Tsinopoulou, Grammatikopoulou, Stylianou, Kokka, & Emmanouilidou, 2009), more than 20% of participants were overweight or obese. One of the intervention studies recruited only obese participants (Thomas-Dobersen, Butler-Simon, & Fleshner, 1993). Participant and study characteristics are identified in Table 3.1.

Physical activity ($n = 1$) and lifestyle behaviors including sedentary behavior ($n = 2$), sleep ($n = 1$), and diet ($n = 3$) were explored in the observational studies. In one study, three of these health behaviors were examined (Overby et al., 2009). Physical activity and overweight/obesity in youth with T1D was considered only in one study in which moderate to vigorous activity was assessed with a self-report questionnaire followed by the allocation of metabolic equivalent values to activities (Overby et al., 2009). No association was found with time spent on physical activity and overweight; however, the study is limited by the use of a self-report questionnaire that had not been validated across the entire age span of the sample.

The relationship between sedentary behavior and overweight/obesity was reported in two of the observational studies. In both studies, self-report

TABLE 3.1

Articles Meeting Inclusion Criteria for Overweight/Obesity in Youth With Type 1 Diabetes

Authors, Country	Primary Aim	Study Design	Participant Characteristics[a]	Health Behavior, Measurement	Results[a]
Observational Studies					
Estrada et al., 2012 USA	To examine sleep in families of individuals with T1D and the relationship of sleep with obesity, diabetes, and insulin resistance	Cohort/ Cross-sectional	N: 78 Girls (%): 53 Age (mean, yr): 14.4±6.3 Race/Ethnicity: 36% Non-Hispanic White; 24% Non-Hispanic Black; 13% Hispanic; 5% Other Diabetes Duration (yr): NR HbA1c (mean %): NR BMI (mean): 21.2 Overweight (%): 33.3%	Sleep; self-report of previous day's sleep and wake times and frequency of daytime naps	Irregular napping was associated with overweight/obese BMI (vs. normal BMI, $OR=0.19$, $p<0.01$), higher body fat (per 10 unit increase, $OR=0.39$, $p<0.01$), and ≥85th percentile WC (vs. <85th percentile WC, $OR=0.20$, $p=0.05$)
Galli-Tsinopoulou et al., 2009 Greece	To assess body composition, nutritional status, and diabetes control in youth with T1D	Case-control	N: 24 Girls (%): 50 Age (mean, yr): 4–18 Race/Ethnicity: NR Diabetes Duration (yr): 3.7±2.0 HbA1c (mean %): 7.6±1.5 BMI (mean): 20.0±3.3 Overweight (%): 12.5	Diet; self-report 3-day food diary	3 overweight participants had dietary fat that ranged from ~100g to ~138g

Author, Year, Country	Aim	Study design	Sample characteristics	Measures	Results
Heyman et al., 2012 France	To examine the relationship of both physical activity and dietary composition with body composition, and markers of lipid and apolipoprotein profiles and insulin resistance in T1D adolescent girls	Case-control	N: 19 Girls (%): 100 Age (mean, yr): 15.9±1.3 Race/Ethnicity: 100% Caucasian Diabetes Duration (yr): 7.4±4.5 HbA1c (mean %): 8.1±1.3 BMI (mean): 24.6±3.9 Overweight (%): NR	Sedentary behavior; self-report questionnaire	Girls who watched more TV/videos had higher BMI ($r=0.61$, $p<0.01$), higher body fat ($r=0.60$, $p<0.01$), lower levels of protective lipoproteins (HDL-C, $r=-0.68$, $p<0.001$) and apolipoproteins (ApoA1, $r=-0.74$, $p<0.001$), and higher risk of insulin resistance (leptin, $r=0.46$, $p<0.05$; adiponectin, $r=-0.53$, $p<0.05$).
Overby et al., 2008 Norway	To describe characteristics related to skipping meals and snacking events in youth with T1D after the general introduction of insulin pumps and multiple injection treatments	Case-control	N: 665 Girls (%): 50 Age (mean, yr): 11.4±3.5 Race/Ethnicity: NR Diabetes Duration (yr): 3.8±3.1 HbA1c (mean %): 7.9±1.1 BMI (mean): 19.8±3.8 Overweight (%): 26.0	Diet; self-report questionnaire of the number of meals per day, TV viewing, personal computer use, and parents' education	Youth who skipped breakfast had higher odds of overweight compared with those who had breakfast almost every day (Adj. $OR=2.8$, 95% CI 1.1–7.2, $p<0.05$)

(Continued)

TABLE 3.1

Articles Meeting Inclusion Criteria for Overweight/Obesity in Youth With Type 1 Diabetes (Continued)

Authors, Country	Primary Aim	Study Design	Participant Characteristics[a]	Health Behavior, Measurement	Results[a]
Overby et al., 2009 Norway	To describe the physical activity and inactivity and parameters associated with overweight in T1D youth using intensified insulin treatment	Cohort/ cross-sectional	N: 723 Girls (%): 48 Age (mean, yr): 12.0 Race/Ethnicity: NR Diabetes Duration (yr): 4.6 HbA1c (mean %): 7.5–8.2 BMI (mean): 17.3–21.3 Overweight (%): 21.4	Physical activity, sedentary behavior, and diet; self-report questionnaires of the number of meals per day, frequency and intensity of activity, and transportation time. The questionnaire could estimate total amount of time spent on inactivity and light, moderate and vigorous activity	More than 1 hour of TV was associated with higher odds of overweight than TV less than 1 hour per day (Adj. $OR=2.52$, 95% CI 1.40–4.54, $p<0.01$); the same was observed for more than 2 hours of TV per day ($OR=2.30$, 95% CI 1.25–4.24, $p=0.01$). Eating breakfast 6–7 times a week had lower odds of overweight than eating breakfast 0–5 times per week ($OR=0.48$, 95% CI 0.23–0.99, $p<0.05$); the same was observed for eating dinner 6–7 times a week relative to eating dinner 0–5 times per week ($OR=0.50$, 95% CI 0.30–0.85, $p=0.01$). Physical activity was not associated with overweight

Intervention Studies

Source	Purpose	Design	Characteristics	Variables	Results
Semiz et al., 2000 Turkey	To evaluate the effectiveness of diabetes camp on diabetic children	Pretest–post-test evaluation without a comparison group. Intervention: 10-day camp with educational and social activity programs	N: 28 Girls (%): NR Age (mean, yr): 13.6±2.9 Race/Ethnicity: NR Diabetes Duration (yr): 5.1±3.3 HbA1c (mean %): 10.2±2.3 BMI (mean): NR Overweight (%): 28.6	Physical activity and diet; 10-day camp protocol aimed to balance insulin dosage with activity level (facilitated by social exercise programs) and food intake (facilitated by education program)	Mean decrement of 0.9 Kg in weight of the overweight children was detected at the end of the first camp (10 days)
Thomas-Dobersen et al., 1993 USA	To apply a family-based behavior-modification program (SHAPEDOWN) adapted for T1D to a group of obese adolescents with T1D	Two-group repeated measures design. Intervention: Adapted 14-session behavior-modification program focusing on diet, exercise, and metabolic control Comparison: Standard nutrition care from diabetes clinic	N: 19 Girls (%): 95 Age (mean, yr): 13.9 (intervention), 15.2 (comparison) Race/Ethnicity: NR Diabetes Duration (yr): 4.6 (intervention), 6.5 (comparison) HbA1c (mean %): 12.2 (intervention), 13.1 (comparison) Overweight (%): 100.0	Physical activity and diet; self-report questionnaire of weight-related behaviors and nutrition knowledge	Intervention group increased weight management knowledge compared to comparison group ($p<0.01$). No change in relative weight at 3 months between groups; at 15 months the intervention group lost 3.0% and comparison group gained 0.9% of relative weight ($p=NS$)

Abbreviations: N = sample size; NR = not reported; BMI = body mass index; WC = waist circumference; T1D = type 1 diabetes; OR = odds ratio; CI = confidence interval; NS = not significant

[a]Only characteristics and results tangential to the chapter's purpose were included.

questionnaires were used to estimate the duration and frequency of screen time in youth with T1D. More time watching television and videos was correlated with a higher BMI, higher percentage of body fat, lower levels of protective lipoproteins and apolipoproteins, and higher risk of insulin resistance in a sample of girls (Heyman et al., 2012). Similarly, in another study of boys and girls, youth who watched more than 1 hr of television per day had higher odds of being overweight than those who watched television less than 1 hr per day, even after adjustment for age, gender, physical activity, and having breakfast and dinner (Overby et al., 2009).

Sleep behavior was examined in one study to determine its relationship with obesity, diabetes, and insulin resistance. More than one-third of the participants in this study were found to be overweight or obese, the highest prevalence found across the studies in this review. Using a self-report questionnaire, the authors established that regular napping was significantly and inversely associated with characteristics of overweight, including high BMI, high percentage of body fat, and high waist circumference (Estrada et al., 2012).

Dietary intake was the most often studied obesity-related lifestyle behavior. In all three studies that investigated diet, a self-report measure was used to obtain dietary intake estimates. Two of these studies resulted in the finding that youth who skipped breakfast had higher odds of being overweight compared to those who had breakfast almost every day (Overby et al., 2009; Overby et al., 2008). Similarly, those who had a regular meal pattern of eating dinner 6–7 times per week had lower odds of being overweight than those who ate dinner 0–5 times per week (Overby et al., 2009), and some show that regular meals are also related to metabolic control (Overby, Margeirsdottir, Brunborg, Andersen, & Dahl-Jorgensen, 2007). In another study, it was found that when dietary fat intake was plotted against BMI, overweight youth had a dietary fat range from approximately 100 to 138 g, which is higher than the recommended daily intake (Bantle et al., 2006; Galli-Tsinopoulou et al., 2009).

Two intervention studies were included in this review, and the outcomes of both studies included physical activity and dietary intake. In one study, a 14-week family-based behavior modification program adapted for obese adolescents with T1D was evaluated (Thomas-Dobersen et al., 1993). The intervention employed cognitive, behavioral, and affective techniques to promote modifications in diet, exercise, communication, and affect among obese youth (95% girls) and their parents with T1D (Mellin, Slinkard, & Irwin, 1987). Participants were recruited from a diabetes clinic, with 11 participants enrolled in the intervention arm and nine controls were matched from those who received routine care from the clinic. All participants were obese at baseline and data were collected at baseline, 3 months and 15 months. At the 3- and 15-month intervals, the intervention group reported improved weight management knowledge ($p < .01$) and obesity-related behavior changes, including better dietary intake and physical activity ($p < .05$); the comparison group indicated improved obesity-related behaviors at both time points ($p < .05$). Although there was no difference between groups on weight loss at 3 months, there was a mean 3% relative weight loss at the 15-month time point in the intervention group, whereas the comparison group gained 0.9% relative weight (Thomas-Dobersen et al., 1993). Although this weight loss outcome appears promising, the small number of participants, retention issues, high variability of total weight loss, and the lack of a randomized design limit the applicability of findings.

The effectiveness of a Turkish diabetes camp for youth with T1D aimed to balance insulin dosage with activity levels and food intake was evaluated in the other intervention study reviewed. Using a pretest–posttest design without a comparison group, the intervention delivered during a 10-day camp used social physical activities and food educational programs. There were 28 adolescents enrolled, 8 of whom were overweight or obese. The mean weight loss was 0.9 kg after the first 10 days of camp (Semiz et al., 2000). Gender and statistical significance of the weight loss or sustainability was not reported.

SUMMARY AND IMPLICATIONS

Although based on a small number of observational and intervention studies included in this review, the data indicate that both overweight and obesity are rising in the population of youth with T1D and that the rates now mirror that of the general population (Liu et al., 2010). Indeed, the more recent studies included in this review demonstrated a high prevalence of overweight/obesity among youth with T1D, ranging from 12.5% to 33.3%. However, the prevalence may be less variable than this range suggests because all but one study had a mean overweight rate of 20.0% or more, although an epidemiologic review is needed to confirm this observation. Nevertheless, the high prevalence of overweight is concerning in that overweight/obesity in combination with T1D might contribute to development of double diabetes, in addition to other obesity-related complications.

Despite the limited number of studies, this review has identified what is known about obesity-related risk factors, including physical activity, sedentary behavior, sleep, and diet in youth with T1D. In brief, the observational studies yielded findings that overweight in youth with T1D was associated with infrequent napping (Estrada et al., 2012), increased screen time (Heyman et al., 2012; Overby et al., 2009), and skipping breakfast (Overby et al., 2009; Overby et al., 2008) and dinner (Overby et al., 2009) but was surprisingly not related to time spent engaging in physical activities (Overby et al., 2008). With the exception of the latter finding, these observations are largely congruent with youth in general, but must be interpreted with caution because objective measures were not used to assess behavior, sample sizes were generally small, and important participant characteristics were not reported. Nevertheless, the identification of these obesity-related behaviors in the real-world setting points to potential lifestyle modification targets for weight prevention and management in youth with T1D.

Two intervention studies were also identified in which physical activity and dietary change were used to improve weight and glycemic control in youth with T1D (Semiz et al., 2000; Thomas-Dobersen et al., 1993). In both studies, a modest weight loss of 0.9 kg after 10 days and 3% of relative weight after 15 months were reported (Semiz et al., 2000; Thomas-Dobersen et al., 1993). Again, however, the studies were limited by small sample sizes, retention issues, and missing participant characteristics that challenge the applicability of the results to a larger population. Nonetheless, these two studies suggest that weight-related interventions can have a positive impact on health behaviors and weight loss, along with other diabetes-specific health outcomes, such as improved glycemic control.

As is inherent with any review, several limitations exist. Although we believe we have conducted an exhaustive search, it is possible that some studies were not included either because of publication or selection bias. However, this may be mitigated since no additional manuscripts were identified from searching the reference lists. As mentioned before, one should take caution in the generalizability of many of these findings because they may have been compromised because of poor study quality.

Implications for Future Research and Practice

In light of this review, it is clear that more research is needed to address the role of the entire "activity spectrum," including physical activity, sedentary behavior, and sleep on youth with T1D who are overweight or obese. For instance, although it is known that fear of hypoglycemia is a common barrier to participation in physical activity (Brazeau et al., 2008; Di Battista et al., 2009; Nordfeldt & Ludvigsson, 2005), its effects may be compounded for youth who are overweight or obese and already have a less positive attitude toward physical activity (Deforche, De Bourdeaudhuij, & Tanghe, 2006). Furthermore, youth with T1D may actually be predisposed to excess weight gain by merit of supplementing carbohydrates before, during, and after engagement with physical activities in order to avoid a hypoglycemic event. Understanding the role of sedentary behaviors, and decreasing screen time in particular, may be one intervention pathway that leads to expending calories without compromising variability in blood glucose levels. Overweight and obesity may also have unique implications for sleep in youth with T1D as well. Studies of children and adolescents have found that sleep duration is inversely associated with overweight in youth (Eisenmann, Ekkekakis, & Holmes, 2006), and excessive weight is related to an increased risk of sleep problems (Beebe et al., 2007). Youth with T1D frequently report altered sleep patterns because of nocturnal hypoglycemia (Beregszaszi et al., 1997) and variation in blood glucose (Pillar et al., 2003), and thus they may be at higher risk for overweight than those without diabetes, or alternatively may experience poor sleep quality because of both excessive weight and having T1D.

In the future, studies in the field need to assure adequate representation of boys and girls from geographically diverse locations. Furthermore, use of objective measures of health behaviors in addition to self-report measures is highly recommended. Although T1D is less common in Black and Latino populations, compared to T2D, it will be important to study these questions in youth from various backgrounds because insulin resistance tends to be worse at higher BMI in obese Latino and Black youth compared to White youth, and they have among the highest prevalence of overweight (Holl, Jaser, Womack, Jefferson, & Grey, 2011; Ogden, Flegal, Carroll, & Johnson, 2002). Indeed, only one study in our sample reported an ethnically diverse sample (Estrada et al., 2012). To build the foundation for robust and efficacious interventions, various study designs should be considered, including qualitative, descriptive, correlational, and longitudinal designs.

Nurses and diabetes educators play a critical role in helping youth develop positive lifestyle behaviors to address the prevalent problem of overweight and obesity in youth with T1D. Because the problem of overweight in these youth is relatively new, clinical care has focused more on assuring good metabolic control and accurate carbohydrate counting than weight control. Less attention has been paid to issues related to physical activity, sedentary behavior, and sleep. For preventive efforts to avoid the deleterious effects of overweight and obesity in youth with T1D, health professionals should incorporate health-promoting guidelines that are recommended for all youth, while being especially attentive to the specific concerns of already overweight and obese youth and with T1D treatment. These recommendations include 60 min or more of moderate to vigorous physical activity per day (Strong et al., 2005; World Health Organization, 2010), fewer than 2 hr of screen time per day (American Academy of Pediatrics, 2001), and more than 9 hr of sleep per night (National Sleep Foundation, 2013). Furthermore, assessment of such health behaviors should be conducted regularly using standardized assessment tools so that youth and parents can be helped to promote and integrate health behaviors into their lives. Nurse scientists are also poised to conduct this type of research, yet only 1.5% of the 542 abstracts were published in nursing journals.

In summary, given the high prevalence of overweight and obesity in youth with T1D, there is a need for further research to explore the antecedents and consequences of excessive weight gain in youth with T1D. Although this review has identified potential lifestyle modification targets for weight prevention and management—including physical activity, sedentary behavior, and sleep—additional studies are needed to inform effective interventions for this vulnerable population.

ACKNOWLEDGMENTS

KEM is supported by an NIH/NIDDK pre-doctoral fellowship, T32-DK097718, Multidisciplinary Behavioral Research Training in Type 1 Diabetes to Margaret Grey, Program Director.

REFERENCES

(*Articles that met inclusion criteria and underwent review)
American Academy of Pediatrics. (2001). American Academy of Pediatrics: Children, adolescents, and television. *Pediatrics, 107*, 423–426.
American Diabetes Association. (1993). Implications of the Diabetes Control and Complications Trial. *Diabetes, 42*, 1555–1558. http://dx.doi.org/10.2337/diab.42.11.1555
American Diabetes Association. (2002). Diabetes mellitus and exercise. *Diabetes Care, 25*, s64. http://dx.doi.org/10.2337/diacare.25.2007.S64
Bandura, A. (2004). Health promotion by social cognitive means. *Health Education & Behavior, 31*, 143–164. http://dx.doi.org/10.1177/1090198104263660
Bantle, J. P., Wylie-Rosett, J., Albright, A. L., Apovian, C. M., Clark, N. G., Franz, M. J., . . . Wheeler, M. L. (2006). Nutrition recommendations and interventions for diabetes—2006: A position statement of the American Diabetes Association. *Diabetes Care, 29*, 2140–2157. http://dx.doi.org/10.2337/dc06-9914
Beebe, D. W., Lewin, D., Zeller, M., McCabe, M., MacLeod, K., Daniels, S. R., & Amin, R. (2007). Sleep in overweight adolescents: shorter sleep, poorer sleep quality, sleepiness, and sleep-disordered breathing. *Journal of Pediatric Psychology, 32*, 69–79. http://dx.doi.org/10.1093/jpepsy/jsj104
Bell, R. A., Mayer-Davis, E. J., Beyer, J. W., D'Agostino, R. B., Jr., Lawrence, J. M., Linder, B., . . . Dabelea, D. (2009). Diabetes in non-Hispanic white youth: Prevalence, incidence, and clinical characteristics: The SEARCH for Diabetes in Youth Study. *Diabetes Care, 32*(Suppl. 2), S102–111. http://dx.doi.org/10.2337/dc09-S202
Beregszaszi, M., Tubiana-Rufi, N., Benali, K., Noel, M., Bloch, J., & Czernichow, P. (1997). Nocturnal hypoglycemia in children and adolescents with insulin-dependent diabetes mellitus: Prevalence and risk factors. *Journal of Pediatrics, 131*, 27–33.
Blair, S. N., & Connelly, J. C. (1996). How much physical activity should we do? The case for moderate amounts and intensities of physical activity. *Research Quarterly for Exercise & Sport, 67*, 193–205.
Brazeau, A.-S., Rabasa-Lhoret, R., Strychar, I., & Mircescu, H. (2008). Barriers to physical activity among patients with type 1 diabetes. *Diabetes Care, 31*, 2108–2109. http://dx.doi.org/10.2337/dc08-0720
Cardwell, C. R., Stene, L. C., Joner, G., Bulsara, M. K., Cinek, O., Rosenbauer, J., . . . Patterson, C. C. (2010). Maternal age at birth and childhood type 1 diabetes: A pooled analysis of 30 observational studies. *Diabetes, 59*, 486–494. http://dx.doi.org/10.2337/db09-1166

Cardwell, C. R., Stene, L. C., Joner, G., Davis, E. A., Cinek, O., Rosenbauer, J., . . . Patterson, C. C. (2010). Birthweight and the risk of childhood-onset type 1 diabetes: A meta-analysis of observational studies using individual patient data. *Diabetologia, 53,* 641–651.

Chimen, M., Kennedy, A., Nirantharakumar, K., Pang, T. T., Andrews, R., & Narendran, P. (2012). What are the health benefits of physical activity in type 1 diabetes mellitus? A literature review. *Diabetologia, 55,* 542–551. http://dx.doi.org/10.1007/s00125-011-2403-2

Conway, B., Miller, R. G., Costacou, T., Fried, L., Kelsey, S., Evans, R. W., & Orchard, T. J. (2010). Temporal patterns in overweight and obesity in type 1 diabetes. *Diabetic Medicine, 27,* 398–404. http://dx.doi.org/10.1111/j.1464-5491.2010.02956.x

Daniels, S. R. (2006). The consequences of childhood overweight and obesity. *Future Child, 16,* 47–67.

DCCT Research Group. (1988). Weight gain associated with intensive therapy in the diabetes control and complications trial. The DCCT Research Group. *Diabetes Care, 11,* 567–573.

DCCT Research Group. (1993). The effect of intensive treatment of diabetes on the development and progression of long-term complications in insulin-dependent diabetes mellitus. *New England Journal of Medicine, 329,* 977–986. http://dx.doi.org/10.1056/NEJM199309303291401

Deforche, B. I., De Bourdeaudhuij, I. M., & Tanghe, A. P. (2006). Attitude toward physical activity in normal-weight, overweight and obese adolescents. *Journal of Adolescent Health, 38,* 560–568. http://dx.doi.org/10.1016/j.jadohealth.2005.01.015

Di Battista, A. M., Hart, T. A., Greco, L., & Gloizer, J. (2009). Type 1 diabetes among adolescents: Reduced diabetes self-care caused by social fear and fear of hypoglycemia. *Diabetes Educator, 35,* 465–475. http://dx.doi.org/10.1177/0145721709333492

Donga, E., van Dijk, M., van Dijk, J. G., Biermasz, N. R., Lammers, G. J., van Kralingen, K., . . . Romijn, J. A. (2010). Partial sleep restriction decreases insulin sensitivity in type 1 diabetes. *Diabetes Care, 33,* 1573–1577. http://dx.doi.org/10.2337/dc09-2317

Eaton, D. K., Kann, L., Kinchen, S., Shanklin, S., Ross, J., Hawkins, J., . . . Wechsler, H. (2010). Youth risk behavior surveillance—United States, 2009. *Mortality and Morbidity Weekly Report MWR Surveillance Summary, 59,* 1–142.

Einhorn, D., Stewart, D., Erman, M., Gordon, N., Philis-Tsimikas, A., & Casal, E. (2007). Prevalence of sleep apnea in a population of adults with type 2 diabetes mellitus. *Endocrine Practice, 13,* 355–362. http://dx.doi.org/10.4158/ep.13.4.355

Eisenmann, J. C., Ekkekakis, P., & Holmes, M. (2006). Sleep duration and overweight among Australian children and adolescents. *Acta Pædiatrica, 95,* 956–963. http://dx.doi.org/10.1080/08035250600731965

*Estrada, C. L., Danielson, K. K., Drum, M. L., & Lipton, R. B. (2012). Insufficient sleep in young patients with diabetes and their families. *Biological Research for Nursing, 14,* 48–54. http://dx.doi.org/10.1177/1099800410395569

Faulkner, M. S. (2010). Cardiovascular fitness and quality of life in adolescents with type 1 or type 2 diabetes. *Journal for Specialists in Pediatric Nursing, 15,* 307–316. http://dx.doi.org/10.1111/j.1744-6155.2010.00254.x

Faulkner, M. S., Chao, W. H., Kamath, S. K., Quinn, L., Fritschi, C., Maggiore, J. A., . . . Reynolds, R. D. (2006). Total homocysteine, diet, and lipid profiles in type 1 and type 2 diabetic and nondiabetic adolescents. *Journal of Cardiovascular Nursing, 21,* 47–55.

Faulkner, M. S., Michaliszyn, S. F., & Hepworth, J. T. (2010). A personalized approach to exercise promotion in adolescents with type 1 diabetes. *Pediatric Diabetes, 11,* 166–174.

Field, A. E., Cook, N. R., & Gillman, M. W. (2005). Weight status in childhood as a predictor of becoming overweight or hypertensive in early adulthood. *Obesity Research, 13,* 163–169. http://dx.doi.org/10.1038/oby.2005.21

Galler, A., Lindau, M., Ernert, A., Thalemann, R., & Raile, K. (2011). Associations between media consumption habits, physical activity, socioeconomic status, and glycemic control in children, adolescents, and young adults with type 1 diabetes. *Diabetes Care, 34*, 2356–2359.

*Galli-Tsinopoulou, A., Grammatikopoulou, M. G., Stylianou, C., Kokka, P., & Emmanouilidou, E. (2009). A preliminary case-control study on nutritional status, body composition, and glycemic control of Greek children and adolescents with type 1 diabetes. *Journal of Diabetes, 1*, 36–42.

Gillespie, S. J., Kulkarni, K. D., & Daly, A. E. (1998). Using carbohydrate counting in diabetes clinical practice. *Journal of the American Dietetic Association, 98*, 897–905.

Han, J. C., Lawlor, D. A., & Kimm, S. Y. S. (2010). Childhood obesity. *Lancet, 375*, 1737–1748.

*Heyman, E., Berthon, P., Youssef, H., Delamarche, A., Briard, D., Gamelin, F. X., . . . de Kerdanet, M. (2012). Metabolic dysfunction in late-puberty adolescent girls with type 1 diabetes: Relationship to physical activity and dietary intakes. *Diabetes & Metabolism, 38*, 337–342.

Hill, A. L., Rand, D. G., Nowak, M. A., & Christakis, N. A. (2010). Infectious disease modeling of social contagion in networks. *PLoS Computational Biology, 6*, e1000968. http://dx.doi.org /10.1371/journal.pcbi.1000968

Holl, M. G., Jaser, S. S., Womack, J. A., Jefferson, V. L., & Grey, M. (2011). Metabolic risk and health behaviors in minority youth at risk for type 2 diabetes. *Diabetes Care, 34*, 193–197. http:// dx.doi.org/10.2337/dc10-1197

Imperatore, G., Boyle, J. P., Thompson, T. J., Case, D., Dabelea, D., Hamman, R. F., . . . SEARCH for Diabetes in Youth Study Group. (2012). Projections of type 1 and type 2 diabetes burden in the U.S. population aged <20 years through 2050: Dynamic modeling of incidence, mortality, and population growth. *Diabetes Care, 35*, 2515–2520. http://dx.doi.org/10.2337 /dc12-0669

Jack, A. (2007). Time to supersize control efforts for obesity. *Lancet, 370*, 1521. http://dx.doi .org/10.1016/S0140-6736(07)61639-0

Janssen, I., & Leblanc, A. G. (2010). Systematic review of the health benefits of physical activity and fitness in school-aged children and youth. *International Journal of Behavioral Nutrition and Physical Activity, 7*, 40. http://dx.doi.org/10.1186/1479-5868-7-40

Knip, M., Veijola, R., Virtanen, S. M., Hyöty, H., Vaarala, O., & Åkerblom, H. K. (2005). Environmental triggers and determinants of type 1 diabetes. *Diabetes, 54*, S125–S136. http:// dx.doi.org/10.2337/diabetes.54.suppl_2.S125

Krishnan, S., & Short, K. R. (2009). Prevalence and significance of cardiometabolic risk factors in children with type 1 diabetes. *Journal of the Cardiometabolic Syndrome, 4*, 50–56. http:// dx.doi.org/10.1111/j.1559-4572.2008.00034.x

Laing, S. P., Swerdlow, A. J., Slater, S. D., Burden, A. C., Morris, A., Waugh, N. R., . . . Patterson, C. C. (2003). Mortality from heart disease in a cohort of 23,000 patients with insulin-treated diabetes. *Diabetologia, 46*, 760–765. http://dx.doi.org/10.1007/s00125-003-1116-6

Lawrence, J. M., Liese, A. D., Liu, L., Dabelea, D., Anderson, A., Imperatore, G., & Bell, R. (2008). Weight-loss practices and weight-related issues among youth with type 1 or type 2 diabetes. *Diabetes Care, 31*, 2251–2257. http://dx.doi.org/10.2337/dc08-0719

Libman, I. M., & Becker, D. J. (2003). Coexistence of type 1 and type 2 diabetes mellitus: "Double" diabetes? *Pediatric Diabetes, 4*, 110–113. http://dx.doi.org/10.1034/j.1399-5448.2003.00012.x

Libman, I. M., Pietropaolo, M., Arslanian, S. A., LaPorte, R. E., & Becker, D. J. (2003). Changing prevalence of overweight children and adolescents at onset of insulin-treated diabetes. *Diabetes Care, 26*, 2871–2875.

Liese, A. D., Ma, X., Maahs, D. M., & Trilk, J. L. (2013). Physical activity, sedentary behaviors, physical fitness, and their relation to health outcomes in youth with type 1 and type 2 diabetes: A review of the epidemiologic literature. *Journal of Sport and Health Science, 2*, 21–38. http://dx.doi.org/10.1016/j.jshs.2012.10.005

Lipman, T. H., Levitt Katz, L. E., Ratcliffe, S. J., Murphy, K. M., Aguilar, A., Rezvani, I., . . . Suarez, E. (2013). Increasing incidence of type 1 diabetes in youth: Twenty years of the Philadelphia Pediatric Diabetes Registry. *Diabetes Care, 36*(6), 1597–1603. http://dx.doi.org/10.2337/dc12-0767

Liu, L. L., Lawrence, J. M., Davis, C., Liese, A. D., Pettitt, D. J., Pihoker, C., . . . SEARCH for Diabetes in Youth Study Group. (2010). Prevalence of overweight and obesity in youth with diabetes in USA: The SEARCH for Diabetes in Youth study. *Pediatric Diabetes, 11*, 4–11.

Mark, A. E., & Janssen, I. (2008). Relationship between screen time and metabolic syndrome in adolescents. *Journal of Public Health, 30*, 153–160. http://dx.doi.org/10.1093/pubmed/fdn022

Matyka, K. A., Crawford, C., Wiggs, L., Dunger, D. B., & Stores, G. (2000). Alterations in sleep physiology in young children with insulin-dependent diabetes mellitus: Relationship to nocturnal hypoglycemia. *Journal of Pediatrics, 137*, 233–238. http://dx.doi.org/10.1067/mpd.2000.107186

Mayer-Davis, E. J., Nichols, M., Liese, A. D., Bell, R. A., Dabelea, D. M., Johansen, J. M., . . . Williams, D. (2006). Dietary intake among youth with diabetes: The SEARCH for Diabetes in Youth Study. *Journal of the American Dietetic Association, 106*, 689–697.

Mellin, L. M., Slinkard, L. A., & Irwin, C. E., Jr. (1987). Adolescent obesity intervention: Validation of the SHAPEDOWN program. *Journal of the American Dietetic Association, 87*, 333–338.

Michaliszyn, S., & Faulkner, M. (2010). Physical activity and sedentary behavior in adolescents with type 1 diabetes. *Research in Nursing & Health, 33*, 441–409.

Michaliszyn, S. F., Shaibi, G. Q., Quinn, L., Fritschi, C., & Faulkner, M. S. (2009). Physical fitness, dietary intake, and metabolic control in adolescents with type 1 diabetes. *Pediatric Diabetes, 10*, 389–394.

Moher, D., Liberati, A., Tetzlaff, J., & Altman, D. G. (2009). Preferred reporting items for systematic reviews and meta-analyses: The PRISMA statement. *Annals of Internal Medicine, 151*, 264–269. http://dx.doi.org/10.1371/journal.pmed.1000097

National Sleep Foundation. (2013). *Children and sleep*. Retrieved from www.sleepfoundation.org/article/sleep-topics/children-and-sleep

Nordfeldt, S., & Ludvigsson, J. (2005). Fear and other disturbances of severe hypoglycaemia in children and adolescents with type 1 diabetes mellitus. *Journal of Pediatric Endocrinology & Metabolism, 18*, 83–91.

Ogden, C. L., Flegal, K. M., Carroll, M. D., & Johnson, C. L. (2002). Prevalence and trends in overweight among U.S. children and adolescents, 1999–2000. *Journal of the American Medical Association, 288*, 1728–1732. http://dx.doi.org/10.1001/jama.288.14.1728

Olshansky, S. J., Passaro, D. J., Hershow, R. C., Layden, J., Carnes, B. A., Brody, J., . . . Ludwig, D. S. (2005). A potential decline in life expectancy in the United States in the 21st century. *New England Journal of Medicine, 352*, 1138–1145. http://dx.doi.org/10.1056/NEJMsr043743

Onkamo, P., Vaananen, S., Karvonen, M., & Tuomilehto, J. (1999). Worldwide increase in incidence of type 1 diabetes—The analysis of the data on published incidence trends. *Diabetologia, 42*, 1395–1403. http://dx.doi.org/10.1007/s001250051309

Overby, N. C., Margeirsdottir, H. D., Brunborg, C., Andersen, L. F., & Dahl-Jorgensen, K. (2007). The influence of dietary intake and meal pattern on blood glucose control in children and adolescents using intensive insulin treatment. *Diabetologia, 50*, 2044–2051.

*Overby, N. C., Margeirsdottir, H. D., Brunborg, C., Anderssen, S. A., Andersen, L. F., Dahl-Jorgensen, K., & Norwegian Study Group for Childhood Diabetes. (2009). Physical activity and overweight in children and adolescents using intensified insulin treatment. *Pediatric Diabetes, 10*, 135–141.

*Overby, N. C., Margeirsdottir, H. D., Brunborg, C., Dahl-Jorgensen, K., Andersen, L. F., & Norwegian Study Group for Childhood Diabetes. (2008). Sweets, snacking habits, and skipping meals in children and adolescents on intensive insulin treatment. *Pediatric Diabetes, 9*, 393–400.

Padez, C., Mourao, I., Moreira, P., & Rosado, V. (2009). Long sleep duration and childhood overweight/obesity and body fat. *American Journal of Human Biology, 21,* 371–376. http://dx.doi.org/10.1002/ajhb.20884

Pate, R. R., O'Neill, J. R., & Lobelo, F. (2008). The evolving definition of "sedentary." *Exercise and Sport Sciences Reviews, 36,* 173–178. http://dx.doi.org/10.1097/JES.0b013e3181877d1a

Patrick, K., Norman, G. J., Calfas, K. J., Sallis, J. F., Zabinski, M. F., Rupp, J., & Cella, J. (2004). Diet, physical activity, and sedentary behaviors as risk factors for overweight in adolescence. *Archives of Pediatrics & Adolescent Medicine, 158,* 385–390.

Patterson, C., Gyürüs, E., Rosenbauer, J., Cinek, O., Neu, A., Schober, E., . . . Soltész, G. (2012). Trends in childhood type 1 diabetes incidence in Europe during 1989–2008: Evidence of non-uniformity over time in rates of increase. *Diabetologia, 55*(8), 2142–2147.

Perfect, M. M., Patel, P. G., Scott, R. E., Wheeler, M. D., Patel, C., Griffin, K., . . . Quan, S. F. (2012). Sleep, glucose, and daytime functioning in youth with type 1 diabetes. *Sleep, 35,* 81–88. http://dx.doi.org/10.5665/sleep.1590

Pillar, G., Schuscheim, G., Weiss, R., Malhotra, A., McCowen, K. C., Shlitner, A., . . . Shehadeh, N. (2003). Interactions between hypoglycemia and sleep architecture in children with type 1 diabetes mellitus. *Journal of Pediatrics, 142,* 163–168. http://dx.doi.org/10.1067/mpd.2003.66

Pozzilli, P., Guglielmi, C., Caprio, S., & Buzzetti, R. (2011). Obesity, autoimmunity, and double diabetes in youth. *Diabetes Care, 34*(Suppl. 2), S166–S170. http://dx.doi.org/10.2337/dc11-s213

Purnell, J. Q., Zinman, B., & Brunzell, J. D. (2013). The effect of excess weight gain with intensive diabetes mellitus treatment on cardiovascular disease risk factors and atherosclerosis in type 1 diabetes mellitus: Results from the Diabetes Control and Complications Trial/Epidemiology of Diabetes Interventions and Complications Study (DCCT/EDIC) Study. *Circulation, 127*(2), 180–187. http://dx.doi.org/10.1161/circulationaha.111.07748

Purnell, J., Hokanson, J. E., Marcovina, S. M., Steffes, M. W., Cleary, P. A., & Brunzell, J. D. (1998). Effect of excessive weight gain with intensive therapy of type 1 diabetes on lipid levels and blood pressure: Results from the DCCT. *Journal of the American Medical Association, 280,* 140–146. http://dx.doi.org/10.1001/jama.280.2.140

Robertson, K., Adolfsson, P., Scheiner, G., Hanas, R., & Riddell, M. C. (2009). Exercise in children and adolescents with diabetes. *Pediatric Diabetes, 10,* 154–168. http://dx.doi.org/10.1111/j.1399-5448.2009.00567.x

Russell-Jones, D., & Khan, R. (2007). Insulin-associated weight gain in diabetes—Causes, effects and coping strategies. *Diabetes, Obesity and Metabolism, 9,* 799–812. http://dx.doi.org/10.1111/j.1463-1326.2006.00686.x

Schilling, L. S., Grey, M., & Knafl, K. A. (2002). The concept of self-management of type 1 diabetes in children and adolescents: An evolutionary concept analysis. *Journal of Advanced Nursing, 37,* 87–99. http://dx.doi.org/10.1046/j.1365-2648.2002.02061.x

Schweiger, B., Klingensmith, G., & Snell-Bergeon, J. K. (2010). Physical activity in adolescent females with type 1 diabetes. *International Journal of Pediatrics, 328318.* http://dx.doi.org/10.1155/2010/328318

SEARCH for Diabetes in Youth Study Group. (2006). The burden of diabetes mellitus among US youth: Prevalence estimates from the SEARCH for Diabetes in Youth Study. *Pediatrics, 118,* 1510–1518. http://dx.doi.org/10.1542/peds.2006-0690

SEARCH for Diabetes in Youth Study Group. (2007). Incidence of diabetes in youth in the United States. *The Journal of the American Medical Association, 297,* 2716–2724. http://dx.doi.org/10.1001/jama.297.24.2716

*Semiz, S., Bilgin, U. O., Bundak, R., & Bircan, I. (2000). Summer camps for diabetic children: An experience in Antalya, Turkey. *Acta Diabetologica, 37,* 197–200.

Silverstein, J., Klingensmith, G., Copeland, K., Plotnick, L., Kaufman, F., Laffel, L., . . . Clark, N. (2005). Care of children and adolescents with type 1 diabetes: A statement of the American Diabetes Association. *Diabetes Care, 28,* 186–212.

Soedamah-Muthu, S. S., Fuller, J. H., Mulnier, H. E., Raleigh, V. S., Lawrenson, R. A., & Colhoun, H. M. (2006). High risk of cardiovascular disease in patients with type 1 diabetes in the U.K.: A cohort study using the General Practice Research Database. *Diabetes Care, 29,* 798–804. http://dx.doi.org/10.2337/diacare.29.04.06.dc05-1433

Soltesz, G., Patterson, C. C., Dahlquist, G., & Eurodiab Study Group. (2007). Worldwide childhood type 1 diabetes incidence—What can we learn from epidemiology? *Pediatric Diabetes, 8,* 6–14. http://dx.doi.org/10.1111/j.1399-5448.2007.00280.x

Spiegel, K., Knutson, K., Leproult, R., Tasali, E., & Cauter, E. V. (2005). Sleep loss: A novel risk factor for insulin resistance and type 2 diabetes. *Journal of Applied Physiology, 99,* 2008–2019. http://dx.doi.org/10.1152/japplphysiol.00660.2005

Strong, W. B., Malina, R. M., Blimkie, C. J. R., Daniels, S. R., Dishman, R. K., Gutin, B., . . . Trudeau, F. (2005). Evidence based physical activity for school-age youth. *Journal of Pediatrics, 146,* 732–737. http://dx.doi.org/10.1016/j.jpeds.2005.01.055

*Thomas-Dobersen, D. A., Butler-Simon, N., & Fleshner, M. (1993). Evaluation of a weight management intervention program in adolescents with insulin-dependent diabetes mellitus. *Journal of the American Dietetic Association, 93,* 535–540.

Touchette, E., Petit, D., Tremblay, R. E., Boivin, M., Falissard, B., Genolini, C., & Montplaisir, J. Y. (2008). Associations between sleep duration patterns and overweight/obesity at age 6. *Sleep, 31,* 1507–1514.

Tremblay, M. S., LeBlanc, A. G., Kho, M. E., Saunders, T. J., Larouche, R., Colley, R. C., . . . Connor, G. S. (2011). Systematic review of sedentary behaviour and health indicators in school-aged children and youth. *International Journal of Behavioral Nutrition & Physical Activity, 8,* 98. http://dx.doi.org/10.1186/1479-5868-8-98

Troiano, R. P., Berrigan, D., Dodd, K. W., Masse, L. C., Tilert, T., & McDowell, M. (2008). Physical activity in the United States measured by accelerometer. *Medicine and Science in Sports and Exercise, 40,* 181–188. http://dx.doi.org/10.1249/mss.0b013e31815a51b3

Van Vliet, M., Van Der Heyden, J. C., Diamant, M., Von Rosenstiel, I. A., Schindhelm, R. K., Heymans, M. W., . . . Veeze, H. J. (2012). Overweight children with type 1 diabetes have a more favourable lipid profile than overweight non-diabetic children. *European Journal of Pediatrics, 171,* 493–498.

Vgontzas, A. N., Liao, D., Pejovic, S., Calhoun, S., Karataraki, M., & Bixler, E. O. (2009). Insomnia with objective short sleep duration is associated with type 2 diabetes: A population-based study. *Diabetes Care, 32,* 1980–1985. http://dx.doi.org/10.2337/dc09-0284

Villa, M. P., Multari, G., Montesano, M., Pagani, J., Cervoni, M., Midulla, F., . . . Ronchetti, R. (2000). Sleep apnoea in children with diabetes mellitus: Effect of glycaemic control. *Diabetologia, 43,* 696–702. http://dx.doi.org/10.1007/s001250051365

Warburton, D. E. R., Nicol, C. W., & Bredin, S. S. D. (2006). Health benefits of physical activity: The evidence. *Canadian Medical Association Journal, 174,* 801–809. http://dx.doi.org/10.1503/cmaj.051351

Wild, S., Roglic, G., Green, A., Sicree, R., & King, H. (2004). Global prevalence of diabetes: Estimates for the year 2000 and projections for 2030. *Diabetes Care, 27,* 1047–1053.

Wilkin, T. J. (2001). The accelerator hypothesis: Weight gain as the missing link between type I and type II diabetes. *Diabetologia, 44,* 914–922. http://dx.doi.org/10.1007/s001250100548

World Health Organization. (2010). *Global recommendations on physical activity for health.* Geneva, Switzerland: Author.

CHAPTER 4

Physical Activity Intervention Studies and Their Relationship to Body Composition in Healthy Women

Susan Weber Buchholz, JoEllen Wilbur, Shannon Halloway, Judith H. McDevitt, and Michael E. Schoeny

ABSTRACT

Engaging in regular physical activity is a key component for maintaining a healthy weight and preventing overweight and obesity. Obesity continues to be a concern globally, especially for women, and women are less physically active than men. This systematic review examined current research on physical activity interventions designed for healthy community dwelling women and assessed the effects of those interventions on physical activity and body composition. Three author-developed data collection tools were used to extract and examine study variables. For studies with suitable data, effect sizes were obtained. The initial search identified 1,406 titles published between 2000 and 2012, of which 40 randomized clinical trials met inclusion criteria. Of these 40 studies, 16 had a physical activity intervention that did not have a diet component and 24 had a physical activity intervention along with a diet component. The overall weighted mean effect was $d = .21$, 95% CI [0.06, 0.36] for physical activity outcomes ($n = 18$ studies) and $d = -.16$, 95% CI [-0.22, -0.09] for body composition outcomes ($n = 24$ studies). Both physical activity interventions without and

© 2013 Springer Publishing Company
http://dx.doi.org/10.1891/0739-6686.31.71

with a diet component were effective in promoting physical activity and improving body composition. Physical activity interventions without a diet component were more effective than physical activity interventions with a diet component at promoting physical activity. The most effective interventions need to be adapted for dissemination into practice.

PHYSICAL ACTIVITY INTERVENTION STUDIES AND THEIR RELATIONSHIP TO BODY COMPOSITION IN HEALTHY WOMEN

Physical activity (PA) is critical for maintaining a healthy weight and preventing overweight and obese states. According to the U.S. Department of Health and Human Services (USDHHS), women are less physically active then men and are at increased risk for obesity (USDHHS, 2012). The purpose of this chapter is to provide a systematic review of current research on PA interventions designed for healthy, community dwelling women and to assess the effects of those interventions on PA and body composition (BC).

The first part of the chapter provides background information on the prevalence of overweight and obesity in women and how BC is measured. Background information on PA levels in women and how PA is measured follows. The background concludes with an overview of previously published systematic reviews of PA interventions and examines to what extent they have included interventions specifically for healthy women. In the second part of this chapter, we present the methods used to conduct this systematic review. We then present the results of the review, focusing on the extent to which PA interventions change PA behavior and BC and the characteristics of these effective PA interventions. In the discussion, we first address conceptual and methodological issues associated with PA interventions in women. We conclude with a discussion of research, theory, public health, and dissemination implications.

BACKGROUND

Obesity

Obesity has become a significant health concern worldwide. In the past 30 years, the incidence of obesity has nearly doubled. Women are at disproportionate risk for being overweight or obese. Globally, 34% of men and 35% of women are overweight, whereas 10% of men and 14% of women are actually obese (World Health Organization, 2011). In the United States, two-thirds of adults are overweight or obese and obesity rates are higher than they are globally, with 34% of men and 36% of women being obese (USDHHS, 2012). Increased adiposity, especially central adiposity (women >35 in. or 88 cm and men >40 in. or 102 cm), places adults at increased risk for diabetes and cardiovascular disease (USDHHS, 2006). In general, women have a higher body fat percentage than men (Blaak, 2001). When they become postmenopausal, women are at particular risk for weight gain and changes in BC, especially abdominal fat accumulation, thus increasing their risk for diabetes and cardiovascular disease (Davis et al., 2012).

Determining BC is critical in assessing for overweight, obesity, and weight loss in adults (American College of Sports Medicine [ACSM], 2010; Bray, 2013; Heyward, 2006). BC is generally expressed as the relative percentage of body mass that is fat and fat-free tissue, with field methods the most commonly used as measures (ACSM, 2010). Field methods include anthropometric methods and bioelectrical impedance analysis (BIA). Briefly, anthropometry is the measurement of the size and proportions of the body. The accuracy and reliability of anthropometric measures relies on client factors and the equipment and skill of the assessor. Body mass index (BMI) is obtained from height and weight measures, and circumferences measure the girth of the waist, hip, arm, and/or thigh. Skinfolds are an indirect measure of the thickness of subcutaneous fat that is proportional to the total amount of body fat and require a stringent protocol (ACSM, 2010; Heyward, 2006). Last, BIA indirectly estimates the volume of the body's total body water and free fat mass. As with skinfolds, BIA also requires a stringent protocol.

Laboratory methods for determining BC provide criterion measures for the derivation and evaluation of BC field methods and predictive equations (ACSM, 2010; Heyward, 2006). Although laboratory methods provide greater accuracy, they require highly trained personnel, are inconvenient for participants, and generally are more expensive and time consuming than field methods. Laboratory methods include dual-energy x-ray absorptiometry (DXA), hydrodensitometry (hydrostatic weighing or underwater weighing), and air displacement plethysmography. Less commonly used laboratory methods are computed tomography (CT) and magnetic resonance imaging (MRI; ACSM, 2010; Bray, 2013).

Physical Activity

One health behavior that can play an important role in maintaining a healthy weight and maintaining weight loss in previously overweight or obese individuals is PA (USDHHS, 2008). PA is any bodily movement that involves skeletal muscle use and increases energy expenditure. It consists of activities that people participate in throughout the day, including but not limited to scheduled exercise sessions during which individuals engage in PA to specifically improve health and fitness (Jonas, 2009). PA has been demonstrated to have an effect on BC levels. Increased

PA levels contribute to higher muscle mass and, equally important, to decreased fat mass (Donnelly, Jacobsen, Heelan, Seip, & Smith, 2000; Strasser, 2013).

Current PA recommendations for adults 18–64 years old are 150 min of moderate-intensity aerobic PA or at least 75 min of vigorous-intensity aerobic PA per week. In addition, muscle strengthening exercises are recommended on at least 2 days/week (World Health Organization, 2010). These recommendations have influenced numerous PA intervention studies designed to encourage sedentary people to be more physically active, with the goal being to eventually achieve the recommended level of PA. However, despite several decades of research in PA (Centers for Disease Control and Prevention, 1996), PA levels have risen only slightly. In the United States, women continue to have lower PA levels than men and as they age, their levels of PA decrease (USDHHS, 2012). These disheartening trends can also be seen worldwide, with 31.1% of adults not obtaining recommended PA levels per public health guidelines (Hallal et al., 2012) and physical inactivity now ranked fourth as a risk factor for global mortality (World Health Organization, 2010). As in the United States, global physical inactivity levels disproportionately affect women, with women having a higher rate of physical inactivity (33.9%) compared to men (27.9%; Hallal et al., 2012).

Both self-report and objective measures of PA are used in research studies. More than 80 self-report PA questionnaires are available and include those targeted to specific populations such as children, women, adults, or the elderly (Helmerhorst, Brage, Warren, Besson, & Ekelund, 2012; van Poppel, Chinapaw, Mokkink, van Mechelen, & Terwee, 2010). Total PA, leisure time PA, household PA, occupational PA, and transportation PA are various PA dimensions that can be captured. Recall can be elicited for the past day's activity to a lifetime of activity, although many PA questionnaires have a 7-day recall period. The number of items in PA questionnaires can range from 1 to more than 100. Estimates of metabolic equivalent of task (MET), kcal $\cdot$ kg^{-1} $\cdot$ week^{-1}, and minutes of moderate and high intensity activity per week are among the most common units of measurement.

Self-report measures are particularly prone to measurement error because of biased misreporting, social desirability reporting, and problems with recall. Furthermore, it is difficult for respondents to estimate highly variable PA such as the free-living activity that occurs in the household and occupational domains. Psychometrically, although the reliability of self-report measures is acceptable (adults 0.64–0.79), the validity of self-report in quantifying PA is limited (Helmerhorst et al., 2012; van Poppel et al., 2010). Self-report measures are better used to simply rank PA. The decision about which self-report measure to use is dependent on the sample and setting of the study (Helmerhorst et al., 2012; van Poppel et al., 2010).

Accelerometers, PA monitors that can detect or record the actual magnitude of acceleration, offer a robust, objective alternative to self-report (Hawkins et al.,

2009). They are small and unobtrusive and can be worn throughout the day without interfering with everyday movement. Another unique feature is their ability to capture light-intensity PA, which is difficult to recall on self-report questionnaires. Accelerometers show a valid assessment of PA in adult men and women during treadmill walking or running and daily activity (Hendelman, Miller, Baggett, Debold, & Freedson, 2000). Pedometers record only steps taken and are useful objective measures when the activity of interest is walking (Helmerhorst et al., 2012). However, in addition to capturing steps, recently, accelerometers have become available to measure individuals when swimming or biking.

The current recommendation for measuring PA in research is to use both self-report and objective measures. A combination of motion sensor (e.g., accelerometer, pedometer) and self-report measures may enhance the rigor of research by quantifying PA behavior and providing the domain in which that PA occurred (Ju, Wilbur, Lee, & Miller, 2011).

Cardiorespiratory fitness provides an indirect measure of PA. Higher levels of cardiorespiratory fitness are associated with higher levels of PA (ACSM, 2010). Such PA involves large muscle groups and develops the ability to perform dynamic, moderate- to high-intensity PA for prolonged times (ACSM, 2010). Maximal oxygen uptake (VO_{2max}) is the criterion measure. Field tests including walking tests performed in a given time frame can be used to classify cardiorespiratory fitness level. Treadmill and cycle ergometer tests also can be used for either maximal or submaximal testing (Heyward, 2006). However, they are more expensive and time-consuming than field tests and require a specific level of expertise to administer and supervise.

Systematic Reviews of Physical Activity Interventions

Twenty-one earlier systematic reviews of PA interventions in samples of healthy, community-based adults and published between 2005 and 2012 were identified for background review (see Table 4.1). We assessed the methods and outcomes of previous reviews and identified studies with women only that had outcomes for both PA and BC. Twelve of the 21 reviews identified were of studies in both women and men with PA change as the primary outcome. These 12 were site specific, such as worksite (Benedict & Arterburn, 2008; Conn, Hafdahl, Cooper, Brown, & Lusk, 2009; Orrow, Kinmonth, Sanderson, & Sutton, 2012) and primary care settings (Orrow et al., 2012; Williams, Hendry, France, Lewis, & Wilkinson, 2007); population specific, such as in minorities or low-income persons (Cleland, Tully, Kee, & Cupples, 2012; Conn, Phillips, Ruppar, & Chase, 2012; Ickes & Sharma, 2012; Whitt-Glover & Kumanyika, 2009); PA type or mode specific, such as walking (Ogilvie et al., 2007); or were general reviews

TABLE 4.1

Systematic Reviews of Physical Activity Interventions Focused Primarily on Healthy Adults Published 2005–2013

	Purpose	Key Findings	Studies of Women, Physical Activity (PA), and Body Composition (BC)
Worksite			
Anderson et al. (2009)	Examine the effectiveness of worksite nutrition and PA programs to promote healthy weight among employees.	Modest improvement in weight status for men and women at 6- to 12-month follow-up.	—
Benedict & Arterburn (2008)	Assess the quality and effectiveness of worksite interventions for weight control.	Worksite programs can result in modest short improvements in body weight.	—
Conn et al. (2009)	Examine the effects of workplace interventions to increase PA on PA behavior, health, and work-related outcomes.	Significantly positive effects were observed for PA behavior, fitness, and anthropometric measures.	Campbell et al. (2002)
Primary care site			
Orrow et al. (2012)	Determine whether primary care based PA interventions for sedentary adults show sustained effects on PA.	Promotion of PA to sedentary adults recruited from primary care significantly increases PA levels at 12 months.	Keyserling et al. (2008) Yancey et al. (2006) Hovell et al. (2008)
Williams et al. (2007)	Assess whether primary-care-initiated exercise referral schemes were effective in improving exercise participation in sedentary adults.	Seventeen sedentary adults would need to be referred for one to become moderately active (poor uptake and adherence).	—

TABLE 4.1

Systematic Reviews of Physical Activity Interventions Focused Primarily on Healthy Adults
Published 2005–2013   (Continued)

	Purpose	Key Findings	Studies of Women, Physical Activity (PA), and Body Composition (BC)
Minority/low-income			
Cleland et al. (2012)	Examine the effectiveness of interventions to promote PA in socioeconomically disadvantaged communities.	Multicomponent group-based interventions with theoretical frameworks were most effective in increasing PA.	Keyserling et al. (2008) Yancey et al. (2006) Hovell et al. (2008)
Conn et al. (2012)	Examine overall effects of supervised PA intervention with verified PA performance on physical fitness, anthropometric measures, diabetes risk, and mood outcome among health minority adults.	Interventions designed to motivate minority adults to increase PA changed subsequent PA behavior and anthropometric outcomes.	Keller & Cantue (2008) Wilbur et al. (2008) Fitzgibbon et al. (2005) Campbell et al. (2002) Staten et al. (2004) Poston et al. (2001) Santa-Clara et al. (2006)
Ickes & Sharma (2012)	Summarize existing evidence related to PA intervention with goal of obesity prevention in Hispanic adults.	Intervention effects were successful for PA and/or BMI.	Keller & Cantue (2008) Hayashi et al. (2010) Hovell et al. (2008) Poston et al. (2001)
Whitt-Glover & Kumanyika (2009)	Identify characteristics of effective interventions designed to increase PA or fitness among African Americans.	Most studies showed significant within group pre–post improvements in PA, but fewer found differences between intervention and comparison groups.	Campbell et al. (2002) Yanek et al. (2001) Fitzgibbon et al. (2005)

(Continued)

TABLE 4.1

Systematic Reviews of Physical Activity Interventions Focused Primarily on Healthy Adults Published 2005–2013   (Continued)

	Purpose	Key Findings	Studies of Women, Physical Activity (PA), and Body Composition (BC)
Type of activity			
Ogilvie et al. (2007)	Characterize interventions effective in promotion walking and effect of interventions on overall PA and health.	Evidence that people can be encouraged to walk more by interventions tailored to their needs, targeted at the most sedentary or most motivated to change (individual and group based).	Nies et al. (2003)
General PA			
Conn et al. (2011)	Examine overall effects of PA intervention on PA behavior after completion of intervention.	Interventions designed to increase PA were moderately effective.	Keller & Cantue (2008)
Muller-Riemenschneider et al. (2008)	Summarize the evidence for the long-term effectiveness of PA interventions.	There is evidence for long-term increases in PA behavior and physical fitness.	Yancey et al. (2006) Campbell et al. (2002) Eiben & Lissner (2006)
PA and weight			
Foster et al. (2005)	Compare effectiveness of interventions for PA promotion in adults not living in an institution, with no intervention, minimal intervention, or attention control.	The effect of interventions on self-reported PA was positive and moderate as was the effect on cardiorespiratory fitness.	—

TABLE 4.1

Systematic Reviews of Physical Activity Interventions Focused Primarily on Healthy Adults Published 2005–2013   (Continued)

	Purpose	Key Findings	Studies of Women, Physical Activity (PA), and Body Composition (BC)
Kay & Fiatarone Singh (2006)	Examine PA interventions and abdominal fat.	Studies suggest a beneficial influence of PA on reduction in abdominal and visceral fat in overweight and obese subjects.	Donnelly et al. (2000) Ross et al. (2004)
Ohkawara et al. (2007)	Establish whether reduction of visceral fat by aerobic exercise has a dose-response relationship.	At least 10 MET hours per week in aerobic exercise is required for visceral fat reduction.	Ross et al. (2004) Irwin et al. (2003)
Shaw et al. (2009)	Assess exercise interventions as a means of achieving weight loss in people with overweight or obesity.	Exercise combined with diet resulted in greater weight reduction than diet alone.	Janssen et al. (2002) Asikainen et al. (2002)
Laska et al. (2012)	Review weight gain prevention interventions among young adults.	Studies showed promising results as small-scale pilot studies but lacked data from fully powered randomized trials.	—
Weinheimer et al. (2010)	Evaluate intervention effects on weight loss induced via energy restriction, energy restriction combined with exercise, and exercise alone.	Exercise groups had modest body weight and fat-free mass changes.	Nicklas et al. (2009)

(Continued)

TABLE 4.1
Systematic Reviews of Physical Activity Interventions Focused Primarily on Healthy Adults Published 2005–2013   (Continued)

	Purpose	Key Findings	Studies of Women, Physical Activity (PA), and Body Composition (BC)
Women			
Brown (2006)	Examine the effectiveness of lifestyle interventions designed to produce weight loss in postmenopausal women.	All active treatment arms had significant improvements in weight and BC.	Asikainen et al. (2002) Carels et al. (2004) Irwin et al. (2003)
Perez et al. (2010)	Examine PA interventions that include Hispanic women.	Few studies documented positive change in PA but significant changes were noted in health outcomes including BMI, waist–hip ratio, and skin fold sums.	Keller & Cantue (2008) Hovell et al. (2008) Poston et al. (2001) Staten et al. (2004)
Sharma (2008)	Review existing community-based PA interventions done in apparently healthy Hispanic girls and women.	Half of the interventions were successful in improving PA and/or nutritional behaviors.	Staten et al. (2004) Poston et al. (2001)

Note. BMI = body mass index; METs = metabolic equivalent of tasks.

(Conn, Hafdahl, & Mehr, 2011; Muller-Riemenschneider, Reinhold, Nocon, & Willich, 2008; see Table 4.1).

Examination of these 12 reviews revealed that 9 included one to seven studies published since 2000 reporting interventions specifically designed for women and that included PA change and BC as outcomes, yielding 26 (13 unduplicated) studies for inclusion in this systematic review. These 12 previous reviews did not separately analyze change in PA or BC in women as intervention outcomes.

Six additional reviews focused on PA interventions for men and women and had control or changes in BC as a main outcome. Of these reviews, four focused primarily on the effects of PA alone (Foster, Hillsdon, & Thorogood, 2005; Kay & Fiatarone Singh, 2006; Ohkawara, Tanaka, Miyachi, Ishikawa-Takata, & Tabata, 2007; Shaw, Gennat, O'Rourke, & Del Mar, 2009), although two focused on the effect of lifestyle interventions on BC and had both PA and dietary components (Laska, Pelletier, Larson, & Story, 2012; Weinheimer, Sands, & Campbell, 2010). Only four of the six reviews included studies that had interventions specifically developed for women, yielding seven unduplicated studies for inclusion in the present systematic review. Again, none of these four reviews analyzed intervention outcomes specifically pertaining to women such as change in PA or BC.

Last, three reviews focused on PA interventions for specific groups of healthy women including postmenopausal women (Brown, 2006) and Latinas (Brown, 2006; Perez, Fleury, & Keller, 2010; Sharma, 2008). Because of their restricted inclusion criteria, these reviews of studies in women provide only limited information about the effects of PA interventions designed for healthy women generally. However, the reviews yielded nine (seven unduplicated) PA intervention studies focused on change in PA and BC that were deemed suitable for inclusion in the present systematic review.

There were 27 studies in women identified from these three groups of earlier systematic reviews. After removing 6 duplications from the groups mentioned earlier, 21 studies remained for inclusion in this review.

Overall, this series of earlier PA intervention reviews suggests the positive benefits of PA interventions on both changes in PA behavior and in BC. Although most of the reviews included studies with interventions for women, only three reviews compared outcomes in terms of change in PA and BC in women, and these reviews were narrowly focused on subpopulations such as Latinas or postmenopausal women. There remains a need to reanalyze the 21 studies of women identified from these earlier systematic reviews along with studies from the most recent literature to obtain a better understanding of the extent to which and how PA interventions change PA behavior and BC. Therefore, this systematic review sought to answer two research questions: (a) What are the effects of PA interventions on change in PA behavior and BC in healthy women? and (b) What are the characteristics of PA interventions that change PA behavior in healthy women?

METHODS

Design and Sample

This systematic review used guidelines from the Centre for Review and Dissemination (Centre for Reviews and Dissemination, University of York, 2009). These guidelines cover how to specify the review question(s), cite inclusion and exclusion criteria, identify the literature to be searched, select studies for inclusion, extract data from the studies, and synthesize the results (Centre for Reviews and Dissemination, University of York, 2009). Inclusion criteria for this review were (a) randomized clinical trials (RCTs); (b) female-only studies in healthy, community-dwelling women (18–64 years old); (c) PA as an outcome variable; (d) BC as an outcome variable; (e) published in English; and (f) published after January 1, 2000. Studies were excluded if they included any pharmacological component in addition to a diet and/or PA intervention for weight loss. Studies were excluded if they focused strictly on women with significant chronic or life-threatening diseases beyond obesity and metabolic syndrome because PA guidelines can vary depending on the seriousness of the disease, for example, chronic obstructive pulmonary disease and breast cancer (Goris, Vermeeren, Wouters, Schols, & Westerterp, 2003; Pinto, Clark, Maruyama, & Feder, 2003). Studies were also excluded if they focused on pregnant women because of the unique exercise recommendations applying during pregnancy (Nascimento, Surita, & Cecatti, 2012).

The authors searched the literature using search terms of woman, women, female, and adult as keywords (all MeSH terms). Outcomes included the two broad categories of PA and BC. In the first category, PA, exercise, and motor activity (all MeSH terms) were used. In the second category, BC, body weight, BMI, waist-to-hip ratio, waist circumference, skinfold thickness, anthropometry, tomography, CT and imaging, and MRI (all MeSH terms) were used. For the design, clinical trial (MeSH) was used.

The authors methodically searched multiple databases, starting with the Cumulative Index to Nursing and Allied Health Literature (CINAHL) and continuing on to Ovid MEDLINE, SciVerse Scopus, Health Source Academic Edition, and PsycINFO. To find studies including unpublished studies that may not have been located in these databases, the authors searched ProQuest Dissertations and Theses as well as Google Scholar. Historical searches were conducted on all papers that met the study criteria. As described in the "Background" section earlier, the authors also searched reference lists from systematic reviews of PA interventions and PA and BC outcomes in healthy adults.

There were 1,406 titles retrieved after removing duplicates (see Figure 4.1). Two of the authors used a three-step process to select studies for inclusion. At each step, the reviewers conducted an independent review and then came back together to discuss their results. First, the titles were assessed for inclusion criteria. This resulted in 1,250 that did not meet inclusion criteria. Next, abstracts of the resulting 156 publications were reviewed to determine if they met the inclusion criteria, resulting in 63 potentially eligible papers. Full-text retrieval was then conducted to determine which of the remaining 63 papers met the inclusion criteria. After reviewing the full texts, it was determined that 40 papers met the inclusion criteria (see Table 4.2), with 21 of these being the papers identified in the previous systematic reviews.

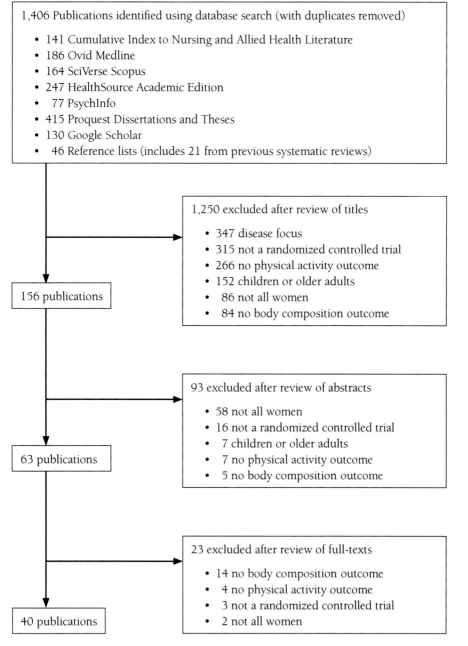

1,406 Publications identified using database search (with duplicates removed)

- 141 Cumulative Index to Nursing and Allied Health Literature
- 186 Ovid Medline
- 164 SciVerse Scopus
- 247 HealthSource Academic Edition
- 77 PsychInfo
- 415 Proquest Dissertations and Theses
- 130 Google Scholar
- 46 Reference lists (includes 21 from previous systematic reviews)

156 publications

1,250 excluded after review of titles

- 347 disease focus
- 315 not a randomized controlled trial
- 266 no physical activity outcome
- 152 children or older adults
- 86 not all women
- 84 no body composition outcome

63 publications

93 excluded after review of abstracts

- 58 not all women
- 16 not a randomized controlled trial
- 7 children or older adults
- 7 no physical activity outcome
- 5 no body composition outcome

40 publications

23 excluded after review of full-texts

- 14 no body composition outcome
- 4 no physical activity outcome
- 3 not a randomized controlled trial
- 2 not all women

FIGURE 4.1 Flow chart of search and retrieval process and results.

TABLE 4.2.

Sample Characteristics and Setting in 40 Studies of Women Stratified by Physical Activity Interventions With and Without Diet

Author/Year	Country	N	Inclusion Criteria	Age (Years)	Ethnicity	Setting
Physical activity without diet						
Asikainen et al. (2002)	Finland	134	Healthy, postmenopausal, sedentary, nonsmoker, no regular medication, body mass index (BMI) <32 kg/m²	48–63		Supervised indoor track, sidewalks, streets, trails, parks
Byrne & Wilmore (2001)	USA	28	Premenopausal, sedentary, ≥30% body fat, weight stable for past year (≤3 kg)	18–45 M (SD) 38.0 ± 9.0	White (96%), African American (4%)	Supervised gym, home
Cox et al. (2001)	Australia	126	Healthy, sedentary	40–65 M (SD) 48.5 ± 5.6	White (97%), Asian (3%)	Center, home
Donnelly et al. (2000)	USA	22	Sedentary, BMI ≥25 kg/m²	Age by condition: M (SD) 54.0 ± 9.0, 49.0 ± 8.0		Laboratory setting at university
Hemmingsson et al. (2009)	Sweden	120	Waist circumference 88–120 cm	30–60 M (SD) 48.2 ± 7.4		Clinic, home
Hovell et al. (2008)	USA	151	Healthy, sedentary	18–55 M (SD) 31.4 ± 6.2	Latina	Storefront exercise site
Irwin et al. (2003)	USA	173	Sedentary, postmenopausal, nonsmoker, no diagnosis of diabetes, BMI ≥24 kg/m², body fat >33%	50–75	White (86%), African American (4%), Asian (6%), Other (4%)	University; commercial gym

Study	Country	N	Criteria	Age	Ethnicity	Setting
Keller & Cantue (2008)	USA	18	Sedentary, BMI $\geq$30 kg/m^2	45–70	Mexican American	Community center
Kraemer et al. (2001)	USA	35	Healthy, active	Age by condition: M (SD) 31.0 $\pm$ 7.9, 33.0 $\pm$ 8.1, 37.3 $\pm$ 8.0, 27.8 $\pm$ 6.9		University laboratory
Lawton et al. (2009)	New Zealand	1,089	Sedentary	40–74 M (SD) 58.9 $\pm$ 7.0	European (78%), Maori/Pacific Islander (13%)	Clinic
Nies et al. (2003)	USA	197	Sedentary	30–60	African American (48%), European American (52%)	Home
Park et al. (2003)	South Korea	30	Obese, healthy	40–45		College of physical education
Poston et al. (2001)	USA	379	BMI between 25 and 40 kg/m^2	18–65	Mexican American	Community setting, home
Santa-Clara (2006)	USA	47	Healthy, sedentary, postmenopausal, nonsmoker	40–70	African American (51%), White (49%)	Supervised exercising setting, home
Swearingin (2008)	USA	45	Healthy, sedentary, overweight women	22–55	African American	Community group meetings, home
Wilbur et al. (2008)	USA	281	Sedentary	40–65	African American	Community health centers, home

(Continued)

TABLE 4.2

Sample Characteristics and Setting in 40 Studies of Women Stratified by Physical Activity Interventions With and Without Diet   *(Continued)*

Author/Year	Country	N	Inclusion Criteria	Age (Years)	Ethnicity	Setting
Physical activity with diet						
Adachi et al. (2007)	Japan	205	BMI $\geq$24 kg/m^2 or BMI $\geq$23 kg/m^2 and hypertension, hyperlipidemia, or diabetes	20–65 M (SD) 46.00 ± 2.95		Home
Bacon et al. (2002)	USA	78	Healthy, nonsmoker, BMI $\geq$30 kg/m^2 with history of chronic dieting	30–45 M (SD) 39.3 ± 4.5	White	Free-living, general community
Campbell et al. (2002)	USA	660	Employed in rural blue-collar worksite	$\geq$18	White non-Hispanic (39%), African American (58%), Other (3)	Worksites in rural counties
Carels et al. (2004)	USA	44	Sedentary, postmenopausal, nonsmoker, BMI $\geq$30 kg/m^2	M (SD) 54.7 ± 7.9	Majority White	Community, home
Eiben & Lissner (2006)	Sweden	40	Had at least one severely obese parent, BMI $\geq$18, 5kg/m^2	18–28		Laboratory setting at university hospital
Fitzgibbon et al. (2005)	USA	59	BMI $\geq$25 kg/m^2	$\geq$20	African American	Hospital setting
Fitzgibbon et al. (2010)	USA	213	BMI $\geq$30 and $\leq$50 kg/m^2	30–50 M (SD) 46.0 ± 8.4	African American	University
Folta et al. (2009)	USA	96	Sedentary, BMI $\geq$24 kg/m^2	$\geq$40	White (98%), American Indian (2%)	Community center

Grant et al. (2004)	United Kingdom	44	Sedentary, BMI ≥25 kg/m²	55–70 M (SD) 63.0 ± 4.0		Community center
Hayashi et al. (2010)	USA	869	Low-income; blood pressure or total cholesterol levels considered at risk for cardiovascular disease	40–64	Hispanic	Health centers
Jakicic et al. (2003)	USA	201	Healthy, sedentary, BMI 27–40 kg/m²	21–45 M (SD) 37.0 ± 5.7	White (81%), Hispanic (8%), African American (8%), Other (3%)	University
Janssen et al. (2002)	Canada	38	Premenopausal, no regular medications, BMI ≥27 kg/m², waist-to-hip ratio >0.85, stable weight (+2 kg)	Age by condition: M (SD) 40.1 ± 6.7, 37.5 ± 6.0, 34.8 ± 5.8		Supervised exercise setting, community setting
Keyserling et al. (2008)	USA	236	Healthy, low-income	40–64	White (58%), African American (40.5%)	Community health center
Lombard et al. (2010)	Australia	250	Mothers with school-aged children	25–51 M (SD) 40.4 ± 4.77		Elementary school
Nicklas et al. (2009)	USA	112	Postmenopausal, sedentary BMI 25–40 kg/m², waist circumference >88 cm, weight stable for ≥6 months (<5% weight change)	50–70	White (65%), African American (34%), Other (1%)	Clinic
Nieman et al. (2002)	USA	121	Healthy, BMI ≥25 to ≤65 kg/m²	25–75 M (SD) 46.0 ± 1.1		Indoor track, home

(Continued)

TABLE 4.2

Sample Characteristics and Setting in 40 Studies of Women Stratified by Physical Activity Interventions With and Without Diet *(Continued)*

Author/Year	Country	N	Inclusion Criteria	Age (Years)	Ethnicity	Setting
O'Toole et al. (2003)	USA	40	Postpartum, sedentary, self-report BMI 25–29.9 kg/m²	Age by condition: M (SD) 32.2 ± 4.9, STR 30.8 ± 4.2	White (98%), African American (2%)	Research laboratory
Rosamond et al. (2000)	USA	1,957	Low-income at risk for cardiovascular disease	≥50	White, African American, Other	County health departments
Ross et al. (2004)	Canada	104	Sedentary, premenopausal, nonsmoker, BMI >27 kg/m², waist circumference >88 cm, weight stable for 6 months (≤2 kg)	Age by condition M (SD): 43.7 ± 6.4, 43.9 ± 4.9, 43.2 ± 5.1, 41.3 ± 7.2		School of physical and health education
Samuel-Hodge et al. (2009)	USA	143	Low-income, BMI 25–45 kg/m²	40–64 M (SD) 52.8 ± 0.6	African American (38%), White (60%)	Church located near clinic
Staten et al. (2004)	USA	217	Uninsured	>50 M (SD) 57.2 ± 4.8	Hispanic (74%), White (25%), African American (1%)	Clinic
Walker et al. (2009)	USA	225	Lived in rural community	50–69	White (94%), Hispanic (4%), American Indian/ Alaska Native (2%)	Home
Yancey et al. (2006)	USA	366	Healthy, nonsmoker	21–77	African American	Community health club
Yanek et al. (2001)	USA	529	≥40 years old, required physician permission to participate	≥40	African American	Church, home

Measures

The authors developed three data collection tools to extract data for this review (Joanna Briggs Institute, 2011). The first tool included the primary author, year of publication and country, sample size, inclusion criteria, demographics, and setting (see Table 4.2). The second data collection tool included the study design and duration, the type of PA intervention and control conditions, and the theoretical framework used (see Table 4.3). The third data collection tool included PA and BC measures and the relationship between PA and BC (see Table 4.4).

Analytic Strategy

Each of the first three authors reviewed the abstractions of the 40 papers in the tables and checked for inconsistencies in coding of study characteristics (e.g., design, type of intervention, outcome measures). When adequate data were available, effect sizes were calculated to determine the intervention effect on PA and BC. In some instances, the data needed to calculate effect sizes was incomplete and assumptions were made to estimate effect sizes. In studies that presented pre–post change scores but omitted the pre–post correlations for the outcome measures, a conservative estimate of $r = .80$ was used to estimate the effect sizes. For studies that presented means and standard deviations by wave without change scores, posttest means and standard deviations were used to estimate effect sizes. In these cases, if the group means at baseline were different from one another (e.g., the mean weight for the treatment group was lower than the mean weight for the control group), effect size estimates were omitted. Consequently, the estimated effect sizes were likely conservative estimates (i.e., erring toward zero effect).

Because of the reliance on estimated effect sizes for many studies, a formal meta-analysis was not conducted. For studies with multiple effect sizes as presented in Table 4.4, a single effect size was selected for each study to calculate a weighted mean effect. For PA, objective measures were used followed by self-report if there was no objective measure available. For BC, BMI was used followed by body weight. Fixed-effect models were generally used to calculate weighted mean effect sizes; however, random-effect models were used when significant heterogeneity existed.

RESULTS

Sample Characteristics and Setting

Of the 40 RCTs (see Table 4.2) that met inclusion criteria, 16 were PA interventions without a diet component (Asikainen et al., 2002; Byrne & Wilmore, 2001; Cox et al., 2001; Donnelly et al., 2000; Hemmingsson, Uddén, Neovius,

TABLE 4.3

Design, Duration, Intervention, and Control in 40 Studies of Women Stratified by Physical Activity Interventions With and Without Diet

Study	Design	Duration (Months)	Intervention(s) and Control	Theoretical Framework
Physical activity without diet				
Asikainen et al. (2002)	RCT	4	Interventions Exercise 5 days/week (65% VO_{2max} for weekly exercise volume of 1,500 kcal total) • One daily continuous walking sessions (2 supervised, 3 home-based) • Two daily walking sessions (4 supervised, 8 home-based) Control • Once a month attended lectures on health and flexibility exercises	Theory of exercise accumulation
Byrne & Wilmore (2001)	RCT	5	Interventions • Group resistance training 4 times/week (3 sets of 8 exercises) • Group resistance training 4 times/week + walking unsupervised 3 times/week (graded walking starting with 20 min at 50% VO_{2max}, increased to 40 min at 70% VO_{2max} (predetermined) Control • No intervention control	No known

Cox et al. (2001)	RCT	18	Interventions • Moderate (40%–55% HR$_{res}$) exercise, highly monitored center-based program (3 times/week, 30 min) • Vigorous (65%–80% HR$_{res}$) exercise, highly monitored center-based program (3 times/week, 30 min) • Moderate exercise, home-based program (3 times/week, 30 min) • Vigorous exercise, home-based program (3 times/week, 30 min)	No known
Donnelly et al. (2000)	RCT	18	Interventions • Continuous exercise group—exercised for 30 min/ sessions or 3 days/week (at 60%–75% of maximal aerobic capacity) • Intermittent brisk walking group—exercised using brisk walking for two 15-min sessions or 5 days/week (at 50%–65% of maximal heart rate reserve)	No known
Hemmingsson et al. (2009)	RCT	18	Interventions • Added care—2-hr group counseling at baseline and 6 months to increase steps walked (increase of 5,000) with pedometer + 3 individual sessions with physician (baseline, 6 months, 12 months) on PA prescription, changing behavior + two 2-hr group counseling during cycling season + a free bicycle • Standard care—2-hr group counseling at baseline and 6 months to increase steps walked (increase of 5,000) with pedometer	Transtheoretical model

(Continued)

TABLE 4.3

Design, Duration, Intervention, and Control in 40 Studies of Women Stratified by Physical Activity Interventions With and Without Diet   *(Continued)*

Study	Design	Duration (Months)	Intervention(s) and Control	Theoretical Framework
Hovell et al. (2008)	RCT	6	Intervention • Three sessions per week of supervised aerobic dancing - 10 min of warm-up stretching; 10-min aerobic component (gradually increasing by 3 min/week to a maximum of 40 min); and 10 min of cool-down - Aerobic component was conducted to aim for 70% of age-predicted maximum HR Control • 18 safety education sessions	No known
Irwin et al. (2003)	RCT	12	Intervention • 45-min moderate intensity (60%–75% HR_{max}) PA (walking, treadmill, cycle) and strength-training sessions - Months 1–3: 3 group exercise sessions/week, 2 home-based exercise sessions/week - Months 4–12: 1 group exercise session/week, 4 home-based exercise sessions/week + individualized attention in classes, behavior change education, weekly calls to promote adherence, incentives, quarterly newsletters, and group activities Control • Stretching: 45-min group session once a week for 12 weeks	No known

Keller & Cantue (2008)	RCT	9	Intervention 30 min of group walking with a promotora at pace of 20-min mile • Group 1—3 days a week • Group 2—5 days a week	No known
Kraemer et al. (2001)	RCT	3	Intervention 3 group sessions/week • 25-min Bench-Step Aerobics (BSA; intensity to target 80%–90% of HR_{max}) • 25-min BSA + resistance exercise program (target 10 repetitions of each exercise before fatigue) • 40-min BSA Control • No intervention control	No known
Lawton et al. (2009)	RCT	9	Intervention • Brief PA intervention ("green script") delivered by nurse, with on average five motivational interviewing phone calls over 9 months, and 30 min nurse visit at 6 months (recommended goal of moderate-intensity exercise [brisk walking encouraged] for 30 min 5 times a week) Control • No intervention control	No known

(Continued)

TABLE 4.3

Design, Duration, Intervention, and Control in 40 Studies of Women Stratified by Physical Activity Interventions With and Without Diet   *(Continued)*

Study	Design	Duration (Months)	Intervention(s) and Control	Theoretical Framework
Nies et al. (2003)	RCT	7	Intervention • 16 telephone calls over 24 weeks delivered by trained interventionists—once a week for 8 weeks, and then every other week for the remaining 16 weeks to assess PA levels and problem solve regarding how to fit adequate walking activity into their week, using intervention script (encouraged to walk 90 min/week) Controls • Attention control—same number of telephone calls as intervention group (only asked for PA report) • No intervention control	Author developed
Park et al. (2003)	RCT	6	Interventions • Aerobic training group—6 days a week, 60 min sessions designed to reach 60%–70% HR_{max} • Combined training group—aerobic training for 3 days a week + resistance training Control • No intervention control	No known

Poston et al. (2001)	RCT Block preexisting networks	10	Intervention • Weekly culturally appropriate group meetings held to increase PA—for the first 6 months, the groups were led by bilingual Mexican American health care professionals; in the second 6 months, weekly peer-led maintenance groups were provided + 6 monthly meetings with health care professionals (goal is to increase PA to a minimum of 30 min 5 times a week [either brisk walking during group sessions or walking clubs]) Control • Delayed control	Social cognitive theory
Santa-Clara (2006)	RCT	6	Intervention • Supervised group exercise (treadmill walking/jogging, cycling, rowing) 3–4 sessions/week at 70%–85% of maximum HR intensity (gradually increased in length until 45–60 min) Control • No intervention control	No known

(Continued)

TABLE 4.3

Design, Duration, Intervention, and Control in 40 Studies of Women Stratified by Physical Activity Interventions With and Without Diet   *(Continued)*

Study	Design	Duration (Months)	Intervention(s) and Control	Theoretical Framework
Swearingin (2008)	RCT	4	**Interventions** • Traditional group exercise (treadmill, elliptical cycle): 4 sessions/week for 150 min/week (intensity, 50%–65% HR_{max}) • Lifestyle activity: weekly educational group sessions by the researcher for 6 weeks, then biweekly group sessions for last 6 weeks (to complete at least 150 min of PA/week and incorporate lifestyle PA daily) **Control** • No intervention control	CDC Guide for Community Action, Division of Nutrition & PA
Wilbur et al. (2008) USA	RCT Condition to site	12	**Interventions** Individualized orientation (walking 3 times a week at individual moderate intensity target HR range): • Tailored walking prescription, health information, goal-setting, problem solving + PA manual + four 60-min targeted workshops on PA facilitated by an African American staff member involved in the target community (including videos with African American female role models) + Tailored phone motivational calls gradually decreasing from weekly to monthly (walking 3 times a week at individual moderate-intensity target HR range) • PA manual	Interaction Model of Client Health Behavior

PA with diet

				Behavioral therapy
Adachi et al. (2007)	RCT	7	Interventions To increase walking by self-monitor walking steps with a pedometer • KM-Kenkou-tatsujins® (KT) gives 2 interactive letters with computer tailored advice on behavioral modification for diet & PA) + weight and behavior self-monitoring • KT only • BM-KT—self-help booklet + self-monitoring • B-KT—self-help booklet only program	
Bacon et al. (2002)	RCT	6	Interventions • Diet group-eating behaviors, attitudes, nutrition, social support, and exercise (walk at intensity by training heart rate; weekly 90-min sessions led by registered dietician for 24 weeks, monthly group support for 6 months after the program) • Nondiet group health-centered wellness program facilitated by a counselor experienced in psychotherapeutic workshops—topics included body acceptance, eating behavior, activity, nutrition, and social support (weekly 90-min sessions for 24 weeks, monthly group support for 6 months after the program)	No known

(Continued)

TABLE 4.3

Design, Duration, Intervention, and Control in 40 Studies of Women Stratified by Physical Activity Interventions With and Without Diet   (Continued)

Study	Design	Duration (Months)	Intervention(s) and Control	Theoretical Framework
Campbell et al. (2002)	RCT to 1 of 9 worksites	18	Intervention • Two computer-tailored women's magazines with personalized feedback, strategies for behaviors (health concerns and health behaviors including dietary and leisure-time PA, smoking, cancer screening), strategies for change and community resources (baseline, 6 months) + natural helpers (women at worksite had training session bimonthly for 18 months) diffused information and provided support (encouraged to increase leisure time PA including aerobic and strength/flexibility) Control • Delayed intervention (after 6 months received one individually tailored magazine)	Social cognitive theory, Transtheoretical framework
Carels et al. (2004)	RCT	6	Interventions • Lifestyle change intervention—24 weekly 60–75 min group sessions led by a clinical health psychologist and psychology graduate student (LEARN program, which is a weight management and PA approach) • Lifestyle change with self-control skills intervention—24 weekly 90–120 min group sessions led by a clinical health psychologist and psychology graduate student with didactic instruction, activities, and out-of-class assignments (LEARN program + self-control skills training)	Lifestyle change approach, self-control

Eiben & Lissner (2006)	RCT	12	Interventions • Customized support package for PA, diet, and weight control (decided by themselves when to focus on each section) • Delivered by one face-to-face session followed by regular contact via phone, e-mail, occasional group session, or dietician visit Control • Delay control received information on Internet after the program was over	No known
Fitzgibbon et al. (2005)	RCT	3	Interventions • Culturally tailored weight loss intervention (ORBIT)—focused on changes in lifestyle diet and PA; small group meetings 2 times a week for 12 weeks with 45-min interactive didactic component and 45-min structured aerobic exercise • Faith-based weight loss intervention—culturally tailored intervention + integration of scripture readings to group meetings facilitated by a woman experienced in faith-based health risk reduction interventions	Social cognitive theory

(Continued)

TABLE 4.3

Design, Duration, Intervention, and Control in 40 Studies of Women Stratified by Physical Activity Interventions With and Without Diet   (Continued)

Study	Design	Duration (Months)	Intervention(s) and Control	Theoretical Framework
Fitzgibbon et al. (2010)	RCT	18	**Intervention** • Group meetings twice weekly led by female role model interventionist to discuss behavioral strategies for weight loss/maintenance, 45-min structured aerobic sessions + monthly motivational interview session addressing diet or PA (encouraged to walk >10,000 steps/day with self-monitoring logs and pedometers to guide activity) **Control** • Weekly general health and safety newsletter + monthly phone calls to discuss newsletter by trained interventionists	Social cognitive theory
Folta et al. (2009)	RCT	3	**Intervention** • Group based 60-min walking/aerobic dance session and strength + behavioral and diet strategy discussion and goal setting twice weekly (encouraged to increase lower-intensity activity outside of class) facilitated by Cooperative State Research, Education, and Extension Service (CSREES) educators **Control** • Delay	Social cognitive theory

			Interventions	Theory
Grant et al. (2004)	RCT	3	Interventions • Individual dietary advice with nurse + group-based 40-min group functional exercise sessions 2 times a week (10-min warm-up, 20 min of continuous aerobic exercise with multiple intensity options, 5 min strength/endurance activities, and 5 min of stretching) • Individual dietary advice with nurse	No known
Hayashi et al. (2010)	RCT	12	Intervention • WISEWOMAN: lifestyle intervention with three face-to-face sessions with a community health worker for nutritional and PA assessment and counseling (1, 2, and 6 months after enrollment) Control • Usual care with educational pamphlets on high blood pressure and high cholesterol	Transtheoretical model
Jakicic et al. (2003)	RCT	12	Interventions Behavioral group meetings (weekly for 24 weeks, then biweekly for remainder) + biweekly phone calls from intervention team member from months 7 to 12 + prescribed diet (1,200–1,500 kcal/day intake) + exercise, 5 times a week unsupervised treadmill (prescribed intensity for targeted energy expenditure) • Vigorous intensity/high duration (VI/HD) • Moderate intensity/high duration (MI/HD) • Moderate intensity/moderate duration (MI/MD) • Vigorous intensity/moderate duration (VI/MD)	Social cognitive theory

(Continued)

TABLE 4.3

Design, Duration, Intervention, and Control in 40 Studies of Women Stratified by Physical Activity Interventions With and Without Diet   (Continued)

Study	Design	Duration (Months)	Intervention(s) and Control	Theoretical Framework
Janssen et al. (2002)	RCT	3	Intervention • Dietary protocol (calorie reduction by 1,000 kcal/day, weekly meetings for dietary counsel, daily diet records, limit dietary fat to <30%) • Dietary protocol + aerobic protocol, group exercise stair stepping, treadmill, and cycling five 60-min sessions/week (aerobic intensity starting at 15 min and gradually increasing to 60 min at 50%–85% HR_{max}) supervised by a physical educator • Dietary protocol + resistance training protocol, three 30-min resistance exercise training sessions/week (7 exercises, 8–12 repetitions) supervised by a physical educator	No known
Keyserling et al. (2008)	RCT	12	Interventions • WISEWOMAN: enhanced intervention—6-month intensive Phase 2 individual counseling sessions with health counselor, 3 group sessions and 3 phone calls by community health advisors; followed by a 6-month maintenance phase, 1 individual counseling session, 7 phone calls (15-min chair exercise component in group sessions) • Minimal intervention—one-time mailing of pamphlets on diet and PA	Social cognitive theory, transtheoretical model, behavior modification

			Interventions	
Lombard et al. (2010) Australia	Randomized to group based on geographic location	12	Interventions • To self-monitor activity with a pedometer • Four 1-hr group sessions behavioral change skills for PA/diet education with goal setting led by a trained dietician + motivational text messaging monthly • One 30-min lecture on diet and PA guidelines with brochure	Social cognitive theory
Nicklas et al. (2009)	RCT	5	Interventions • Calorie restriction (CR): all meals and snacks provided, calorie deficit of 2,800 kcal/week • CR + 3 moderate-intensity (45%–50% HR_{max}) aerobic exercise sessions/week supervised by an exercise physiologist (progressing from 20 to 55 min) to account for 700 kcal/week energy expenditure • CR + 3 vigorous-intensity (70%–75% HR_{max}) aerobic supervised exercise sessions/week (progressing from 10 to 30 min) to account for 700 kcal/week energy expenditure	No known
Nieman et al. (2002)	RCT	3	Interventions • Exercise five 45-min walks/week, 4 supervised group walks, 1 individual (intensity gradually increased from 25–30 min at 60%–65% HR_{max} to 45 min at 70%–80% HR_{max}) + energy-restricted diet • Exercise only • Diet + stretching (five 45-min stretching sessions/week, 4 group, 1 individual) • Stretching only	No known

(Continued)

TABLE 4.3

Design, Duration, Intervention, and Control in 40 Studies of Women Stratified by Physical Activity Interventions With and Without Diet   (Continued)

Study	Design	Duration (Months)	Intervention(s) and Control	Theoretical Framework
O'Toole et al. (2003)	RCT	12	Interventions Goal: to create a caloric deficit of at least 500 calories/ day, gradual increase of PA from 100 kcal/day of energy expenditure because of PA to 150 kcal/day (>1,050 kcal/week) based on HR • Individualized dietary and PA prescription + group educational meeting once a week for 12 weeks, biweekly for 2 months, and monthly for 1 year • Individualized dietary and PA prescription + one education session with dietician and exercise physiologist at baseline	No known
Rosamond et al. (2000)	Treatment randomly assigned to site	6	Interventions • WISEWOMAN: 3 counseling sessions with tailored diet/PA interventions (increase lifestyle PA) • Enhanced intervention: health department usual counseling and education materials and were referred + 3 counseling sessions with a tailored, culturally appropriate structured assessment and intervention program ("New Leaf") facilitated by trained health professionals • Minimum intervention: health department usual counseling and education materials and were referred	Social cognitive theory, transtheoretical model, behavior modification

			Interventions	
Ross et al. (2004)	RCT	3.5	Interventions Four groups all received 1-hr weekly seminars led by a dietician in proper food selection and preparation. Different goals: • Diet weight loss (reduction of 500 kcal/day) • Diet weight loss + supervised exercise (treadmill exercise to burn 500 kcal/day, brisk walking or jogging at 80% HR_{max}) • Exercise • Maintain weight	No known
Samuel-Hodge et al. (2009)	RCT	4	Intervention • 16 weekly group education sessions led by a registered nurse health counselor trained in motivational interviewing (weigh-in, group sharing, goal-setting, weight management related to diet and PA, goal setting problem solving) Goal: 7 servings fruits/vegetables and 150 min/week PA, diet reduction of 500 kcal/day Control • Two educational newsletters (skin health and back pain)	Adapted from Diabetes Prevention Program, DASH, Premier trials

(Continued)

TABLE 4.3

Design, Duration, Intervention, and Control in 40 Studies of Women Stratified by Physical Activity Interventions With and Without Diet (*Continued*)

Study	Design	Duration (Months)	Intervention(s) and Control	Theoretical Framework
Staten et al. (2004)	RCT	12	Interventions • WISEWOMAN • Provider counseling on PA (moderate-vigorous PA at three 10-min sessions) and fruit/vegetable consumption at three clinic visits • Provider counseling PA + 2 health education classes + monthly health newsletter • Provider counseling PA + 2 health education classes + monthly health newsletter + phone calls by community health workers semiweekly or monthly (PA/diet strategy discussion, invitation for scheduled bimonthly walk)	Social cognitive theory
Walker et al. (2009)	Treatment randomized to geographic area	12	Interventions To choose 1–2 activities and designate frequency • 18 participant newsletters (advice on healthy eating & PA) + computer-selected text messages tailored to participant—selected needs and asked to designate frequency for 1–2 PA and choose 1 healthy eating behavior + videotape and companion manual + feedback on assessments at baseline, 3, 6, and 9 months • 18 newsletters without tailored messages + videotape, manual + feedback on assessments	Pender's health promotion model

| Yancey et al. (2006) | RCT | 2 | Intervention
• 8 weekly 2-hr interactive group sessions led by project staff on skills in regular exercise regimen and nutrition education + lifestyle integration of PA + free gym membership

Control
• 8 weekly 2-hr interactive group session on women's health topics (screening, menopause, depression) led by project staff without external social support | Social support |
| Yanek et al. (2001) | Randomized by 16 church sites | 8 | Interventions
Goal of at least 30 min of PA daily
• Standard group methods with weekly sessions—weekly sessions conducted for 20 weeks by African American health educators on nutrition and PA (each session included taste test or cooking demonstration and a 30 min aerobic activity session); lay leaders offered weekly sessions for the next 20 weeks
• Standard group methods supplemented with a spiritual and church cultural component which included group prayers and health messages enriched with scripture, PA-incorporated gospel music and worship dance
• Nonspiritual, self-help interventions—Handouts (including American Heart Association, Project Joy, NIH, and YMCA educational material), feedback given on personal screening, a place to list goals was provided to allow self-monitoring, hotline number available for consultation with Project Joy health educators | Behavioral model, community action, and social marketing model developed originally by the Health and Religion Project of the Pawtucket Heart Health Program |

Note. CDC = Centers for Disease Control and Prevention; DASH = Dietary Approaches to Stop Hypertension; HR_{max} = maximum heart rate; HR_{res} = resting heart rate; LEARN = lifestyle exercise attitudes relationships nutrition; NIH = National Institutes of Health; ORBIT = obesity reduction black intervention trial; PA= physical activity; RCT = randomized clinical trial; $VO2_{max}$ = maximal oxygen uptake; WISEWOMAN = Well-Integrated Screening and Evaluation for Women Across the Nation.

TABLE 4.4

Physical Activity (PA) and Body Composition (BC) Measures, Intervention Effect Sizes, and Relationship Between PA and BC in 40 Studies of Women Stratified by PA Interventions With and Without Diet

Author/Year	PA Measures	Intervention Effect on PA		BC Measures	Intervention Effect on BC		Relationship Between PA and BC
		1-session group	2-session group		1-session group	2-session group	
Physical activity without diet							
Asikainen et al. (2002)	• Self-reported PA score (1 = no regular PA weekly to 5 = PA ≥3 times/week)	—	—	• Body weight	−0.39	−0.33	—
				• BMI	−0.42	−0.34	
	• Treadmill			• Skinfold thickness (% body fat)	−0.68	−0.55	
	- HR at 75% VO_{2max}	−0.13	−0.25				
	- HR at 65% VO_{2max}	−0.09	−0.17				
Byrne & Wilmore (2001)	• Treadmill	—		• Body weight	—		RMR associated with FFM
	- Walk time (graded treadmill test with increasing incline and speed until exhaustion)			• Hydrostatic weight (fat mass, fat free mass [FFM])			
	- Average HR						
	- Relative lung volume						
	- RMR						
	- VO_{2max}						

Cox et al. (2001)	Cycle ergometer	6 mo	12 mo	18 mo
	- HR	—	—	—
	- VO$_{2max}$			
	• Body weight	0.00	0.00	−0.08
	• BMI	0.21	0.21	−0.40
	• Skinfold thickness	0.03	−0.02	−0.39
	• WHR	0.20	0.36	0.48

Donnelly et al. (2000)	• Adherence to exercise session, as monitored by research team (distance walked, HR, duration)	—
	- Distance walked (miles)	
	- HR at end	
	- Duration of exercise	
	- Rating of perceived exertion	
	• Treadmill	—
	- HR	
	- VO$_{2max}$	
	• Body weight	
	• BMI	
	• Waist circumference	
	• WHR	
	• Hydrostatic weight	
	- Fat mass	
	- FFM	

Hemmingsson et al. (2009)		6 mo	18 mo
	• Self-reported commuting mode (walking, cycling)	0.11	
	• Body weight	−0.12	−0.02
	• Waist circumference	−0.08	0.06
	• Pedometer steps (18 months)	—	
	• Cycling trip meter (18 months)	1.06	
	• Sagittal abdominal diameter	−0.05	0.05

(Continued)

TABLE 4.4

Physical Activity (PA) and Body Composition (BC) Measures, Intervention Effect Sizes, and Relationship Between PA and BC in 40 Studies of Women Stratified by PA Interventions With and Without Diet   (Continued)

Author/Year	PA Measures	Intervention Effect on PA	BC Measures	Intervention Effect on BC		Relationship Between PA and BC
Hovell et al. (2008)	• 7-day PAR and 23 specific PA questions (over past 2 weeks) • Treadmill - VO_{2max}	—	• BMI	—		—
Irwin et al. (2003)	• Minnesota PA Questionnaire • Activity log of sports & recreational activities (recreational/household, past 3 months) • Treadmill - HR - VO_{2max}	—	• Body weight • Waist circumference • DXA whole-body scanner - Total body fat - Total body fat % • CT - Intra-abdominal - Subcutaneous fat	3 mo −0.10 −0.06 	12 mo −0.19 −0.14 −0.24 −0.25 −0.14 −0.23	Change in body fat associated with changes in duration of sports activities and cardiovascular fitness

Keller & Cantue (2008)	• 7-day PAR (time spent sleeping, doing activities, intensity, and duration of activities)	• BMI • WHR • BIA	—	—

Kraemer et al. (2001)	• Cycle ergometer (peak aerobic power)
	• Strength/power tests (plyometric power system)
	• Vertical jump power performance
		• Body weight
		• Hydrodensitometry
		  - FFM
		  - Percent body fat)
		• Skinfold thickness
		• MRI
		  - Muscle cross-sectional area
			—	—

Lawton et al. (2009)	• PA questionnaire (PA in past 7 days in relation to activity type, context, intensity, and duration)	• Body weight • Waist circumference	—	—

(Continued)

TABLE 4.4

Physical Activity (PA) and Body Composition (BC) Measures, Intervention Effect Sizes, and Relationship Between PA and BC in 40 Studies of Women Stratified by PA Interventions With and Without Diet   (Continued)

Author/Year	PA Measures	Intervention Effect on PA	BC Measures	Intervention Effect on BC	Relationship Between PA and BC
Nies et al. (2003)	• Self-report measure of average minutes walked per day • Rockport 1-mile walk test - VO_{2max} estimate	—	• BMI	—	—
Park et al. (2003)	• Treadmill - VO_{2max}	2.61	• Body weight • BMI • CT - Visceral fat/subcutaneous fat	−1.05 — −6.61	—
Poston et al. (2001)	• 7-day PAR	—	• BMI • WHR	−0.16[a] —	—
Santa-Clara (2006)	• Treadmill - maximum HR - VO_{2max} RMR - maximum respiratory quotient	—	• Body weight • BMI • Plethysmography - Fat mass - % body fat	—	—

| Swearingin (2008) | • Stanford 7-day PAR
• Pedometer steps
• Cycle ergometer
  - HR
  - VO_{2max} | — | • BMI
• Waist circum-ference
• Skinfold thickness
• BIA
  - % body fat | — | — |
| Wilbur et al. (2008) | • BRFSS (self-report of vigorous or moderate household, work, leisure, or transportation activity; women were grouped into meets recommendation, insufficiently active, and not active)
• Polar heart rate monitor (mean number minutes waked within prescribed intensity)
• Treadmill test of aerobic fitness | —

—

0.05 | • BMI
• Waist circum-ference | −0.05
0.01 | |

(Continued)

TABLE 4.4

Physical Activity (PA) and Body Composition (BC) Measures, Intervention Effect Sizes, and Relationship Between PA and BC in 40 Studies of Women Stratified by PA Interventions With and Without Diet   (Continued)

Author/Year	PA Measures	Intervention Effect on PA	BC Measures	Intervention Effect on BC	Relationship Between PA and BC
Physical activity with diet					
Adachi et al. (2007)	• 3 Lifestyle PA questions (shopping, stair use, watch TV) • Pedometer steps (7 months)	—	• Body weight • BMI	1 mo 3 mo 7 mo −0.43 −0.40 −0.41 −0.44 −0.40 −0.39	—
Bacon et al. (2002)	• Stanford 7-day PAR energy expenditure in: - light - moderate - hard - very hard PA	24 weeks 52 weeks .16[b] −.03 −.34 −.18 .30 −.17 −.67 −.15	• Body weight • BMI	24 weeks 52 weeks −0.28[b] −0.40 −0.30 −0.42	—
Campbell et al. (2002)	• PA leisure time (women were first assessed yes/no; if yes, then completed a 10-item checklist) - Duration of PA - Frequency of PA • MET values	—	• BMI	—	—

Study	PA measures	BC measures	Correlation	Correlation	Notes
Carels et al. (2004)	• Paffenbarger PA Questionnaire (leisure time PA) • Accelerometers • Treadmill - time (s) - VO$_{2max}$	• Body weight • BMI • BIA - Body fat - FFM - Fat mass estimates	—	—	Change in body weight significantly associated with changes in time on treadmill, controlling for intervention group
Eiben & Lissner (2006)	• Point-based work, commuting, and leisure PA scale (kcal/week) • Treadmill - VO$_{2max}$	• BMI • Waist circumference • WHR • DXA - Total BC	0.31[c] · 0.42	−0.51[c] · −0.26 · −0.59 · −0.46	—
Fitzgibbon et al. (2005)	• Stanford 7-Day PAR kcal/kg per day: - energy expenditure - moderate - vigorous PA	• Body weight • BMI	−0.27 · −0.20 · −0.14	−0.14 · −0.13	—
Fitzgibbon et al. (2010)	• IPAQ—long format (min/day, 7 days)	• Body weight • BMI	—	6 mo: −0.37, −0.37; 18 mo: −0.21, −0.23	—

(Continued)

TABLE 4.4

Physical Activity (PA) and Body Composition (BC) Measures, Intervention Effect Sizes, and Relationship Between PA and BC in 40 Studies of Women Stratified by PA Interventions With and Without Diet (Continued)

Author/Year	PA Measures	Intervention Effect on PA	BC Measures	Intervention Effect on BC	Relationship Between PA and BC
Folta et al. (2009)	• Pedometer steps (7 days) • Walking test - Estimated VO_{2max} (based on time to walk 2 km, age, BMI)	0.38 —	• Body weight • BMI • Waist circumference	−0.41 −0.49 −0.26	—
Grant, et al. (2004)	Functional status tests: • 20-min walk • Chair rise • "Up and go" test • Lifting of 1- and 2-kg bag on shelf • Stair walking • "Sit and reach" flexibility test	−0.30 −0.19 −0.34 −0.20 −0.11 0.09	• Body weight • BMI • Skinfold thickness	−0.38 −0.32 −0.23	—
Hayashi et al. (2010)	• Stage of readiness to change behavior—improvement in PA	0.34	• Body weight • BMI	—	

Jakicic et al. (2003)

Vigorous vs. moderate intensity:

	Month 0–6	Month 7–12
• PA log		
- duration	−0.13	−0.42
- frequency	0.13	0.20
- perceived exertion	0.67	0.89
- 7-Day PAR—Total duration of leisure PA	−0.07	−0.25

	6 Months	12 Months
• Treadmill submaximal		
- VO$_{2max}$ (perceived exertion)	0.17	0.22
- HR	0.33	0.17

Vigorous vs. moderate intensity:

	6 mo	18 mo
• Body weight	−0.02	0.01
• BMI	−0.01	0.02

Janssen et al. (2002)

• Treadmill		
- VO$_{2max}$	—	
• Energy expenditure		

	DA vs. DQ	DA vs. DQ
• Body weight	−0.17[c]	0.00
• BMI	−0.10	0.05
• WHR	0.00	0.00
• Waist circumference (cm)	0.03	−0.18
• MRI		
- Total fat (kg)	−0.35	−0.18
- Abdominal subcutaneous fat (kg)	−0.39	−0.27
- L4–L5 (cm^2)	0.27	0.76
- Intermuscular fat (kg)	0.38	−0.32

(Continued)

TABLE 4.4

Physical Activity (PA) and Body Composition (BC) Measures, Intervention Effect Sizes, and Relationship Between PA and BC in 40 Studies of Women Stratified by PA Interventions With and Without Diet   (Continued)

Author/Year	PA Measures	Intervention Effect on PA	BC Measures	Intervention Effect on BC	Relationship Between PA and BC
Keyserling et al. (2008)	• New Leaf PA assessment (light, moderate or vigorous activity) • Accelerometer	—	• Body weight	—	—
Lombard et al. (2010)	• IPAQ—short version (7 days) (MET/min/wk) - walking - moderate activity - vigorous activity • Pedometer steps	−0.07 0.12 0.11 −0.03	• Body weight • BMI • Waist circumference • Hip circumference	−0.13 — −0.08 —	—
Nicklas et al. (2009)	• Treadmill - VO_{2max}	Moderate Vigorous −0.12 −0.41	• Body weight • Total fat mass • % Body Fat • Waist Circumference • WHR	Moderate Vigorous −0.06[c] −0.07 −0.17 −0.21 −0.24 −0.30 −0.06 −0.15 0.08 −0.07	"changes in visceral fat were inversely related to increases in relative VO_{2max}" (p. 1049)

	Exercise measures	Exercise and Exercise + Diet vs. Control	Body composition measures	Exercise and Exercise + Diet vs. Control	
Nieman et al. (2002)	• Treadmill - VO_{2max}	.54	• Body weight • BMI • X-ray absorptiometry (fat mass, % body fat)	−0.37 −0.23 −0.25	—
O'Toole (2003)	• YPAS (kcal/week, lifestyle, typical week) • Treadmill - VO_{2max}	—	• Body weight • Plethysmography (% body fat)	—	Weight loss significantly associated with average PA kcal/week and with YVAS score
Rosamond et al. (2000)	• PA self-report (single question, participate in moderate/vigorous physical active ≥30 minutes most days of week)	−.12	• Body weight • BMI	6 mo 12 mo −0.07[c] −0.09 −0.08 −0.08	—
Ross et al. (2004)	• Treadmill - VO_{2max}	—	Combined 3 tx groups vs. control • Body weight • BMI • Waist circumference • MRI - % body fat	−0.59[d] −0.47 −0.57 −0.86	—

(Continued)

TABLE 4.4

Physical Activity (PA) and Body Composition (BC) Measures, Intervention Effect Sizes, and Relationship Between PA and BC in 40 Studies of Women Stratified by PA Interventions With and Without Diet   (Continued)

Author/Year	PA Measures	Intervention Effect on PA		BC Measures	Intervention Effect on BC		Relationship Between PA and BC
Samuel-Hodge et al. (2009)	• Self-reported PA Assessment - Moderate PA - Vigorous PA • Self-reported weekly PA minutes	0.34 0.08 —		• Body weight • BIA - % body fat	−0.67 −0.27		Weight loss associated with group attendance and recorded PA minutes
Staten et al. (2004)	• Arizona Activity Frequency Questionnaire (moderate-to-vigorous PA minutes/week) • Health and lifestyle questionnaire based on BRFSS (self-report of vigorous or moderate household, work, leisure, or transportation activity)	PC + HE vs. PC only 0.06 —	PC + HE + CHW vs. PC 0.07 —	• Body weight • BMI • Waist circumference	PC+HE vs. PC only 0.12c 0.18 0.20	PC+HE+ CHW vs. PC only 0.06 0.06 0.00	

Walker et al. (2009)	• Modified 7-day activity recall (minutes/day)	0.29	• BMI	0.00	—
	• Sit-and-reach test	0.20	• BIA - % body fat	−0.41	
	• Timed chair stands	0.59			
	• 1 mile walk test - Estimate VO_{2max}	0.20			
Yancey et al. (2006)	• Leisure time PA-4 items (no PA, only light PA, vigorous PA 20 min, 2 times a week, vigorous PA ≥3 times a week)	—	• BMI • WHR • BIA	—	—
	• Treadmill - Time to walk 1 mile				
Yanek et al. (2001)	• YPAS (kcal/week, lifestyle, typical week)	—	• Body weight • BMI • Waist circumference • BIA - total body fat	—	—

Note. BIA = body impedance analysis; BMI = body mass index; BRFSS = Behavioral Risk Factor Surveillance Survey; CHW = community health workers; CT = computed tomography; DXA = dual-energy x-ray absorptiometry; HE = health education; HR = heart rate; IPAQ = International Physical Activity Questionnaire; MET = metabolic equivalent of task; MRI = magnetic resonance imaging; PC = provider counseling; PAR = Physical Activity Recall; RMR = resting metabolic rate; VO_{2max} = maximal oxygen uptake; WHR = waist-to-hip ratio; YPAS = Yale Physical Activity Survey.
[a]6-month only because of differential attrition at 12 months. [b]Effect sizes based on posttest comparisons only. [c]Estimate assuming a pre–post correlation of .80 for the outcome measures. [d]Using posttest data only.

Ekelund, & Rössner, 2009; Hovell et al., 2008; Irwin et al., 2003; Keller & Cantue, 2008; Kraemer et al., 2001; Lawton et al., 2009; Nies, Chruscial, & Hepworth, 2003; Park et al., 2003; Poston et al., 2001; Santa-Clara, Szymanski, Ordille, & Fernhall, 2006; Swearingin, 2008; Wilbur et al., 2008). The other 24 RCTs were PA interventions with a diet component (Adachi et al., 2007; Bacon et al., 2002; Campbell et al., 2002; Carels, Darby, Cacciapaglia, & Douglass, 2004; Eiben & Lissner, 2006; Fitzgibbon et al., 2005; Fitzgibbon et al., 2010; Folta et al., 2009; Grant, Todd, Aitchison, Kelly, & Stoddart, 2004; Hayashi, Farrell, Chaput, Rocha, & Hernandez, 2010; Jakicic, Marcus, Gallagher, Napolitano, & Lang, 2003; Janssen, Fortier, Hudson, & Ross, 2002; Keyserling et al., 2008; Lombard, Deeks, Jolley, Ball, & Teede, 2010; Nicklas et al., 2009; Nieman, Brock, Butterworth, Utter, & Nieman, 2002; O'Toole, Sawicki, & Artal, 2003; Rosamond et al., 2000; Ross et al., 2004; Samuel-Hodge et al., 2009; Staten et al., 2004; Walker et al., 2009; Yancey et al., 2006; Yanek, Becker, Moy, Gittelsohn, & Koffman, 2001).

Of the 40 studies in this review, 31 were conducted in North America, 4 in Europe, 3 in Oceania, and 2 in Asia. The number of participants varied significantly. Sample sizes ranged from 18 to 1,957 participants, with a mean (SD) of 242 (361) and a median of 130 participants. In the lowest quartile, sample sizes ranged from 18 to 44. The second quartile had sample sizes from 45 to 126. The third quartile had sample sizes from 134 to 225. In the highest quartile, sample sizes ranged from 250 to 1,957. Of the 28 studies that identified ethnicity of the participants, 6 had African American women only, 7 had both African American and White American women, and 4 had Hispanic women only. The remainder was predominately non-Latino White or had a variety of ethnic groups.

In not quite half of the studies (18), being sedentary was an inclusion criterion, whereas being active was an inclusion criterion in only one study. A specific BMI was required in more than half of the studies, with 8 requiring a BMI of ≥ 25 kg/m^2 or more, 3 requiring a BMI of ≥ 27 kg/m^2, and 4 requiring a BMI of ≥ 30 kg/m^2. Additional BC criteria were having at least 30% body fat or a waist measurement of >35 in. BMI levels were capped in 7 studies, ranging from 29.9 to 65.0. Participants in 3 studies included postmenopausal women only, whereas 2 included premenopausal women only and 1 study had postpartum women only. Five studies included low-income or uninsured women only.

Studies took place in many different settings within the community. Many studies (13) used more than one type of site, for example, a home setting and a gym setting. Thirteen of the 40 studies had at least part or all of the intervention being conducted at or around the participants' home. Other settings included gyms of health clubs (7), clinics (7), universities or colleges (5), exercise labs (4), community centers (3), worksite (1), and church (1).

Intervention Characteristics

The following are the characteristics of the interventions in the PA studies with and without diet.

Physical Activity Without Diet

Of the 16 intervention studies that focused on PA without a diet component, 14 were RCTs with random assignment of participants to either one or more interventions or to an intervention and a control condition (see Table 4.3). Poston et al. (2001) used block randomization of preexisting networks and Wilbur et al. (2008) used random assignment of interventions to community health centers. Only 5 interventions lasted 12 months or longer (Cox et al., 2001; Donnelly et al., 2000; Hemmingsson et al., 2009; Irwin et al., 2003; Wilbur et al., 2008). Eight studies compared one or more interventions to untreated controls (Byrne & Wilmore, 2001; Kraemer et al., 2001; Lawton et al., 2009; Nies et al., 2003; Park et al., 2003; Poston et al., 2001; Santa-Clara et al., 2006; Swearingin, 2008), 3 studies compared one or more treatment to an attention control (Asikainen et al., 2002; Hovell et al., 2008; Irwin et al., 2003), whereas 5 studies compared multiple treatment conditions (Cox et al., 2001; Donnelly et al., 2000; Hemmingsson et al., 2009; Keller & Cantue, 2008; Wilbur et al., 2008).

Examination of the interventions revealed that most (nine) used structured exercise groups (Asikainen et al., 2002; Byrne & Wilmore, 2001; Cox et al., 2001; Donnelly et al., 2000; Hovell et al., 2008; Keller & Cantue, 2008; Kraemer et al., 2001; Park et al., 2003; Santa-Clara et al., 2006). Most of these interventions had a maximum of three group sessions per week with recommendations for home-based PA on other days of the week. Not surprisingly, eight of the nine interventions with structured exercise groups had specific exercise prescriptions related to duration and intensity of aerobic activity. The one study that did not was a walking program for Latinas with a promotora (lay coach) who led walking at a pace of a 20-min mile (Keller & Cantue, 2008).

The other 7 studies all had a behavioral component in addition to PA. These included a variety of approaches, including group-based programs on strategies for changing behavior (Kraemer et al., 2001; Swearingin, 2008); individual sessions with an interventionist on strategies for changing behavior (Lawton et al., 2009; Nies et al., 2003); and a combination of both group-based and individual behavioral change sessions delivered in person or over the phone (Hemmingsson et al., 2009; Poston et al., 2001; Wilbur et al., 2008). Of these 7 studies, 2 also included a structured exercise group component (Irwin et al., 2003; Poston et al., 2001), whereas the others encouraged home-based PA

(Hemmingsson et al., 2009; Lawton et al., 2009; Nies et al., 2003; Swearingin, 2008; Wilbur et al., 2008). Although 2 of the behavioral interventions were very prescriptive in terms of duration and intensity of PA (Irwin & Supplee, 2012; Wilbur et al., 2008), others encouraged increasing steps walked (Hemmingsson et al., 2009), brisk walking for 30 min a day (Lawton et al., 2009; Poston et al., 2001), or obtaining PA for a specific number of minutes a week (150 min; Nies et al., 2003; Swearingin, 2008). The background of the interventionist was provided for 3 of the 7 studies and, in all cases, it was a health care provider (Hemmingsson et al., 2009; Lawton et al., 2009; Poston et al., 2001). Overall, 6 of the 16 intervention studies focusing on PA without diet provided a theoretical model or framework.

Physical Activity With Diet

Of the 24 intervention studies that had PA with a diet component, 19 were RCTs with random assignment of participants to one or more interventions or to an intervention or control condition. Other studies used random assignment to a geographic area (Lombard et al., 2010; Walker et al., 2009) or sites such as worksites (Campbell et al., 2002), health departments (Rosamond et al., 2000), or churches (Yanek et al., 2001). This set of studies primarily compared various versions of interventions, including interventions with different strategies or different strategies were added to a base strategy that participants in all interventions received. Only 6 studies compared an intervention to a control, either a no intervention control (Campbell et al., 2002; Folta et al., 2009) or an attention control (Fitzgibbon et al., 2010; Hayashi et al., 2010; Samuel-Hodge et al., 2009; Yancey et al., 2006). Only 9 of the 24 studies lasted 12 months or longer.

Of the 24 intervention studies, all but 2 had a behavioral component focused on PA and BC. One of the exceptions was the study by Nicklas et al. (2009), in which all meals and snacks along with a group-based exercise program were provided but which did not mention behavioral strategies. Likewise, Nieman et al. (2002) delivered a group-based exercise intervention but did not mention behavioral strategies. The most frequent approach for delivering the behavioral component was use of the group or seminar (14/22). Ten studies used the group or seminar alone (Bacon et al., 2002; Carels et al., 2004; Fitzgibbon et al., 2005; Folta et al., 2009; Janssen et al., 2002; Lombard et al., 2010; O'Toole et al., 2003; Ross et al., 2004; Yancey et al., 2006; Yanek et al., 2001), but 4 used a combination of group and individual delivery via phone or face-to-face (Fitzgibbon et al., 2010; Jakicic, Marcus, Lang, & Janney, 2008; Keyserling et al., 2008; Samuel-Hodge et al., 2009). The 8 without a group or seminar had individual delivery only (Campbell et al., 2002; Eiben & Lissner, 2006; Grant et al., 2004; Hayashi et al., 2010; Rosamond et al., 2000; Staten et al., 2004) or used a newsletter or magazine alone (Adachi et al., 2007; Walker et al., 2009).

Newsletters and magazines were frequently used to supplement both group and individually delivered behavioral interventions.

Overall, only 7 of the 22 studies with a behavioral component had a structured exercise group component (Bacon et al., 2002; Fitzgibbon et al., 2005; Fitzgibbon et al., 2010; Folta et al., 2009; Grant et al., 2004; Janssen et al., 2002; Yanek et al., 2001). All of the 7 structured exercise group interventions included two or more components of a PA prescription including frequency, duration, and intensity. The remaining 13 studies with a behavioral component used home-based PA. Of these, only three PA included a PA prescription (Jakicic et al., 2003; Ross et al., 2004; Staten et al., 2004). The other home-based interventions primarily encouraged an increase in PA without being prescriptive. Half of the studies provided the background of the interventionist including physicians or nurses (Grant et al., 2004; Samuel-Hodge et al., 2009; Staten et al., 2004), dieticians (Bacon et al., 2002; Eiben & Lissner, 2006; Lombard et al., 2010; O'Toole et al., 2003), a psychologist (Carels et al., 2004), and a health educator (Yanek et al., 2001). Only 2 studies used community workers (Campbell et al., 2002; Hayashi et al., 2010). Others noted they used trained interventionists but did not provide their background. Overall, 16 of the 24 intervention studies focusing on PA with diet provided a theoretical model or framework.

Characteristics of the Study Physical Activity and Body Composition Measures

The following are the characteristics of the PA and BC measures used in the PA studies with and without diet.

Physical Activity Without Diet

Of the 16 intervention studies that focused on PA without diet, 10 used one or more self-report PA measures (see Table 4.4). Although a variety of measures was used, 7 used a standard PA questionnaire. Six of these were identified in Helmerhorst et al.'s (2012) systematic review of PA questionnaires (Hovell et al., 2008; Irwin et al., 2003; Keller & Cantue, 2008; Poston et al., 2001; Swearingin, 2008; Wilbur et al., 2008). The seventh was reported elsewhere (Lawton et al., 2009). The other 3 studies using self-report measures had very brief questionnaires with four questions or less (Asikainen et al., 2002; Hemmingsson et al., 2009; Nies et al., 2003). Overall, 7 of the self-report measures included both lifestyle PA and exercise (Hovell et al., 2008; Irwin et al., 2003; Keller & Cantue, 2008; Lawton et al., 2009; Poston et al., 2001; Swearingin, 2008; Wilbur et al., 2008).

Objective measures of PA included the direct measures of distance cycled using a trip meter and pedometers (Hemmingsson et al., 2009) or pedometers only (Swearingin, 2008). None of these studies used an accelerometer. When measuring PA objectively, however, most studies (11) used indirect measurement with cardiorespiratory (aerobic) fitness tests. Treadmill tests were performed in 7 of the 16 studies and were used to obtain a variety of measures including VO_{2max}, heart rate, and maximum respiratory quotient (Asikainen et al., 2002; Byrne & Wilmore, 2001; Donnelly et al., 2000; Irwin et al., 2003; Park et al., 2003; Santa-Clara et al., 2006; Wilbur et al., 2008). Three studies used a cycle ergometer to obtain estimated VO_{2max} and heart rate (Cox et al., 2001; Kraemer et al., 2001; Swearingin, 2008). One study had participants complete a 1-mile walk test to obtain estimated VO_{2max} (Nies et al., 2003).

Of the 16 PA intervention studies focusing on PA without diet, most (15) used field measures of BC, including BMI, weight, waist or waist-to-hip circumference, or skinfold thickness. BMI or weight or both were reported in all 15 studies. Waist or waist-to-hip measures or both were given in 9 studies (Cox et al., 2001; Donnelly et al., 2000; Hemmingsson et al., 2009; Irwin et al., 2003; Keller & Cantue, 2008; Lawton et al., 2009; Poston et al., 2001; Swearingin, 2008; Wilbur et al., 2008), skinfold thickness in 4 studies (Asikainen et al., 2002; Cox et al., 2001; Kraemer et al., 2001; Swearingin, 2008), and BIA in 2 studies (Keller & Cantue, 2008; Swearingin, 2008).

Seven studies combined field with other measures of BC or used other measures of BC only. These included DXA (Irwin et al., 2003), CT (Irwin et al., 2003; Park et al., 2003), MRI (Kraemer et al., 2001), hydrostatic weighing (Byrne & Wilmore, 2001; Donnelly et al., 2000; Kraemer et al., 2001), and plethysmography (Santa-Clara et al., 2006).

Physical Activity With Diet

Of the 24 intervention studies that had PA with a diet component, 18 used a PA self-report tool. Of these, 11 used a standard PA questionnaire identified in the systematic review by Helmerhorst et al. (2012; Bacon et al., 2002; Carels et al., 2004; Fitzgibbon et al., 2005; Fitzgibbon et al., 2010; Hayashi et al., 2010; Jakicic et al., 2003; Lombard et al., 2010; O'Toole et al., 2003; Staten et al., 2004; Walker et al., 2009; Yanek et al., 2001). Four used very brief questionnaires (four questions or less; Adachi et al., 2007; Hayashi et al., 2010; Rosamond et al., 2000; Yancey et al., 2006). An additional 3 used questionnaires developed for the study (Campbell et al., 2002; Eiben & Lissner, 2006; Keyserling et al., 2008). Overall, 12 of the 18 self-report tools measured both lifestyle PA and exercise (Bacon et al., 2002; Eiben & Lissner, 2006; Fitzgibbon et al., 2005; Fitzgibbon et al., 2010; Jakicic et al., 2003; Keyserling et al., 2008; Lombard et al., 2010; O'Toole et al., 2003; Samuel-Hodge et al., 2009; Staten et al., 2004; Walker et al., 2009; Yanek et al., 2001).

Three studies used pedometers to measure PA objectively (Adachi et al., 2007; Folta et al., 2009; Lombard et al., 2010), and two used accelerometers (Carels et al.,

2004; Keyserling et al., 2008). Indirect objective measures of PA included aerobic fitness tests with a treadmill (9/24; Carels et al., 2004; Eiben & Lissner, 2006; Jakicic et al., 2003; Janssen et al., 2002; Nicklas et al., 2009; Nieman et al., 2002; O'Toole et al., 2003; Ross et al., 2004; Yancey et al., 2006) or walking tests (Folta et al., 2009; Walker et al., 2009) to determine estimated VO$_{2max}$. Two studies tested various aspects of functional status (Grant et al., 2004; Walker et al., 2009).

All 24 intervention using PA with diet used field measures of BC, with all reporting BMI or weight or both. Other field measures were skinfold thickness (Grant et al., 2004; Janssen et al., 2002) and waist or waist-to-hip circumference or both (Eiben & Lissner, 2006; Folta et al., 2009; Lombard et al., 2010; Nicklas et al., 2009; Ross et al., 2004; Staten et al., 2004; Yancey et al., 2006; Yanek et al., 2001). Other measures of BC included BIA (Carels et al., 2004; Samuel-Hodge et al., 2009; Walker et al., 2009; Yancey et al., 2006; Yanek et al., 2001), DXA (Eiben & Lissner, 2006; Nicklas et al., 2009; Nieman et al., 2002), MRI (Janssen et al., 2002; Ross et al., 2004), and plethysmography (O'Toole et al., 2003).

Intervention Effects

Across all 40 studies, effect sizes for PA outcomes were calculated for 18 (45%) and effect sizes for BC were calculated for 24 (60%) studies (see Table 4.5). After calculating these separate intervention effect sizes, weighted mean effects were examined. The weighted mean effect was $d = .21$, 95% CI [0.06, 0.36] for PA outcomes and $d = -.16$, 95% CI [−0.22, −0.09] for BC outcomes.

Physical Activity Without Diet

Of the 16 intervention studies of PA without diet, effect sizes for PA outcomes were calculated for 4 (25%) of the studies (Asikainen et al., 2002; Hemmingsson et al., 2009; Park et al., 2003; Wilbur et al., 2008). The weighted mean effect for these studies was $d = .70$, 95% CI [0.02, 1.38]. Effect sizes for BC outcomes were calculated for 7 (44%) of the studies (Asikainen et al., 2002; Cox et al., 2001; Hemmingsson et al., 2009; Irwin et al., 2003; Park et al., 2003; Poston et al., 2001; Wilbur et al, 2008). The weighted mean effect for these studies was $d = -.21$, 95% CI [−0.34, −0.07].

Of the nine studies that had the structured exercise group component only (Asikainen et al., 2002; Byrne & Wilmore, 2001; Cox et al., 2001; Donnelly et al., 2000; Hovell et al., 2008; Keller & Cantue, 2008; Kraemer et al., 2001; Park et al., 2003; Santa-Clara et al., 2006), effect sizes for intervention impact on PA were estimated for two studies (Asikainen et al., 2002; Park et al., 2003). The weighted mean effect for these two studies was $d = 1.29$, 95% CI [−1.07, 3.65]. Of the remaining seven studies that had a behavioral component in addition to PA (Hemmingsson et al., 2009; Irwin et al., 2003; Lawton et al., 2009; Nies et al., 2003; Poston et al., 2001; Swearingin, 2008; Wilbur et al., 2008), effect sizes for intervention impact on

TABLE 4.5
Weighted Mean Effect Sizes of Selected Physical Activity Intervention
of Women With and Without Diet

Study Characteristics (n of studies)	PA Outcome		BC Outcome	
	n (%)[a]	M [95% CI]	n (%)[a]	M [95% CI]
All studies (N = 40)	18 (45)	0.21 [0.06, 0.36][b]	24 (60)	−0.16 [−0.22, −0.09]
PA without diet (n =16)	4 (25)	0.70 [0.02, 1.38][2]	7 (44)	−0.21 [−0.34, −0.07]
Structured exercise group component only (n = 9)	2 (22)	1.29 [−1.07, 3.65][b]	3 (33)	−0.48 [−0.76, −0.20]
Behavioral component in addition to PA (n = 7)	2 (29)	0.37 [−0.25, 0.98][b]	4 (57)	−0.13 [−0.28, 0.03]
PA with diet (n =24)	14 (58)	0.14 [0.01, 0.27][b]	17 (71)	−0.14 [−0.22, −0.07]
Behavioral program that includes group or seminar (n = 14)	6 (43)	0.12 [−0.02, 0.26]	9 (64)	−0.24 [−0.36, −0.11]
Behavioral program that did not include group or seminar (n = 8)	6 (75)	0.15 [−0.06, 0.36][b]	6 (75)	−0.09 [−0.18, 0.00]

Note. BC = body composition; PA = physical activity.
[a]Number of studies for which effect sizes could be calculated. [b]Random-effect model used because of significant heterogeneity.

PA were estimated for two studies (Hemmingsson et al., 2009; Wilbur et al., 2008). The weighted mean effect for these two studies was $d = .37$, 95% CI [−0.25, 0.98].

Of the nine studies that had the structured exercise group component, only effect sizes for intervention impact on BC were estimated for three studies (Asikainen et al., 2002; Cox et al., 2001; Park et al., 2003). The weighted mean effect for these three studies was $d = −.48$, 95% CI [−0.76, −0.20]. Of the studies with a behavioral component in addition to PA effect sizes for intervention impact on BC were estimated for four studies (Hemmingsson et al., 2009; Irwin et al., 2003; Poston et al., 2001; Wilbur et al., 2008). The weighted mean effect for these four studies was $d = −.13$, 95% CI [−0.28, 0.03].

Physical Activity With Diet
Of the 24 intervention studies that had PA with diet, effect sizes for PA outcomes were calculated for 14 (58%) studies (Bacon et al., 2002; Carels et al., 2004; Fitzgibbon et al., 2005; Fitzgibbon et al., 2010; Folta et al., 2009; Jakicic et al., 2008; Janssen et al., 2002; Keyserling et al., 2008; Lombard et al., 2010; O'Toole et al., 2003; Ross et al., 2004; Samuel-Hodge et al., 2009; Yancey et al., 2006; Yanek et al., 2001). The weighted mean effect for these 14 studies was $d = .14$, 95% CI [0.01, 0.27]. For BC outcomes, effect sizes were calculated for 17 (71%) of the 24 studies. The weighted mean effect for these studies was $d = -.14$, 95% CI [−0.22, −0.07].

Of the 14 studies that included group behavioral programs, effect sizes for intervention impact on PA were estimated for 6 (Bacon et al., 2002; Fitzgibbon et al., 2005; Folta et al., 2009; Jakicic et al., 2008; Lombard et al., 2010; Samuel-Hodge et al., 2009) studies. The weighted mean effect for these 6 studies was $d = .12$, 95% CI [−0.02, 0.26]. Of the 8 studies that did not include group behavioral programs, effect sizes for intervention impact on PA were estimated for 6 studies (Eiben & Lissner, 2006; Grant et al., 2004; Hayashi et al., 2010; Nieman et al., 2002; Rosamond et al., 2000; Staten et al., 2004). The weighted mean effect for these 6 studies was $d = .15$, 95% CI [−0.06, 0.36]. Of the 14 studies that included group behavioral programs, effect sizes for intervention impact on BC were estimated for 9 studies (Bacon et al., 2002; Fitzgibbon et al., 2005; Fitzgibbon et al., 2010; Folta et al., 2009; Janssen et al., 2002; Jakicic et al., 2008; Lombard et al., 2010; Ross et al., 2004; Samuel-Hodge et al., 2009). The weighted mean effect for these 9 studies was $d = -.24$, 95% CI [−0.36, −0.11]. Of the 8 studies that did not include group behavioral programs, effect sizes for intervention impact on BC were estimated for 6 studies (Eiben & Lissner, 2006; Grant et al., 2004; Nieman et al., 2002; Rosamond et al., 2000; Staten et al., 2004; Walker et al., 2009). The weighted mean effect for these 6 studies was $d = -.09$, 95% CI [−0.18, 0.00].

Relationship Between Physical Activity and Body Composition
Across all 40 studies in this review, only 6 (15%) addressed the relationship between PA and BC. These 6 studies found associations between PA and BC such that changes in PA were associated with changes in BC.

DISCUSSION

This review of interventions for women to increase PA and improve BC addresses several objectives of the 2008–2013 Action Plan for the Global Strategy for the Prevention and Control of Noncommunicable Diseases to target physical inactivity in and its role in obesity (World Health Organization, 2008). This review also addresses a primary theme of the NIH Strategic Plan for Obesity Research, which is to design obesity prevention and treatment interventions to promote a healthy weight (USDHHS, 2012).

All studies in this review were RCTs, with some randomizing by site or community rather than by participants. As Wilbur et al. (2008) pointed out, randomizing by site avoids the problem of treatment contamination that can occur when participants who know each other are randomized to different interventions. Most of the studies had moved away from the use of a no intervention control, now considered to be unethical by some researchers (Conn et al., 2009), because the positive effects of PA interventions are known to be beneficial. Instead, these studies tested against an attention control group or compared different interventions or intervention components to each other.

Intervention Effects

The findings of this review are consistent with those of previous reviews (Conn et al., 2009; Conn et al., 2011; Ickes & Sharma, 2012; Weinheimer et al., 2010). When participants engaged in a PA intervention, whether alone or in combination with a diet intervention, PA levels increased and weight was maintained or decreased. Our moderate weighted effect size on PA of .21 (for the 18 studies for which effect sizes could be calculated) is identical to the .21 found in a prior review of worksite PA programs (Conn et al., 2009) and similar to the .19 found in a review of PA interventions with healthy adults (Conn et al., 2011). Our moderate weighted effect size of −.16 on BC is weaker than the −.73 weighted effect on BC of two studies in the review of Shaw et al. (2009) comparing a structured exercise intervention to a no intervention control. As noted earlier, many of the studies in our review compared two different interventions or levels/intensities of a similar intervention. Therefore, it is not unexpected that the reported effects appear weaker in our review as a result of comparing to groups that received an intervention rather than a no intervention control condition.

Interestingly, the studies of PA without diet had a stronger effect on PA than did the studies of PA with diet. When the primary outcome is weight, PA change has not been a focus. For example, Shaw et al. (2009) did not mention PA outcomes in their review of PA interventions for with and without diet when the primary outcome was weight. We speculate that studies targeting behavioral change in PA and diet for the purposes of achieving weight loss may put less emphasis on changing PA behavior than changing dietary behavior. In addition, there is a lack of consensus regarding the benefits of introducing simultaneous multiple behavior change (PA and diet; Prochaska, Spring, & Nigg, 2008). Findings here suggest that a single focus on PA may be more effective in improving PA.

In contrast, there were no differences between studies of PA with and without diet on BC change. This differs from earlier reviews suggesting that improvements in BC are primarily garnered when exercise or PA is combined with dietary interventions (Shaw et al., 2009). It is possible that when women participating solely in a PA intervention see success, they may be encouraged to change dietary behavior as well (Parekh, Vandelanotte, King, & Boyle, 2012).

Among the studies with PA as the sole intervention, there was a small to medium effect size for PA and BC among the interventions with a behavioral component compared to a large effect size among those using structured exercise groups only. The success of the interventions with structured exercise groups may be related to the provision of graduated exercise prescriptions with supervision available for feedback. In contrast, most of the studies with a behavioral component and no group exercise did not provide as much structure or feedback to guide people that are exercising on their own. Home-based exercise interventions can be strengthened with personalized exercise prescriptions and the use of heart rate monitors or accelerometers to provide needed structure and feedback. These strategies may well prove to be a viable alternative to on-site supervision. Follow-up focus groups to one of the home-based interventions (Wilbur et al., 2008) suggested that the women valued and used the feedback they received from wearing heart rate monitors to assess their achievement of their prescribed intensity of exercise (Ingram, Wilbur, McDevitt, & Buchholz, 2011). In addition, the larger average effects for the supervised exercise studies may be because measures were primarily taken at the end of the intervention. Although not reported, those studies that had a home-based walking component and were designed to motivate or increase PA may have had a longer lag time from intervention end to return for assessment.

A prior study comparing structured exercise with lifestyle or home-based interventions found comparable benefits for both strategies immediately following the intervention but greater maintenance of increased PA among lifestyle or home-based groups after long-term follow-up (Dunn et al., 1998). It is possible that lifestyle or home-based interventions are better at teaching PA self-management; however, information about long-term maintenance is sparse. Overall, in this review only 7 of the 40 studies (Bacon et al., 2002; Carels et al., 2004; Fitzgibbon et al., 2005; Hovell et al., 2008; Lawton et al., 2009; Rosamond et al., 2000; Yancey et al., 2006) followed the women 6 or more months after the end of the intervention, which points out the need for better understanding of long-term maintenance in future studies.

Examination of group versus individual or other behavioral approaches for PA with diet interventions revealed that all approaches had small effects on PA. However, the group approach may provide some relative advantage over the individual approach for BC. Although details regarding the interventions were not always provided, group behavioral interventions may have included dietary demonstrations not feasible with face-to-face individual delivery. These in turn may have changed dietary behavior not examined here. Additional study is needed to tease out the intervention approaches that have the most impact on both PA and BC.

Measurement

Although more than half of the studies (63%, or 25/40) used a standardized PA questionnaire, closer examination revealed that only 2 (Fitzgibbons et al., 2010; Lombard et al., 2010) used one of the four questionnaires deemed to have good results for both reliability and validity in a recent systematic review of PA questionnaires (Helmerhorst et al., 2012). Considering the generally low reliability and poor validity of most self-report measures, the reliance solely on self-report in 10 of the studies in this review is concerning because overestimating as well as underestimating PA can occur (Prince et al., 2008).

Of the 30 studies in this review that used an objective measure, only 2 used an accelerometer. An accelerometer can detect and record the actual magnitude of acceleration, providing a more accurate assessment of incidental activity and consequently a more accurate representation of PA in minutes per day. Because accelerometers allow investigators to objectively assess the influence of PA of various intensities on health outcomes such as BC (Tryon & Williams, 1996), we expect to see greater use of these devices in the future.

Theoretical Approaches

Slightly more than half of the studies reviewed were guided by a theory (21/40), with social cognitive theory (Bandura, 1997) the most frequently used. However, none operationalized the constructs of the theory to determine which constructs were affecting behavioral change as recommended by Sharma (2008). Providing a framework could also promote appropriate tailoring of the intervention by identifying possible constructs for purposeful adaptation. Although all of the studies in this review included women, it was primarily studies that provided a theory that noted how the intervention was tailored or targeted to meet women's needs. Whitt-Glover & Kumanyika (2009) has suggested it is possible that some interventions may spontaneously adapt to meet the needs of women, particularly when the adaptation is not a deliberate part of the intervention. This practice could interfere with study fidelity.

Public Health Implications

Significant but generally modest improvements in PA and BC were found in the studies that had adequate data for effect size determination. From a public health perspective, small, incremental changes in PA are important, especially in sedentary individuals. Although everyone benefits from engaging in PA, sedentary individuals who incrementally increase their PA decrease mortality rates more than do already moderately active individuals who become more active (Löllgen, Böckenhoff, & Knapp, 2009). Regular PA has also been found critical in preventing weight gain and maintaining weight loss (Donnelly et al., 2000; Shaw et al., 2009). Furthermore, adults typically gain about 1 lb/year, leading to overweight and obesity within two to three decades (Mozaffarian, Hao, Rimm, Willett, & Hu, 2011). This set of studies suggests that PA can abate this chronic gradual weight gain. In addition, nonsignificant results derived via body weight or BMI cannot be interpreted as an absence of effect of PA on abdominal fat. This is important because abdominal fat is associated with glucose tolerance and insulin sensitivity (Kay & Fiatarone Singh, 2006).

In addition to the important health benefits of losing weight when obese, medical expenditures related to obesity may also be decreased when weight loss occurs. It is estimated that annual medical expenditures would be 6.7%–10.7% lower if patients were not obese (Trogdon, Finkelstein, Feagan, & Cohen, 2012). The monetary costs of weight management interventions would be pertinent in this regard because they may indicate potential treatment costs. Cost-effective analyses of PA interventions are needed to assess the feasibility of disseminating selected strategies on a broad population basis.

Dissemination

Scant attention has been focused on developing and evaluating obesity prevention strategies that can be widely disseminated. Most interventions in this review were not focused on dissemination. Exceptions were the WISEWOMAN studies that demonstrate research dissemination (Hayashi et al., 2010; Keyserling et al., 2008; Rosamond et al., 2000; Staten et al., 2004). Although the WISEWOMAN program was specifically designed to be delivered to low-income women, information for the public and for health care providers on how to decrease cardiovascular disease risk in women and promote PA is readily available at the Centers for Disease Control and Prevention Website (Centers for Disease Control and Prevention, 2010).

Researchers need to examine the costs associated with interventions prior to dissemination. Although no cost analyses were provided in any of the studies reviewed, the inclusion criteria for this review did not specify cost and additional studies may be available. The monetary costs of PA and BC interventions are pertinent for developing useful dissemination packages. For example, 12 of 14 studies in this review that identified the interventionist used highly trained health professionals. To reduce costs, successful interventions must be streamlined and protocols made available in manuals (paper or digital media) so they can be easily delivered by lay health advisors or community health workers in clinical and community settings (Sharma, 2008). Another potentially cost-effective strategy to increase PA and improve BC is the greater use of rapidly growing mobile health communication technologies, now commonly referred to as mHealth technology (Roess & Sikka, 2012). Only one of the studies used a sophisticated mobile technology now available, such as text messaging (Lombard et al., 2010).

Limitations

This systematic review was limited by the primary studies located. Although multiple databases, related systematic reviews, and reference lists were methodically searched, some studies that met the inclusion criteria may not have been located. Of the studies that were located and met the inclusion criteria, not all of them presented adequate data to calculate or estimate effect sizes. More than half of the studies ($n = 22$) did not report adequate data to be able to determine a PA outcome effect size. Forty percent ($n = 16$) of the studies did not provide adequate data to be able to determine a BC outcome effect size. Even if these studies noted statistical significance, without data to support effect size calculation, they cannot be easily compared with outcomes of other studies. In addition, there may be bias in our reported mean effect sizes because nearly half of the studies were excluded from the calculations. This potential bias limits generalizations that can be made from the study findings. Furthermore, as noted previously (see "Analytic Strategy" section), incomplete data to calculate effect sizes for several studies necessitated assumptions that may have resulted in underestimated intervention effects.

In future studies, it is recommended that either effect sizes are presented along with statistical significance or sufficient statistical data is provided to allow accurate calculation of effect sizes. This is of particular relevance given the increasing prevalence of complex research designs and analytic approaches, including cluster randomized designs and longitudinal studies that employ growth modeling.

CONCLUSION

Although PA has many benefits for women, including playing a critical role in the management of maintaining a healthy weight as well as weight loss; PA levels have remained relatively stagnant. In addition, overweight and obesity levels have continued to rise. In this review of the recent literature, it is evident that many rigorous PA interventions designed specifically for women to improve their PA and BC have been conducted. Diversity was seen in the design of the studies and in the delivery of the interventions that incorporated lifestyle PA or structured exercise. As congruent with other PA literature reviews, most studies in this review had significant findings that demonstrated that PA interventions did improve PA levels and impact BC. Equally important, many of the effective interventions conducted resulted in increased PA levels among sedentary women. Also, many of the studies demonstrated that women that were overweight or obese were able to increase their level of PA and decrease their weight.

As a result of these PA interventions, modest overall effect sizes were seen with both PA and BC outcomes. In this review, PA interventions without a diet intervention added were more effective in improving PA and BC than PA interventions with a diet component. PA interventions with diet should consider either enhancing the PA component or introducing diet and PA sequentially. In the case of home-based exercise, the use of an exercise prescription and self-monitoring (e.g., pedometer or accelerometer) may offer a realistic and cost-effective alternative to group-based structured exercise programs. The group behavioral approach may be more effective than the individual approach for delivering the behavioral component when BC is the focus. However, individual approaches may be just as effective as the group approach for PA. Finally, the next stage is to move these studies into dissemination. To effectively do this, interventions must have the following components: (a) program materials or manuals and support services (e.g., training and technical support), (b) cost information, and (c) tools or measures for monitoring impact (Flay et al., 2005). Given the dire statistics of physical inactivity and overweight and obesity in women, it is critical that successful PA interventions are carried over into practice settings.

ACKNOWLEDGMENTS

We appreciate the formatting assistance provided by Alexis F. Manning, MA, and Edith Ocampo, MS, Rush University College of Nursing.

REFERENCES

Adachi, Y., Sato, C., Yamatsu, K., Ito, S., Adachi, K., & Yamagami, T. (2007). A randomized controlled trial on the long-term effects of a 1-month behavioral weight control program assisted by computer tailored advice. *Behaviour Research and Therapy*, 45(3), 459–470. http://dx.doi .org/10.1016/j.brat.2006.03.017

American College of Sports Medicine. (2010). *ACSM's resource manual for guidelines for exercise testing and prescription* (6th ed.). Philadelphia, PA: Lippincott Williams and Wilkins.

Anderson, L. M., Quinn, T. A., Glanz, K., Ramirez, G., Kahwati, L. C., Johnson, D. B., . . . Task Force on Community Preventive Services. (2009). The effectiveness of worksite nutrition and physical activity interventions for controlling employee overweight and obesity: A systematic review. *American Journal of Preventive Medicine*, 37(4), 340–357. http://dx.doi.org/10.1016/j .amepre.2009.07.003

Asikainen, T. M., Miilunpalo, S., Oja, P., Rinne, M., Pasanen, M., & Vuori, I. (2002). Walking trials in postmenopausal women: Effect of one vs. two daily bouts on aerobic fitness. *Scandinavian Journal of Medicine & Science in Sports, 12*(2), 99–105. http://dx.doi.org /10.1034/j.1600-0838.2002.120206.x

Bacon, L., Keim, N. L., Van Loan, M. D., Derricote, M., Gale, B., Kazaks, A., & Stern, J. S. (2002). Evaluating a 'non-diet' wellness intervention for improvement of metabolic fitness, psychological well-being and eating and activity behaviors. *International Journal of Obesity and Related Metabolic Disorders: Journal of the International Association for the Study of Obesity, 26*(6), 854–865. http://dx.doi.org/10.1038/sj.ijo.0802012

Bandura, A. (1997). *Self-efficacy: The exercise of control.* New York, NY: W. H. Freeman.

Benedict, M. A., & Arterburn, D. (2008). Worksite-based weight loss programs: A systematic review of recent literature. *American Journal of Health Promotion, 22*(6), 408–416. http://dx.doi .org/10.4278/ajhp.22.6.408; 10.4278/ajhp.22.6.408

Blaak, E. (2001). Gender differences in fat metabolism. *Current Opinion in Clinical Nutrition and Metabolic Care, 4*(6), 499–502. http://dx.doi.org/10.1097/00075197-200111000-00006

Bray, G. A. (2013). *Determining body composition in adults.* Retrieved from http://www.uptodate .com/contents/determining-body-composition-in-adults?source=search_result&search= determining+body+composition+in+adults&selectedTitle=1%7E150

Brown, T. J. (2006). Health benefits of weight reduction in postmenopausal women: A systematic review. *The Journal of the British Menopause Society, 12*(4), 164–171. http://dx.doi .org/10.1258/136218006779160599

Byrne, H. K., & Wilmore, J. H. (2001). The effects of a 20-week exercise training program on resting metabolic rate in previously sedentary, moderately obese women. *International Journal of Sport Nutrition and Exercise Metabolism, 11*(1), 15–31. Retrieved from http://journals .humankinetics.com/ijsnem

Campbell, M. K., Tessaro, I., DeVellis, B., Benedict, S., Kelsey, K., Belton, L., & Sanhueza, A. (2002). Effects of a tailored health promotion program for female blue-collar workers: Health works for women. *Preventive Medicine, 34*(3), 313–323. http://dx.doi.org/10.1006/pmed.2001.0988

Carels, R. A., Darby, L. A., Cacciapaglia, H. M., & Douglass, O. M. (2004). Reducing cardiovascular risk factors in postmenopausal women through a lifestyle change intervention. *Journal of Women's Health (2002), 13*(4), 412–426. http://dx.doi.org/10.1089/154099904323087105

Centers for Disease Control and Prevention. (1996). *Physical activity and health at-a-glance.* Retrieved from http://www.cdc.gov/nccdphp/sgr/pdf/sgraag.pdf

Centers for Disease Control and Prevention. (2010). *WISEWOMAN: Well-Integrated Screening and Evaluation for Women Across the Nation.* Retrieved from http://www.cdc.gov/wisewoman/

Centre for Reviews and Dissemination, University of York. (2009). *Systematic reviews: CRD's guidance for undertaking reviews in health care.* York, United Kingdom: Author.

Cleland, C. L., Tully, M. A., Kee, F., & Cupples, M. E. (2012). The effectiveness of physical activity interventions in socio-economically disadvantaged communities: A systematic review. *Preventive Medicine, 54*(6), 371–380. http://dx.doi.org/10.1016/j.ypmed.2012.04.004

Conn, V. S., Hafdahl, A. R., Cooper, P. S., Brown, L. M., & Lusk, S. (2009). Meta-analysis of workplace physical activity interventions. *American Journal of Preventive Medicine, 37*(4), 330–339. http://dx.doi.org/10.1016/j.amepre.2009.06.008

Conn, V., Hafdahl, A., & Mehr, D. (2011). Interventions to increase physical activity among healthy adults: Meta-analysis of outcomes. *American Journal of Public Health, 101*(4), 751–758. http:// dx.doi.org/10.2105/AJPH.2010.194381

Conn, V., Phillips, L., Ruppar, T., & Chase, J. (2012). Physical activity interventions with healthy minority adults: Meta-analysis of behavior and health outcomes. *Journal of Health Care for the Poor and Underserved, 23*(1), 59–80. http://dx.doi.org/10.1353/hpu.2012.0032

Cox, K. L., Burke, V., Morton, A. R., Gillam, H. F., Beilin, L. J., & Puddey, I. B. (2001). Long-term effects of exercise on blood pressure and lipids in healthy women aged 40–65 years: The sedentary women exercise adherence trial (SWEAT). *Journal of Hypertension, 19*(10), 1733–1743. http://dx.doi.org/10.1097/00004872-200110000-00006

Davis, S. R., Castelo Branco, C., Chedraui, P., Lumsden, M. A., Nappi, R. E., Shah, D., & Villaseca, P. (2012). Understanding weight gain at menopause. *Climacteric, 15*(5), 419–429. http://dx.doi.org/10.3109/13697137.2012.707385

Donnelly, J. E., Jacobsen, D. J., Heelan, K. S., Seip, R., & Smith, S. (2000). The effects of 18 months of intermittent vs. continuous exercise on aerobic capacity, body weight and composition, and metabolic fitness in previously sedentary, moderately obese females. *International Journal of Obesity and Related Metabolic Disorders, 24*(5), 566–572. http://dx.doi.org/10.1038/sj.ijo.0801198

Dunn, A. L., Garcia, M. E., Marcus, B. H., Kampert, J. B., Kohl, H. W. & Blair, S. N. (1998). Six-month physical activity and fitness changes in Project Active, a randomized trial. *Medicine Science Sports Exercise, 30*(7), 1076–1083. http://dx.doi.org/10.1097/00005768-199807000-00009

Eiben, G., & Lissner, L. (2006). Health hunters: An intervention to prevent overweight and obesity in young high-risk women. *International Journal of Obesity, 30*(4), 691–696. http://dx.doi.org/10.1038/sj.ijo.0803167

Fitzgibbon, M., Stolley, M., Ganschow, P., Schiffer, L., Wells, A., Simon, N., & Dyer, A. (2005). Results of a faith-based weight loss intervention for black women. *Journal of the National Medical Association, 97*(10), 1393–1402. Retrieved from http://www.nmanet.org/index.php/Publications_Sub/jnma

Fitzgibbon, M., Stolley, M., Schiffer, L., Sharp, L., Singh, V., & Dyer, A. (2010). Obesity reduction black intervention trial (ORBIT): 18-month results. *Obesity, 18*(12), 2317–2325. http://dx.doi.org/10.1038/oby.2010.47

Flay, B. R., Biglan, A., Boruch, R. F., Castro, F. G., Gottfredson, D., Kellam, S., . . . Ji, P. (2005). Standards of evidence: Criteria for efficacy, effectiveness and dissemination. *Prevention Science: The Official Journal of the Society for Prevention Research, 6*(3), 151–175.

Folta, S., Lichtenstein, A., Seguin, R., Goldberg, J., Kuder, J., & Nelson, M. (2009). The StrongWomen-healthy hearts program: Reducing cardiovascular disease risk factors in rural sedentary, overweight, and obese midlife and older women. *American Journal of Public Health, 99*(7), 1271–1277. http://dx.doi.org/10.2105/AJPH.2008.145581

Foster, C., Hillsdon, M., & Thorogood, M. (2005). Interventions for promoting physical activity. *Cochrane Database of Systematic Reviews,* (1), CD003180. http://dx.doi.org/10.1002/14651858.CD003180.pub2

Goris, A. H. C., Vermeeren, M. A. P., Wouters, E. F. M., Schols, A. M. W. J., & Westerterp, K. (2003). Energy balance in depleted ambulatory patients with chronic obstructive pulmonary disease: The effect of physical activity and oral nutritional supplementation. *British Journal of Nutrition, 89*(5), 725–731. http://dx.doi.org/10.1079/BJN2003838

Grant, S., Todd, K., Aitchison, T. C., Kelly, P., & Stoddart, D. (2004). The effects of a 12-week group exercise programme on physiological and psychological variables and function in overweight women. *Public Health, 118*(1), 31–42. http://dx.doi.org/10.1016/S0033-3506(03)00131-8

Hallal, P., Andersen, L., Bull, F., Guthold, R., Haskell, W., & Ekelund, U. (2012). Global physical activity levels: Surveillance progress, pitfalls, and prospects. *Lancet, 380*(9838), 247–257. http://dx.doi.org/10.1016/S0140-6736(12)60646-1

Hawkins, M., Storti, K., Richardson, C., King, W., Strath, S., Holleman, R., & Kriska, A. (2009). Objectively measured physical activity of USA adults by sex, age, and racial/ethnic groups: A cross-sectional study. *The International Journal of Behavioral Nutrition and Physical Activity, 6*, 31. http://dx.doi.org/10.1186/1479-5868-6-31

Hayashi, T., Farrell, M. A., Chaput, L. A., Rocha, D. A., & Hernandez, M. (2010). Lifestyle intervention, behavioral changes, and improvement in cardiovascular risk profiles in the California WISEWOMAN project. *Journal of Women's Health, 19*(6), 1129–1138. http://dx.doi.org/10.1089/jwh.2009.1631

Helmerhorst, H. J. F., Brage, S., Warren, J., Besson, H., & Ekelund, U. (2012). A systematic review of reliability and objective criterion-related validity of physical activity questionnaires. *The International Journal of Behavioral Nutrition and Physical Activity, 9*, 103. http://dx.doi.org/10.1186/1479-5868-9-103

Hemmingsson, E., Uddén, J., Neovius, M., Ekelund, U., & Rössner, S. (2009). Increased physical activity in abdominally obese women through support for changed commuting habits: A randomized clinical trial. *International Journal of Obesity, 33*(6), 645–652. http://dx.doi.org/10.1038/ijo.2009.77

Hendelman, D., Miller, K., Baggett, C., Debold, E., & Freedson, P. (2000). Validity of accelerometry for the assessment of moderate intensity physical activity in the field. *Medicine and Science in Sports and Exercise, 32*(Suppl. 9), S442–S449. http://dx.doi.org/10.1097/00005768-200009001-00002

Heyward, V. H. (2006). *Advanced fitness assessment and exercise prescription* (5th ed.). Champaign, IL: Human Kinetics.

Hovell, M. F., Mulvihill, M. M., Buono, M. J., Liles, S., Schade, D. H., Washington, T. A., . . . Sallis, J. F. (2008). Culturally tailored aerobic exercise intervention for low-income Latinas. *American Journal of Health Promotion, 22*(3), 155–163. http://dx.doi.org/10.4278/ajhp.22.3.155

Ickes, M. J., & Sharma, M. (2012). A systematic review of physical activity interventions in Hispanic adults. *Journal of Environmental and Public Health, 2012*, 156435. http://dx.doi.org/10.1155/2012/156435

Ingram, D., Wilbur, J., McDevitt, J., & Buchholz, S. (2011). Women's walking program for African American women: Expectations and recommendations from participants as experts. *Women Health, 51*(6), 566–582. http://dx.doi.org/10.1080/03630242.2011.606357

Irwin, M., & Supplee, L. (2012). Directions in implementation research methods for behavioral and social science. *The Journal of Behavioral Health Services Research, 39*(4), 339–342. http://dx.doi.org/10.1007/s11414-012-9293-z

Irwin, M., Yasui, Y., Ulrich, C., Bowen, D., Rudolph, R., Schwartz, R., . . . McTiernan, A. (2003). Effect of exercise on total and intra-abdominal body fat in postmenopausal women: A randomized controlled trial. *The Journal of the American Medical Association, 289*(3), 323–330. http://dx.doi.org/10.1001/jama.289.3.323

Jakicic, J. M., Marcus, B. H., Gallagher, K. I., Napolitano, M., & Lang, W. (2003). Effect of exercise duration and intensity on weight loss in overweight, sedentary women: A randomized trial. *The Journal of the American Medical Association, 290*(10), 1323–1330. http://dx.doi.org/10.1001/jama.290.10.1323

Jakicic, J., Marcus, B., Lang, W., & Janney, C. (2008). Effect of exercise on 24-month weight loss maintenance in overweight women. *Archives of Internal Medicine, 168*(14), 1550–1559. Retrieved from http://archinte.jamanetwork.com/journal.aspx

Janssen, I., Fortier, A., Hudson, R., & Ross, R. (2002). Effects of an energy-restrictive diet with or without exercise on abdominal fat, intermuscular fat, and metabolic risk factors in obese women. *Diabetes Care, 25*(3), 431–438. http://dx.doi.org/10.2337/diacare.25.3.431

Joanna Briggs Institute. (2011). The systematic review and synthesis of quantitative data. *Joanna Briggs Institute reviewers' manual*. Adelaide, Australia: Author.

Jonas, S. (2009). Introduction: What this book is about. In S. Jonas & E. M. Phillips (Eds.), *ACSM's exercise is medicine: A clinician's guide to exercise prescription* (pp. 1–12). Philadelphia, PA: Lippincott Williams & Wilkins.

Ju, S., Wilbur, J., Lee, E., & Miller, A. (2011). Lifestyle physical activity behavior of Korean American dry cleaner couples. *Public Health Nursing, 28*(6), 503–514. http://dx.doi .org/10.1111/j.1525-1446.2011.00952.x

Kay, S. J., & Fiatarone Singh, M. A. (2006). The influence of physical activity on abdominal fat: A systematic review of the literature. *Obesity Reviews, 7*(2), 183–200. http://dx.doi .org/10.1111/j.1467-789X.2006.00250.x

Keller, C., & Cantue, A. (2008). Camina por salud: Walking in Mexican-American women. *Applied Nursing Research, 21*(2), 110–113. http://dx.doi.org/10.1016/j.apnr.2006.12.003

Keyserling, T., Samuel-Hodge, C. D., Jilcott, S., Johnston, L., Garcia, B., Gizlice, Z., . . . Ammerman, A. (2008). Randomized trial of a clinic-based, community-supported, lifestyle intervention to improve physical activity and diet: The North Carolina enhanced WISEWOMAN project. *Preventive Medicine, 46*(6), 499–510. http://dx.doi.org/10.1016/j.ypmed.2008.02.011

Kraemer, W. J., Keuning, M., Ratamess, N. A., Volek, J. S., McCormick, M., Bush, J. A., . . . Häkkinen, K. (2001). Resistance training combined with bench-step aerobics enhances women's health profile. *Medicine and Science in Sports and Exercise, 33*(2), 259–269. http:// dx.doi.org/10.1097/00005768-200102000-00015

Laska, M. N., Pelletier, J. E., Larson, N. I., & Story, M. (2012). Interventions for weight gain prevention during the transition to young adulthood: A review of the literature. *The Journal of Adolescent Health: Official Publication of the Society for Adolescent Medicine, 50*(4), 324–333. http://dx.doi.org/10.1016/j.jadohealth.2012.01.016

Lawton, B. A., Rose, S. B., Raina Elley, C., Dowell, A. C., Fenton, A., & Moyes, S. A. (2009). Exercise on prescription for women aged 40–74 recruited through primary care: Two year randomised controlled trial. *British Journal of Sports Medicine, 43*(2), 120–123. http://dx.doi .org/10.1136/bmj.a2509

Löllgen, H., Böckenhoff, A., & Knapp, G. (2009). Physical activity and all-cause mortality: An updated meta-analysis with different intensity categories. *International Journal of Sports Medicine, 30*(3), 213–224. http://dx.doi.org/10.1055/s-0028-1128150

Lombard, C., Deeks, A., Jolley, D., Ball, K., & Teede, H. (2010). A low intensity, community based lifestyle programme to prevent weight gain in women with young children: Cluster randomised controlled trial. *British Medical Journal, 341*, c3215.

Mozaffarian, D., Hao, T., Rimm, E., Willett, W., & Hu, F. (2011). Changes in diet and lifestyle and long-term weight gain in women and men. *The New England Journal of Medicine, 364*(25), 2392–2404. http://dx.doi.org/10.1056/NEJMoa1014296

Muller-Riemenschneider, F., Reinhold, T., Nocon, M., & Willich, S. N. (2008). Long-term effectiveness of interventions promoting physical activity: A systematic review. *Preventive Medicine, 47*(4), 354–368. http://dx.doi.org/10.1016/j.ypmed.2008.07.006

Nascimento, S., Surita, F., & Cecatti, J. (2012). Physical exercise during pregnancy: A systematic review. *Current Opinion in Obstetrics Gynecology, 24*(6), 387–394. http://dx.doi.org/10.1097/ GCO.0b013e328359f131

Nicklas, B., Wang, X., You, T., Lyles, M., Demons, J., Easter, L., . . . Carr, J. J. (2009). Effect of exercise intensity on abdominal fat loss during calorie restriction in overweight and obese postmenopausal women: A randomized, controlled trial. *The American Journal of Clinical Nutrition, 89*(4), 1043–1052. http://dx.doi.org/10.3945/ajcn.2008.26938

Nieman, D., Brock, D., Butterworth, D., Utter, A., & Nieman, C. (2002). Reducing diet and/or exercise training decreases the lipid and lipoprotein risk factors of moderately obese women. *Journal of the American College of Nutrition, 21*(4), 344–350. Retrieved from http://www.jacn.org/

Nies, M. A., Chruscial, H. L., & Hepworth, J. T. (2003). An intervention to promote walking in sedentary women in the community. *American Journal of Health Behavior, 27*(5), 524–535. http://dx.doi.org/10.5993/AJHB.27.5.4

Ogilvie, D., Foster, C., Rothnie, H., Cavill, N., Hamilton, V., Fitzsimons, C., & Mutrie, N. (2007). Interventions to promote walking: Systematic review. *British Medical Journal, 334*(7605), 1204–1204. http://dx.doi.org/10.1136/bmj.39198.722720.BE

Ohkawara, K., Tanaka, S., Miyachi, M., Ishikawa-Takata, K., & Tabata, I. (2007). A dose-response relation between aerobic exercise and visceral fat reduction: Systematic review of clinical trials. *International Journal of Obesity, 31*(12), 1786–1797. http://dx.doi.org/10.1038/sj.ijo.0803683

Orrow, G., Kinmonth, A. L., Sanderson, S., & Sutton, S. (2012). Effectiveness of physical activity promotion based in primary care: Systematic review and meta-analysis of randomised controlled trials. *British Medical Journal, 344*, e1389. http://dx.doi.org/10.1136/bmj.e1389

O'Toole, M., Sawicki, M., & Artal, R. (2003). Structured diet and physical activity prevent postpartum weight retention. *Journal of Women's Health, 12*(10), 991–998. http://dx.doi.org/10.1089/154099903322643910

Parekh, S., Vandelanotte, C., King, D., & Boyle, F. M. (2012). Improving diet, physical activity and other lifestyle behaviours using computer-tailored advice in general practice: A randomised controlled trial. *The International Journal of Behavioral Nutrition and Physical Activity, 9*, 108. http://dx.doi.org/10.1186/1479-5868-9-108

Park, S. K., Park, J. H., Kwon, Y. C., Kim, H. S., Yoon, M. S., & Park, H. T. (2003). The effect of combined aerobic and resistance exercise training on abdominal fat in obese middle-aged women. *Journal of Physiological Anthropology and Applied Human Science, 22*(3), 129–135. http://dx.doi.org/10.2114/jpa.22.129

Perez, A., Fleury, J., & Keller, C. (2010). Review of intervention studies promoting physical activity in Hispanic women. *Western Journal of Nursing Research, 32*(3), 341–362. http://dx.doi.org/10.1177/0193945909351300

Pinto, B., Clark, M., Maruyama, N., & Feder, S. (2003). Psychological and fitness changes associated with exercise participation among women with breast cancer. *Psycho-Oncology, 12*(2), 118–126. http://dx.doi.org/10.1002/pon.618

Poston, W. S., Haddock, C. K., Olvera, N. E., Suminski, R. R., Reeves, R. S., Dunn, J. K., . . . Foreyt, J. P. (2001). Evaluation of a culturally appropriate intervention to increase physical activity. *American Journal of Health Behavior, 25*(4), 396–406. Retrieved from http://www.ajhb.org/

Prince, S., Adamo, K., Hamel, M., Hardt, J., Gorber, S., & Tremblay, M. (2008). A comparison of direct versus self-report measures for assessing physical activity in adults: A systematic review. *The International Journal of Behavioral Nutrition and Physical Activity, 5*, 56–56. http://dx.doi.org/10.1186/1479-5868-5-56

Prochaska, J., Spring, B., & Nigg, C. (2008). Multiple health behavior change research: An introduction and overview. *Preventive Medicine, 46*(3), 181–188. http://dx.doi.org/10.1016/j.ypmed.2008.02.001

Roess, A., & Sikka, N. (2012). The use of mobile communication technologies to improve the health of individuals and populations has great potential. Introduction. *Journal of Health Communication, 17*(Suppl. 1), 4. http://dx.doi.org/ 10.1080/10810730.2012.667715

Rosamond, W. D., Ammerman, A. S., Holliday, J. L., Tawney, K. W., Hunt, K. J., Keyserling, T. C., . . . Mokdad, A. H. (2000). Cardiovascular disease risk factor intervention in low-income women: The North Carolina WISEWOMAN project. *Preventive Medicine, 31*(4), 370–379. http://dx.doi.org/10.1006/pmed.2000.0726

Ross, R., Janssen, I., Dawson, J., Kungl, A., Kuk, J., Wong, S., . . . Hudson, R. (2004). Exercise-induced reduction in obesity and insulin resistance in women: A randomized controlled trial. *Obesity Research, 12*(5), 789–798. http://dx.doi.org/ 10.1038/oby.2004.95

Samuel-Hodge, C., Johnston, L., Gizlice, Z., Garcia, B., Lindsley, S., Bramble, K., . . . Keyserling, T. (2009). Randomized trial of a behavioral weight loss intervention for low-income women: The Weight Wise Program. *Obesity, 17*(10), 1891–1899. http://dx.doi.org/10.1038/oby.2009.128

Santa-Clara, H., Szymanski, L., Ordille, T., & Fernhall, B. (2006). Effects of exercise training on resting metabolic rate in postmenopausal African American and Caucasian women. *Metabolism: Clinical and Experimental*, 55(10), 1358–1364. http://dx.doi.org/10.1016/j .metabol.2006.06.006

Sharma, M. (2008). Physical activity interventions in Hispanic American girls and women. *Obesity Reviews: An Official Journal of the International Association for the Study of Obesity*, 9(6), 560–571. http://dx.doi.org/10.1111/j.1467-789X.2008.00501.x

Shaw, K., Gennat, H., O'Rourke, P., & Del Mar, C. (2009). Exercise for overweight or obesity. *The Cochrane Database of Systematic Reviews*, (3), CD003817. http://dx.doi.org/10.1002/ 14651858.CD003817.pub3

Staten, L. K., Gregory-Mercado, K. Y., Ranger-Moore, J., Will, J. C., Giuliano, A. R., Ford, E. S., & Marshall, J. (2004). Provider counseling, health education, and community health workers: The Arizona WISEWOMAN project. *Journal of Women's Health*, 13(5), 547–556. http:// dx.doi.org/10.1089/1540999041281133

Strasser, B. (2013). Physical activity in obesity and metabolic syndrome. *Annals of the New York Academy of Sciences*, 1281, 141–159. http://dx.doi.org/10.1111/j.1749-6632.2012.06785.x

Swearingin, B. (2008). *The comparison of the effects of lifestyle activity and structured cardiovascular exercise on obesity-related risk factors of African-American women ages 22–55* (Doctoral dissertation). Retrieved from ProQuest Dissertations and Theses. (304535313)

Trogdon, J., Finkelstein, E., Feagan, C., & Cohen, J. (2012). State- and payer-specific estimates of annual medical expenditures attributable to obesity. *Obesity*, 20(1), 214–220. http://dx.doi .org/10.1038/oby.2011.169

Tryon, W. W., & Williams, R. (1996). Fully proportional actigraphy: A new instrument. *Behavior Research Methods Instruments & Computers*, 28, 392–403. http://dx.doi.org/10.3758/BF03200519

U.S. Department of Health and Human Services. (2006). *Facts about healthy weight*. Retrieved from http://www.nhlbi.nih.gov/health/prof/heart/obesity/aim_kit/healthy_wt_facts.pdf

U.S. Department of Health and Human Services. (2008). *2008 physical activity guidelines for Americans*. Retrieved from http://www.health.gov/paguidelines/pdf/paguide.pdf

U.S. Department of Health and Human Services. (2012). *Health, United States, 2011*. Retrieved from http://www.cdc.gov/nchs/data/hus/hus11.pdf#073

van Poppel, M. N., Chinapaw, M. J., Mokkink, L., van Mechelen, W., & Terwee, C. (2010). Physical activity questionnaires for adults: A systematic review of measurement properties. *Sports Medicine*, 40(7), 565–600. http://dx.doi.org/10.2165/11531930-000000000-00000

Walker, S., Pullen, C., Boeckner, L., Hageman, P., Hertzog, M., Oberdorfer, M., & Rutledge, M. (2009). Clinical trial of tailored activity and eating newsletters with older rural women. *Nursing Research*, 58(2), 74–85. http://dx.doi.org/10.1097/NNR.0b013e31818fcee1

Weinheimer, E., Sands, L., & Campbell, W. (2010). A systematic review of the separate and combined effects of energy restriction and exercise on fat-free mass in middle-aged and older adults: Implications for sarcopenic obesity. *Nutrition Reviews*, 68(7), 375–388. http://dx.doi .org/10.1111/j.1753-4887.2010.00298.x

Whitt-Glover, M. C., & Kumanyika, S. K. (2009). Systematic review of interventions to increase physical activity and physical fitness in African-Americans. *American Journal of Health Promotion*, 23(6), S33–S56. http://dx.doi.org/10.4278/ajhp.070924101

Wilbur, J., McDevitt, J., Wang, E., Dancy, B., Miller, A., Briller, J., . . . Lee, H. (2008). Outcomes of a home-based walking program for African-American women. *American Journal of Health Promotion*, 22(5), 307–317. http://dx.doi.org/10.4278/ajhp.22.5.307

Williams, N. H., Hendry, M., France, B., Lewis, R., & Wilkinson, C. (2007). Effectiveness of exercise-referral schemes to promote physical activity in adults: Systematic review. *The British Journal of General Practice*, 57(545), 979–986. http://dx.doi.org/10.3399/096016407782604866

World Health Organization. (2008). *2008–2013 action plan for the global strategy for the prevention and control of noncommunicable diseases.* Geneva, Switzerland: Author.

World Health Organization. (2010). *Global recommendations on physical activity for health.* Geneva, Switzerland: Author.

World Health Organization. (2011). *Global status report on noncommunicable diseases 2010.* Retrieved from http://whqlibdoc.who.int/publications/2011/9789240686458_eng.pdf

Yancey, A. K., McCarthy, W. J., Harrison, G. G., Wong, W. K., Siegel, J. M., & Leslie, J. (2006). Challenges in improving fitness: Results of a community-based, randomized, controlled lifestyle change intervention. *Journal of Women's Health, 15*(4), 412–429. http://dx.doi.org/10.1089/jwh.2006.15.412

Yanek, L. R., Becker, D. M., Moy, T. F., Gittelsohn, J., & Koffman, D. M. (2001). Project joy: Faith based cardiovascular health promotion for African American women. *Public Health Reports, 116*(Suppl. 1), 68–81. http://dx.doi.org/10.1093/phr/116.S1.68

CHAPTER 5

The Effects of Exercise During Pregnancy

Theories, Evidence, and Interventions

SeonAe Yeo

ABSTRACT

Physical activities provide women a way to improve their health and intervene in disease processes during pregnancy. This chapter briefly describes pathophysiological models and then examines current research on the effects of physical activity on prevention and treatment of gestational diabetes and preeclampsia. The chapter then reviews cognitive behavioral theories and current literature on the effects of behavioral interventions on physical activity in pregnancy. The literature helps to explain the pathophysiological mechanisms through which physical activity mediates disease processes and the behavioral interventions through which physical activity can be introduced and sustained during pregnancy. Throughout the chapter, both pathophysiological models and behavioral theories are viewed as part of a socioecologic model that encompasses pregnancy and physical activity.

INTRODUCTION

Social Meaning of Pregnancy—Sociological, Feminist View

Pregnancy is a unique biological and social stage of women of reproductive ages. It introduces significant changes in their physiological, psychological, sociopolitical, and cultural environments. Such profound and multilevel changes come with stress, fatigue, psychological ambivalence, and even confusion. Many societies celebrate pregnancy with rites and provide protection for women during this period through social customs or policies. Unfortunately, the United States provides the least protection at a policy level—for example, it is the only industrialized nation not to mandate paid parental leave (Sekoff, 2013). Furthermore, understanding of the diverse cultural customs of immigrants to the United States, some racial or ethnic minorities, is limited.

Historically, pregnant women received minimum guidance or counseling about being active during pregnancy (Oxford Companion to Canadian History, 2004), in part, because of concerns for fetal safety. In the United States as well as other industrialized countries, studies of physical exercise in pregnancy during the 1980s and 1990s mainly addressed fetal safety relative to types and intensity of exercises (Downs, Chasan-Taber, Evenson, Leiferman, & Yeo, 2012). Heat stress, shunting blood flow from the fetus via the placenta, and mechanical impacts were among the concerns (Clapp, Lopez, & Harcar-Sevcik, 1999; Yeo, 1994, 1996; Yeo, Hayashi, Wan, & Dubler, 1995). Many obstetricians and scientists viewed pregnancy as consisting of a woman and a child—two independent bodies incased in one body, and thus two entities competing for limited resources.

For example, pregnant women were advised to avoid exercising in a hot and humid environment, fearing potential heat stress for the fetus (Lindqvist, Marsal, Merlo, & Pirhonen, 2003). This advice was based on the assumption that increased core body temperature of women was dissipated to the fetus by diffusion (from high to low gradient), and the heat stress generated could be teratogenic. A substantial number of studies, however, found that pregnant women adjusted to physiological modifications during exercise. These studies confirmed that as exercise intensified, the core temperature remained relatively constant, although the skin temperature rose significantly (Clapp, Wesley, & Sleamaker, 1987; Jones, Botti, Anderson, & Bennett, 1985; Lindqvist et al., 2003). This makes sense, when pregnancy is viewed as one biological system rather than a conflict between a mother and a fetus. Clearly, many assumptions about pregnancy have not been examined, even though physiological models for pregnancy are often the products of such assumptions.

For example, pregnancy-specific diseases such as preeclampsia and gestational diabetes have been understood primarily through pathophysiological models, without examining behavioral, social, and cultural frameworks. The lack of consideration of frameworks other than biological models has delayed the development of behavioral interventions such as exercise interventions to mitigate these pregnancy-specific diseases, particularly among at risk groups, who are often racial or ethnic minorities and low-income women.

Consideration of sociopolitical and cultural environments is particularly important for physical activities, which are behaviors influenced by one's view of self, friends, family, health care providers, workplace, community, and others. The studies to date, however, have rarely addressed these factors in a systematic fashion. In addition, the studies of exercise and physical activity for pregnant women have often failed to consider pregnancy-specific influences on women's views of exercise and physical activities at interpersonal levels (e.g., prenatal care providers, peers, and significant others), sociocultural levels (e.g., financial strain, cultural restrictions, unstable relationships with partners), and environmental levels (e.g., sidewalks, parks, child care), making it more difficult to design effective exercise and physical activity interventions for pregnant women in the United States.

Physical Activity and Exercise

Symptoms and problematic psychological states are often effectively remediated by physical activity. Defined as "any bodily movement produced by the contraction of skeletal muscles that results in a substantial increase over resting energy expenditure" (Pate et al., 1995, p. 402), the term considers physical activity as a physiological event, with no reference to psychobehavioral or sociocultural factors in physical activity. Thus, studies in which physical activity or exercise has been hypothesized to mitigate or prevent pathological processes or mechanisms have mainly applied exercise physiology models and pathophysiological models.

The term *exercise*, which is planned and structured physical activity (i.e., a subcategory of physical activity) is often used interchangeably with *physical activity*. *Physical activities* take place in various domains, including domestic (child care, adult care, household activities), occupational, transportation, and recreational activities. Although the first three domain activities are carried out to accomplish social tasks, exercises or sports are planned and structured physical activities done for their own right. In this chapter, physical activity is used when activities involve all four domains, and *exercise* is used when a physical activity is planned and structured. Sports are thus considered as exercise.

Fortunately, recent studies of physical activity in pregnancy have focused on behavioral interventions to manage pregnant women's lifestyle to increase daily physical activity and sustain the increased physical activity. Although some studies have used pathophysiological models as a theoretical basis (Brankston, Mitchell, Ryan, & Okun, 2004; Davenport, Mottola, McManus, & Gratton, 2008; de Barros, Lopes, Francisco, Sapienza, & Zugaib, 2010), more recent studies have begun to examine pregnant women's lifestyles based on behavioral theories. These studies have applied behavioral interventions to influence pregnant women's cognitive behaviors to increase and sustain the targeted physical activities

(Asbee et al., 2009; Huang, Yeh, & Tsai, 2011; Phelan et al., 2011; Polley, Wing, & Sims, 2002). Unfortunately, most studies have either used biological models only or behavioral theories only, although researchers perhaps need to apply both models to elucidate possible interaction effects.

Guidelines for Exercise During Pregnancy

In 2009, the American Congress of Obstetricians and Gynecologists (ACOG) reaffirmed the guidelines for exercise for pregnant women, originally issued in 2002 (ACOG, 2002). The guidelines say, "In the absence of either medical or obstetric complications, *30 minutes* or more of *moderate exercise* a day on *most*, if not all, *days* of the week is recommended for pregnant women." This recommendation provides the basis for clinicians to suggest physical activity during pregnancy. However, although recommendations for moderate exercise exist, there are no specific guidelines for either vigorous exercise or low or light exercise. The U.S. Department of Health and Human Services (USDHHS) has noted, "The effects of vigorous-intensity aerobic activity during pregnancy have not been studied carefully, so there is no basis for recommending that women should begin vigorous-intensity activity during pregnancy" (USDHHS, 2008). However, the USDHHS does not say that women should or should not engage in vigorous intensity activity. It simply says there is not enough evidence to support or refute the importance of beginning a program of vigorous activity for pregnant women. There are no behavioral strategies for pregnant women or no effective intervention strategies for providers.

The guidelines are also rather ambiguous about the effects of different types of exercise. Moderate exercise is generally interpreted as moderate-intensity aerobic exercise such as brisk walking (Ainsworth et al., 2000). Other types of exercise, such as resistant circuit exercises, have been reported effective in delaying insulin treatment for women with gestational diabetes (Brankston et al., 2004; de Barros et al., 2010), but no specific recommendations are given for resistance exercise. Similarly, light- or low-intensity exercises are not mentioned at all, even though one study (Yeo et al., 2008) found that low intensity stretching exercises were more effective than moderate intensity walking exercise in reducing the rate of preeclampsia. In this study, pregnant women who were assigned to stretching exercise were instructed to follow the study video, wearing a portable heart rate monitor, and called in after the exercise throughout the intervention period. Low- or light-intensity exercise, stretching exercise in particular, may be more effective during pregnancy because of possible interactions between pregnancy and low- or light-intensity aerobic exercise. These exercises need to be incorporated in the guidelines to promote wide range of safe and effective exercises for pregnant women.

Although beyond the scope of this chapter, the evidence is even more inconclusive on *postpartum* physical activity. After birth, women, particularly lactating women, may need information on energy balance because both physical activities and lactation result in a negative balance. Vigorous and prolonged physical activities are also reported to negatively affect the infant's taste of breast milk because of lactic acid (Carey, Quinn, & Goodwin, 1997). This, however, can be easily avoided if mothers breastfeed or pump milk before they engage in vigorous physical activity for extended periods. Moderate- and low-intensity exercises do not increase lactic acid. Physical activity may also have a significant role in postpartum weight and in the prevention of diabetes and hypertension in subsequent pregnancies. However, many women are overwhelmed by numerous stresses with their new roles and tasks as mothers. Thus, effective interventions at multiple levels are needed to promote a physically active lifestyle for women after birth.

In summary, physical activities provide women a viable tool for improving their health and intervening to prevent or ameliorate diseases during perinatal period. This chapter examines the current literature on the effectiveness of physical activity in preventing and treating gestational diabetes and preeclampsia. The chapter also reviews the current literature on the effectiveness of behavioral intervention in increasing physical activity to avoid obesity or excessive gestational weight gain (GWG). The literature in these two areas will enable us to understand the pathophysiological mechanisms by which physical activity mediates disease processes and the behavioral interventions through which physical activity can be introduced and sustained during the perinatal period. The relationships between pathophysiological models and behavioral theories are not explicitly discussed, other than the fact that behavioral theories are required to understand the implementation of physical activity interventions. However, throughout the paper, both models are considered as part of a socioecologic model that encompasses pregnancy and physical activity.

EFFECTIVENESS OF REGULAR EXERCISE IN PREVENTING OR TREATING PREGNANCY-SPECIFIC DISEASES
Pathophysiologic Models
Preeclampsia, a syndrome characterized by the sudden onset of hypertension and proteinuria in the latter half of pregnancy, accounts for 22% of maternal deaths and 18% of premature births (Sibai, 2008). It also increases maternal risk of future cardiovascular disease (Magnussen, Vatten, Smith, & Romundstad, 2009; McDonald, Malinowski, Zhou, Yusuf, & Devereaux, 2008). Preceding the clinical manifestation of this disease is a period of largely asymptomatic gradual

decline in health, beginning in early pregnancy, characterized by autonomic dysregulation, labile blood pressure, insulin resistance, and oxidative stress (Yeo, 2010). Numerous studies have documented these pathologic changes in maternal systems, although the etiology of preeclampsia remains unknown and most likely multifactorial. Risk factors include certain genetic traits, obesity, and nulliparous status, history of preeclampsia, diabetes, hypertension, and sedentary lifestyle (Yeo, 2010).

Based on observations indicating that oxidative stress with enhanced lipid peroxide formation in cells could lead to endothelial dysfunction in preeclampsia, Yeo and Davidge proposed in 2001 that regular exercise would enhance antioxidative enzymes in pregnant women, reducing oxidative stress and, thus, the incidence of preeclampsia. In their model (see Figure 5.1), they noted that other conditions, such as increased transferrin saturation and decreased iron-binding capacity, directly and indirectly promote the process of oxidative stress and subsequent endothelial dysfunction.

They also noted that exercise increases oxidative metabolism and produces a prooxidant environment. This acidic environment during exercise (at or beyond anaerobic threshold) promotes oxygen release from hemoglobin, increases partial pressure of oxygen (PO2) in the blood in tissues, and releases iron from transferrin. Although exercise creates oxidative stress during and immediately after the exercise, Yeo and Davidge (2001), and others (Alessio, 1993; Goto et al., 2003), suggested that when exercise is repeated regularly, the body promptly adjusts so that oxidative stress is eliminated or reduced. Thus, they hypothesized that the body's adaptations to regular exercise produces an antioxidant effect (see Figure 5.1).

Some studies have found that cardiovascular characteristics observed among women with preeclampsia, particularly those who develop the disease after 34 weeks, are similar to those observed among obese people; thus the authors hypothesized that controlling weight gain during pregnancy might reduce the risk for late-onset preeclampsia (Magnussen et al., 2009; Valensise, Vasapollo, Gagliardi, & Novelli, 2008).

Because the autonomic nervous system is important in controlling cardiovascular system adjustments, other investigators have hypothesized that late-onset preeclampsia occur as the result of poor autonomic regulation, when it fails to adjust from a lower sympathetic and higher vagal modulation to higher sympathetic and lower vagal modulation (Eneroth-Grimfors, Westgren, Ericson, Ihrman-Sandahl, & Lindblad, 1994; Fischer et al., 2004; Khatun et al., 1999; Yang, Chao, Kuo, Yin, & Chen, 2000). Overstimulation of the sympathetic nervous system, when it is mediated not by healthy but by weakened parasympathetic control, may cause damage to the vascular lining, resulting in activation of the immune system and an increase in oxidative stress—a known pathway

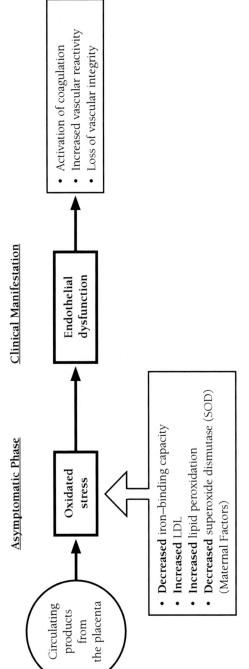

FIGURE 5.1 Development of preeclampsia and the role of oxidative stress.
Note. LDL = low-density lipoprotein.

to preeclampsia (Brown, 1997; Fischer et al., 2004; Kaaja & Pöyhönen-Alho, 2006). Altogether, these findings highlight the characteristics of a systemic inflammatory response, which in turn increases systemic oxidative stress. Of note, in the case of preeclampsia, once the diagnosis is made, it is still standard practice for women to be put in bed rest or have immediate delivery of the child (Stella & Sibai, 2006).

Gestational diabetes mellitus (GDM) is a disorder of pregnancy characterized by insulin resistance accompanied by elevated blood glucose. The normal processes of pregnancy create a state of insulin resistance in the latter half of pregnancy, when placental hormones increase insulin resistance to help increase glucose availability for the fetus during the rapid anabolic state. When the woman's metabolic system already has diminished insulin secretion or impaired glucose tolerance and thus increased insulin resistance, this results in hyperglycemia similar to type 2 diabetes (American Diabetes Association [ADA], 2003; Han, Middleton, & Crowther, 2012).

Unlike preeclampsia, GDM generally has few symptoms and it is often diagnosed only by a detailed history and 1-hr glucose challenge test (a 50-g oral glucose intake and assessment of blood glucose level in 1 hr) at 24–28 weeks gestation (ADA, 2007). Typically, GDM is diagnosed when a 50-g glucose challenge test has values greater than 130–140 mg/dl, followed by a 100-g 3-hr glucose tolerance test with two or more values higher than cutoff values (95 mg/dl fasting; 180 mg/dl 1 hr; 155 mg/dl 2 hr; and 140 mg/dl 3 hr).

Unlike women with preeclampsia, those with GDM have a relatively long period of pregnancy after the diagnosis is made. This provides an opportunity to apply exercise interventions for treatment.

Like preeclampsia, the pathophysiologic pathways leading to GDM involve oxidative stress and autonomic nervous system dysregulation (Anim-Nyame et al., 2004; D'Anna et al., 2006; Forest et al., 2005; Kaaja, Laivuori, Laakso, Tikkanen, & Ylikorkala, 1999; Kaaja & Pöyhönen-Alho, 2006). Also, high comorbidity between preeclampsia (PE) and GDM has been reported. Women who are at risk for one disease are at high risk for the other. Thus the biological models describing the protective mechanisms of exercise against these two diseases are often similar. However, there is a difference in the way exercise exerts its influence on glucose metabolism.

Exercise or contraction in skeletal muscle activates the metabolic system by consuming energy stored in cells (Kahn, Alquier, Carling, & Hardie, 2005). The degree of metabolic system activation depends on the intensity of the exercise. Exercise also activates enzymes in the liver and adipose tissue causes systemic alterations in substrate availability (Kelly et al., 2004). Even one time exercise has a direct effect, lowering blood glucose via improvement of insulin sensitivity and glucose absorption. This effect has been observed with even low intensity exercise, such as slow walking. One study reported that slow walking produced a significant reduction in postprandial glucose level among pregnant women (Nygaard, Tomten, & Høstmark, 2009).

Evidence

During the last decade, epidemiologic studies have reported protective effects of exercise on preeclampsia (Sorensen et al., 2003; Weissgerber, Wolfe, & Davies, 2004) and gestational diabetes (Tobias, Zhang, van Dam, Bowers, & Hu, 2011). However, although correlational studies have indicated associations between physical activity and these diseases, randomized trials have provided inconclusive findings (Han et al., 2012; Kasawara, do Nascimento, Costa, Surita, & e Silva, 2012). Recent findings on the effects of exercise and physical activity are briefly described in the following text.

Exercise and Preeclampsia

Electronic databases (Ovid MEDLINE and other nonindexed citations) were searched using the keywords preeclampsia or preeclampsia and exercise or physical activity for the years 2008–2013. The results were limited to studies published in English. Of 49 citations identified, 11 reported the results of either correlational studies or randomized trials.

Correlational Studies. Seven studies reported an association between physical activity and the incidence of preeclampsia. The directions of the association were not consistent. Table 5.1 gives summaries of these seven studies. Surprisingly, only one study reported a significant protective effect of physical activities during pregnancy (Magnus, Trogstad, Owe, Olsen, & Nystad, 2008). Other studies reported moderate trends that failed to reach statistical significance (Fortner et al., 2011; Hegaard et al., 2010; Østerdal et al., 2009; Rudra et al., 2006; Tyldum, Romundstad, & Slørdahl, 2010; Vollebregt et al., 2006). One study (Østerdal et al., 2009) even reported a negative effect of physical activity. Østerdal et al. (2009) found that high physical activity levels (>270 min/week) were associated with a greater risk of severe preeclampsia than in the nonexercising group (adjusted $OR = 1.65, 95\%$ CI [1.11–2.43]).

Randomized Trials. Yeo and Davidge (2001) conducted a randomized controlled trial (RCT) to test the effectiveness of regular exercise in preventing preeclampsia (Yeo et al., 2008). Application of regular exercise to lower the risk of recurring preeclampsia among women at risk was a provocative idea at the time, when bed rest was generally prescribed for pregnant women with signs of preeclampsia or other symptoms (Maloni, 2011). Regular exercise habit was an unconventional but viable option for promoting a positive and healthy lifestyle without concern about

TABLE 5.1
Studies of Exercise/Physical Activity and Preeclampsia

Author (reference)	Study Design	Sample	Exercise/Physical Activity	Outcome
(Fortner et al., 2011)	Prospective cohort study Latina Gestational Diabetes Mellitus Study	1,043 Puerto Rican pregnant women	Physical activity during pregnancy	Increasing sports/exercise in early pregnancy was modestly associated with lower rate of preeclampsia (OR = 0.4, 95% CI* = 0.1–1.1).
(Tyldum, Romundstad, & Slordahl, 2010)	Prospective cohort study Medical Birth Registry of Norway	3,656 singleton pregnant women	Physical activity prior to pregnancy	Only among the women physically active for 120 min/week or more, a tendency for reduced risk was found. Adjusted OR = 0.6; 95% CI 0.3–1.2.
(Hegaard et al., 2010)	Prospective cohort study Danish Birth Registry	2,793 healthy pregnant women	Physical activity during pregnancy	Pre-eclampsia: 4.2%, 4.2% and 3.1% of women with sedentary, light and moderate-to-heavy leisure time physical activity. Differences were not statistically significant.
(Vollebregt et al., 2006)	Prospective cohort study Amsterdam Population Study	3,679 nulliparous women with a singleton pregnancy	Leisure time physical activity of the past week	The amount of time or intensity of physical activity in leisure time was not associated with a difference in risk of preeclampsia.
(Osterdal et al., 2009)	Prospective cohort study Danish population	85,139 pregnant Danish women	Physical activity in early pregnancy	High physical activity levels (> 270 min/week) were associated with increased risk of severe pre-eclampsia compared with the nonexercising group. Adjusted OR = 1.65 (95% CI: 1.11–2.43).

Study	Study type	Sample	Measure/Intervention	Results
(Rudra et al., 2006)	Prospective cohort study US-Washington State	2,241 pregnant women	Physical activity in before and during pregnancy	Leisure physical activity before or during early pregnancy lowered the risk non-significantly ($OR = 0.73$, 95% $CI = 0.30–1.77$)
(Magnus, Trogstad, Owe, Olsen, & Nystad, 2008)	Prospective cohort study Norwegian Mother and Child Cohort Study	59,573 Norwegian pregnant women	Physical activity during pregnancy	Adjusted $OR = 0.79$ 95% CI: 0.64–0.96. The effect was stronger among women with BMI < 25 kg/m^2.
(Sankaralingam, Jiang, Davidge, & Yeo, 2011)	Randomized trial	Sedentary pregnant women with history of preeclampsia. Stretching ($n = 6$) Walking ($n = 5$)	40 minutes of moderate walking exercise 5 times/ week vs. 40 minutes of stretching exercise 5 times/ week	Super oxide dismutase expression was increased ($p < 0.05$) in stretchers (106.3 [interquatile range 84.2 to 127.8 arbitrary unite [AU]) when compared with that of walker (56.92 [interqualite range 46.35 to 82.32 AU]). Transferrin levels continued to increase throughout pregnancy only among the stretcher.
(Yeo et al., 2008)	Randomized trial	Sedentary pregnant women with history of preeclampsia. Stretching ($n = 38$) Walking ($n = 41$)	40 minutes of moderate walking exercise 5 times/ week vs. 40 minutes of stretching exercise 5 times/ week	The incidence of preeclampsia was 14.6% (95% CI: 5.6–29.2) among the walkers and 2.6% (95% CI: 0.07–13.8) among the stretchers.

side effects. The randomized trial with 124 sedentary pregnant women compared the effects of a walking exercise (the intervention) and a stretching exercise (the control) on preeclampsia. Contrary to their expectations, the incidence of preeclampsia was higher among the walkers (14.6%; 95% CI [5.6–29.2]) than among the stretchers (2.6%; 95% CI [0.07–13.8]; p = .07 for group difference; Yeo et al., 2008). The expected rate of preeclampsia among women with a history of preeclampsia, which was the main inclusion criterion for the study, was 15% (Caritis et al., 1998). It appeared that walking exercise did not change this rate. That finding was further confirmed by a follow-up study. Vascular superoxide dismutase expression and transferrin, biomarkers for enhanced antioxidant cells, taken from the participants' vasculature membranes via biopsy and systemic levels in red blood cells were also lower among stretchers than walkers (Sankaralingam, Jiang, Davidge, & Yeo, 2011). The control condition group (stretching) was designed in such a way that participants believed that they were engaged in a regular exercise program. Anecdotally, women in the control group stated that doing stretching exercises almost every day at home and attending supervised stretching exercise once a week were helpful. Participants' exercise logs also showed that the control group "exercised" more often than the intervention group (Yeo, Cisewski, Lock, & Marron, 2010). These results forced the investigators to look for other explanations for the outcomes. The theoretical framework was further revisited (Yeo, 2010, 2011).

Exercise and Gestational Diabetes
Electronic databases (Ovid MEDLINE and other nonindexed citation) were searched with the keywords gestational diabetes mellitus or gestational diabetes and exercise or physical activity for the years 2008–2013. The results were limited to studies published in English. Of 100 citations identified, 10 reported the results of correlational studies (n = 7), 1 case control study, and randomized trials (n = 2).

Correlational Studies. Five studies reported significant associations between physical activity during pregnancy and lower risk of hyperglycemia (Deierlein, Siega-Riz, & Evenson, 2012), reduced insulin response (Gradmark et al., 2011), and lower risk of GDM (Chasan-Taber et al., 2008; Harizopoulou et al., 2010; Liu, Laditka, Mayer-Davis, & Pate, 2008). Table 5.2 summarizes these results. Among those which reported significant results, two also reported an interaction effect between physical activity and obesity (BMI ≥ 25 kg/m^2; Chasan-Taber et al., 2008; Deierlein et al., 2012). Two studies reported no associations between physical activity and GDM (Harizopoulou et al., 2010; Snapp & Donaldson, 2008).

Randomized Trials and a Case Control Study. Three trials are summarized in Table 5.3. One randomized trial determined whether counseling on physical

TABLE 5.2

Correlational Studies of Exercise/Physical Activity and Gestational Diabetes/Insulin Resistance

Author (reference)	Study Design	Sample	Exercise/Physical Activity	Outcome
(Deierlein, Siega-Riz, & Evenson, 2012)	Survey U.S. – North Carolina (PIN3 data)	1,437 pregnant women	Physical activity during pregnancy	Women who reported any recreational activity had a 27% lower risk of hyperglycemia (adjusted RR [aRR] 0.73, 95% confidence interval [95% CI] 0.54–0.99) compared to women who reported no recreational activity. Interaction terms were significant for pregnancy BMI and recreational activity ($p = 0.01$). Women with prepregnancy BMI < 25 kg/m^2, who reported any recreational activity had a nearly 50% lower risk of hyperglycemia compared to those who reported none (aRR 0.52, 95% CI 0.33–0.83).
(Harrison, Lombard, & Teede, 2012)	Observational study in Australia	97 pregnant women	Physical activity	No association between physical activity and GDM. PA assessed by a pedometer
(Gradmark et al., 2011)	Observational study in Sweden	35 non-obese pregnant women	Physical activity	Activity was associated with reduced insulin response (Regression $r^2 = 0.11$; Spearman $r = -0.47$; $p = 0.007$). PA assessed by accelerometer, heart rate monitor, doubly-labeled water and expired gas indirect calorimeter.
(Harizopoulou et al., 2010)	Case-control study	160 postpartum women (40 with GDM and 120 without)	Physical activity before and during pregnancy	Women who were "inactive" before or during early pregnancy had odds ratio (OR) 7.9 [95% confidence interval (CI) 3.7–16.56] and 1.3 (95% CI 1.2–1.4) of developing GDM, compared to "minimally active" or "active" women, respectively.

(Continued)

TABLE 5.2

Correlational Studies of Exercise/Physical Activity and Gestational Diabetes/Insulin Resistance   (Continued)

Author (reference)	Study Design	Sample	Exercise/Physical Activity	Outcome
(Liu, Laditka, Mayer-Davis, & Pate, 2008)	Survey 1988 National Maternal and Infant Survey (NMIHS)	4,813 women who were physically inactive before pregnancy with singleton birth and no history of previous diabetes	Physical activity	Women who became physically active had 57 percent lower adjusted odds of developing gestational diabetes than those who remained inactive (OR = 0.43, 95% CI 0.20–0.93). Women who had done brisk walking during pregnancy had a lower adjusted risk of gestational diabetes (OR = 0.44, CI 0.19–1.02).
(Snapp & Donaldson, 2008)	Survey 1988 National Maternal and Infant Survey (NMIHS)	Women with GDM (n = 105,600) and without GDN (n = 2,952,482)	Physical activity and exercise	The non-GDM and GDM groups of pregnant women were not different in physical activity. No difference between exercise and no exercise during pregnancy.
(Chasan-Taber et al., 2008)	Prospective cohort study	1,006 Hispanic pregnant women	Physical activity before and during pregnancy	Women in the highest quartile of prepregnancy (OR = 0.2, 95% CI 0.1–0.8) and midpregnancy (OR = 0.2, 95% CI 0.1–0.8) household/caregiving activities as well as midpregnancy sports/exercise (OR = 0.1, 95% CI 0.0–0.7) had a reduced risk of GDM compared with women in the lowest quartile, after controlling for age and prepregnancy body mass index (BMI).

TABLE 5.3

Randomized Trials of Exercise and Gestational Diabetes Mellitus (Prevention and Treatment)

Author (reference)	Study Design	Sample	Exercise/Physical Activity	Outcome
Prevention				
(Luoto et al., 2011)	Randomized trial	399 Finn pregnant women with GDM risk	Intensified counseling on physical activity as a part of lifestyle counseling.	15.8% (34/216) of women in the intervention group and 12.4% (22/179) in the usual care group developed GDM (absolute effect size 1.36, 95% confidence interval [CI] 0.71–2.62, $p = 0.36$). Non significant.
Treatment				
(de Barros, Lopes, Francisco, Sapienza, & Zugaib, 2010)	Randomized trial	64 sedentary women with GDM.	Circuit resistance exercise (3/wk at home + 1/wk supervised) + Diet + glucose monitor (4/d) vs. Diet + glucose monitor (4/d)	18/32 women in control and 7/32 women in exercise required insulin Time spent in glucose target range: 41% control and 63% exercise. No difference in amount of insulin required (0.49 units/kg for control and 0.44 units/kg for exercise) or time to requirement (2.11 weeks control and 1.85 weeks exercise).
(Davenport, et al., 2008)	Case control matched (2:1)	30 women with GDM. BMI > 25 kg/m^2	Walking program started with 25 min/d, increased by 2 min per wk to 40 min 3–4/wk ($n = 10$) + Diet vs. Diet ($n = 20$)	Walking group had significantly lower mean glucose levels at the end of pregnancy and required significantly fewer units of insulin (0.16 units/kg) than control (0.50 units/kg). No difference in incidence of starting insulin (70% both groups) or time to insulin use (29 weeks for control and 28.5 weeks for walking).

activity *prevented* GDM among an at-risk group (Luoto et al., 2011). Pregnant women with a risk of GDM (*n* = 399) were randomly assigned to receive either intensified counseling to increase physical activity or usual care at prenatal clinics. Although GDM cases in the counseling group were lower (12%) than in the control group (16%), the difference was not statistically significant.

Two trials specifically tested exercise as a treatment modality to control glucose level and minimize or delay exogenous insulin administration (Davenport, Giroux, Sopper, & Mottola, 2011; Davenport et al., 2008; de Barros et al., 2010). One study, by de Barros et al. (2010), was an RCT and one, by Davenport, was a case control trial. Davenport randomized women into low- and moderate-intensity walking exercise, and selected matched cases from other pool as a non-exercise control. The RCT applied circuit resistance exercise and reported that the exercise group showed a longer latency to insulin use; fewer women started insulin; and they stayed at a normal glucose level longer (de Barros et al., 2010). Davenport found that walking exercise lowered mean glucose levels at the end of pregnancy and women required fewer units of insulin (Davenport et al., 2008).

Both circuit resistance exercise and walking exercise were low intensity, with average frequencies 2–3 times per week. In addition, one study (Brankston et al., 2004) reported a dose effect. Brankston et al. (2004) found that those who exercised more frequently experienced larger effects in indices of glucose control. These study results suggest a need to better understand nonaerobic type exercises (i.e., circuit resistance exercise) and lower intensity and less frequent exercises than recommended in current exercise guidelines.

CONTROLLING WEIGHT GAIN BY REGULAR EXERCISE

During the 9 months of pregnancy, women gain from as little as 10.0 lb to as much as 40.0 lb. This gained weight at term include 7.5 lb for the fetus, 3.0 lb for the placenta and amniotic fluid, 3.0–4.0 lb for additional blood volume, 1.0–2.0 lb for increased breasts size and density, 4.0–6.0 lb for maternal fat, and 2.0 lb for the uterus (Cunningham & Williams, 2010). With the dynamic and anabolic changes, avoidance of excessive GWG is often difficult to attain.

In 2009, the Institute of Medicine (IOM) issued guidelines for "healthy" weight gain for pregnant women (IOM, 2009). The recommended weight gain ranges during pregnancy are based on prepregnancy body mass index (BMI [m/kg^2])—25–35 lb gain for normal prepregnant BMIs (18.8–24.9); 15–25 lb gain for overweight prepregnant BMIs (25.0–29.9); and 11–20 lb gain for obese prepregnant BMIs (≥30.0). It has been reported that obese women (prepregnant BMI ≥30 kg/m^2) are 6.5 times more likely to develop gestational diabetes, 7.9 times more likely to develop hypertension, and 3.7 times more likely to develop preeclampsia during pregnancy than normal-weight women (prepregnant BMI = 18.8–24.9; Doherty, Magann, Francis, Morrison, & Newnham, 2006). In addition, the IOM has reported that those who gain more weight than recommended not only increase their risk for gestational diabetes and preeclampsia with the index pregnancy, but they are also more likely to retain substantially higher weight during the postpartum period and hence to increase their risk for obesity in subsequent pregnancies (IOM, 2009).

Clearly, there is a critical need for pregnant women to control weight gain. "Weight" appears to be influenced not only by biological but also by psychological, social, and environmental factors. Weight control interventions during pregnancy aim at both prevention and treatment, and may include prevention of adverse pregnancy outcomes in the index pregnancy; prevention of obesity in the subsequent pregnancy; and treatment of obesity in the index pregnancy, intervening with insulin and glucose dysregulation.

The studies to date aiming to control GWG have, by and large, applied behavioral theories or frameworks rather than biological models. Clearly, to see meaningful weight changes over the period of pregnancy, exercise and other physical activities need to be a part of daily living. However, enactment of daily regular exercises requires lifestyle changes. Yet there is not much cross-pollination between biological models and behavioral models in physical activity studies with pregnant women.

Social Cognitive Behavior Models Encompassing Lifestyle Interventions

A lifestyle typically reflects an individual's attitudes, values, or views, which seem to forge a sense of self and "to create cultural symbols that resonate with personal identity and surrounded by social and technical environments" (Spaargaren & VanVliet, 2000,). Trials of social cognitive interventions combine physical activity promotion with healthy eating (Althuizen, van der Wijden, van Mechelen, Seidell, & van Poppel, 2013; Claesson et al., 2008; Ferrara et al., 2011; Phelan et al., 2011; Ruchat et al., 2012).

Effective lifestyle interventions successfully affect the pregnant woman's sense of self through intervening to change ideas about physical activity and weight gain during pregnancy that are influenced by her identity and cultural symbols. Lifestyle interventions are administered through various modes including counseling, group sessions, phone calls, e-mails, and text messages to name a few. The interactions are hypothesized to influence a person's attitudes and intention, and eventually the targeted behavior, that is, physical activity and healthy eating.

Intensive interventions apply multiple modes repeatedly and usually include individual counseling. Although intensive behavioral weight management interventions are known to be effective in reducing obesity-related chronic disease risk among high-risk adults (U.S. Preventive Services Task Force, 2003), only a few studies have been conducted with pregnant women. The following section discusses theoretical approaches to lifestyle interventions, focusing on the application of different frequencies and intensities of interactions for pregnant women.

A milestone study for nonpregnant populations was conducted by the Diabetes Prevention Program (DPP), which produced a 58% reduction in the incidence of diabetes in 3 years (DPP Research Group, 2004). The study set a goal of 150 min/week of physical activity. Goal achievement was assessed at the end of the 6-month core intervention and after the final intervention visit following a maintenance phase. Seventy-four percent of participants met the activity goal initially, whereas 67% met the goal long-term. The methods used to achieve lifestyle changes were intensive: 16 weekly group sessions using behavior modification strategies, supervised physical activities, and self-monitoring for a period of 6 months. The main mode of exercise was a brisk walk at least 10 min per session and 3 times a week—moderate intensity exercise. Throughout the program, participants had an option of exercising independently or attending group and supervised exercise up to twice a week.

The key components of this and other lifestyle interventions are informed by constructs and behavioral approaches from social cognitive theory (SCT), the socioecological model, (Fisher et al., 2005; McLeroy, Bibeau, Strecker, & Glanz, 1988), the transtheoretical stages of change model, (Prochaska & DiClemente, 1983), self-applied behavior modification (Watson & Tharp, 1989), motivational counseling (Rollnick, Mason, & Butler, 1999), and problem-solving techniques (D'Zurilla, Nezu, & Maydeu-Olivares, 2002). SCT emphasizes that behaviors are shaped by both cognitive and social factors. Key constructs from SCT include self-efficacy, social support, outcome expectations, self-control, behavioral capacity, and emotional coping responses.

Behavioral Interventions for Pregnant Women's Physical Activity

The theory of planned behavior (TPB) is most often applied to understand and predict pregnant women's exercise behavior. This is a belief-based social cognitive theory of intention (motivation/plan) to perform or not perform a behavior (Ajzen, 1991). The premise of TPB is that people will intend to engage in a behavior when they evaluate it positively (attitude), believe that significant others want them to participate in it (subjective norm), and perceive it to be under their control (perceived behavioral control). Although TPB focuses on individual and interpersonal factors leading to exercise behavior, people's beliefs and behaviors are also influenced by other factors.

The socioecological model recognizes the importance of both individual and social environmental factors as targets for health promotion interventions. Specifically, the model posits that the most effective approach to healthy behaviors includes interventions directed at individual, interpersonal, organizational, community, and public policy levels (Fisher et al., 2005).

The transtheoretical model emphasizes that behavior change is a dynamic process, with different stages of readiness to change requiring different strategies to promote sustained behavior change. Thus, throughout the intervention, different behavioral strategies are emphasized to match the participant's stage of behavior change (Prochaska & DiClemente, 1983).

Techniques such as motivational counseling, which stresses the need for pregnant women to be active participants in decision making, problem solving, and goal setting; and problem-solving strategies that specify how to define a problem and generate, implement, and evaluate possible solutions, are integral parts of all contacts with pregnant women (Rollnick et al., 1999). Cognitive behavioral approaches, such as problem solving and cognitive restructuring (dealing with negative thoughts that in turn prompt non-health-promoting behaviors), can be incorporated into implementation of individual and group-based contacts, session activities, and materials (D'Zurilla et al., 2002).

Behavioral intervention is still relatively new, let alone lifestyle intervention, when it comes to physical activity among pregnant women. One study examined exercise intention and behavior among pregnant women and found that attitude was the strongest determinant of exercise intention and exercise behavior (Downs & Hausenblas, 2003). Perceived behavioral control and subjective norm were less effective predictors.

Attitude, a key construct of lifestyle, is a disposition or tendency to respond positively or negatively toward a certain idea, object, person, or situation. Attitudes are products of the social environment, are closely related to our opinions and beliefs, and are based on our experiences. For example, among those who are inactive, the experience of initial enactment of exercise can have a significant influence on beliefs about exercise and intention (Festinger & Carlsmith, 1959). Thus, immediate feedback on each exercise and active intervention to improve the experience of exercise at each session are needed.

There are other behavioral theories that may be relevant to pregnancy, physical activity, and the interactions between them. They include social modeling theory (i.e., behavior is influenced by *modeling processes*), social pressure theory (i.e., there is explicit social pressure for "eating for two"), and social norm theory (i.e., perceptions, whether accurate or not, can serve as a form of social influence if individuals adopt health-related behaviors that they perceive to be approved by their social reference group). More research is needed to deepen our understanding of how to engage pregnant women in a given situation, in a given community, and in a given society to exercise regularly. The evidence suggests that effective strategies for behavioral interventions outside of pregnancy may also be effective during pregnancy (Artinian et al., 2010; Donnelly et al., 2009; Phelan et al., 2011). Key components of effective interventions include self-monitoring of daily physical activity, goal setting, feedback on progress, frequent follow-up contacts, strategies that build self-efficacy, and motivational interviewing strategies to facilitate lifestyle behavior change.

Evidence is limited on how multiple models influence specific populations. Interventions that may be effective for pregnant women who are highly educated and earn a decent living may not be effective for pregnant women who are low income or those of racial or ethnic minority groups. Although the need for effective programs is similar, if not greater for pregnant women who are low income or those of racial or ethnic minority groups. For example, it is often argued that exercise interventions for pregnant women, particularly low-income women, should be home-based, use a telephone call instead of face-to-face interaction, and involve less frequent visits (Ferrara et al., 2011; Phelan et al., 2011); but these may provide a relatively weak influence on factors related to attitude changes. If pregnant women are physically inactive, then a higher intensity of behavioral intervention must be introduced.

Evidence

Electronic databases (Ovid MEDLINE and other nonindexed citation) were searched using the keywords gestational weight gain and exercise or physical activity for the years 2008–2013. The results were limited to studies published in English. Of 46 citations identified, 10 reported the results of either correlational studies ($n = 4$) or randomized trials ($n = 6$).

Correlational Studies

Four studies examined the associations between physical activity and excessive GWG (Althuizen, van Poppel, Seidell, & van Mechelen, 2009; Herring et al., 2012; Jiang et al., 2012; Stuebe, Oken, & Gillman, 2009).

Two studies reported that being inactive during pregnancy increased the odds of excessive GWG using the IOM's guidelines (Althuizen et al., 2009; Stuebe et al., 2009). During midpregnancy, pregnant women who exercised (i.e., walked 30 min a day) had an 8% lower risk for excessive weight gain. Those who reported vigorous physical activities during the same period had a 25% lower risk for excessive weight gain. Another study that reported daily pedometer steps found that the highest quartile women had 40% less risk for excessive GWG than the lowest quartile group (Jiang et al., 2012). Table 5.4 summarizes these studies.

TABLE 5.4

Correlational Studies of Exercise/Physical Activity and Gestational Weight Gain

Author (reference)	Study Design	Sample	Exercise/Physical Activity	Outcome
(Herring et al., 2012)	Prospective cohort study in US (Philadelphia)	94 pregnant women	Physical activities	Engaging in regular physical activity during pregnancy (OR, 0.35; 95% CI, 0.11–1.09) was suggestive of a reduced risk of excessive gain.
(Jiang et al., 2012)	Prospective cohort study in China	862 pregnant women	Physical activity by pedometers	The adjusted odds ratio (OR) was 0.59 (95%CI: 0.36 ~ 0.95) for excessive GWG in the Active group and 0.66 (95% CI: 0.43 ~ 1.00) in the Somewhat Active group, compared with the Sedentary group respectively.
(Althuizen, van Poppel, Seidell, & van Mechelen, 2009)	Observational study in Netherland	144 pregnant women	Physical activities	Being overweight, judging yourself to be less physically active than others, and a perceived elevated food intake during pregnancy were significantly associated with excessive weight gain (odds ratio [OR] = 6.33, 95% confidence interval [CI]: 2.01–19.32; OR = 3.96, 95% CI: 1.55l, 10.15; and OR = 3.14, 95% CI: 1.18, 8.36, respectively).
(Stuebe, Oken, & Gillman, 2009)	Prospective cohort study Project Viva (US)	1388 pregnant women	Physical activity	First trimester vegetarian diet (OR, 0.46; 95% CI, 0.28–0.78) and midpregnancy walking (OR, 0.92; 95% CI, 0.83–1.01, per 30 minutes per day) and vigorous physical activity (OR, 0.76; 95% CI, 0.60–0.97, per 30 minutes per day) were inversely associated with excessive GWG

Randomized Trials

The interventions in six studies tested physical activity and healthy eating for pregnant women (see Table 5.5). Phelan et al. (2011) tested the effectiveness of a *low-intensity lifestyle intervention* with 401 pregnant women (201 normal prepregnant weight and 200 overweight prepregnant weight). The intervention consisted of one individual counseling session followed by three phone calls. If a participant gained more than recommended, she received two additional phone follow-ups. The authors reported that more women in the intervention group than in the control group returned to their prepregnant weight level, even though no intervention was continued after the birth. No difference was detected in GWG between the two groups. Three other lifestyle intervention studies also reported no group differences in GWG or physical activity levels (Althuizen et al., 2013; Ferrara et al., 2011; Guelinckx, Devlieger, Mullie, & Vansant, 2010; Hui et al., 2012). Althuizen et al. (2013) used four counseling sessions by midwives, who also provided prenatal care, but the authors did not report how these midwives were trained in behavioral intervention counseling. The other two studies that did not find group differences were also low-intensity interventions (Ferrara et al., 2011; Guelinckx et al., 2010). These studies did not report how the interventionists were trained. Lack of information about fidelity of the intervention makes it difficult to judge whether low intensity or infidelity to the intervention resulted in nonsignificant results.

One study by Hui et al. (2012) used an intensive intervention; the core of the program was weekly exercise group sessions held in the community. The study reported a significant increase in physical activity. Lastly, Huang et al. (2011) reported a difference in GWG between the intervention and control groups. The interventionists in this study were master's-prepared nurses with special training in diet and physical activity during pregnancy. Individual sessions were used to set up individual participant's goals for weight retention and examples were provided of a healthy diet and appropriate physical activity plan. After clinic visits, participants in the intervention group received a personalized graph of their weight changes via e-mail. At the following session, pregnant women in the intervention group submitted a report of self-monitored physical activity. Each woman received detailed feedback on her progress based on self-monitoring data. Those whose weight exceeded the recommended levels were provided an additional assessment of physical activity, problem solving, and goal setting for physical activity.

In summary, the results of these six trials show, in essence, that low intensity lifestyle interventions have failed to produce significant effects (Althuizen et al., 2013; Ferrara et al., 2011; Guelinckx et al., 2010; Phelan et al., 2011), whereas intensive interventions with either individual counseling at a clinic or

TABLE 9.5
Randomized Trials of Exercise and Gestational Weight Gain

Author (reference)	Study Design	Sample	Intervention Components					Outcome
			# of Individual counseling	# of group session	# of phone call follow up	Other		
(Phelan et al., 2011)	RCT in US	401 (201 NW and 200 OW/OB) pregnant women	1		3 for feedback + 2 more if high weight gain	Weekly printed materials via mailing		NW women who exceeded IOM recommendation were less than OW/OB women who exceeded (40.2% vs. 52.1%; $p = 0.003$) No difference in physical activity
(Ferrara et al., 2011)	RCT in US	197 pregnant women	1		2	Printed material provided		No difference in GWG
(Althuizen, van der Wijden, van Mechelen, Seidell, & van Poppel, 2013)	RCT in Netherland	229 healthy nulliparous	4					No difference in GWG
(Hui et al., 2012)	RCT in Canada	190 (102 in intervention; 88 in control) pregnant women	1 dietary counseling	Weekly exercise sessions at community		Home exercise instructed		Higher physical activity in 2 months compared to the control.
(Huang, Yeh, & Tsai, 2011)	RCT in Taiwan	189 pregnant women	Counseling as a part of prenatal care visit			Personalized graph of weight change sent after each visit		GWG: 14.02 kg for the intervention vsl. 16.22 kg for the control.
(Guelinckx, Devlieger, Mullie, & Vansant, 2010)	RCT in Belgium	195 white, obese pregnant women	3			Printed material provided		No difference in physical activities; No difference in GWG

Note. RCT = Randomized clinical trial; NW = normal weight; OW = overweight; OB = obese (all categories were based on pre-pregnant BMI used by IOM); GWG = gestational weight gain group sessions in community have reported significant effects (Huang et al., 2011; Hui et al., 2012).

FUTURE RESEARCH DIRECTIONS

The state of science on the application of physical activity indicates that the most effective interventions to prevent or treat pregnancy-specific health conditions are intensive behavior interventions. Such interventions have been effective in increasing physical activities and improving some outcomes.

Behavioral interventions for pregnant women have put less emphasis on group sessions, although there is a growing interest in group prenatal care (Novick et al., 2013).

As described, the studies that failed to achieve significant results through behavioral interventions intentionally avoid or did not emphasize group sessions, even though frequent group sessions have produced significantly improved outcomes among nonpregnant women of low-income backgrounds (Samuel-Hodge et al., 2009). Although it may seem logical to avoid group sessions for pregnant women, particularly low-income pregnant women because of concerns for lack of resources and time, group sessions can empower pregnant women to exercise for their health. Translation of effective weight control interventions into clinic-based programs, particularly in a form of group prenatal care, is warranted.

Another important area to explore includes use of commercially available high technologies to monitor physical activities and other behaviors. Availability of remote monitoring of physical activity and body weight with smaller and lighter machines often through smartphones makes studies to closely monitor biological and behavioral data possible with less burden to participants than ever.

In conclusion, this chapter has reviewed the state of science in physical activity and pregnancy. Most pregnant women know that being physically active is important for their health, yet many pregnant women remain inactive. Although biological models suggest benefit of physical activity, only limited studies demonstrate proposed effects, in part because of the lack of incorporation of behavioral models and the lack of a report of the fidelity. When behavioral interventions are considered in future studies, factors unique to pregnancy at individual, family, institutional, community, and policy levels must be incorporated in the models.

REFERENCES

Ainsworth, B. E., Haskell, W. L., Whitt, M. C., Irwin, M. L., Swartz, A. M., Strath, S. J., . . . Leon, A. S. (2000). Compendium of physical activities: An update of activity codes and MET intensities. *Medicine and Science in Sports and Exercise*, *32*(Supp. 9), S498–S504.

Ajzen, I. (1991). The theory of planned behavior. *Organizational Behavior and Human Decision Processes, 50*(2), 179–211.

Alessio, H. M. (1993). Exercise-induced oxidative stress. *Medicine and Science in Sports and Exercise, 25*(2), 218–224.

Althuizen, E., van der Wijden, C. L., van Mechelen, W., Seidell, J. C., & van Poppel, M. N. (2013). The effect of a counselling intervention on weight changes during and after pregnancy: A randomised trial. *British Journal of Obstetrics and Gynaecology, 120*(1), 92–99. http://dx.doi.org/10.1111/1471-0528.12014

Althuizen, E., van Poppel, M. N., Seidell, J. C., & van Mechelen, W. (2009). Correlates of absolute and excessive weight gain during pregnancy. *Journal of Women's Health, 18*(10), 1559–1566. http://dx.doi.org/10.1089/jwh.2008.1275

American Congress of Obstetricians and Gynecologists. (2002). Exercise during pregnancy and the postpartum period, Committee Opinion No. 267. Committee on Obstetric Practice. *International Journal of Gynaecology and Obstetrics, 77*(1), 79–81.

American Diabetes Association. (2003). Report of the expert committee on the diagnosis and classification of diabetes mellitus. *Diabetes Care, 26*(Supp. 1), S5–S20.

American Diabetes Association. (2007). Standards of medical care in diabetes—2007. *Diabetes Care, 30*(Supp. 1), S4–S41.

Anim-Nyame, N., Sooranna, S. R., Jones, J., Alaghband-Zadeh, J., Steer, P. J., & Johnson, M. R. (2004). Insulin resistance and pre-eclampsia: A role for tumor necrosis factor-alpha? *Gynecological Endocrinology, 18*(3), 117–123.

Artinian, N. T., Fletcher, G. F., Mozaffarian, D., Kris-Etherton, P., Van Horn, L., Lichtenstein, A. H., . . . Burke, L. E. (2010). Interventions to promote physical activity and dietary lifestyle changes for cardiovascular risk factor reduction in adults: A scientific statement from the American Heart Association. *Circulation, 122*(4), 406–441. http://dx.doi.org/10.1161/CIR.0b013e3181e8edf1

Asbee, S. M., Jenkins, T. R., Butler, J. R., White, J., Elliot, M., & Rutledge, A. (2009). Preventing excessive weight gain during pregnancy through dietary and lifestyle counseling: A randomized controlled trial. *Obstetrics and Gynecology, 113*(2, Pt. 1), 305–312. http://dx.doi.org/10.1097/AOG.0b013e318195baef

Brankston, G. N., Mitchell, B. F., Ryan, E. A., & Okun, N. B. (2004). Resistance exercise decreases the need for insulin in overweight women with gestational diabetes mellitus. *American Journal of Obstetrics and Gynecology, 190*(1), 188–193.

Brown, M. A. (1997). Pre-eclampsia: A case of nerves? *Lancet, 349*(9048), 297–298. http://dx.doi.org/10.1016/S0140-6736(05)62819-X

Carey, G. B., Quinn, T. J., & Goodwin, S. E. (1997). Breast milk composition after exercise of different intensities. *Journal of Human Lactation, 13*(2), 115–120.

Caritis, S., Sibai, B., Hauth, J., Lindheimer, M. D., Klebanoff, M., Thom, E., . . . Thurnau, G. (1998). Low-dose aspirin to prevent preeclampsia in women at high risk. National Institute of Child Health and Human Development Network of Maternal-Fetal Medicine Units. *New England Journal of Medicine, 338*(11), 701–705.

Chasan-Taber, L., Schmidt, M. D., Pekow, P., Sternfeld, B., Manson, J. E., Solomon, C. G., . . . Markenson, G. (2008). Physical activity and gestational diabetes mellitus among Hispanic women. *Journal of Women's Health, 17*(6), 999–1008. http://dx.doi.org/10.1089/jwh.2007.0560

Claesson, I. M., Sydsjö, G., Brynhildsen, J., Cedergren, M., Jeppsson, A., Nyström, F., . . . Josefsson, A. (2008). Weight gain restriction for obese pregnant women: A case-control intervention study. *British Journal of Obstetrics and Gynaecology, 115*(1), 44–50. http://dx.doi.org/10.1111/j.1471-0528.2007.01531.x

Clapp, J. F., III, Lopez, B., & Harcar-Sevcik, R. (1999). Neonatal behavioral profile of the offspring of women who continued to exercise regularly throughout pregnancy. *American Journal of Obstetrics and Gynecology, 180*(1, Pt. 1), 91–94.

Clapp, J. F., III, Wesley, M., & Sleamaker, R. H. (1987). Thermoregulatory and metabolic responses to jogging prior to and during pregnancy. *Medicine and Science in Sports and Exercise, 19*(2), 124–130.

Cunningham, F. G., & Williams, J. W. (2010). *Williams obstetrics* (23rd ed.). New York, NY: McGraw-Hill.

D'Anna, R., Baviera, G., Corrado, F., Giordano, D., De Vivo, A., Nicocia, G., & Di Benedetto, A. (2006). Adiponectin and insulin resistance in early- and late-onset pre-eclampsia. *British Journal of Obstetrics and Gynaecology, 113*(11), 1264–1269.

Davenport, M. H., Giroux, I., Sopper, M. M., & Mottola, M. F. (2011). Postpartum exercise regardless of intensity improves chronic disease risk factors. *Medicine and Science in Sports and Exercise, 43*(6), 951–958. http://dx.doi.org/10.1249/MSS.0b013e3182051155

Davenport, M. H., Mottola, M. F., McManus, R., & Gratton, R. (2008). A walking intervention improves capillary glucose control in women with gestational diabetes mellitus: A pilot study. *Applied Physiology, Nutrition, and Metabolism, 33*(3), 511–517. http://dx.doi.org/10.1139/H08-018

de Barros, M. C., Lopes, M. A., Francisco, R. P., Sapienza, A. D., & Zugaib, M. (2010). Resistance exercise and glycemic control in women with gestational diabetes mellitus. *American Journal of Obstetrics and Gynecology, 203*(6), e551–e556. http://dx.doi.org/10.1016/j.ajog.2010.07.015

Deierlein, A. L., Siega-Riz, A. M., & Evenson, K. R. (2012). Physical activity during pregnancy and risk of hyperglycemia. *Journal of Women's Health, 21*(7), 769–775. http://dx.doi.org/10.1089/jwh.2011.3361

Diabetes Prevention Program Research Group. (2004). Achieving weight and activity goals among diabetes prevention program lifestyle participants. *Obesity Research, 12*(9), 1426–1434.

Doherty, D. A., Magann, E. F., Francis, J., Morrison, J. C., & Newnham, J. P. (2006). Pre-pregnancy body mass index and pregnancy outcomes. *International Journal of Gynaecology and Obstetrics, 95*(3), 242–247. http://dx.doi.org/10.1016/j.ijgo.2006.06.021

Donnelly, J. E., Blair, S. N., Jakicic, J. M., Manore, M. M., Rankin, J. W., & Smith, B. K. (2009). American College of Sports Medicine Position Stand. Appropriate physical activity intervention strategies for weight loss and prevention of weight regain for adults. *Medical and Science in Sports and Exercise, 41*(2), 459–471. http://dx.doi.org/10.1249/MSS.0b013e3181949333

Downs, D. S., Chasan-Taber, L., Evenson, K., Leiferman, J. A., & Yeo, S. (2012). Physical activity and pregnancy: Past and present evidence and future recommendations. *Research Quarterly for Exercise and Sport, 83*(4), 485–502.

Downs, D. S., & Hausenblas, H. A. (2003). Exercising for two: Examining pregnant women's second trimester exercise intention and behavior using the framework of the theory of planned behavior. *Women's Health Issues, 13*(6), 222–228.

D'Zurilla, T. J., Nezu, A. M., & Maydeu-Olivares, A. (2002). *Social Problem-Solving Inventory—Revised (SPSI-R): Technical manual.* North Tonawanda, NY: Multi-Health Systems.

Eneroth-Grimfors, E., Westgren, M., Ericson, M., Ihrman-Sandahl, C., & Lindblad, L. E. (1994). Autonomic cardiovascular control in normal and pre-eclamptic pregnancy. *Acta Obstetricia et Gynecologica Scandinavica, 73*(9), 680–684.

Ferrara, A., Hedderson, M. M., Albright, C. L., Ehrlich, S. F., Quesenberry, C. P., Jr., Peng, T., . . . Crites, Y. (2011). A pregnancy and postpartum lifestyle intervention in women with gestational diabetes mellitus reduces diabetes risk factors: A feasibility randomized control trial. *Diabetes Care, 34*(7), 1519–1525. http://dx.doi.org/10.2337/dc10-2221

Festinger, L., & Carlsmith, J. M. (1959). Cognitive consequences of forced compliance. *Journal of Abnormal Psychology, 58*(2), 203–210.

Fischer, T., Schobel, H. P., Frank, H., Andreae, M., Schneider, K. T., & Heusser, K. (2004). Pregnancy-induced sympathetic overactivity: A precursor of preeclampsia. *European Journal of Clinical Investigation*, 34(6), 443–448. http://dx.doi.org/10.1111/j.1365-2362.2004.01350.x

Fisher, E. B., Brownson, C. A., O'Toole, M. L., Shetty, G., Anwuri, V. V., & Glasgow, R. E. (2005). Ecological approaches to self-management: the case of diabetes. *American Journal of Public Health*, 95, 1523–1535.

Forest, J.-C., Girouard, J., Massé, J., Moutquin, J.-M., Kharfi, A., Ness, R. B., . . . Giguere, Y. (2005). Early occurrence of metabolic syndrome after hypertension in pregnancy. *Obstetrics and Gynecology*, 105(6), 1373–1380.

Fortner, R. T., Pekow, P. S., Whitcomb, B. W., Sievert, L. L., Markenson, G., & Chasan-Taber, L. (2011). Physical activity and hypertensive disorders of pregnancy among Hispanic women. *Medicine and Science in Sports and Exercise*, 43(4), 639–646. http://dx.doi.org/10.1249/MSS.0b013e3181f58d3e

Goto, C., Higashi, Y., Kimura, M., Noma, K., Hara, K., Nakagawa, K., . . . Nara, I. (2003). Effect of different intensities of exercise on endothelium-dependent vasodilation in humans: Role of endothelium-dependent nitric oxide and oxidative stress. *Circulation*, 108(5), 530–535.

Gradmark, A., Pomeroy, J., Renström, F., Steiginga, S., Persson, M., Wright, A., . . . Franks, P. W. (2011). Physical activity, sedentary behaviors, and estimated insulin sensitivity and secretion in pregnant and nonpregnant women. *BioMed Central Pregnancy and Childbirth*, 11, 44. http://dx.doi.org/10.1186/1471-2393-11-44

Guelinckx, I., Devlieger, R., Mullie, P., & Vansant, G. (2010). Effect of lifestyle intervention on dietary habits, physical activity, and gestational weight gain in obese pregnant women: A randomized controlled trial. *The American Journal of Clinical Nutrition*, 91(2), 373–380. http://dx.doi.org/10.3945/ajcn.2009.28166

Han, S., Middleton, P., & Crowther, C. A. (2012). Exercise for pregnant women for preventing gestational diabetes mellitus. *Cochrane Database of Systematic Reviews*, 7, CD009021. http://dx.doi.org/10.1002/14651858.CD009021.pub2

Harizopoulou, V. C., Kritikos, A., Papanikolaou, Z., Saranti, E., Vavilis, D., Klonos, E., . . . Goulis, D. G. (2010). Maternal physical activity before and during early pregnancy as a risk factor for gestational diabetes mellitus. *Acta Diabetologica*, 47(Supp. 1), 83–89. http://dx.doi.org/10.1007/s00592-009-0136-1

Harrison, C. L., Lombard, C. B., & Teede, H. J. (2012). Understanding health behaviours in a cohort of pregnant women at risk of gestational diabetes mellitus: an observational study. [Research Support, Non-U.S. Gov't]. *BJOG : an international journal of obstetrics and gynaecology*, 119(6), 731-738. doi: 10.1111/j.1471-0528.2012.03296.x

Hegaard, H. K., Ottesen, B., Hedegaard, M., Petersson, K., Henriksen, T. B., Damm, P., & Dykes, A. K. (2010). The association between leisure time physical activity in the year before pregnancy and pre-eclampsia. *Journal of Obstetrics and Gynaecology*, 30(1), 21–24. http://dx.doi.org/10.3109/01443610903315686

Herring, S. J., Nelson, D. B., Davey, A., Klotz, A. A., Dibble, L. V., Oken, E., & Foster, G. D. (2012). Determinants of excessive gestational weight gain in urban, low-income women. *Women's Health Issues*, 22(5), e439–e446. http://dx.doi.org/10.1016/j.whi.2012.05.004

Huang, T. T., Yeh, C. Y., & Tsai, Y. C. (2011). A diet and physical activity intervention for preventing weight retention among Taiwanese childbearing women: A randomised controlled trial. *Midwifery*, 27(2), 257–264. http://dx.doi.org/10.1016/j.midw.2009.06.009

Hui, A., Back, L., Ludwig, S., Gardiner, P., Sevenhuysen, G., Dean, H., . . . Shen, G. X. (2012). Lifestyle intervention on diet and exercise reduced excessive gestational weight gain in pregnant women under a randomised controlled trial. *British Journal of Obstetrics and Gynaecology*, 119(1), 70–77. http://dx.doi.org/10.1111/j.1471-0528.2011.03184.x

Institute of Medicine. (2009). *Weight gain during pregnancy: Reexamining the guidelines*. Washington, DC: The National Academies Press.

Jiang, H., Qian, X., Li, M., Lynn, H., Fan, Y., Jiang, H., . . . He, G. (2012). Can physical activity reduce excessive gestational weight gain? Findings from a Chinese urban pregnant women cohort study. *The International Journal of Behavioral Nutrition and Physical Activity, 9*, 12.

Jones, R. L., Botti, J. J., Anderson, W. M., & Bennett, N. L. (1985). Thermoregulation during aerobic exercise in pregnancy. *Obstetrics and Gynecology, 65*(3), 340–345.

Kaaja, R., Laivuori, H., Laakso, M., Tikkanen, M. J., & Ylikorkala, O. (1999). Evidence of a state of increased insulin resistance in preeclampsia. *Metabolism: Clinical and Experimental, 48*(7), 892–896.

Kaaja, R. J., & Pöyhönen-Alho, M. K. (2006). Insulin resistance and sympathetic overactivity in women. *Journal of Hypertension, 24*(1), 131–141.

Kahn, B. B., Alquier, T., Carling, D., & Hardie, D. G. (2005). AMP-activated protein kinase: ancient energy gauge provides clues to modern understanding of metabolism. *Cell Metabolism, 1*(1), 15–25. http://dx.doi.org/10.1016/j.cmet.2004.12.003

Kasawara, K. T., do Nascimento, S. L., Costa, M. L., Surita, F. G., & e Silva, J. L. (2012). Exercise and physical activity in the prevention of pre-eclampsia: Systematic review. *Acta Obstetricia et Gynecologica Scandinavica, 91*(10), 1147–1157. http://dx.doi.org/10.1111/j .1600-0412.2012.01483.x

Kelly, M., Keller, C., Avilucea, P. R., Keller, P., Luo, Z., Xiang, X., . . . Ruderman, N. B. (2004). AMPK activity is diminished in tissues of IL-6 knockout mice: The effect of exercise. *Biochemical and Biophysical Research Communications, 320*(2), 449–454. http://dx.doi.org/10.1016/j.bbrc.2004.05.188

Khatun, S., Kanayama, N., Belayet, H. M., Masui, M., Sugimura, M., Kobayashi, T., & Terao, T. (1999). Induction of preeclampsia like phenomena by stimulation of sympathetic nerve with cold and fasting stress. *European Journal of Obstetrics, Gynecology, and Reproductive Biology, 86*(1), 89–97.

Lindqvist, P. G., Marsal, K., Merlo, J., & Pirhonen, J. P. (2003). Thermal response to submaximal exercise before, during and after pregnancy: A longitudinal study. *The Journal of Maternal-Fetal and Neonatal Medicine, 13*(3), 152–156. http://dx.doi.org/10.1080/jmf .13.3.152.156

Liu, J., Laditka, J. N., Mayer-Davis, E. J., & Pate, R. R. (2008). Does physical activity during pregnancy reduce the risk of gestational diabetes among previously inactive women? *Birth, 35*(3), 188–195. http://dx.doi.org/10.1111/j.1523-536X.2008.00239.x

Luoto, R., Kinnunen, T. I., Aittasalo, M., Kolu, P., Raitanen, J., Ojala, K., . . . Tulokas, S. (2011). Primary prevention of gestational diabetes mellitus and large-for-gestational-age newborns by lifestyle counseling: A cluster-randomized controlled trial. *Public Library of Science Medicine, 8*(5), e1001036. http://dx.doi.org/10.1371/journal.pmed.1001036

Magnus, P., Trogstad, L., Owe, K. M., Olsen, S. F., & Nystad, W. (2008). Recreational physical activity and the risk of preeclampsia: A prospective cohort of Norwegian women. *American Journal of Epidemiology, 168*(8), 952–957. http://dx.doi.org/10.1093/aje/kwn189

Magnussen, E. B., Vatten, L. J., Smith, G. D., & Romundstad, P. R. (2009). Hypertensive disorders in pregnancy and subsequently measured cardiovascular risk factors. *Obstetrics and Gynecology, 114*(5), 961–970. http://dx.doi.org/10.1097/AOG.0b013e3181bb0dfc

Maloni, J. A. (2011). Lack of evidence for prescription of antepartum bed rest. *Expert Review of Obstetrics & Gynecology, 6*(4), 385–393. http://dx.doi.org/10.1586/eog.11.28

McDonald, S. D., Malinowski, A., Zhou, Q., Yusuf, S., & Devereaux, P. J. (2008). Cardiovascular sequelae of preeclampsia/eclampsia: A systematic review and meta-analyses. *American Heart Journal, 156*(5), 918–930. http://dx.doi.org/10.1016/j.ahj.2008.06.042

McLeroy, K., Bibeau, D., Strecker, A., & Glanz, K. (1988). An ecological perspective on health promotion programs. *Health Education Quarterly*, 15(4), 351–377.

Novick, G., Reid, A. E., Lewis, J., Kershaw, T. S., Rising, S. S., & Ickovics, J. R. (2013). Group prenatal care: Model fidelity and outcomes. *American Journal of Obstetrics and Gynecology*. Advance online publication. http://dx.doi.org/10.1016/j.ajog.2013.03.026

Nygaard, H., Tomten, S. E., & Høstmark, A. T. (2009). Slow postmeal walking reduces postprandial glycemia in middle-aged women. *Applied Physiology, Nutrition, and Metabolism*, 34(6), 1087–1092. http://dx.doi.org/10.1139/h09-110

Østerdal, M. L., Strøm, M., Klemmensen, A. K., Knudsen, V. K., Juhl, M., Halldorsson, T. I., . . . Olsen, S. F. (2009). Does leisure time physical activity in early pregnancy protect against preeclampsia? Prospective cohort in Danish women. *British Journal of Obstetrics and Gynaecology*, 116(1), 98–107. http://dx.doi.org/10.1111/j.1471-0528.2008.02001.x

Oxford Companion to Canadian History. (2004). *Women and medicine*. Retrieved from http://www.answers.com/topic/women-and-medicine

Pate, R. R., Pratt, M., Blair, S. N., Haskell, W. L., Macera, C. A., Bouchard, C., . . . Wilmore, J. H. (1995). Physical activity and public health. A recommendation from the Centers for Disease Control and Prevention and the American College of Sports Medicine. *Journal of the American Medical Association*, 273, 402–407.

Phelan, S., Phipps, M. G., Abrams, B., Darroch, F., Schaffner, A., & Wing, R. R. (2011). Randomized trial of a behavioral intervention to prevent excessive gestational weight gain: The fit for delivery study. *The American Journal of Clinical Nutrition*, 93(4), 772–779. http://dx.doi.org/10.3945/ajcn.110.005306

Polley, B. A., Wing, R. R., & Sims, C. J. (2002). Randomized controlled trial to prevent excessive weight gain in pregnant women. *International Journal of Obesity and Related Metabolic Disorders*, 26(11), 1494–1502. http://dx.doi.org/10.1038/sj.ijo.0802130

Prochaska, J. O., & DiClemente, C. C. (1983). Stages and processes of self-change of smoking: Toward an integrative model of change. *Journal of Consulting and Clinical Psychology*, 51(3), 390–395.

Rollnick, S., Mason, P., & Butler, C. (Eds.). (1999). *Health behavior change: A guide for practioners*. London, United Kingdom: Churchill Livingstone.

Ruchat, S. M., Davenport, M. H., Giroux, I., Hillier, M., Batada, A., Sopper, M. M., . . . Mottola, M. F. (2012). Nutrition and exercise reduce excessive weight gain in normal-weight pregnant women. *Medicine and Science in Sports and Exercise*, 44(8), 1419–1426. http://dx.doi.org/10.1249/MSS.0b013e31825365f1

Rudra, C. B., Qiu, C., David, R. M., Bralley, J. A., Walsh, S. W., & Williams, M. A. (2006). A prospective study of early-pregnancy plasma malondialdehyde concentration and risk of preeclampsia. *Clinical Biochemistry*, 39(7), 722–726.

Samuel-Hodge, C. D., Johnston, L. F., Gizlice, Z., Garcia, B. A., Lindsley, S. C., Bramble, K. P., . . . Keyserling, T. C. (2009). Randomized trial of a behavioral weight loss intervention for low-income women: The weight wise program. *Obesity*, 17(10), 1891–1899. http://dx.doi.org/10.1038/oby.2009.128

Sankaralingam, S., Jiang, Y., Davidge, S. T., & Yeo, S. (2011). Effect of exercise on vascular superoxide dismutase expression in high-risk pregnancy. *American Journal of Perinatology*, 28(10), 803–810. http://dx.doi.org/10.1055/s-0031-1284230

Sekoff, R. (2013). Paid parental leave: U.S. vs. the world (Infographic). *Parents*. Retrieved from http://www.huffingtonpost.com/2013/02/04/maternity-leave-paid-parental-leave-_n_2617284.html

Sibai, B. M. (2008). Maternal and uteroplacental hemodynamics for the classification and prediction of preeclampsia. *Hypertension*, 52(5), 805–806. http://dx.doi.org/10.1161/HYPERTENSIONAHA.108.119115

Snapp, C. A., & Donaldson, S. K. (2008). Gestational diabetes mellitus: Physical exercise and health outcomes. *Biological Research for Nursing, 10*(2), 145–155. http://dx.doi.org/10.1177/1099800408323728

Sorensen, T. K., Williams, M. A., Lee, I. M., Dashow, E. E., Thompson, M. L., & Luthy, D. A. (2003). Recreational physical activity during pregnancy and risk of preeclampsia. *Hypertension, 41*(6), 1273–1280.

Spaargaren, G., & Van Vliet, B. (2000). Lifestyle, consumption and environment: The ecological medernisation of domestic consumption. *Environmental Politics, 9*(1), 50–75.

Stella, C. L., & Sibai, B. M. (2006). Preeclampsia: Diagnosis and management of the atypical presentation. *The Journal of Maternal-Fetal and Neonatal Medicine, 19*(7), 381–386. http://dx.doi.org/10.1080/14767050600678337

Stuebe, A. M., Oken, E., & Gillman, M. W. (2009). Associations of diet and physical activity during pregnancy with risk for excessive gestational weight gain. *American Journal of Obstetrics and Gynecology, 201*(1), e1–e8. http://dx.doi.org/10.1016/j.ajog.2009.02.025

Tobias, D. K., Zhang, C., van Dam, R. M., Bowers, K., & Hu, F. B. (2011). Physical activity before and during pregnancy and risk of gestational diabetes mellitus: A meta-analysis. *Diabetes Care, 34*(1), 223–229. http://dx.doi.org/10.2337/dc10-1368

Tyldum, E. V., Romundstad, P. R., & Slørdahl, S. A. (2010). Pre-pregnancy physical activity and preeclampsia risk: A prospective population-based cohort study. *Acta Obstetricia et Gynecologica Scandinavica, 89*(3), 315–320. http://dx.doi.org/10.3109/00016340903370106

U.S. Department of Health and Human Services. (2008). *Physical activity guidelines advisory committee report.* Washington, DC: Author.

U.S. Preventive Services Task Force. (2003). Behavioral counseling in primary care to promote a healthy diet: Recommendations and rationale. *The American Journal of Nursing, 103*(8), 81–92.

Valensise, H., Vasapollo, B., Gagliardi, G., & Novelli, G. P. (2008). Early and late preeclampsia: Two different maternal hemodynamic states in the latent phase of the disease. *Hypertension, 52*(5), 873–880. http://dx.doi.org/10.1161/HYPERTENSIONAHA.108.117358

Vollebregt, K. C., Klijn, N., van der Wal, M., Boer, K., Wolf, H., & Bonsel, G. (2006). Does physical exercise in the beginning of pregnancy reduce the incidence of preeclampsia? *Hypertension in Pregnancy, 25*, 205.

Watson, D. L., & Tharp, R. G. (1989). *Self-directed behavior: Self-modification for personal adjustment.* Pacific Grove, CA: Brooks/Cole.

Weissgerber, T. L., Wolfe, L. A., & Davies, G. A. L. (2004). The role of regular physical activity in preeclampsia prevention. *Medicine and Science in Sports and Exercise, 36*(12), 2024–2031.

Yang, C. C., Chao, T. C., Kuo, T. B., Yin, C. S., & Chen, H. I. (2000). Preeclamptic pregnancy is associated with increased sympathetic and decreased parasympathetic control of HR. *American Journal of Physiology. Heart and Circulatory Physiology, 278*(4), H1269–H1273.

Yeo, S. (1994). Exercise guidelines for pregnant women. *Image—The Journal of Nursing Scholarship, 26*(4), 265–270.

Yeo, S. (1996). Exercise during pregnancy. *The Female Patient, 21*(8), 25–38.

Yeo, S. (2010). Prenatal stretching exercise and autonomic responses: Preliminary data and a model for reducing preeclampsia. *Journal of Nursing Scholarship, 42*(2), 113–121. http://dx.doi.org/10.1111/j.1547-5069.2010.01344.x

Yeo, S. (2011). A risk reduction model for late-onset preeclampsia: A theory for using low-intensity exercises to enhance cardiac homeostasis in nursing research and practice. *Advances in Nursing Science, 34*(1), 78–88. http://dx.doi.org/10.1097/ANS.0b013e3182094387

Yeo, S., Cisewski, J., Lock, E. F., & Marron, J. S. (2010). Exploratory analysis of exercise adherence patterns with sedentary pregnant women. *Nursing Research, 59*(4), 280–287. http://dx.doi.org/10.1097/NNR.0b013e3181dbbd61

Yeo, S., & Davidge, S. T. (2001). Possible beneficial effect of exercise, by reducing oxidative stress, on the incidence of preeclampsia. *Journal of Women's Health & Gender-Based Medicine, 10*(10), 983–989.

Yeo, S., Davidge, S. T., Ronis, D. L., Antonakos, C. L., Hayashi, R., & O'Leary, S. (2008). A comparison of walking versus stretching exercise to reduce the incidence of preeclampsia: A randomized clinical trial. *Hypertension in Pregnancy, 27*(2), 113–130.

Yeo, S., Hayashi, R. H., Wan, J. Y., & Dubler, B. (1995). Tympanic versus rectal thermometry in pregnant women. *Journal of Obstetric, Gynecologic, and Neonatal Nursing, 24*(8), 719–724.

CHAPTER 6

Using Function-Focused Care to Increase Physical Activity Among Older Adults

Barbara Resnick and Elizabeth Galik

ABSTRACT

Despite the known benefits of physical activity for older adults, adherence to regular physical activity recommendations is poor. Less than half of adults in this country meet physical activity recommendations with reasons for lack of adherence including such things as access, motivation, pain, fear, comorbidities, among others. To overcome these challenges, function-focused care was developed. Function-focused care is a philosophy of care that focuses on evaluating the older adult's underlying capability with regard to function and physical activity and helping him or her optimize and maintain physical function and ability and continually increase time spent in physical activity. Examples of function-focused care include such things as using verbal cues during bathing, so the older individual performs the tasks rather than the caregiver bathing the individual; walking a resident or patient to the bathroom rather than using a urinal, or taking a resident to an exercise class. There are now over 20 studies supporting the benefits of function-focused care approaches across all settings and different types of patient groups (i.e, those with mild versus moderate-to-severe cognitive impairment). The approaches for implementation of function-focused care have also been well supported and have moved beyond establishing

© 2013 Springer Publishing Company
http://dx.doi.org/10.1891/0739-6686.31.175

effectiveness to considering dissemination and implementation of this approach into real world clinical settings. The process of dissemination and implementation has likewise been articulated and supported, and ongoing work needs to continue in this venue across all care settings.

It is well known that there are significant benefits to engaging in physical activity for older adults. Exercise, defined as moderate level physical activity (e.g., 50%–70% of maximum heart rate; or in lay terms, an increase in your heart rate and breathing rate, sweating but still being able to carry on a conversation, but not being able to sing), is a subset of all physical activity. Repeatedly, exercise—specifically aerobic and resistance exercise—has been noted to result in improvements in functional performance (e.g., gait and balance; ability to get up from a chair) and activities of daily living (Chang, Pan, Chen, Tsai, & Huang, 2012; Chou, Hwang, & Wu, 2012; Simek, McPhate, & Haines, 2012; Valenzuela, 2012; Wilhelm et al., 2012). These benefits are noted regardless of cognitive status, age, comorbidities, or living location. There is less evidence, however, to support the quality of life or mental health benefits associated with exercise.

In addition to benefits noted following moderate level physical activity, there is evidence to support the many benefits of overall time spent in physical activity during the course of a day (Allen & Morey, 2010; Aoyagi & Shephard, 2009; Diehr & Hirsch, 2010; Hughes et al., 2011; Kolt, Schofield, Kerse, Garrett, Ashton, & Patel, 2012; Rueggeberg, Wrosch, & Miller, 2012; Snyder, Colvin, & Gammack, 2011; Thompson, Zack, Krahn, Andresen, & Barile, 2012; Virtuoso et al., 2012). Consistently, those who engage in more time in overall physical activity have less functional impairment, better perceived health, better adherence to preventive cardiovascular outcomes (i.e., blood pressure), better mood, and better quality of life. There is even some evidence to suggest that as little as 40 min/day in overall physical activity results in functional benefits for older adults (Virtuoso et al., 2012) and a small increase in walking activity (4 blocks/day) have positive health benefits (Diehr & Hirsch, 2010).

The benefits of physical activity have likewise been noted for older adults who are in long-term care facilities. Repeatedly in these settings, studies have indicated that increasing participation in functional and physical activity results in improved gait and balance, improved mood, and fewer disruptive behaviors (Galik et al., 2008; Galik, Resnick, & Pretzer-Aboff, 2009; Resnick, Galik, Gruber-Baldini, & Zimmerman, 2009, 2011, 2012; Resnick, Galik, Pretzer-Aboff, Rogers, & Gruber-Baldini, 2008; Resnick, Gruber-Baldini, et al., 2009). In addition, residents that are encouraged to optimize their function and physical activity are less likely to be transferred to the emergency room for episodes of care associated with nonfall related problems such as infections (Resnick et al., 2011). Thus, there is sufficient support to engage older adults in physical activity and discourage them from participating in sedentary behaviors such as lying in bed or sitting for long periods.

Unfortunately, despite the known benefits of physical activity for older adults, adherence to regular physical activity is poor (Bergman, Grjibovski, Hagströmer, Bauman, Sjöström, 2008; Matthews et al., 2008; Netz, Goldsmith, Shimony, Ben-Moshe, & Zeev, 2011; Tak et al., 2012; Troiano et al., 2008). Less than half of adults in this country meet physical activity recommendations set out by groups such as the American Heart Association (Matthews et al., 2008). The numbers of active adults obtained in epidemiological research is likely an inflated rate of adherence given the likelihood that individuals overreport physical activity (Troiano et al., 2008). Unfortunately, after starting a physical activity program, only about a fourth of those who enroll voluntarily continue with the program (Tak et al., 2012). Older adults who are institutionalized spend very little time in physical activity (Galik et al., 2008; Resnick, Boltz, Galik, & Wells, 2013), with rates of moderate level of physical activity being less than a minute (Resnick et al., 2011). Among older adults with cognitive impairment, time spent in physical activity is even lower, particularly among those who exhibit problematic behaviors (Kalinowski et al., 2012; Scherder, Bogen, Eggermont, Hamers, & Swaab, 2010). It is critical, therefore, that innovative approaches be used to increase the amount of physical activity that older adults engage in across all settings. To that end, a function-focused care approach to interacting with older adults regardless of age, clinical status, or setting was established.

FUNCTION-FOCUSED CARE

Function-focused care, also commonly referred to as restorative care, is a philosophy of care that focuses on evaluating the older adult's underlying capability with regard to function and physical activity and helping him or her optimize and maintain physical function and ability and continually increase time spent in physical activity. This philosophy of care is one that views physical function as a dynamic process with opportunities for clinicians to promote function for patients of varying levels of capability. Examples of function-focused care (see Table 6.1) interactions include such things as using verbal cues during bathing so the older individual performs the tasks rather than the direct care worker (DCW) bathing the individual; walking a resident or patient to the bathroom rather than the nurse, DCW, or family caregiver giving him or her a urinal or having him or her sit on a commode chair; or taking the patient or resident to an exercise class.

TABLE 6.1
Examples of Function-Focused Care Activities

Function	Example of Function-Focused Care Performed	Examples of When Function-Focused Care Is Not Performed
Bed mobility	Asks or encourages older adult to move in bed and give him or her time to move.	Asks or encourages older adult to move in bed but does not allow time for older adult to respond.
	Gives step-by-step cues on how to move in bed—for example, put your right hand on the rail and pull yourself over on your left side.	Moves older adult without asking older adult to help.
		Pulls older adult up fully on bed without asking older adult to help.
	Places older adult's hands to facilitate independent movement (e.g., on guard rail).	Discourages or stops older adult from performing activity.
		Older adult performed activity but with no involvement or encouragement from direct care worker (DCW).
Transfer from one surface to another	Asks or encourages older adult to transfer and waits for older adult to move.	Asks or encourages older adult to transfer but does not wait for older adult to initiate the transfer and just starts to pull him/her up.
	Gives step-by-step cues on how to transfer (e.g., "slide to the edge of the chair").	Transfers/lifts older adult fully with no encouragement by DCW to have older adult perform any of the transfer.
	Places hands to facilitate independent movement (e.g., places hands on walker).	Discourages or stops older adult from performing activity.
		Older adult performed activity but with no involvement or encouragement from DCW.
Mobility (ambulation/ wheelchair)	Asks or encourages older adult to walk or independently propel wheelchair and gives him or her time to perform activity.	Uses wheelchair instead of encouraging ambulation and does not encourage older adult to self-propel (even short distance/ even with one hand).
	Gives step-by-step cues to get older adult to walk (e.g., "move your left foot forward, now move your right foot").	Discourages or stops older adult from performing activity.
	Assist, ask, and/or encourage use of assistive devices (e.g., Merry Walker, rolling walker, and standing table).	Older adult performed activity but with no involvement or encouragement from DCW.

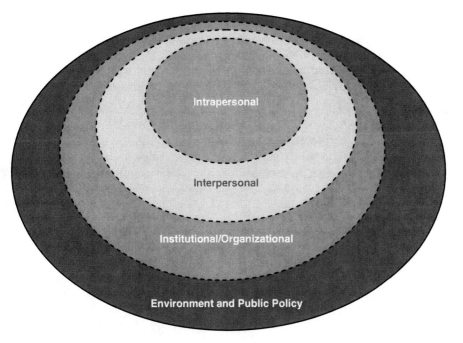

FIGURE 6.1 Social-Ecological Model.

THEORETICAL MODEL TO GUIDE INTEGRATION OF THE FUNCTION-FOCUSED CARE APPROACH

Evidence and knowledge of the benefits of engaging in physical activity or providing care using a function-focused care approach are not sufficient to assure that this will occur in real-world clinical settings. Using a social ecological model (SEM; see Figure 6.1) to guide the implementation of the function-focused care philosophy is necessary as it provides an overarching framework for understanding the interrelations among diverse personal and environmental factors in human health and illness that influence behavior. Specifically, the SEM considers intrapersonal, interpersonal, environmental, and policy factors that can be used to ensure successful implementation of new philosophies of care aligned with health-promoting behaviors. There is increasing recognition that this type of multilevel perspective is needed to address health behavior change and facilitate changes in current care philosophies and care practices (Haughton & Stang, 2012; Li et al., 2012; Pronk & Kottke, 2009).

There are several intrapersonal factors that are relevant to consider as part of the SEM because they can lead to functional limitation, disability, and low physical activity in older adults. These factors include comorbidities, acute medical problems, and psychological factors (e.g., mood and motivation). There are also nonmodifiable intrapersonal factors that should be considered including variables such as age, gender, and race.

Although there is likely an intrapersonal aspect of motivation based on intrinsic personality factors and genetic and epigenetic influences, motivation is also influenced by variables extrinsic to the individual. Bandura (1997, 2004; Bandura & Locke, 2003) conceptualized motivation within the broader spectrum of the theory of self-efficacy. The theory of self-efficacy suggests that the stronger the individual's self-efficacy and outcome expectations, the more likely it is that he or she will initiate and persist with a given activity. Self-efficacy expectations are the individuals' beliefs in their capabilities to perform a course of action to attain a desired outcome; and outcome expectations are the beliefs that a certain consequence will be produced by personal action. Efficacy expectations are dynamic and are both appraised and enhanced by four mechanisms: (a) enactive mastery experience or successful performance of the activity of interest; (b) verbal persuasion or verbal encouragement given by a credible source that the individual is capable of performing the activity of interest; (c) vicarious experience or seeing individuals perform a specific activity; and (d) physiological and affective states such as pain, fatigue, or anxiety associated with a given activity.

At the interpersonal level, the theory of self-efficacy can be used to guide interventions that will strengthen efficacy beliefs among older adults and their caregivers and thereby increase the likelihood that caregivers will implement function-focused care and older adults will engage in functional tasks and physical activity. Specifically, interventions such as the use of verbal encouragement, goal setting, role modeling, mastery or successful performance of an activity, and decreasing or eliminating unpleasant sensations associated with an activity are all ways in which to motivate older adults to engage in physical activity (Galik et al, 2008; Judge, Jackson, Shaw, Scott, & Rich, 2007; McAuley et al., 2006; McAuley et al., 2007; Qi, Resnick, Smeltzer, & Bausell, 2011; Resnick et al., 2008; Resnick et al., 2007).

Environments that facilitate physical activity can reduce functional decline and enable people to achieve their highest level of function and well-being (Bjornsdottir, Arnadottir, & Halldorsdottir, 2012; Carlson et al., 2012; Kalinowski et al., 2012; Rodiek, 2006; Tsunoda et al., 2012). This is true of community-based settings that provide more accessible, pleasant, and safe walking areas as well as nursing home settings that encourage physical activity by providing open walking areas and role models with others walking and exercising, and pleasant destinations to motivate individuals to set as goals (e.g., walking to the coffee shop). Unfortunately, designated exercise space is generally limited in health care settings and the hallways, common areas, and outdoor walkways are seldom used to promote physical activity (Kalinowski et al., 2012; Rodiek, 2006). When environments are evaluated, it is generally only for safety or efficiency of the staff rather than optimizing function or increasing physical activity among residents and patients. Policy initiatives have been successful in changing behaviors in areas such as wearing seat belts and smoking cessation (Castle, 2000; Salzberg & Moffat, 2004). There are currently no specific national policies related to physical activity. Organizational policies, however, within settings of care for older adults that address such things as use of shared space areas, how care is provided, and what expectations are of residents in terms of going to the dining room for meals, having a wheelchair in the dining room, or even having flexible bathing and eating schedules can impact physical activity among residents. If outdoor space for walking is locked and made inaccessible, or if the underlying philosophy or culture within the facility is to provide care rather than optimize function, perceptions and expectations among older adults, staff, and families can be affected, which can lead to functional dependency. Understanding the policies and informal structures in care facilities is a necessary first step to identifying barriers to implementing a function-focused care philosophy and function-focused care relevant interventions.

IMPLEMENTING FUNCTION-FOCUSED CARE

Implementation of function-focused care philosophy into any setting requires an organized approach and the willingness and ability of a champion within the setting to initiate and support the process. The champion might be a nurse, a DCW, or a family member or a friend in the home setting. Regardless of setting or the champion, implementation of this philosophy of care requires a thoughtful process and organized approach. This is best done using the four components (Resnick, Galik, & Boltz, 2013). These components have been used successfully on an individual basis but are most effective when initiated sequentially and used continually until a function-focused care philosophy is integrated into routine care.

The four recommended components include (a) assessment of the environment and policies/procedures or culture within the site of care; (b) education of caregivers, families, and older individuals; (c) establishing function-focused care goals; and (d) motivating and mentoring caregivers, families, and older individuals. An implementation plan can be established to best fit with the needs of each setting.

Component I: Assessment of the Environment and Policies/Procedures

Environment and policy assessments (see Tables 6.2 and 6.3) can be done using brief 19-item checklists and a focus on specific well-known environmental challenges to physical activity such as clutter or inappropriate bed and chair heights. Following

TABLE 6.2

General Assessment of Environment for Function and Physical Activity

Item	Present	Not Present
1. Evidence of area for walking that is clear of clutter		
2. Evidence of area for walking that has rest spots available		
3. Evidence of area for walking that is pleasant		
4. Evidence of area for walking that has pleasant destination areas		
5. Evidence of cues in the environment to encourage physical activity		
6. Evidence of supplies (i.e., safe assistive devices) to encourage function and activity		
7. Chair height appropriate (between 80% and 120% of lower leg length)		
8. Bed height appropriate (between 80% and 120% of lower leg length)		
9. Toilet height appropriate (between 80% and 120% of lower leg length)		
10. Evidence of cues in the environment to encourage functional activity		
11. Access to age appropriate exercise equipment		
12. Access to pleasant outdoor areas		
13. Access to places to sit/rest when walking outdoors		
14. Evidence of poor lighting		
15. Evidence of slippery floors		
16. Evidence of uneven surfaces		
17. Evidence of items that could cause a trip		
18. Evidence of unsafe footwear		

TABLE 6.3

Assessment of Policy/Protocols for Function and Physical Activity

Item	Present	Not Present	Not Applicable
1. Evidence of policy regarding physical restraints that optimizes function and physical activity.			
2. Evidence of policy regarding Foley catheters that optimizes function and physical activity.			
3. Evidence of policy related to use of free space (corridors, kitchens) that optimizes function and physical activity.			
4. Evidence of policy around ambulation that optimizes function and physical activity.			
5. Evidence of policy associated with transportation (in sites) that optimizes function and physical activity.			
6. Evidence of policy associated with bed/chair/toilet height that optimizes function and physical activity.			
7. Evidence of policy change associated with "hand-off" communication that optimizes function and physical activity.			
8. Evidence of policy associated with discharge instructions that optimizes function and physical activity.			
9. Evidence of policy associated with pressure ulcer prevention that optimizes function and physical activity.			
10. Evidence of policy associated with falls prevention that optimizes function and physical activity.			
11. Evidence of policy associated with nursing assessment that addresses and optimizes function and physical activity.			
12. Evidence of policy associated with change in patient condition that addresses and optimizes function and physical activity.			

(Continued)

TABLE 6.3

Assessment of Policy/Protocols for Function and Physical Activity   (Continued)

Item	Present	Not Present	Not Applicable
13. Evidence of policy associated with evaluation of nursing competencies to address function and physical activity of patients.			
14. Evidence of policy associated with documentation of function and physical activity.			
15. Evidence of policy associated with patient/family information that optimizes function and physical activity.			

assessments, recommendations can be made and should include the following evidence-based interventions: visibility of exercise-related areas, walkable spaces, safe walking areas, interesting destinations, appropriate lighting and signage, cues for participating in physical activity (e.g., posters), and availability of age-appropriate exercise equipment(Alessi et al., 2005). Outdoor improvements include ensuring that sidewalks and stairs are safe and accessible, providing greenery and interesting destinations, and assuring adequate shade and seating so older individuals using these areas will feel comfortable outdoors. Policy assessments focus on such things as disclosure statements if in a long-term care setting, individualized plans of care, and policies around falls and fall prevention so that physical activity is encouraged within the messages presented in each of the policies or procedures.

Following assessment of the environment and policies, education about function-focused care should be provided. There are no known best practices with regard to implementation of education for function-focused care (Resnick, Cayo, Galik, & Pretzer-Aboff, 2009). Multiple approaches should be considered (formal and informal education, written information, and face-to-face interactive lectures) and implemented depending on setting and learners.

Although cognitive ability may vary among individuals, older adults across all settings should be provided with a basic review of the philosophy of function-focused care and the benefits of engaging in this type of care. As part of the education, it is helpful to provide families with specific tips about ways in which they can help their family member engage in functional and physical activity. The tips (see Table 6.4) include asking about and reinforcing participation in exercise classes, giving gifts that facilitate function (comfortable sweat pants to wear

TABLE 6.4
10 Tips for Family to Help Promote Restorative Care

1. Ask your family member about setting goals for fitness or activities of daily living (dressing, etc.). Such as going to an exercise class regularly.

2. Find out when exercise classes are held. Help remind them to go—see attached schedule.

3. Try to avoid visits during these times so they can attend class.

4. Or if you come during these times attend the classes with them.

5. Tell them how important exercise is for them to promote overall health; increase strength; reduce falls, fractures, and hospitalizations; and ultimately preventing pain.

6. Tell them about how you like to exercise and what it has done for you.

7. When you come and visit your family member, exercise with them. Go for a walk, do basic range of motion exercises with them, such as rotating their joints (ankles, shoulders, knees, and wrists).

8. For birthday and holiday season, buy them gifts that promote their independence such as scrub mitts for residents that have problems with dexterity, zipper extenders for those that have trouble putting on clothes, and be sure to buy clothes that are easier to put on such as elastic banded pants and pull on shirts or zippered shirts. Hand weights will increase strength.

9. If they have a decline in function, don't think "do everything" for them is the best for them. It is important to promote their function and help them to get back to their baseline as much as possible.

10. Tell them you know they can reach their goals, "You can do it!"; "You look great!"; and that you are proud of them for their effort. A little goes a long way!

during exercise), calling and reminding their loved one to go to exercise class, and using visit time to walk together or engage in some type of physical activity. Once the caregivers and older adults have received some exposure to and information about function-focused care, older individuals receiving function-focused care should be helped to establish appropriate goals. The physical capability assessment (Resnick, Boltz, et al., 2013) considers the underlying capability of the older individual and provides guidance in terms of what should be expected from the individual in terms of participation in routine activities of daily living (bathing, dressing) as well as other types of physical activity (e.g., walking, dancing). To complete the capability assessment (see Table 6.5), the older adult is asked to perform a few simple functional tasks: follow one-, two-, or three-step

TABLE 6.5

Physical Capability Scale

Item	Able to Perform	Not Able to Perform	Directions to Participant	Scoring
Upper extremity range of Motion			The evaluator demonstrates the task for the participant and asks them to do the same thing.	
Full flexion (hands over head)	1	0	The evaluator demonstrates and says, "put your hands over your head like this."	1 = range to 160–180 degrees; 0 = inability to range at least to 160–180 degrees
Full external rotation (hands behind head)	1	0	The evaluator demonstrates and says, "put your hands behind your head like this."	1 = ability to put hands behind head; 0 = inability to put hands behind head.
Full internal rotation and adduction (hands in small of back)	1	0	The evaluator demonstrates and says, "put your hands behind your back this."	1 = ability to put hands together in small of back; 0 = inability to put hands together in small of back.
Lower Extremity Range of Motion				
Able to flex ankle	1	0	When lying or sitting, the participant is asked to point his or her toes to ceiling and to the foot of the bed.	1 = ability to point toes to the ceiling; 0 = inability to point toes to the ceiling.
Able to point toe	1	0	When lying or sitting, the participant asked to point his or her toes to ceiling and to the foot of the bed.	1 = ability to point toes to the foot of the bed/floor; 0 = inability to point toes to the foot of the bed/floor.

TABLE 6.5

Physical Capability Scale   (Continued)

Item	Able to Perform	Not Able to Perform	Directions to Participant	Scoring
Able to flex knees and march	1	0	When sitting the participant is asked to march with knees flexed at 90 degrees.	1 = ability to march with knees flexed; 0 = inability to march.
Chair rise			The participant is asked to rise independently (with or without the use of arm strength) from a standard 18 in. hard back chair with arms and stand.	
How many tries does it take	1–3 tries = 1	Unable to rise with 3 tries = 0		A try is defined as any attempt to push up from the chair. 1 = 1–3 attempts to push up from the chair with success occurring by the third try; 0 = unable to rise even on the third try.
Does the participant use arms to get up from the chair	0	1		1 = ability to get up without arms; 0 = inability to get up without arms.
Can the participant make it to a full stand and stand independently for 1 min	1	0		1 = ability to come to stand for a full minute; 0 = inability to come to stand and stay there for a full minute.

(Continued)

TABLE 6.5

Physical Capability Scale   (Continued)

Item	Able to Perform	Not Able to Perform	Directions to Participant	Scoring
Ability to Follow Commands			The participant is asked to take a towel, fold it in half, and put it on the table (bedside table or bed or whatever appropriate source is available).	
Follows a one-step verbal command	1	0		1 = picks up the towel; 0 = does not pick up the towel.
Follows a two-step verbal command	1	0		1 = picks up the towel and folds it half; 0 = does not pick up the towel or fold it in half.
Follows a three-step verbal command	1	0		1 = picks up the towel, folds it half, and puts it on the table; 0 = does not pick up the towel, fold it in half or put it on the bed.
Follows a three-step visual command			The evaluator demonstrates for the participant how to take a towel, fold it in half and put it on the table (bedside table or bed or whatever source is available).	

TABLE 6.5

Physical Capability Scale   (Continued)

Item	Able to Perform	Not Able to Perform	Directions to Participant	Scoring
Follows a one-step visual command	1	0		1 = picks up the towel; 0 = does not pick up the towel.
Follows a two-step visual command	1	0		1 = picks up the towel and folds it half; 0 = does not pick up the towel or fold it in half.
Follows a three-step visual command	1	0		1 = picks up the towel, folds it half, and puts it on the table; 0 = does not pick up the towel, fold it in half or put it on the bed.

Total score _____

commands; perform upper and lower extremity range of motion; transfer and bear weight bilaterally on lower extremities; and demonstrate normal standing balance. If, for example, the individual has full range of motion and is able to follow at least a one-step command, he or she should be performing bathing and dressing with verbal cues as needed.

Once the other components of function-focused care have been initiated, the champions (or ideally a champion on each unit) provides ongoing motivating and mentoring of caregivers as well as ongoing motivating of older adults (residents and patients) to engage in functional and physical activity. Interventions known to strengthen self-efficacy and outcome expectations in older adults include having the individual successfully perform a recommended physical activity (e.g., walking to the bathroom); verbal encouragement to perform functional and physical activities and positive reinforcement for all efforts; providing positive role models of other similar individuals going to an exercise class or walking to the dining room; and decreasing unpleasant sensations associated with the physical activity (e.g., preventing pain or fear from occurring during the activity or eliminating pain prior to the activity) and increasing positive sensations associated with function and physical activity such as feeling good, less pain, and less shortness of breath with activity. Interventions to increase the self-efficacy and outcome expectations of caregivers to provide function-focused care include working with them to successfully help engage a resident in bathing or dressing or walking; providing verbal encouragement and positive reinforcement for walking a resident; highlighting role models or other caregivers who have provided function-focused care to residents successfully; and decreasing any unpleasant sensations associated with function-focused care such as focusing more on safety than function, requiring burdensome paperwork associated with function-focused care.

Interpersonal interactions are important with regard to motivating older adults to engage in physical activity level. Social support networks that can provide positive interpersonal interactions include family, friends, peers, and health care providers (Resnick, Galik, Gruber-Baldini, & Zimmerman, 2010). Repeatedly, motivation to perform physical activity and exercise has been found to be influenced by the social milieu of the care setting and social interactions and support (Carlson et al., 2012; Martin & Woods, 2012; Singh et al., 2012). Social interactions can influence self-efficacy and outcome expectations and can alter the downward trajectory in function commonly noted among older adults. *Bradykinesia* associated with Parkinson's disease, for example, may have less of an impact on dressing for individuals whose family/caregivers patiently encourage them to dress versus family/caregivers who simply want the task completed in the quickest manner possible. The influence of any member of the resident's social network can be positive or negative depending on his or her philosophy and beliefs related to function-focused care. In some situations, families advocate for maximal care to be provided to their loved one (Resnick et al., 2008; Resnick, Simpson, Galik, et al., 2006). This propagates sedentary behavior, decreases self-efficacy related to function, and can reduce participation in physical activity. In addition to motivating residents, the champion must provide ongoing support and positive reinforcement to all the individuals in the patients'/residents' social network to be sure that they provide and/or support function-focused care during all care and relevant interactions.

EVIDENCE OF EFFECTIVENESS OF FUNCTION-FOCUSED CARE

A recent review (Resnick, Galik, & Boltz, 2013) of function-focused care identified 20 published studies testing this approach (Beck et al., 1995; Blair, Glaister, Brown, & Phillips, 2007; Bonanni et al., 2009; Coyne & Hoskins, 1997; Engelman, Mathews, & Altus, 2002; Galik et al., 2008; Kerse et al., 2008;

Lim, 2003; Morris et al., 1999; Peri et al., 2007; Pretzer-Aboff, Galik, & Resnick, 2011; Remsburg, Armacost, Radu, & Bennett, 1999; Resnick, Simpson, Bercovitz, et al., 2006; Resnick et al., 2011; Resnick, Galik, et al., 2009; J. C. Rogers et al., 1999; Shanti et al., 2004; Tappen, 1994; Tinetti et al., 2002). Of these, 50% were done in a single site and were pilot or descriptive in nature and the other 50% used an experimental design (randomized controlled trials or quasi-experimental design). The studies included all settings of care (acute, assisted living, skilled nursing facilities, etc.) and ranged in size from 3 to 480 older individuals. Most studies ($n = 16$ [80%]), as part of the intervention, provided some education to the caregivers. Nine (45%) of the studies addressed only specific activities of daily living (e.g., bathing or dressing), 2 (10%) addressed physical activity in general, and the remaining 9 (45%) studies considered both activities of daily living and physical activity. Close to half ($n = 9$ [45%]) of the studies addressed motivational issues and implemented approaches to increase motivation to participate in physical activity. The remaining 11 studies (55%) focused the intervention on teaching caregivers skills needed to help the older individual perform an activity (e.g., increasing independence in feeding or dressing).

Most studies ($n = 15$ [75%]) noted some positive outcome/outcomes associated with implementation of a function-focused care approach. Outcomes included activities of daily living, time in physical activity, quality of life, mood, or anxiety. Evaluation of activities of daily living was considered in 15 (75%) of the studies with improvement noted in 9 (60%) of those 15 studies. Depression was considered as an outcome in 9 (45%) of the studies and this was noted to improve in 1 (11%) of the studies, get worse in 2 (22%) of the studies, and remain unchanged in the remaining 6 (67%) studies in which depression was considered. Quality of life was considered in 8 (40%) of the studies and this did not improve in any of the studies. Specifically, quality of life got worse in 1 (12%) of the studies and remained unchanged in 7 (88%) of the studies in which quality of life was considered. Gait and balance was addressed in 7 (35%) of the studies with no change noted in 5 (71%) of the studies and 2 (29%) reporting a significant improvement.

Falls were considered in seven (35%) of the studies and decreased in one (14%) study and remained unchanged either over time or when compared to treatment groups in the other six (86%) studies in which falls were considered. Additional outcomes considered in just few of the studies included such things as grooming, anxiety, and disruptive behavior; motivational factors such as self-efficacy and outcome expectations; and goal attainment. There were no significant differences in terms of demonstrating a positive outcome (of any nature) from function-focused care based on use of an integrated or designated approach ($\chi^2 = .39$, $p = .53$).

EVIDENCE OF EFFECTIVENESS OF FUNCTION-FOCUSED CARE AMONG THOSE WITH MODERATE TO SEVERE COGNITIVE IMPAIRMENT

Three of the studies in the review article (Beck et al., 1995; Coyne & Hoskins, 1997; Galik et al., 2008) focused on those with moderate to severe cognitive impairment. Implementation of function-focused care among these individuals generally resulted in improvements in disruptive behaviors and improvement in mood. Two recently completed randomized controlled trials tested the effectiveness of function-focused care for cognitively impaired nursing home and assisted living residents using a social–ecological approach and facility-based champions to better address system issues and adoption of the intervention by facility staff (Galik, Resnick, Hammersla, & Brightwater, in press; Galik, Resnick, Hammersla, & Lerner, in press). The intervention was implemented more than 6 months and addressed environmental- and policy-related barriers. Resident outcomes in these studies focused on function, physical activity, mood, behavior, antipsychotic medication use, and adverse events.

Results from the nursing home study demonstrated significant improvements in the amount and intensity of resident physical activity (by survey and actigraphy) and physical function in the treatment group, and a decrease in the number of falls. Residents in control sites were more likely to have more symptoms of depression compared to the treatment sites. Generalized behavioral symptoms and psychotropic medication use in both control and treatment sites were lower than the national average for nursing home residents and did not change significantly during the 6-month study. Resistance to care was not objectively measured in these prior studies. Nursing staff in treatment sites, however, reported that engaging cognitively impaired residents in activities of daily living increased their cooperation and decreased their resistance (e.g., turning away, pushing, or hitting) during these care interactions.

However, in the assisted living study, there was no significant difference between the two groups with regard to function (i.e., performance of activities of daily living) over the 6-month study period with the exception of an improvement in self-feeding among those in the treatment group. There were no significant differences between treatment and control sites in terms of overall physical function, physical activity measured by actigraphy, falls, depression, agitation, and psychotropic medication use. Residents in the control group showed an increase in overall time spent in physical activity based on survey results; however, the different subscales evaluated in the physical activity survey indicated that repetitive behaviors were increasing in the control group whereas these repetitive behaviors actually decreased among those in the treatment group with difference being significant at 6 months ($p = .05$). In the assisted living study, there was an additional challenge of staff turnover, particularly in the treatment group. Twenty-two (30%) DCWs left employment (16 [21%] in treatment group) and (6 [8%] in the control group). This made it challenging in terms of consistent delivery of the study intervention. DCW positions remained vacant for some time and current staff was stressed with increased resident assignments. Although the function-focused care nurse provided training to new employees, many new employees were less engaged because they felt "overwhelmed" with just beginning a new job.

The recruited residents of the four dementia special care assisted living facilities had severe cognitive impairment (mean minimum mean square error [MMSE] = 6), had moderate levels of behavioral symptoms that challenged the DCWs in their care delivery. The prevalence of psychotropic medication use at baseline was high with 62% of residents in the treatment group and 38% of in the control group receiving an antipsychotic. In addition, 32% of residents in the treatment group and 68% of residents in the control group were receiving anxiolytics at baseline. The high prevalence of psychotropic medication use likely had an adverse effect on the achievement of functional and physical activity resident goals.

EVIDENCE FOR DISSEMINATION AND IMPLEMENTATION OF FUNCTION-FOCUSED CARE

Dissemination focuses on the distribution of information, whereas implementation is the process through which an intervention such as function-focused care is communicated over time through certain channels of a social system (E. M. Rogers, 2003). Disseminating and implementing innovative approaches to nursing care across any setting is challenging and associated with many factors. As per the dissemination of innovation (DOI) theory, these include attributes of the innovation, communication channels within settings, timing, and social systems within which the intervention is implemented (E. M. Rogers, 2003).

DOI suggests that the following four key components influence implementation and therefore should be carefully considered when implementing any new type of care innovation:

1. Attributes of the innovation—(a) relative advantage, or the degree to which the innovation is perceived to be better than prior care/activity; (b) compatibility, or the degree to which an innovation fits with existing values, experiences, and needs of adopters; (c) complexity, or the degree to which an innovation is perceived as difficult to understand and use; (d) trialability, or the ability to experiment with an intervention on a limited basis; and (e) observability, which is evidence of positive outcomes associated with the intervention.

2. Communication through certain channels (e.g., interpersonal, mass media).
3. Timing of the intervention.
4. The structure and impact of the social system that includes change agents, opinion leaders, and champions.

An opinion leader is an individual who is able to influence other individuals with regard to attitudes or behavior in a desired way with relative frequency. This is not the "job" of the opinion leader in a specific setting but more of an assumed or acquired role. Change agents are individuals who influence others to make innovative decisions in a direction that is believed to be desirable. Change agents and opinion leaders often work together in settings to facilitate the changes desired to occur. A champion is a charismatic individual who is dedicated to the innovation and overcoming indifference or resistance among others. Addressing these factors is critical to successful implementation of a function-focused care approach.

CHALLENGES TO DISSEMINATION AND IMPLEMENTATION OF FUNCTION-FOCUSED CARE

There are many challenges and barriers to dissemination and implementation of evidence-based interventions such as function-focused care into any care setting or with any population. In health care facilities, when implementing interventions that require involvement of nursing staff, the challenges have included such things as beliefs about the use and feasibility of the new approach, insufficient training, insufficient recognition and support from administration, inadequate staffing, workload concerns, staff turnover, costs, lack of fit between the intervention and culture or philosophy of care within the community, lack of appropriate resources, inappropriate policies, fear and focus on protecting oneself and the residents from a possible fall, and the physical environment (e.g., bed and chair height, open walkways; Beck et al., 2005; Lekan-Rutledge, Palmer, & Belyea, 1998; Resnick, Galik, Gruber-Baldini, & Zimmerman, 2013; Schnelle et al., 2002). When trying to implement an approach that increases time spent in physical activity, there are also challenges to changing the behavior of the residents or patients. Barriers to engaging older patients or residents in physical activity include such things as their underlying cognitive and physical abilities, delirium, depressed mood, poor perceived health status, lack of motivation, cultural expectations, pain, fear of falling, body mass index, and polypharmacotherapy and drug side effects, nutritional status and expectations of the health care system and caregivers (Brown, Williams, Woodby, Davis, & Allman, 2007; Ouslander, Griffiths, McConnell, Riolo, Kutner, & Schnelle, 2005; Resnick et al., 2008).

DISSEMINATION AND IMPLEMENTATION APPROACH

To address the many potential barriers at the staff, resident, and community level, a dissemination and implementation approach was developed incorporating the previously described SEM and social cognitive theory to facilitate the necessary behavior change and change in philosophy of care needed to successfully implement function-focused care among caregivers and older adults (Resnick et al., in press). Guided by these multiple frameworks, function-focused care was disseminated and implemented into 4 and then into 20 assisted living facilities in Maryland (Resnick, Boltz, et al., 2013; Resnick, Galik, Vigne, in press). The approach used to disseminate and implement function-focused care across multiple sites is shown in Table 6.6. To evaluate the dissemination and implementation approach, the Reach, Effectiveness, Adoption, Implementation and Maintenance (RE-AIM) model (Glasgow, Toobert, Hampson, & Strycker, 2002) was used. Components of the model and how each component was evaluated in the 4 sites and the 20 sites dissemination and implementation studies are shown in Table 6.7.

DISSEMINATION AND IMPLEMENTATION IN THE FOUR-SITE STUDY

The four-site study included four assisted living facilities that had at least 100 residents each. Reach was demonstrated by our ability to recruit about 50% of the eligible residents. Across all sites, we recruited 65%of the DCWs into the study. None of the residents or DCWs requested to be removed from the study. In all sites, all DCWs were invited and encouraged to attend the educational sessions, information about function-focused care was provided for all staff, and all residents were exposed to function-focused care approaches. Our reach in these sites was further supported by evidence of participation in function-focused care activities among residents and staff who did not consent to the research evaluation. For example, all DCWs, even those who had not consented to participate in the study, documented when they provided function-focused care, helped develop function-focused goals for residents, and rewarded residents when they engaged in physical activity. Nonconsented residents likewise participated in exercise classes offered and associated function-focused care activities. Furthermore, qualitative reports indicated that nonconsented residents spoke with administrative staff in the communities to make sure that all new physical activity programs started during the study would continue after the study's termination.

Efficacy/Effectiveness was established based on the major study outcomes. Observations of DCWs during care interactions provided evidence that the

TABLE 6.6

Description of the Dissemination and Implementation Process of Function-Focused Care

Implementation Process	Description of Activities
Identification and training of champions	Part of the eligibility criteria for sites was that they had to identify an inhouse champion to work with us to implementation function-focused care in their settings.

Half day face-to-face training of the champions by the function-focused nurse facilitator (an individual with experience implementing function-focused care). Training focused on learning the four components used to implement function-focused care.

I. Environmental and Policy Assessments	• Champions were taught to use the Environment and Policy/Procedures for Function and Physical Activity Evaluation Forms to assess their physical environments and policies.
II. Education	• Champions were provided with resources and taught how to educate nursing staff, other members of the interdisciplinary team (e.g., social work, physical therapy), residents and families about function-focused care. As requested, the nurse facilitator would also help with staff and family education.
III. Establishing Function-Focused Care Goals for Residents	• Champions were taught to evaluate residents underlying physical capability using the Physical Capability Assessments and develop goals for residents using the Goal Attainment Forms and/or to incorporate the goals into the service plan.
	• Champions were given the resources to teach staff how to do these assessments as well.

TABLE 6.6

Description of the Dissemination and Implementation Process of
Function-Focused Care   (Continued)

Implementation Process	Description of Activities
IV. Mentoring and Motivating	• The champions were taught the techniques to motivate resident and motivate their staff to engage in function-focused care approaches: (a) observe performance of caregivers and residents and provide one-on-one mentoring of the caregivers to incorporate function-focused care into routine care; (b) provided caregivers with positive reinforcement for providing function-focused care and residents for engaging in physical activity; (b) talk with caregivers about their beliefs related to function-focused care and their experiences in providing this type of care; (c) reinforce benefits of function-focused care to caregivers and residents; (d) highlight role models; (e) identify change aides and positive opinion leaders; and (f) eliminate the influence of negative opinion leaders.

Monthly Face-to-Face Follow Up Visits by the Nurse Facilitator

• Environment and policy findings were reviewed during the first face-to-face meeting with the nurse facilitator.

• The nurse facilitator worked with the champion to identify appropriate and affordable interventions to alter environments and policies/procedures to optimize function and physical activity of residents.

• Education of staff, residents, and families was reviewed with the nurse facilitator during face-to-face visits and the nurse facilitator helped with education as needed.

• Monthly visits focused motivational challenges among staff and residents, sharing of innovative approaches to integrate physical activity into routine activities within the setting, and ongoing education about assessment of residents and identification of goals.

• Weekly e-mails were sent to all champions that provided additional resources and information about function focus and encouraged champions to share their successes and get help with their challenges.

TABLE 6.7

RE-AIM Evaluation Process for Dissemination and Implementation Studies

RE-AIM Model	4-Site Study	20-Site Study
Reach refers to the proportion of representativeness of the population targeted by the innovation.	Study consent/ recruitment rates Class sign in lists for the staff Qualitative data and reports of involvement of non-consented residents and staff.	Site recruitment rates and training class participation by the champions; total number of residents potentially impacted by function-focused care.
Efficacy refers to the extent to which the intervention improved outcomes of participants.	Measurement of function of residents using the Barthel Index; Actigraphy data from residents wearing the ActiGraph; observation of staff during care interactions using the Restorative Care Behavior Checklist.	Pre and post 12 months period assessments of the environment, policy, and service plans; measurement of resident falls and hospital transfers prior to and at the end of the study period.
Adoption refers to the proportion of organizations or settings that adopt the innovation.	Community identification of a champion; adherence of champion to meetings and participation in function-focused care activities; Evidence of changes in environment based on Person–Environment Fit scores for residents and community wide changes in policy and environment.	Setting identification of a champion and adherence of the champion to meetings and participation in function-focused care activities; Evidence of changes in environment, policies, and service plans.

TABLE 6.7

RE-AIM Evaluation Process for Dissemination and Implementation Studies   (Continued)

RE-AIM Model	4-Site Study	20-Site Study
Implementation is the assessment of treatment fidelity or assurance that function-focused care has been implemented as intended	Delivery: Evidence of delivery of Components I–IV. Receipt: Evidence of increased knowledge on the part of the direct care workers. Enactment: Documentation that function-focused care was provided on a daily basis.	Delivery was based on evidence that the initial face-to-face training of champions was completed and that all champions (often with the help of the nurse facilitator) provided education in their settings; that environment and policy assessments were completed and reviewed; that residents were evaluated for capability and service plans adjusted; that mentoring and motivating of the champions continued with weekly e-mails and monthly visits to settings; and champions motivated staff in their settings.
Maintenance refers to the long-term adherence to the intervention and transition of the intervention into routine care.	Review of environment and policy changes that reflected ongoing changes to integrate function-focused care. Evidence that function-focused care activities initiated were maintained over time in the settings (e.g., education of new staff, exercise classes for residents, motivational interventions).	Review of environment and policy changes that reflected ongoing changes to integrate function-focused care. Evidence that function-focused care activities were maintained over time in the settings (e.g., exercise classes for residents, motivational interventions).

DCWs increased the amount of time they spent providing function-focused care approaches during routine care activities (Resnick, Boltz, et al., 2013). Outcome findings related to residents were based on functional outcomes and time spent in physical activity. Residents in both treatment and control groups showed a decline in function over 12 months, with the decline significantly larger in the control versus the treatment group (Resnick, Boltz, et al., 2013). There were no significant differences between treatment groups with regard to actigraphy (objective monitoring of physical activity), although positive trends were noted. Residents in the intervention group showed a greater increase in the amount of time spent in moderate level physical activity at 4 months ($p = .08$).

There was some evidence of adoption of the intervention in that all organization leaders of the communities approached were willing to participate in the study and identified a champion to work with the research supported nurse facilitator. In both treatment communities, however, the champions who were initially identified resigned (not because of their role in Function Focused Care for Assisted Living [FFC-AL]) and new champions were identified by administration. The champions' greatest challenges to more active involvement were other job demands and not because they disagreed with the purpose and content of the program. Although it took approximately six months to establish regular meetings with community champions, by the end of the 12-month intervention period the champions were able to perform oversight of function-focused care activities and there were plans in place for future activities (e.g., ongoing exercise classes).

Adoption of function-focused care was further supported based on evidence of changes in the physical environments of communities with resultant improvements in residents' personal environment and assuring that their fit with the environment optimized physical activity (e.g., more appropriate bed and chair height, removal of clutter). There was, over the 12-month intervention period, a significant decrease in environmental barriers to physical activity with regard to the outside environment, entrances, and indoor environments. The changes resulted in allowing residents easier access in and out of the buildings and more opportunities to engage in physical activity outside of the facility (e.g., safe walking paths were developed).

Treatment fidelity, or implementation of the intervention as intended, was demonstrated based on the ability of the nurse facilitator to work with site champions and implement all components of function-focused care. Starting with Component I, the comprehensive assessment of the environment and community-based policies and culture of care were evaluated at the onset of the intervention activities and information used to make changes in the settings to encourage physical activity among the residents. Component II focused on education of staff, families, and residents and was delivered as intended via face-to-face encounters or by providing written materials. Receipt of the intervention (following delivery of the educational component of function-focused care) was evaluated using a paper and pencil test to consider if DCWs demonstrate an increase in their knowledge about function-focused care. All of the DCWs demonstrated an increase in their knowledge over the 12-month study period.

Component III, completing resident assessments and developing goals and changing service plans was implemented in a collaborative effort by the nurse facilitator, site champion, resident, staff, and physical therapist as appropriate (i.e., if the therapist had recently worked with the resident). Goals were established for all participating residents and reevaluated monthly throughout the course of the intervention period. Approximately 10% of study participants did not establish goals with the nurse facilitator and/or site champion because of cognitive challenges or refusal.

Lastly, there was evidence that Component IV, which focused on mentoring and motivating staff, was successfully implemented. Motivational feedback was provided formally to the DCWs during monthly observations of each consented DCW during caregiver interactions. DCWs were recognized with gold stars on a bulletin board to indicate exemplary performance of function-focused care during these observations. To motivate residents, a reward program, "Gifts of the Heart," was initiated. This involved giving tokens to residents who engaged in functional tasks or other types of physical activity (e.g., a resident who walked to the dining room or attended an exercise class).

Maintenance of function-focused care over time in these settings was demonstrated based on permanent changes in the physical environment of the sites, service plan forms, marketing materials, and job descriptions of the DCWs. Environmental changes included such things as flyers and bulletin boards in treatment communities reflecting the positive benefits of physical activity and encouraging residents to engage in these activities. In addition, as recommended by the nurse facilitator and site champions, chairs were strategically placed along clear pathways appropriate for walking to encourage residents to walk these areas and yet provide appropriate rest areas. Treatment sites explored affordable ways in which to alter their outdoor environments to be safer and allow for and encourage walking. Another way in which maintenance of the intervention was demonstrated was based on continuation of exercise classes initiated during the study. The activities staff incorporated combined aerobic and resistive exercise programs, initiated during the study by the nurse facilitator, into their activity programming. Furthermore, dance classes and a walking club replaced more sedentary activities. The Gifts of the Heart program was also adopted by the staff and supported by administration financially by supplying the gifts. Lastly, maintenance of a function-focused care approach was further demonstrated through changes in marketing materials, staff orientation, and service plans. Marketing materials were revised to reflect a care approach that facilitated physical activity versus just providing services. Anticipating the high turnover of staff commonly noted in long-term care environments, we worked with appropriate organizational leaders to develop educational materials that were incorporated into new staff orientation. Lastly, service plan forms were revised to include a section on function-focused care activities.

EVALUATION OF DISSEMINATION AND IMPLEMENTATION IN THE 20-SITE STUDY

Reach in the 20-site dissemination and implementation study was based on being able to recruit these sites from the approximately 170 settings reached via e-mail invitations. Initially, 23 sites were interested and 20 volunteered to participate in the study, identified a champion, and attended the face-to-face training. Working with these 20 assisted living facilities, approximately 1,000 residents were impacted.

Efficacy/effectiveness in these sites was based on demonstrating change in the environments and the policies within settings to make them more likely to encourage residents to engage in physical activity. Objective evidence of improvement was noted with overall improved scores on both assessments. In addition, there was an overall decrease in the number of falls that occurred in these settings and no change in hospitalizations and emergency room visits.

Adoption of function-focused care was noted based on the willingness of the 20 sites to send a champion to attend the face-to-face education. Of these initial 20, 18 champions were willing to work with the nurse facilitator during monthly visits to complete the environment and policy assessments and participate in staff, family, and resident education and ongoing implementation of integrating a function-focused care approach. The champions worked with the nurse facilitator and identified site change agents and positive opinion leaders and brainstormed on ways to manage negative opinion leaders. Two sites refused to meet with the nurse facilitator monthly, complete the environment and policy assessment forms, and address function and physical activity of their residents. These sites were willing, however, to remain on the listserv and receive weekly information about function-focused care. Their reasons for not participating were time constraints given other initiatives within the settings.

Implementation of the function-focused care approach was done as intended in the 18 sites willing to work with the nurse facilitator. Setting up monthly meetings was more challenging in some of the sites than others and in several the nurse facilitator simply visited monthly without setting an appointment with the champion. The sites varied in terms of how they educated staff, residents, and families. Some did this during in-service educational sessions and had the nurse facilitator attend and help with the education. Others provided written materials to staff and smaller settings provided informal education by the champion to staff, residents, and families. Evaluation of the environment and policies was done in all settings and these findings were reviewed with the nurse facilitator and changes made. Champions found it challenging to evaluate residents underlying capability and establish goals and ongoing training at the bedside during monthly visits was done to try and facilitate this process. Sites found it easier to implement multicomponent interventions (i.e., interventions that are implemented throughout the setting for all residents) such as requiring that *all* residents walk or self-propel to meals and increasing physical activity options for activities during the course of the day and setting up walking paths within and around the facility.

As intended, weekly e-mails were sent to all champions during the course of the 12-month intervention period. Feedback from champions indicated that the information was shared with other facilities that were owned and operated by the same individual or organization. Approximately half of the sites responded to e-mails and participated in contests held via our weekly e-mails during the course of the study (e.g., picture contests at holiday time for the best pictures of residents in holiday-related physical activities).

Maintenance of function-focused care over time was based on integrating enduring changes in service plans, marketing materials, policy, and environmental changes and altering the culture to one in which there was a focus on increasing physical activity among the residents. Objectively, the sites made significant changes in their environments that we considered evidence of maintenance of function-focused care. Examples of changes included development of pleasant walking paths, rest areas to encourage safe walking across long walkways or outdoors, and availability of resources that encourage physical activities (e.g., resistance weights, ergometers, and games such as golf or bean bag toss). Sites varied greatly in terms of the type of forms used for service plans and the sophistication of the marketing materials. Most sites handwrote their service plans and were not willing to change items on the forms. Wording changes were made, however, in many of these sites so that the care provided would encourage the resident to engage in an activity versus simply stating what the caregiver would do for the resident (e.g., dress, brush teeth, put on shoes). In several sites, we recommended wording and formatting changes in their service forms to encourage staff to provide care that would increase physical activity. With regard to marketing materials, some sites had very well developed glossy marketing materials and others had simple printed flyers. Marketing flyers in a group of the smaller sites were changed to indicate that the site provided a philosophy of care that would "maintain the resident's independence by sustaining independent or semi-independent functioning in a daily living environment." In addition, one of the sites provided evidence of maintenance of a function-focused care approach in that the owners were opening a new facility and the facility was to be one that specifically provided function-focused care for older adults with cognitive impairment.

CONCLUSION

Function-focused care is an approach to care that is evidence based in terms of physical and mental health benefits for older adults and the negative impact that sedentary behavior has in terms of contributing to deconditioning, pressure ulcers, falls, infections, and exacerbation of underlying comorbidities such as osteoarthritis. There are now more than 20 studies supporting the benefits of function-focused care approaches across all settings and different types of patient groups (i.e., those with mild vs. moderate to severe cognitive impairment). The approaches for implementation of function-focused care have also been well supported and have moved beyond establishing effectiveness to considering dissemination and implementation of this approach into real world clinical settings. The process of dissemination and implementation has likewise been articulated and supported and ongoing work needs to continue in this venue across all settings of care.

REFERENCES

Alessi, C. A., Martin, J. L., Webber, A. P., Cynthia Kim, E., Harker, J. O., & Josephson, K. R. (2005). Randomized, controlled trial of a nonpharmacological intervention to improve abnormal sleep /wake patterns in nursing home residents. *Journal of the American Geriatrics Society*, *53*(5), 803–810.

Allen, K., & Morey, M. C. (2010). Physical activity and adherence. In H. Bosworth (Ed.), *Improving patient treatment adherence*. New York, NY: Springer Science+Business Media, LLC.

Aoyagi, Y., & Shephard, R. J. (2009). Steps per day: The road to senior health? *Sports Medicine*, *39*(6), 423–438.

Bandura, A. (1997). *Self-efficacy: The exercise of control*. New York, NY: W. H. Freeman and Company.

Bandura, A. (2004). Health promotion by social cognitive means. *Health Education & Behavior*, *31*(2), 143–164.

Bandura, A., & Locke, E. A. (2003). Negative self-efficacy and goal effects revisited. *Journal of Applied Psychology*, *88*(1), 17–99.

Beck, C., Heacock, P., Mercer, S., Doan, R., O'Sullivan, P., Stevenson, J., . . . Hoskins, J. (2005). Sustaining a best-care practice in a nursing home. *Journal of Healthcare Quality*, *27*(4), 5–16.

Beck, C., Heacock, P., Mercer, S., Walls, R. C., Rapp, C. G., & Vogelpohl, T. S. (1995). Dressing behavior in nursing home residents. *Nursing Research*, *46*(3), 126–132.

Bergman, P., Grjibovski, A. M., Hagströmer, M., Bauman, A., & Sjöström, M. (2008). Adherence to physical activity recommendations and the influence of socio-demographic correlates—A population-based cross-sectional study. *BMC Public Health*, *8*, 367. http://dx.doi. org/10.1186/1471-2458-8-367

Bjornsdottir, G., Arnadottir, S. A., & Halldorsdottir, S. (2012). Facilitators of and barriers to physical activity in retirement communities: Experiences of older women in urban areas. *Physical Therapy*, *92*(4), 551–562.

Blair, C. E., Glaister, J., Brown, A., & Phillips, C. (2007). Fostering activities of daily living by intact nursing home residents. *Educational Gerontology, 33*, 679–699.

Bonanni, D. R., Devers, G., Dezzi, K., Duerr, C., Durkin, M., Hernan, J., & Joyce, C. (2009). A dedicated approach to restorative nursing. *Journal of Gerontological Nursing, 35*(1), 37–44.

Brown, C. J., Williams, B. R., Woodby, L. L., Davis, L. L., & Allman, R. M. (2007). Barriers to mobility during hospitalization from the perspectives of older patients and their nurses and physicians. *Journal of Hospital Medicine, 2*(5), 305–313.

Carlson, J. A., Sallis, J. F., Conway, T. L., Saelens, B. E., Frank, L. D., Kerr, J., . . . King, A. C. (2012). Interactions between psychosocial and built environment factors in explaining older adults' physical activity. *Preventive Medicine, 54*(1), 68–73.

Castle, N. G. (2000). Differences in nursing homes with increasing and decreasing use of physical restraints. *Medical Care, 38*(12), 1154–1163.

Chang, Y., Pan, C., Chen, F. Z., Tsai, C. L., & Huang, C. C. (2012). Effect of resistance-exercise training on cognitive function in healthy older adults: A review. *Journal of Aging & Physical Activity, 20*(4), 497–517.

Chou, C., Hwang, C. L., & Wu, Y. T. (2012). Effect of exercise on physical function, daily living activities, and quality of life in the frail older adults: A meta-analysis. *Archives of Physical Medicine & Rehabilitation, 93*(2), 237–244.

Coyne, M. L., & Hoskins, L. (1997). Improving eating behaviors in dementia using behavioral strategies. *Clinical Nursing Research, 6*(3), 275–290.

Diehr, P., & Hirsch, C. (2010). Health benefits of increased walking for sedentary, generally healthy older adults: Using longitudinal data to approximate an intervention trial. *Journals of Gerontology. Series A, Biological Sciences and Medical Sciences, 65*(9), 982–989.

Engelman, K. K., Mathews, R. M., & Altus, D. E. (2002). Restoring dressing independence in persons with Alzheimer's disease: A pilot study. *American Journal of Alzheimer's Disease and Other Dementias, 17*(1), 37–43.

Galik, E. M., Resnick, B., Gruber-Baldini, A., Nahm, E. S., Pearson, K., & Pretzer-Aboff, I. (2008). Pilot testing of the restorative care intervention for the cognitively impaired. *Journal of the American Medical Directors Association, 9*(7), 516–522.

Galik, E., Resnick, B., Hammersla, M., & Brightwater, J. (in press). Testing the impact of Res-Care-CI among cognitively impaired nursing home residents. Manuscript submitted for publication.

Galik, E., Resnick, B., Hammersla, M., & Lerner, N. (in press). Testing the impact of Res-Care-CI among residents in assisted living. Manuscript submitted for publication.

Galik, E. M., Resnick, B., & Pretzer-Aboff, I. (2009). Knowing what makes them tick: Motivating cognitively impaired older adults to participate in restorative care. *International Journal of Nursing Practice, 15*(1), 48–55.

Glasgow, R. E., Toobert, D. J., Hampson, S. E., & Strycker, L. A. (2002). Implementation, generalization and long-term results of the "choosing well" diabetes self-management intervention. *Patient Education and Counseling, 48*(2), 115–122.

Haughton, B., & Stang, J. (2012). Population risk factors and trends in health care and public policy. *Journal of the Academy of Nutrition & Dietetics, 112*(3), S35–S46.

Hughes, S., Leith, K. H., Marquez, D. X., Moni, G., Nguyen, H. Q., Desai, P., & Jones, D. L. (2011). Physical activity and older adults: Expert consensus for a new research agenda. *The Gerontologist, 51*(6), 822–832.

Judge, T. A., Jackson, C. L., Shaw, J. C., Scott, B. A., & Rich, B. L. (2007). Self-efficacy and work related performance: The integral role of individual differences. *Journal of Applied Psychology, 92*(1), 107–127.

Kalinowski, S., Wulff, I., Kölzsch, M., Kopke, K., Kreutz, R., & Dräger, D. (2012). Physical activity in nursing homes—Barriers and facilitators: A cross-sectional study. *Journal of Aging and Physical Activity, 20*(4), 421–441.

Kerse, N., Peri, K., Robinson, E., Wilkinson, T., von Randow, M., Kiata, L., . . . Arroll, B. (2008). Does a functional activity programme improve function, quality of life, and falls for residents in long term care? Cluster randomised controlled trial. *British Medical Journal, 337*, a1445.

Kolt, G., Schofield, G. M., Kerse, N., Garrett, N., Ashton, T., & Patel, A. (2012). Healthy steps trial: Pedometer-based advice and physical activity for low-active older adults. *Annals of Family Medicine, 10*(3), 206–212.

Lekan-Rutledge, D., Palmer, M. H., & Belyea, M. (1998). In their own words: Nursing assistants' perceptions of barriers to implementation of prompted voiding in long-term care. *The Gerontologist, 38*(3), 370–378.

Li, K., Seo, D. C., Torabi, M. R., Peng, C. Y. J., Kay, N. S., & Kolbe, L. J. (2012). Social-ecological factors of leisure-time physical activity in Black adults. *American Journal of Health Behavior, 36*(6), 797–810.

Lim, Y. (2003). Nursing intervention for grooming of elders with mild cognitive impairments in Korea. *Geriatric Nursing, 24*(1), 11–15.

Martin, A., & Woods, C. B. (2012). What sustains long-term adherence to structured physical activity after a cardiac event? *Journal of Aging and Physical Activity, 20*(2), 135–147.

Matthews, C., Chen, K. Y., Freedson, P. S., Buchowski, M. S., Beech, B. M., Pate, R. R., & Troiano, R. P. (2008). Amount of time spent in sedentary behaviors in the United States, 2003–2004. *American Journal of Epidemiology, 167*(7), 875–881.

McAuley, E., Konopack, J. F., Motl, R. W., Morris, K. S., Doerksen, S. E., & Rosengren, K. R. (2006). Physical activity and quality of life in older adults: Influence of health status and self-efficacy. *Annals of Behavioral Medicine, 31*(1), 99–103.

McAuley, E., Morris, K. S., Doerksen, S. E., Motl, R. W., Liang, H., White, S. M., . . . Rosengren, K. (2007). Effects of change in physical activity on physical function limitations in older women: Mediating roles of physical function performance and self-efficacy. *Journal of the American Geriatrics Society, 55*(12), 1967–1973.

Morris, J. N., Fiatarone, M., Kiely, D. K., Belleville-Taylor, P., Murphy, K., Littlehale, S., . . . Doyle, N. (1999). Nursing rehabilitation and exercise strategies in the nursing home. *Journal of Gerontology. Series A, Biological Sciences and Medical Sciences, 54*, M494–M500.

Netz, Y., Goldsmith, R., Shimony, T., Ben-Moshe, Y., & Zeev, A. (2011). Adherence to physical activity recommendations in older adults: An Israeli national survey. *Journal of Aging and Physical Activity, 19*(1), 30–47.

Ouslander, J. G., Griffiths, P., McConnell, E., Riolo, L., Kutner, M., & Schnelle, J. (2005). Functional incidental training: A randomized, controlled, crossover trial in Veterans Affairs nursing homes. *Journal of the American Geriatrics Society, 53*, 1091–1100.

Peri, K., Kerse, N., Robinson, E., Parsons, M., Parsons, J., & Latham, N. (2007). Does functionally based activity make a difference to health status and mobility? A randomised controlled trial in residential care facilities (The Promoting Independent Living Study; PILS). *Age Ageing, 10*, 1–7.

Pretzer-Aboff, I., Galik, E., & Resnick, B. (2011). Testing the impact of Res-Care Parkinson's disease. *Nursing Research, 60*(4), 276–283.

Pronk, N., & Kottke, T. E. (2009). Physical activity promotion as a strategic corporate priority to improve worker health and business performance. *Preventive Medicine, 49*(4), 316–320.

Qi, B., Resnick, B., Smeltzer, S., & Bausell, B. (2011). Self-efficacy enhanced education program in preventing osteoporosis among Chinese immigrants: A randomized controlled trial. *Nursing Research, 60*, 393–404.

Remsburg, R., Armacost, K., Radu, C., & Bennett, R. (1999). Two models of restorative nursing care in the nursing home: Designated versus integrated restorative nursing assistants. *Geriatric Nursing, 20*, 321–326.

Resnick, B., Boltz, M., Galik, E., & Wells, C. (2013). Reliability and validity of the physical capability assessment. *Clinical Nursing Research, 22*, 7–29.

Resnick, B., Cayo, J., Galik, E., & Pretzer-Aboff, I. (2009). Implementation of the 6-week educational component in the Res-Care intervention: Process and outcomes. *Journal of Continuing Education*, 40, 353–360.

Resnick, B., Galik, E., & Boltz, M. (2013). Function focused care approaches: Literature review of progress and future possibilities. *Journal of the American Medical Directors Association*, 14(5), 313–318.

Resnick, B., Galik, E., Gruber-Baldini, A., & Zimmerman, S. (2009). Implementing a restorative care philosophy of care in assisted living: Pilot testing of Res-Care-AL. *Journal of the American Academy of Nurse Practitioners*, 21(2), 123–133.

Resnick, B., Galik, E., Gruber-Baldini, A., & Zimmerman, S. (2010). Perceptions and performance of function and physical activity in assisted living communities. *Journal of the American Medical Directors Association*, 11(6), 406–414.

Resnick, B., Galik, E., Gruber-Baldini, A., & Zimmerman, S. (2011). Testing the effect of function-focused care in assisted living. *Journal of the American Geriatrics Society*, 59(12), 2233–2240.

Resnick, B., Galik, E., Gruber-Baldini, A., & Zimmerman, S. (2012). Falls and fall-related injuries associated with function-focused care. *Clinical Nursing Research*, 21, 34–54.

Resnick, B., Galik, E., Gruber-Baldini, A., & Zimmerman, S. (2013). Understanding dissemination and implementation of a new intervention in assisted living settings: The case of function-focused care. *Journal of Applied Gerontology*, 32(3), 280–301.

Resnick, B., Galik, E., Petzer-Aboff, I., Rogers, V., & Gruber-Baldini, A. (2008). Testing the reliability and validity of self-efficacy and outcome expectations of restorative care performed by nursing assistants. *Journal of Nursing Care Quality*, 23(2), 162–169.

Resnick, B., Galik, E., & Vigne, E. (in press). Dissemination and implementation of function focused care to assisted living facilities. Manuscript submitted for publication.

Resnick, B., Gruber-Baldini, A., Galik, E., Pretzer-Aboff, I., Russ, K., Hebel, J., & Zimmerman, S. I. (2009). Changing the philosophy of care in long-term care: Testing of the restorative care intervention. *The Gerontologist*, 49(2), 175–184.

Resnick, B., Orwig, D., Hawkes, W., Hebel, R., Zimmerman, S., Golden, J., & Magaziner, J. (2007). Testing the reliability and validity of the self-efficacy and outcome expectation measures for exercise in older women post hip fracture. *Western Journal of Nursing Research*, 28(5), 586–601.

Resnick, B., Pretzer-Aboff, I., Galik, E., Russ, K., Cayo, J., Simpson, M., & Zimmerman, S. (2008). Barriers and benefits to implementing a restorative care intervention in nursing homes. *Journal of the American Medical Directors Association*, 9(2), 102–108.

Resnick, B., Simpson, M., Bercovitz, A., Galik, E., Gruber-Baldini, A., Zimmerman, S., & Magaziner, J. (2006). Pilot testing of the restorative care program: Impact on residents. *Journal of Gerontological Nursing*, 2, 11–14.

Resnick, B., Simpson, M., Galik, E., Bercovitz, A., Gruber-Baldini, A., Zimmerman, S., & Magaziner, J. (2006). Making a difference: Nursing assistants' perspectives of restorative care nursing. *Rehabilitation Nursing*, 31(2), 78–86.

Rodiek, S. (2006). Resident perceptions of physical environment features that influence outdoor usage at assisted living facilities. *Journal of Housing for the Elderly*, 19(3–4), 95–107.

Rogers, E. M. (2003). *Diffusion of innovations, 5th Edition*. New York, NY: Free Press.

Rogers, J. C., Holm, M., Burgio, L., Granieri, E., Hsu, C., Hardin, J., & McDowell, B. (1999). Improving morning care routines of nursing home residents with dementia. *Journal of the American Geriatrics Society*, 47, 1049–1057.

Rueggeberg, R., Wrosch, C., & Miller, G. E. (2012). The different roles of perceived stress in the association between older adults' physical activity and physical health. *Health Psychology*, 31(2), 164–171.

Salzberg, P., & Moffat, J. M. (2004). Ninety five percent: An evaluation of law, policy, and programs to promote seat belt use in Washington state. *Journal of Safety Research*, 35(2), 215–222.

Scherder, E. J. H., Bogen, T., Eggermont, L. H. P., Hamers, J. P. H., & Swaab, D. F. (2010). The more physical inactivity, the more agitation in dementia. *International Psychogeriatrics / IPA*, 22(8), 1203–1208.

Schnelle, J. F., Alessi, C. A., Simmons, S. F., Al-Samarrai, N. R., Beck, J. C., & Ouslander, J. G. (2002). Translating clinical research into practice: A randomized controlled trial of exercise and incontinence care with nursing home residents. *Journal of the American Geriatrics Society*, 50, 1476–1483.

Shanti, C., Johnson, J., Meyers, A. M., Jones, G. R., Fitzgerald, C., Lazowski, D. A., . . . Ecclestone, N. A. (2004). Evaluation of the restorative care education and training program for nursing homes. *Canadian Journal on Aging*, 24(2), 115–126.

Simek, E., McPhate, L., & Haines, T. P. (2012). Adherence to and efficacy of home exercise programs to prevent falls: A systematic review and meta-analysis of the impact of exercise program characteristics. *Preventive Medicine*, 55(4), 262–275.

Singh, N. A., Quine, S., Clemson, L. M., Williams, E. J., Williamson, D. A., Stavrinos, T. M., . . . Singh, M. A. (2012). Effects of high-intensity progressive resistance training and targeted multidisciplinary treatment of frailty on mortality and nursing home admissions after hip fracture: A randomized controlled trial. *Journal of the American Medical Directors Association*, 13(1), 24–30.

Snyder, A., Colvin, B., & Gammack, J. K. (2011). Pedometer use increases daily steps and functional status in older adults. *Journal of the American Medical Directors Association*, 12(8), 590–594.

Tak, E., van Uffelen, J. G. Z., Mai, J. M., Chin, A. P., van Mechelen, W., & Hopman-Rock, M. (2012). Adherence to exercise programs and determinants of maintenance in older adults with mild cognitive impairment. *Journal of Aging & Physical Activity*, 20(1), 32–46.

Tappen, R. (1994). The effect of skill training on functional abilities of nursing home residents with dementia. *Research in Nursing and Health*, 17(3), 159–165.

Thompson, W., Zack, M. M., Krahn, G. L., Andresen, E. M., & Barile, J. P. (2012). Health-related quality of life among older adults with and without functional limitations. *American Journal of Public Health*, 102(3), 496–502.

Tinetti, M. E., Baker, D., Gallo, W. T., Nanda, A., Charpentier, P., & O'Leary, J. (2002). Evaluation of restorative care vs usual care for older adults receiving an acute episode of home care. *Jounal of the American Medical Association*, 287(16), 2098–2105.

Troiano, R., Berrigan, D., Dodd, K. W., Masse, L. C., Tilert, T., & McDowell, M. (2008). Physical activity in the United States measured by accelerometer. *Medicine and Science in Sports and Exercise*, 40, 181–188.

Tsunoda, K., Tsuji, T., Kitano, N., Mitsuishi, Y., Yoon, J. Y., Yoon, J., & Okura, T. (2012). Associations of physical activity with neighborhood environments and transportation modes in older Japanese adults. *Preventive Medicine*, 55(2), 113–118.

Valenzuela, T. (2012). Efficacy of progressive resistance training interventions in older adults in nursing homes: A systematic review. *Journal of the American Medical Directors Association*, 13(5), 418–428.

Virtuoso, J., Jair, S., Tribess, S., De Paulo, T. R. S., Martins, C. A., & Romo-Perez, V. (2012). Physical activity as an indicator of predictive functional disability in elderly. *Revista Latino-Americana de Enfermagem (RLAE)*, 20(2), 259–265.

Wilhelm, M., Roskovensky, G., Emery, K., Manno, C., Valek, K., & Cook, C. (2012). Effect of resistance exercises on function in older adults with osteoporosis or osteopenia: A systematic review. *Physiotherapy Canada*, 64(4), 386–394.

CHAPTER 7

Hispanic Women and Physical Activity

An Integrative Review

Karen T. D'Alonzo and Marie K. Saimbert

ABSTRACT

Hispanics/Latinos represent the largest, fastest growing, and youngest minority group in the United States. Although data suggest that most Hispanics/Latinos in the United States tend to be in better health than non-Hispanic Whites (the so-called "Hispanic Paradox"), these relative advantages in health status decrease markedly with the number of years of residence in the United States. Hispanic women or Latinas, in general, report less than recommended levels of physical activity (PA), putting them at greater risk for the development of cardiovascular disease (CVD) and other chronic illnesses associated with sedentary lifestyles.

This chapter presents an integrative review of the topic of PA among Latinas and examines a wide variety of experimental, nonexperimental, qualitative, and theoretical studies that examine the topic. Facilitators and barriers to participation in PA among Latinas are presented, as well as a summary of various types of interventions designed to increase PA among Hispanic women. Lastly, recommendations for future research in this area are presented.

© 2013 Springer Publishing Company
http://dx.doi.org/10.1891/0739-6686.31.209

HISPANIC WOMEN AND PHYSICAL ACTIVITY— AN INTEGRATIVE REVIEW

In the first two decades of the third millennium, perhaps no racial or ethnic group has grown as rapidly or has influenced life in the United States more profoundly than Hispanics/Latinos.[1] Defined as individuals who can trace their ancestry to Spain, Mexico, or any of the Spanish speaking countries of Central and South America and the Caribbean, Hispanics are now the nation's largest minority group at 17% of the U.S. population (Pew Hispanic Center, 2013). This gives the United States the second largest Hispanic population in the world, second only to Mexico (U.S. Census Bureau, 2013). The nation's largest and fastest growing minority group is also the youngest; Latinos now account for about one in four people younger than 18 years. As a result, Hispanic immigrants and their U.S.-born descendants are expected to provide much of the growth of the U.S. population in the decades to come. In the United States, most Hispanics reside in urban areas and poverty rates for Hispanic families are substantially higher than those of non-Hispanic Whites (Macartney, Bishaw, & Fontenot, 2013).

Although the interaction of ethnicity, immigration, geography, and poverty places many Hispanics at risk for multiple health problems, decades of data suggest most Hispanics/Latinos in the United States tend to be in better health than non-Hispanic Whites. Although this trend varies according to the country of birth, it is particularly true with regard to preventable chronic diseases such as cancer, cardiovascular disease (CVD) and cerebrovascular disease, HIV/AIDS, diabetes, and renal disease (Ruiz, Steffen, & Smith, 2013). This phenomenon has been referred to as the "Hispanic Paradox" (Markides & Coreil, 1986) and is most evident among immigrant Latinos. Unfortunately, these relative advantages in health status decrease markedly with the number of years of residence in the United States, so that over time, the risk for chronic diseases among these groups meets or exceeds that of U.S.-born non-Hispanics.

One health promoting lifestyle behavior linked to good health is physical activity (PA). Although the benefits of an active lifestyle are well documented, there is evidence that sedentarism is more profound among Hispanic women (Latinas) when compared to both White non-Hispanic women and other minority groups. Less than 10% of Hispanic women in the United States currently meet the 2008 Federal Physical Activity Guidelines for adults ≥ 18 years of age (U.S. Department of Health and Human Services [USDHHS], 2008). Sedentarism among Hispanic women places them at significantly higher risk for the development of largely preventable chronic illnesses, including hypertension, type 2 diabetes mellitus, and CVD.

This chapter presents an integrative review of the topic of PA among Latinas. This approach was chosen because it allows for a review of various experimental, nonexperimental, qualitative, and theoretical studies that examine the topic. The chapter reviews demographic information regarding the size and diversity of the Hispanic population in the United States. A review of various definitions of PA is included and how these definitions affect the interpretation of data concerning rates of PA and inactivity in this population. A review of the literature surrounding facilitators and barriers to participation in PA among Latinas is presented, including cultural perspectives on the traditional role of women in Hispanic society and how these factors may impact participation in PA. Next, we review a summary of various types of interventions designed to increase PA among Hispanic women. Lastly, recommendations for future research in this area are presented.

METHODS

Inclusion Criteria

This integrative review focuses on a compilation of research regarding PA among healthy adult Hispanic women/Latinas. Articles from searches of two large bibliographic health science databases, PubMed and Cumulative Index to Nursing and Allied Health Literature (CINAHL), were included in the review. Articles reflecting a wide interpretation of the terms "Hispanic" or "Latina" were considered, including studies concerning new immigrant women as well as first, second, and subsequent generation Hispanic American women from several Latin American countries. Additional inclusion criteria for articles included English language studies of adults (18 years and older), and qualitative and quantitative studies, including trials. Studies that included both minority and majority subjects were included if 25% or more of the subjects in the sample were Hispanic females. PA studies among Hispanic women with specific health conditions, such as breast cancer, were excluded from analysis, as were studies of pregnant women and girls. No date limit was set for retrieved citations; the final pool of articles from the databases noted earlier spanned from 1987 to 2013.

Search Heuristics

Preliminary searches for literature on Hispanic Americans and exercise included databases such as Cochrane Library (John Wiley and Sons), Academic Search Premier (EBSCO Industries), ERIC (U.S. Department of Education), Indices Bibliografico Espanol en Ciencias de la Salud (IBECS), Latin American and Caribbean Center on Health Sciences Information (LILACS), and Proquest Social Sciences Premium Collection. The authors then decided that the pool of citations on this topic appeared large, but a focus on literature on Latinas and exercise was desired. Towards those ends, a final set of searches was performed in PubMed and CINAHL. A search of the PubMed database, with citations from 1940s to present (U.S. National Library of Medicine, 2011) yielded 1,156 citations using the search strategy ("Hispanic Americans" OR "Latina") AND ("Exercise" OR "physical fitness" OR "physical activity"). The search engine behind the PubMed database expanded the search statement earlier to include MeSH (Medical Subject Heading) terms such as motor activity [MeSH] for the term physical activity. There was expansion of truncated terms such as Latina to the terms Latina, Latino/American, Latina/Carribean, and Latina/Latino. In addition, per PubMed's search algorithm, terms related to those in the original query were part of the final search details. A basic and advance search of the CINAHL database was performed and search queries employed in CINAHL were similar to that used in PubMed.

FINDINGS—THE STATE OF THE SCIENCE

Latinos in the United States

Increased rates of immigration from Latin America, coupled with higher than average birth rates among Hispanics, have resulted in a major demographic shift in the U.S. population since the year 2000. According to the U.S. Census Bureau, Hispanic population growth between 2000 and 2010 accounted for more than half of the nation's population growth (Passel, Cohn, & Lopez, 2011). In the decades to come, the percentage of Hispanics in the United States will continue to climb. Current projections estimate that by the year 2050, Hispanics will comprise 30% of the nation's population (Passel & Cohn, 2008); Hispanics are already expected to surpass White non-Hispanics as the plurality in California by 2014 (California Department of Finance, 2011).

Hispanic/Latino origin is based on self-reported ancestry or place of birth. Collectively, the Hispanic population in the United States can be divided into (a) native Hispanics (persons born in the country who are of Hispanic ancestry) and (b) foreign-born Hispanics who have immigrated to the United States and who may or may not have acquired U.S. citizenship (Motel & Patten, 2013). Currently, nearly two-thirds of Hispanics are considered native-born U.S. citizens and the remaining 37.4% are immigrants. Immigrant Latinos are a heterogeneous group; 92.0% of these immigrants come from 1 of 10 Latin American countries including Mexico, Puerto Rico, Cuba, El Salvador, Dominican Republic, Guatemala, Colombia, Honduras, Ecuador, and Peru (Motel & Patten, 2013). Although illegal immigration from Latin American countries has decreased since 2007 (Passel & Cohn, 2012), nearly half of the nation's 40 million immigrants are Hispanic (Motel & Patten, 2013). Demographically, the Hispanic population in the United States is younger (27 years vs. 37 years of age) than the median age of the U.S. population as a whole (Pew Hispanic Center, 2013).

Definitions of Physical Activity

Although the terms "physical activity" and "exercise" are often used interchangeably, they are in fact two very distinct constructs. As Redeker and Musanti (2002) have discussed, this conceptual ambiguity may impact the ability to promote PA as a healthy lifestyle behavior among minority women. In the literature, PA has been defined as movement of one's skeleton that leads to variations (low or high) in energy expenditure (kilocalories) and is correlated with positive physical fitness (Caspersen, Powell, & Christenson, 1985). Exercise not only contains all the elements of PA but also involves planning of a PA regimen with the goal of improving or maintaining one's physical fitness. The Physical Activity Guidelines for Americans (USDHHS, 2008) broadly define PA as "any bodily movement produced by contraction of skeletal muscle that raises energy expenditure above a basal level" (pp. 8–9). PA can be divided into two types: (a) baseline PA or light-intensity activities of daily living (ADLs) and (b) health enhancing PA or moderate to vigorous PA, which increases the heart rate and respirations. This type of activity is usually thought of as leisure-time PA or exercise. Because little is known about the health effects of enhancing baseline PA, attempts to quantify and to encourage PA among subgroups of the population have historically focused on measurement of exercise. This is true even though among many Hispanic women, PA is more likely to consist of light-intensity ADL, interspersed with periods of moderate- to vigorous-intensity activities (e.g., climbing stairs, lifting groceries, or playing with children; Brownson et al., 2000; Hawkins, Cockburn, Hamilton, & Mack, 2004; Marquez & McAuley, 2006a). Given the fact that work is seen as a survival strategy among immigrant populations, and that jobs requiring hard, physical labor are most often held by poor and minority populations, the phrase "leisure-time physical activity" can be seen to reflect an elitist mindset (D'Alonzo & Sharma, 2010). Thus, total PA levels of Hispanic women may be substantially higher if work-related PA is included in the calculation (Brownson et al., 2000).

Statistics—Latinas and Physical Activity

Several large epidemiological studies have noted Hispanic women, in general, report less than recommended levels of PA. The Centers for Disease Control and Prevention (CDC, 2005) National Center for Health Statistics reported that for 2007–2008, only 9.5% of all Hispanic women engaged in adequate amounts of PA, defined as 2.50 hr/week of moderate-intensity activity or 1.25 hr/week of vigorous-intensity activity, or an equivalent combination of both, plus muscle-strengthening activities on 2 or more days per week (USDHHS, 2008). In this study, Hispanic women were the least active racial or ethnic group studied. Even more troublesome is the percentage of Hispanic women who do not engage in any form of PA. In the 2009 Racial and Ethnic Approaches to Community Health across the U.S. (REACH U.S.) Risk Factor Survey, almost one-third of Hispanic women reported no leisure time PA during the preceding month (Liao et al., 2011). There is evidence that factors such as country of origin, age, and level of acculturation may affect Latinas' participation of PA. Neighbors, Marquez, and Marcus (2008) noted leisure-time PA varied significantly among Hispanic subgroups. Cuban and Dominican women were the least active, whereas Mexican American women were the most active. In an analysis of National Health and Nutrition Examination Survey (NHANES) data from 2003 to 2004 by Hawkins et al. (2009), Latinas were more active at middle age (40–59 years) compared to younger or older age and not significantly less active than men in middle or older age groups (i.e., age 40–59 years or age 60 years and older). Likewise, Gaskins, Baskin, and Person (2012) noted that although Hispanic women as a whole did not mean PA recommendations, from this data, it is apparent that they may be at high risk for CVD and other chronic illnesses associated with sedentary lifestyles.

Facilitators and Barriers to Participation in PA Among Latinas

In the theoretical and empirical literature, there are several personal (intrinsic) and environmental (extrinsic) factors found to play a key role in determining the extent to which Latinas participate in PA. These factors may be broadly categorized as either facilitators or barriers. Several of the facilitators and barriers listed in the following text are similar to those noted in the literature among majority populations (Bragg, Tucker, Kaye, & Desmond, 2009; Heesch, Brown, & Blanton, 2000). In addition, there are other facilitators and barriers that appear to be unique to Latinas or are based on Hispanic cultural constructs. We have labeled these "culture-specific" factors.

Intrinsic Facilitators

Self-Efficacy

Self-efficacy has been studied as a correlate or predictor of PA for more than three decades. As has been demonstrated in majority populations (Trost, Owen, Bauman, Sallis, & Brown, 2002), self-efficacy has been shown to be a powerful predictor of PA among Hispanic women. Numerous studies have identified exercise self-efficacy as the most common facilitator of participation in PA in Latinas across the lifespan (D'Alonzo, Stevenson, & Davis, 2004; Kohlbry & Nies, 2010; Laffrey, 2000; Y. Lee & Laffrey, 2008; Marquez & McAuley, 2006b; Marquez, McAuley, & Overman, 2004; Wilbur, Chandler, Dancy, & Lee, 2003). Self-efficacy has been broadly defined as "an individual's judgment of their capability to organize and execute actions needed to perform an activity, even among conflicting circumstances" (Bandura, 1997, pp. 8–9). Rodgers, Wilson, Hall,

Fraser, and Murray (2008) identified three behavioral domains of self-efficacy: task, scheduling, and coping. Thus an individual will feel self-efficacious with regard to participation in PA if he/she perceives they are capable of performing selected activities regularly, under challenging conditions, and in spite of other time demands. In comparing Hispanic and non-Hispanic college students, Ryan (2005) reported that task efficacy was a significant predictor of reported PA for Latino subjects, but scheduling efficacy was not. This finding may mean that Hispanic women may be more strongly committed to begin a program of exercise than sustaining it and may require additional support to strengthen skills in goal-setting, self-monitoring, planning, and problem solving (Rovniak, Anderson, Winett, & Stephens, 2002). Although self-efficacy is an intrinsic facilitator, the construct is influenced by external and cultural factors as well. For example, Hispanic women who have traditionally been encouraged to avoid vigorous, more "masculine" forms of activity (Im et al., 2010) may feel little sense of self-efficacy to perform these activities. Given that overt mastery experience and vicarious experience are the two strongest sources of Self-efficacy (SE) information (Bandura, 1997), Hispanic women who did not participate in PA as young girls and who lacked role models for physically active lifestyles are less likely to be active as adults (D'Alonzo & Fischetti, 2008; Hoebeke, 2008). Ironically, self-efficacy has not been universally found to be associated with PA among Hispanic women. Collins, Lee, Albright, and King (2004) reported that exercise self-efficacy did not improve among low-income Latinas following a preintervention PA course and Voorhees and Rohm Young (2003) found that for urban Latinas, exercise self-efficacy was negatively correlated with exercise and PA behaviors. These results suggest that with regard to PA and exercise, there may be other factors that take precedence over self-efficacy among Latinas. For example, in a study of PA among African American women, Fallon, Wilcox, and Ainsworth (2005) reported self-efficacy for PA was higher among women who reported fewer social role constraints and had a more positive sense of community.

Education

In the empirical literature, total number of years of education is most often associated with greater levels of PA, but there are conflicting reasons for this finding. Because there is a large body of evidence linking education with health, even when other factors such as income are taken into account (Mirowsky & Ross, 2005), education may indeed be an independent predictor of PA among Hispanic women, and there is ample evidence to support this relationship (Evenson, Sarmiento, Tawney, Macon, & Ammerman, 2003; Eyler et al., 2003a; Giardina et al., 2009; King et al., 2000; Willey, Paik, Sacco, Elkind, & Boden-Albala, 2010). Through this pathway, it is posited that education may increase an individual's knowledge and cognitive skills, enabling them to make better informed choices about their health (Cutler, Deaton, & Lleras-Muney, 2006). An alternative explanation of the link between education and PA may be that education is seen as a proxy variable for socioeconomic status (SES). Thus, years of education are linked to better jobs with higher wages and more control over one's working hours, leaving more discretionary time for exercise. Hispanic women with higher SES tend to participate in more vigorous PA and do it more frequently than Hispanic women with lower SES (Coleman, Gonzalez, & Cooley, 2000). In a photovoice study of low-income immigrant Hispanic women (D'Alonzo & Sharma, 2010), economic pressures forced the women to make money by piecing together work from a series of low-paying, unskilled jobs, which left them little time for health promoting behaviors such as PA. Lastly, among Latinos, education is sometimes seen as evidence of English language proficiency and may therefore be more indicative of acculturation. Because acculturation is a complex process, for the purposes of this review, acculturation will be examined separately as a culture-specific independent factor associated with PA.

Extrinsic Facilitators
Social Support
Social support is also strongly associated with participation in PA among Hispanic women. Social support is broadly defined as the perception and actuality that one is cared for, has assistance available from other people, and that one is part of a supportive social network (Cohen & Wills, 1985). Resources in the social network can provide various forms of assistance including emotional support (e.g., nurturance), tangible support (e.g., financial assistance), informational support (e.g., advice), or companionship (e.g., sense of belonging; House & Kahn, 1985). Hovell et al. (1991) first reported that the emotional support of friends who encourage or exercise with you was a stronger predictor of vigorous PA among Latino men and women than family support or exercise self-efficacy. Likewise, physical inactivity was found to be associated with having fewer friends (Shelton et al., 2011; Willey et al., 2010), whereas women who were physically active were more likely to have "supportive others" (Ashida, Wilkinson, & Koehly, 2012; Belza et al., 2004; Fleury, Keller, Perez, & Castro, 2009; Im, Chee, Lim, Liu, & Kim, 2008; Wilcox, Castro, King, Houseman, & Brownson, 2000). In a qualitative study by Gonzalez and Keller (2004), participants described the importance of having a *gran amiga* (great friend) who shared their interest in PA. Evenson et al. (2002) noted that Latinas who did not have the support of a spouse who approved of exercise or who could help with child care were less likely to be physically active. Juarbe, Turok, and Warda (2003) noted that Mexican and Central American women used problem-focused coping strategies to obtain informational support for exercise from friends and extended

family members. Lastly, social support may come in the form of camaraderie or "cultural unity" (Melillo et al., 2001) with other Latinas in pursuit of healthier lifestyles. Such groups may help to relieve feelings of *aislamiento* (isolation; D'Alonzo, 2012), particularly for immigrant Latinas.

Environmental Factors

For women of all races and ethnicities, the physical environment is a major contributing factor to participation in PA. Safety is a primary consideration for women; several studies reported that Hispanic women who perceived they had access to safe places to walk and exercise were more likely to be physically active (Belza & Baker, 2000; Brown et al., 2008; Brown et al., 2011; Bungum, Thompson-Robinson, Moonie, & Lounsbery, 2011; Evenson et al., 2003; Im et al., 2008; R. E. Lee et al., 2012; Lees et al., 2007; López, Bryant, & McDermott, 2008; Melillo et al., 2001; Taylor et al., 2007; Voorhees & Rohm Young, 2003). Several of these studies referred to specific supportive aspects of the built environment, such as the presence of sidewalks and affordable public recreation facilities, greater traffic control devices and crossing aids (R. E. Lee et al., 2012), more street lights (Taylor et al., 2007), and access to safe, clean public parks (Cronan, Shinew, & Stodolska, 2008). Many of the concerns about safety were strongest among elderly Hispanic women. In other studies, the presence of informal social ties with neighbors was important, as evidenced by seeing other people exercise in the neighborhood (Evenson et al., 2003; Lees et al., 2007) or the presence of homes with "welcoming" architectural features such as porches and stoops (Brown et al., 2008).

Culture-Specific Facilitators

Acculturation

Immigration, or the act of moving from one country to another, may be viewed as a complex, transitional process (Jones, Zhang, & Meleis, 2003), which frequently results in alterations in lifestyle. Acculturation has been defined as a normative process that occurs when a person from one culture comes in contact with another culture (Berry, 1989). To date, measurement of acculturation, particularly among Hispanics, has been dominated by two distinct theoretical frameworks. Acculturation can be viewed as a unidimensional construct that can be measured along a continuum from immersion in the culture of origin to immersion in the culture of the host country (Gordon, 1995). Alternatively, acculturation can be seen as a bidimensional construct which simultaneously consists of two distinct dimensions, adherence to the dominant culture, and maintenance of the culture of origin (Marín & Gamba, 1996). Language use (English or Spanish) is a prominent feature of both models of acculturation, although other factors such as generation status, length of time living in the United States, country of origin of friends, preferences for music and food, perceived discrimination, knowledge of the history of the United States and home country, and ethnic identity may also be included (Cabassa, 2003). One health-promoting lifestyle that is profoundly affected by immigration and the acculturation process is PA. Most studies indicate that the acculturation process has a positive influence on participation in leisure time and household forms of PA, particularly when English language acquisition is used as a measure of acculturation (Berrigan, Dodd, Troiano, Reeve, & Ballard-Barbash, 2006; Crespo, Smit, Carter-Pokras, & Anderson, 2001; Evenson, Sarmiento, & Ayala, 2004; Fitzgerald et al., 2006; Ghaddar, Brown, Pagán, & Díaz, 2010; Guinn & Vincent, 2008; Ham, Yore, Kruger, Heath, & Moeti, 2007; He & Baker, 2005; King et al., 2000; Pichon et al., 2007; Slattery et al., 2006; van Rompay et al., 2012; Van Wieren, Roberts, Arellano, Feller, & Diaz, 2011). In one study, Spanish-speaking women reported being afraid to venture outside the house for PA for fear of becoming lost because of language barriers (Vaughn, 2009). This association did not hold true in all studies, however. Cantero, Richardson, Baezconde-Garbanati, and Marks (1999) noted that although acculturation appeared to positively affect the health practices of middle-aged Latinas, it had no effect on Hispanic women aged 75 years and older. In particular, subjects in several qualitative studies have reported a marked decline in PA since coming to the United States, except for work activities (D'Alonzo, 2012; D'Alonzo & Sharma, 2010; Hartweg & Isabelli-García, 2007; Hartweg, Isabelli-García, McEwen, & Piper, 2012). It may be that acculturation is positively associated with PA only for those women for whom acculturation results in a higher standard of living. In a study of Hispanic and Anglo women in El Paso, Texas, Coleman et al. (2000) noted that although Hispanic women's choices to exercise were independent of acculturation, those of higher SES were more physically active than those of lower SES.

Barriers to Physical Activity

It is obvious from the previous discussion of facilitators that Hispanic women with low levels of self-efficacy, little social support, fewer years of education, or who lack safe, affordable places to exercise are likely to lack the tools needed to become physically active on a regular basis. There are also several additional intrinsic, extrinsic, and culture-specific factors identified in the literature that appear to serve as barriers to participation in PA among Latinas.

Intrinsic Barriers

Fatigue. Many women of all races and ethnicities report simply feeling too tired to be physically active. The literature suggests this is particularly true for immigrant women who are juggling home and work responsibilities, often without the social support they experienced in their home countries (D'Alonzo, 2012; D'Alonzo & Sharma, 2010; Juarbe, Lipson, & Turok, 2003; Juniu 2000). Many immigrant women perceive they engage in sufficient amounts of PA at work and prefer to spend their leisure time in relatively sedentary activities, such as watching telenovelas (a type of television programming popular in Latin America and elsewhere; Berg, Cromwell, & Arnett, 2002). Even women who did not work outside the home described their days as tiring, "being in constant motion" (Hartweg et al., 2012). Subjects in a study by Im et al. (2010) noted that some of these sentiments may be a reflection of the older generation's response to years of hard physical labor. Interestingly, two studies have reported that actual time commitments did not match the perceived lack of time available for PA among Hispanic women (Heesch & Mâsse, 2004; Tudor-Locke, Leonardi, Johnson, & Katzmarzyk, 2011).

Extrinsic and Culture-Specific Barriers
Several extrinsic barriers to participation in PA, such as lack of child care and family care giving responsibilities are inextricably linked to culture-specific issues among Hispanic women. For this reason, we have grouped these factors together for discussion. Many of the studies addressing these culture-specific issues have qualitative designs.

Cultural Traditions That Discourage PA in Hispanic Women. Dating back to the time of the conquistadores, Hispanic culture in the Americas has been associated with the assignment of distinct gender roles for men and women. In many Latin American countries, the primary role of males has historically been economic protection, whereas the primary role of females is as caregivers and mothers. These roles vary with the level of acculturation, education, and SES. Because of the emphasis on performance of domestic responsibilities, Latinas have traditionally spent much of their day in the company of other women, who in turn provide support for activities such as childrearing and family caregiving. This arrangement has afforded women some periods of discretionary time during which they can pursue health promoting activities such as PA. Because women (particular those who immigrate to the United States) enter the workforce to add to the family income, this system of female-centered social support diminishes. Many immigrant Latinas lament the loss of such support and describe the difficulty of finding time for themselves (D'Alonzo, 2012; A. Gonzales & Keller, 2004; Hoebeke, 2008).

The term most frequently used to describe the constellation of culturally specified behaviors considered appropriate for Hispanic women is *marianismo* (Stevens, 1973). *Marianismo* can be seen as the feminine counterpart to machismo; women are expected to be sexually chaste, to defer to their husbands in all decisions, and to put the needs of the family ahead of their own. Latinas with strong *marianismo* beliefs may feel that some forms of vigorous PA are unfeminine or that it is inappropriate to take time away from the family to such pursuits. Several studies have reported how the cultural beliefs of spouses, partners, or parents discourage vigorous PA for women because of concerns about reproductive health (D'Alonzo & Fischetti, 2008; Juarbe, Lipson, et al., 2003) or seeking only sexual attractiveness (Juarbe, Lipson, et al., 2003). Many Latinas report exercise was not considered a priority for women when they were growing up (Hartweg et al., 2012).

Overwhelmingly, the strongest cultural barrier to participation in PA among Latinas in the literature is time for family responsibilities. There are several Hispanic cultural beliefs that support the notion that a woman's primary role is to prioritize the needs of her spouse, children, parents, and other family members ahead of her own needs. Immigrant women raised with strong *marianismo* beliefs may feel the woman is the center of the family, "the oil that keeps the home running" (D'Alonzo, 2012). Time taken away for individual pursuits such as PA may be seen as a selfish indulgence (D'Alonzo & Sharma, 2010) or a waste of time (Im et al., 2010). This concern is tied to the theme of *familismo* (familism), considered to be a core characteristic of Hispanic culture. Sabogal, Marin, Otero-Sabogal, Marin, & Perez-Stable (1987) have defined three aspects of familism: (a) *Familial obligations* or the belief that family members have a responsibility to provide economic and emotional support to each other; (b) *perceived support and emotional closeness*—family members are dependable sources of assistance to each other, should be united, and have close relationships and (c) *family as referent*, the belief that behavior of each member of the family should meet with overall familial expectations. Using this framework, the family is viewed as an extension of oneself and the behavior of one individual is a reflection of the entire family. In addition, "family" is conceptualized more broadly in many Latin American countries than the traditional nuclear family epitomized in the United States and may include extended family members, long-time family friends, neighbors, and beloved members of the community. Data from several studies indicate Latinas often feel guilty making time for themselves for PA (Berg, 2003; Berg et al., 2002; D'Alonzo, 2012; A. Gonzales & Keller, 2004; B. C. Gonzales & Jivovec, 2001; Hartweg et al., 2012; Im et al., 2010). Cantu (2011) and Cantu and Fleuriet (2008) described how physical presence or "being there" was important in Latino families and how PA might make Hispanic women unavailable for caregiving activities within the family unit. Some researchers have capitalized on these values to explore how women can use PA as a way to stay healthy and remain caring for their family (Berg et al., 2002; Cantu & Fleuriet, 2008; Collins et al., 2004; Gonzalez & Keller, 2004) or how family members can exercise together to promote healthy lifestyles for all (Columna, Pyfer, & Senne, 2011; Sallis, Patterson, Buono, Atkins, & Nader, 1988). *Fatalismo* (fatalism), or the sense that an individual has very little personal control over health and illness, is common in Hispanic culture (Abraído-Lanza et al., 2007; Otero-Sabogal, Stewart, Sabogal, Brown, & Perez-Stable, 2003) and is evidenced in every day expressions such as *Si Dios quiere* (if God wills it) and *De algo se tiene que morir uno* (You have to die of something). Thus, Hispanic women may not readily acknowledge the importance of PA as a health promoting behavior. It has been demonstrated that compared to White women, Mexican women self-report not only a lower frequency of PA but also a lower sense of control over their health (Sallis et al., 1988; Vega, Warhiet, Buhl-Auth, & Meinhardt, 1984). Because the cultural concepts of *marianismo, familismo,* and *fatalismo* appear to diminish with acculturation (Comas-Diaz, 1988; Cuéllar, Arnold, & González, 1995), women who are new immigrants may find these cultural traditions to be greater barriers to PA than U.S.-born Latinas.

PHYSICAL ACTIVITY INTERVENTIONS

This review specifically focuses on interventions to increase PA behaviors among healthy adult Hispanic women. For the purposes of this review, the interventions included studies that used (a) behavioral and/or social approaches to facilitate behavior change and/or (b) environmental and policy approaches to provide access to places for PA. Qualitative and quantitative studies were included with results of quantitative studies explored in depth if at least 25% of a study's sample was Hispanic women. The outcome variables used most often to measure intervention effectiveness were changes in PA behavior and aerobic capacity. Sixteen studies that met these criteria were included in the analysis. Studies were selected after reviewing 43 citations that had been added into an electronic citation manager and initially categorized as general citations dealing with PA interventions. Full text for citations with abstracts were further reviewed by hand for selection of studies on PA interventions, including at least 25% Latinas in the sample. Although other studies had been located from the final searches on PA interventions for Latinas with specific conditions such as cardiovascular events, depression, diabetes, and menopause symptoms, those studies were omitted in this review because researchers felt those studies often included populations motivated to exercise and wanted to focus on studies testing PA interventions in Latinas in general.

Final searches for citations on Hispanic women and PA were performed in PubMed and CINAHL. A search of the PubMed database, with citations from 1940s to present (U.S. National Library of Medicine, 2011) yielded

1,156 citations using the search strategy ("Hispanic Americans" *OR* "Latina") *AND* ("Exercise" *OR* "physical fitness" *OR* "physical activity"). The search engine behind the PubMed database expanded the search statement mentioned earlier to include *MeSH* terms such as motor activity [MeSH] for the term physical activity. There was expansion of truncated terms such as Latina to the terms Latina, Latino/American, Latina/Caribbean, and Latina/Latino. In addition, per PubMed's search algorithm, terms related to those in the original query were part of the final search details. A basic and advance search of the CINAHL database was performed and search queries employed in CINAHL were similar to that used in PubMed. In addition, two PubMed Alerts of final searches in that database were constructed and citations on PA culled as published in the literature between February 2, 2013 and April 7, 2013.

PubMed Alert 1—Hispanics and Exercise
Search: ("Hispanic Americans" *OR* "Latin") *AND* ("Exercise" *OR* "physical fitness" *OR* "physical activity")
PubMed Alert 2—Hispanics and Exercise *and* Randomized Control Trials
Search: ("Hispanic Americans" *OR* "latin") *AND* ("Exercise" *OR* "physical fitness" *OR* "physical activity") *AND* ("randomized controlled trial"[pt] *OR* "controlled clinical trial"[pt] *OR* "randomized"[tiab] *OR* "randomised"[tiab] *OR* "randomization"[tiab] *OR* "randomisation"[tiab] *OR* "placebo"[tiab] *OR* "drug therapy"[sh] *OR* "randomly"[tiab] *OR* "trial"[tiab] *OR* "groups"[tiab]) *NOT* ("animals"[mh] *NOT* "humans"[mh]) **NOT** ("Editorial"[ptyp] *OR* "Letter"[ptyp] *OR* "Case Reports"[ptyp] *OR* "Comment"[ptyp])

Aerobic Exercise

Most intervention studies among Latinas tested the use of a walking intervention (Avila & Hovell, 1994; Grassi, Gonzalez, Tello, & He, 1999; Keller & Cantue, 2008; Poston et al., 2001; Staten et al., 2004). All of these studies used community partnership approaches in the design and/or implementation of the intervention. Other approaches focused on Latin and aerobic dancing (Hovell et al., 2008; N. Olvera et al., 2010) or other culturally appropriate approaches.

Community-Based

Community-based interventions have been tested to combat sedentary behavior. Although such studies show positive outcomes from the intervention itself, they often include few Latinas in the sample (Shaw & Page, 2008). Some share results that are not statistically significant. For example, in the BOUNCE (Behavior Opportunities Uniting Nutrition, Counseling, and Exercise) study, mother–daughter groups in either the experimental or control group did not show statistically significant changes in PA or body mass index (BMI) after the 12-week intervention. In another study by Grassi et al. (1999) involving walking clubs, Hispanic women composed approximately 90% of the participants from four rural cities in Central California. Mean hours of walking were decreased among participants in the La Vida Caminando club. Significant barriers identified by participants included cost, child care, neighborhood safety, and transportation.

Environment-Based

Interventions that result in environment changes contribute to a milieu supporting engagement in PA. In one study, Spanish signage was added to a local Young Men's Christian Association (YMCA) and a five-way intersection modified with addition of lights and crossing cues making it safer for residents to use a park nearby (Ziebarth et al., 2012). Hispanic women have expressed the need for PA options that are affordable and accessible in their neighborhoods (Berg et al., 2002).

Faith-Based

A multifocal faith-based intervention was tested on church members, primarily Mexican American (81.1%). The study included an 8-week walking contest, health fair or fiesta, and Spanish language materials. Although the program seemed feasible, significance was not concluded and there was a relatively small sample size ($n = 50$; Bopp, Fallon, & Marquez, 2011). In another study with 48.0% sedentary Hispanic women between ages 17 and 70 years, women in the 50- to 70-year-old age bracket were found to engage in more exercise sessions in a church-based program compared to those in the 17- to 27-year-old age bracket (Dornelas, Stepnowski, Fischer, & Thompson, 2007). The researchers highlight that it was not clear whether having the sessions in a church truly made a difference or if another predictor variable mediated the effects of the intervention. This issue needs to be explored in future research. In addition, there was a relatively high attrition rate in the study, which is common in PA intervention studies.

Home-Based

In the IMPACT (Increasing Motivation for Physical ACTivity) trial, approximately 70% of the sample was composed of Mexican American women. Subjects participated in an 8-week behavioral modification program and then were part of a group receiving phone calls plus mail counseling for up to 10 weeks or mail support on PA topics including barriers to PA (Albright et al., 2005). According to analysis of completed Stanford Physical Activity Recall (PAR) log, the group randomized to phone calls plus mail counseling expended energy higher than their baseline and maintained that over time. These findings were in contrast to the mail support group whose energy expenditure decreased to their prebehavioral program activity levels or even lower by the end of 12 months. Comparisons of the slopes between groups revealed a significant difference ($p < .045$).

Family-Focused

Capitalizing on the cultural concept of *familismo*, PA interventions for Latinas and/or their families have been explored in the literature. The programs described were multifocal, designed to increase PA knowledge and promote PA behaviors. An 8-week PA intervention, "We Can!" (Ziebarth et al., 2012), was tested among Mexican Americans in Wisconsin. The program curriculum was translated into Spanish and included culturally sensitive diet and PA interventions for families. One participant highlighted the program's emphasis on promotion of health and family unity in diet management and engagement in PA. In a convenience sample of 47 families, 89% of the women were followed over the course of a 4-year period. There were statistically significant decreases in adult waist circumference ($M = -0.54$ in., $p < .03$), weight ($M = -2.03$ lb, $p < .002$), and BMI ($M = -0.35$ kg/m^2, $p < .01$). It was not clear from the study if the significance was correlated with changes in diet alone, PA alone, or the combination of study interventions.

Older Latinas

The PA patterns of older Hispanic American women (50 years of age and older), have been the focus of several studies. In a study of PA among older Mexican American women, Cromwell and Berg (2006) reported that most women were sedentary and lacked knowledge regarding PA and age-appropriate options for engaging in PA. The women were mostly comfortable with walking and dancing (Cromwell & Berg, 2006). The researchers suggest tai chi or yoga exercises as potential PA options to investigate for older Latinas (Cromwell & Berg, 2006).

Theoretical Frameworks for Intervention Studies

Several of the interventions focused on increasing PA using Hispanic cultural values, such as *familismo*. In addition, most interventions were designed using theoretical models, including Behavioral Economics (Coleman et al., 2000), Self-Management Model, Social Cognitive Theory (N. Olvera et al., 2008; Poston et al., 2001), Social Learning Theory (Nader et al., 1989), and the Transtheoretical Model (Ayala, 2011; Collins et al., 2004; Crespo, Keteyian, Heath, & Sempos, 1996; Pekmezi et al., 2009). However, several studies did not include a theoretical model or did not explain the model well enough so that it was clear how the model informed the PA intervention (Perez, Fleury, & Keller, 2010; Sharma & Romas, 2008).

In summary, interventions to decrease Latinas' sedentary behavior include education (e.g., print materials, PA workshops), moderate- to high-activity sessions (e.g., walking, dance, aerobics), and social support modalities. Interventions are often tailored to participants according to age (e.g., midlife, elderly), acculturation level, beliefs and behaviors regarding PA, and Spanish language preference. Several researchers have emphasized that successful PA interventions among Hispanic women may also need to be low cost (Pekmezi et al., 2012; Ziebarth et al., 2012).

LIMITATIONS

The studies summarized in this chapter are part of a growing body of knowledge regarding how to best encourage Hispanic women to engage in PA. However, the studies suffer from several limitations. First, most studies focused on Mexican and Mexican American women (Bopp et al., 2011), whereas few studies have addressed PA in other subgroups of Latinas. Because Hispanic women are a heterogeneous group of women and there are large differences in the risk for chronic illness among subgroups of Latinas (Ai, Appel, Huang, & Lee, 2012), such studies are sorely needed. Similarly, in virtually all of these studies, the acculturation level or even the generation of the subjects is not disclosed, so study findings should not be generalized to Hispanic women in general.

Many of the descriptive and intervention studies reviewed were also limited because of small sample size (Dornelas et al., 2007) and high dropout rates (Collins et al., 2004; Poston et al., 2001). In some of these studies, the calculation of effect sizes when statistical significance could not be quantified would have been an added strength. In addition, a significant number of intervention studies relied on convenience samples and were not true randomized controlled clinical trials. Many of the interventions were cross-sectional in nature (Ashing-Giwa, Lim, & Gonzales, 2010; Wilbur et al., 2012) and relatively short-term (3–6 months); additional longitudinal studies are needed that follow subjects for at least 1 year to assess the subjects' ability to sustain newly acquired PA behaviors. Likewise, virtually all of the studies relied on subjects' self-reports of PA. In future studies, researchers need to incorporate more objective methods for assessing PA, involving the measurement of physiological or biomechanical parameters. A significant number of qualitative, descriptive, and intervention studies targeted various groups of low-income minority women. Given the importance of cultural practices that may alternatively discourage or promote PA, it may be more appropriate to target the specific needs of Hispanic women in future studies. A few studies made use of community health workers or *promotores de salud* to assist in carrying out the PA intervention. Although such approaches may be culturally appropriate, it is important that such laypersons be adequately trained in data collection procedures. Ayala (2011) noted that in one intervention, data analysis was hampered because it was difficult to distinguish dropouts from those subjects who remained enrolled in the study (Ayala, 2011).

Lastly, it has been customary to limit integrative reviews to manuscripts published in English, yet there is good evidence that there is high-quality studies published in Spanish and Portuguese language journals. Such manuscripts may add to the development of transnational collaborations to deal with the increasingly global impact of obesity and sedentary lifestyles.

DISCUSSION

The body of knowledge regarding ways to promote PA among Hispanics is growing and as evidenced in this chapter, is no longer limited to a discussion of factors frequently attributed to majority populations. As the Hispanic/Latino population of the United States continues to grow, it is imperative that we develop culturally relevant methods to improve healthy lifestyle behaviors such as PA among Hispanic women. This is particularly important for Latinos to avoid the onset of chronic diseases such as diabetes, hypertension, and CVD, which are more prevalent with acculturation. Although traditional Hispanic cultural values may impose barriers on participation in PA for women, as the center of the family, Latinas are the gatekeepers of their family's health and are in an ideal position to serve as role models for physically active lifestyles. By using examples of learned resourcefulness (Rosenbaum, 1990), Cantu (2011) described situations where physically active older Mexican women were able to leverage their role as caregiver and matriarch to justify the importance of exercise to continue meeting the needs of others in the family. Such progressive approaches circumvent the need for immigrant woman to abandon the cultural values of their home country, by instead adopting a pattern of selective acculturation (Portes & Rumbaut, 2006), which combines salutogenic aspects of both the home and the host culture. Thus, selective acculturation may be a useful framework for future interventions to improve PA among Latinas (Yeh, Viladrich, Bruning, & Roye, 2009).

NOTE

1. In keeping with the terminology used by the U.S. Census Bureau, the terms "Hispanic" and "Latino/Latina" are used interchangeably here).

REFERENCES

Abraído-Lanza, A. E., Viladrich, A., Flórez, K. R., Céspedes, A., Aguirre, A. N., & De La Cruz, A. A. (2007). Commentary: Fatalismo reconsidered: A cautionary note for health-related research and practice with Latino populations. *Ethnic Disease, 17*, 153–158.

Ai, A. L., Appel, H. B., Huang, B., & Lee, K. (2012). Overall health and healthcare utilization among Latino American women in the United States. *Journal of Women's Health, 21*(8), 878–885. http://dx.doi.org/10.1089/jwh.2011.3431

Albright, C. L., Pruitt, L., Castro, C., Gonzalez, A., Woo, S., & King, A. C. (2005). Modifying physical activity in a multiethnic sample of low-income women: One-year results from the IMPACT (Increasing Motivation for Physical ACTivity) project. *Annals of Behavioral Medicine*, *30*(3), 191–200. http://dx.doi.org/10.1207/s15324796abm3003_3

Ashida, S., Wilkinson, A. V., & Koehly, L. M. (2012). Social influence and motivation to change health behaviors among Mexican-origin adults: Implications for diet and physical activity. *American Journal of Health Promotion*, *26*(3), 176–179.

Ashing-Giwa, K. T., Lim, J. W., & Gonzalez, P. (2010). Exploring the relationship between physical well-being and healthy lifestyle changes among European- and Latina-American breast and cervical cancer survivors. *Psychooncology*, *19*(11), 1161–1170. http://dx.doi.org/10.1002/pon.1687

Avila, P., & Hovell, M. F. (1994). Physical activity training for weight loss in Latinas: A controlled trial. *International Journal of Obesity Related Metabolic Disorders*, *18*(7), 476–482.

Ayala, G. X. (2011). Effects of a promotor-based intervention to promote physical activity: Familias Sanas y Activas. *American Journal of Public Health*, *101*(12), 2261–2268. http://dx.doi.org/10.2105/ajph.2011.300273

Bandura, A. (1997). *Self-efficacy: The exercise of control*. New York, NY: W.H. Freeman.

Belza, B., Walwick, J., Shiu-Thornton, S., Schwartz, S., Taylor, M., & LoGerfo, J. (2004). Older adult perspectives on physical activity and exercise: Voices from multiple cultures. *Preventing Chronic Disease*, *1*(4), A09.

Belza, B., & Baker, M. W. (2000). Maintaining health in well older adults: Initiatives for schools of nursing and the John A. Hartford Foundation for the 21st century. *Journal of Gerontological Nursing*, *26*(7), 8–17.

Berg, J. A. (2003). Mexican American women's willingness to promote health. *Journal of Multicultural Nursing & Health*, *9*(2), 34–43.

Berg, J. A., Cromwell, S. L., & Arnett, M. (2002). Physical activity: Perspectives of Mexican American and Anglo American midlife women. *Health Care for Women International*, *23*(8), 894–904. http://dx.doi.org/10.1080/07399330290112399

Berrigan, D., Dodd, K., Troiano, R. P., Reeve, B. B., & Ballard-Barbash, R. (2006). Physical activity and acculturation among adult Hispanics in the United States. *Research Quarterly for Exercise and Sport*, *77*(2), 147–157.

Berry, J. W. (1989). Psychology of acculturation. In J. Berman (Ed.), *Cross-cultural perspectives: Nebraska symposium on motivation* (Vol. 37, pp. 201–234). Lincoln, NE: University of Nebraska.

Bopp, M., Fallon, E. A., & Marquez, D. X. (2011). A faith-based physical activity intervention for Latinos: Outcomes and lessons. *American Journal of Health Promotion*, *25*(3), 168–171. http://dx.doi.org/10.4278/ajhp.090413-ARB-138

Bragg, M. A., Tucker, C. M., Kaye, L. B., & Desmond, F. (2009). Motivators of and barriers to engaging in physical activity: Perspectives of low-income culturally diverse adolescents and adults. *American Journal of Health Education*, *40*(3), 146–154.

Brown, S. C., Mason, C. A., Perrino, T., Lombard, J. L., Martinez, F., Plater-Zyberk, E., & Szapocznik, J. (2008). Built environment and physical functioning in Hispanic elders: The role of "eyes on the street." *Environmental Health Perspectives*, *116*(10), 1300–1307.

Brown, S. C., Huang, S., Perrino, T., Surio, P., Borges-Garcia, R., Flavin, K., & Szapocznik, J. (2011). The relationship of perceived neighborhood social climate to walking in Hispanic older adults: A longitudinal, cross-lagged panel analysis. *Journal of Aging and Health*, *23*(8), 1325–1351. http://dx.doi.org/10.1177/0898264311418502

Brownson, R. C., Eyler, A. A., King, A. C., Brown, D. R., Shyu, Y. L., & Sallis, J. F. (2000). Patterns and correlates of physical activity among U.S. women 40 years and older. *American Journal of Public Health*, *90*(2), 264–270.

Bungum, T. J., Thompson-Robinson, M., Moonie, S., & Lounsbery, M. A. (2011). Correlates of physical activity among Hispanic adults. *Journal of Physical Activity and Health*, *8*(3), 429–435.

Cabassa, L. J. (2003). Measuring acculturation: Where we are and where we need to go. *Hispanic Journal of Behavioral Sciences*, 25, 127–146. http://dx.doi.org/10.1177/07399863 03025002001

California Department of Finance. (2011). *New population projections: California to surpass 50 million in 2049*. Retrieved from http://ucanr.edu/blogs/blogcore/postdetail.cfm?postnum=9210

Cantero, P. J., Richardson, J. L., Baezconde-Garbanati, L., & Marks, G. (1999). The association between acculturation and health practices among middle-aged and elderly Latinas. *Ethnic Disease*, 9(2), 166–180.

Cantu, A. G. (2011). Exploring intra-person mediators of older Mexican American women who exercise: A life history approach. *Hispanic Health Care International*, 9(2), 99–108. http://dx.doi.org/10.1891/1540-4153.9.2.99

Cantu, A. G., & Fleuriet, K. J. (2008). The sociocultural context of physical activity in older Mexican American women. *Hispanic Health Care International*, 6(1), 27–40.

Caspersen, C. J., Powell, K. E., & Christenson, G. M. (1985). Physical activity, exercise, and physical fitness: Definitions and distinctions for health-related research. *Public Health Reports*, 100(2), 126–131.

Centers for Disease Control and Prevention. (2005). Trends in leisure-time physical inactivity by age, sex, and race/ethnicity—United States, 1994–2004. *MMWR Morbidity and Mortality Weekly Report*, 54(39), 991–994.

Hawkins, S. A., Cockburn, M. G., Hamilton, A. S., & Mack, T. M. (2004). An estimate of physical activity prevalence in a large population-based cohort. *Medicine & Science in Sports & Exercise*, 36(2), 253–260.

Cohen, S., & Wills, T. A. (1985). Stress, social support, and the buffering hypothesis. *Psychological Bulletin*, 98, 310–357.

Coleman, K. J., Gonzalez, E. C., & Cooley, T. (2000). An objective measure of reinforcement and its implications for exercise promotion in sedentary Hispanic and Anglo women. *Annals of Behavioral Medicine*, 22(3), 229–236.

Collins, R., Lee, R. E., Albright, C. L., & King, A. C. (2004). Ready to be physically active? The effects of a course preparing low-income multiethnic women to be more physically active. *Health Education Behavior*, 31(1), 47–64. http://dx.doi.org/10.1177/1090198103255529

Columna, L., Pyfer, J., & Senne, T. A. (2011). Physical recreation among immigrant Hispanic families with children with disabilities. *Therapeutic Recreation Journal*, 45(3), 214–233.

Comas-Diaz, L. (1988). *Feminist therapy with Hispanic/Latina women: Myth or reality?* Binghampton, NY: Hayworth Press.

Crespo, C. J., Keteyian, S. J., Heath, G. W., & Sempos, C. T. (1996). Leisure-time physical activity among U.S. adults. Results from the Third National Health and Nutrition Examination Survey. *Archives of Internal Medicine*, 156(1), 93–98.

Crespo, C. J., Smit, E., Carter-Pokras, O., & Andersen, R. (2001). Acculturation and leisure-time physical inactivity in Mexican American adults: Results from NHANES III, 1988–1994. *American Journal of Public Health*, 91(8), 1254–1257.

Cromwell, S. L., & Berg, J. A. (2006). Lifelong physical activity patterns of sedentary Mexican American women. *Geriatric Nursing*, 27(4), 209–213.

Cronan, M. K., Shinew, K. J., & Stodolska, M. (2008). Trail use among Latinos: Recognizing diverse uses among a specific population. *Journal of Park & Recreation Administration*, 26(1), 62–86.

Cuéllar, I., Arnold, B., & González, G. (1995). Cognitive referents of acculturation: Assessment of cultural constructs in Mexican Americans. *Journal of Community Psychology*, 23, 339–356.

Cutler, D. M., Deaton, A., & Lleras-Muney, A. (2006). The determinants of mortality. *Journal of Economic Perspectives*, 20(3), 97–120.

D'Alonzo, K. T. (2012). The influence of *marianismo* beliefs on physical activity of immigrant Latinas. *Journal of Transcultural Nursing*, 23(2), 124–133. http://dx.doi.org/10.1177/1043659611433872

D'Alonzo, K. T., & Fischetti, N. (2008). Cultural beliefs and attitudes of Black and Hispanic college-age women toward exercise. *Journal of Transcultural Nursing, 19*(2), 175–183. http://dx.doi .org/10.1177/1043659607313074

D'Alonzo, K. T., & Sharma, M. (2010). The influence of *marianismo* beliefs on physical activity of mid-life immigrant Latinas: A Photovoice study. *Qualitative Research in Sport and Exercise, 2*(2), 229–249. http://dx.doi.org/10.1080/193984412010.488031

D'Alonzo, K. T., Stevenson, J. S., & Davis, S. E. (2004). Outcomes of a program to enhance exercise self-efficacy and improve fitness among Black and Hispanic college-age women. *Research in Nursing and Health, 27*, 357–369. http://dx.doi.org/10.1002/nur.20029

Dornelas, E. A., Stepnowski, R. R., Fischer, E. H., & Thompson, P. D. (2007). Urban ethnic minority women's attendance at health clinic vs. church based exercise programs. *Journal of Cross Cultural Gerontology, 22*(1), 129–136. http://dx.doi.org/10.1007/s10823-006-9023-1

Evenson, K. R., Sarmiento, O. L., & Ayala, G. X. (2004). Acculturation and physical activity among North Carolina Latina immigrants. *Social Science and Medicine, 59*(12), 2509–2522. http:// dx.doi.org/10.1016/j.socscimed.2004.04.011

Evenson, K. R., Sarmiento, O. L., Tawney, K. W., Macon, M. L., & Ammerman, A. S. (2003). Personal, social, and environmental correlates of physical activity in North Carolina Latina immigrants. *American Journal of Preventive Medicine, 25*(3, Suppl. 1), 77–85.

Evenson, K. R., Wilcox, S., Pettinger, M., Brunner, R., King, A. C., & McTiernan, A. (2002). Vigorous leisure activity through women's adult life: The Women's Health Initiative Observational Cohort Study. *American Journal of Epidemiology, 156*(10), 945–953.

Eyler, A. A., Matson-Koffman, D., Young, D. R., Wilcox, S., Wilbur, J., Thompson, J. L., . . . Evenson, K. R. (2003a). Quantitative study of correlates of physical activity in women from diverse racial/ethnic groups: Women's Cardiovascular Health Network Project—Introduction and methodology. *American Journal of Preventive Medicine, 25*(3, Suppl. 1), 5–14.

Eyler, A. A., Matson-Koffman, D., Young, D. R., Wilcox, S., Wilbur, J., Thompson, J. L., . . . Evenson, K. R. (2003b). Quantitative study of correlates of physical activity in women from diverse racial/ethnic groups: The Women's Cardiovascular Health Network Project—Summary and conclusions. *American Journal of Preventive Medicine, 25*(3, Suppl. 1), 93–103. http://dx.doi .org/10.1016/S0749-3797(03)00170-3

Fallon, E. A., Wilcox, S., & Ainsworth, B. E. (2005). Correlates of self-efficacy for physical activity in African American women. *Women and Health, 41*(3), 47–62.

Fitzgerald, N., Himmelgreen, D., Damio, G., Segura-Pérez, S., Peng, Y., & Pérez-Escamilla, R. (2006). Acculturation, socioeconomic status, obesity and lifestyle factors among low-income Puerto Rican women in Connecticut, U.S., 1998–1999. *Revista Panamericana de Salud Publica, 19*(5), 306–313.

Fleury, J., Keller, C., Perez, A., & Castro, F. (2009). A multi-level analysis of physical activity in Hispanic women: Toward foundational science. *Communicating Nursing Research, 42*, 95.

Gaskins, R. B., Baskin, M. L., & Person, S. D. (2012). Language, duration of United States residency, and leisure time physical activity among women from the Third National Health and Nutrition Examination Survey (NHANES III). *Journal of Women's Health, 21*(11), 1170–1179. http://dx.doi.org/10.1089/jwh.2012.3477

Ghaddar, S., Brown, C. J., Pagán, J. A., & Díaz, V. (2010). Acculturation and healthy lifestyle habits among Hispanics in United States-Mexico border communities. *Revista Panamericana de Salud Pública, 28*(3), 190–197.

Giardina, E. V., Laudano, M., Hurstak, E., Saroff, A., Fleck, E., Sciacca, R., & Cassetta, J. (2009). Physical activity participation among Caribbean Hispanic women living in New York: Relation to education, income, and age. *Journal of Women's Health, 18*(2), 187–193. http:// dx.doi.org/10.1089/jwh.2008.0946

Gonzales, A., & Keller, C. (2004). Mi familia viene primero (My family comes first): Physical activity issues in older Mexican American women. *Southern Online Journal of Nursing Research, 5*(4), 1–21.

Gonzales, B. C., & Jirovec, M. M. (2001). Elderly Mexican women's perception of exercise and conflicting role responsibilities. *International Journal of Nursing Studies, 38*, 45–49.

Gordon, M. (1995). Assimilation in America: Theory and reality. In A. Aguirre & E. Baker (Eds.), *Notable selections in race and ethnicity* (pp. 91–101). Guilford, CT: Dushkin.

Grassi, K., Gonzalez, G., Tello, P., & He, G. (1999). La Vida Caminando: A community-based physical activity program designed by and for rural Latino families. *Journal of Health Education, 30*(2), S13–S17.

Guinn, B., & Vincent, V. (2008). Activity determinants among Mexican American women in a border setting. *American Journal of Health Education, 39*(3), 148–154.

Ham, S. A., Yore, M. M., Kruger, J., Heath, G. W., & Moeti, R. (2007). Physical activity patterns among Latinos in the United States: Putting the pieces together. *Prevention of Chronic Disease, 4*(4), A92.

Hartweg, D. L., & Isabelli-García, C. (2007). Health perceptions of low-income, immigrant Spanish-speaking Latinas in the United States. *Hispanic Health Care International, 5*(2), 53–63.

Hartweg, D., Isabelli-García, C., McEwen, M., & Piper, R. (2012). Being physically active: Perceptions of recent Mexican immigrant women on the Arizona-Mexico border. *Hispanic Health Care International, 10*(3), 127–136.

Hawkins, M. S., Storti, K. L., Richardson, C. R., King, W. C., Strath, S. J., Holleman, R. G., & Kriska, A. M. (2009). Objectively measured physical activity of USA adults by sex, age, and racial/ethnic groups: A cross-sectional study. *International Journal of Behavioral Nutrition and Physical Activity, 6*, 31. http://dx.doi.org/10.1186/1479-5868-6-31

He, X. Z., & Baker, D. W. (2005). Differences in leisure-time, household, and work-related physical activity by race, ethnicity, and education. *Journal of General Internal Medicine, 20*(3), 259–266. http://dx.doi.org/10.1111/j.1525-1497.2005.40198.x

Heesch, K. C., Brown, D. R., & Blanton, C. J. (2000). Perceived barriers to exercise and stage of exercise adoption in older women of different racial/ethnic groups. *Women Health, 30*(4), 61–76. http://dx.doi.org/10.1300/J013v30n04_05

Heesch, K. C., & Mâsse, L. C. (2004). Lack of time for physical activity: Perception or reality for African American and Hispanic women? *Women Health, 39*(3), 45–62.

Hoebeke, R. (2008). Low-income women's perceived barriers to physical activity: Focus group results. *Applied Nursing Research, 21*(2), 60–65.

House, J. S., & Kahn, R. L. (1985). Measures and concepts of social support. In S. Cohen & S. L. Syme (Eds.), *Social support and health* (pp. 83–108). New York, NY: Academic Press.

Hovell, M. F., Mulvihill, M. M., Buono, M. J., Liles, S., Schade, D. H., Washington, T. A., . . . Sallis, J. F. (2008). Culturally tailored aerobic exercise intervention for low-income Latinas. *American Journal of Health Promotion, 22*(3), 155–163. http://dx.doi.org/10.4278/ajhp.22.3.155

Hovell, M., Sallis, J., Hofstetter, R., Barrington, E., Hackley, M., Elder, J., . . . Kilbourne, K. (1991). Identification of correlates of physical activity among Latino adults. *Journal of Community Health, 16*(1), 23–36.

Im, E., Chee, W., Lim, H., Liu, Y., & Kim, H. K. (2008). Midlife women's attitudes toward physical activity. *Journal of Obstetric, Gynecologic & Neonatal Nursing, 37*(2), 203–213. http://dx.doi.org/10.1111/j.1552-6909.2008.00219.x

Im, E. O., Lee, B., Hwang, H., Yoo, K. H., Chee, W., Stuifbergen, A., . . . Chee, E. (2010). "A waste of time": Hispanic women's attitudes toward physical activity. *Women Health, 50*(6), 563–579. http://dx.doi.org/10.1080/03630242.2010.510387

Jones, P. S., Zhang, X. E., & Meleis, A. I. (2003). Transforming vulnerability. *Western Journal of Nursing Research, 25*(7), 835–853.

Juarbe, T. C., Lipson, J. G., & Turok, X. (2003). Physical activity beliefs, behaviors, and cardiovascular fitness of Mexican immigrant women. *Journal of Transcultural Nursing, 14*(2), 108–116.

Juarbe, T. C., Turok, X. P., & Warda, M. R. (2003). Coping strategies associated with physical activity and healthy dietary practice barriers among Mexican and Central American women. *Hispanic Health Care International, 2*(2), 51–61.

Juniu, S. (2000). The impact of immigration: Leisure experience in the lives of South American immigrants. *Journal of Leisure Research, 32*(3), 358–381.

Keller, C. S., & Cantue, A. (2008). Camina por Salud: Walking in Mexican American women. *Journal of Applied Nursing, 21*(2), 110–113.

King, A. C., Castro, C., Wilcox, S., Eyler, A. A., Sallis, J. F., & Brownson, R. C. (2000). Personal and environmental factors associated with physical inactivity among different racial-ethnic groups of U.S. middle-aged and older women. *Health Psychology, 19*(4), 354–364.

Kohlbry, P., & Nies, M. A. (2010). Hispanic women and physical activity: A community approach. Home Health Care Management & Practice, 22(2), 89–95. http://dx.doi.org/10.1177/1084822309331576

Laffrey, S. C. (2000). Physical activity among older Mexican American women. *Research in Nursing and Health, 23*(5), 383–392.

Lee, R. E., O'Connor, D. P., Smith-Ray, R., Mama, S. K., Medina, A. V., Reese-Smith, J. Y., . . . Estabrooks, P. A. (2012). Mediating effects of group cohesion on physical activity and diet in women of color: Health is power. *American Journal of Health Promotion, 26*(4), e116–e125. http://dx.doi.org/10.4278/ajhp.101215-QUAN-400

Lee, Y., & Laffrey, S. C. (2008). Exercise and self-efficacy among employed Hispanic men and women. *Hispanic Health Care International, 6*(1), 21–26.

Lees, E., Taylor, W. C., Hepworth, J. T., Feliz, K., Cassells, A., & Tobin, J. N. (2007). Environmental changes to increase physical activity: Perceptions of older urban ethnic-minority women. *Journal of Aging and Physical Activity, 15*(4), 425–438.

Liao, Y., Bang, D., Cosgrove, S., Dulin, R., Harris, Z., Taylor, A., . . . Giles, W. (2011). Surveillance of health status in minority communities—Racial and Ethnic Approaches to Community Health Across the U.S. (REACH U.S.) Risk Factor Survey, Unites States, 2009. *MMWR Morbidity and Mortality Weekly Report, 60*(SS06), 1–41.

López, I. A., Bryant, C. A., & McDermott, R. J. (2008). Influences on physical activity participation among Latinas: An ecological perspective. *American Journal of Health Behavior, 32*(6), 627–639.

Macartney, S., Bishaw, A., & Fontenot, K. (2013). Poverty rates for selected detailed race and hispanic groups by state and place: 2007–2011. *American community survey brief.* Retrieved from http://www.census.gov/prod/2013pubs/acsbr11-17.pdf

Marín, G. S., & Gamba, R. J. (1996). A new measurement of acculturation for Hispanics: The Bidimensional Acculturation Scale for Hispanics (BAS). *Hispanic Journal of Behavioral Sciences, 18*(3), 297–316.

Marquez, D. X., & McAuley, E. (2006a). Gender and acculturation influences on physical activity in Latino adults. *Annals of Behavioral Medicine, 31*(2), 138–144. http://dx.doi.org/10.1207/s15324796abm3102_5

Marquez, D. X., & McAuley, E. (2006b). Social cognitive correlates of leisure time physical activity among Latinos. *Journal of Behavioral Medicine, 29*(3), 281–289. http://dx.doi.org/10.1007/s10865-006-9055-6

Marquez, D. X., McAuley, E., & Overman, N. (2004). Psychosocial correlates and outcomes of physical activity among Latinos: A review. *Hispanic Journal of Behavioral Science, 26*(2), 195–229.

Markides, K. S., & Coreil, J. (1986). The health of Hispanics in the south Western United States: An epidemiological paradox. *Public Health Reports, 101*(3), 253–265.

Melillo, K. D., Williamson, E., Houde, S. C., Futrell, M., Read, C. Y., & Campasano, M. (2001). Perceptions of older Latino adults regarding physical fitness, physical activity, and exercise. *Journal of Gerontological Nursing, 27*(9), 38–46.

Mirowsky, J., & Ross, C. E. (2005). "Education, cumulative advantage and health." *Aging International*, 30(1), 27–62.

Motel, S., & Patten, E. (2013). *Statistical Portrait of Hispanics in the United States, 2011.* Retrieved from: http://www.pewhispanic.org/2013/02/15/statistical-portrait-of-hispanics-in-the-united-states-2011/

Nader, P. R., Sallis, J. F., Patterson, T. L., Abramson, I. S., Rupp, J. W., Senn, K. L., . . . Wallace, J. P. (1989). A family approach to cardiovascular risk reduction: Results from the San Diego Family Health Project. *Health Education Quarterly*, 16(2), 229–244.

Neighbors, C. J., Marquez, D. X., & Marcus, B. H. (2008). Leisure-time physical activity disparities among Hispanic subgroups in the United States. *American Journal of Public Health*, 98(8), 1460–1464. http://dx.doi.org/10.2105/ajph.2006.096982

Olvera, N., Knox, B., Scherer, R., Maldonado, G., Sharma, S. V., Alastuey, L., & Bush, J. A. (2008). A healthy lifestyle program for Latino daughters and mothers: The BOUNCE overview and process evaluation. *American Journal of Health Education*, 39(5), 283–295.

Olvera, N., Scherer, R., McLeod, J., Graham, M., Knox, B., Hall, K., . . . Bloom, J. (2010). BOUNCE: An exploratory healthy lifestyle summer intervention for girls. *American Journal of Health Behavior*, 34(2), 144–155.

Otero-Sabogal, R., Stewart, S., Sabogal, F., Brown, B. A., & Perez-Stable, E. J. (2003) Access and attitudinal factors related to breast and cervical cancer rescreening: Why are Latinas still underscreened? *Health Education Behavior*, 30, 337–359.

Passel, J., & Cohn, D. (2008). *U.S. population projections: 2005–2050.* Retrieved from http://www.pewhispanic.org/2008/02/11/us-population-projections-2005-2050/

Passel, J., & Cohn, D. (2012). *Unauthorized immigrants: 11.1 million in 2011.* Retrieved from http://www.pewhispanic.org/2013/02/15/statistical-portrait-of-hispanics-in-the-united-states-2011/

Passel, J., Cohn, D., & Lopez, M. J. (2011). *Hispanics Account for More than Half of Nation's Growth in Past Decade.* Retrieved from http://www.pewhispanic.org/2011/03/24/hispanics-account-for-more-than-half-of-nations-growth-in-past-decade/

Pekmezi, D., Dunsiger, S., Gans, K., Bock, B., Gaskins, R., Marquez, B., . . . Marcus, B. (2012). Rationale, design, and baseline findings from Seamos Saludables: A randomized controlled trial testing the efficacy of a culturally and linguistically adapted, computer-tailored physical activity intervention for Latinas. *Contemporary Clinical Trials*, 33(6), 1261–1271. http://dx.doi.org/10.1016/j.cct.2012.07.005

Pekmezi, D. W., Neighbors, C. J., Lee, C. S., Gans, K. M., Bock, B. C., Morrow, K. M., . . . Marcus, B. H. (2009). A culturally adapted physical activity intervention for Latinas: A randomized controlled trial. *American Journal of Preventive Medicine*, 37(6), 495–500. http://dx.doi.org/10.1016/j.amepre.2009.08.023

Perez, A., Fleury, J., & Keller, C. (2010). Review of intervention studies promoting physical activity in Hispanic women. *Western Journal of Nursing Research*, 32(3), 341–362. http://dx.doi.org/10.1177/0193945909351300

Pew Hispanic Center. (2013). *A statistical portrait of U.S. Hispanics.* Retrieved from http://www.pewhispanic.org/2013/02/15/hispanic-population-trends/ph_13-01-23_ss_hispanics1/

Pichon, L. C., Arredondo, E. M., Roesch, S., Sallis, J. F., Ayala, G. X., & Elder, J. P. (2007). The relation of acculturation to Latinas' perceived neighborhood safety and physical activity: A structural equation analysis. *Annals of Behavioral Medicine*, 34(3), 295–303. http://dx.doi.org/10.1080/08836610701677618

Portes, A., & Rumbaut, R. (2006). *Immigrant America: A portrait* (3rd ed.). Berkeley, CA: University of California Press.

Poston, W. S., II, Haddock, C. K., Olvera, N. E., Suminski, R. R., Reeves, R. S., Dunn, J. K., . . . Foreyt, J. P. (2001). Evaluation of a culturally appropriate intervention to increase physical activity. *American Journal of Health Behavior*, 25(4), 396–406.

Redeker, N., & Musanti, R. (2002). Women's physical activity: Conceptual issues. *Topics in Geriatric Rehabilitation, 18*(1), 1–8.

Rodgers, W. M., Wilson, P. M., Hall, C. R., Fraser, S. N., & Murray, T. C. (2008). Evidence for a multidimensional self-efficacy for exercise scale. *Research Quarterly for Exercise and Sport, 79*(2), 222–234.

Rosenbaum, M. (1990).The role of learned resourcefulness in self-control of health behavior. In M. Rosenbaum (Ed.), *Learned resourcefulness: On coping skills, self-control and adaptive behavior* (pp. 4–25). New York, NY: Springer Publishing.

Rovniak, L. S., Anderson, E. S., Winett, R. A., & Stephens, R. S. (2002). Social cognitive determinants of physical activity in young adults: A prospective structural equation analysis. *Annals of Behavioral Medicine, 24*(2), 149–156.

Ruiz, J. M., Steffen, P., & Smith, T. B. (2013). Hispanic mortality paradox: A systematic review and meta-analysis of the longitudinal literature. *American Journal of Public Health, 103*(3), e52–e60. http://dx.doi.org/10.2105/AJPH.2012.301103

Ryan, M. P. (2005). Physical activity levels in young adult Hispanics and Whites: Social cognitive theory determinants. *Psychology & Health, 20*(6), 709–727.

Sabogal, F., Marin, G., Otero-Sabogal, R., Marin, B. V., & Perez-Stable, E. (1987). Hispanic familism and acculturation: What changes and what doesn't? *Hispanic Journal of Behavioral Sciences, 9*, 397–412.

Sallis, J. F., Patterson, T. L., Buono, M. J., Atkins, C. J., & Nader, P. R. (1988). Aggregation of physical activity habits in Mexican-American and Anglo families. *Journal of Behavioral Medicine, 11*(1), 31–41.

Sharma, M., & Romas, J. A. (2008). *Theoretical foundations of health education and health promotion.* Sudbury, MA: Jones and Bartlett.

Shaw, K. L., & Page, C. (2008). A pilot community-based walking-for-exercise program for senior women. *Topics in Geriatric Rehabilitation, 24*(4), 315–324.

Shelton, R. C., McNeill, L. H., Puleo, E., Wolin, K. Y., Emmons, K., & Bennett, G. G. (2011). The association between social factors and physical activity among low-income adults living in public housing. *American Journal of Public Health, 101*(11), 2102–2110. http://dx.doi .org/10.1126/science.277.5328.918

Slattery, M. L., Sweeney, C., Edwards, S., Herrick, J., Murtaugh, M., Baumgartner, K., . . . Byers, T. (2006). Physical activity patterns and obesity in Hispanic and non-Hispanic white women. *Medicine and Science in Sports and Exercise, 38*(1), 33–41.

Staten, L. K., Gregory-Mercado, K. Y., Ranger-Moore, J., Will, J. C., Giuliano, A. R., Ford, E. S., & Marshall, J. (2004). Provider counseling, health education, and community health workers: The Arizona WISEWOMAN project. *Journal of Women's Health, 13*(5), 547–556. http:// dx.doi.org/10.1089/1540999041281133

Stevens, E. D. (1973). Marianismo: The other face of machismo in Latin America. In A. Decastello (Ed.), *Female and male in Latin America.* Pittsburgh, PA: University of Pittsburgh Press.

Taylor, W. C., Sallis, J. F., Lees, E., Hepworth, J. T., Feliz, K., Volding, D. C., . . . Tobin, J. N. (2007). Changing social and built environments to promote physical activity: Recommendations from low income, urban women. *Journal of Physical Activity and Health, 4*(1), 54–65.

Trost, S. G., Owen, N., Bauman, A. E., Sallis, J. F., & Brown, W. (2002). Correlates of adults' participation in physical activity: Review and update. *Medicine and Science in Sport and Exercise, 34*(12), 1996–2001.

Tudor-Locke, C., Leonardi, C., Johnson, W. D., & Katzmarzyk, P. T. (2011). Time spent in physical activity and sedentary behaviors on the working day: The American time use survey. *Journal of Occupational and Environmental Medicine, 53*(12), 1382–1387. http://dx.doi.org/10.1097 /JOM.0b013e31823c1402

U.S. Census Bureau. (2013). *International Programs.* Retrieved from http://www.census.gov/population /international/

U.S. Department of Health and Human Services. (2008). *Physical Activity Guidelines for Americans*. Retrieved from http://www.health.gov/paguidelines/guidelines/

U.S. National Library of Medicine. (2011). *PubMed Help- NCBI Bookshelf*. Retrieved from http://www.ncbi.nlm.nih.gov/books/NBK3827/-pubmedhelp.PubMed_Coverage

van Rompay, M. I., McKeown, N. M., Castaneda-Sceppa, C., Falcon, L. M., Ordovas, J. M., & Tucker, K. L. (2012). Acculturation and sociocultural influences on dietary intake and health status among Puerto Rican adults in Massachusetts. *Journal of the Academy of Nutrition and Dietetics, 112*(1), 64–74. http://dx.doi.org/10.1016/j.jada.2011.08.049

Van Wieren, A. J., Roberts, M. B., Arellano, N., Feller, E. R., & Diaz, J. A. (2011). Acculturation and cardiovascular behaviors among Latinos in California by country/region of origin. *Journal of Immigrant and Minority Health, 13*(6), 975–981. http://dx.doi.org/10.1007/s10903-011-9483-4

Vaughn, S. (2009). Factors influencing the participation of middle-aged and older Latin-American women in physical activity: A stroke-prevention behavior. *Rehabilitation Nursing, 34*(1), 17–23.

Vega, W., Warhiet, G., Buhl-Auth, J., & Meinhardt, K. (1984). The prevalence of depressive symptoms among Mexican Americans and Anglos. *American Journal of Epidemiology, 120*, 592–607.

Voorhees, C. C., & Rohm Young, D. (2003). Personal, social, and physical environmental correlates of physical activity levels in urban Latinas. *American Journal of Preventive Medicine, 25*(3, Suppl. 1), 61–68.

Wilbur, J., Chandler, P. J., Dancy, B., & Lee, H. (2003). Correlates of physical activity in urban Midwestern Latinas. *American Journal of Preventive Medicine, 25*(3, Suppl. 1), 69–76.

Wilbur, J., Marquez, D. X., Fogg, L., Wilson, R. S., Staffileno, B. A., Hoyem, R. L., . . . Manning, A. F. (2012). The relationship between physical activity and cognition in older Latinos. *Journals of Gerontology Series B: Psychological Sciences and Social Sciences, 67*(5), 525–534. http://dx.doi.org/10.1093/geronb/gbr137

Wilcox, S., Castro, C., King, A. C., Housemann, R., & Brownson, R. C. (2000). Determinants of leisure time physical activity in rural compared with urban older and ethnically diverse women in the United States. *Journal of Epidemiology and Community Health, 54*(9), 667–672.

Willey, J. Z., Paik, M. C., Sacco, R., Elkind, M. S. V., & Boden-Albala, B. (2010). Social determinants of physical inactivity in the Northern Manhattan Study (NOMAS). *Journal of Community Health, 35*(6), 602–608. http://dx.doi.org/10.1007/s10900-010-9249-2

Yeh, M. C., Viladrich, A., Bruning, N., & Roye, C. (2009). Determinants of Latina obesity in the United States: The role of selective acculturation. *Journal of Transcultural Nursing, 20*(1), 105–115. http://dx.doi.org/10.1177/1043659608325846

Ziebarth, D., Healy-Haney, N., Gnadt, B., Cronin, L., Jones, B., Jensen, E., & Viscuso, M. (2012). A community-based family intervention program to improve obesity in Hispanic families. *World Medical Journal, 111*(6), 261–266.

CHAPTER 8

Exercise Therapy in Individuals With Chronic Kidney Disease

A Systematic Review and Synthesis of the Research Evidence

Pelagia Koufaki, Sharlene A. Greenwood, Iain C. Macdougall, and Thomas H. Mercer

ABSTRACT

Chronic kidney disease (CKD) is becoming a serious health problem throughout the world and is one of the most potent known risk factors for cardiovascular disease (CVD) which is considered the leading cause of morbidity and mortality in this cohort of patients. Additional independent risk factors for poor health outcomes among many include diabetes, physical inactivity and physical dysfunction. Physical inactivity partly contributes to the accelerated deterioration of physical function in people in all stages of CKD, to levels that significantly impact on clinically and patient important outcomes such as morbidity, employment, quality of life (QoL) and ultimately survival. Ongoing research aims to determine the effectiveness and impact of exercise rehabilitation on reducing/ managing the risk of CVD, alleviating physical function limitations, preventing disability and enhancing QoL. Current research also aims to elucidate the

© 2013 Springer Publishing Company
http://dx.doi.org/10.1891/0739-6686.31.235

mechanisms via which exercise therapy may contribute to clinically relevant benefits.

An evaluative overview of the available evidence from experimental interventions to modify PA levels, highlights the huge variability in exercise training and assessment protocols utilised and inconsistency in reporting procedures that hampers, systematic synthesis of the evidence. Nonetheless, the general conclusion that can be deciphered is that a mixed cardiovascular and resistance training programme that lasts at least 4-6 months, results in significant improvements in cardiorespiratory fitness. However, this level of improvement, does not consistently and meaningfully translates into enhanced CV risk profile or renal function, or QoL, even in the presence of improved physical function as a result of increased PA levels. The relatively short duration of interventions as well as the extremely small sample sizes, combined with the inherent large variability in individual responses and progression, may be partially responsible for the lack of a systematic and consistent effect. Moreover, the dose of exercise may have not been sufficient to produce larger effects in relatively short periods of time. Thus, although the research evidence base needs more work, that should incorporate more accurate and systematic approaches in the prescription and delivery of exercise dosage, the association between exercise and some enhanced outcomes in the CKD population is sufficiently strong to recognise the potential importance of this area of renal care and further invest in it.

BACKGROUND AND RATIONALE
Chronic Kidney Disease and Cardiovascular Disease Risk

Cardiovascular disease (CVD) is a common concomitant of chronic kidney disease (CKD) and the leading cause of morbidity and mortality in this cohort of patients. Although many patients with CKD have other risk factors for CVD (e.g., diabetes, smoking, sedentary lifestyle, hypertension), and part of the increased risk is attributable to these risk factors, studies demonstrate that CKD itself is a major independent risk factor. As renal function declines, the association with CVD increases, and patients with non-dialysis-requiring CKD are more likely to die from CVD than develop end-stage renal disease (ESRD; Sarnak et al., 2003). *Diabetes* is identified as the single most common cause of gradual loss of kidney function and the prevalence and incidence of CKD not yet requiring renal replacement therapy is on the rise worldwide as a direct and indirect consequence of the increasing prevalence/incidence of obesity, diabetes, and hypertension (Zhang & Rothenbacher, 2008). In addition, survival once on dialysis is poor. The Scottish

Renal Registry Report (NHS Scotland, 2012) notes that the median life expectancy of a patient with primary renal disease (glomerulonephritis) aged 45 years commencing dialysis is 6.8 years, and for a person with diabetes, this figure falls to 2.5 years, compared with >30 years for age-matched healthy adults. The incidence of new patients accepted for renal replacement therapy in the United Kingdom has almost doubled in the last 10 years from 60 patients per million population (pmp) to 110 pmp (The Renal Association, U.K. Renal Registry, 2010). This may reflect the rising prevalence of diabetes and impaired renal function in the general population. The Health Survey for England (2009) reported that out of the 8% of the population that reported having been screened for renal function, about 50% were diagnosed with abnormal kidney function (glomerular filtration rate [GFR] less than 90 ml/min/1.73m^2) and, overall, 6% of the population were in stages 2–4 (GFR less than 60 ml/min/1.73m^2). The prevalence of CKD stages 2–5 increased with age, and the median age for all new patients starting dialysis now stands at ~65 years, permitting classification of a large proportion of patients on dialysis as elderly. Similar patterns of prevalence and incidence are reported among U.S. adults, with a 51% increase in prevalence of kidney failure and with an estimated 19 million people having CKD in the predialysis stages (Coresh et al., 2005).

Observations, mainly from the dialysis population, indicate that risk factors such as hypertension, endothelial dysfunction, increased oxidative stress, inflammation, and insulin resistance may contribute further to the amplified CVD risk associated with CKD (Himmelfarb, 2004). The development of these additional cardiovascular (CV) risk factors may start early in the disease trajectory and, therefore, any therapeutic strategies that can favorably modify these risk factors at the early stages may have a significant impact on CV and metabolic outcome and thus in the overall management and progression of CKD.

Physical Function and Related Health Outcomes in CKD

The severity of physical dysfunction in people receiving dialysis has been well documented. Severely deconditioned patients on dialysis are more likely to stop working, more frequently become hospitalized, reach disability levels, suffer from depression and other mental health problems, and use a greater proportion of the renal care team's time and resources (Blake, Codd, Cassidy, & O'Meara, 2000; Johansen, Chertow, Jin, & Kutner, 2007; Tentori et al., 2010). In contrast, physical function levels in predialysis patients are much less defined. Cardiorespiratory fitness, as measured by the integrated index of peak oxygen uptake (VO_{2peak}) and habitual levels of physical activity (PA), as measured using self-report questionnaires, are linked to CV risk. Both low VO_{2peak} and physical inactivity have been identified as strong independent risk factors for CV morbidity and mortality in the general population (Myers et al.,

2002) and have been identified as prognostically important for CVD and all-cause mortality in patients with CKD stage 5 (O'Hare, Tawney, Bacchetti, & Johansen, 2003; Sietsema, Amato, Adler, & Brass, 2004) and in patients with CKD stages 2–4 (Odden, Whooley, & Shlipak, 2004; Shlipak et al., 2005). PA, physical function limitations, muscle mass, and muscle function related measures have also been identified as strong predictors of disease progression and survival in patients in all stages of CKD (Fried et al., 2006; Kurella et al., 2004; Kurella Tamura et al., 2009; Robinson-Cohen et al., 2009; Stengel, Tarver-Carr, Powe, Eberhardt, & Bracati, 2003; Stenvinkel, Barany, Chung, Lindholm, & Heimbürger, 2002). Even self-reported physical function, as evaluated using the physical component score (PCS) from the Short Form 36 (SF-36) questionnaire, has been shown to carry a significant hospitalization and survival prognostic value for patients on dialysis. These studies suggest that a one point increase in the PCS translated into a 2% reduction in mortality rate and that a total PCS <25 was also associated with 93% increased risk of dying and 56% increased risk of hospitalization (Lowrie, Curtin, LePain, & Schatell, 2003; Mapes et al., 2003). Investigators have drawn some attention to observations that there is a "dose response" relationship between the PCS and mortality risk (Mapes et al., 2003) especially in the patient group of 55 years or younger. This predictive power for mortality was not observed in the older dialysis patients, indicating that aging and associated side effects perhaps overrides the protective effect of adequate physical function.

Reduced levels of muscular fitness—as reflected by muscle strength/power, endurance, and flexibility—have also been associated with the early detection of adverse clinical outcomes such as severe muscle loss and malnutrition in people in predialysis CKD stages (Heimbürger, Qureshi, Blaner, Berglund, & Stenvinkel, 2000). Patients with advanced CKD have a reduction in muscle strength comparable to patients on dialysis (being reduced by up to 63% compared to healthy controls). Cardiorespiratory exercise capacity has also been shown to be reduced by 40% in this group and by 45% in CKD stage 5 (Johansen & Painter, 2012). Measures of habitual physical activity (HPA) levels, physical function, and functional limitations such as grip strength, rising from a chair, walking performance, and self-care were also significantly reduced when compared with healthy population norms (Brodin, Ljungman, & Sunnerhagen, 2008; Kurella et al., 2004; Padilla et al., 2008). Low levels of PA, smoking, and morbid obesity (body mass index [BMI] >35 kg/m^2) were strong predictors of developing CKD in a cohort population of 9,250 individuals (Stengel et al., 2003). In a statistical model that controlled for diabetes, CV disease, hypertension, and abnormal lipid metabolism, individuals in the low PA group were, on average, 10 times more likely to develop CKD. This was a significant increase from the relative risk of 2.2 in a model that only adjusted for age, gender, and race, indicating that perhaps PA becomes a more important determinant of renal function in people with CVD and diabetes, which are common occurrence in the CKD population (Stengel et al., 2003). In a different longitudinal cohort study, more than 4,000 people older than 65 years of age were followed for 7 years and had at least two measures of kidney function analyzed as well as detailed information on type and amount of PA collected (Robinson-Cohen et al., 2009). This study reported that people who were in the highest PA group and spent more than 2,000 kcal/week on PA had the greatest reductions in the risk of rapid kidney function decline (RKFD) by 25%–37%. In addition, patients who could walk at a speed of 1.3 m/s had a significantly reduced risk of RKFD by 18%–26%. It is noteworthy again that the aforementioned risk reductions were present even after adjustments for age, sex, presence of CV disease, diabetes, and BMI, indicating a strong and independent effect of regular and specific dose of PA on preventing rapid kidney function loss.

Odden et al. (2004) reported significant associations between physical function and stage of renal impairment. This study showed that when objective measures of physical function were used in contrast to self-reported questionnaires, decreased levels of physical function were present even at minor levels of renal impairment. A recent study by Greenwood et al. (2012) that directly compared physical function outcomes in predialysis, dialysis, and transplanted patients demonstrated that objectively measured physical function and self-reported ability to perform activities of daily living and self-care were equally reduced across the CKD spectrum, indicating that physical dysfunction and disability starts early and persists even after successful transplantation. Physical function and ability to perform activities of daily living seem to decline with worsening renal function. Leikis et al. (2006) followed 12 patients in CKD stages 3–4 over a 2-year period and recorded a significant 9% reduction in VO_{2peak} and isokinetic muscle strength, whereas creatinine clearance significantly fell from 35 to 25 ml/min. Kurella Tamura et al. (2009) demonstrated significant associations between decline in the Duke's Activity Status Index (DASI) score (a self-reported level of ability to perform activities of daily living) and decline in estimated GFR values. They followed female patients in CKD stages 2–4 over a 4-year period and recorded a drop in the mean DASI score of 8.7 points (± 14.9) from a baseline score of 33.8 (± 11) points, whereas GFR declined on average by 4.2 (± 11.0) ml/min/1.73m². A longitudinal cohort study by Fried and colleagues (2006), based on 2,135 older individuals (mean age 73.5 years) and followed for a year, reported that GFR <60.0 ml/min/1.73m² was associated with significantly increased risk (~1.5 times higher risk) of developing functional limitations, which is considered a precursor of disability. Over a year, 36.3% of all individuals followed and 62.0% of those who died had developed physical limitations.

Therefore, one might speculate that physical dysfunction caused by physical inactivity may be at least partially responsible for some of the acceleration of CVD and kidney disease progression. Although many pharmacological strategies target some of the underlying causes of CVD and muscle wasting (metabolic acidosis, the microinflammatory and pro-oxidant state, endothelial dysfunction, hypertension, atherosclerosis, anemia, etc.) in CKD, therapeutic interventions such as exercise may further inhibit or minimize the risks of developing functional limitations, disability, worsening CV function, and residual renal function if applied early enough in the disease trajectory.

Exercise as a Potential Intervention
There are more than 30 years of research investigations into the efficacy and effectiveness of exercise training interventions on various physiological and patient relevant outcomes. Because of space limitations and to avoid reproduction of information already extensively covered in the published literature, we decided to provide a brief synthesized overview of the current research evidence from the published systematic and meta-analytic reviews on the effects of exercise interventions in patients on dialysis (Cheema & Singh, 2005; Heiwe & Jacobson, 2011; Segura-Orti, 2010; Smart & Steele, 2011). An extensive range of review papers is available in the link provided for the more interested readers (http://www.britishrenal.org/Physical-Activity/Physical-activity-resources-for-PAMs.aspx). Currently, there is limited information on the effectiveness of exercise training interventions on health-related outcomes, which are strong determinants of kidney disease progression and morbidity in patients with CKD stages 2–4. Although the general consensus and recent clinical practice guidelines for CV disease produced by the U.K. Renal Association (Holt & Goldsmith, 2011) suggest that exercise should be encouraged and that patients should participate in regular exercise programs, practical recommendations on the optimum dose and mode of therapeutic exercise cannot really be produced based on the available research evidence. Therefore, the aim of this systematic review is to attempt to summarize and evaluate the existing evidence for the effectiveness of exercise interventions in patients in predialysis CKD stages and following kidney transplantation (KTx).

OVERVIEW OF EXERCISE THERAPY FOR PATIENTS IN RENAL REPLACEMENT THERAPY (SUMMARY OF EVIDENCE BASED ON EXISTING SYSTEMATIC REVIEWS AND META-ANALYSES)

Aerobic-only-based exercise training performed during dialysis or on an off dialysis day significantly and to a large extend, improves indices of CV fitness (mainly measured VO_2 during various levels of physical stress). Significant improvements are noted after 3 months of exercise training but the largest amount of improvement in CV fitness is noted after at least six months of exercise training. The average improvement in CV fitness indices ranges from 17% to 50% in some reports. Although, on average, there are significant and large effects, careful examination of data when possible indicates large variability in patients' responses. Variability in assessment and training protocols, baseline levels of fitness, overall training stimulus in relation to patients' energy requirements, age, overall clinical status, and dialysis vintage are some of the most likely reasons to explain the large heterogeneity observed. Studies have evaluated the effect of exercise on VO_{2peak} comparing the effectiveness of exercise programs implemented during dialysis or on a nondialysis day. Although exercise training on a nondialysis day seemed to produce larger improvements in aerobic capacity (43%), compared with home exercise (37%) and exercise-on-dialysis (33%), it also demonstrated a larger dropout rate (24% vs. 17% vs. 17%, respectively). It should however be acknowledged that it may be slightly unrealistic to expect patients receiving hospital-delivered hemodialysis (HD) therapy to attend additional hospital or community-based exercise classes on nondialysis days at least in the United Kingdom environment.

Unfortunately, aerobic-only-based exercise did not seem to significantly improve indices of objectively measured functional capacity that relates to activities of daily living such as walking capacity, ability to stand up from a chair, stair climbing, and so forth based on the pooled data analysis performed by Heiwe and Jacobson (2011). A likely reason for this surprising lack of effect could be the relatively small number of studies (four) and thus patients who were analyzed ($n = 71$). The reasons suggested earlier as responsible for the variability in responses may become more prominent in small sample sizes, which may explain this lack of benefit following aerobic-based exercise training. It should also be noted that the principle of specificity of training is a factor that is often overlooked by researchers in the discussion of findings. It is reasonable to assume that physical function outcomes such as walking capacity or climbing stairs, for example, will require some specialized training that imitates the assessed activity, if any significant improvements are to be expected. Exercise interventions that have used cycling regimens are unlikely to produce immediate and large improvements in walking times for instance because the patterns of muscular activity are different.

Quality of life indices seem to be improved overall, following aerobic-based exercise, but most studies consistently report improvements in the physical component subscores of the questionnaires, with only random improvements in other elements of quality of life such as vitality, social function, general health, and so forth.

Few (four) randomized controlled trials (RCTs) using *resistance-only* training prescription have been included in the meta-analyses. Unfortunately, none had an index of CV fitness as an outcome and, thus, currently we do not know whether resistance training (RT) on its own can affect this important component of health-related fitness. Muscle strength and mid-thigh muscle cross-sectional area were, however, significantly and to a large extent improved, as indicated by the meta-analysis of Heiwe and Jacobson (2011) but not confirmed in the meta-analysis by Segura-Ortí (2010). The reason for this could be that Segura Ortí included two studies in the analysis ($n = 44$ patients), whereas Heiwe and Jacobson analyzed results from 111 to 135 patients altogether. Interestingly, the studies that were included in the meta-analysis by Segura-Ortí did not show significant changes in any strength and functional capacity outcomes but reported a really large and significant improvement in health-related quality of life indices, which seem to be driven by the self-reported physical function components of the SF-36 questionnaire that was used. This observation highlights the discrepancy between objectively measured and subjectively perceived ability to perform physical tasks that relate to activities of daily living. This dissociation between objective and subjective measures of functional limitations does not minimize the importance of someone's perceived ability to perform a task because the individual is more likely to actually perform a task if she or he thinks is achievable and therefore is more likely to engage in active living.

Separate analyses have been performed for data from studies that have combined exercise interventions of *resistance and aerobic training*. In summary, nine studies that have used combination training regimens demonstrated significant and large effects on indices of CV fitness especially after 6 months of training intervention. These large improvements in CV fitness did not seem to be accompanied by significant changes in functional capacity indices such as sit-to-stand (STS) transfers and walking performance. A closer examination of the data indicates that the large changes in CV indices are driven by several studies by the same research group who report substantially larger percentage changes in VO_{2peak} indices compared to the average values reported in the literature. Unfortunately, they do not report accompanying indices of functional capacity from their patients to allow evaluation of the relationship between large CV fitness improvement and the extent of corresponding functional capacity improvements. Quality of life indices did not significantly improve following combination training programs as indicated from the pooled analysis by Segura Ortí (2010). The meta-analysis by Heiwe and Jacobson (2011) also reports significant and substantial improvements in resting diastolic blood pressure (DBP) and systolic blood pressure (SBP) following any type of exercise training for at least six months. When combined resistance and aerobic training modalities were examined, significant improvements were noted only in DBP after 7 months of training.

All four systematic reviews highlight the scarcity of information from well-designed RCTs on primary outcomes relating to cardiometabolic health such as glucose metabolism, endothelial function, inflammation, and oxidative stress. They also highlight the huge variability in exercise training protocols used, assessment protocols, and inconsistency in reporting procedures that makes review summary and synthesis difficult. Nonetheless, the general conclusion that can be deciphered from these reviews is that a mixed CV and RT program that lasts at least four to six months results in greater improvements in aerobic exercise capacity (11%–45%). Such an improvement in aerobic exercise capacity if it exceeds 1 metabolic equivalent of task (MET; 3.5 ml of $O_2 \cdot kg^{-1} \cdot min^{-1}$) is associated with a significant ~9% reduction in risk of death in people with CVD (Myers et al., 2002).

EXERCISE THERAPY IN CKD STAGES 2–4
Search Strategy
One nonblinded author (PK) searched and summarized the information from exercise interventions involving individuals with CKD stages 2–5. Extracted data were entered into an excel spreadsheet database for further analysis. A literature search was conducted using the following databases: MEDLINE, BioMed Central, Directory of Open Access Journals (DOAJ), Google Scholar, Web of Knowledge, PubMed, ScienceDirect, SPORTDiscus, and a Heriot-Watt University-based search tool (Discovery) that combines searching several different databases simultaneously. The key concepts searched included "exercise therapy," "exercise training," "chronic kidney disease," and "predialysis" with associated MESH terms as defined by PubMed: ("exercise therapy"[MeSH Terms] *OR* "exercise"[All Fields]) *AND* ("therapy" [All Fields] *OR* "exercise therapy"[All Fields]) *AND* (chronic[All Fields]) *AND* ("kidney diseases"[MeSH Terms] *OR* "kidney"[All Fields]) *AND* ("diseases"[All Fields] *OR* "kidney diseases"[All Fields] *OR* "kidney"[All Fields]) *AND* ("disease"[All Fields] *OR* "kidney disease"[All Fields]) *AND* ("humans"[MeSH Terms]) *AND* (English; Colangelo, Stillman, Kessler-Fogil, & Kessler-Hartnett, 1997) *AND* ("adult"[MeSH Terms]). Filters used in all databases searched included English language only, humans, adults, and no time restrictions. Reference lists of papers retrieved were scrutinized for additional relevant references. Search histories were saved for future reference.

Inclusions
Only studies that had at least one structured exercise or lifestyle PA intervention components of any duration were considered. Also, studies had to have

a separate comparison group that included patients with CKD stages 2–5 but not yet on dialysis. Studies with mixed patient groups were excluded from the analysis (Cook, MacLaughlin, & Macdougall, 2008; MacLaughlin et al., 2010).

Literature Search Results

Between 305 and 700 records were identified that included the exact or combinations of the search terms used, following different database searches. All abstracts and, where appropriate, full text papers were reviewed to determine suitability for inclusion in the current systematic review synthesis. There were 19 reports identified that met our inclusion criteria. Out of these reports, 7 were full text published prospective RCTs with an exercise/PA intervention component, 8 were prospective nonrandomized controlled trials (NRCTs) with an exercise/PA intervention component, and 4 were prospective uncontrolled clinical trials (UCTs) with an exercise/PA intervention component. Out of the 7 RCTs identified, 3 separate full text publications (Balakrishnan et al., 2010; Castaneda et al., 2004; Castaneda et al., 2001) reported data from the same clinical trial based on the same participants so, in effect, there were only 5 independent RCTs identified.

Systematic Synthesis and Evaluation of Research Evidence
Exercise Training Studies' Characteristics

Based on the studies that have reported some details on the recruitment process (Balakrishnan, 2010; Castaneda et al., 2004; Castaneda et al., 2001; Leehey et al., 2009; Mustata et al., 2011), less than 50% of eligible patients started the exercise intervention. Patients were generally deemed noneligible to participate if they had uncontrolled comorbid conditions or if they had any orthopedic or other conditions that would not permit them to execute the physical component of the interventions (i.e., severe musculoskeletal pain, amputations, etc.). In total, 108 men and women in CKD stages 2–4 with mean ages ranging from 44 to 66 years have been randomized to either an exercise training (ET) group ($n = 56$) or to a usual care (UC)/attention control group ($n = 52$) at baseline. The dropout rates at follow-up assessments ranged from 10.0% (Mustata et al., 2011) to 23.3% (Eidemak, Haaber, Feldt-Rasmussen, Kanstrup, & Strandgaard, 1997), leaving 92 patients with complete data at reassessment time points (see Table 8.1). The reported reasons for loss to follow up included loss of interest and changes in personal circumstances, start of dialysis, investigators' decision, and refusal of muscle biopsies. All patients were receiving medication and none of the studies reported changes in medication, or any adverse effects associated with the exercise intervention. Out of the five RCTs that were conducted on independent population samples, only one research group used supervised progressive RT only (Balakrishnan et al., 2010; Castaneda et al., 2004; Castaneda et al., 2001). One study used a

TABLE 8.1

Summary of Exercise/PA Training Interventions in Patients With CKD Stages 2–4

Studies	ET (n)	CON (n)	Age (Years) ET/CON	Intervention/ Control Descriptions	Exercise Training Characteristics (FITT)	Duration (Weeks)	VO$_{2peak}$ (%Δ in ET vs. CON)	Functional Limitation Index (%Δ)	Disability Index (%Δ)	eGFR Difference (ml/ min/1.73m^2)
Randomized Controlled Clinical Trials										
Eidemak et al. (1997)	12	13	45	Unsupervised/ self-managed vs. usual care	• 7x/week • 60%–75% VO$_{2peak}$ • C,W, R, S • 30 min	78	8.0 vs. −9.5			−0.27 vs. −0.28
Castaneda et al. (2001)[a]	14	12	65	Supervised PRT + low protein diet vs. low protein diet + sham exercise	• 3x/week	12		32.00 vs. −13.00		1.65 vs. −1.98
Castaneda et al. (2004)[a]					• 80% 1RM					
Balakrishnan et al. (2010)[a]	13	10			• 3 sets × 8 reps • 45 min					
Leehey et al. (2009)	7	4	66	Supervised for 6 weeks + home-based for 18 weeks vs. usual care	• 3x/week • 45%–85% VO$_{2peak}$ • W • 30–40 min	24	4.7 vs. 9.1			

(Continued)

TABLE 8.1
Summary of Exercise/PA Training Interventions in Patients With CKD Stages 2–4   (Continued)

Studies	ET (n)	CON (n)	Age (Years) ET/CON	Intervention/ Control Descriptions	Exercise Training Characteristics (FITT)	Duration (Weeks)	VO$_{2peak}$ (%Δ in ET vs. CON)	Functional Limitation Index (%Δ)	Disability Index (%Δ)	eGFR Difference (ml/ min/1.73m^2)
Mustata et al. (2011)	10	10	64/72.5	2 supervised sessions + 1 home-based vs. usual care	• 2–3x/week • 40%–60% VO$_{2peak}$ • W, C, elliptical trainer	52	15.0 vs. 4.6	10.90 vs. 3.60	No change	No change
Gregory et al. (2011)	10	11	57/52	Supervised aerobic + RT after 24 weeks + nutritional counseling vs. usual care	• 3x/week • 50%–60% VO$_{2peak}$ • W, C, ST, elliptical trainer, RT • 55 min	48	12.7 vs. −13.9			6.00 vs. 6.00
Nonrandomized Controlled Clinical Trials										
Clyne et al. (1991)	10	9	46	Supervised calisthenics vs. usual care	• 3x/week • 60%–70% peak power output • Calisthenics • 45 min	12		9.40 vs. 0.00		
Boyce et al. (1997)	9	9	50	Supervised vs. usual care	• 3x/week • 50%–70% HRR • C, W • 60 min	16	12.0 vs. 3.0			Significantly declined after training and detraining

Study	n			Intervention	Details				
Fitts et al. (1999)	13	13	50/44	Rehabilitation counseling + "simplecise" routine vs. usual care	• 1x/week for the first 3 months and then 1x/month for the next 3 months • Self-regulated • Calisthenics • 60 min	24		0.67 vs. 0.13	No change (Karnofsky index)
Heiwe et al. (2001)[b]	16	10	76/72	Supervised strength training vs. usual care	• 3x/week • 60% 1RM • Knee extensions and weight-bearing exercises • 45 min	12		15.90 vs. NR	
Pechter et al. (2003)	11	9	52/48	Supervised aqua aerobics vs. usual care	• 2x/week • Aqua aerobics • 30 min	12	2.1 vs. 1.4	4.00 vs. −2.60	
Heiwe et al. (2005)[b]	7	5	71	Supervised strength training vs. usual care	• 3x/week • 60% 1RM • Knee extensions and weight-bearing exercises • 45 min	12		−40 vs. 60 (in median kilogram)	

(Continued)

TABLE 8.1
Summary of Exercise/PA Training Interventions in Patients With CKD Stages 2–4   (*Continued*)

Studies	ET (n)	CON (n)	Age (Years) ET/CON	Intervention/ Control Descriptions	Exercise Training Characteristics (FITT)	Duration (Weeks)	VO_{2peak} (%Δ in ET vs. CON)	Functional Limitation Index (%Δ)	Disability Index (%Δ)	eGFR Difference (ml/ min/1.73m^2)
Toyama et al. (2010)	10	9	71	Cardiac rehab 1x/week supervised and daily walk vs. usual care	• 7x/week • 12–13 RPE • Cardiac rehab and W • 30 min	12	1.0 vs. −1.0 in VO_2-VT			8.20 vs. −3.30
Kosmadakis et al. (2012)	18	16	61/56	Walking + high target bicarbonate vs. high target bicarbonate	• 5x/week • 12–14 RPE • W • 30 min	24				
Uncontrolled Observations										
Leaf et al. (2003)	5		57	Localized isometric handgrip training with heating	• 1 supervised session and 3 at home • 30%–40% MVC • Handgrip training • 1–6 min	6				
Venkataraman et al. (2005)	115		66	Cardiac rehabilitation/ individual counseling, group education	NR	29 sessions in total		17.30 (6MWT)	24.4 (PCS)	

Study								
Greenwood et al. (2012)	46	58	Renal rehabilitation + education	• 2 supervised + 1 home-based • 13–15 RPE • C, W, strength • 60 min	12		60.00 (ISWT) −29.50 (3-m TUG) 24.60 (STS60)	32.0 (DASI)
Aoike et al. (2012)	10	50	NR	• 3x/week • HR at VT	12	19.4	9.10 (6MWT) 34.60 (STS30)	8.5 (SF36-PF)

Note. Data are presented as means unless otherwise indicated. C = cycling; CON = control group with n = number of control participants who had follow-up data; DASI = Duke's Activity Status Index; Δ = positive changes unless otherwise indicated by the preceding sign; eGFR = estimated glomerular filtration rate; ET = exercise training group with n = number of exercising patients that had follow-up data; FITT = frequency/week, intensity as %, type, time (session duration in minutes); HR = heart rate; HRR = heart rate reserve; ISWT = Incremental Shuttle Walk Test; MVC = maximum voluntary contraction; NR = not reported; 1RM = one repetition maximum; PCS = Physical Composite Score from SF-36 questionnaire; RT = resistance training; R = running; RPE = rated perceived exertion; S = swimming; SF-36-PF = physical function component from SF-36 questionnaire; STS = sit-to-stand; 6MWT = 6-min walk test; 3-m TUG = 3-meter Up & Go test; VO_{2peak} = peak oxygen uptake; VO_2-VT = VO_2 at ventilatory threshold; VT = ventilatory threshold; W = walking.

[a]Publications from the same sample population. [b]publications from the same sample population.

combination of supervised aerobic and RT intervention (Gregory et al., 2011), and all the rest used a mixture of supervised and unsupervised aerobic-based exercise interventions (Eidemak et al., 1997; Leehey et al., 2009; Mustata et al., 2011). Compliance to the prescribed exercise sessions, defined as percentage of attended sessions out of all possible ones, ranged from 91% (Castaneda et al., 2004; Castaneda et al., 2001) to 74% for the aerobic component and 50% for the RT component in the study by Gregory et al. (2011). Exercise intervention durations ranged from 12 weeks (Balakrishnan et al., 2010; Castaneda et al., 2004; Castaneda et al., 2001) to 78 weeks (Eidemak et al., 1997). The average number of prescribed exercise sessions per week was three, but some studies had a home-based session for at least once per week (Leehey et al., 2009; Mustata et al., 2011). Compliance rates to the prescribed sessions have not been reported by these authors, and thus we cannot determine whether patients in fact completed all elements of the prescribed intervention. Eidemak et al. (1997) prescribed unsupervised PA on a daily basis for at least 30 min, but then again compliance with the exercise prescription was not reported. All exercise interventions that had an aerobic component prescribed walking, cycling, stepping, or exercising on an elliptical trainer at low to moderate intensity (40%–70% of VO_{2peak}). Castaneda and colleagues (Balakrishnan et al., 2010; Castaneda et al., 2004; Castaneda et al., 2001) prescribed RT for various upper and lower body muscle groups at 80% of one repetition maximum (1RM) with regular reassessments and adjustments of the resistance load. The progression of the exercise stimulus has not been clearly explained in any other studies. The exercise session durations ranged from 30 to 60 min in all studies.

Effects on Physiological Impairment: Cardiorespiratory and Muscular Fitness
Four RCTs reported objectively measured VO_{2peak} on a cycle (Eidemak et al., 1997; Mustata et al., 2011) or treadmill ergometer (Leehey et al., 2009; Gregory et al., 2011). The combined mean VO_{2peak} changed from 18.2 to 20.0 ml $\cdot$ kg^{-1} $\cdot$ min^{-1} in the ET groups and from a mean of 16.7 to 16.0 ml $\cdot$ kg^{-1} $\cdot$ min^{-1} in the control (CON) groups (see Table 8.1). The average increase in VO_{2peak} ($\sim$9%) was less than 1 MET (3.50 ml $\cdot$ kg^{-1} $\cdot$ min^{-1}), which is lower compared to the overall improvement observed following exercise rehabilitation during dialysis (11%–43%). This level of improvement, however, is similar to the amount of natural decline in VO_{2peak} observed in predialysis patients by Leikis et al. (2006), indicating that a decline in CV fitness could be at least halted by exercise interventions such as the ones described here. The CON groups also appeared to have substantially different baseline VO_{2peak} values compared to the ET groups (Eidemak et al., 1997; Leehey et al., 2009; Gregory et al., 2011), but studies did not report any statistical differences at baseline. However, the difference in VO_{2peak} following exercise

training widened substantially between the intervention and CON groups rang-ing from 2.20 (Gregory et al., 2011) to 8.00 ml $\cdot$ kg^{-1} $\cdot$ min^{-1} in the youngest patients (Eidemak et al., 1997) with the average difference being around 4.35 ml $\cdot$ kg^{-1} $\cdot$ min^{-1} by the end of the observation periods, indicating that although patients following the exercise interventions improved from baseline, patients in the CON group remained the same or, in some cases, deteriorated. The study by Gregory et al. (2011) reported that at baseline, about 500 kcal/week were expended during exercise and after about a year of combined aerobic and RT exer-cise, the energy expenditure via exercise was estimated to be around 1,000 kcal/week. This amount of exercise, which corresponds to the minimum amount of exercise necessary for health benefits to be realized (U.K. Department of Health, 2011; American College of Sports Medicine [ACSM] & American Diabetes Association [ADA], 2010), was associated with a 2.2 ml $\cdot$ kg^{-1} $\cdot$ min^{-1} increase in VO$_{2peak}$. Eidemak et al. (1997) aimed to achieve an energy expenditure of around 2,000 kcal/week during their 78-week home-based intervention, but they did not report whether this target was fully or partially achieved. VO$_{2peak}$ increased on average by about 2 ml $\cdot$ kg^{-1} $\cdot$ min^{-1} by the end of their intervention period (see Table 8.1). In our evaluation, it was not clearly reported whether and to what extent patients had complied with the overall exercise prescription. Therefore, the overall exercise volume may have not been of sufficient dose or overall duration to produce a clinically meaningful effect that can translate into an enhanced CV fit-ness and morbidity or mortality outcome in this group of patients. Future studies should aim to accurately quantify and report the amount of exercise prescribed versus the amount achieved in conjunction with associated research outcomes.

Data on muscular strength are reported in one RCT that included a resistance-based exercise training program (Balakrishnan et al., 2010; Castaneda et al., 2004; Castaneda et al., 2001; see Table 8.1). This well-designed and pro-gressive RT stimulus resulted in significant group interactions in all muscular strength assessment outcomes (1RM) for the upper and lower body, with average percentage improvements ranging from 29% to 47% in the ET group whereas the CON group experienced changes in the same measurements ranging from −9% to 2%. The 1RM of the quadriceps muscle group was also assessed in the non-RCT study by Heiwe, Clyne, Tollbäck, and Borg (2005) and Heiwe, Tollbäck, and Clyne (2001), which was primarily a resistance-based exercise training inter-vention. Data presented should be evaluated with caution because an increase in the median score of the ET of 2.0 kg (from 5.0 to 7.0 kg postintervention) was deemed significant, whereas an increase of 4.5 kg in the CON group (from 7.5 to 12.0 kg) was deemed as nonsignificant even though both groups had similar ranges in scores. At the same time, muscle fiber distribution based on muscle biopsy analyses did not significantly differ between the ET and CON groups.

Clyne, Ekholm, Jogestrand, Lins, and Pehrsson (1991) and Pechter et al. (2003) also reported peak power output (PPO) at the time of exhaustion during cycling ergometry as an indicator of peak muscle performance. The ET group improved PPO from 159 to 174 watts (about 9% improvement) following a general callisthenics-based training regimen, whereas the CON group remained at 171 watts at both assessment points. Patients in that study were achieving more than 90% of the expected norm at baseline (Clyne et al., 1991). Patients of similar age in the study by Pechter et al. underwent an aqua aerobic training program and were assessed using cycle ergometry. The ET group surprisingly increased PPO from 96.5 to 110.9 watts (about 15% improvement), whereas the CON group went from 127.8 watts at baseline to 124.4 watts following a 12-week follow-up. Although the authors did not comment on any significant differences for assessed outcomes at baseline, groups do not appear to be comparable in terms of physical function. It should be noted that in principle, people with lower physical function capacity to start with experience greater and quicker improvements following an exercise program, compared to "fitter" individuals.

Functional Limitations and Disability

Comprehensive and accurate measurement and reporting of physical function is very important if we want to determine physiological impairment and how this may lead to functional limitations and inevitably disability (Koufaki & Kouidi, 2010). The characterization and monitoring of physical function becomes even more important in the context of a highly prevalent frailty phenotype in patients in all stages of CKD that is apparent only in elderly patients (Blake & O'Meara, 2004; Johansen et al., 2007). The clinical use and discriminatory value of physical function outcomes for future adverse health events in patients with CKD, although limited, has also been noted (see the "Background" section earlier in this chapter).

Unfortunately, only one RCT has included outcomes that reflect functional limitations or disability levels (Mustata et al., 2011). In this study, the EuroQol (EQ-5D) and the SF-36 questionnaires were used to monitor changes in self-reported mobility, self-care, pain/discomfort (EQ-5D), and physical function (PCS from the SF-36 questionnaire). No statistically significant differences were observed between the ET and CON groups in pre–post evaluations. The authors claim a clinically important change in the "role physical" domain, but it should be noted that on average, the ET group physical function perceptions appeared lower compared to the CON group, and thus the nonsignificant changes noted may just reflect normal variation or regression to the mean trends. Two non-RCTs report data on the 6-min walk test (6MWT) and 3-m Timed Up & Go (TUG) test that are indicators of objectively measured functional limitations (Fitts, Guthrie,

& Blagg, 1999; Heiwe et al., 2001; see Table 8.1). Fitts et al. (1999) observed an increase of 3.90 m from a baseline distance of 581.00 m in their predialysis patients over a period of 6 months (gait speed of 1.61–1.62 m/s) and Heiwe et al. (2001) noted an increase of 62.00 m from a baseline value of 390.00 m (1.00–1.25 m/s). None of the two studies reported the data from their CON groups for comparison purposes, making it difficult to fully evaluate the true magnitude of change attributable to the exercise intervention. However, in both studies, CKD patients were well above the gait speed threshold of <0.65m/s, that is proposed as a criterion to classify patients at increased risk of developing functional dependencies (Painter & Marcus, 2013). The 3-m TUG score decreased from 11 to 9 s in the study by Fitts et al., but no comparative data from the CON group was provided. Three non-RCTs assessed self-reported physical function and disability via the use of the Karnofsky Index of Disability (KID), Sickness Impact Profile (SIP; Fitts et al., 1999; Heiwe et al., 2001), and the Functional Assessment of Chronic Illness Therapy—Spiritual Well-Being Scale (FACIT-Sp; Kosmadakis et al., 2012). The physical SIP scores were significantly different after 6 and 12 months of rehabilitation in the predialysis group compared to the CON group (0.2 vs. 1.9) as reported by Fitts et al. and it did not change in the study by Heiwe et al. The PCS of the FACIT-Sp questionnaire as presented in a graph in the study by Kosmadakis et al. (2012) had a similar pattern and magnitude of response in both exercise and CON groups. Overall, results on functional limitations and disability outcomes are extremely limited, highly variable, and thus inconclusive at this point of time, regarding the effectiveness of exercise interventions in preventing or alleviating functional dependencies. Future studies should aim to accurately and clearly report data on physical function outcomes reflecting functional limitations and disability that clearly link to clinically important benefits.

Residual Kidney Function and CV Risk Factors
There have been 4 RCTs (Castaneda et al., 2004; Castaneda et al., 2001; Eidemak et al., 1997; Gregory et al., 2011; Leehey et al., 2009) and 1 non-RCT (Toyama, Sugiyama, Oka, Sumida, & Ogawa, 2010) that have reported GFR as a secondary outcome. When all available data were pooled together, mean GFR changed on average from 36.9 to 42.4 ml/min/1.73m^2 in the ET groups and from 40.9 to 39.9 ml/min/1.73m^2 in the CON groups during the observation periods. Only the study by Toyama et al. (2010) reported a statistically significant increase in estimated GFR (eGFR) from baseline 47.0 (±13.7) ml/min/1.73m^2 to 52.2 (±16.9) ml/min/1.73m^2 postintervention in the ET group. This is surprising given the extremely small size ($n = 10$ vs. 9), the short intervention period (12 weeks), and the nature of the intervention (1 supervised cardiac rehabilitation session/week and self-managed daily walking for 30 min). However, they

did report significant improvements in lipid metabolism and submaximal aerobic metabolism (VO_2 at ventilator threshold) following comprehensive cardiac rehabilitation that included diet advice and behavior modification. Three of the longest in duration RCTs (48–78 weeks) showed no changes in eGFR even though they demonstrated significant but small improvements in cardiorespiratory fitness, but no other significant improvements in lipid and glucose metabolism or other biochemistry and CV outcomes. The research group by Castaneda et al. (Balakrishnan et al., 2010; Castaneda et al., 2004; Castaneda et al., 2001) that employed a progressive resistance-based exercise training program with low protein diet versus low protein diet alone for 12 weeks reported significant group interactions for eGFR (ET: 24.76–26.35 vs. CON: 30.01–28.03 ml/min/1.73m²), accompanied with significant improvements in muscle protein metabolism, mitochondrial content, muscle fiber area and strength, and reduction in inflammation markers such as C-reactive protein (CRP) and serum interleukin-6 (IL-6).

Traditional CVD risk factors such as those involved in the metabolic syndrome (i.e., hypertension, elevated fasting glucose, high cholesterol levels, and elevated free triglycerides) have long been implicated in the development and progression of kidney function loss and poor CV outcome in patients with established CKD. The rationale that exercise training may be able to favorably modify these CV risk factors and by extension improve the prognosis of patients with CKD is supported by available literature in other chronic CV and metabolic conditions (Heran et al., 2011; Orozco et al., 2008). It remains to be seen whether these observations can be confirmed in people with CKD. None of the RCTs that assessed blood pressure (BP) reported any significant favorable adaptations. Two non-RCTS reported significant reductions in SBP and DBP (Boyce et al., 1997; Pechter et al., 2003). On average, SBP decreased from 146.0 to 131.0 mmHg in the ET group and from 148.0 to 143.5 mmHg in the CON groups. In contrast, DBP decreased from 88.0 to 81.0 mmHg in the ET group and from 90.0 to 87.0 mmHg in the CON groups. Although changes in medications and health status were noted in the study by Boyce et al. (1997), BP medication doses were not increased. Caution should be applied in the interpretation of these findings because none of the studies was really powered or executed to assess BP responses. For example, although Boyce et al. did perform multiple BP measurements at different time points to establish a stable baseline value, repeat values after the training and detraining periods were based only on a single measurement. The same critical comment applies to the study by Pechter et al. (2003), where no information regarding how BP was assessed or changes in medication and health status was provided. Overall, no favorable responses to exercise training were reported for cholesterol, triglycerides, and fasting glucose levels in the studies that provided information on these outcomes (Boyce et al., 1997;

Eidemak et al., 1997; Gregory et al., 2011; Leehey et al., 2009; Pechter et al., 2003). Averaged total cholesterol remained around 5.20 mmol/L preexercise and postexercise training in the ET group and about the same in the CON groups before and after the interventions. Triglycerides remained around 1.90 mmol/L in the ET groups and around 2.10 mmol/L in the CON groups. Fasting glucose was at 1.90 mmol/L at baseline in the ET groups, and following the interventions, this was at 6.45 mmol/L, whereas in the CON group it went from 7.20 to 7.40 mmol/L. Two studies (Kosmadakis et al., 2012; Mustata et al., 2011) have reported the augmentation index (AI; %) as an indicator of arterial stiffness, a potent determinant and precursor of hypertension and of compromised vascular health, that strongly predicts CV outcome in patients with CKD (Mark et al., 2008). The averaged AI (%) remained the same in the ET groups (25.4%) and in the CON groups (24.2%) pre–post the intervention/observation periods.

Conclusion

There is some evidence from longitudinal observations that suggest a strong and independent reverse association between PA levels, functional capacity, and progression of kidney function loss (see the "Background" section earlier in this chapter) that even appears stronger in the more comorbid subgroup of this population. These relationships become apparent following observation of many thousand people over several years to monitor kidney function loss. Experimental interventions to modify PA levels have not consistently and meaningfully altered CV risk factors or renal function, even in the presence of improved physical function as a result of increased PA levels. The relatively short duration of interventions as well as the extremely small sample sizes, combined with the inherent large variability in individual kidney function loss progression, may be partially responsible for the lack of a systematic and consistent effect. Moreover, the dose of exercise may have not been sufficient to produce a larger effect in relatively short periods. According to Robinson-Cohen et al. (2009), the minimum amount of PA that was associated with significant reductions in kidney function decline was 1,012–2,088 kcal/week in models controlling only for race, age, and sex. The beneficial effect at this level was lost in analysis models that controlled for diabetes, CV disease, smoking, BMI, and medication use, suggesting perhaps that a greater amount of PA may be needed for people with these risk factors present. With these observations in mind and given the nature of exercise interventions employed as described in the published reports, it would be reasonable to speculate that the overall dose of exercise was not sufficient or effective in favorably modifying CV risk factors and thus residual renal function in people with CKD stages 3–4 even though it did result into meaningful physical function benefits. Future studies should aim to accurately quantify and prescribe exercise dosage that at least meets the minimum PA recommendation levels for health-related benefits.

EXERCISE THERAPY FOLLOWING
KIDNEY TRANSPLANTATION

KTx is an effective treatment option for life-threatening end-stage kidney disease and becomes a cost-effective treatment option over the average lifespan of the transplant, although it is not without associated risk (Garcia, Harden, & Chapman, 2012). The use of modern immunosuppression therapies have improved the life expectancy of kidney grafts; however, secondary complications such as diabetes, CVD, and obesity (Friedman, Miskulin, Rosenberg, & Levey, 2003; Gordon, Prohaska, Siminoff, Minich, & Sehgal, 2005) are an associated risk. CVD remains the leading cause of death in in KTx. It has been established that recipients of KTx increase their PA level in the subsequent years after transplantation because of improved quality of life; however, within that time, they do not reach the level of PA of those of age-matched healthy controls (Nielens et al, 2001). A reason for this may be that despite the reversal of many of the prevailing uremic symptoms following KTx, functional capacity remains compromised because of the combined effects of prior deconditioning, uremic myopathy, muscle atrophy, and also partly exacerbated by immunosuppression therapy. As a result, many of the CV and cardiometabolic risks/comorbidities that exist pretransplant will still be there even after KTx.

KTx may prove to be an ideal time point for health care providers to counsel patients on improving PA and maximizing their physical potential; however, there is limited data to support the provision of exercise therapy for these patients into routine patient care, and little evidence to suggest which type of exercise training therapy may be most beneficial.

Search Strategy

One nonblinded author (SG) identified potential studies by a systematic search of Ovid MEDLINE (1950–March 2013), Embase.com (1974–March 2013), Cochrane Central Register of Controlled Trials, Cumulative Index to Nursing and Allied Health Literature (CINAHL), Physiotherapy Evidence Database (PEDro), and Web of Science. The search strategy used the search terms chronic renal failure, chronic kidney disease, kidney transplantation, renal transplantation, exercise training, physical activity, aerobic exercise, resistance exercise, physical function, cardiovascular fitness, and cardiorespiratory fitness. Reference lists of papers found were scrutinized for new references.

Inclusion or Exclusion Criteria

Because of the limited number of published studies, we included RCTs, NRCTs, and UCTs where participants were older than 18 years of age and had a functioning graft. Studies were required to have a PA or exercise intervention component. Studies with prospective designs were included.

Animal studies, studies on joint kidney–pancreas transplants, and review papers were excluded. Studies that did not have an exercise or PA intervention or studies in languages other than English were also excluded.

Literature Search Results

There were 17 studies identified that met the inclusion criteria. There were six RCTs with an exercise intervention; however, two of these publications (Painter et al., 2002; Painter et al., 2003) report data from one RCT, so in fact there are five RCTs that were included in this review. There were three non-RCTs and eight uncontrolled observations (see Table 8.2). This review will concentrate on reporting the findings of the RCTs but will draw on the results of remaining studies where information may be clinically relevant. Any information garnered from these studies must, however, be interpreted with caution.

Systematic Synthesis and Evaluation of Research Evidence

Exercise Training Studies' Characteristics

In total, 304 men and women who had received a kidney transplant (mean ages ranging from 31 to 56 years) have been randomized to either an ET group ($n = 148$) or to a UC/attention control group ($n = 156$) at baseline. A further 506 men and women (465 KTx, 25 HD, and 4 liver transplant), mean ages ranging from 34 to 55 years, were involved in non-RCTs.

The kidney transplant vintage ranged from 2 days to 52 months. Exclusion criteria were not well-reported, but contraindications to the various training programs included CVD and diabetes. Seven studies reported a percentage dropout ranging from 4.2% to 43.0%. Compliance to the exercise programs ranged from 75.0% (Kempeneers et al, 1990) in a supervised exercise program for potential transplant games participants to 67.0% in a home exercise program for kidney transplant patients with a 12-month duration (Painter et al., 2002; Painter et al., 2003). The exercise or PA training programs are detailed in Table 8.2.

Effects on Physiological Impairment—Cardiorespiratory and Muscular Fitness

A recent small, nonrandomized study by Painter, Krasnoff, Kuskowski, Frassetto, and Johansen (2011) compared VO_{2peak} in patients on HD, kidney transplant recipients, and a sedentary CON group. Kidney transplant recipients improved their VO_{2peak} as a result of modality change, irrespective of any

TABLE 8.2

Summary of Exercise/PA Training Interventions in Kidney Transplant Recipients (Continued)

Studies	ET (n)	CON (n)	Age (Years)	Intervention/ Control Descriptions	Exercise Training Characteristics (FITT)	Exercise Duration (Weeks)	VO_{2peak} (%Δ in ET vs. CON)	Functional Limitation Index (%Δ)	Disability Index (%Δ)	eGFR Difference (ml/min/ 1.73m^2)
Randomized Controlled Clinical Trials										
Kouidi et al. (2012)	11	12	52	Supervised aerobic and strength training	4x/week 65%–85% HRmax C 60–90 min	24 weeks	15.8 vs. 0.0			
You et al. (2008)	15	14	NR	DanJeon Breathing Exercise Program—once weekly contact and daily at home	4–6x/week No intensity reported 60 min	10 weeks				
Korabiewska et al. (2007)	35	32	49	First 24 weeks: supervised and unsupervised— upper and lower limb strengthening, relaxation Last 24 weeks: walking	2–3x/week No intensity reported RT 20–30 min 1–3x/week Submaximal W 10–20 min	26 weeks 26 weeks		Handgrip: 16.0 vs. 6.0		27.0 vs. 41.0

Study				Intervention	Protocol	Duration				
Juskowa et al. (2006)	32	37	44, 46	Supervised and unsupervised inpatient program	7x/week ? intensity RT 30 min	4–6 weeks				
Painter et al. (2003)[a]	51	45	42	Home exercise program	<4x/week 60%–80% HRmax C, W <30 min	48 weeks				
Painter et al. (2002)[a]	54	43	42	Home-based to include cardiovascular (W/C)	<4x/week 60%–80% HRmax C, W <30 min	48 weeks	25.0 vs. 7.0	32.0 vs. 19.0	SF-36-PF: 25.0 vs. 14.0	−12.0 vs. 13.0

Nonrandomized Controlled Clinical Trials and Uncontrolled Observations

Study				Intervention	Protocol	Duration				
Greenwood et al. (2012)	77 (16 KTx, 29 HD, and 32 predialysis)	55		Supervised aerobic program	2–3x/week RPE 13–15 C, W, R, RT 60 min	12 weeks	ISWT: 31.0 3-m TUG: 15.0 SCD: 19.0	DASI: 30.0		
Romano et al. (2010)	8	52		Supervised aerobic exercise	3x/week 50%–90% HRmax C 40 min	10 weeks or 30 sessions 13.0	SF-36-PF (total value): 40.0			

(Continued)

TABLE 8.2
Summary of Exercise/PA Training Interventions in Kidney Transplant Recipients   (Continued)

Studies	ET (n)	CON (n)	Age (Years)	Intervention/Control Descriptions	Exercise Training Characteristics (FITT)	Exercise Duration (Weeks)	VO_{2peak} (%Δ in ET vs. CON)	Functional Limitation Index (%Δ)	Disability Index (%Δ)	eGFR Difference (ml/min/1.73m²)
Sharif et al. (2008)	Glucose intolerant + exercise (36) Glucose tolerant + no exercise (79)			Unsupervised, home-based program	1x/week ? intensity W, R, S 120 min	26 weeks				−2.0
van den Ham et al. (2007)	35 KTx, 16 HD	21	52	Supervised resistance training, aerobic exercise	2x/week 70% peak watts C, W, S, RT, gymnastics		10.0	10.0		
Violan et al. (2002)	12 KTx, 9 HD		35	Supervised aerobic exercise	3x/week 60% HRmax W, R, ball games 50 min	26 weeks	18.0			

Author						
Surgit et al. (2001)	16 (12 KTx, 4 liver)	NR	Supervised aerobic	3x/week NR intensity C 45 min	9 weeks	11.0
Kempeneers et al. (1990)	24 KTx, detailed = 16	Tx 33, control: 24	Supervised aerobic	3x/week 80% HRmax calisthenics, ball games 60 min	26 weeks	26.0	22.0
Triolo et al. (1989)	26 low protein diet with exercise	26 control with exercise	NR	Diet and home-based exercise program	NR W, C, stair climb, RT	26 weeks
Horber et al. (1987)	9	34	Supervised outpatient program	3x/week 8–10 repetitions or exhaustion RT 20 min	6 weeks	15.0
Miller et al. (1987)	1	32	Supervised and unsupervised and home-based aerobic exercise	3x/week 40%–60% HRmax W, C 25–40 min	108–113 weeks	Multiples resting metabolic rate— 114.0	17.0

(Continued)

TABLE 8.2
Summary of Exercise/PA Training Interventions in Kidney Transplant Recipients   (Continued)

Studies	ET (n)	CON (n)	Age (Years)	Intervention/Control Descriptions	Exercise Training Characteristics (FITT)	Exercise Duration (Weeks)	VO_{2peak} (%Δ in ET vs. CON)	Functional Limitation Index (%Δ)	Disability Index (%Δ)	eGFR Difference (ml/min/1.73m²)
Horber et al. (1985)	12	12 healthy	37	supervised outpatient program	3x/week 8–10 repetitions max or exhaustion RT 20 min	8 weeks	22.0		Thigh muscle cross-sectional area exercise vs. nonexercised leg—8.0	

Note. Data are presented as means unless otherwise indicated. C = cycling; CON = control group with n = number of control participants who had follow-up data; Δ = positive changes unless otherwise indicated by the preceding sign; ET = exercise training group with n = number of exercising patients that had follow-up data; FITT = frequency/week, intensity as %, type, time (session duration in minutes); HRmax = maximum heart rate; ISWT = Incremental Shuttle Walk Test; KTx = kidney transplant; NR = not reported; PCS = Physical Composite Score from SF-36 questionnaire; R = running; RT = resistance training; S = swimming; SCD = stair climb and descent; SF-36-PF = physical function component from SF-36 questionnaire; 6MWT = 6-min walk test; STS = sit-to-stand; 3-m TUG = 3-m Up & Go test; Tx = treatment; W = walking.
[a]Publications from the same sample population.

other intervention, although the resultant VO_{2peak} remained only 79.0% of age predicted. An earlier study by Painter, Hanson, Messer-Rehak, Zimmerman, and Glass (1987) confirms this finding, with VO_{2peak} increasing by 27.0% without exercise intervention. The addition of an exercise intervention to further improve on VO_{2peak} that is achieved with transplant alone and to aid individuals to achieve closer to normal age-predicted values post-KTx may be warranted. VO_{2peak} was assessed in two of the five independent RCTs that included an exercise intervention (Kouidi, Vergoulas, Anifanti, & Deligiannis, 2012; Painter et al., 2002; Painter et al., 2003). Both of these trials report significant improvements in VO_{2peak} of 15.8% (Kouidi et al., 2012) and 25.0% (Painter et al., 2002; Painter et al., 2003) when compared with a comparable CON group, following an exercise intervention. The exercise ($n = 11$), sedentary ($n = 12$), and healthy ($n = 12$) groups in the study by Kouidi et al. report similar baseline exercise testing values and a significant difference in VO_{2peak} of 5.5 ml · kg^{-1} · min^{-1} in the exercise versus sedentary group and 5.6 ml · kg^{-1} · min^{-1} in the exercise versus healthy group. The supervised exercise intervention in the 6-month, 4 times a week program was designed with sufficient overload and intensity (50%–75% VO_{2peak} or 65%–85% maximum heart rate [HRmax]) to elicit this response. However, because of the small number of participants, there is limited generalizability of these results. The RCT by Painter et al. (2002) and Painter et al. (2003) randomized 52 patients to an individualized, aerobic, 12-month duration home exercise program, and 46 patients received usual care. The home exercise program used walking and cycling at 60%–65% of HRmax, which was progressed until a target of 75%–80% was reached. The baseline exercise testing values were similar between the exercise and UC group. At 6 months, the exercise group had achieved a mean improvement in VO_{2peak} of 3.8 ml · kg^{-1} · min^{-1}, whereas the UC group improved by a mean of 3.6 ml · kg^{-1} · min^{-1}. Self-reported regular exercise participation at this time point was 58% and 42% respectively. At 12 months, a mean change in VO_{2peak} of 6.1 ml · kg^{-1} · min^{-1} from baseline measures was elicited in the exercise intervention (EX) group, compared with a mean improvement of only 1.8 ml · kg^{-1} · min^{-1} in the UC group. The mean VO_{2peak} declined between 6- and 12-month testing in the UC group, corresponding with a reduction in the amount of self-reported PA in this group (36%). Sixty-seven percent of the exercise group were reported to be still exercising regularly at 12 months showing very good compliance to this type of exercise intervention. At 12-month testing, the percentage of age-predicted values for the EX group was 85% compared with 77% in the UC group. It was suggested by Painter et al. (2011) that improvements in muscle metabolism may be necessary to increase the arterial venous oxygen difference, which in turn may further improve VO_{2peak} in the kidney transplant recipient population.

Cardiorespiratory exercise capacity was reported in seven of the interventional studies without a comparable CON group (Greenwood et al., 2012; Kempeneers et al., 1990; Miller et al., 1987; Romano et al., 2010; Surgit, Ersoz, G., Gursel, & Ersoz, S., 2001; van den Ham et al., 2007; Violan et al., 2002). The incremental shuttle walk test (ISWT; Greenwood et al., 2012) improved by 88.1 m (31%) following an individually prescribed 12-week, aerobic and strengthening program at a rated perceived exertion (RPE) of 13–16. The study by Romano et al. (2010) used a supervised, 30-min interval training routine at 90% of peak heart rate for 30 sessions, and demonstrated that maximal oxygen uptake (VO_{2max}) increased significantly from 27.58 ± 4.82 ml · kg^{-1} · min^{-1} to 31.31 ± 4.65 ml · kg^{-1} · min^{-1}, accompanied by a significant increase in maximum working capacity from 90 ± 14 to 115 ± 15 watts. Van den Ham et al. (2007) used an exercise training program that consisted of both endurance (cycling) and RT. The cycling was prescribed at 60%–70% of participants' peak workload, resulting in a significant increase in VO_{2peak} from 21.6 (±6.3) to 23.8 (±6.1) ml · min^{-1} · kg^{-1}. In a study by Violan et al. (2002), VO_{2peak} is reported to have improved by 18% in the kidney transplant recipients trained in a supervised program of walking, jogging, and ball games at 60% of HRmax; however, no actual values are reported. VO_{2peak} improvements of 11% are reported in the study by Surgit et al. (2001). This gain was achieved with a thrice-weekly 45-min supervised cycling program. No actual values or intensity is described in the publication. Kempeneers et al. (1990) trained very motivated kidney transplant recipients thrice-weekly for 6 months using a combination of jogging, walking, calisthenics, and ball games at an intensity that progressed to 90% of their HRmax. VO_{2max} improved from 29.0 (±7.8) to 37.5 (±4.8) ml · min^{-1} · kg^{-1}. The posttraining levels, even at this intensity of training, only reached the upper range for healthy persons starting exercise. Lastly, Miller et al. (1987) report an improvement in metabolic equivalents from a baseline value of 5.1 to 9.7 METs following a 2-month supervised cycle and treadmill program prescribed at an intensity of 40%–60% of HRmax. These favorable improvements in cardiorespiratory parameters are in agreement with the previously discussed RCTs (Kouidi et al., 2012; Painter et al., 2002; Painter et al., 2003) and are clinically interesting in the absence of more RCTs in this area, but the absence of a comparable CON group does not allow us to use this data to draw any firm conclusions.

Only one of the RCTs (Painter et al., 2002; Painter et al., 2003) objectively measured muscle strength (quadriceps peak torque) reporting statistically significant improvements of 8.0 ft.lbs/kg (32%) versus 3.5 ft.lbs/kg (19%) between their EX group when compared with the CON group. This finding was surprising because the exercise intervention was aerobic home-based exercise. However, the reported improvements in muscle strength remained lower than normal values suggesting the need for inclusion of RT to elicit the amount of improvement that would translate into meaningful functional improvements. Korabiewska, Lewandowska, Juskowa, and Bialoszewski (2007) used a supervised RT program, followed by a submaximal walking program, and described a significant improvement in handgrip strength from 15.99 (4.42) to 18.56 (2.36) PSI in their intervention group versus only a modest increase from 15.89 (6.01) to 16.88 (4.34) PSI in the CON group.

Muscle strength was reported in four uncontrolled observations (Horber et al., 1987; Horber, Scheidegger, Grunig, & Frey, 1985; Kempeneers et al., 1990; van den Ham et al., 2007). These studies showed significant mean increases of between 10% and 22% in upper and lower limb muscle strength following an exercise intervention. The largest improvements were noted in those exercise studies with a specific strength training component. The only observational study of habitual PA that assessed muscle strength (van den Ham et al., 2005) reported no independent effect of habitual PA on muscle strength.

Functional Limitations and Disability
Greenwood et al. (2012) was the only interventional study, albeit without a comparable CON group, which assessed objective physical function outcomes other than muscle strength. In this study, the 3-m TUG time decreased significantly from 8.10 s (2.83) to 6.90 s (1.60), and the time to complete the stair climb or descent test decreased significantly from 25.75 s (9.47) to 21.00 s (6.90) in the kidney transplant subgroup (see Table 8.2).

Painter et al. (2002) evaluated quality of life with the SF-36 questionnaire. There was no difference at 12 months follow-up in self-reported physical function in the EX group when compared with UC (baseline: EX 68.1 ± 19.5, UC 64.1 ± 19.7; 12 months: EX 84.8 ± 21.6, UC 73.2 ± 29.4; $p = .06$). Although both groups improved in role limitations relating to physical health (RP) section of the questionnaire during the 12 months (baseline: EX 39.0 ± 37.5, UC 542.9 ± 37.4; 12 months: EX 59.4 ± 40.5, UC 60.6 ± 39.5), it remained low compared with the general population (average for general population is 83). General health scores remained similar across both groups. The uncontrolled interventional study by Romano et al. (2010) assessed quality of life with the SF-36 questionnaire. Significant mean improvements of 40% were reported in this outcome, although the results were not described according to the individual components of the scale, and therefore we were unable to determine the effect of the exercise intervention on each component. The uncontrolled pragmatic renal rehabilitation study described by Greenwood et al. (2012) reports a significant improvement in the DASI, following an exercise intervention that was individually prescribed to kidney transplant recipients according to their baseline scores.

The DASI improved from 26.1 in RP section of the questionnaire ($\pm$11.8) to 33.8 ($\pm$12.9) following the 12-week intervention.

A study by Painter et al. (1987), an observational study of habitual PA in a highly motivated group of organ transplant recipients participating in transplant games, reported that health-related fitness and quality of life, as measured with the self-reported SF-36, were near normal levels for those participants who participated in regular PA. This highly select group is however not representative of the general kidney transplant population.

Residual Kidney Function and CV Risk Factors

Serum creatinine levels were reported in two of the controlled interventional studies (Korabiewska et al., 2007; You, Chung, So, & Choi, 2008). The study by You et al. (2008) reported significant improvements in kidney function but did not report the actual values. Korabiewska et al. (2007) and three of the uncontrolled interventional studies (Painter et al., 2003; Romano et al., 2010; Sharif, Moore, & Baboolal, 2008) showed no significant improvements in kidney function. Miller et al. (1987) demonstrated a nonsignificant increase in serum creatinine during the exercise intervention. None of the studies had a sufficiently long enough follow-up period to assess the effect of the intervention on the long-term outcome of kidney function, and no study used the gold standard method of inulin clearance to ascertain kidney function.

An RCT by Juskowa et al. (2006) evaluated the effect of early physical rehabilitation (2 days posttransplantation, continuing for 5 weeks during hospitalization) and risk of atherosclerosis after successful kidney transplantation. The authors found an inverse correlation between total homocysteine as well as interleukin-18 (IL-18) levels and muscle strength of the upper limbs, and reported a positive correlation between muscle strength and improved graft function in the EX group versus the CON group. The uncontrolled study by Romano et al. (2010) reported a significant mean reduction in IL-6, a proinflammatory cytokine, following an exercise intervention (1.1 pg/ml). It has been widely recognized that IL-6 plays a significant role in the progression of mesangial proliferative glomerulonephritis (Horii et al., 1993), and that it is a risk factor for relapse of IgA nephropathy in transplanted patients (Odum et al., 1994). The study by Romano et al. is the first study, albeit uncontrolled, that has reported the effect of IL-6 lowering in kidney transplant recipients. Surgit et al. (2001), in an uncontrolled interventional study, reported a statistically significant enhanced immune response (peripheral T-helper cells, IgG, and IgM levels) following an exercise program, but reported no graft dysfunction in the short-term. Further studies examining the role of exercise and its influence on inflammatory markers may be especially pertinent given the inherent CV risk and associated mortality in this population. The influence of exercise on nitric oxide levels, reactive oxygen species, and the resultant effect this may have on the vasculature of kidney transplant recipients certainly also warrants further investigation in future studies.

Cardiac autonomic function following an exercise intervention in kidney transplant recipients was reported for the first time in the RCT by Kouidi et al. (2012). Heart rate variability and baroreflex sensitivity (BRS) were significantly improved by an exercise training intervention. This study was adequately powered to confidently report the improvements in BRS of 43.7% in transplant recipients who followed the aerobic training program and suggest that improvements in CV efficiency may lead to a better CV prognosis in kidney transplant recipients.

BP was assessed in two RCTs (Kouidi et al., 2012; Painter et al., 2003) and was not significantly altered by the exercise programs used in these studies. It is suggested that it may be unreasonable to expect exercise training alone to overcome the secondary effects of medications, such as immunosuppressive medication that is known to contribute to elevated BP, and underlying renal pathological states (Painter et al., 2011). However, an uncontrolled study by Romano et al. (2010) did report a significant improvement in resting mean arterial pressure of 13 mmHg following 30 sessions of exercise training. This study prescribed a supervised aerobic exercise program (interval cycling at a moderate to high intensity), which may have achieved the appropriate dosage of exercise required to elicit an improvement in this parameter. This result is corroborated by Kempeneers et al. (1990) who also demonstrated improvements in BP following a high-level 6-month training program designed for 16 kidney transplant patients who wished to partake in the transplant games. BP was a secondary outcome in both of these studies, and the small sample size and lack of a comparable CON group in either study means that these results must be interpreted with caution. As in the HD population, further large-scale trials that are adequately powered to detect changes in BP are required, and the type of exercise intervention which may be required must be assessed in RCTs.

Blood lipid measures were reported in two of the interventional RCTs (Juskowa et al., 2006; Painter et al., 2003). Neither study showed significant reductions in total cholesterol and high-density lipid cholesterol. The controlled study by You et al. (2008) reports improvements in serum cholesterol; however, the improvement is incalculable because of poor reporting. Of the remaining uncontrolled observations (Sharif et al., 2008; Triolo et al., 1989), only Triolo and colleagues (1989) reports a significant reduction in both total cholesterol and high-density lipoprotein cholesterol. The study by Triolo et al. evaluated the effects of PA, in conjunction with two different dietary approaches (unsaturated and polyunsaturated lipids compared with an animal protein diet with less than 300 mg cholesterol/day). The results of this combined approach of diet and exercise suggest the importance of multiple lifestyle intervention modifications when aiming for outcomes such as dyslipidemia.

Conclusion

The supporting literature for using exercise as part of a lifestyle modification program in patients with CKD is hampered by the large variety of exercise prescriptions, inconsistent reporting of methodology, and a lack of trials that use a training program that is designed with specificity and correct overload to address the specific physical and CV shortcomings that are inherent in this patient population. There is perhaps also a requirement to investigate a multiple risk modification program, with exercise prescription as a component, to achieve really meaningful changes in the CV risk associated with the kidney transplant population. There is, however, a need to explore the potential value of exercise training modalities to counter the reduced physical function (associated with muscle problems) and also CV risk (including VO_{2peak} and vascular dysfunction) in large scale, adequately powered RCTs. Until we have supporting data from some large RCTs, with these specific targets as the primary focus, we cannot expect commissioning bodies to invest money in facilities and exercise-trained personnel to provide this part of patient care.

The Way Forward—Translational Rehabilitation

The evidence for the benefits of PA for patients with CKD is accumulating, and encouragement to exercise and lead a physically active lifestyle is included in the national CKD management guidelines (U.K. Department of Health, 2005). The challenge is, quite clearly, how to translate the research findings outlined previously into routine clinical practice.

Strong evidence for the beneficial effects of exercise in nonresearch settings at least for patients receiving dialysis comes from the Dialysis Outcomes and Practice Patterns Study (DOPPS) published in 2010. A cross-section of 20,920 DOPPS participants in 12 countries from 1996 to 2004 were reviewed. Regular exercise was associated with higher health-related quality of life, better physical functioning, fewer limitations in physical functioning, better sleep quality, less intrusiveness of body pain or anorexia, a more positive affect, and fewer depressive symptoms. The offering of exercise in a unit was associated with 38% higher odds of exercising patients. Finally, overall mortality risk was lower in those units with more exercisers.

The following are suggestions for ways that might be adopted to facilitate the incorporation of exercise rehabilitation into routine care:

- Education, support, and advocacy should be offered to nephrologists, nurses, and other health care professionals caring for CKD patients.
- Exercise promotion, advice, or services should be offered as part of routine care in all renal units by specially trained personnel who understand the "art and science" of sufficient and effective exercise prescription.
- Standards of care relating to exercise rehabilitation endorsed by national and professional bodies should be developed with an agreed timescale for their implementation. The participation of representative patients' groups (National Kidney Federation in the United Kingdom and similar organizations in the United States and elsewhere) should be part of these activities.
- The documentation of functional capacity initially and serially after the start of formal renal treatment should exist in all national registries. In addition, every unit undertaking exercise promotion and delivery should document its effects and associations as part of routine care in an accurate and standardized way.
- Funding of well-designed, multicenter research continues to be crucial to provide a better evidence base. Future larger research trials should aim to specifically address the relationship between changes in physiological function and whether these translate into changes in functional outcome benefits, less morbidity and disability, and improved quality of life.

Thus, although the research evidence base needs more work, the association between exercise and better outcomes in the CKD population is sufficiently strong to state the following: It is now time, as has been stated by several authors of previous reviews, for nephrologists and nurses and their colleagues, for their professional bodies, and for government health departments to recognize the potential importance of this area of renal care and further invest in it.

ACKNOWLEDGMENT

The first two authors contributed to this chapter equally as co-lead authors.

REFERENCES

American College of Sports Medicine, & American Diabetes Association. (2010). Exercise and type 2 diabetes. The American College of Sports Medicine and the American Diabetes Association: Joint position statement. *Medicine and Science in Sports and Exercise*, 42(12), 2282–2303.

Aoike, D. T., Baria, F., Rocha, M. L., Kamimura, M. A., Mello, M. T., Tufik, S., . . . Cuppari, L. (2012). Impact of training at ventilatory threshold on cardiopulmonary and functional capacity in overweight patients with chronic kidney disease. *Journal Brasileiro de Nefrologia*, 34(2), 139–147.

Balakrishnan, V. S., Rao, M., Menon, V., Gordon, P. L., Pilichowska, M., Castaneda, F., & Castaneda-Sceppa, C. (2010). Resistance training increases muscle mitochondrial biogenesis in patients with chronic kidney disease. *Clinical Journal of the American Society of Nephrology, 5*(6), 996–1002.

Blake, C., Codd, M. B., Cassidy, A., & O'Meara, Y. M. (2000). Physical function, employment and quality of life in end-stage renal disease. *Journal of Nephrology, 13*(2), 142–149.

Blake, C., & O'Meara, Y. M. (2004). Subjective and objective physical limitations in high-functioning renal dialysis patients. *Nephrology, Dialysis, Transplantation, 19*(12), 3124–3129.

Boyce, M. L., Robergs, R. A., Avasthi, P. S., Roldan, C., Foster, A., Montner, P., . . . Nelson, C. (1997). Exercise training by individuals with predialysis renal failure: Cardiorespiratory endurance, hypertension, and renal function. *American Journal of Kidney Diseases, 30*(2), 180–192.

Brodin, E., Ljungman, S., & Sunnerhagen, K. S. (2008). Rising from a chair: A simple screening test for physical function in predialysis patients. *Scandinavian Journal of Urology and Nephrology, 42*(3), 293–300.

Castaneda, C., Gordon, P. L., Parker, R. C., Uhlin, K. L., Roubenoff, R., & Levey, A. S. (2004). Resistance training to reduce the malnutrition-inflammation complex syndrome of chronic kidney disease. *American Journal of Kidney Diseases, 43*(4), 607–616.

Castaneda, C., Gordon, P. L., Uhlin, K. L., Levey, A. S., Kehayias, J. J., Dwyer, J. T., . . . Singh, M. F. (2001). Resistance training to counteract the catabolism of a low-protein diet in patients with chronic renal insufficiency. A randomized, controlled trial. *Annals of Internal Medicine, 135*(11), 965–976.

Cheema, B. S., & Singh, M. A. (2005). Exercise training in patients receiving maintenance hemodialysis: A systematic review of clinical trials. *American Journal of Nephrology, 25*(4), 352–364.

Clyne, N., Ekholm, J., Jogestrand, T., Lins, L. E., & Pehrsson, S. K. (1991). Effects of exercise training in predialytic uremic patients. *Nephron, 59*(1), 84–89.

Colangelo, R. M., Stillman, M. J., Kessler-Fogil, D., & Kessler-Hartnett, D. (1997). The role of exercise in rehabilitation for patients with end-stage renal disease. *Rehabilitation Nursing, 22*(6), 288–292.

Cook, S. A., MacLaughlin, H., & Macdougall, I. C. (2008). A structured weight management programme can achieve improved functional ability and significant weight loss in obese patients with chronic kidney disease. *Nephrology, Dialysis, Transplantation, 23*(1), 263–268.

Coresh, J., Byrd-Holt, D., Astor, B. C., Briggs, J. P., Eggers, P. W., Lacher, D. A., & Hostetter, T. H. (2005). Chronic kidney disease awareness, prevalence, and trends among U.S. adults, 1999 to 2000. *Journal of the American Society of Nephrology, 16*(1), 180–188.

Eidemak, I., Haaber, A. B., Feldt-Rasmussen, B., Kanstrup, I. L., & Strandgaard, S. (1997). Exercise training and the progression of chronic renal failure. *Nephron, 75*(1), 36–40.

Fitts, S. S., Guthrie, M. R., & Blagg, C. R. (1999). Exercise coaching and rehabilitation counseling improve quality of life for predialysis and dialysis patients. *Nephron, 82*(2), 115–121.

Fried, L. F., Lee, J. S., Shlipak, M., Chertow, G. M., Green, C., Ding, J., . . . Newman, A. B. (2006). Chronic kidney disease and functional limitation in older people: Health, aging and body composition study. *Journal of the American Geriatrics Society, 54*(5), 750–756.

Friedman, A. N., Miskulin, D. C., Rosenberg, I. H., & Levey, A. S. (2003). Demographics and trends in overweight and obesity in patients at time of kidney transplantation. *American Journal of Kidney Diseases, 41*(2), 480–487.

Garcia, G. G., Harden, P., & Chapman, J. (2012). The global role of kidney transplantation. *Current Opinion in Nephrology and Hypertension, 21*(3), 229–234.

Gordon, E. J., Prohaska, T., Siminoff, L. A., Minich, P. J., & Sehgal, A. R. (2005). Needed: Tailored exercise regimens for kidney transplant recipients. *American Journal of Kidney Diseases, 45*(4), 769–774.

Greenwood, S. A., Lindup, H., Taylor, K., Koufaki, P., Rush, R., Macdougall, I. C., & Mercer, T. H. (2012). Evaluation of a pragmatic exercise rehabilitation programme in chronic kidney disease. *Nephrology, Dialysis, Transplantation, 27*(Suppl. 3), iii126–iii134.

Gregory, S. M., Headley, S. A., Germain, M., Flyvbjerg, A., Frystyk, J., Coughlin, M. A., . . . Nindl, B. C. (2011). Lack of circulating bioactive and immunoreactive IGF-1 changes despite improved fitness in chronic kidney disease patients following 48 weeks of physical training. *Growth Hormone & IGF Research, 21*(1), 51–56.

Health Survey for England. (2009). *Volume 1: Health and Lifestyles.* Available from: http://www.hscic.gov.uk/pubs/hse09report

Heimbürger, O., Qureshi, A. R., Blaner, W. S., Berglund, L., & Stenvinkel, P. (2000). Hand-grip muscle strength, lean body mass, and plasma proteins as markers of nutritional status in patients with chronic renal failure close to start of dialysis therapy. *American Journal of Kidney Diseases, 36*(6), 1213–1225.

Heiwe, S., Clyne, N., Tollbäck, A., & Borg, K. (2005). Effects of regular resistance training on muscle histopathology and morphometry in elderly patients with chronic kidney disease. *American Journal of Physical Medicine & Rehabilitation, 84*(11), 865–874.

Heiwe, S., & Jacobson, S. H. (2011). Exercise training for adults with chronic kidney disease. *The Cochrane Database of Systematic Reviews,* Oct 5(10), CD003236.

Heiwe, S., Tollbäck, A., & Clyne, N. (2001). Twelve weeks of exercise training increases muscle function and walking capacity in elderly predialysis patients and healthy subjects. *Nephron, 88*(1), 48–56.

Heran, B. S., Chen, J. M. H., Ebrahim, S., Moxham, T., Oldridge, N., Rees, K., . . . Taylor, R. S. (2011). Exercise-based cardiac rehabilitation for coronary heart disease. *The Cochrane Database of Systematic Reviews,* Jul 6(7), CD001800.

Himmelfarb, J. (2004). Linking oxidative stress and inflammation in kidney disease: Which is the chicken and which is the egg? *Seminars in Dialysis, 17*(6), 449–454.

Holt, S., & Goldsmith, D. (2011). Renal Association Clinical Practice Guideline on cardiovascular disease in CKD. *Nephron. Clinical Practice, 118*(Supp. 1), c125–c144.

Horber, F. F., Hoopeler, H., Scheidegger, J. R., Grünig, B. E., Howald, H., & Frey, F. J. (1987). Impact of physical training on the ultrastructure of midthigh muscle in normal subjects and in patients treated with glucocorticoids. *The Journal of Clinical Investigation, 79*(4), 1181–1190.

Horber, F. F., Scheidegger, J. R., Grunig, B. E., & Frey, F. J. (1985). Thigh muscle mass and function in patients treated with glucocorticoids. *European Journal of Clinical Investigation, 15*(6), 302–307.

Horii, Y., Iwano, M., Hirata, E., Shiiki, M., Fujii, Y., Dohi, K., & Ishikawa, H. (1993). Role of interleukin-6 in the progression of mesangial proliferative glomerulonephritis. *Kidney International. Supplement, 39,* S71–S75.

Johansen, K. L., Chertow, G. M., Jin, C., & Kutner, N. G. (2007). Significance of frailty among dialysis patients. *Journal of the American Society of Nephrology, 18*(11), 2960–2967.

Johansen, K. L., & Painter, P. (2012). Exercise in individuals with CKD. *American Journal of Kidney Diseases, 59*(1), 126–134.

Juskowa, J., Lewandowska, M., Bartlomiejczyk, I., Foroncewicz, B., Korabiewska, I., Niewczas, M., & Sierdziński, J. (2006). Physical rehabilitation and risk of atherosclerosis after successful kidney transplantation. *Transplantation Proceedings, 38*(1), 157–160.

Kempeneers, G., Noakes, T. D., van Zyl-Smit, R., Myburgh, K. H., Lambert, M., Adams, B., & Wiggins, T. (1990). Skeletal muscle limits the exercise tolerance of renal transplant recipients: Effects of a graded exercise training program. *American Journal of Kidney Diseases, 16*(1), 57–65.

Korabiewska, L., Lewandowska, M., Juskowa, J., & Bialoszewski, D. (2007). Need for rehabilitation in renal replacement therapy involving allogeneic kidney transplantation. *Transplantation Proceedings, 39*(9), 2776–2777.

Kosmadakis, G. C., John, S. G., Clapp, E. L., Viana, J. L., Smith, A. C., Bishop, N. C., . . . Freehally, J. (2012). Benefits of regular walking exercise in advanced pre-dialysis chronic kidney disease. *Nephrology, Dialysis, Transplantation, 27*(3), 997–1004.

Koufaki, P., & Kouidi, E.(2010) Current best evidence recommendations on measurement and interpretation of physical function in patients with chronic kidney disease. *Sports Medicine, 40*(12), 1055–1074.

Kouidi, E., Vergoulas, G., Anifanti, M., & Deligiannis, A. (2012). A randomized controlled trial of exercise training on cardiovascular and autonomic function among renal transplant recipients. *Nephrology, Dialysis, Transplantation, 28*(5), 1294–1305.

Kurella, M., Ireland, C., Hlatky, M. A., Shlipak, M. G., Yaffe, K., Hulley, S. B., & Chertow, G. M. (2004) Physical and sexual function in women with chronic kidney disease. *American Journal of Kidney Diseases, 43*(5), 868–876.

Kurella Tamura, M., Covinsky, K. E., Chertow, G. M., Yaffe, K., Landefeld, C. S., & McCulloch, C. E. (2009). Functional status of elderly adults before and after initiation of dialysis. *The New England Journal of Medicine, 361*(16), 1539–1547.

Leehey, D. J., Moinuddin, I., Bast, J. P., Qureshi, S., Jelinek, C. S., Cooper, C., . . . Collins, E. G. (2009). Aerobic exercise in obese diabetic patients with chronic kidney disease: A randomized and controlled pilot study. *Cardiovascular Diabetology, 8*, 62.

Leikis, M. J., McKenna, M. J., Petersen, A. C., Kent, A. B., Murphy, K. T., Leppik, J. A., . . . McMahon, L. P. (2006). Exercise performance falls over time in patients with chronic kidney disease despite maintenance of hemoglobin concentration. *Clinical Journal of the American Society of Nephrology, 1*(3), 488–495.

Lowrie, E. G., Curtin, R. B., LePain, N., & Schatell, D. (2003). Medical outcomes study short form-36: A consistent and powerful predictor of morbidity and mortality in dialysis patients. *American Journal of Kidney Diseases, 41*(6), 1286–1292.

Macdonald, J. H., Kirkman, D., & Jibani, M. (2009). Kidney transplantation: A systematic review of interventional and observational studies of physical activity on intermediate outcomes. *Advances in Chronic Kidney Disease, 16*(6), 482–500.

MacLaughlin, H. L., Cook, S. A., Kariyawasam, D., Roseke, M., van Niekerk, M., & Macdougall, I. C. (2010). Nonrandomized trial of weight loss with orlistat, nutrition education, diet, and exercise in obese patients with CKD: 2-year follow-up. *American Journal of Kidney Diseases, 55*(1), 69–76.

Mapes, D. L., Lopes, A. A., Satayathum, S., McCullough, K. P., Goodkin, D. A., Locatelli, F., . . . Port, F. K. (2003). Health-related quality of life as a predictor of mortality and hospitalization: The Dialysis Outcomes and Practice Patterns Study (DOPPS). *Kidney International, 64*(1), 339–349.

Mark, P. B., Doyle, A., Blyth, K. G., Patel, R. K., Weir, R. A. P., Steedman, T., . . . Jardine, A. G. (2008). Vascular function assessed with cardiovascular magnetic resonance predicts survival in patients with advanced chronic kidney disease. *Journal of Cardiovascular Magnetic Resonance, 10*, 39.

Miller, T. D., Squires, R. W., Gau, G. T., Ilstrup, D. M., Frohnert, P. P., & Sterioff, S. (1987). Graded exercise testing and training after renal transplantation: A preliminary study. *Mayo Clinic Proceedings, 62*(9), 773–777.

Mustata, S., Groeneveld, S., Davidson, W., Ford, G., Kiland, K., & Manns, B. (2011). Effects of exercise training on physical impairment, arterial stiffness and health-related quality of life in patients with chronic kidney disease: A pilot study. *International Urology and Nephrology, 43*(4), 1133–1141.

Myers, J., Prakash, M., Froelicher, V., Do, D., Partington, S., & Atwood, J. E. (2002). Exercise capacity and mortality among men referred for exercise testing. *The New England Journal of Medicine*, 346(11), 793–801.

NHS Scotland. (2012, October). The Scottish Renal Registry Report 2011, With demographic data to 2011 and audit data to 2012. Available from: http://www.srr.scot.nhs.uk/

Nielens, H., Lejeune, T. M., Lalaoui, A., Squifflet, J. P., Pirson, Y., & Goffin, E. (2001). Increase of physical activity level after successful renal transplantation: A 5-year follow-up study. *Nephrology, Dialysis, Transplantation*, 16(1), 134–140.

Odden, M. C., Whooley, M. A., & Shlipak, M. G. (2004). Association of chronic kidney disease and anemia with physical capacity: The heart and soul study. *Journal of the American Society of Nephrology*, 15(11), 2908–2915.

Odum, J., Peh, C. A., Clarkson, A. R., Bannister, K. M., Seymour, A. E., Gillis, D., . . . Woodroffe, A. J. (1994). Recurrent mesangial IgA nephritis following renal transplantation. *Nephrology, Dialysis, Transplantation*, 9(3), 309–312.

O'Hare, A. M., Tawney, K., Bacchetti, P., & Johansen, K. L. (2003). Decreased survival among sedentary patients undergoing dialysis: Results from the dialysis morbidity and mortality study wave 2. *American Journal of Kidney Diseases*, 41(2), 447–454.

Orazio, L., Hickman, I., Armstrong, K., Johnson, D., Banks, M., & Isbel, N. (2009). Higher levels of physical activity are associated with a lower risk of abnormal glucose tolerance in renal transplant recipients. *Journal of Renal Nutrition*, 19(4), 304–313.

Orozco, L. J., Buchleitner, A. M., Gimenez-Perez, G., Roqué i Figuls, M., Richter, B., & Mauricio, D. (2008). Exercise or exercise and diet for preventing type 2 diabetes mellitus. *The Cochrane Database of Systematic Reviews*, 16(3), CD003054.

Padilla, J., Krasnoff, J., Da Silva, M., Hsu, C. Y., Frassetto, L., Johansen, K. L., & Painter, P. (2008). Physical functioning in patients with chronic kidney disease. *Journal of Nephrology*, 21(4), 550–559.

Painter, P., Hanson, P., Messer-Rehak, D., Zimmerman, S. W., & Glass, N. R. (1987). Exercise tolerance changes following renal transplantation. *American Journal of Kidney Diseases*, 10(6), 452–456.

Painter, P. L., Hector, L., Ray, K., Lynes, L., Dibble, S., Paul, S. M., . . . Ascher, N. L. (2002). A randomized trial of exercise training after renal transplantation. *Transplantation*, 74(1), 42–48.

Painter, P. L., Hector, L., Ray, K., Lynes, L., Paul, S. M., Dodd, M., . . . Ascher, N. L. (2003). Effects of exercise training on coronary heart disease risk factors in renal transplant recipients. *American Journal of Kidney Diseases*, 42(2), 362–369.

Painter, P., Krasnoff, J. B., Kuskowski, M., Frassetto, L., & Johansen, K. L. (2011). Effects of modality change and transplant on peak oxygen uptake in patients with kidney failure. *American Journal of Kidney Diseases*, 57(1), 113–122.

Painter, P., & Marcus, R. L. (2013). Assessing physical function and physical activity in patients with CKD. *Clinical Journal of the American Society of Nephrology*, 8(5), 861–872.

Pechter, U., Ots, M., Mesikepp, S., Zilmer, K., Kullissaar, T., Vihalemm, T., . . . Maaroos, J. (2003). Beneficial effects of water-based exercise in patients with chronic kidney disease. *International Journal of Rehabilitation Research*, 26(2), 153–156.

The Renal Association, UK Renal Registry. (2010). The Thirteenth Annual Report. Available from: http://www.renalreg.com

Robinson-Cohen, C., Katz, R., Mozaffarian, D., Dalrymple, L. S., de Boer, I., Sarnak, M., . . . Kestenbaum, B. (2009). Physical activity and rapid decline in kidney function among older adults. *Archives of Internal Medicine*, 169(22), 2116–2123.

Romano, G., Simonella, R., Falleti, E., Bortolotti, N., Deiuri, E., Antonutto, G., . . . Montanaro, D. (2010). Physical training effects in renal transplant recipients. *Clinical Transplantation*, 24(4), 510–514.

Sarnak, M. J., Levey, A. S., Schoolwerth, A. C., Coresh, J., Culleton, B., Hamm, L. L., . . . Wilson, P. W. (2003). Kidney disease as a risk factor for development of cardiovascular disease: A statement from the American Heart Association Councils on Kidney in Cardiovascular Disease, High Blood Pressure Research, Clinical Cardiology, and Epidemiology and Prevention. *Circulation, 108*(17), 2154–2169.

Segura-Ortí, E. (2010). Exercise in haemodyalisis patients: A literature systematic review. *Nefrología, 30*(2), 236–246.

Sharif, A., Moore, R., & Baboolal, K. (2008). Influence of lifestyle modification in renal transplant recipients with postprandial hyperglycemia. *Transplantation, 85*(3), 353–358.

Shlipak, M. G., Fried, L. F., Cushman, M., Manolio, T. A., Peterson, O., Stehman-Breen, C., . . . Psaty, B. (2005). Cardiovascular mortality risk in chronic kidney disease. Comparison of traditional and novel risk factors. *Journal of the American Medical Association, 293*(14),1737–1745.

Sietsema, K. E., Amato, A., Adler, S. G., & Brass, E. P. (2004). Exercise capacity as a predictor of survival among ambulatory patients with end-stage renal disease. *Kidney International, 65*(2), 719–724.

Smart, N., & Steele, M. (2011). Exercise training in haemodialysis patients: A systematic review and meta-analysis. *Nephrology, 16*(7), 626–632.

Stengel, B., Tarver-Carr, M. E., Powe, N. R., Eberhardt, M. S., & Bracati, F. (2003), Lifestyle factors, obesity and the risk of chronic kidney disease. *Epidemiology, 14*(4), 479–487.

Stenvinkel, P., Barany, P., Chung, S. H., Lindholm, B., & Heimbürger, O. (2002). A comparative analysis of nutritional parameters as predictors of outcome in male and female ESRD patients. *Nephrology, Dialysis, Transplantation, 17*(7), 1266–1274.

Surgit, O., Ersoz, G., Gursel, Y., & Ersoz, S. (2001). Effects of exercise training on specific immune parameters in transplant recipients. *Transplantation Proceedings, 33*(7–8), 3298.

Tentori, F., Elder, S. J., Thumma, J., Pisoni, R. L., Bommer, J., Fissell, R. B., . . . Robinson, B. M. (2010). Physical exercise among participants in the Dialysis Outcomes and Practice Patterns Study (DOPPS): Correlates and associated outcomes. *Nephrology, Dialysis, Transplantation, 25*(9), 3050–3062.

Toyama, K., Sugiyama, S., Oka, H., Sumida, H., & Ogawa, H. (2010). Exercise therapy correlates with improving renal function through modifying lipid metabolism in patients with cardiovascular disease and chronic kidney disease. *Journal of Cardiology, 56*(2), 142–146.

Triolo, G., Segoloni, G. P., Tetta, C., Vercellone, A., Cassader, M., Boggio-Bertinet, D., & Schieroni, M. P. (1989). Effect of combined diet and physical exercise on plasma lipids of renal transplant recipients. *Nephrology, Dialysis, Transplantation, 4*(3), 237–238.

U.K. Department of Health. (2005). *The National Service Framework for Renal Services part two: Chronic kidney disease, acute renal failure and end of life care.* Retrieved from http://www.dh.gov.uk/en/Publicationsandstatistics/Publications/PublicationsPolicyAndGuidance/DH_4101902

U.K. Department of Health. (2011). *Start active, stay active: A report on physical activity from the four home countries' Chief Medical Officers.* Retrieved from http://www.dh.gov.uk/en/Publicationsandstatistics/Publications/PublicationsPolicyAndGuidance/DH_128209

van den Ham, E. C., Kooman, J. P., Christiaans, M. H., & van Hooff, J. P. (2000). Relation between steroid dose, body composition and physical activity in renal transplant patients. *Transplantation, 69*(8), 1591–1598.

van den Ham, E. C., Kooman, J. P., Schols, A. M., Nieman, F. H., Does, J. D., Akkermans, M. A., . . . van Hooff, J. P. (2007). The functional, metabolic, and anabolic responses to exercise training in renal transplant and hemodialysis patients. *Transplantation, 83*(8), 1059–1068.

van den Ham, E. C., Kooman, J. P., Schols, A. M., Nieman, F. H., Does, J. D., Franssen, F. M., . . . van Hooff, J. P. (2005). Similarities in skeletal muscle strength and exercise capacity between renal transplant and hemodialysis patients. *American Journal of Transplantation, 5*(8), 1957–1965.

Venkataraman, R., Sanderson, B., & Bittner, V. (2005). Outcomes in patients with chronic kidney disease undergoing cardiac rehabilitation. *American Heart Journal, 150*(6), 1140–1146.

Violan, M. A., Pomes, T., Maldonado, S., Roura, G., De la Fuente, I., Verdaguer, T., . . . Campistol, J. M. (2002). Exercise capacity in hemodialysis and renal transplant patients. *Transplantation Proceedings, 34*(1), 417–418.

You, H. S., Chung, S. Y., So, H. S., & Choi, S. J. (2008). Effect of a DanJeon Breathing Exercise Program on the quality of life in patients with kidney transplants. *Transplantation Proceedings, 40*(7), 2324–2326.

Zhang, Q. L., & Rothenbacher, D. (2008). Prevalence of chronic kidney disease in population-based studies: Systematic review. *BMC Public Health, 8,* 117.

CHAPTER 9

Effect of Exercise on Cardiac and Metabolic Outcomes in People Living With HIV

Anella Yahiaoui, Barbara A. Smith, and Joachim G. Voss

ABSTRACT

Poorly controlled HIV infection and antiretroviral therapy, especially the use of protease inhibitors, are among the causes that contribute to the development of cardiovascular disease in people living with HIV (PLWH). Poor lifestyle choices (smoking, lack of physical activity, poor diet) and individual factors such as high stress, physical or emotional trauma, depression, and so forth contribute to the overall risk of developing cardiovascular disease. The purpose of this review was to critically evaluate the more recent aerobic and resistance exercise studies and their impact on cardiovascular and metabolic risk factors in PLWH.

Using the PubMed database, we searched for the keywords "HIV and exercise" and "HIV and physical exercise" published in the year 2000 or later and found 557 articles. We further limited the search to include only clinical trials and review articles, which yielded 217 publications. Of those 217 publications, 8 studies addressed the effect of aerobic and/or resistance exercise on body composition, cardiac, and metabolic outcomes, and were included in this review.

© 2013 Springer Publishing Company
http://dx.doi.org/10.1891/0739-6686.31.277

Most studies using aerobic exercise documented a modest yet significant increase in either measured or estimated maximal oxygen uptake (VO_{2max}) while the effect on body composition and metabolic variables were somewhat mixed. Most studies using resistive exercise documented significant improvements in muscle strength and metabolic function.

In the future, improved rigor in study design, measurement, and consistency in the reporting of data is essential. Longer-term studies will allow us to understand whether aerobic or resistive exercise has benefits that extend beyond the life of the individual studies. Finally, a careful exploration of the dosage of exercise needed to bring about change and a focus on the mechanisms of how aerobic and/or resistive exercise improve cardiometabolic variables during HIV infection and antiretroviral treatment would advance the science.

INTRODUCTION

The HIV-1 virus is a retrovirus that can infect a wide array of cells and organs including the brain, nerve, liver, gut, lung, immune, vascular, endothelial, and mucosal cells (Schiralli, Lester, & Henderson, 2012). The pathophysiology of the mechanisms of how viral RNA is integrated into immune and tissue cells continues to be an exciting field for discovery (Louboutin & Strayer, 2012). The HIV virus, on the other hand, has never been known to infect skeletal or cardiac myocytes directly (Otis et al., 2008). Yet, resident macrophages and other immune cells in skeletal or cardiac muscle have been found to carry the HIV virus most likely affecting skeletal muscle function as the HIV virus is transcribed, and transactivation protein (TAT) and HIV envelope glycoprotein 120 (gp120) proteins are expressed.

We are beginning to form a basic understanding of the mechanisms involved by which TAT impacts skeletal and cardiac muscle. For that, we need to take a closer look at the transcription of certain genes responsible for the differentiation of muscle cells (O'Brien, Knight, & Rana, 2012). The positive transcription elongation factor b (P-TEFb) participates in the activation of expression of many genes transcribed by RNA polymerase II (Pol II). Pol II controls the step of RNA elongation and activates the largest subunit of RNA II. The inhibition or overexpression of P-TEPb by TAT in the skeletal muscle or the heart potentially deregulates the transcription of several muscle genes and may partially explain some of the mechanisms for skeletal muscle atrophy or cardiac hypertrophy in people living with HIV (PLWH; Rice, 2009). We know little about how these mechanisms are impacted by different types of exercise, or if different types of HIV treatment impact the regulation of skeletal muscle genes. A second potential mechanism under investigation is the role of genes related to early muscle senescence and fibrosis, such as HIV associated upregulation of the senescence factor p16INK4a (CDKN2A) and fibrosis associated transforming growth factor beta 1 (TGFβ1), connective tissue growth factor (CTGF) and both forms 1 and 2 of collagen 1 A (COL1A1) and (COL1A2; Kusko et al., 2012). Again, little is known whether there is an impact of exercise or different types of highly active anti-retroviral therapy (HAART) on the expression of those genes.

Although we are just beginning to understand the complex genetic factors that are related to TAT expression and skeletal muscle differentiation, we have seen and documented the decline in muscle mass and strength in PLWH for almost three decades. The muscle loss caused by the decline in muscle function leaves PLWH feeling weak, fatigued, and exhausted. Sleep and rest do not alleviate these symptoms and they can persist for a long time and this constellation of symptoms has been classified as HIV-related fatigue (Darko, McCutchan, Kripke, Gillin, & Golshan, 1992). The constant urge to rest, sleep longer, and do less physical activity causes many HIV patients to decondition even further (Taibi, Price, & Voss, 2012), which impacts skeletal muscle strength and the cardiopulmonary system. Other reasons for the cardiovascular system to suffer from the effects of chronic HIV infection are the antiretroviral medications that cause or promote metabolic syndrome and insulin resistance, which in turn impacts the heart and the vasculature (Gibellini et al., 2012; Goldhaber & Philipson, 2013).

One way to improve cardiovascular and metabolic function and fight the persistent fatigue is to recommend regular forms of aerobic and resistance exercise to the PLWH. Exercise trials using various forms and doses of exercise have been conducted with variable success rates. We have critically reviewed the current understanding of factors contributing to increased cardiometabolic risks in PLWH. Furthermore, we have examined the effects of aerobic and resistance exercise studies published since 2000 that were directed at ameliorating cardiovascular and metabolic changes in PLWH.

BACKGROUND

The risk for and the development of cardiovascular disease (CVD) is a combination of factors ranging from negative health behavior, HIV infection, HIV treatment, and their impact on metabolic function. Metabolic complications associated with HIV demand a significant amount of provider time during the management of HIV infection, and often include cardiac risk factors leading to myocardial infarction (Friis-Møller et al., 2003). These abnormalities include body composition changes, lipoatrophy (loss of adipose tissue in face, extremities, and buttocks), lipodystrophy (accumulation of central fat and loss of subcutaneous fat), lipid abnormalities, abnormal glucose metabolism, and insulin resistance (Morse & Kovacs, 2006). This section will provide a brief overview of the literature.

Consequences of Negative Health Behavior

There are many health behaviors contributing to the early onset of CVD that have a significant role in the overall health and quality of life of an individual (Fisher et al., 2011). For example, in a simian model of HIV (simian immuno-deficiency virus [SIV]), stable versus unstable social conditions in monkeys and the genotype of the serotonin receptor affected the viral setpoint in SIV-infected monkeys (Capitanio et al., 2008). What this means is that the social environment can interact with the hosts' neurogenetic and personality characteristics to create an environment of joint risk factors that influence the trajectory of a chronic disease. Chronic depression and chronic stress, stressful life events, and trauma have been found to negatively impact HIV disease progression as well (Leserman, 2008 Reiche, Nunes, & Morimoto, 2004). In the United States, behaviors such as smoking are twofold to threefold higher in PLWH compared to the general population. A recent study in New York among HIV infected individuals reported a smoking rate of 59% compared to a 20% rate in the overall U.S. population (Tesoriero, Geiryic, Carrascal, & Lavigne, 2010). Cigarette smoking has been linked to negative effects on physical functioning and is an independent cofactor to prematurely developing cardiovascular disease in HIV infected persons (Bozzette, Ake, Tam, Chang, & Louis, 2003; Burke, Nelson, Kwong, & Cook, 2012; Turner et al., 2011).

Prior to Highly Active Anti-Retroviral Therapy (HAART)

Before 1996 and the introduction of HAART, cardiovascular diseases related to HIV manifested mainly as inflammatory-related processes including cardiomyopathy with pericardial effusion, endocarditis, or pulmonary hypertension (Barbaro & Barbarini, 2011). Before the onset of combination therapy, cardiomyopathies were observed in the autopsies of 40%–52% of all HIV patients who died from AIDS (Barbaro, Di Lorenzo, Grisorio, & Barbarini, 1998), which means the damage to the heart was likely caused by the HIV virus itself. A second cause of cardiomyopathy in HIV patients was the use of zidovudine (AZT), the first antiretroviral treatment available. The use of high dose AZT was associated with significant mitochondrial dysfunction and inhibition of mitochondrial DNA replication, all of which contributed to myocardial cell dysfunction (Lewis et al., 2000). Nutritional deficiencies in PLWH including B^{12}, selenium, carnitine, as well as deficiencies in growth and thyroid hormones have all been associated with left ventricular dysfunction (Hoffman, Lipschutz, & Miller, 1999).

The development of endocarditis was mainly related to intravenous drug use and has not changed in prevalence before or after the introduction of ARTs. According to the Centers for Disease Control and Prevention (CDC) (2008), in 2006, 12% of estimated new HIV infections were attributed to injection drug users. The most frequent agents to infect the tricuspid valve are *Staphylococcus aureus* (>75% of cases), *Streptococcus pneumoniae*, *Haemophilus influenzae*, *Candida albicans*, *Aspergillus fumigatus*, and *Cryptococcus neoformans* (Barbaro et al., 1998). Other causal agents for endocarditis can be *Haemophilus* species, *Actinobacillus actinomycetemcomitans*, *Cardiobacterium hominis*, *Eikenella corrodens*, and *Kingella kingae*—all of which are bacteria from the endogenous flora of the mouth (Klatt, 2003).

The incidence of pulmonary hypertension increased in PLWH after the introduction of HAART. For PLWH, the estimates of developing pulmonary hypertension are currently 1/200 compared to 1/200,000 in the general population (Barbaro, 2003). To understand the mechanisms of this condition, we need to focus on the pulmonary dendritic cells infected with HIV. They are not sensitive to HAART and may express HIV viruses on their surface for prolonged periods of time. Those cells chronically release cytotoxic cytokines (e.g., endothelin-1, interleukin-6, interleukin-1 beta, and tumor necrosis factor alpha). Exposure to these cytokines in the lungs can lead to vascular damage, progressive tissue damage, and lead to congestive heart failure (Barbaro, 2003).

HIV and Metabolic Function in the Post-HAART Era

HAART was first reported during the 1996 Vancouver AIDS Conference, where the successful implementation of combination therapy was shown (Vella, Schwartlander, So, Eholie & Murphy, 2012). That was the year that indinavir, a protease inhibitor (PI), was approved and quickly became an integral part of antiretroviral therapy because of the dramatic decrease in morbidity and mortality among the HIV-infected population (Vella et al., 2012). PIs prevent viral replication by binding to viral protease and blocking cleavage of viral polyproteins after viral budding (Anuurad, Bremer, & Berglund, 2010). Although abnormalities in lipid metabolism were observed prior to the introduction of HAART, primarily low high-density lipoprotein (HDL), the introduction of PIs led to a substantial increase in adverse metabolic side effects (Brown et al., 2005; Grinspoon, 2009; Grunfeld, 2002; Murata, Hruz, & Mueckler, 2000). PIs induce metabolic changes in the body which contribute to insulin resistance, and the centralization of fat in the viscera led to an increase in total and low-density lipoprotein (LDL) cholesterol in PLWH.

The link between HAART and metabolic complications remains unclear, however, and may be caused by the direct effect of drug toxicity, immune reconstitution, or a longer life span in PLWH (Robinson, Quinn, & Rimmer, 2007). PIs have been shown to affect the transport of glucose by inhibiting glucose transporter 4 (Glut4) receptors, which impair glucose signaling (Murata et al., 2000). Glut4 activation by insulin is crucial for glucose storage in muscle and fat after a meal (Grunfeld, 2002).

Changes in body fat distribution are commonly referred to as HIV/HAART-associated lipodystrophy, and tend to occur after 6–12 months of PI therapy (Anuurad et al., 2010). Patients treated with HAART often demonstrate a dyslipidemic profile of low HDL cholesterol (HDL-C), increased triglyceride levels, and increased levels of LDL cholesterol (LDL-C; Stanley & Grinspoon, 2012). Results from the Swiss HIV Cohort Study found PIs to be associated with an increase in triglycerides and in plasma total cholesterol in patients starting HAART therapy, which is often associated with a rise in cardiovascular risk (Young et al., 2005). Iloeje and colleagues (2005) also found that patients exposed to a PI have an increased risk of CVD. This has been confirmed by the Data Collection on Adverse Events of Anti-HIV Drugs (D:A:D) study, a prospective, multicohort study that found a 17% increase in the risk of myocardial infarction with each twofold increase in triglyceride levels (Giannarellia, Klein, & Badimona, 2011; Feeney & Mallon, 2011).

Obesity

Several studies have shown a rise in obesity in HIV-positive patients (Amorosa et al., 2005; Engelson et al., 2006). HIV-associated obesity generally refers to the abnormal redistribution of fat, including "buffalo hump" and truncal obesity (Anuurad et al., 2010). A cross-sectional study by Amorosa and colleagues (2005) found that obesity and overweight were more prevalent than wasting in an HIV-positive cohort. They additionally reported that although women and men were about equally overweight (30% vs. 31%), they found a higher level of obesity in women than men (28% vs. 11%). Lakey, Yang, Yancy, Chow, and Hicks (2013) found a 27% relative increase in overweight/obesity prevalence in HIV-infected participants during 12 months of initial HAART, whereas no significant change was found in the HIV seronegative control group.

Diabetes

The underlying cause of diabetes mellitus type 2 (DM2) in PLWH may be different than that of non-HIV-infected patients. In PLWH, DM is known to result from PIs inhibiting Glut4 receptors (Murata et al, 2000), which affect glucose transport, and lead to an increase in fat in the liver and muscle (Grinspoon, 2009). A longitudinal cohort study found that subjects receiving HAART were 3.1 times more likely to develop DM2 than control subjects (Grinspoon & Carr, 2005). As in the general population, Worm and colleagues (2009) found that DM is an important risk factor for coronary heart disease and noted that the prevalence of DM2 is likely to increase as a result of the aging HIV population. Furthermore, the risk of myocardial infarction among PLWH is more than doubled in those with DM2 (Worm et al., 2009). Brown and colleagues (2005) conducted an analysis in the Multicenter AIDS Cohort Study and found a 14% prevalence of DM2 at baseline in HIV-infected men, compared to 5% in the HIV-seronegative control group. They also found more than a fourfold increase in incidence of DM2 in HIV-infected men exposed to HAART than that of the HIV-seronegative male control group (Brown et al., 2005).

Research findings have documented the benefits of exercise on cardiometabolic function in PLWH (Driscoll et al., 2004; Engelson et al., 2006; Scevola et al., 2003; Terry et al., 2006). Exercise improves myocardial circulation, which protects the heart from hypoxic stress (Scevola et al., 2003). Resting heart rate and blood pressure are also reduced after exercise, which leads to a significant reduction in the work of the myocardium at rest (Scevola et al., 2003). Studies have shown that moderate- to high-intensity aerobic exercise conducted 2–3 times per week may have a significant impact on increased maximum oxygen consumption (VO_{2max}) in PLWH (Dolan et al., 2006; Hand et al., 2008; Mutimura, Stewart, et al., 2008). Other benefits of exercise documented in apparently healthy adults and PLWH may include an increased plasma volume, increased cardiac output, decreased body mass index (BMI), subcutaneous fat, and abdominal girth (Cade, Peralta, & Keyser, 2004; McArdle, Katch, & Katch, 2010; Smith et al., 2001). Thoni and colleagues (2002) reported significant decreases in total abdominal adipose tissue, total cholesterol, and triglycerides, and significant increases in HDL cholesterol. A study by Driscoll et al. (2004) found that aerobic and resistance exercise, coupled with the use of metformin, decreased muscle adiposity in PLWH, which improves hyperinsulinemia and visceral adiposity in this population (Feigenbaum & Longstaff, 2010).

Recommendations for Aerobic Exercise

Aerobic exercise interventions typically include walking, jogging, cycling, swimming, stair stepping, and rowing. The American College of Sports Medicine (ACSM) recommends that apparently healthy adults engage in at least 150 min of moderate-intensity exercise per week and reducing the total time engaged in sedentary activities. Exercise recommendations can be met through 30–60 min of moderate-intensity aerobic exercise 5 days/week or 20–60 min of vigorous-intensity aerobic exercise 3 days/week (Garber et al., 2011). After extensive review of current exercise literature for adults living with HIV, the Cochrane Collaboration found that aerobic exercise conducted for at least 5 weeks, 3 times per week for at least 20 min may lead to significant improvements in cardiopulmonary fitness and body composition outcomes (O'Brien, Nixon, Tynan, & Glazier, 2010).

Recommendations for Resistance Exercise

Resistance exercise includes muscle-strengthening activities such as weight training and weight bearing calisthenics (Nelson et al., 2007). The ACSM recommends training each major muscle group (chest, shoulders, back, hips, legs, trunk, and arms) 2 or 3 days each week for two to four sets of each exercise (Garber et al., 2011). They recommend 8–12 repetitions to improve strength and power; 10–15 repetitions to improve strength in middle-aged, frail, and older persons beginning exercise; and 15–20 repetitions to improve muscular endurance. One of the most important benefits of strength training is an increase in lean tissue (mostly muscle), which is more metabolically active than adipose tissue and can lead to better glucose control (Westcott, 2012).

Cardiac Measure

Maximal aerobic capacity is the maximum amount of oxygen consumed by the body during maximal exertion (VO_{2max}) and is expressed in milliliters of oxygen per kilogram of body weight per minute ($ml \cdot kg^{-1} \cdot min^{-1}$) or liters of oxygen consumed per minute (L/min; Wilmore & Costill, 2004, p. 707). The Fick principle was first described by Adolf Fick in the 19th century as a way of measuring of cardiac output. The principle applied to VO_2 equals the product of cardiac output (oxygen delivery to muscles) and the ability of the muscle to extract and use the oxygen to produce energy (Cade et al., 2004; McArdle et al., 2010). Many sedentary individuals or those with a chronic disease or disability are often unable to reach maximal exertion. For cases, when the person is unable to continue during a graded exercise test (GXT) because of symptoms or exhaustion and a plateau in oxygen use has not been achieved, the term *peak VO_2* is used to describe what the person achieved (Durstine et al., 2003).

Resistance Measure

One of four methods are typically used to measure strength: tensitometry, dynamometry, one-repetition maximum (1-RM), and computer-assisted methods such as the isokinetic dynamometer that can measure maximum force through full range of motion at a given velocity (McArdle et al., 2010). Two widely used methods that do not require expensive testing equipment include the handgrip dynamometer, which measures static strength of the hand via compression and 1-RM testing, which can be described as the maximum amount of weight that can be lifted in one time (McArdle et al., 2010).

Metabolic Measures

Metabolic markers of interest in this review include total cholesterol, HDL-C, LDL-C, triglycerides, glucose, and insulin levels. These are typically measured in serum collected from subjects while fasting and analyzed in a laboratory using standard clinical procedures.

Risk of Exercise

Generally, there is little risk with moderate forms of exercise by PLWH if they are under the supervision of a competent provider and exercise professional. Training partners can motivate PLWH to continue exercising and are effective for a long-term commitment to behavior change (Yahiaoui, McGough, & Voss, 2012). There is general agreement that moderate aerobic and/or resistance exercise does not negatively impact viral load or CD4 T cell counts (Clem & Borchers, 2007; Smith et al., 2001).

However, high-intensity aerobic exercise has been found to activate the immune system leading not only to leukocytosis but also to neutrophilia and leucopenia. Because of the reduction in white blood cells, many endurance athletes are at higher risk for contracting viral respiratory infections and have higher degrees of proinflammatory cytokines (interleukin-1 beta and interleukin-6) in their serum, which is associated with elevated levels of HIV virus replication in PLWH (Dudgeon et al., 2010). Furthermore, exposing HIV-infected endurance athletes to bacterial infections can lead to an increased risk to infectious myocarditis/cardiomyopathy (Friman & Wesslen, 2000).

High-impact athletes may also be exposed to increased cardiovascular disease risk through chronic steroid use. In a sample of British gay men participating in high-intensity resistive exercise, 31.7% of the HIV positive men used anabolic steroids whereas only 14.5% of the HIV negative men used steroids. This exposed the men using the steroids to all the negative side effects of chronic steroid use (Bolding, Sherr, & Elford, 2002).

Finally, regardless of age, being HIV-infected is correlated with up to a 42% reduction in cardiorespiratory fitness (Ferrand et al., 2012; Oursler, Sorkin, Smith, & Katzel, 2006). Hsue and colleagues (2010) and Oursler and colleagues (2009) demonstrated that PLWH are at a 2.5 times greater risk for developing diastolic dysfunction and hypertension and experienced lower VO_{2peak} than those without hypertension. In summary, there is a multitude of risks to develop cardiovascular and metabolic changes for PLWH. Some are driven by disease factors, treatment factors, or by lifestyle choices that individuals make. We know little about how the cumulative evidence guides the decisions to recommend an aerobic and/or resistance exercise program to reduce the risks and improve vascular, pulmonary, and skeletal muscle function in PLWH.

METHODS

This review systematically searched the PubMed database for the keywords "HIV and exercise" and "HIV and physical exercise" published in the year 2000 or later and found 557 articles. We then set the limit to include only clinical trials and review articles, which yielded 217 publications. Of those, 14 trials addressed exercise and cardiac outcomes and were selected for further scrutiny. Eight studies matched all of our inclusion criteria including

a. subjects were HIV positive adults 18 years or older,
b. study included weekly aerobic and/or resistive exercise training,
c. study included cardiac, metabolic, and/or strength measurements; and
d. study included two groups (exercise vs. control or strength vs. aerobic).

RESULTS

Several studies have shown that aerobic and resistance exercise can improve cardiac and metabolic outcomes in people living with and without HIV. Of the eight studies included in this review, all of them tested the effects of aerobic exercise on cardiopulmonary and/or metabolic indices in PLWH. Duration, intensity, and frequency varied from study to study and included primarily treadmill, brisk walking, jogging, running, and stair climbing. Two of the eight trials also conducted resistance exercise training, which included upper and lower extremity exercises such as bench press, leg press, knee extension, shoulder abduction, and arm curls. Two of the studies were led by a nurse investigator (Baigis et al., 2002; Smith et al., 2001).

Cardiac Outcomes

Of the eight studies in this review, only four measured VO_2 directly (Baigis et al., 2002; Lindegaard et al., 2008; Smith et al., 2001; Terry et al., 2006). The other four studies in this review estimated VO_2 using treadmill speed and grade or resistance and revolutions per minute on a cycle ergometer (Dolan et al., 2006; Hand et al., 2008; Mutimura, Stewart, et al., 2008; Ogalha et al., 2011). Of those who measured VO_2 directly, two studies documented significant improvements in VO_{2max} in the exercise groups compared to control or comparison groups (Lindegaard et al., 2008; Terry et al., 2006), one approached significance ($p = .09$; Smith et al, 2001) and one showed no improvement (Baigis et al., 2002). Lindegaard and colleagues had no control group but rather evaluated the difference between aerobic and resistance exercise training.

Of the four studies in this review that estimated VO_{2max}, Hand et al. (2008) and Mutimura, Stewart, et al., (2008) reported a significant increase in estimated VO_{2max}. Hand and colleagues demonstrated a 21% increase in estimated VO_{2max} (31.6–39.9 ml $\cdot$ kg^{-1} $\cdot$ min^{-1}; $p < .01$) in the exercise compared to the control group. Furthermore, they reported that female exercisers in the cohort showed a 24% improvement in VO_{2max} from baseline, whereas male exercisers improved by 20%. No significant changes were seen in the control group. Mutimura, Stewart, et al., (2008) found that after the 6-month study, the exercise group experienced a change of 4.7 ± 3.9 ml $\cdot$ kg^{-1} $\cdot$ min^{-1} in VO$_{2max}$ (24.3–29.0 ml $\cdot$ kg^{-1} $\cdot$ min^{-1}; $p <$ .0001) compared to 0.5 ± 0.3 ml $\cdot$ kg^{-1} $\cdot$ min^{-1} for the control group (23.9–24.4 ml $\cdot$ kg^{-1} $\cdot$ min^{-1}; $p <$ .05). Dolan et al. (2006) showed an increase of 1.5 ml $\cdot$ kg^{-1} $\cdot$ min^{-1} in the exercise group (16.9–18.4 ml $\cdot$ kg^{-1} $\cdot$ min^{-1}) while there was a -2.5ml $\cdot$ kg^{-1} $\cdot$ min^{-1} decline in the control group (15.3–12.8 ml $\cdot$ kg^{-1} $\cdot$ min^{-1}), which could explain the significant difference in the two groups in part. Comparing baseline and posttest values of Ogalha and colleagues (2011), there was a decline in VO$_2$. Lindegaard and colleagues (2008), who measured VO$_2$ directly had a robust 14.4% increase in VO$_{2max}$ when the aerobic exercise group was compared to the resistance exercise group. A trial conducted by Terry and colleagues (2006) showed an 8 ml $\cdot$ kg^{-1} $\cdot$ min^{-1} increase in VO$_{2peak}$ (32–40 ml $\cdot$ kg^{-1} $\cdot$ min^{-1}; $p <$ .001) in the exercise and diet group compared to an insignificant increase (34–35 ml $\cdot$ kg^{-1} $\cdot$ min^{-1}; $p <$ .05) in the diet-only group. Although Smith and colleagues (2001) showed an increase of 2.6 ml $\cdot$ kg^{-1} $\cdot$ min^{-1} in the exercise group, this did not achieve significance in part because the control group also improved ($p =$ .09). Baigis and colleagues (2002) did not find a notable improvement in VO$_{2\ max}$ between the exercise group (30.2–30.5 ml $\cdot$ kg^{-1} $\cdot$ min^{-1}) and the control group (32.0–30.8 ml $\cdot$ kg^{-1} $\cdot$ min^{-1}). The authors included several potential reasons to explain the lack of VO$_{2max}$ improvement in the exercise group. These included (a) exercise prescription of only 20 min, 3 times per week, and a lack of progressively increasing the intensity, frequency, and duration; (b) missed sessions that reduced frequency of exercise to an average of 2 times per week; (c) length of intervention (15 weeks) may have been too short; and (d) the individuals with lower levels of initial fitness demonstrated most significant increase in VO$_{2max}$; however, many of her participants were fit at baseline.

Heart Rate

A decline in resting heart rate is sometimes used as a surrogate for fitness. Ogalha and colleagues (2011) reported a significant improvement in resting heart rate in the exercise group (74.1–70.5 bpm) compared to the control group (71.4–70.5 bpm; $p <$ .001).

Metabolic Outcomes

Five studies in this review tested the effect of exercise on some measures of metabolic function. Mutimura, Crowther, et al., (2008) reported significant improvements in waist circumference, waist-to-hip ratio, sum of skin folds, and percentage of body fat. Mutimura, Crowther, et al., 2008 also found a significant decrease in fasting plasma glucose in the exercise group compared to the control group ($p < .0001$), and a decrease in total cholesterol levels in the exercise group compared to the control group ($p < .05$), although no significant changes were found in HDL-C or LDL-C. Ogalha and colleagues (2011) found no changes in lipodystrophy in the patients and no improvement in HDL-C or LDL-C levels. They noted an improvement in muscle mass ($p = .001$) and hip circumference ($p = .001$) in the exercise group compared to the control group. Lindegaard and colleagues (2008) compared an aerobic-only training group to a resistance-only training group and found that insulin-mediated glucose uptake increased with both aerobic ($p = .02$) and strength ($p = .05$) training. The study showed aerobic exercise reduced total cholesterol, LDL-C, free fatty acids, and increased HDL-C. Only resistance training caused an improvement in triglycerides ($p < .001$). The study by Dolan and colleagues (2006) demonstrated no significant change in results for lipid levels, glucose levels, blood pressure, and abdominal visceral fat between the exercise and control groups. This may be in part because of the fact that the exercise group only improved VO_2 1.5 ml · kg^{-1} · min^{-1}.

Terry and colleagues (2006) found no significant change in triglyceride, cholesterol, or HDL-C levels between exercise and control groups. After 15 weeks, they found that both the diet-only group and the diet and exercise group produced the same weight loss results. They conclude that changes in body composition were mainly attributed to the dietary intervention, with little contribution from aerobic exercise (Terry et al., 2006). Smith and colleagues (2001) demonstrated a significant reduction in BMI, weight, and waist circumference, an important predictor of visceral adipose tissue in HAART-associated fat redistribution.

Strength Outcomes

Two of the six studies in this review included resistance exercise training (Dolan et al., 2006; Lindegaard et al., 2008). Lindegaard and colleagues found that 3–4 sets of 8–12 repetitions of progressive upper extremity (UE) and lower extremity (LE) exercises led to a an increase in strength of 30%, a decrease in body weight, an increase in lean body mass, a decrease in total fat mass ($p = .023$) and limb fat mass ($p = .003$) compared to the aerobic only group. Triglycerides and free fatty acids decreased, and HDL-C increased after resistance training. Dolan and colleagues (2006) demonstrated that 3–4 sets of 8–10 repetitions at 60%–80% of 1-RM led to significant improvement in the UE and LE muscle groups tested. The study showed an increase in total muscle area ($p = .02$) and total muscle attenuation ($p = .03$) in the exercise group compared to the control group. BMI, abdominal fat, and total fat neither change between groups nor did lipid levels or glucose.

DISCUSSION

There is a paucity of data related to body composition and cardiometabolic outcomes from well-designed RCTs of exercise in those infected with HIV. This was made even more apparent when we were able to identify only eight RCTs since 2000 that met our inclusion/exclusion criteria. Although most of the eight RCTs we identified reported that aerobic exercise improved VO_{2max}, the change in many was modest at best and in some could have been explained more by a decline in VO_{2max} in the control or comparison group rather than in a significant improvement in the intervention group. In addition, a number of the studies also reported small sample sizes, attrition, various degrees of adherence to the exercise interventions, and in the most cases lacked direct comparability of study designs.

Almost all studies that included resistance exercise reported improvements in muscle strength. Long term studies are needed to determine if resistance exercise benefits can be extended beyond the life of the trial and what dose would be necessary to continue these benefits for PLWH.

Besides correcting some of these studies' shortcomings, future studies should explore why VO_{2max}/VO_{2peak} are lower in PLWH. Is skeletal mitochondrial damage still occurring and does it affect oxygen extraction in the muscles? Does damage to the lung tissue from the HIV virus prevent rapid oxygen diffusion across the alveolar membrane contributing to a decrease in VO_2? If so, is this damage preventable with early onset of HAART, and could exercise play an additional role in this process. If newer medication regimens could prevent the lung damage, the decline in VO_2 could be prevented. Or is the reduction in VO_2 caused by a reduction in cardiac function that could be improved with exercise?

Methodologically, one of the more important questions is how can changes of oxygen consumption be measured or estimated accurately in PLWH without being invasive, requiring specialized equipment and specialized expertise?

In addition, future studies need to focus on identifying the basic mechanisms by which aerobic and resistance exercise change physiology in the presence of the HIV virus and antiretroviral treatment. More knowledge is needed to understand the basic mechanisms by which the newer antiretroviral therapies impact cardiac and skeletal muscle mitochondrial function especially in PLWH over the age of 50 years.

Early exercise studies in PLWH contained mostly male participants (Rigsby, Dishman, Jackson, MacLean, & Raven, 1992; MacArthur, Levine, & Birk, 1993; Lox, McAuley, & Tucker, 1995; Sattler et al., 1999, Bhasin et al., 2000). All but three of the studies in this review had a significantly higher proportion of male to female participants, with as little as 13% females in one study (Smith et al., 2001). Recent trials have begun to close the gender gap by including more female participants (Mutimura, Stewart, et al., 2008; Ogalha et al., 2011).

HAART has led to a growing number of older PLWH. Aging, HIV infection, and HAART oftentimes has a cumulative effect on physical function and metabolic parameters (Souza et al., 2008). Certain age-associated factors such as osteopenia/osteoporosis, osteoarthritis, and frailty may contribute to a further decline in physical function. Clinical presentations of frailty include loss of muscle mass, loss of weight and energy, slow walking speed, and a decrease in overall physical activity (Fried et al., 2001). Studies have shown that the aging process also affects the body's ability to metabolize nutrients, which can result in poor absorption and further loss of skeletal muscle mass (Brant, 2010), which can decrease strength makes exercise a burden. Most participants in the review were between 35 and 45 years of age. However, ages ranged from 28 to 61 years. Future studies must be done to evaluate the impact of exercise in the aging, HIV-infected population in particular focusing on cardiac and metabolic factors.

Exercising in a group or with a training partner may be a good way to improve the psychological well-being of an individual. Six of the eight studies in this review conducted supervised, group training sessions in a fitness center or outdoor setting. Only two studies conducted supervised, home-based exercise training (Baigis et al., 2002; Dolan et al., 2006). The dropout rates for the six studies that employed group exercise ranged from 3% to 38%, yet the methods for reporting dropout were not clearly explicated in all studies. Although the dropout rate was only 4% and 21% in the home-based studies, one home-based study showed no change in VO_{2max} (Baigis et al., 2002) and the difference in VO_{2max} in the other could have been explained more by a decline in VO_{2max} in the control or comparison group rather than in a significant improvement in the intervention group (Dolan et al., 2006). Thus, patient supervision or monitoring during exercise appears to be an important factor in the training outcome of an intervention. More consistent calculation and reporting of attrition are essential and further studies are needed to investigate the impact of group or home-based exercise outcomes.

CONCLUSION

Small sample sizes, attrition, various degrees of adherence to the exercise interventions, and in the most cases lacked direct comparability of study designs

In summary, HIV and its treatment can have a positive effect on cardiopulmonary function, change the metabolic profile and influence other variables in PLWH. Aerobic and resistance exercise used on a regular basis have few risks and many benefits. The risks associated with exercise come from the initiation of exercise in a sedentary population with comorbid conditions, prolonged vigorous exercise that reduces immune system function in even healthy adults, or through other high risk behaviors such as the use of anabolic steroids to increase muscle strength and size. The benefits include cardiopulmonary, metabolic, and psychosocial improvements. What less clear is whether the modestly statistical significance improvements brought about by exercise translates into clinically meaningful changes in the short run or improved morbidity and mortality in the long run. In addition, future studies must be properly powered, report findings consistently so studies can be replicated, attend to high rates of attrition, examine adherence to the interventions, take into consideration training specificity, and be certain that the exercise prescription be of the appropriate intensity, frequency, and duration to bring about needed change.

REFERENCES

Amorosa, V., Synnestvedt, M., Gross, R., Friedman, H., MacGregor, R. R., Gudonis, D., . . . Tebas P. (2005). A Tale of 2 epidemics: The intersection between obesity and HIV infection in Philadelphia. *Journal of Acquired Immune Deficiency Syndromes, 39*, 557–561.

Anuurad, E., Bremer, A., & Berglund, L. (2010). HIV protease inhibitors and obesity. *Current Opinion in Endocrinology, Diabetes, and Obesity, 17*, 478–485.

Baigis, J., Korniewicz, D. M., Chase, G., Butz, A., Jacobson, D., & Wu, A. W. (2002). Effectiveness of a home-based exercise intervention for HIV-infected adults: A randomized trial. *Journal of the Association of Nurses in AIDS Care, 13*, 33–34. http://dx.doi.org/10.1016/S1055-3290(06)60199-4

Barbaro, G. (2003). Long-term effects of protease-inhibitor-based combination therapy. *Lancet, 363*(9412), 900.

Barbaro, G., & Barbarini, G. (2011). Human immunodeficiency virus & cardiovascular risk. *Indian Journal of Medical Research, 134*(6), 898–903.

Barbaro, G., Di Lorenzo, G., Grisorio, B., & Barbarini, G. (1998). Cardiac involvement in the acquired immunodeficiency syndrome: A multicenter clinical-pathological study. Gruppo Italiano per lo Studio Cardiologico dei pazienti affetti da AIDS Investigators. *AIDS Research and Human Retroviruses, 14*, 1071–1077.

Bhasin, S., Storer, T. W., Javanbakht, M., Berman, N., Yarasheski, K. E., Phillips, J., & Beall, G. (2000). Testosterone replacement and resistance exercise in HIV-infected men with weight loss and low testosterone levels. *Journal of the American Medical Association, 283*, 763–770. http://dx.doi.org/10. 1001/jama.283.6.763

Bolding, G., Sherr, L., & Elford, J. (2002). Use of anabolic steroids and associated health risks among gay men attending London gyms. *Addiction, 97*(2), 195–203.

Bozzette, S. A., Ake, C. F., Tam, H. K., Chang, S. W., & Louis, T. A. (2003). Cardiovascular and cerebrovascular events in patients treated for human immunodeficiency virus infection. *New England Journal of Medicine, 348*, 702–710.

Brant, J. M. (2010). Practical approaches to pharmacologic management of pain in older adults with cancer. *Oncology Nursing Forum, 37*(Suppl.), 17–26. http://dx.doi.org/10.1188/10.ONF.S1

Brown, T. T., Cole, S. R., Li, X., Kingsley, L. A., Palella, F. J., Riddler, S. A., . . . Dobs, A. S. (2005). Antiretroviral therapy and the prevalence and incidence of diabetes mellitus in the Multicenter AIDS Cohort Study. *Archives of Internal Medicine, 165*, 1179–1184.

Burke, E. G., Nelson, J., Kwong, J., & Cook, P. F. (2012). Cardiovascular risk assessment for persons living with HIV. *Journal of the Association of Nurses in AIDS Care, 23*(2), 134–145. http://dx.doi.org/10.1016/j.jana.2011.08.001

Cade, T. W., Peralta, L., & Keyser, R. E. (2004). Aerobic exercise dysfunction in human immunodeficiency virus: A potential link to physical disability. *Physical Therapy, 84*, 655–664.

Capitanio, J. P., Abel, K., Mendoza, S. P., Blozis, S. A., McChesney, M. B., Cole, S. W., & Mason, W. A. (2008). Personality and serotonin transporter genotype interact with social context to affect immunity and viral set-point in simian immunodeficiency virus disease. *Brain, Behavior, and Immunity, 22*, 676–689.

U.S. Centers for Disease Control and Prevention. (2008). *Estimates of new HIV infections in the United States.* Retrieved from http://www.cdc.gov/nchhstp/newsroom/docs/Fact-Sheet-on-HIV-Estimates.pdf

Clem, K. L., & Borchers, J. R. (2007). HIV and the athlete. *Clinics in Sports Medicine, 26*, 413–424.

Darko, D. F., McCutchan, J. A., Kripke, D. F., Gillin, J. C., & Golshan, S. (1992). Fatigue, sleep disturbance, disability, and indices of progression of HIV infection. *American Journal of Psychiatry, 149*(4), 514–520.

Dolan, S. E., Frontera, W., Librizzi, J., Ljungquist, K., Juan, S., Dorman, R., & Grinspoon, S. (2006). Effects of a supervised home-based aerobic and progressive resistance training regimen in women infected with human immunodeficiency virus: A randomized trial. *Archives of Internal Medicine, 166*, 1225–1231.

Driscoll, S. D., Meininger, G. E., Ljungquist, K., Hadigan, C., Torriani, M., Klibanski, A., . . . Grinspoon, S. (2004). Differential effects of metformin and exercise on muscle adiposity and metabolic indices in human immunodeficiency virus-infected patients. *Journal of Clinical Endocrinology & Metabolism, 89*, 2171–2178. http://dx.doi.org/10.1210/jc.2003-031858

Dudgeon, W. D., Phillips, K. D., Durstine, J. L., Burgess, S. E., Lyerly, G. W., Davis, J. M., & Hand, G. A. (2010). Individual exercise sessions alter circulating hormones and cytokines in HIV-infected men. *Applied Physiology and Nutritional Metabolism, 35*(4), 560–568. http://dx.doi.org/10.1139/H10-045

Durstine, L., Moore, G. E., & Bayles, C. (2003). *ACSM's exercise management for persons with chronic diseases and disabilities* (2nd ed.). Champaign, IL: Human Kinetics.

Engelson, E. S., Agin, D., Kenya, S., Werber-Zion, G., Luty, B., Albu, J. B., & Kotler, D. P. (2006). Body composition and metabolic effects of a diet and exercise weight loss regimen on obese, HIV-infected women. *Metabolism: Clinical and Experimental, 55*, 1327–1336. http://dx.doi.org/10.1016/j.metabol.2006.05.018

Feeney, E. R., & Mallon, P. W. G. (2011). HIV and HAART-associated dyslipidemia. *The Open Cardiovascular Medicine Journal, 5*, 49–63.

Feigenbaum, K., & Longstaff, L. (2010). Management of the metabolic syndrome in patients with human immunodeficiency virus. *The Diabetes Educator, 36*(3), 457–464. http://dx.doi.org/10.1177/0145721710363619

Ferrand, R. A., Desai, S. R., Hopkins, C., Elston, C. M., Copley, S. J., Nathoo, K., & Ndhlovu, C. E. (2012). Chronic lung disease in adolescents with delayed diagnosis of vertically acquired HIV infection. *Clinical Infectious Diseases, 55*(1), 145–152. http://dx.doi.org/10.1093/cid/cis271

Fisher, E. B., Fitzgibbon, M. L., Glasgow, R. E., Haire-Joshu, D., Hayman, L. L., Kaplan, R. M., . . . Ockene, J. K. (2011). Behavior matters. *American Journal of Preventative Medicine, 40*, e15–e30.

Fried, L. P., Tangen, C. M., Walston, J., Newman, A. B., Hirsch, C., Gottdiener, J., & McBurnie, M. A. (2001). Frailty in older adults: Evidence for a phenotype. *Journals of Gerontology, 56A*, M146–M156. http://dx.doi.org/10.1093/gerona/56.3.M146

Friis-Møller, N., Weber, R., Reiss, P., Thiebaut, R., Kirk, O., d'Arminio Monforte, A., & Lundgren, J. D. (2003). Cardiovascular disease risk factors in HIV patients—Association with antiretroviral therapy. Results from the DAD study. *AIDS, 17,* 1179–1193. http://dx.doi.org/10.1097/01. aids.0000060358.78202.c1

Friman, G., & Wesslen, L. (2000). Infections and exercise in high-performance athletes. *Immunology and Cell Biology, 78*(5), 510–522.

Garber, C. E., Blissmer, B., Deschenes, M. R., Franklin, B. A., Lamonte, M. J., Lee, I.-M., . . . Swain, D. P. (2011). American College of Sports Medicine position stand. Quantity and quality of exercise for developing and maintaining cardiorespiratory, musculoskeletal, and neuromotor fitness in apparently healthy adults: Guidance for prescribing exercise. *Medicine & Sciences in Sports & Exercise, 43*(7), 1334–1359.

Giannarellia, C., Klein, R. S., & Badimona, J. J. (2011). Cardiovascular implications of HIV-induced dyslipidemia. *Atherosclerosis, 219,* 384–389.

Gibellini, D., Borderi, M., Clò, A., Morini, S., Miserocchi, A., Bon, I., & Re, M. C. Antiretroviral molecules and cardiovascular diseases. (2012). *The New Microbiologica, 35*(4) 359–375.

Goldhaber, J. I., & Philipson, K. D. (2013). Cardiac sodium-calcium exchange and efficient excitation-contraction coupling: Implications for heart disease. *Advances in Experimental Medicine and Biology, 961,* 355–364. http://dx.doi.org/10.1007/978-1-4614-4756-6_30

Grinspoon, S. (2009). Diabetes mellitus, cardiovascular risk, and HIV disease. *Circulation, 119,* 770–772.

Grinspoon, S., & Carr, A. (2005). Cardiovascular risk and body-fat abnormalities in HIV-infected adults. *New England Journal of Medicine, 352,* 48–62.

Grunfeld, C. (2002). HIV protease inhibitors and glucose metabolism. *AIDS, 16,* 925–926.

Hand, G. A., Phillips, K. D., Dudgeon, W. D., Lyerly, G. W., Durstine, J. L., & Burgess, S. E. (2008). Moderate intensity exercise training reverses functional aerobic impairment in HIV-infected individuals. *AIDS Care, 20,* 1066–1074. http://dx.doi.org/10.1080/09540120701796900

Hoffman, M., Lipshultz, S. E., & Miller, T. L. (1999). Malnutrition and cardiac abnormalities in the HIV-infected patients. In: T. L. Miller & S. Gorbach (Eds.). *Nutritional Aspects of HIV Infection* (pp. 33–39). London, United Kingdom: Arnold.

Hsue, P. Y., Hunt, P. W., Ho, J. E., Farah, H. H., Schnell, A., Hoh, R., & Martin, J. N. (2010). Impact of HIV infection on diastolic function and left ventricular mass. *Circulation. Heart Failure, 3*(1), 132–139. http://dx.doi.org/10.1161/CIRCHEARTFAILURE.109.854943

Iloeje, U. H., Yuan, Y., L'Italien, G., Mauskopf, J., Holmberg, S. D., Moorman, A. C., . . . Moore, R. D. (2005). Protease inhibitor exposure and increased risk of cardiovascular disease in HIV-infected patients. *HIV Medicine, 6,* 37–44.

Klatt, E. C. (2003). Cardiovascular pathology in AIDS. *Advances in Cardiology, 40,* 23–48.

Kusko, R. L., Banerjee, C., Long, K. K., Darcy, A., Otis, J., Sebastiani, P., & Melov, S. (2012). Premature expression of a muscle fibrosis axis in chronic HIV infection. *Skeletal Muscle, 2*(1), 10. http://dx.doi.org/10.1186/2044-5040-2-10

Lakey, W., Yang, L. Y., Yancy, W., Chow, S. C., & Hicks, C. (2013). Short communication from wasting to obesity: Initial antiretroviral therapy and weight gain in HIV-infected persons. *AIDS Research and Human Retroviruses, 23,* 435–440.

Leserman, J. (2008). Role of depression, stress, and trauma in HIV disease progression. *Psychosomatic Medicine, 70,* 539–545.

Lewis, W., Grupp, I. L., Grupp, G., Hoit, B., Morris, R., Samarel, A. M., . . . Klotman, P. (2000). Cardiac dysfunction in the HIV-1 transgenic mouse treated with zidovudine. *Laboratory Investigation, 80,* 187–197.

Lindegaard, B., Hansen, T., Hvid, T., van Hall, G., Plomgaard, P., Ditlevsen, S., . . . Pedersen, B. K. (2008). The effect of strength and endurance training on insulin sensitivity and fat distribution in human immunodeficiency virus-infected patients with lipodystrophy. *Journal of Clinical Endocrinology & Metabolism*, 93(10), 3860–3869.

Louboutin, J. P., & Strayer, D. S. (2012). Blood-brain barrier abnormalities caused by HIV-1 gp120: Mechanistic and therapeutic implications. *Scientific World Journal*, 2012:482575. http://dx.doi.org/10.1100/2012/482575

Lox, C. L., McAuley, E., & Tucker, R. S. (1995). Exercise as an intervention for enhancing subjective well-being in an HIV-1 population. *Journal of Sport and Exercise Psychology*, 17, 346–362.

MacArthur, R. D., Levine, S. D., & Birk, T. J. (1993). Supervised exercise training improves cardiopulmonary fitness in HIV-infected persons. *Medicine and Science in Sports and Exercise*, 25, 684–688.

McArdle, W., Katch, F., & Katch, V. (2010). *Exercise physiology: Energy, nutrition, and human performance* (7th ed.). Philadelphia, PA: Williams and Wilkins.

Morse, C. G., & Kovacs, J. A. (2006). Metabolic and skeletal complications of HIV infection. *Journal of the American Medical Association*, 296, 844–854. http://dx.doi.org/10.1001/jama.296.7.844

Murata, H., Hruz, P. W., & Mueckler, M. (2000). The mechanism of insulin resistance caused by HIV protease inhibitor therapy. *Journal of Biological Chemistry*, 275, 20251–20254.

Mutimura, E., Crowther, N. J., Cade, T. W., Yarasheski, K. E., & Stewart, A. (2008). Exercise training reduced central adiposity and improves metabolic indices in HAART-treated HIV-positive subjects in Rwanda: A randomized controlled trial. *AIDS Research and Human Retroviruses*, 24, 15–23.

Mutimura, E., Stewart, A., Crowther, N. J., Yarasheski, K. E., & Cade, W. T. (2008). The effects of exercise training on quality of life in HAART-treated HIV-positive Rwandan subjects with body fat redistribution. *Quality of Life Research*, 17, 377–385. http://dx.doi.org/10.1007/s11136-008-9319-4

Nelson, M. E., Rejeski, W. J., Blair, S. N., Duncan, P. W., Judge, J. O., King, A. C., & Castaneda-Sceppa, C. (2007). Physical activity and public health in older adults: Recommendation from the American College of Sports Medicine and the American Heart Association. *Medicine and Science in Sports and Exercise*, 39, 1435–1445. http://dx.doi.org/10.1161/CIRCU-LATIONAHA.107.185650

O'Brien, S. K., Knight, K. L., & Rana, T. M. (2012). Phosphorylation of histone H1 by P-TEFb is a necessary step in skeletal muscle differentiation. *Journal of Cellular Physiology*, 227(1), 383–389. http://dx.doi.org/10.1002/jcp.22797

O'Brien, K., Nixon, S., Tynan, A. M., & Glazier, R. (2010). Aerobic exercise interventions for adults living with HIV/AIDS. *Cochrane Database Systematic Reviews*, (8), CD001796.

Ogalha, C., Luz, E., Sampaio, E., Souza, R., Zarife, A., Neto, M. G., . . . Brites, C. (2011). A randomized, clinical trial to evaluate the impact of regular physical activity on the quality of life, body morphology and metabolic parameters of patients with AIDS in Salvador, Brazil. *Journal of Acquired Immune Deficiency Syndromes*, 57(Suppl. 3), S179–S185.

Otis, J. S., Ashikhmin, Y. I., Brown, L. A., & Guidot, D. M. (2008). Effects of HIV-1-related protein expression on cardiac and skeletal muscles from transgenic rats. *AIDS Research and Therapy*, 5, 8.

Oursler, K. K., Sorkin, J. D., Smith, B. A., & Katzel, L. I. (2006). Reduced aerobic capacity and physical functioning in older HIV-infected men. *AIDS Research and Human Retroviruses*, 22, 1113–1121. http://dx.doi.org/10.1089/aid.2006.22.1113

Oursler, K. K., Katzel, L. I., Smith, B. A., Scott, W. B., Russ, D. W., & Sorkin, J. D. (2009). Prediction of cardiorespiratory fitness in older men infected with the human immunodeficiency virus: Clinical factors and value of the six-minute walk distance. *Journal of the American Geriatric Society*, 57(11), 2055–2061.

Reiche, E. M., Nunes, S. O., & Morimoto, H. K. (2004). Stress, depression, the immune system, and cancer. *Lancet Oncology*, 5(10), 617–625.

Rice, A. P. (2009). Dysregulation of positive transcription elongation factor B and myocardial hypertrophy. *Circulation Research, 104*(12), 1327–1329.

Rigsby, L. W., Dishman, R. K., Jackson, A. W., Maclean, G. S., & Raven, P. B. (1992). Effects of exercise training on men seropositive for the human immunodeficiency virus-1. *Medicine and Science in Sports and Exercise, 24,* 6–12.

Robinson, F. P., Quinn, L. T., & Rimmer, J. H. (2007). Effects of high-intensity endurance and resistance exercise on HIV metabolic abnormalities: A pilot study. *Biological Research for Nursing, 8,* 177–185.

Sattler, F. R., Jaque, S. V., Schroeder, E. T., Olson, C., Dube, M. P., Martinez, C., . . . Azen, S. (1999). Effects of pharmacological doses of nandrolone decanoate and progressive resistance training in immunodeficient patients infected with HIV. *Journal of Clinical End & Met, 84*(4), 1268–1276.

Scevola, D., Di Matteo, A., Lanzarini, P., Uberti, F., Scevola, S., Bernini, V., . . . Faga, A. (2003). Effect of exercise and strength training on cardiovascular status in HIV-infected patients receiving highly active antiretroviral therapy. *AIDS, 17,* S123–S129.

Schiralli Lester, G. M., & Henderson, A. J. (2012). Mechanisms of HIV transcriptional regulation and their contribution to latency. *Molecular Biology International,* 2012, 614120. http://dx.doi.org/10.1155/2012/614120

Smith, B. A., Neidig, J. L., Nickel, J. T., Mitchell, G. L., Para, M. F., & Fass, R. J. (2001). Aerobic exercise: Effects on parameters related to fatigue, dyspnea, weight and body composition in HIV-infected adults. *AIDS, 15,* 693–701.

Souza, P. M., Jacob-Filho, W., Santarem, J. M., Silva, A. R., Li, H. Y., & Burattini, M. N. (2008). Progressive resistance training in elderly HIV-positive patients: Does it work? *Clinics, 63,* 619–624. http://dx.doi.org/10.1590/S1807-59322008000500009

Stanley, T. L., & Grinspoon, S. K. (2012). Body composition and metabolic changes in HIV-infected patients. *Journal of Infectious Diseases, 205,* S383–S390. http://dx.doi.org/10.1093/infdis/jis205

Taibi, D. M., Price, C., & Voss, J. (2012). A pilot study of sleep quality and rest-activity patterns in persons living with HIV. *Journal of the Association of Nurses in AIDS Care.* Advance online publication. http://dx.doi.org/10.1016/j.jana.2012.08.001

Terry, L., Sprinz, E., Stein, R., Medeiros, N. B., Oliveira, J., & Ribeiro, J. P. (2006). Exercise training in HIV-1-infected individuals with dyslipidemia and lipodystrophy. *Medicine and Science in Sports and Exercise, 38,* 411–417. http://dx.doi.org/10.1249/01.mss.0000191347.73848.80

Tesoriero, J. M., Gieryic, S. M., Carrascal, A., Lavigne, H. E. (2010). Smoking among HIV positive New Yorkers: Prevalence, frequency, and opportunities for cessation. *AIDS and Behavior, 14,* 824–835.

Thoni, G. J., Fedou, C., Brun, J. F., Fabre, J., Renard, E., Reynes, J., . . . Mercier, J. (2002). Reduction of fat accumulation and lipid disorders by individualized light aerobic training in human immunodeficiency virus infected patients with lipodystrophy and/or dyslipidemia. *Diabetes & Metabolism, 28,* 397–404.

Turner, J., Page-Shafer, K., Chin, D. P., Osmond, D., Mossar, M., Markstein, L., . . . Chesney, M. (2011). Adverse impact of cigarette smoking on dimensions of health-related quality of life in persons with HIV infection. *AIDS Patient Care STDS, 15,* 615–624.

Vella, S., Schwartländer, B., Sow, S. P., Eholie, S. P., & Murphy, R. L. (2012). The history of antiretroviral therapy and of its implementation in resource-limited areas of the world. *AIDS, 26,* 1231–1241.

Westcott, W. L. (2012). Resistance training is medicine: Effects of strength training on health. *Current Sports Medicine Reports, 11*(4), 209–216. http://dx.doi.org/10.1249/JSR.0b013e31825dabb8.

Wilmore, J. H., & Costill, D. L. (2004). *Physiology of sport and exercise* (3rd ed.). Champaign, IL: Human Kinetics.

Worm, S. W., De Wit, S., Weber, R., Sabin, C. A., Reiss, P., El-Sadr, W., . . . Friis-Møller, N. (2009). Diabetes mellitus, preexisting coronary heart disease, and the risk of subsequent coronary heart disease events in patients infected with human immunodeficiency virus: The Data Collection on Adverse Events of Anti-HIV Drugs (D:A:D Study). *Circulation, 119,* 805–811.

Yahiaoui, A., McGough, E. L., & Voss, J. G. (2012). Development of evidence-based exercise recommendations for older HIV-infected patients. *Journal of the Association of Nurses in AIDS Care, 23*(3), 204–219. http://dx.doi.org/10.1016/j.jana.2011.06.001

Young, J., Weber, R., Rickenbach, M., Furrer, H., Bernasconi, E., Hirschel, B., . . . Bucher, B. C. (2005). Lipid profiles for antiretroviral-naive patients starting PI- and NNRTI-based therapy in the Swiss HIV cohort study. *Antiviral Therapy, 10,* 585–591.

CHAPTER 10

Interventions to Increase Physical Activity in People With COPD

Systematic Review

Janet L. Larson, Carol M. Vos, and Dena Fernandez

ABSTRACT

People with chronic obstructive pulmonary disease (COPD) are very sedentary and this contributes to their health problems. The aim of this systematic review was to examine the effects of interventions designed to increase physical activity (PA) in people with COPD. Studies were included when PA was the primary outcome and measured objectively. Six databases were searched and 15 studies with a total of 761 subjects were identified that met inclusion criteria. Nine of the studies were quasi-experimental (QE) and six were randomized controlled trials (RCT). Interventions included pulmonary rehabilitation ($n = 7$), exercise only ($n = 2$), behavioral only ($n = 2$) and a combination of both behavioral and pulmonary rehabilitation/exercise interventions ($n = 4$). Methodological quality was evaluated using the Downs and Black checklist. The quality of the pulmonary rehabilitation studies was the lowest with a fair rating and the quality of exercise only studies was the highest with a good rating. Eight of the 15 studies demonstrated statistically significant increases in PA: two pulmonary rehabilitation (QE = 2), two exercise only (RCT = 2), two behavioral only (RCT = 1, QE = 1), and two combined behavioral and pulmonary rehabilitation/exercise (RCT = 2). The magnitude of increase was modest in all but one study; and in many studies the increase in PA was not clinically meaningful. Longer interventions demonstrated a higher success rate and only three studies examined longer term effects of the interventions. Existing interventions are promising, but the small number of randomized controlled trials makes it difficult to draw conclusion. Further research is needed to identify a range of interventions that are effective and could be used to promote PA in people with COPD.

Chronic obstructive pulmonary disease (COPD) is the fourth leading cause of disability (Centers for Disease Control and Prevention, 2009) for adults ≥ 65 years of age in the United States. An extremely sedentary lifestyle contributes to the disability of COPD. People with COPD have lower levels of physical activity (PA) compared to healthy older adults, 40%–60% lower (Pitta et al., 2005; Sandland, Singh, Curcio, Jones, & Morgan, 2005; Schonhofer, Ardes, Geibel, Kohler, & Jones, 1997; Singh & Morgan, 2001; Waschki et al., 2012); and this is consistent for accelerometer-based measures of activity counts (Sandland et al., 2005; Schonhofer et al., 1997; Singh & Morgan, 2001), pedometer measures of step counts (Tudor-Locke, Washington, & Hart, 2009), smart monitors that identify types of activities (Pitta et al., 2005), and self-report measures of PA (Hirayama, Lee, Binns, Leong, & Hiramatsu, 2008). In one study, people with COPD spent a mean of 44 ($SD = 26$) min/day walking as compared to 81 ($SD = 26$) min/day for healthy older adults (Pitta et al., 2005). People with COPD are also less active than people with other chronic diseases (Tudor-Locke et al., 2009).

Increasing PA can improve functional status and has the potential to improve respiratory health. Growing evidence suggests that higher levels of PA are associated with better lung health for people with COPD, including a slower rate of decline in lung function (Garcia-Aymerich, Lange, Benet, Schnohr, & Anto, 2007) and fewer acute exacerbations of COPD (Garcia-Aymerich et al., 2003; Waschki et al., 2012). In a prospective study of 340 people with COPD, physically active people had a reduced risk of hospital admission because of acute exacerbation of COPD and this relationship held true when controlling for severity of COPD (Garcia-Aymerich et al., 2003).

Pulmonary rehabilitation and exercise interventions improve physical fitness and physical function (Lacasse, Goldstein, Lasserson, & Martin, 2006; Ng, Mackney, Jenkins, & Hill, 2012), but less is known about the effects of pulmonary rehabilitation on PA, especially long term maintenance of PA. A recent systematic review examined the effects of exercise interventions designed to increase PA in COPD, studies reviewed employed objective measures of PA and were published through the first half of 2010 (Ng et al., 2012). Results were disappointing. Two randomized trials compared two interventions (de Blok et al., 2006;

Sewell, Singh, Williams, Collier, & Morgan, 2005), both designed to improve PA, and five quasi-experimental studies tested a single intervention comparing subjects before and after the intervention (Dallas, McCusker, Haggerty, Rochester, & ZuWallack, 2009; Pitta et al., 2008; Steele et al., 2010; Steele et al., 2003; Walker, Birmett, Flavahan, & Calverley, 2008). The combined effect size was small, equivalent to an increase in PA of approximately 5 min of walking a day (Ng et al., 2012).

The aim of this systematic review is to further examine the effects of interventions designed to increase PA in people with COPD when PA is treated as either a primary or a secondary outcome. We have expanded the review to include behavioral interventions.

METHODS

We searched the following computerized databases: MEDLINE, PubMed, CINAHL, Cochrane Central Register of Controlled Trials, Cochrane Systematic Reviews, and Cochrane Database of Abstracts of Effect. Search strategies were developed with a reference librarian and included terms for participants, interventions, and outcome variables. Major subject headings used in the search included "chronic obstructive pulmonary disease" or "chronic bronchitis" or "bronchiolitis" or "pulmonary emphysema" and "exercise therapy" or "therapeutic exercise" or "exercise tolerance" or "motor activity" or "lung" or "pulmonary" and "rehabilitation." Title or abstract terms included "COPD" or "chronic" and "bronchitis" or "bronchiolitis" and "lung" or "pulmonary" and "rehabilitation" or "pulmonary rehabilitation" or "physical activity" or "physical activities" or "pedometer."

Published reports were screened for eligibility by two investigators independently and disagreements were reviewed and judged by a third investigator. Abstracts were reviewed for 319 reports and the full manuscript was reviewed for 55. Forty were discarded because there was no objective measure of PA or the measure of PA did not meet inclusion criteria and 15 reports remained to be included in this systematic review (see Figure 10.1).

Studies were included if they met the following criteria: (a) subjects had COPD documented by pulmonary function tests, (b) the intervention was designed to increase PA as either a primary or secondary outcome, (c) the intervention included exercise and/or behavioral strategies, and (d) PA was objectively measured with a monitor for at least 3 days. Studies that measured PA with self-report were excluded because of the biases associated with self-reported PA (Tucker, Welk, & Beyler, 2011).

The following data were extracted from each record: research design, sample characteristics, description of the intervention, length of intervention and

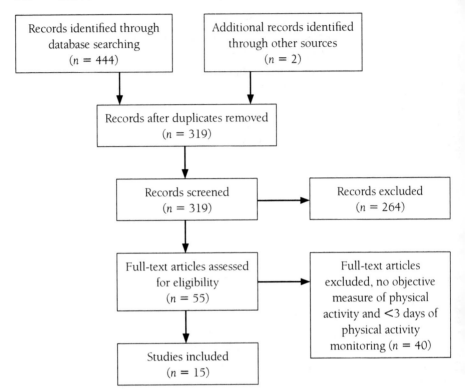

FIGURE 10.1 Flow diagram for retrieval of records.

length of follow-up after completing the intervention, equipment and procedures used to measure PA, and PA outcomes. Sample characteristics included sample size, gender, age, and forced expiratory volume in 1 s (FEV_1).

Interventions were categorized as pulmonary rehabilitation, exercise only, or behavioral only interventions. Pulmonary rehabilitation generally includes a multidisciplinary approach with exercise training and patient education (Troosters, Casaburi, Gosselink, & Decramer, 2005). The educational component may include psychosocial support, an emphasis on functional independence and encouragement to continue exercising, but typically does not include a focused behavioral strategy for increasing PA. So studies of pulmonary rehabilitation were not considered to have a behavioral component unless a behavioral strategy was clearly described. To the extent possible, we described each intervention using the published description (see Tables 10.1 and 10.2).

We evaluated the methodological quality of each study using the Downs and Black Checklist (Downs & Black, 1998). The checklist comprises 27 items

TABLE 10.1

Pulmonary Rehabilitation (n = 7) and Exercise Only (n = 2): Description of Study Participants, Physical Activity Monitoring and Intervention

Study	Sample Size Enrolled (*n*) Country of Origin	Gender Age, Years Disease Severity[a] Mean (*SD*)	Activity Monitor, Days Monitored	Intervention
Egan et al., 2012	47[b] Ireland	Males reported as slightly <50% of the sample Age not reported FEV$_1$ % pred. 48.6 (16.6)	Sense Wear Pro Armbands, 7 days	*Pulmonary rehabilitation.* Included aerobic and resistance training and interdisciplinary education. Two sessions a week for 7 weeks.
Mador et al., 2011	24 US, VA[c]	Gender not reported Age 71.90 (7.70) FEV$_1$ % pred. 44.1 (17.9)	RT3 accelerometer, 7 days	*Pulmonary rehabilitation.* Included calisthenics with and without weights, cycle ergometry and treadmill exercises, and education. Three sessions a week for 8 weeks.
Steele et al., 2010	146[d] US, VA[c]	Gender not reported Age[d] AECOPD 67.0 (9.0) No AECOPD 66.8 (10.4) FEV$_1$ % pred. AECOPD 36.3 (14.9) No AECOPD 39.8 (15.8)	RT3 accelerometer, 6 days	*Pulmonary rehabilitation.* Comprehensive outpatient pulmonary rehabilitation included progressive resistance exercises with hand weights, elastic resistance tubing, and/or weight machines; cardiovascular/endurance training with the treadmill, cycle ergometer, NuStep and upper extremity ergometers. Two sessions a week for 8 weeks.

(Continued)

TABLE 10.1

Pulmonary Rehabilitation (n = 7) and Exercise Only (n = 2): Description of Study Participants, Physical Activity Monitoring and Intervention   (Continued)

Study	Sample Size Enrolled (n) Country of Origin	Gender Age, Years Disease Severity[a] Mean (SD)	Activity Monitor, Days Monitored	Intervention
Dallas et al., 2009	59[c] US	M/F = 21/24 Age 69.00 (8.00) FEV$_1$ % pred. 45.0 (18.0)	NL-2000 Activity Monitor pedometer, 7 days	*Pulmonary rehabilitation.* Results are from four different programs and each met established guidelines for PR. Programs included multimodality aerobic and strength exercise training of the lower and upper extremities, education and psychosocial support. Promotion of exercise and physical activity at home was a part of each program. Two to three sessions a week for 6–12 weeks.
Walker et al., 2008	23 United Kingdom	M/F = 12/11 Age 66.00 (9.00) FEV$_1$ % pred. 36.4 (11.6)	Actiwatch Uniaxial Accelerometer worn at the ankle, 3 weekdays	*Pulmonary rehabilitation.* With individualized aerobic exercises of upper and lower limbs, peripheral muscle strengthening, and whole body endurance exercises. Three sessions a week (two supervised and one at home) for 8 weeks.
Pitta et al., 2008	41[c] Belgium	M/F = 23/6 Age 67.00 (8.00) FEV$_1$ % pred. 48.0 (16.0)	DynaPort Activity Monitor, 5 days	*Pulmonary rehabilitation.* Included exercise, education, and counseling regarding the importance of exercising regularly and how to be more active in their daily lives. Three sessions a week for 12 weeks followed by two sessions a week for another 12 weeks.

Steele et al., 2003	41[c] US, VA[c]	M/F = 37/1 Age 63.70 (7.80) FEV$_1$ % pred. 39.0 (17.0)	Tritrac R3D triaxial accelerometer, 5 days	*Pulmonary rehabilitation.* In addition to the standard supervised exercise sessions, subjects were encouraged to exercise 3 additional days a week at home. Two sessions a week for 8 weeks.
Effing et al., 2011	80[e] Netherlands	M/F = 45/32 Age 62.90 (8.10) FEV$_1$ % pred. 49.6 (14.2)	Ymax Digi-Walker pedometer, 7 days	*Exercise.* Intervention group received self-management sessions, once a week for 4 weeks. This was followed by a community-based physiotherapeutic exercise (COPE-active) program focused on activities considered to be challenging for people with COPD, specifically walking or cycling, strength exercises for upper and lower extremities. Intensity was consistent with established recommendations for pulmonary rehabilitation. The first 6 months of training were considered compulsory and the last 5 months were considered optional but recommended, emphasizing maintenance. Exercise diaries were reviewed every week. Three sessions a week (2 laboratory and 1 at home) for 24 weeks compulsory phase. This was followed by two sessions a week (1 laboratory and 1 at home) for 20 weeks, labeled voluntary phase.
	79[e]	M/F = 44/32 Age 63.90 (7.80) FEV$_1$ % pred. 50.5 (17.0)		*Control group.* Received self-management sessions, once a week for 4 weeks. Subjects were allowed to attend regular, non-COPE-active physiotherapy sessions if prescribed as part of regular care. One session a week for 4 weeks.

(Continued)

TABLE 10.1

Pulmonary Rehabilitation (n = 7) and Exercise Only (n = 2): Description of Study Participants, Physical Activity Monitoring and Intervention (Continued)

Study	Sample Size Enrolled (n) Country of Origin	Gender Age, Years Disease Severity[a] Mean (SD)	Activity Monitor, Days Monitored	Intervention
Breyer et al., 2010	30 Austria	M/F = 14/16 Age 61.90 (8.87) FEV$_1$ % pred. 48.1 (19.1)	DynaPort Activity Monitor; 3 weekdays	*Exercise.* Nordic walking for 1 hr each session at a target heart rate of 75% of initial maximum heart rate. Three sessions a week for 12 weeks.
	30	M/F = 13/17 Age 59.00 (8.02) FEV$_1$ % pred. 47.1 (16.3)		*No treatment control.*

[a]Disease severity is reflected by the forced expiratory volume in 1 s (FEV$_1$) and reported as a percentage of predicted normal values
[b]A total of 47 subjects were enrolled, 34 completed 7 weeks of the intervention, and 22 completed 13 additional weeks of follow-up and provided physical activity data.
[c]Subjects were recruited predominantly or exclusively from a United States Veterans Health Administration clinical setting.
[d]A total of 146 subjects initiated pulmonary rehabilitation and 112 subjects completed the post-PR intervention described in this study. Subjects were described according to whether or not they experienced an acute exacerbation of COPD (AECOPD) during pulmonary rehabilitation. This description is for 136 subjects who completed the study or dropped out for reasons other than an AECOPD.
[e]The difference between the number of subjects enrolled and the number of subjects described in the next column (M/F) was caused by subject attrition.

TABLE 10.2

Behavioral Interventions (n = 2) and Combined Behavioral and Pulmonary Rehabilitation or Exercise Interventions (n = 4):
Description of Study Participants, Physical Activity Monitoring, and Intervention

Study	Sample Size Enrolled (n) Country of Origin	Gender Age, Years Disease Severity[a] Mean (SD)	Activity Monitor, Days Monitored	Intervention
Moy et al., 2012	27 US, VA[b]	M/F = 27/0 Age 72.0 (8.0) FEV$_1$ % pred. 55.0 (16.0)	Omron HJ-720ITC pedometer, 5–7days	Behavioral. Every step counts walking program combines pedometer with a website to support walking. Pedometer data were uploaded to the website on a regular basis. The data were displayed graphically on the subjects' individual webpages and subjects received realistic walking goals, motivational messages, and educational tips weekly via e-mail. One interaction a week for 12 weeks.
Hospes et al., 2009	20[c] Netherlands	M/F = 10/8 Age 63.1 (8.3) FEV$_1$ % pred. 67.4 (17.5)	Ymax Digi-Walker SW-2000 pedometer, 14 days	Behavioral. Customized exercise counseling program designed to enhance daily physical activity and motivate people to establish a more physically active lifestyle. The program employed principles of goal setting and implementation of goals. Motivational interviewing was used as a counseling technique. Pedometers were worn all day during the intervention period. Total of five sessions.
	19[c]	M/F = 11/6 Age 61.2 (9.1) FEV$_1$ % pred. 61.8 (14.4)		Usual care control.

(Continued)

TABLE 10.2

Behavioral Interventions (n = 2) and Combined Behavioral and Pulmonary Rehabilitation or Exercise Interventions (n = 4): Description of Study Participants, Physical Activity Monitoring, and Intervention   (Continued)

Study	Sample Size Enrolled (n) Country of Origin	Gender Age, Years Disease Severity[a] Mean (SD)	Activity Monitor, Days Monitored	Intervention
Pomidori et al., 2012	18 Italy	M/F = 13/5 Age 70.0 (9.0) FEV$_1$ % pred. 48.0 (13.0)	SenseWear armband, 7 days	*Combined behavioral and exercise.* Speed walking paced by a metronome. Subjects were instructed to walk 20–30 min a day at the prescribed speed. Prescribed walking speed was based on a maximal walking test. A metronome was used to pace walking. Weekly supervised sessions for 4 weeks followed by phone calls twice a month for 12 months.
	18	M/F = 14/4 Age 74.0 (7.0) FEV$_1$ % pred. 49.0 (12.0)		*Exercise control group.* Walking a known distance in a given period. An equivalent distance was calculated using the maximal walking test and subjects were instructed to walk the fixed distance using a walking path located near their home. Weekly supervised sessions for 4 weeks followed by phone calls twice a month for 12 months.
Nguyen et al., 2009	9 US	M/F = 3/6 Age 64.0 (12.0) FEV$_1$ % pred. 34.4 (15.0)	Stepwatch® 3 Activity Monitor worn at the ankle, 14 days	*Combined behavioral and pulmonary rehabilitation.* Randomized after 8 weeks of pulmonary rehabilitation. Mobilizing Support for Long-term Exercise—coached (MOBILE-C), a cell phone mediated cognitive-behavioral exercise persistence intervention with weekly coaching for 36 weeks that includes motivational feedback and assistance with problem solving to develop self-regulatory capacity for exercise persistence.

	8	MF = 3/5 Age 72.0 (9.0) FEV$_1$ % pred. 46.7 (18.7)		*Combined behavioral and pulmonary rehabilitation.* Randomized after 8 weeks of pulmonary rehabilitation. Mobilizing Support for Long-term Exercise—self-monitoring (MOBILE-SM), an active control intervention that includes the cell phone supported intervention for self-monitoring for 36 weeks. Pedometers were used as part of this intervention.
Steele et al., 2008	54[c] US, VA[b]	Gender not reported Mean age = 67 for total sample (*SD* not reported) No COPD N = 12[d] GOLD stage II N = 8 GOLD stage III n = 24 GOLD stage IV n = 8	RT3 accelerometer, 6 days	*Combined behavioral and pulmonary rehabilitation.* Randomized after 8 weeks of pulmonary rehabilitation. Home-based exercise adherence intervention was delivered with weekly phone calls and one home visit over 3 months. The intervention emphasized self-monitoring and recording of exercise sessions, problem-solving skills to prevent or manage exercise lapses, and encouragement to participate in exercise outside the home at least once a week.
	57[c]	No COPD N = 9[d] GOLD stage II N = 7 GOLD stage III n = 22 GOLD stage IV n = 16		*Usual care control group.* Included continuing care with referring provider and individual recommendations for continuation of the exercise program. All were invited to attend the lung club group sessions.

(Continued)

TABLE 10.2

Behavioral Interventions (n = 2) and Combined Behavioral and Pulmonary Rehabilitation or Exercise Interventions (n = 4): Description of Study Participants, Physical Activity Monitoring, and Intervention   (Continued)

Study	Sample Size Enrolled (n) Country of Origin	Gender Age, Years Disease Severity[a] Mean (SD)	Activity Monitor, Days Monitored	Intervention
de Blok et al., 2006	10 Netherlands	M/F = 5/5 Age 65.7 (10.4) FEV$_1$ % pred. 52.0 (22.0)	Digi-Walker SW-200 pedometer, 7 days	*Combined behavioral and pulmonary rehabilitation.* Standard pulmonary rehabilitation plus lifestyle physical activity counseling with pedometer feedback. Subjects were encouraged to incorporate activities such as walking, cycling, stair-climbing, and gardening into daily life. Motivational interviewing techniques were used. Four counseling session.
	11	M/F = 4/7 Age 62.5 (12.3) FEV$_1$ % pred. 43.0 (13.0)		*Pulmonary rehabilitation control group.* Standard pulmonary rehabilitation included exercise training, dietary intervention, and psychoeducational modules.

Note. GOLD = Global Initiative for Chronic Obstructive Lung Disease.

[a]Disease severity is reflected by the forced expiratory volume in one second (FEV$_1$) and reported as a percentage of predicted normal values.

[b]Subjects were recruited predominantly or exclusively from a U.S. Department of Veterans Health Administration clinical setting.

[c]The difference between the number of subjects enrolled and the number of subjects described in the next column (M/F) was caused by subject attrition.

[d]These subjects had interstitial lung disease, apnea-hypoventilation syndrome, or sleep apnea.

that address the quality of reporting, external validity, internal validity—bias, internal validity—confounding (selection bias) and power. Item 27 was designed to measure power in qualitative studies and controlled clinical trials, and for purposes of this review, we used a modified scoring system that has been used by others (Deshpande et al., 2009; Samoocha, Bruinvels, Elbers, Anema, & van der Beek, 2010). Item 27 was scored as "1" if the author reported statistical power in the original article and as "0" if not. The total possible score was 28 and quality was considered excellent (26–28), good (20–25), fair (15–19), and poor (<14). Each study was evaluated by two people independently and disagreements were discussed to come to a consensus.

RESULTS

Fifteen studies met inclusion criteria and were examined in this review. A description of the subjects and interventions is provided in Tables 10.1 and 10.2. There were 761 subjects with COPD represented in this body of research. Disease severity ranged from moderate to very severe with mean FEV_1 ranging from 67.4% to 36.3% of predicted normal values. In three studies, the mean FEV_1 percentage predicted was <40, and in one study it was >60. Seven of the studies were conducted in the United States, five of these in Veterans Health Administration settings. Three were conducted in the Netherlands and one was conducted in Austria, Belgium, Ireland, Italy and United Kingdom. Ten studies used accelerometers and five used pedometers to measure PA. The monitoring frame ranged from 3 to 14 days.

The quality of the studies varied with Downs and Black scores ranging from 12 to 23 and an overall mean score of 17.33 (SD = 2.92). The interventions fell into three categories: (a) pulmonary rehabilitation (n = 7) or exercise only (n = 2), (b) behavioral only interventions (n = 2), and (c) the combination of behavioral and pulmonary rehabilitation or exercise interventions (n = 4). The Black and Downs scores were somewhat lower for the pulmonary rehabilitation studies, mean 15.58 (SD = 2.37). Scores for the remaining categories were exercise only, 20.0 (SD = 2.83), behavioral only, 17.5 (SD = 2.12), and combination behavioral and pulmonary rehabilitation or exercise, 18 (SD = 2.94).

Studies included six experimental and nine quasi-experimental research designs. The six experimental studies were randomized trials, three of which employed a usual care or no-treatment control group (Breyer et al., 2010; Effing, Zielhuis, Kerstjens, van der Valk, & van der Palen, 2011; Hospes, Bossenbroek, Ten Hacken, van Hengel, & de Greef, 2009) and one compared two active interventions (Pomidori, Contoli, Mandolesi, & Cogo, 2012). In two randomized trials, subjects were randomized to groups immediately after they completed

pulmonary rehabilitation and for purposes of this research, they were classified as combined behavioral and pulmonary rehabilitation interventions, one
compared two active interventions (Nguyen, Gill, Wolpin, Steele, & Benditt,
2009) and the other employed a usual care control group (Steele et al., 2008).
The quasi-experimental studies all employed a one-group before–after research
design. Results are presented in Tables 10.3 and 10.4.

The effects of pulmonary rehabilitation were examined in seven studies;
only two observed significant increases in PA and the observed increases were
modest (Pitta et al., 2008; Walker et al., 2008). In most studies, pulmonary
rehabilitation was implemented for 8 weeks, but in one study from Belgium,
subjects completed 6 months of pulmonary rehabilitation (Pitta et al., 2008). In
this study, subjects demonstrated no increase in PA at 3 months, but a significant
increase in PA at 6 months, walking time increased by a mean of 10 min a day
($p = .008$) and movement intensity during walking increased by 7% ($p = .002$;
Pitta et al., 2008). After 8 weeks of pulmonary rehabilitation, Walker and colleagues (2008) observed a mean increase of 5% time spent mobile ($p = .014$)
and a 33% increase in movement intensity ($p = .001$).

Two reports examined the effects of exercise-only interventions and both
observed modest but significant increases in PA. Breyer et al. (2010) observed
an increase in walking time, 14.9 ($SD = 1.9$) min a day, and a larger increase
in standing time, 129 ($SD = 26$) min a day, after completing 12 weeks of
Nordic walking and the improvements persisted for 6 months after the completion of the structured Nordic walking program. Note the activity monitoring
did not include the time spent Nordic walking. Effing et al. (2011) observed
a 20% increase in steps per day after 4 weeks of self-management followed
by 48 weeks of community-based physiotherapeutic exercise (COPE-active).
Subjects in the treatment group started with a mean of 4,472 steps/day and
increased by a mean of 815 steps/day.

The effects of behavioral only interventions were examined in two studies and both demonstrated increases in the number of steps per day. One was
a web-based intervention designed with feedback and goal setting activities
to support walking over a 12-week period and subjects increased their steps
per day by 43% (Moy, Weston, Wilson, Hess, & Richardson, 2012). The
other was five sessions of face-to-face counseling with an emphasis on goal
setting and implementation of goals with pedometer feedback. Motivational
interviewing techniques were employed. Subjects in the counseling group
increased their steps per day by 11% (Hospes et al., 2009). Subjects in the
first study started at a very low level of activity, 2,908 ($SD = 2,416$) steps/
day, compared to subjects in the second study, 7,087 ($SD = 4,058$) steps/day.
In both of these studies, the mean scores for FEV_1 (percentage of predicted

TABLE 10.3

Results of Pulmonary Rehabilitation (n = 7) and Exercise Only (n = 2) Interventions

Study	Duration of Intervention[a] (Weeks)	Duration of Follow-up[b] (Weeks)	Intervention	PA Outcome (+ or −)[c]	Baseline Total PA Change in Total PA	Other Dimensions of PA
Egan et al., 2012	7	13	PR	−	Baseline step count, mean = 3,611 (SD = 2,863) steps/day Within group effects, NS	
Mador et al., 2011	8	0	PR	−	Baseline total VMU/min, mean = 116 (SD = 62.70) Within group effects, NS	Baseline time spent at VMU >500/min, mean = 39.4 (SD = 43) min/day Within group effects, NS
Steele et al., 2010	8	0	PR	−	Baseline total VMU/min, mean = 164.9 (SD = 142.90) for subjects with AECOPD Baseline total VMU/min, mean = 162.8 (SD = 89.20) for subjects with no AECOPD Within group effects, NS	
Dallas et al., 2009	6–12	0	PR	−	Baseline pedometer count, mean = 207 (SD = 139.00) counts/hour Within group effects, NS	

(Continued)

TABLE 10.3

Results of Pulmonary Rehabilitation (n = 7) and Exercise Only (n = 2) Interventions   (Continued)

Study	Duration of Intervention[a] (Weeks)	Duration of Follow-up[b] (Weeks)	Intervention	PA Outcome (+ or −)[c]	Baseline Total PA Change in Total PA	Other Dimensions of PA
Walker et al., 2008	8	0	PR	+	Baseline activity ($\times 10^3$ counts/hr), mean = 82 (SE = 53) End of PR vs. baseline Δ activity ($\times 10^3$ counts/hr), mean = +35.7 (SE = 49), $p = .002$	Baseline mean % time mobile, mean = 50 (SE = 13.90) Intensity of activity during active times ($\times 10^3$ counts/hr), mean = 156 (SE = 69.00) End of PR vs. baseline Δ % time mobile, mean = +5.2 (SE = 9.4), $p = .014$ Δ intensity of activity during active times ($\times 10^3$ counts/hr), mean = +52.5 (SE = 74.2), $p = .001$

| Pitta et al., 2008 | 36 Measures were taken at baseline, 3 months and 6 months. | 0 | PR | – and + | Baseline walking time, mean = 55 (SD = 26.00) min/day Baseline standing time, mean = 227 (SD = 92.00) min/day 3 months vs. baseline Δ walking time, NS Δ standing time, NS 6 months vs. baseline Δ walking time, mean = +10 min/day min greater than baseline, p = .008 Δ Standing time, NS | Baseline movement intensity, mean = 1.81 (SD = 0.24) m/s² 3 months vs. baseline Δ movement intensity during walking, mean = +0.07 m/s², p = .046 6 months vs. baseline Δ movement intensity during walking, mean = +0.33 m/s² greater than baseline, p = .0002 |
| Steele et al., 2003 | 8 | 0 | PR | – | Baseline VMU/min, mean = 82.4 (SD = 34.10) Within group effect, NS | |

(Continued)

TABLE 10.3

Results of Pulmonary Rehabilitation (n = 7) and Exercise Only (n = 2) Interventions   (Continued)

Study	Duration of Intervention[a] (Weeks)	Duration of Follow-up[b] (Weeks)	Intervention	PA Outcome (+ or −)[c]	Baseline Total PA Change in Total PA	Other Dimensions of PA
Breyer et al., 2010	12	36 Measures were taken at 3 months and 6 months after completion of the intervention	Nordic walking	+	Baseline walking time, mean = 46.7 (SD = 35.20) min/day End of training, 3 months and 6 months follow-up vs. baseline: Walking time between group effects, p = .034 Standing time between group effects, $p < .05$. End of training vs. baseline Δ walking time, mean = +14.9 (SD = 1.90) min/day, $p < .01$ Δ standing time, mean + 129.0 (SD = 26.00) min/day; $p < .01$ 3 months vs. baseline Δ walking time, mean = +12.7 (SD = 1.80) min/day, p = .024 Δ standing time, mean = +133.0 (SD = 14.00) min/day, $p < .01$ 6 months vs. baseline Δ walking time, mean = +9.2 (SD = 2.90) min/day, p = .036 Δ standing time, mean = +105.0 (SD = 4.00) min/day; $p < .01$	Baseline movement intensity, mean = 1.59 (SD = 0.47) m/s^2 End of training, 3 months and 6 months follow-up vs. baseline: Between groups effect, $p < .01$ Within group effect, $p < .01$. Baseline to 6 months follow-up Δ movement intensity, mean = +.25 (SD = 0.09) m/s^2, $p < .01$

		−	No treatment control	Baseline walking time, mean = 42.3 (SD = 36.50) min/day Baseline standing time, mean = 222 (SD = 169) min/day No change in walking or standing time, data not reported	Baseline movement intensity, mean = 1.50 (SD = 0.29) m/s² Movement intensity slowly declined and was below baseline at 6 months after completion of the intervention, $p < 0.01$ (data not reported).
Effing et al., 2011	52 Measures were taken at 7 months and 12 months	0	+	Self-management plus COPE-active	Baseline step count, mean = 4,472 (SD = 2,715) steps/day Overall Δ in step count, treatment vs. control, mean = +876.6, 95% CI (95.4–1,657.7) steps/day in favor of treatment.
			−	Self-management sessions	Baseline step count, mean = 5,224 (SD = 3,464) steps/day Within group effect, NS

Note. AECOPD = acute exacerbation of chronic obstructive pulmonary disease; PR = pulmonary rehabilitation; VMU = vector magnitude unit.
[a]Measures were taken before and after the intervention unless otherwise noted.
[b]Duration of follow-up after completion of intervention.
[c]PA outcome (+ or −), refers to the primary PA outcome by group and whether it was positive or negative.

TABLE 10.4

Results of Behavioral Interventions (n = 2) and Combined Behavioral and Pulmonary Rehabilitation or Exercise Interventions (n = 4)

Study	Duration of Intervention[a] (Weeks)	Duration of Follow up[b] (Weeks)	Intervention	PA Outcome (+ or −)[c]	Baseline Total PA Change in Total PA	Other Dimensions of PA
Moy et al., 2012	12	0	Every step counts walking program	+	Baseline step count, mean = 2,908 (SD = 2,416) steps/day Δ step count, mean = +1,263 steps/day; $p = .0054$	
Hospes et al., 2009	12	0	Customized exercise counseling program designed to enhance daily physical activity	+	Baseline step count, mean = 7,087 (SD = 4,058) steps/day Group × time interaction, $p = .01$ Δ step count, mean = +785 steps/day	
			Usual care	−	Baseline step count, mean = 7,539 (SD = 3,945) steps/day Δ step count, mean = −1,367 steps/day	
Pomidori et al., 2012	52 Measures were taken at 6 months and 12 months	0	Speed walking paced by a metronome and phone calls twice a month	+	Baseline METs daily average, mean = 1.22 (SD = 0.13) 12 months vs. baseline Δ METs daily average, mean = +0.17 (SD = 0.14), $p < .05$ Within group effects, $p < .05$, Between group effects, $p < .05$	

Nguyen et al., 2009	After PR 36	Walking a known distance in a given period of time and phone calls twice a month	−	Baseline METs daily average, mean = 1.29 (SD = 0.21) 12 months vs. baseline Δ METs daily average, mean = +0.04 (SD = 0.13), Within group effects, NS	
	0	Mobilizing Support for Long-term Exercise—coached (MOBILE-C)	−	Baseline step count, mean = 6,692 (SD = 1,007) steps/day Group × time interaction, p = .04 Δ step count, mean = −1,017 steps/day	Baseline % active time (moderate to high), mean = 27.1 (SD = 2.60) Group × time interaction, p = .003 Δ % active time, mean = −3.5
		Mobilizing Support for Long-term Exercise—self-monitoring (MOBILE-SM)	+	Baseline step count, mean = 5,229 (SD = 1,068) steps/day Δ step count, mean = +609 steps/day	Baseline % active time (moderate to high), mean = 19.1 (SD = 2.70) Δ % active time, mean = +4.4
Steele et al., 2008	PR = 8 weeks Behavioral intervention = 12 weeks	32 Measures were taken after PR, week 8; after behavioral	Home-based exercise adherence intervention, phone calls	−	Baseline before PR VMU/min, mean = 177 (SD = 123.00)

(Continued)

TABLE 10.4

Results of Behavioral Interventions (n = 2) and Combined Behavioral and Pulmonary Rehabilitation or Exercise Interventions (n = 4)   (Continued)

Study	Duration of Intervention[a] (Weeks)	Duration of Follow up[b] (Weeks)	Intervention	PA Outcome (+ or −)[c]	Baseline Total PA Change in Total PA	Other Dimensions of PA
Steele et al., 2008		intervention, week 20; and 32 weeks after behavioral intervention, week 52.	Usual care	−	Baseline before PR VMU/min, mean = 143 (SD = 63.00) Between group comparisons controlled for measures taken at baseline and at the end of PR, NS	
de Blok et al., 2006	9	0	PR plus lifestyle physical activity counseling with pedometer feedback	−	Baseline step count, mean = 2,082 (95% CI, 1,139–3,025) steps/day Group × time interaction, NS Δ step count, mean = +1,438 steps/day Within group effect, NS	
			PR	−	Baseline step count, mean = 2,377 (95% CI, 1,370–3,384) steps/day Δ step count, mean = +455 steps/day, +19.1% Within group effect, NS	

Note. MET = metabolic equivalent of task; PA physical activity; = PR = pulmonary rehabilitation; VMU = vector magnitude unit.
[a]Measures were taken before and after the intervention unless otherwise noted.
[b]Duration of follow-up after completion of intervention.
[c]PA outcome (+ or −), refers to the primary PA outcome by group and whether it was positive or negative.

normal value) suggested that the sample was on the healthier end of the spectrum with predominantly moderate airflow obstruction, FEV_1 % pred. = 55.0 (SD = 16; Moy et al., 2012) and FEV_1 % pred. = 67.4 (SD = 17.5) and 61.8 (SD = 14.4; Hospes et al., 2009).

The effects of a combination of behavioral and either pulmonary rehabilitation or exercise interventions were examined in four studies, two of which demonstrated an increase in PA. In two studies, the behavioral intervention was delivered simultaneously with the exercise intervention and in the other two the behavioral intervention was delivered after the completion of an 8-week pulmonary rehabilitation program. The behavioral component of the interventions ranged from 4 months to 52 months in duration. They included lifestyle PA counseling with pedometer feedback (de Blok et al., 2006), phone calls twice a month (Pomidori et al., 2012), self-monitoring and coaching with a pedometer feedback delivered via a mobile phone (Nguyen et al., 2009), and 3 months of weekly phone calls focusing on overcoming barriers and self-monitoring with one home visit to address safety issues (Steele et al., 2010). All but one used a pedometer for feedback. The magnitude of improvement varied for the two successful interventions (Nguyen et al., 2009; Pomidori et al., 2012). In one paced walking with a metronome and phone calls twice a month for 1 year increased PA from a mean of 23 (SD = 22) to 58 (SD = 38) min spent in activities >3.00 metabolic equivalent of tasks (METs) and increased MET daily average from 1.22 to 1.33 (Pomidori et al., 2012). In the other study, walking increased by a mean of 609 step/day and percentage time active in the moderate to high range increased by 4.4% (Nguyen et al., 2009).

One study demonstrated no significant effect of the lifestyle PA counseling intervention in combination with pulmonary rehabilitation compared to a control group with only pulmonary rehabilitation (deBlock et al., 2006). The interaction effect was not significant (p = .11) in part because both groups demonstrated an increase in PA. The mean steps increased from 2,082 to 3,512 steps/day in the combined group and from 2,377 to 2,832 step/day in the control group that received only pulmonary rehabilitation.

Longer interventions were more successful in increasing PA. Shorter interventions, 6–12 weeks long, were examined in 11 studies and 4 demonstrated increases in PA (Breyer et al., 2010; Hospes et al., 2009; Moy et al., 2012; Walker et al., 2008). Longer interventions, 36–52 weeks, were examined in 4 studies and all 4 demonstrated increases in PA (Effing et al., 2011; Nguyen et al., 2009; Pitta et al., 2008; Pomidori et al., 2012).

Only three studies examined long term effects after completion of the intervention (Breyer et al., 2010; Egan et al., 2012; Steele et al., 2008) and only one of them demonstrated a long term increase in PA (Breyer et al., 2010).

DISCUSSION

We identified and assessed 15 studies designed to test interventions to increase daily PA in people with COPD. Interventions included pulmonary rehabilitation ($n = 7$) or exercise ($n = 2$), behavioral interventions ($n = 2$) and a combination of both behavioral and pulmonary rehabilitation/exercise interventions ($n = 4$). The quality of the pulmonary rehabilitation studies was the lowest with a fair rating and the quality of exercise only studies was the highest with a good rating. Eight of the 15 studies demonstrated significant increases in PA, 2 pulmonary rehabilitation, 2 exercise only, 2 behavioral, and 2 combined behavioral and pulmonary rehabilitation/exercise interventions. The magnitude of increase was modest in all but one study; and in many studies the increase in PA may not be clinically meaningful. Longer interventions demonstrated a higher success rate and only 3 studies examined longer term effects of the interventions.

Low PA is a serious health problem for people with COPD and sedentary behavior patterns are well entrenched and difficult to change after three to four decades of a very sedentary lifestyle. Efforts to establish a more active lifestyle are particularly challenging for people with COPD because of the day-to-day fluctuations in symptoms (dyspnea and fatigue) that affect energy levels (Kessler et al., 2011) and periodic acute exacerbations of COPD that interrupt PA patterns (Borges & Carvalho, 2012; Kessler et al., 2006; Pitta et al., 2006). This complicates the situation and makes it difficult to establish long term changes in PA patterns. For healthy older adults, the PA guidelines recommend 150 min a week of moderate-intensity exercise such as brisk walking (Physical Activity Guidelines Advisory Committee, 2008), and when this is added to the typical background of PA that is associated with daily living (5,000 steps/day), it is equivalent to approximately 7,000–10,000 steps/day (Tudor-Locke et al., 2011). Some people with chronic disease live with a much lower background level of PA and their total recommended steps per day would be lower, somewhere in the range of 7,000–8,000 counts/day (Rowe, Kemble, Robinson, & Mahar, 2007; Tudor-Locke et al., 2011).

Most of the subjects represented in this review were sedentary. Six investigators reported step counts and the mean ranged from 2,082 steps/day to 7,539 steps/day at baseline. Based on the mean data, subjects in only one of these studies met guidelines recommended for PA (Hospes et al., 2009) and another was close but steps were measured with an ankle monitor that is more sensitive to slow walking and tends to produce higher step counts compared to waist-mounted devices (Nguyen et al., 2009). Three investigators reported the mean time subjects' spent walking with a range of 39–55 min/day (Breyer et al., 2010; Mador, Patel, & Nadler, 2011; Pitta et al., 2008). These data represent total volume of walking, but it is not possible to determine if these subjects met PA guidelines. One investigator reported that subjects spent 50% of their time mobile during daytime hours (Walker et al., 2008). They used an ankle-mounted accelerometer that is sensitive to slow walking and they set the threshold very low at ≥1 activity count per 30 s epoch, which means it is possible that movement of the leg during sitting could be counted as mobile time. So again, it is not possible to determine the extent to which they met PA guidelines. As stated earlier, it is reasonable to conclude that subjects in only one study met the recommended guidelines for PA and this is not surprising given the severity of COPD.

With the exception of the pulmonary rehabilitation category, no other category of interventions performed noticeably better or worse than the other. The magnitude of effect was very modest with the most successful interventions, those with significant increases in PA, demonstrating an increase of approximately 10 min of walking per day. This was consistent across all categories of interventions and regardless of measurement device, accelerometer or pedometer. An increase of 1,000 steps/day is considered to be equivalent to 10 min of brisk walking or moderate PA (Tudor-Locke, Hart, & Washington, 2009; Tudor-Locke, Sisson, Collova, Lee, & Swan, 2005). We could not estimate changes in time spent in PA for two of the studies that demonstrated significant effects (Pomidori et al., 2012; Walker et al., 2008). It is further noted that in two of these studies, the control group decreased their PA (Hospes et al., 2009; Nguyen et al., 2009). This is not surprising because people with COPD typically experience a gradual decline in functioning. In fact, for some people with COPD, the benefit of an intervention may be to prevent or slow the rate of decline without actually producing an increase in performance.

One of the combined behavioral and exercise interventions outperformed the others. Speed walking with a metronome demonstrated better results than the other interventions, with a mean increase of 35 min a day of walking at a rate equal to >3 METs (Pomidori et al., 2012). This was a powerful intervention and it enabled people to meet recommended levels of PA. Two other factors may account for the success of this intervention. It was a long intervention, lasting 1 year, and after the completion of 4 weeks of supervised training, subjects received phone calls twice a month for the rest of the year. It appears that the phone calls were helpful in sustaining subjects' commitment to the program.

Total steps per day and total activity counts are indicators of the volume of walking and does not address the issues of PA intensity. Three studies examined the intensity of PA and all three demonstrated improvements (Breyer et al., 2010; Pitta et al., 2008; Walker et al., 2008). This moved people in the right direction, but it is not clear that improvements were clinically meaningful.

Pulmonary rehabilitation studies had the lowest success rate with respect to increasing PA and we do not have an obvious explanation for this. It could be the lack of a behavioral strategy to change PA behavior. Alternatively, it could be related to heterogeneity among pulmonary rehabilitation programs and/or inconsistency in the implementation of exercise training, possibly related to the intensity of training. Of the studies in this review, most were described as multidisciplinary programs that included exercise and educational classes. Many reported that their pulmonary rehabilitation program met standard guidelines, but it is difficult to assess the variability among programs without a detailed description. The intensity of the exercise training could vary among programs, but this seems unlikely because most programs reported increases in measures of functional capacity and this suggests that the intensity of training was sufficient. It is probably unrealistic to think that an intervention such as pulmonary rehabilitation might make a meaningful change in PA behavior on an ongoing basis. Pulmonary rehabilitation includes education but does not include structured behavioral interventions to change PA behavior. Pulmonary rehabilitation does increase exercise capacity, but an increase in exercise capacity will not necessarily change long standing sedentary habits.

The rigor of PA monitoring was similar across studies. In studies that did not demonstrate an increase in PA, five used accelerometers and two used pedometers to measure PA. In those that demonstrated an increase in PA, five used accelerometers and three used pedometers to measure PA. Accelerometers and pedometers were of similar quality. However, it can be difficult to compare the output of different monitors. Two of the studies monitored PA with accelerometers mounted at the ankle (Nguyen et al., 2009; Walker et al., 2008) and activity counts taken from the ankle are not necessarily comparable to those acquired with waist-mounted accelerometers. Ankle monitors are more sensitive to slow walking than waist-mounted monitors, thereby increasing the likelihood of observing a higher step count in sedentary people with COPD, many of whom have slow walking speeds (Karabulut, Crouter, & Bassett, 2005).

The overall quality of this body of research is fair to good. The large number of quasi-experimental studies with no control group is problematic and could bias the results. In general, for studies of an active intervention and a research design with no control group, one is concerned about the potential for a positive bias in favor of the intervention. For people with COPD, it is also possible that studies without a control group could be negatively biased against the intervention. This is because people with COPD experience a gradual decline in PA over time and a control group is needed to account for this effect. Two controlled studies in this review demonstrated a decrease in PA for the control group (Hospes et al., 2009; Nguyen et al., 2009). It was noted that the quality of pulmonary rehabilitation studies was lower than studies that examined other interventions, mostly because of the quasi-experimental research designs. This is influenced by ethical concerns and it is not likely to change in the future. Because pulmonary rehabilitation with physical exercise is known to be effective in improving exercise capacity (Troosters et al., 2005), many consider it to be unethical to use a control group that would include withholding pulmonary rehabilitation for purposes of research. This is a limitation of the existing research.

There are several limitations and strengths of this body of research. There are a limited number of randomized trials and this can bias results. Many of the studies had very small samples, making it difficult to identify significant effects when they exist. Studies were conducted in seven countries and this strengthens the external validity of the work, but at the same time there are cultural differences with respect to attitudes about PA and this could bias results in selected studies. The results of individual studies must be interpreted with this in mind. Also, the fact that five of the seven studies from the United States were from Veterans Health Administration, facilities limit the generalizability of results from those studies. It is difficult to compare the results across studies because of the differences in equipment and the units of measure. And finally, this body of research includes a limited number of behavioral interventions. One of the major strengths of this body of research is the use of reliable and valid objective measures of PA, thereby avoiding the measurement error associated with self-reported measures of PA. In addition, measures were taken over at least 3 days of monitoring, thereby providing stable results.

In this body of research, there was one fairly powerful intervention and several interventions that produced promising but suboptimal results. This suggests that the field is making progress, but additional research is needed to further improve outcomes. In addition, a variety of effective interventions are needed because it is not likely that one intervention will be appropriate for all people with COPD. Making long term changes in PA patterns is difficult for habitually sedentary people, perhaps as difficult as it is for obese people to make long term changes in eating patterns. Similarly, it may require repeated exposures over time to multiple interventions that employ different strategies, much like the different weight-loss approaches. With repeated experiences, the individual will gradually build the skill, knowledge, and attitude required to make a sustainable change in PA patterns. Taking this perspective, one will evaluate an intervention in terms of the extent of forward progress that was achieved in PA, not expecting that any one intervention will accomplish the goal of meeting PA guidelines. This is a pragmatic and reasonable approach given the state of the science.

CONCLUSION

Most but not all of the COPD subjects reflected in this review were sedentary. To date, a relatively small number and limited variety of interventions have been tested. The interventions that were examined are promising, but results are suboptimal and little is known about long term effects. To advance the science, a greater number of controlled studies are needed—testing a wider variety of interventions. At this point, three categories of interventions appear to hold the most promise: (a) exercise, (b) behavioral, and (c) the combination of behavioral and exercise interventions.

REFERENCES

Borges, R., & Carvalho, C. (2012). Physical activity in daily life in Brazilian COPD patients during and after exacerbation. *COPD, 9*(6), 596–602.

Breyer, M., Breyer-Kohansal, R., Funk, G., Dornhofer, N., Spruit, M., Wouters, E., . . . Hartl, S. (2010). Nordic walking improves daily physical activities in COPD: A randomised controlled trial. *Respiratory Research, 11*, 112.

Center for Disease Control and Prevention. (2009). Prevalence and most common causes of disability among adults—United States, 2005. *MMWR. Morbidity and Mortality Weekly Report, 58*, 421–426.

Dallas, M., McCusker, C., Haggerty, M., Rochester, C., & ZuWallack, R. (2009). Using pedometers to monitor walking activity in outcome assessment for pulmonary rehabilitation. *Chronic Respiratory Disease, 6*(4), 217–224.

de Blok, B., de Greef, M., ten Hacken, N., Sprenger, S., Postema, K., & Wempe, J. (2006). The effects of a lifestyle physical activity counseling program with feedback of a pedometer during pulmonary rehabilitation in patients with COPD: A pilot study. *Patient Education and Counseling, 61*(1), 48–55.

Deshpande, A., Khoja, S., Lorca, J., Mckibbon, A., Rizo, C., Husereau, D., & Jadad, A. (2009). Asynchronous telehealth: A scoping review of analytic studies. *Open Medicine, 3*(2), e69–e91.

Downs, S., & Black, N. (1998). The feasibility of creating a checklist for the assessment of the methodological quality both of randomised and non-randomised studies of health care interventions. *Journal of Epidemiology & Community Health, 52*(6), 377–384.

Effing, T., Zielhuis, G., Kerstjens, H., van der Valk, P., & van der Palen, J. (2011). Community based physiotherapeutic exercise in COPD self-management: A randomised controlled trial. *Respiratory Medicine, 105*(3), 418–426.

Egan, C., Deering, B., Blake, C., Fullen, B., McCormack, N., Spruit, M., & Costello, R. (2012). Short term and long term effects of pulmonary rehabilitation on physical activity in COPD. *Respiratory Medicine, 106*(12), 1671–1679.

Garcia-Aymerich, J., Farrero, E., Félez, M., Izquierdo, J., Marrades, R., & Antó, J. (2003). Risk factors of readmission to hospital for COPD exacerbation: A prospective study. *Thorax, 58*(2), 100–105.

Garcia-Aymerich, J., Lange, P., Benet, M., Schnohr, P., & Anto, J. (2007). Regular physical activity modifies smoking-related lung function decline and reduces risk of chronic obstructive pulmonar disease: A population-based cohort study. *American Journal of Respiratory and Critical Care Medicine, 175*(5), 458–463.

Hirayama, F., Lee, A., Binns, C., Leong, C., & Hiramatsu, T. (2008). Physical activity of patients with chronic obstructive pulmonary disease. *Journal of Cardiopulmonary Rehabilitation, 28*(5), 330–334.

Hospes, G., Bossenbroek, L., Ten Hacken, N., van Hengel, P., & de Greef, M. (2009). Enhancement of daily physical activity increases physical fitness of outclinic COPD patients: Results of an exercise counseling program. *Patient Education and Counseling, 75*(2), 274–278.

Karabulut, M., Crouter, S., & Bassett, D. (2005). Comparison of two waist-mounted and two ankle-mounted electronic pedometers. *European Journal Applied Physiology, 95*(4), 335–343.

Kessler, R., Partridge, M., Miravitlles, M., Cazzola, M., Vogelmeier, C., Leynaud, D., & Ostinelli, J. (2011). Symptom variability in patients with severe COPD: A Pan-European cross-sectional study. *European Respiratory Journal, 37*(2), 264–272.

Kessler, R., Stahl, E., Vogelmeier, C., Haughney, J., Trudeau, E., Lofdahl, C.-G., & Partridge, M. (2006). Patient understanding, detection, and experience of COPD exacerbations: An observational, interview-based study. *Chest*, *130*(1), 133–142.

Lacasse, Y., Goldstein, R., Lasserson, T., & Martin, S. (2006). Pulmonary rehabilitation for chronic obstructive pulmonary disease. *Cochrane Database of Systematic Reviews*.

Mador, M., Patel, A., & Nadler, J. (2011). Effects of pulmonary rehabilitation on activity levels in patients with chronic obstructive pulmonary disease. *Journal of Cardiopulmonary Rehabilitation and Prevention*, *31*(1), 52–59.

Moy, M., Weston, N., Wilson, E., Hess, M., & Richardson, C. (2012). A pilot study of an Internet walking program and pedometer in COPD. *Respiratory Medicine*, *106*(9), 1342–1350.

Ng, L., Mackney, J., Jenkins, S., & Hill, K. (2012). Does exercise training change physical activity in people with COPD? A systematic review and meta-analysis. *Chronic Respiratory Disease*.

Nguyen, H., Gill, D., Wolpin, S., Steele, B., & Benditt, J. (2009). Pilot study of a cell phone-based exercise persistence intervention post-rehabilitation for COPD. *International Journal of Chronic Obstructive Pulmonary Disease*, *4*, 301–313.

Physical Activity Guidelines Advisory Committee. (2008). *Physical Activity Guidelines Advisory Committee Report, 2008*. Washington, DC: U.S. Department of Health and Human Services.

Pitta, F., Troosters, T., Probst, V. S., Langer, D., Decramer, M., & Gosselink, R. (2008). Are patients with COPD more active after pulmonary rehabilitation? *Chest*, *134*(2), 273–280.

Pitta, F., Troosters, T., Probst, V. S., Spruit, M., Decramer, M., & Gosselink, R. (2006). Physical activity and hospitalization for exacerbation of COPD. *Chest*, *129*(3), 536–544.

Pitta, F., Troosters, T., Spruit, M., Probst, V., Decramer, M., & Gosselink, R. (2005). Characteristics of physical activities in daily life in chronic obstructive pulmonary disease. *American Journal of Respiratory and Critical Care Medicine*, *171*(9), 972–977.

Pomidori, L., Contoli, M., Mandolesi, G., & Cogo, A. (2012). A simple method for home exercise training in patients with chronic obstructive pulmonary disease: One-year study. *Journal of Cardiopulmonary Rehabilitation and Prevention*, *32*(1), 53–57.

Rowe, D., Kemble, C., Robinson, T., & Mahar, M. (2007). Daily walking in older adults: Day-to-day variability and criterion-referenced validity of total daily step counts. *Journal of Physical Activity Health*, *4*(4), 434–446.

Samoocha, D., Bruinvels, D., Elbers, N., Anema, J., & van der Beek, A. (2010). Effectiveness of web-based interventions on patient empowerment: A systematic review and meta-analysis. *Journal of Medical Internet Research*, *12*(2), e23.

Sandland, C., Singh, S., Curcio, A., Jones, P., & Morgan, M. (2005). A profile of daily activity in chronic obstructive pulmonary disease. *Journal of Cardiopulmonary Rehabilitation*, *25*(3), 181–183.

Schonhofer, B., Ardes, P., Geibel, M., Kohler, D., & Jones, P. (1997). Evaluation of a movement detector to measure daily activity in patients with chronic lung disease. *European Respiratory Journal*, *10*(12), 2814–2819.

Sewell, L., Singh, S., Williams, J., Collier, R., & Morgan, M. (2005). Can individualized rehabilitation improve functional independence in elderly patients with COPD? *Chest*, *128*(3), 1194–1200.

Singh, S., & Morgan, M. (2001). Activity monitors can detect brisk walking in patients with chronic obstructive pulmonary disease. *Journal of Cardiopulmonary Rehabilitation*, *21*(3), 143–148.

Steele, B., Belza, B., Cain, K., Coppersmith, J., Lakshminarayan, S., Howard, J., & Haselkorn, J. (2008). A randomized clinical trial of an activity and exercise adherence intervention in chronic pulmonary disease. *Archives of Physical Medicine and Rehabilitation*, *89*(3), 404–412.

Steele, B., Belza, B., Cain, K., Coppersmith, J., Lakshminaryan, S., Howard, J., & Haselkorn, J. (2010). The impact of chronic obstructive pulmonary disease exacerbation on pulmonary rehabilitation participation and functional outcomes. *Journal of Cardiopulmonary Rehabilitation and Prevention*, *30*(1), 53–60.

Steele, B., Belza, B., Hunziker, J., Holt, L., Legro, M., Coppersmith, J., . . . Lakshminaryan, S. (2003). Monitoring daily activity during pulmonary rehabilitation using triaxial accelerometer. *Journal of Cardiopulmonary Rehabilitation, 23*(2), 139–142.

Troosters, T., Casaburi, R., Gosselink, R., & Decramer, M. (2005). Pulmonary rehabilitation in chronic obstructive pulmonary disease. *American Journal of Respiratory and Critical Care Medicine, 172*(1), 19–38.

Tucker, J., Welk, G., & Beyler, N. (2011). Physical activity in U.S. adults compliance with the physical activity guidelines for Americans. *American Journal of Preventive Medicine, 40*(4), 454–461.

Tudor-Locke, C., Craig, C., Aoyagi, Y., Bell, R., Croteau, K., De Bourdeaudhui, I., . . . Blair, S. (2011). How many steps/day are enough? For older adults and special populations. *International Journal of Behavioral Nutrition and Physical Activity, 8,* 80.

Tudor-Locke, C., Hart, T., & Washington, T. (2009). Expected values for pedometer-determined physical activity in older populations. *International Journal of Behavioral Nutrition and Physical Activity, 6,* 59.

Tudor-Locke, C., Sisson, S., Collova, T., Lee, S., & Swan, P. (2005). Pedometer-determined step count guidelines for classifying walking intensity in a young ostensibly healthy population. *Canadian Journal Applied Physiology, 30*(6), 666–676.

Tudor-Locke, C., Washington, T., & Hart, T. (2009). Expected values for steps/day in special populations. *Preventive Medicine, 49*(1), 3–11.

Walker, P., Birmett, A., Flavahan, P., & Calverley, P. (2008). Lower limb activity and its determinants in COPD. *Thorax, 63,* 683–689.

Waschki, B., Spruit, M., Watz, H., Albert, P., Shrikrishna, D., Groenen, M., . . . Wouters, E. (2012). Physical activity monitoring in COPD: Compliance and associations with clinical characteristics in multicenter study. *Respiratory Medicine, 106*(4), 522–530.

CHAPTER 11

Exercise and Cancer

M. Tish Knobf and Kerri Winters-Stone

ABSTRACT

There are an estimated 13.7 million cancer survivors in the United States. Persistent and late effects of cancer therapy have contributed to an increased risk for co-morbid illness and higher all-cause mortality. Physical exercise is a targeted rehabilitative intervention following cancer therapy and a health promotion risk reduction intervention for patients as they transition into survivorship. This chapter provides a brief overview of the research on exercise and cancer survivor outcomes with a specific focus on randomized controlled trials (RCT) on the effects of exercise on body composition and bone health. There were 17 RCT trials that were identified with body composition outcomes. There was no change in weight in 16/17 trials, 4 reported decreases in percent fat mass and 2 reported increases in lean mass. Eight exercise trials were identified with bone outcomes, two of which had pharmacologic comparison arms. These trials demonstrated preservation of bone in the intervention group compared with loss in the usual care or placebo control group. The majority of trials were with breast cancer survivors, the largest survivor group. Many are overweight or obese at diagnosis; weight gain continues to increase after therapy; and treatment is associated with bone loss. The findings of the 25 trials reviewed suggest that exercise maintains weight and bone mass in a high risk population. However, differences in design, measurement of body composition and bone mass and lack of targeted exercise to the specific outcomes warrants additional research to improve the quality of life for survivors.

© 2013 Springer Publishing Company
http://dx.doi.org/10.1891/0739-6686.31.327

The population of 13.7 million cancer survivors today is expected to grow to more than 18.0 million by 2020 (deMoor et al., 2013; Mariotto, Yabroff, Shao, Feuer, & Brown, 2011). Unfortunately, persistent and late effects of cancer treatment influence the quality of life for those survivors and contribute to morbidity and mortality (Institute of Medicine [IOM], 2006). There is a recognized need for a comprehensive rehabilitation model of survivorship care that includes symptom management, prevention and management of long-term and late effects, and health promotion (Alfano, Ganz, Rowland, & Hahn, 2012). Physical exercise is a targeted rehabilitative intervention in the posttreatment phase and a health promotion, risk reduction intervention for patients as they transition into survivorship (Courneya & Friedenreich, 2007). With advances in cancer treatment and prolonged survival, all-cause mortality has increased over cancer-specific mortality in some survivor populations such as breast cancer (Chapman et al., 2008; Patnaik, Byers, DiGuiseppi, Denberg, & Dabelea, 2011). Overweight, obesity (especially central adiposity), sedentary behaviors, bone loss in perimenopausal and postmenopausal women, hypertension, and impaired glucose tolerance significantly increase the risks for cardiovascular disease, diabetes, and osteoporosis. Exercise can reduce or modify preexisting as well as treatment-related comorbid risk factors that may lead to increased morbidity and mortality (Alfano et al., 2012; Knobf & Coviello, 2011; Ligibel, 2012).

The purpose of this chapter is to provide a brief overview of the research on exercise and cancer survivor outcomes with a specific focus on randomized controlled trials (RCTs) on the effects of exercise to optimize body composition and bone health.

EXERCISE AND CANCER SURVIVOR OUTCOMES

Ten meta-analyses (Brown et al., 2011; Conn, Hafdahl, Porock, McDaniel, & Nielsen, 2006; Cramp & Daniel, 2008; Fong et al., 2012; Kim, Kang, & Park, 2009; Markes, Brockow, & Resch, 2006; McNeeley et al., 2006; Stevinson, Lawlor, & Fox, 2004; Schmitz, Holtzman, et al., 2005; Speck, Courneya, Mâsse, Duval, & Schmitz, 2010) and systematic reviews (Bicego et al., 2008; De Backer, Schep, Backx, Vreugdenhil, & Kuipers, 2009; Knobf, Musanti, & Dorward, 2007; Schmitz et al., 2010; Sheehan, Hoskins, & Stolley, 2012) have been published on the effects of exercise on cancer survivor outcomes during or after cancer treatment. Physical activity interventions improve fatigue, quality of life, physical functioning, level of aerobic and cardiovascular fitness, endurance, depression, and some have resulted in weight maintenance, improved body composition, bone mass stabilization, and symptom improvement. Most trials have been conducted with breast cancer survivors (BCS), who constitute 22% of all cancer survivors. There is a growing number of trials, however, that have included patients with colorectal, endometrial, prostate, or mixed cancer diagnoses (Fong et al., 2012). In addition to short-term outcomes, observational studies suggest a benefit of physical activity to both disease-free and overall survival in breast, colorectal, and prostate cancer survivors (Bertram et al., 2011; Hamer, Stamatakis, & Saxton, 2009; Holick et al., 2008; Holmes, Chen, Feskanich, Kroenke, & Colditz, 2005; Irwin et al., 2008; Meyerhardt et al., 2006).

Body Composition and Exercise in Prostate and Breast Cancer Survivors

Exercise intervention studies that included body composition outcomes other than body mass index (BMI) as a single measure included only prostate and BCS (Schmitz et al., 2010). Exercise trials included in this review were "posttreatment"—meaning survivors had completed primary and/or nonhormonal adjuvant therapy. Although the term survivor is broadly accepted as anyone following a cancer diagnosis, targeting health promotion interventions for survivors in the transition phase from therapy is consistent with the IOM's report and recommendations for survivorship care (IOM, 2006).

Prostate Cancer Survivors

Survivors of prostate cancer represent 20% of all survivors—the second largest survivor group following breast cancer (deMoor et al., 2013). Patients with localized prostate cancer at higher risk for recurrence may have hormonal therapy (androgen deprivation therapy [ADT]) recommended as adjuvant therapy. ADT is associated with fatigue, changes in muscle strength, sexuality issues, depression, and body composition changes. Exercise intervention studies found in the literature with PCS following primary therapy (e.g., surgery or radiation therapy) were solely targeted to those survivors receiving ADT. Of the four studies identified (Table 11.1), only one (Galvao, Taafe, Spry, Joseph, & Newton, 2010) restricted eligibility to survivors with localized nonmetastatic disease and the other three had mixed-staged patients (Culos-Reed et al., 2010; Segal et al., 2003; Taylor et al., 2006). The interventions ranged from 3 to 6 months and there were no significant differences in body composition with the exception of improved waist circumference in the intervention group in one trial, which compared a 16-week aerobic and "light resistance" (i.e., bands) exercise program to a wait list control group (Culos-Reed et al., 2010). Only one trial (Galvao et al., 2010) assessed body composition using whole body dual energy x-ray absorptiometry (DXA). In summary, it is difficult to draw conclusions from these studies because of limitations in measurement, mixed-staged samples, lack of data

TABLE 11.1

RCT Exercise Trials in Prostate Cancer Survivors Receiving ADT: Body Composition Outcomes

Author	Design	Sample	Measure	Weight	% Fat Mass	LMM	Adherence
Segal et al (2003)	RCT 12 week supervised resistance exercise 3x/wk vs. wait list control	N = 155 ADT 95/155 curative intent therapy	Weight/BMI WC Skinfold measurement	No difference between groups for weight or WC	No difference	NR	79%
Taylor et al (2006)	RCT 6 month (20 sessions) lifestyle vs. education vs. standard care	N = 134 ADT	Weight/BMI WC HC	No significant differences	No significant differences	NR	70% lifestyle and 82% education subjects attended at least 50% sessions
Galvao et al (2010)	RCT 12 week aerobic resistance exercise 2x/week vs. usual care	N = 57 ADT	Weight/BMI DXA	No significant difference	No significant difference	No change (whole body)	NR
Culos-Reed et al (2010)	RCT 16 week exercise (weekly group sessions + home) vs. wait list control	N = 100 ADT	Weight/BMI WC HC	Weight-NR	Decrease WC intervention group ($p = 0.04$)	NR	NR

ADT = androgen deprivation therapy.
WC = waist circumference.
HC = hip circumference.
BMI = body mass index.
DXA = dual energy x-ray absorptiometry.

on adherence, varied dose, intensity and frequency of the exercise interventions, and unclear linkage between the design of the exercise intervention, recognizing that body composition was not the primary outcome in most of the studies.

Breast Cancer Survivors

BCS outcomes are influenced by preexisting risk factors or comorbid health conditions and effects of cancer therapy. In midlife women not diagnosed with cancer, decreases in lean tissue mass, decreases in resting metabolic rate, increases in fat mass (especially increases in abdominal fat mass), increases in fasting insulin levels, and the diagnosis of metabolic syndrome have been reported during the menopausal transition (Coviello, Knobf, & Laclergue, 2013; Crawford, Casey, Avis, & McKinlay, 2000; Svendson, Hassager, & Christiansen, 1995; Wang, Hassager, Ravn, Wang, & Christiansen, 1994). The hormonal changes of menopause alone cannot fully explain the pattern of weight gain and increasing central adiposity commonly observed in postmenopausal women. Advancing age, sedentary behaviors, and an overall decrease in energy expenditure are thought to contribute to weight gain in postmenopausal women.

Weight and Breast Cancer Survivors. Women newly diagnosed with breast cancer are similar to the larger female population with an increasing proportion who are overweight or obese. In addition, weight gain during and after breast cancer treatment is common (Irwin et al., 2005; Knobf, Mullen, Xistris, & Moritz, 1983; McInnes & Knobf, 2001). In the early years of adjuvant breast treatment, when the duration of chemotherapy was 1–2 years long, average weight gains of 14–17 lb were commonly observed (Knobf et al., 1983; Rock et al., 1999). More recent research suggests that gains of 5–14 lb are more common, but the problem of weight gain persists and has reported to increase over time after therapy (Makari-Judson, Judson, & Mertens, 2007; McInnes & Knobf, 2001; Saquib et al., 2006; Thivat et al., 2010). Overweight and obesity are significantly associated with increased risk for cardiovascular disease and diabetes, which contributes to a higher all-cause mortality for cancer survivors. Furthermore, there is now a growing body of evidence that excess weight after breast cancer therapy is associated with an increased risk of breast cancer recurrence and poorer survival (Chlebowski, Aiello, & McTiernan, 2002; Kroenke, Chen, Rosner, & Holmes, 2005; Protani, Coory, & Martin, 2010; Thivat et al., 2010).

Lean Mass and Adipose Tissue in Breast Cancer Survivors. Several studies have reported increases in body fat and decreases in lean muscle mass over time in women who have received adjuvant chemotherapy for breast cancer (Cheney,

Mahloch, & Freeny, 1997; Demark-Wahnefried et al., 2001; Ingram & Brown, 2004; Irwin et al., 2005). Women with estrogen receptor positive breast cancer who take adjuvant endocrine therapy, specifically the selective estrogen receptor modulator (SERM) tamoxifen, have been reported to increase the percentage of fat mass (Ali, al-Ghorabie, Evans, el-Sharkawi, & Hancock, 1998; Campbell, Lane, Martin, Gelman, & McKenzie, 2007; Ingram & Visovsky, 2007; Knobf, Insogna, DiPietro, Fennie, & Thompson, 2008; Kutynec, McCargar, Barr, & Hislop, 1999; Sheehan et al., 2012). Sheehan and colleagues (2012) recently reviewed 36 studies (15 observational and 21 intervention trials [diet, exercise or diet plus exercise]) that used imaging to quantify lean muscle mass and adipose tissue in BCS. Most studies used DXA, with only three of the observational studies using computerized tomography (CT) to measure body composition. They reported no consistent relationship between body weight and body composition changes, supporting their original hypothesis that body weight does not accurately reflect or predict changes in fat or lean body mass. Some studies supported an increase in body fat and a decrease in lean mass, but menopause appeared to confound interpretation of the findings, particularly the abrupt chemotherapy-induced menopause in younger women. There was a reported relationship, however, for increased fat mass and use of tamoxifen. The effect of interventions on body composition also produced mixed results. Yet, when the subset of studies that included only postmenopausal BCS were reviewed, the interventions were reported to effectively reduce fat mass and increase or maintain lean mass. Limitations of the studies identified included methodologic differences, variation in diet and exercise data collected in intervention trials, mix of menopausal status across studies, and lack of racial and ethnic diversity in the samples.

RCT Exercise Interventions of Posttreatment Breast Cancer Survivors. There were 17 RCT exercise trials identified that had weight, waist and/or hip circumference, and/or fat mass and lean mass as outcomes (Table 11.2; Basen-Engquist et al., 2006; Courneya, Mackey, Bell, Jones, Field, & Fairey, 2003; Daley et al., 2007; DeNysschen, Brown, Cho, & Dodd, 2011; Herrero et al., 2006; Irwin et al., 2009; Ligibel et al., 2008; Ligibel et al., 2012; Matthews et al., 2007; Mefford, Nichols, Pakiz, & Rock, 2007; Nikander, Sievänen, Ojala, Oivanen, Kellokumpu-Lehtinen, & Saarto, 2007; Pinto, Frierson, Rabin, Trunzo, & Marcus 2005; Rogers et al., 2009; Schmitz, Ahmed, Hannon, & Yee, 2005; Schmitz et al., 2009; Segal et al., 2001; Winters-Stone et al., 2011). The designs ranged from individual or group counseling to a supervised fitness center structured program or a mix of fitness center and home activity and included aerobic, resistance, or a combination of exercise. Some studies included counseling for healthy eating, but only

TABLE 11.2

RCT Exercise Trials After Non-Hormonal Treatment in Breast Cancer Survivors: Body Composition Outcomes

Author	Design	Sample	Measure	Weight	% Fat Mass	LMM	Adherence
Segal et al. (2001)	RCT usual care vs self directed exercise (5x/wk at home) vs supervised exercise (3x/wk) for total 26 wks	N = 123	Weight	Decrease in supervised exercise group but NS	NR	NR	71.5%
Courneya et al. (2003)	RCT supervised exercise vs control Cycle ergometers 3x/wk for 15 wks	N = 53	Weight Skinfold measurements	Increase control group but NS	Increase in control group; decrease exercise group but NS	NR	98.4%
Herrero et al. (2006)	RCT pilot aerobic-resistance vs control 3x/wk 8wks	N = 16	Weight Skinfold measurements	Lower exercise group but NS	↓ Exercise p = 0.05	↑ Exercise p = 0.05	91.1% (SD 6.9%)
Schmitz et al. (2005)	RCT 12 month weight training immediate vs delayed (began at 6 mos)	N = 85	Weight DXA	No change weight	→ Immediate group (p = 0.03)	↑ Immediate group (p = 0.008)	Average 80% (92% 0–6 mos, 66% 6–12 mos)
Pinto et al. (2005)	RCT 12 wk telephone exercise counseling vs control	N = 86	Weight Skinfold measurements	Weight not reported, no change BMI	No significant change	NR	Average 11.4 calls over 12 weeks

(Continued)

TABLE 11.2

RCT Exercise Trials After Non-Hormonal Treatment in Breast Cancer Survivors: Body Composition Outcomes   (Continued)

Author	Design	Sample	Measure	Weight	% Fat Mass	LMM	Adherence
Basen-Engquist et al. (2006)	RCT pilot 6 month physical activity vs standard care 1x/wk for 16 wks, every otherweek 8wks (21 sessions)	N = 60	Weight Waist and hip circumference	No change in BMI, waist or hip circumference	NR	NR	69.5%
Matthews et al. (2007)	RCT 12 week home based walking vs wait list control	N = 36	Weight DXA	No change either group	No change either group	No change either group	94%
Nikander et al. (2007)	RCT pilot aerobic circuit training 1x/wk gym 2x/ home/wk for 12 wks	N = 31	Weight	Lower exercise group but NS	NR	NR	78% gym average 2.1 x/home
Mefford et al. (2007)	RCT 16 week CBT reduced calorie + exercise (goal 1 hr/day moderate to vigorous exercise + muscle strengthening 2–3x/wk) vs wait list control	N = 85 overweight or obese	Weight Waist hip circumference DXA	Significant decrease weight, WC, HC intervention group (p = 0.05)	↓ Intervention group (p = 0.01)	No change	80% average

Daley et al. (2007)	RCT 8 wk supervised aerobic vs flexibility/stretching vs usual care	N = 108	Weight Bioimpedance	Weight not reported, no change BMI	No change	NR	70%
Ligibel et al. (2008)	RCT 16 week aerobic strength training exercise vs usual care (2–50 min supervised strength training/wk + 90 min/wk home aerobic exercise)	N = 101 overweight	Weight Waist, hip circumference Bioelectric Impedance	No change weight or WC Exercise group lower HC (p = 0.02)	No change	NR	73% strength training; average 114 min aerobic exercise/wk
Irwin et al. (2009)	RCT exercise (3x/wk gym + 2x/wk home) vs usual care for 6 months	N = 75	Weight Waist + hip circumference DXA	Exercise group lost weight but NS Decrease WC and HC but NS	↓ Exercsie group (p = 0.002)	No change (p = 0.047)	73% completion of 80% of goal (150 min/wk)
Rogers et al. (2009)	RCT 12 week exercise (group counseling and individual exercise sessions) vs usual care	N = 41	Weight Waist + hip circumference DXA	Decrease Waist to hip ratio (p = 0.04)	No change	NR	NR
Schmitz et al. (2009)	RCT 12 month 2x/wk weight training vs control	N = 141 with lymphedema	Weight DXA	Weight decreased exercise group but NS	No significant change	No significant change	96%–75%

(Continued)

TABLE 11.2

RCT Exercise Trials After Non-Hormonal Treatment in Breast Cancer Survivors: Body Composition Outcomes   (Continued)

Author	Design	Sample	Measure	Weight	% Fat Mass	LMM	Adherence
DeNysschen et al. (2011)	RCT to aerobic exercise during or after chemo vs usual care	N = 161	Weight DXA	No change	↑Usual care -NS	p = 0.05 exercise vs usual care	74%–86%
Winters-Stone et al. (2011)	RCT 12 month resistance + impact (jump) 3x/wk vs low intensity stretching	N = 106	Weight DXA	No change	No change	↑Intervention group but NS	57% exercise group, 62% stretching group
Ligibel et al. (2012)	RCT 16 wk telephone based exercise intervention vs usual care. Target: 180 min aerobic activity/wk. Cooperative group trial.	N = 121 Breast (100); colorectal (21)	Weight Waist/hip circumference	No change in weight, WC or HC	NR	NR	Average 153.6 min exercise/wk

BMI = Body Mass Index.
WC = waist circumference; HC = hip circumference.
NS = not significant.
NR = not reported.
*total muscle mass estimated using anthropometric data.

one study included a reduced calorie diet plus exercise intervention (Mefford et al., 2007). Three trials were a year in length (Schmitz, Ahmed, et al., 2005; Schmitz, Ahmed, et al., 2009; Winters-Stone, Dobek, et al., 2011) and the others ranged from 2 to 6 months in duration. Sample size was less than 100 subjects in 10 studies and a range of 101–161 subjects in the remaining 7 studies. Measures for body composition included weight only ($n = 2$), weight and waist and/or hip circumference ($n = 2$), skinfold measurements ($n = 3$), DXA ($n = 8$), and bioimpedance for percentage of fat mass ($n = 2$). Adherence ranged from 57% to 98% and varied by duration of the study— generally a lower adherence over time.

Weight was not changed across the interventions, with the exception of the study by Mefford and colleagues (2007) that combined a reduced calorie diet with exercise (a goal of 1 hr/day of moderate to vigorous activity) in a cognitive-behavioral 16-week intervention for overweight or obese BCS. Of the 14 studies that reported the percentage of fat mass outcomes (3 = DXA, 1 = skinfold measurement), there was a significant difference with resulting decreased fat mass in the intervention group in 4 studies (30.7%). Lean mass was improved in 1 study using DXA measurement (Schmitz, Ahmed, et al., 2005) and in 1 study that estimated total muscle mass from anthropometric data (Herrero et al., 2006).

In summary, the evidence from these 17 RCT exercise trials suggest that weight will not likely change with increase in physical activity levels alone and there is little, if any change, in body composition even in studies that report relatively high adherence rates. Limitations of the studies may explain the results because many interventions did not appear to be designed for weight loss or to directly impact fat or lean mass; duration, dose, intensity, and type of exercise varied; and some studies were pilots with small sample sizes.

BONE HEALTH, FRACTURES, AND INTERVENTIONS FOR CANCER SURVIVORS

In the last decade, the side effects of cancer treatment on the skeleton have become better known (Gaillard & Stearns, 2011; Saad et al., 2008; Santen, 2011) and concerns about elevated fracture risk in cancer survivors have been raised (Gralow et al., 2009; Hadji, Ziller, Albert, & Kalder, 2010). Risk factors for osteoporosis and related fractures have been identified for the general population, and these same risk factors apply to cancer survivors (Hadji et al., 2010; Twiss, Gross, Waltman, Ott, & Lindsey, 2006; Winters-Stone, Nail, Bennett, & Schwartz, 2009), but additional insults on the skeleton related to cancer treatment may increase the risk of osteoporosis and related fractures above that in cancer-free women. Chen and colleagues (2005) reported significantly lower hip bone mineral density (BMD) and a greater prevalence of osteoporosis at any skeletal site (27%) among postmenopausal BCS aged 50–79 years ($N = 209$) compared to women without a diagnosis of cancer (19%; $N = 5,759$). The Cancer and Menopause Study (CAMS) of women aged 50 years or younger at breast cancer diagnosis identified lower z scores, indicating lower than age-expected BMD at the spine among BCS who were postmenopausal at DXA evaluation and who had received chemotherapy, independent of adjuvant tamoxifen use (Crandall, Petersen, Ganz, & Greendale, 2004). Smaller studies have reported greater rates of osteopenia at the spine and hip in BCS compared to age-based norms (Twiss et al., 2001) or cancer-free controls (Winters-Stone et al., 2009), with a single conflicting report that BMD is no worse and possibly better among BCS ($N = 80$) than in matched cancer-free controls (Kalder et al., 2011). We know less about bone health in women with cancers other than the breast; however, data on fractures in women with any cancer type and the common application of some treatments across cancer types suggests that bone health is a relevant issue for all women cancer survivors.

The clinical consequence of osteoporosis and other changes in skeletal health (i.e., increased bone turnover, altered bone architecture) is a fracture, with hip fractures having the greatest impact on morbidity and mortality. In the largest report to date using data from the Women's Health Initiative (WHI) study ($N = 146,959$), Chen, Maricic, Bassford, et al. (2005) reported a significantly elevated hazards ratio of hip fracture of 1.55 (95% confidence interval [95%CI] = 1.13–2.11) in women with incident breast cancer and a nonsignificant increase in risk of vertebral fracture of 1.26 (0.94, 1.69). Hazard rates for fractures in women with cancers other than the breast were even higher, with a significantly elevated hazards ratio for both hip fracture of 2.09 (95% CI = 1.65–2.65) and vertebral fracture of 1.86 (95% CI = 1.49–2.32). Annualized rates of fractures were similar between cancer survivors prior to cancer diagnosis and controls, suggesting that the increase in fracture risk among women with cancer was disease and/or treatment related.

Chemotherapy Effects on Bone

In both women and men, estrogen deprivation has a major impact on bone health, chemotherapy alone can contribute to bone loss even in postmenopausal women (Garnero, 2008; Hadji et al., 2011; Parfitt et al., 1983). Women who are postmenopausal at the time of cancer diagnosis still experience bone loss across the course of chemotherapy (Greep et al., 2003; Rodríguez-Rodríguez et al., 2005) as do cancer patients who never lose ovarian function during chemotherapy treatment (Cameron, Douglas, Brown, & Anderson, 2010).

TABLE 11.3

Summary of Randomized Controlled Trials to Evaluate Efficacy of Exercise to Improve Bone Health of Women Cancer Survivors

Authors, Year	Study Design[a]	Population	Measure	Outcomes (% change)	Retention and Adherence
Irwin (2009)	2-arm RCT: AET vs UC Center + home-based; semi-supervised aerobic free-choice (mostly walking); 5x/wk; 50%–80% age-predicted HRmax; 15–30 minutes; 12 months	Breast >6 months post radiation or chemotherapy Postmenopausal Age: 56 yrs N = 75	BMD by DEXA	*Total body BMD* AET: 0.2%* UC: −1.7%	*Retention:* 92% *Adherence* (self-report exercise): AET: 129 min/wk UC: 45 min/wk
Nikander (2012; substudy from Saarto et al., 2012)	2-arm RCT: AET + impact *vs* UC Center + home-based; semi-supervised aerobic dance or circuit training + impact loading; 4x/ week (1 at center; 3 at home); 11–16 RPE for aerobic / circuit and 4–5x body weight for impact; 30–40 min per session; 12 months	Breast 4+ months post chemotherapy or radiation therapy completion or within 4 months of starting adjuvant endocrine therapy Pre or postmenopausal Age: 53 yrs N = 86	Bone architecture by pQCT (only variables that had significant group × time interactions are presented)	*Femoral neck centroid:* AET + impact: 0.5% UC: 1.8%	*Retention:* 78% *Adherence:* 76% (center)

(Continued)

TABLE 11.3

Summary of Randomized Controlled Trials to Evaluate Efficacy of Exercise to Improve Bone Health of Women Cancer Survivors   (Continued)

Authors, Year	Study Design[a]	Population	Measure	Outcomes (% change)	Retention and Adherence

Saarto (2012)	See Nikander 2012	See Nikander 2012 for eligibility criteria
		Age: 46 yrs (premenopausal); 58 yrs (postmenopausal)
		N = 498
			BMD by DEXA (results only reported separately for pre and postmenopausal women)	*Premenopausal women*
				L_1-L_4 spine BMD
				  AET + Impact: −1.9%
				  UC: −2.2%
				*Femoral neck BMD**
				  AET + impact: −0.2%
				  UC: −1.4%
				Postmenopausal women
				L_1-L_4 spine BMD
				  AET + Impact: −1.6%
				  UC: −2.1%
				Femoral neck BMD
				  AET+impact: −1.1%
				  UC: −1.1%
					Retention: 87%
					Adherence
					(range provided for premenopausal and postmenopausal women):
					58%–63% (class)

Schwartz (2007)	3-arm RCT: AET vs RET vs UC
	Home-based, unsupervised; 4x/wk; moderate intensity; 20–30 min (AET) or 2 sets of 8–10 reps (RET); 6 months
		Breast, lymphoma, colon (all female)
		Pre-postmenopausal
		During chemotherapy
		Age: 48 yrs
		N = 66
			BMD by DEXA	L_2-L_4 Spine BMD:
				  RET: −4.9%*
				  AET: −0.8%*
				  UC: −6.2%
					Retention: 93%
					Adherence: NR

| Swenson (2009) | 2-arm RCT: AET + placebo vs. Bisphosphonate (4 mg zolendronic acid every 3 mos) Home-based, unsupervised walking; 7 d/wk (no intensity reported); 10,000 steps/d;12 months | Breast Stage I-III During chemotherapy Pre, peri- or newly menopausal Age: 46.7 yrs N = 72 | BMD by DEXA | *Total hip BMD* AET: −3.4%* BIS: 0.8% *Femoral neck BMD* AET: −6.0%* BIS −0.2% *L₁-L₄ spine BMD* AET: −6.1%* BIS: 1.6% *Total body BMD* AET: −3.3%* BIS: 0.8% *Remodeling markers* AlkB: AET: 17.8%* BIS: −43.9% NTx AET: 63.0%* BIS: −10.9% | *Retention: 81%* *Adherence (steps/day and % meeting goal):* AET: 9,262 steps/d, 96% |

(Continued)

TABLE 11.3

Summary of Randomized Controlled Trials to Evaluate Efficacy of Exercise to Improve Bone Health of Women Cancer Survivors   (Continued)

Authors, Year	Study Design[a]	Population	Measure	Outcomes (% change)	Retention and Adherence
Waltman (2009)	2-arm RCT: RET + bisphosphonate vs bisphosphonate only Center + home, unsupervised; RET (machine-based); 2x/week; Intensity: not reported; 2–3 sets of 8–12 repetitions; 32 wks @ home + 32 wks @ center	Breast Stage 0-II > 6 mos. post-chemotherapy &/or radiation therapy All participants received daily 5–10 mg alendronate + 1500 mg Ca^{++} + 400 IU Vit D Postmenopausal Age: 59yrs N = 249	BMD by DEXA Bone turnover: Alkaline phosphatase B; N-terminal telopeptide	*Total hip BMD* RET + BIS: 2.2% BIS: 1.8% *Femoral neck BMD* RET + BIS: 0.9% BIS 0.6% *L$_1$-L$_4$ spine BMD* RET + BIS: 3.1% BIS: 1.9% *Forearm BMD* RET + BIS: 0.2% BIS: 0.2% *Remodeling markers* AlkB RET + BIS: −11% BIS: −9% NTx RET + BIS: −23% BIS: −17%	*Retention:* 90% *Adherence (class attendance):* 69.4%

| Winters-Stone (2011) | 2-arm RCT (RET + impact vs. UC). Center + home-based; supervised (center) + unsupervised (home); 3x/week (2x at center; 1x at home); 10%–15% of body weight added for resistance + impact; 40–45 min per session; 12 months | Breast 12+ months post chemotherapy or radiation therapy completion; Postmenopausal Age: 62 yrs $N = 106$ | *Total hip BMD* RET + impact: −0.4% FLEX: −0.8% Femoral neck BMD RET + impact: −1.4% Flex: −2.1% *Greater trochanter BMD* RET + impact: −0.5% Flex: −0.2% L_1-L_4 *spine BMD** RET + Impact: 0.4% Flex: −2.3% *Remodeling markers* Osteocalcin* RET + Impact: 1.6% Flex: 26.5% Dpd RET + Impact: −38.8% Flex: −28.7% | *Retention:* 63% *Adherence (class attendance):* 69.4% |

(Continued)

TABLE 11.3

Summary of Randomized Controlled Trials to Evaluate Efficacy of Exercise to Improve Bone Health of Women Cancer Survivors   *(Continued)*

Authors, Year	Study Design[a]	Population	Measure	Outcomes (% change)	Retention and Adherence
Winters-Stone (2012)	2-arm RCT (RET + impact vs. UC). Center + home-based; supervised (center) + unsupervised (home); 3x/week (2x at center; 1x at home); 10%–15% of body weight added for resistance + impact; 40–45 min per session; 12 months	Breast 6–60 months post onset of chemotherapy-associated menopause; Postmenopausal Age: 47 yrs N = 71		*Total hip BMD* RET+impact: −1.1% FLEX: −0.6% *Femoral neck BMD* RET+impact: −0.9% Flex: −1.0% *Greater trochanter BMD* RET+impact: −1.1% Flex: −0.6% L_1-L_4 *spine BMD* RET+Impact: −1.1% Flex: −1.8% *Remodeling markers* Osteocalcin RET+Impact: −7.7% Flex: −15% Dpd RET+Impact: 21.5% Flex: 5.6%	*Retention:* 68% *Adherence (class attendance):* 68% (class) 34% (home)

[a]Study groups abbreviated as follows: aerobic exercise training (AET), resistance exercise training (RET), physical activity behavior (PA), usual care control (UC), bisphosphonate therapy (BIS).

*exercise group significantly different from controls or pharmacologic comparison group, p < .05.

Chemotherapy-induced bone loss may result from the direct effects of medication on bone cell number and function (Carlson, Simonsson, & Ljunghall, 1996; Friedlaender, Tross, Doganis, Kirkwood, & Baron, 1984; Georgiou et al., 2011) or can have indirect effects through fatigue-induced declines in physical activity (Irwin et al., 2003) and/or from steroids often administered as antiemetics (Kelley, 1998; Ratcliffe, Lanham, Reid, & Dawson, 1992). Women who are premenopausal at cancer diagnosis and who subsequently develop chemotherapy-induced ovarian failure quickly lose bone because of an abrupt onset of estrogen deprivation. Ovarian failure is more common among women who are older than 40 years when treated, but even up to 40% of younger women are affected (Bruning et al., 1990; Goodwin et al., 1999). Annual rates of bone loss in women who become menopausal during treatment average 3%–8% at the spine and 4%–5% at the hip (Delmas et al., 1997; Saarto et al., 1997; Shapiro, Manola, & Leboff, 2001; Vehmanen et al., 2001)—nearly double the rate resulting from natural menopause (Pouilles, Tremollieres, & Ribot 1995; Vehmanen et al., 2001). Administration of gonadotropin-releasing hormone (GnRH) agonists to suppress ovarian function in premenopausal cancer patients results in similar bone loss as that from chemotherapy-induced ovarian failure (Fogelman et al., 2003). Return of ovarian function following cessation of GnRH treatment can lead to some recovery of bone mineral, although recovery values usually remain significantly lower than pretreatment levels (Fogelman et al., 2003).

Adjuvant Endocrine Therapy and Bone

For BCS, treatment with adjuvant endocrine therapy can have independent or additive effects on bone health. Whether the SERM, tamoxifen, has agonist or antagonist effects on bone density depends on the estrogen environment. In postmenopausal women, tamoxifen can reduce or prevent bone loss (Kristensen et al., 1994; Love et al., 1992; Marttunen et al., 1999; Saarto et al., 2001; Sverrisdottir, Fornander, Jacobsson, von Schoultz, & Rutqvist, 2004), but it accelerates loss in premenopausal women (Vehmanen, Elomaa, Blomqvist, & Saarto, 2006). Aromatase inhibitor treatment results in total estrogen depletion that accelerates bone loss and is consistently associated with a twofold to threefold higher risk of fractures when compared to fracture rates in patients treated with tamoxifen (Arimidex, Tamoxifen, Alone or in Combination [ATAC]; Coates et al., 2007; Coleman et al., 2007; Howell et al., 2005). Annual rates of bone loss from aromatase inhibitor (AI) treatment range from 3% to 4% at the spine and 1% to 2% at the hip (Saad et al., 2008). Each of the different types of AIs (i.e., anastrozole, letrozole, or exemestane) has detrimental effects on bone compared to tamoxifen. Only head-to-head trials will ultimately determine if a particular Aromatase inhibitor has more impact on bone density or fracture than another. Whether long-term aromatase inhibitor use significantly increases fracture risk compared to a placebo remains unclear (Santen, 2011). However, a 3-year trial of exemestane versus placebo to prevent breast cancer in postmenopausal women reported no significant increase in fractures (Goss et al., 2011).

Measuring Bone Health to Assess Fracture Risk and Therapeutic Efficacy

Because bone is a dynamic tissue and its strength is determined through both material properties and three-dimensional (3D) architecture, the resistance of a bone to fracture can be evaluated by looking at one or more of these characteristics. Measurement of BMD, bone architecture, and bone turnover provide different views of skeletal health, and each varies with respect to its sensitivity, specificity, and ability to predict fractures. Understanding the different approaches to evaluating bone health is important when interpreting the efficacy of therapeutic interventions, such as exercise, to reduce fracture risk.

Bone Mineral Density

The current standard for osteoporosis evaluation is measurement of BMD (g/cm^2) via DXA (Link, 2012; Bouxsein, Courtney, & Hayes, 1995). Site-specific BMD is the best indicator of fracture risk at a particular skeletal region, and because BMD at the hip and spine can be easily measured and has clinical relevance, both sites should be assessed in response to treatment and/or therapy (Cummings et al., 1993; Eckstein et al., 2002; Marshall, Johnell, & Wedel, 1996). Because the skeleton responds to exercise in a site-specific manner, both hip and spine sites should be included in exercise studies and subregions within the hip (e.g., femoral neck, greater trochanter, total hip)—any of which can indicate a reduction in hip fracture risk—should all be reported. DXA precision error is quite low (CV <1.0%–1.5%), making it an ideal tool to evaluate for small but clinically meaningful changes in BMD. Prediction models estimate that even small changes in BMD ranging from 1% to 2% can reduce the 20-year risk of fracture by 10%–11% (Kelley, Kelley, & Kohrt, 2012). Although BMD remains the most widely used clinical tool for assessing fracture risk and indicating treatment, it is not a perfect predictor of fractures, thus additional measures of bone metabolism and/or bone architecture should be included when resources allow (Kanis, 2002).

Bone Architecture

Bone strength is a function of both bone mass (i.e., BMD) and architecture. The latter property is best assessed using 3D imaging techniques, whereas extrapolation of geometric indices of bone from DXA provides only estimates of the true bone architecture. Alterations in bone geometry indices are associated with fractures in postmenopausal women (Alonso, Curiel, Carranza, Cano, & Perez,

2000). Quantitative computed tomography (QCT) is a technique that can measure both volumetric bone density (g/cm^3) and architecture at the hip and spine using conventional body CT scanners or at peripheral sites (radius, tibia) using smaller, less expensive peripheral QCT scanners (pQCT). The ionizing radiation dose of QCT is higher than for DXA and similar to radiographs, but pQCT doses are similar to DXA (Griffith & Genant, 2008). Although BMD measured by QCT is more precise than DXA, World Health Organization osteoporosis criteria using t scores cannot be applied to QCT-derived data. Currently, QCT is not recommended for fracture prediction because of insufficient evidence that it is superior to DXA (Baim et al., 2008). However, future longitudinal studies including those to evaluate its predictive ability for fractures associated with cancer treatment are of interest. Furthermore, architectural changes may indicate other compensatory mechanisms by which the skeleton responds to mechanical loading in an effort to strengthen bone and improve the tolerance to applied forces, like those resulting from a fall.

Bone Turnover

Bone turnover, as evidenced by biomarkers of both bone formation and resorption, can predict fracture independent of BMD and may assess microarchitectural integrity of bone (Garnero, 2008). Increased osteoclastic activity associated with high levels of bone turnover may lead to perforations in trabeculae that lead to fragility (Parfitt et al., 1983). Bone turnover is significantly elevated in response to chemotherapy-induced ovarian failure (Shapiro et al., 2001) and aromatase inhibitor treatment (Coleman et al., 2007; Hadji et al., 2011), but decreased in response to tamoxifen (Hadji et al., 2011). Biomarkers can be determined from serum or urinary specimens using commercial kits now more routinely available. There are several markers of bone turnover, with the cross-linked telopeptide of type I collagen (CTX), showing the most promise as a monitoring tool (Garnero, 2008). Individuals with both low BMD and high levels of biomarker turnover (higher than premenopausal norms) are considered at higher risk of fracture than those with either condition alone (Riggs & Melton, 2002). Because early reductions in biomarkers successfully predict BMD increases in response to therapeutic agents (Ravn et al., 1999), serial measurement of biomarkers may be a low-cost and convenient means to identify responders and nonresponders to intervention strategies.

Exercise for Bone Health

The skeleton adapts to mechanical usage and forces generated from impact with the ground or against other objects by changing its material and structural properties to better tolerate applied forces (Frost, 1990b). Exercise requires muscular force and depending on the type of exercise, it can also generate impact forces making exercise an appropriate strategy for improving bone health. The bone benefits of exercise in otherwise healthy adult populations have been well studied and numerous systematic reviews and meta-analyses have been published (Beck & Snow, 2003; Frost, 1990a; Kelley, 1998; Martyn-St James & Carroll, 2008, 2009; Wallace & Cumming, 2000). The universal property of effective exercise programs is that they include a core of weight-bearing exercise at a sufficient intensity to overcome the habitual loads imposed on the skeleton from daily movements such as walking (Kohrt, Bloomfield, Little, Nelson, & Yingling, 2004). Although it extends that exercise might also be able to prevent bone loss caused by cancer treatment or restore bone health after treatment has ended, only well-designed controlled trials can determine whether exercise is equally efficacious at improving bone health in people with cancer. These cancer survivors are those who might have less tolerance for the vigorous types of exercise necessary for skeletal adaptations and whose treatment may limit the adaptive capacity of the skeleton to mechanical loading. In addition, the effects of exercise with and without currently recommended pharmacologic therapy with bisphosphonates to reduce bone loss during treatment must be examined to determine the relative benefit of the two interventions used alone and in combination.

Despite the documented effects of cancer treatment on the skeleton and the known increase in fracture risk among women cancer survivors, only a limited number of controlled exercise trials in cancer survivors have included outcomes relative to bone health. Eight controlled trials have been conducted (Irwin et al., 2009; Peppone et al., 2010; Saarto et al., 2012; Schwartz, Winters-Stone, & Galluci, 2007; Swenson et al., 2009; Waltman, Ott, Twiss, Gross, & Lindsey, 2009; Winters-Stone, Dobek, et al., 2012; Winters-Stone, Dobek, et al., 2011), with one trial reporting different bone outcomes in separate publications (Nikander et al., 2012; Saarto et al., 2012) and one trial reporting an additional moderator analysis in another publication (Winters-Stone, Leo, & Schwartz, 2012). Four of the controlled trials compared an exercise group to a usual care comparison group (Irwin et al., 2009; Peppone et al., 2010; Saarto et al., 2012; Schwartz et al., 2007), two compared the experimental exercise group to a placebo-stretching group (Winters-Stone, Dobek, et al., 2011; Winters-Stone, Dobek, et al., 2012), and two had pharmacologic comparison groups with one comparing exercise versus drug therapy (Swenson et al., 2009) with one comparing drug therapy alone to drug therapy plus exercise (Waltman et al., 2010).

Many of the trials were in early stage BCS (Irwin et al., 2009; Swenson et al., 2009; Waltman et al., 2003; Waltman et al., 2010), with one trial also including women with early stage cancers of the lymph or colon (Schwartz et al., 2007). Most trials were conducted in participants who had completed chemotherapy and/or radiation therapy or who had recently begun adjuvant endocrine therapy and two trials were conducted during chemotherapy (Schwartz et al., 2007; Swenson et al., 2009). Participant age varied widely within and across studies, with only two trials including age as an eligibility criteria, one to include only women older than the age of 50 years at cancer diagnosis to evaluate training effects in older women (Winters-Stone, Dobek, et al., 2011), and the other to exclude older women (>65 years of age) so that a more rigorous exercise program could be tested (Saarto et al., 2012). Participants had to be free of conditions that contraindicated participation in moderate-intensity exercise training and obtain physician clearance for exercise participation. Pretrial physical activity eligibility criteria varied widely across studies, with none requiring participants to be completely inactive. Trials targeted postmenopausal women (Irwin et al., 2009; Waltman et al., 2010; Winters-Stone, Dobek, et al., 2012), premenopausal or recently menopausal women (Swenson et al., 2009; Winters-Stone, Dobek, et al., 2012), or included participants of mixed menopausal status (Peppone et al., 2010; Saarto et al., 2012; Swartz et al., 2007) with two of the latter considering premenopausal and postmenopausal women together and separately (Saarto et al., 2012; Schwartz et al., 2007). Trials enrolled small ($N = 16$) to large ($N = 573$) samples, with three of the eight trials enrolling >100 participants (Saarto et al., 2012; Waltman et al., 2010; Winters-Stone, Dobek, et al., 2011). BMD was measured in all but one trial, four trials also included remodeling markers (Swenson, Henley, Shapiro, & Schroeder, 2005; Winters-Stone, Dobek, et al., 2011; Winters-Stone, Dobek, et al., 2012) and one exclusively (Peppone et al., 2010), and one trial reported on a subsample of patients who had additional pQCT measurement of bone architecture (Nikander et al., 2012). In studies reporting on BMD outcomes, five of seven measured more than one clinically relevant skeletal site (hip, spine, forearm; Saarto et al., 2012; Swenson et al., 2009; Waltman et al., 2010; Winters-Stone et al., 2011; Winters-Stone et al., 2012).

The setting of interventions varied with two home-based (Schwartz et al., 2007; Swenson et al., 2009), one center-based (Peppone et al., 2010), and the rest in mixed settings, where participants either exercised at a center plus home each week (Irwin et al., 2009; Saarto et al., 2012; Winters-Stone, Dobek, et al., 2011; Winters-Stone et al., 2012) or at home initially (9 months) before transitioning to a fitness center (Peppone et al., 2010). The level of supervision during center-based exercise sessions varied from three times (Peppone et al., 2010) to twice (Winters-Stone, Dobek, et al., 2011; Winters-Stone, Dobek, et al., 2012) or once weekly (Saarto et al., 2012) or intermittently (Irwin et al., 2009). The types of training consisted of aerobic (Irwin et al., 2009; Saarto et al., 2012;

Schwartz et al., 2007; Swenson et al., 2009), resistance (Schwartz et al., 2007; Waltman et al., 2010; Winters-Stone, Dobek, et al., 2011; Winters-Stone, Dobek, et al., 2012), or tai chi (Peppone et al., 2010), with two trials adding impact exercise, such as jumping to resistance training (Winters-Stone, Dobek, et al.,2011; Winters-Stone, Dobek, et al., 2012) and one including impact exercise as a core component of aerobic training (Saarto et al., 2012). Resistance training was performed using free weights (Winters-Stone, Dobek, et al., 2011; Winters-Stone, Dobek, et al., 2012), free weights plus resistance bands (Schwartz et al., 2007), or free weights and machines (Waltman et al., 2010). Aerobic training consisted of prescribed walking (Swenson et al., 2009), free-choice aerobic activities (Irwin et al., 2009; Schwartz et al., 2007) or aerobic dance alternating with circuit training (Saarto et al., 2012). Although the specific intensity, duration, and frequency of training varied across trials, nearly all met the recommended volume of exercise for improving bone health in adult women, with the exception of the walking-only and tai chi interventions that had loading intensities similar to habitual activity (Peppone et al., 2010; Swenson et al., 2009). Most programs were 12 months long, with two shorter (3 or 6 months; Peppone et al., 2010; Schwartz et al., 2007) and another longer (24 months; Waltman et al., 2010). Most studies had retention rates higher than 80%, although two similar trials by the same group had lower retention (Winters-Stone, Dobek, et al., 2011; Winters-Stone, Dobek, et al., 2012). Among studies reporting session attendance, adherence rates ranged from a low of 58% (Saarto et al., 2012). Only two trials documented cases when participants could not fully comply with the study protocol and the subsequent modifications made to the program (Winters-Stone et al., 2011; Winters-Stone et al., 2012).

In controlled trials of aerobic exercise versus usual care control groups, BMD was maintained at the spine (Schwartz et al., 2007), hip (premenopausal women only; Saarto et al., 2012), or total body (Irwin et al., 2009) in aerobic exercisers compared to losses in controls either during or after adjuvant treatment. The single trial of resistance only training using resistive bands failed to stop spine bone loss during chemotherapy in women with mixed cancer types (Schwartz et al., 2007). On the other hand, when resistance exercise was combined with impact loading, training prevented bone loss at the hip and spine in older women postadjuvant treatment (Winters-Stone, Dobek, et al., 2011) and prevented bone loss at the spine and built BMD at the hip in women who were 1 year past the onset of chemotherapy-induced menopause (Winters-Stone, Dobek, et al., 2012). In the two trials with a pharmacologic comparison group, neither reported a significant benefit of either aerobic or resistance exercise compared to bisphosphonate therapy during (Swenson et al., 2009) or after cancer treatment (Waltman et al., 2010). The only studies with similar exercise groups, populations, skeletal site, and intervention timing had disparate results with Schwartz et al. (2007) reporting a maintenance of BMD at the spine with aerobic exercise and Swenson et al. (2009) reporting a decline of 6% at the same skeletal site from a walking only program.

In most cases, trials that demonstrated a training effect on BMD showed that exercise maintained bone over time compared to losses in usual care or placebo control groups. Only one study reported a small but significant increase in hip BMD from resistance plus impact training among a subgroup of prematurely menopausal BCS that were at least 1 year past the onset of menopause (Winters-Stone, Dobek, et al., 2012). Regardless of the direction of the training effect, the percentage differences between changes in exercise and control groups were usually modest, ranging between 1% and 2%; and, this effect size is similar to that reported in trials in women without cancer (Kelley et al., 2012; Martyn-St James et al., 2008) suggesting that the adaptability of the skeleton to exercise after cancer is not fundamentally altered by disease or treatment. Despite the seemingly small effect of exercise on the skeleton, prediction models suggest that even these small changes could reduce the 20-year relative risk of fracture by 10%–11% (Kelley et al., 2012). This level of change from exercise is smaller than that achieved by bisphosphonate treatment. Because neither of the reviewed studies comparing exercise to bisphosphonates included a nonintervention group, whether exercise had some benefits for bone health compared to no treatment at all remains unclear. Exercise should still be considered for cancer survivors on bisphosphonates, though, because a physically active lifestyle has multiple health benefits, including fall reduction, and because the efficacy of bisphosphonates to reduce fractures in cancer survivors and long-term remains unclear (Valachis, Polyzos, Georgomicronulias, Mavroudis, & Mauri, 2010).

Exercise effects on bone remodeling markers were unremarkable, with either no effect of resistance (Waltman et al., 2010; Winters-Stone, Dobek, et al., 2011; Winters-Stone, Dobek, et al., 2012) or tai chi training (Peppone et al., 2010) on individual bone markers or increases in markers with aerobic exercise compared to decreases with bisphosphonate therapy in the adjuvant setting (Swenson et al., 2009). The single trial that assessed bone architecture among a subsample of participants ($N = 86$) reported a small but statistically significant effect of aerobic plus impact training on bone mass distribution at the femoral neck independent of menopausal status and improved indices of bone strength at the tibial shaft, although a site with limited clinical implications, in postmenopausal women only (Nikander et al., 2012). Unfortunately, the additional clinical impact of changes in bone architecture earlier that implicated from changes in BMD is minimal. Whether changes in architectural indices of bone strength that occur in the absence of BMD changes, such as that observed in postmenopausal BCS, reduces fracture risk remains unclear.

Until the evidence for an exercise prescription to prevent or treat bone loss specifically in women with cancer is sufficiently large, the American College of Sports Medicine (ACSM) exercise recommendations to preserve bone health in the general population should be applied (Kohrt et al., 2004). ACSM recommends that women engage in weight-bearing endurance (if walking, include intermittent jogging), impact and/or resistance exercise, or a combination thereof that produces moderate to high bone loading forces for 3–5 days/week for endurance exercise and 2–3 days/week for resistance and/or impact exercise with the duration of sessions lasting 30–60 min each. Across the reviewed trials, those programs that stuck more closely to the ACSM recommendations had better outcomes. Particularly effective exercise programs *specifically* loaded the clinically relevant hip and spine. Resistance training programs included both upper and lower body movements, whereas aerobic interventions incorporated upper, trunk, and lower body motions (i.e., dance or mixed modes) into exercise. Effective programs applied a level of *overload* to the skeleton that was either sufficiently different from, or greater in intensity than normal daily loading (i.e., walking; Carter, 1984). Only programs that included impact exercise, either by incorporating it into dance programs or assigning intervals of jumping exercise, improved bone outcomes at the hip, thus impact loading may be a critically important feature of training programs to stop cancer-treatment-related bone loss. The duration and frequency of exercise sessions and length of the training program were consistent with ACSM recommendations for bone health, with the exception of a single 3-month tai chi trial that did not measure BMD (Kohrt et al., 2004).

5. Nonskeletal Approaches to Fracture Prevention

Although bone is a logical target for interventions aimed to reduce fracture risk in cancer survivors, preventing falls must also be considered as a target because falls play an important role in fracture etiology (Frost, 2001). All wrist fractures, 90% of hip fractures, and 50% of vertebral fractures are associated with a fall (Frost, 2011). There is increasing evidence that women fall more frequently after cancer treatment than before and compared to women who have never had cancer (Chen, Maricic, Bassford, et al., 2005; Winters-Stone et al., 2009). Cancer treatment could increase fall risk through adverse effects on muscle mass and function (Cheney et al., 1997; Demark-Wahnefried et al., 2001; Freedman et al., 2004; Harvie, Campbell, Baildam, & Howell, 2004; Kutynec et al., 1999), balance (Wampler et al., 2007), neuropathies (Kuroi & Shimozuma, 2004), vision (Eisner & Incognito, 2006; Eisner, Toomey, Falardeau, Samples, & Vetto, 2007), and physical function—which have each been independently linked to falls in cancer (Winters-Stone, Torgrimson, et al., 2011) and noncancer populations (Dargent-Molina et al., 1996; Drinkwater, Grimston, Raab-Cullen, & Snow-Harter, 1995; Lord, Rogers, Howland, & Fitzpatrick, 1999; Mold, Veseley, Keyl, Schenk, & Roberts, 2004). Specific exercise programs have been shown effective at reducing falls in older adults (Sherrington et al., 2008). Studies are needed to further examine falls in cancer populations with a goal to develop specific fall prevention strategies to reduce fracture risk, with a large controlled trial currently underway. Until findings from such trials are underway, fall risk should be considered in care plans for cancer survivors and existing guidelines for preventing falls in older adults could be applied.

FUTURE DIRECTIONS RESEARCH

Obesity and increased central adiposity are known risk factors for chronic illness. In addition, there is growing evidence linking insulin and obesity to adverse breast cancer outcomes (Decensi, 2011). Insulin resistance has been associated with decreased breast cancer survival (Duggan et al., 2010) and data suggest there may be some level of independent influence of overweight/obesity and insulin in breast cancer (Chlebowski, 2012). Hyperinsulinemia and insulin resistance have been reported in healthy nonobese postmenopausal women who gained weight during the first 5 years of menopause (Lemay, Turcot, Dechene, Dodin, & Forest, 2010). This is of interest because many breast cancer patients who experience chemotherapy-induced menopause but were not overweight or obese at diagnosis, gain weight following therapy which may put them at risk for impaired glucose tolerance. Also, more research is needed to understand the biologic mechanisms and potential effect of weight loss with diet and exercise in cancer survivors.

Exercise alone in women without breast cancer fails to result in weight loss or any clinically significant loss, which is similar to the findings of this review. In BCS, a limited number of dietary studies (Pekmezi & Demark-Wahnefried, 2011) have reported weight loss compared to control groups. There have been a small number of trials combining dietary counseling and physical activity for BCS (Demark-Wahnefried et al., 2008; Goodwin et al., 1998; McTiernan et al., 1998; Morey et al., 2009; Stolley, Sharp, & Schiffer, 2009). Three studies, limited by the absence of control groups and small sample sizes revealed some degree of weight loss (Goodwin et al., 1998; McTiernan et al., 1998; Stolley et al., 2009). Of the remaining studies with random assignment, one reported no change in weight (Demark-Wahnefried et al., 2008), one had minimum weight loss at 12 months (Morey et al., 2009), and one reported a 6.8 kg weight loss in the intervention compared to control group (Mefford et al., 2007). The association of excess weight and survival outcomes strongly suggests that future trials need to address energy balance combining diet and exercise designed to produce weight loss.

For bone health, this review suggests that some interesting patterns should be explored in future trials. Although older women (>60 years of age) were included in trials as part of a broader age range of participants, only one trial evaluated whether age influenced the bone response to exercise. The analysis showed that the resistance plus impact training could increase BMD at the hip in women closer to 50 years of age, but that the effectiveness of training diminished with increasing age of participants (Winters-Stone et al., 2012). Because cancer treatment might lead to "accelerated aging," the interplay between exercise and age should be considered in future trials. In practice, older participants might need to exercise harder or longer in order to achieve the same skeletal benefits as young women—although the tradeoff between increased injury risk from more training and skeletal benefits should be weighed carefully. In addition to age, menopausal status and time since menopause onset can reflect the influence of estrogens and the withdrawal thereof on bone in tandem with mechanical loading from exercise. Aerobic plus impact training prevented hip but not spine bone loss in recently treated premenopausal BCS but was ineffective in postmenopausal women (Saarto et al., 2012). On the other hand, resistance plus impact training was only effective stopping spine bone loss or increasing hip BMD in women who were past the acute onset of chemotherapy-induced menopause (Winters-Stone, Dobek, et al., 2012). Results of a recently completed trial of a 12-month aerobic weight-loaded resistance exercise intervention in female cancer survivors who are perimenopausal or in early postmenopause (within first 5 years) may provide additional information on the effect on spine and hip bone mass (Knobf, NIH/NCI R01CA122658 2007-2013). Where menopause appeared to play a moderating role on the responsiveness of bone to exercise, trends remained evident in postmenopausal or acutely menopausal women, thus it is possible that skeletal benefits may require a longer period of training before they manifest.

The goal of exercise is to improve the quality and quantity of cancer survivors' lives. There are other major long-term cancer treatment effects, such as the development of cardiovascular disease associated with chemotherapy and newer molecular targeted agents, which can dramatically and negatively influence outcomes. Our approach to risk reduction with lifestyle behaviors should be broad. Although we await the outcomes of ongoing and future trials, all cancer patients should be encouraged to adopt healthy eating, maintain a healthy weight, and follow the recommended physical activity guidelines for adults of 30 min of moderate activity most days of the week.

ACKNOWLEDGMENTS

This work has been supported in part by Clinical and Translational Science Award (UL1 RR024139) from the National Center for Research Resources (NCRR) and the National Center for Advancing Translational Science (NIH) and NIH/NCI R01CA122658 (Knobf) NIH/NCI R01CA163474 and NIH/NCI R21CA164661 (Winters-Stone).

REFERENCES

Alfano, C. M., Ganz, P. A., Rowland, J. R., & Hahn, E. E. (2012). Cancer survivorship and cancer rehabilitation: Revitalizing the link. *Journal of Clinical Oncology, 30*(9), 904–906.

Ali, P. A., al-Ghorabie, F. H., Evans, C. J., el-Sharkawi, A. M., & Hancock, D. A. (1998). Body composition measurements using DXA and other techniques in tamoxifen-treated patients. *Applied Radiation and Isotopes, 49*(5–6), 643–645.

Alonso, C. G., Curiel, M. D., Carranza, F. H., Cano, R. P., & Perez, A. D. (2000). Femoral bone mineral density, neck-shaft angle and mean femoral neck width as predictors of hip fracture in men and women. Multicenter Project for Research in Osteoporosis. *Osteoporosis International 2000, 11*(8), 714–720.

Anonymous. (2001). Guideline for the prevention of falls in older persons. *Journal of the American Geriatrics Society, 49*(5), 664–672.

Baim, S., Binkley, N., Bilezikian, J. P., Kendler, D. L., Hans, D. B., Lewiecki, E. M., & Silverman, S. (2008). Official Positions of the International Society for Clinical Densitometry and executive summary of the 2007 ISCD Position Development Conference. *Journal of Clinical Densitometry, 11*(1), 75–91.

Basen-Engquist, K., Taylor, C. L, Rosneblum, C., Smith, M. A., Shinn, E. H., Greisinger, A., . . . Rivera, E. (2006). Randomized pilot test of a lifestyle physical activity intervention for breast cancer survivors. *Patient Education and Counseling, 64*(1–3), 225–234.

Bertram, L. A., Stefanik, M. L., Saquib, N., Natarajan, L., Patterson, R. E., Bardwell, W., . . . Pierce, J. P. (2011). Physical activity, additional breast cancer events, and mortality among early-stage breast cancer survivors: Findings from the WHEL study. *Cancer Causes Control, 22*(3), 427–435.

Beck, B. R., & Snow, C. M. (2003). Bone health across the lifespan—Exercising our options. *Exercise and Sport Sciences Reviews, 31*(3), 117–122.

Bicego, D., Brown, K., Ruddick, M., Storey, D., Wong, C., & Harris, S. R. (2008). Effects of exercise on quality of life in women living with breast cancer: A systematic review. *The Breast Journal, 15*(1), 45–51.

Bouxsein, M. L., Courtney, A. C., & Hayes, W. C. (1995). Ultrasound and densitometry of the calcaneus correlate with the failure loads of cadaveric femurs. *Calcified Tissue International, 56*(2), 99–103.

Brown, J. C., Huedo-Medina, T. B., Pescatello, L. S., Pescatello, S. M., Ferrer, R. A., & Johnson, B. T. (2011). Efficacy of exercise interventions in modulating cancer-related fatigue among adult cancer survivors: A meta–analysis. *Cancer Epidemiology, Biomarkers & Prevention, 20*(1), 123–133.

Bruning, P. F., Pit, M. J., de Jong-Bakker, M., van den Ende, A., Hart, A., & van Enk, A. (1990). Bone mineral density after adjuvant chemotherapy for premenopausal breast cancer. *British Journal of Cancer, 61*(2), 308–310.

Cameron, D. A., Douglas, S., Brown, J. E., & Anderson, R. A. (2010). Bone mineral density loss during adjuvant chemotherapy in pre-menopausal women with early breast cancer: Is it dependent on oestrogen deficiency? *Breast Cancer Research and Treatment, 23*(3), 805–814. http://dx.doi.org/10.1007/s10549-010-0899-7

Campbell, K. L., Lane, K., Martin, A. D., Gelman, K. A., & MacKenzie, D. C. (2007). Resting energy expenditure and body mass changes in women during adjuvant chemotherapy for breast cancer. *Cancer Nursing, 30*(2), 95–100.

Carlson, K., Simonsson, B., & Ljunghall, S. (1996). Acute effects of high-dose chemotherapy followed by bone marrow transplantation on serum markers of bone metabolism. *Calcified Tissue International, 55*(6), 408–411.

Carter, D. R. (1984). Mechanical loading histories and cortical bone remodeling. *Calcified Tissue International, 36*(1S), S19–S24.

Chapman, J. A., Meng, D., Shepherd, L., Parulekar, W., Ingle, J. N., Muss, H. B., . . . Goss, P. E. (2008). Competing causes of death from a randomized trial of extended adjuvant endocrine therapy for breast cancer. *Journal of the National Cancer Institute, 100*(4), 252–260.

Chen, Z., Maricic, M., Bassford, T. L., Pettinger, M., Ritenbaugh, C., Lopez, A. M., . . . Leboff, M. S. (2005). Fracture risk among breast cancer survivors: Results from the Women's Health Initiative Observational Study. *Archives of Internal Medicine, 165*(5), 552–558.

Chen, Z., Maricic, M., Pettinger, M., Ritenbaugh, C., Lopez, A., Barad, D., . . . Bassford, T. (2005). Osteoporosis and rate of bone loss among postmenopausal survivors of breast cancer. *Cancer, 104*(7), 1520–1530.

Cheney, C. L., Mahloch, J., & Freeny, P. (1997). Computerized tomography assessment of women with weight changes associated with adjuvant treatment for breast cancer. *American Journal of Clinical Nutrition, 66*(1), 141–146.

Chlebowski, R. T. (2012). Obesity and breast cancer outcome: Adding the evidence. *Journal of Clinical Oncology, 30*(2), 126–128.

Chlebowski, R. T., Aiello, E., & McTiernan, A. (2002). Weight loss in breast cancer patient management. *Journal of Clinical Oncology, 20*(4), 1128–1143.

Coates, A. S., Keshaviah, A., Thurlimann, B., Mouridsen, H., Mauriac, L., Forbes, J. F., . . . Goldhirsch, A. (2007). Five years of letrozole compared with tamoxifen as initial adjuvant therapy for postmenopausal women with endocrine-responsive early breast cancer: Update of study BIG 1-98. *Journal of Clinical Oncology: Official Journal of the American Society of Clinical Oncology, 25*(5), 486–492. http://dx.doi.org/10.1200/JCO.2006.08.8617

Coleman, R. E., Banks, L. M., Girgis, S. I., Kilburn, L. S., Vrdoljak, E., Fox, J., . . . Coombes, R. C. (2007). Skeletal effects of exemestane on bone-mineral density, bone biomarkers, and fracture incidence in postmenopausal women with early breast cancer participating in the Intergroup Exemestane Study (IES): A randomised controlled study. *The Lancet Oncology, 8*(2), 119–127.

Conn, V. S., Haldahl, A. R., Porock, D. C., McDaniel, R., & Nielsen, P. J. (2006). A meta-analysis of exercise interventions among people treated for cancer. *Support Care Cancer, 14*(7), 699–712.

Courneya, K. S., & Friedenreich, C. M. (2007). Physical activity and cancer control. *Seminars in Oncology Nursing, 23*(4), 242–252.

Courneya, K. S., Mackey, J. R., Bell, G. J., Jones, L. W., Field, C. J., Fairey, A. S. (2003). Randomized controlled trial of exercise training in postmenopausal breast cancer survivors: Cardiopulmonary and quality of life outcomes. *Journal of Clinical Oncology 21*(9), 1660–1668.)

Coviello, J. S., Knobf, M. T., & Laclergue, S. (2013). Assessing and managing metabolic syndrome and cardiovascular risk in midlife women. *Journal of Cardiovascular Nursing, 28*(2), 147–156.

Cramp, F., & Daniel, J. (2008). Exercise for management of cancer-related fatigue in adults. *Cochrane Database Systematic Reviews, 16*(2), CD006145.

Crandall, C., Petersen, L., Ganz, P. A., & Greendale, G. A. (2004). Bone mineral density and adjuvant therapy in breast cancer survivors. *Breast Cancer Research and Treatment, 88*(3), 257–261.

Crawford, S. L., Casey, V. A., Avis, N. E., & McKinlay, S. M. (2000). A longitudinal study of weight and menopause transition: Results from the Massachusetts Women's Health Study. *Menopause*, 7(2), 96–104.

Culos-Reed, S. N., Robinson, J. W., Lau, H., Stephenson, L., Keats, M., Norris, S., . . . Faris, P. (2010). Physical activity for men receiving androgen deprivation therapy for prostate cancer: Benefits form a 16-week intervention. *Support Care Cancer*, 18(5), 591–599.

Cummings, S. R., Black, D. M., Nevitt, M. C., Browner, W., Cauley, J., Ensrud, K., . . . Vogt T. M. (1993). Bone density at various sites for prediction of hip fractures. The Study of Osteoporotic Fractures Research Group. *Lancet*, 341(8837), 72–75.

Daley, A. J., Crank, H., Saxton, J. M., Mutrie, N., Colemna, R., & Roalfe, A. (2007). Randomized trial of exercise in women treated for breast cancer. *J Clin Oncol*, 25(13), 1713–1721.

Dargent-Molina, P., Favier, F., Grandjean, H., Baudoin, C., Schott, A., Hausherr, E., . . . Breart, G. (1996). Fall-related factors and risk of hip fracture: The EPIDOS prospective study. *Lancet*, 348(9021), 145–149.

De Backer, I. C., Schep, G., Backx, F. J., Vreugdenhil, G., & Kuipers, H. (2009). Resistance training in cancer survivors: A systematic review. *International Journal of Sports Medicine*, 30(10), 703–712.

Decensi, A. (2011). Insulin breast cancer connection: Confirmatory data set the stage for better care. *Journal of Clinical Oncology*, 29(1), 7–9.

Delmas, P. D., Balena, R., Confravreux, E., Hardouin, C., Hardy, P., & Bremond, A. (1997). Bisphosphonate risedronate prevents bone loss in women with artificial menopause due to chemotherapy of breast cancer: A double-blind, placebo-controlled study. *Journal of Clinical Oncology*, 15(3), 955–962.

Demark-Wahnefried, W., Case, L. D., Blackwell, K., Marcom, P. K., Krause, W., Azix, N., . . . Shaw, E. (2008). Results of a diet/exercise feasibility trial to prevent adverse body composition changes in breast cancer patients on adjuvant chemotherapy. *Clinical Breast Cancer*, 8(1), 70–79.

Demark-Wahnefried, W., Peterson, B. L., Winer, E. P., Marks, L., Aziz, N., Marcom, P. K., . . . Rimer, B. K. (2001). Changes in weight, body composition, and factors influencing energy balance among premenopausal breast cancer patients receiving adjuvant chemotherapy. *Journal of Clinical Oncology*, 19(9), 2381–2389.

deMoor, J. S., Mariotto, A. B., Parry, C., Alfano, C. M., Padgett, L., Kent, E. E., . . . Rowland, J. H. (2013). Cancer survivors in the United States: Prevalence across the survivorship trajectory and implications for care. *Cancer Epidemiology, Biomarkers & Prevention*, 22(4), 561–570.

DeNysschen, C. A., Brown, J. K., Cho, M. H., & Dodd, M. J. (2011). Nutritional symptom and body composition outcomes of aerobic exercise in women with breast cancer. *Clinical Nursing Research*, 20(1), 29–46.

Drinkwater, B. L., Grimston, S. K., Raab-Cullen, D. M., & Snow-Harter, C. M. (1995). American College of Sports Medicine position stand. Osteoporosis and exercise. *Medicine & Science in Sports & Exercise*, 27(4), i–vii.

Duggan, C., Irwin, M. L., Xiao, L., Henderson, K. D., Smith, A. W., Baumgartner, R. N., . . . McTiernan, A. (2010). Associations of insulin resistance and adiponectin with mortality in women with breast cancer. *Journal of Clinical Oncology*, 29(1), 32–39. http://dx.doi.org/10.1200/JCO.2010.32.3022

Eckstein, F., Lochmuller, E. M., Lill, C. A., Kuhn, V., Schneider, E., Delling, G., . . . Muller, R. (2002). Bone strength at clinically relevant sites displays substantial heterogeneity and is best predicted from site-specific bone densitometry. *Journal of Bone and Mineral Research*, 17(1), 162–171.

Eisner, A., & Incognito, L. J. (2006). The color appearance of stimuli detected via short-wavelength-sensitive cones for breast cancer survivors using tamoxifen. *Vision Research, 46*(11), 1816–1822. http://dx.doi.org/10.1016/j.visres.2005.11.003

Eisner, A., Toomey, M. D., Falardeau, J., Samples, J. R., & Vetto, J. T. (2007). Differential effects of tamoxifen and anastrozole on optic cup size in breast cancer survivors. *Breast Cancer Research and Treatment, 106*(2), 161–170. http://dx.doi.org/10.1007/s10549-006-9486-3

Fogelman, I., Blake, G. M., Blamey, R., Palmer, M., Sauerbrei, W., Schumacher, M., . . . Wilpshaar, W. (2003). Bone mineral density in premenopausal women treated for node-positive early breast cancer with 2 years of goserelin or 6 months of cyclophosphamide, methotrexate and 5-fluorouracil (CMF). *Osteoporosis International, 14*(12), 1001–1006. http://dx.doi.org/10.1007/s00198-003-1508-y

Fong, D. Y., Ho, J. W., Hui, B. P., Lee, A. M., MacFarlane, D. J., Leung, S. S., . . . Cheng, K. K. (2012). Physical activity for cancer survivors: Meta-analysis of randomized controlled trials. *British Medical Journal, 344*, e70. http://dx.doi.org/10.1136/bmj.e70

Freedman, R. J., Aziz, N., Albanes, D., Hartman, T., Danforth, D., Hill, S., . . . Yanovski, J. A. (2004). Weight and body composition changes during and after adjuvant chemotherapy in women with breast cancer. *The Journal of Clinical Endocrinology & Metabolism, 89*(5), 2248–2253.

Friedlaender, G. E., Tross, R. B., Doganis, A. C., Kirkwood, J. M., & Baron, R. (1984). Effects of chemotherapeutic agents on bone. I. Short-term methotrexate and doxorubicin (adriamycin) treatment in a rat model. *Journal of Bone and Joint Surgery, 66*(4), 602–607.

Frost, H. M. (1990a). Skeletal structural adaptations to mechanical usage (SATMU). 1. Redefining Wolffe's Law: The bone modeling problem. *Anatomical Record, 226*(4), 403–413.

Frost, H. M. (1990b). Skeletal structural adaptations to mechanical usage (SATMU): 2. Redefining Wolff's law: The remodeling problem. *Anatomical Record, 226*(4), 414–422. http://dx.doi.org/10.1002/ar.1092260403

Frost, H. M. (2001). Should fracture risk-of-fracture analyses include another major risk factor? The case for falls. *Journal of Clinical Densitometry, 4*(4), 381–383.

Gaillard, S., & Stearns, V. (2011). Aromatase inhibitor-associated bone and musculoskeletal effects: New evidence defining etiology and strategies for management. *Breast Cancer Research, 13*(2), 205.

Galvao, D. A., Taafe, D. R., Spry, N., Joseph, D., & Newton, R. U. (2010). Combined resistance and aerobic exercise program reverses muscle loss in men undergoing androgen suppression therapy for prostate cancer without bone metastases: A randomized controlled trial. *Journal of Clinical Oncology, 28*(2), 340–347.

Garnero, P. (2008). Biomarkers for osteoporosis management: Utility in diagnosis, fracture risk prediction and therapy monitoring. *Molecular Diagnosis & Therapy, 12*(3), 157–170.

Georgiou, K. R., Scherer, M. A., Fan, C.-M., Cool, J. C., King, T. J., Foster, B. K., . . . Xian, C. J. (2011). Methotrexate chemotherapy reduces osteogenesis but increases adipogenesis potential in the bone marrow. *Journal of Cellular Physiology, 227*(3), 909–918. http://dx.doi.org/10.1002/jcp.22807

Goodwin, P. J., Ennis, M., Pritchard, K. I., McCready, D., Koo, J., Sidlofsky, S., . . . Redwood, S. (1999). Adjuvant treatment and onset of menopause predict weight gain after breast cancer diagnosis. *Journal of Clinical Oncology, 17*(1), 120–129.

Goodwin, P. J., Esplen, M. J., Butler, K., Winocur, J., Pritchard, K., Brazel, S., & Miller, A. (1998). Multidisciplinary weight management in locoregional breast cancer: Results of a phase II study. *Breast Cancer Research and Treatment, 48*(1), 53–64.

Goss, P. E., Ingle, J. N., Alés-Martínez, J. E., Cheung, A. M., Chlebowski, R. T., Wactawski-Wende, J., . . . Richardson, H. (2011). Exemestane for Breast-Cancer Prevention in Postmenopausal Women. *New England Journal of Medicine, 364*(25), 2381–2391. http://dx.doi.org/10.1056/NEJMoa1103507

Gralow, J. R., Biermann, J. S., Farooki, A., Fornier, M. N., Gagel, R. F., Kumar, R. N., . . . Van Poznak, C. H. (2009). NCCN task force report: Bone health in cancer care. *Journal of the National Comprehensive Cancer Network, 7*(Suppl 3), S1–S32.

Greep, N. C., Giuliano, A. E., Hansen, N. M., Taketani, T., Wang, H.-J., & Singer, F. R. (2003). The effects of adjuvant chemotherapy on bone density in postmenopausal women with early breast cancer. *American Journal of Medicine, 114*(8), 653–659.

Griffith, J. F., & Genant, H. K. (2008). Bone mass and architecture determination: State of the art. *Best Practice & Research. Clinical Endocrinology and Metabolism, 22*(5), 737–764.

Hadji, P., Asmar, L., van Nes, J., Menschik, T., Hasenburg, A., Kuck, J., . . . Ziller, M. (2011). The effect of exemestane and tamoxifen on bone health within the Tamoxifen Exemestane Adjuvant Multinational (TEAM) trial: A meta-analysis of the US, German, Netherlands, and Belgium sub-studies. *Journal of Cancer Research and Clinical Oncology, 137*(6), 1015–1025. http://dx.doi.org/10.1007/s00432-010-0964-y

Hadji, P., Ziller, M., Albert, U. S., & Kalder, M. (2010). Assessment of fracture risk in women with breast cancer using current vs emerging guidelines. *British Journal of Cancer, 102*(4), 645–650.

Hamer, M., Stamatakis, E., & Saxton, J. M. (2009). The impact of physical activity on all-cause mortality in men and women after a cancer diagnosis. *Cancer Causes Control, 20*(2), 225–231.

Harvie, M. N., Campbell, I. T., Baildam, A., & Howell, A. (2004). Energy balance in early breast cancer patients receiving adjuvant chemotherapy. *Breast Cancer Research and Treatment, 83*(3), 201–210.

Herrero, F., San Juan, A. F., Fleck, S. J., Balmer, J., Perez, M., Canete, S., . . . Lucia, A. (2006). Combined aerobic and resistance training in breast cancer survivors: A randomized, controlled pilot trial. *International Journal of Sports Medicine, 27*(7), 573–580.

Holick, C. N., Newcomb, P. A., Trentham-Dietz, A., Titus-Ernstoff, L., Bersch, A. J., Stamfer, M. J., . . . Willett, W. C. (2008). Physical activity and survival after diagnosis of invasive breast cancer. *Cancer Epidemiology, Biomarkers & Prevention, 17*(2), 379–386.

Holmes, M. D., Chen, W. Y., Feskanich, D., Kroenke, C. H., & Coldtiz, G. A. (2005). Physical activity and survival after breast cancer diagnosis. *Journal of the American Medical Association, 293*(20), 2479–2486.

Howell, A., Cuzick, J., Baum, M., Buzdar, A., Dowsett, M., Forbes, J. F., . . . Tobias, J. S. (2005). Results of the ATAC (Arimidex, Tamoxifen, Alone or in Combination) trial after completion of 5 years' adjuvant treatment for breast cancer. *Lancet, 365*(9453), 60–62.

Ingram, C., & Brown, J. K. (2004). Patterns of weight and body composition change in premenopausal women with early stage breast cancer: Has weight gain been overestimated? *Cancer Nursing, 27*(1), 483–490.

Ingram, C. & Visovsky, C. (2007). Exercise intervention to modify physiologic risk factors in cancer survivors. *Seminars in Oncology Nursing 23*(4), 275–284.

Institute of Medicine. (2006). *From cancer patient to cancer survivor: Lost in transition.* Washington, DC: National Academies Press.

Irwin, M. L., Alvarez-Reeves, M., Cadmus, L., Mierzejewski, E., Mayne, S. T., Yu, H., . . . DiPietro, L. (2009). Exercise improves body fat, lean mass, and bone mass in breast cancer survivors. *Obesity (Silver Spring), 17*(8), 1534–1541.

Irwin, M. L., Crumley, D., McTiernan, A., Bernstein, L., Baumgartner, R., Gilliland, F. D., . . . Ballard-Barbash, R. (2003). Physical activity levels before and after a diagnosis of breast carcinoma: the Health, Eating, Activity, and Lifestyle (HEAL) study. *Cancer*, 97(7), 1746–1757.

Irwin, M. L., McTiernan, A., Baumgartner, R. N., Baumgartner, K. B., Bernstein, L., Gilliland, F. D., & Ballard-Barbash, R. (2005). Changes in body fat and weight after a breast cancer diagnosis: Influence of demographic, prognostic and lifestyle factors. *Journal of Clinical Oncology*, 23(4), 774–782.

Irwin, M. L., Smith, A. W., McTiernan, A., Ballard-Barbash, R., Cronin, K., Gilliland, F. D., . . . Bernstein, L. (2008). Influence of pre- and postdiagnosis physical activity mortality in breast cancer survivors: The health, eating, activity and lifestyle study. *Journal of Clinical Oncology*, 26(24), 3958–3964.

Kalder, M., Jäger, C., Seker-Pektas, B., Dinas, K., Kyvernitakis, I., & Hadji, P. (2011). Breast cancer and bone mineral density: The Marburg Breast Cancer and Osteoporosis Trial (MABOT II). *Climacteric*, 14(3), 352–361. http://dx.doi.org/10.3109/13697137.2011.557754

Kanis, J. A. (2002). Diagnosis of osteoporosis and assessment of fracture risk. *Lancet*, 359(9321), 1929–1936.

Kelley, G. A. (1998). Exercise and regional bone mineral density in postmenopausal women: A meta-analytic review of randomized trials. *American Journal of Physical Medicine & Rehabilitation*, 77(1), 76–87.

Kelley, G. A., Kelley, K. S., & Kohrt, W. M. (2012). Effects of ground and joint reaction force exercise on lumbar spine and femoral neck bone mineral density in postmenopausal women: A meta-analysis of randomized controlled trials. *BMC Musculoskeletal Disorders*, 13(1), 177.

Kim, C. J., Kang, D. H., & Park. J. W. (2009). A meta-analysis of aerobic exercise interventions for women with breast cancer. *Western Journal of Nursing Research*, 31(4), 437–461.

Knobf, M. T., Mullen, J., Xistris, D. & Moritz, D. (1983). Weight gain in woman with breast cancer on adjuvant chemotherapy. *Oncology Nursing Forum* 6, 17–20.

Knobf, M. T., & Coviello, J. (2011). Lifestyle interventions for cardiovascular risk reduction in women with breast cancer. *Current Cardiology Reviews*, 7(4), 250–257.

Knobf, M. T., Insogna, K., DiPietro, L., Fennie, C., & Thompson, A. S. (2008). An aerobic weight-loaded pilot exercise intervention for breast cancer survivors: Bone remodeling and body composition outcomes. *Biological Research for Nursing*, 10(1), 34–43.

Knobf, M. T., Mullen, J., Xistris, D., & Moritz, D. (1983). Weight gain in women with breast cancer on adjuvant chemotherapy. *Oncology Nursing Forum*, 10, 28–33.

Knobf, M. T., Musanti, R., & Dorward, J. (2007). Exercise and quality of life outcomes in patients with cancer. *Seminars in Oncology Nursing*, 23(4), 285–296.

Kohrt, W. M., Bloomfield, S. A., Little, K. D., Nelson, M. E., & Yingling, V. R. (2004). American College of Sports Medicine Position Stand: Physical activity and bone health. *Medicine & Science in Sports & Exercise*, 36(11), 1985–1996.

Kristensen, B., Ejlertsen, B., Dalgaard, P., Larsen, L., Holmegaard, S. N., Transbol, I., & Mouridsen, H. T. (1994). Tamoxifen and bone metabolism in postmenopausal low-risk breast cancer patients: A randomized study. *Journal of Clinical Oncology*, 12(5), 992–997.

Kroenke, C. H., Chen, W. Y., Rosner, B., & Holmes, M. D. (2005). Weight, weight gain and survival after breast cancer diagnosis. *Journal of Clinical Oncology*, 23(7), 1370–1378.

Kuroi, K., & Shimozuma, K. (2004). Neurotoxicity of taxanes: Symptoms and quality of life assessment. *Breast Cancer*, 11(1), 92–99.

Kutynec, C. L., McCargar, L., Barr, S. I., & Hislop, T. G. (1999). Energy balance in women with breast cancer during adjuvant treatment. *Journal of the American Dietetic Association*, 99(10), 1222–1227.

Lemay, A, Turcot, L, Dechene, F., Dodin, S., & Forest, J. C. (2010). Hyperinsulinemia in nonobese women reporting a moderate weight gain at the beginning of menopause: A useful early measure of susceptibility to insulin resistance. *Menopause*, 17(2), 321–325.

Ligibel, J. (2012). Lifestyle factors in survivorship. *Journal of Clinical Oncology*, *30*(30), 3697–3704.

Ligibel, J. A., Campbell, N., Partridge, A., Chen, W. Y., Salinardi, T., Chen, H., . . . Winer, E. P. (2008). Impact of a mixed strength and endurance exercise intervention on insulin levels in breast cancer survivors. *Journal of Clinical Oncology*, *26*(6), 907–912.

Ligibel, J. A., Meyerhardt, J., Pierce, J. P., Najita, J., Shockro, L., Campbell, N., . . . Shapiro, C. (2012). Impact of a telephone-based physical activity intervention upon exercise behaviors and fitness in cancer survivors enrolled in a cooperative group setting. *Breast Cancer Research and Treatment*, *132*(1), 205–213.

Link, T. M. (2012). Osteoporosis imaging: State of the art and advanced imaging. *Radiology*, *263*(1), 3–17.

Lord, S. R., Rogers, M. W., Howland, A., & Fitzpatrick, R. (1999). Lateral stability, sensorimotor function and falls in older people. *Journal of the American Geriatrics Society*, *47*(9), 1077–1081.

Love, R. R., Mazess, R. B., Barden, H. S., Epstein, S., Newcomb, P. A., Jordan, V. C., . . . DeMets, D. L. (1992). Effects of tamoxifen on bone mineral density in postmenopausal women with breast cancer. *The New England Journal of Medicine*, *326*(13), 852–856.

Makari-Judson, G., Judson, C. H., & Mertens, W. C. (2007). Longitudinal patterns of weight gain after breast cancer diagnosis: Observations beyond the first year. *The Breast Journal*, *13*(3), 258–265.

Mariotto, A. B., Yabroff, K. R., Shao, Y., Feuer, E. J., & Brown, M. L. (2011). Projections of the cost of cancer care in the United States: 2010–2020. *Journal of the National Cancer Institute*, *103*(2), 117–128.

Markes, M., Brockow, T., & Resch, K. L. (2009). Exercise for women receiving adjuvant therapy for breast cancer. *Cochrane Database of Systematic Reviews*, *18*(4), CD005001. http://dx.doi.org/10.1002/14651858.CD005001.pub2

Marshall, D., Johnell, O., & Wedel, H. (1996). Meta-analysis of how well measures of bone mineral density predict occurrence of osteoporotic fractures. *British Medical Journal*, *312*(7041), 1254–1259.

Marttunen, M. B., Hietanen, P., Titinen, A., Roth, H. J., Viinikka, L., & Ylikorkala, O. (1999). Effects of tamoxifen and toremifene on urinary excretion of pyridinoline and deoxypyridinoline and bone density in postmenopausal patients with breast cancer. *Calcified Tissue International*, *65*(5), 365–368.

Martyn-St James, M., & Carroll, S. (2008). Meta-analysis of walking for preservation of bone mineral density in postmenopausal women. *Bone*, *43*(3), 521–531.

Martyn-St James, M., & Carroll, S. (2009). A meta-analysis of impact exercise on postmenopausal bone loss: The case for mixed loading exercise programmes. *British Journal of Sports Medicine*, *43*(12), 898–908.

Matthews, C. E., Wilcox, S., Hanby, C. L., DerAnanian, C., Heiney, S. P., Gebretsadik, T., & Shintani, A. (2007). Evaluation of a 12-week home-based walking intervention for breast cancer survivors. *Support Care Cancer*, *15*(2), 203–211.

McInnes, J. A., & Knobf, M. T. (2001). Weight gain and quality of life in women treated with adjuvant therapy for breast cancer. *Oncology Nursing Forum*, *28*(4), 675–684.

McNeeley, M. L., Campbell, K. L., Rowe, B. H., Klassen, T. P., Mackey, J. R., & Courneya, K. S. (2006). Effects of exercise on breast cancer patients and survivors: A systematic review and meta-analysis. *Canadian Medical Association Journal*, *175*(1), 34–41.

McTiernan, A., Ulrich, C., Kumai, C., Bean, D., Schwartz, R., Mahloch, J., . . . Potter, J. D. (1998). Anthropometric and hormone effects of an eight-week exercise-diet intervention in breast cancer patients: Results of a pilot study. *Cancer Epidemiology, Biomarkers, & Prevention*, *7*(6), 477–481.

Mefford, K., Nichols, J. F., Pakiz, B., & Rock, C. L. (2007). A cognitive behavioral therapy intervention to promote weight loss improves body composition and blood lipid profiles among overweight breast cancer survivors. *Breast Cancer Research and Treatment*, *104*(2), 145–152.

Meyerhardt, J. A., Giovannucci, E. L., Holmes, M. D., Chan, A. T., Chan, J. A., Coldtiz, G. A., & Fuchs, C. S. (2006). Physical activity and survival after colorectal cancer diagnosis. *Journal of Clinical Oncology, 24*(22), 3527–3534.

Mold, J. W., Vesely, S. K., Keyl, B. A., Schenk, J. B., & Roberts, M. (2004). The prevalence, predictors, and consequences of peripheral sensory neuropathy in older patients. *The Journal of the American Board of Family Medicine, 17*(5), 309–318.

Morey, M. C., Snyder, D. C., Sloane, R., Cohen, H. J., Peterson, B., Hartman, T. J., . . . Demark-Wahnefried, W. (2009). Effects of home-based diet and exercise on functional outcomes among older, overweight long-term cancer survivors: RENEW: A randomized controlled trial. *Journal of the American Medical Association, 301*(18), 1883–1891.

Nikander, R., Sievänen, H., Ojala, K., Oivanen, T., Kellokumpu-Lehtinen, P. L., & Saarto, T. (2007). Effect of a vigorous aerobic regimen on physical performance in breast cancer patients: A randomized controlled pilot trial. *Acta Oncologica, 46,* 181–186.

Nikander, R., Sievanen, H., Ojala, K., Kellokumpu-Lehtinen, P. L., Palva, T., Blomqvist, C., . . . Saarto, T. (2012). Effect of exercise on bone structural traits, physical performance and body composition in breast cancer patients—A 12-month RCT. *Journal of Musculoskeletal and Neuronal Interactions, 12*(3), 127–135.

Parfitt, A. M., Mathews, C. H., Villanueva, A. R., Kleerekoper, M., Frame, B., & Rao, D. S. (1983). Relationships between surface, volume, and thickness of iliac trabecular bone in aging and in osteoporosis. Implications for the microanatomic and cellular mechanisms of bone loss. *Journal of Clinical Investigation, 72*(4), 1396–1409.

Patnaik, J. L., Byers, T., DiGuiseppi, C., Denberg, T. D., & Dabelea, D. (2011). The influence of comorbidities on overall survival among older women diagnosed with breast cancer. *Journal of the National Cancer Institute, 103*(14), 1101–1111.

Pekmezi, D. W., & Demark-Wahnefried, W. (2011). Updated evidence in support of diet and exercise interventions in cancer survivors. *Acta Oncologica, 50*(2), 167–178.

Peppone, L. J., Mustian, K. M., Janelsins, M. C., Palesh, O. G., Rosier, R. N., Piazza, K. M., . . . Morrow, G. R. (2010). Effects of a structured weight-bearing exercise program on bone metabolism among breast cancersurvivors: A feasibility trial. *Clinical Breast Cancer, 10*(3), 224–229.

Pinto, B. M., Frierson, G. M., Rabin, C., Trunzo, J. J., & Marcus, B. H. (2005). Home-based physical activity intervention for breast cancer patients. *Journal of Clinical Oncology, 23*(15), 3577–3587.

Pouilles, J. M., Tremollieres, F., & Ribot, C. (1995). Effect of menopause on femoral and vertebral bone loss. *Journal of Bone and Mineral Research, 10*(10), 1531–1536.

Protani, M., Coory, M., & Martin, J. H. (2010). Effect of obesity on survival of women with breast cancer: Systematic review and meta-analysis. *Breast Cancer Research and Treatment, 123,* 627–635.

Ratcliffe, M. A., Lanham, S. A., Reid, D. M., & Dawson, A. A. (1992). Bone mineral density (BMD) in patients with lymphoma: The effects of chemotherapy, intermittent corticosteroids and premature menopause. *Hematological Oncology, 10,* 181–187.

Ravn, P., Hosking, D., Thompson, D., Cizza, G., Wasnich, R., McClung, M., . . . Christiansen, C. (1999). Monitoring of alendronate treatment and prediction of effect on bone mass by biochemical markers in the early postmenopausal intervention cohort study. *Journal of Clinical Endocrinology & Metabolism, 84*(7), 2363–2368.

Riggs, B. L., & Melton, L. J., III. (2002). Bone turnover matters: The raloxifene treatment paradox of dramatic decreases in vertebral fractures without commensurate increases in bone density. *Journal of Bone and Mineral Research, 17*(1), 11–14.

Rock, C. L., Flatt, S. W., Newman, V., Caan, B. J., Haan, M. N., Stefanick, M. L., . . . Pierce, J. P. (1999). Factors associated with weight gain in women after diagnosis of breast cancer.

Women's Healthy Eating and Living Study Group. *Journal of the American Dietetic Association*, 99(10), 1212–1221.

Rodríguez-Rodríguez, L. M., Rodríguez-Rodríguez, E. M., Oramas-Rodríguez, J. M., Santolaria-Fernandez, F., Llanos, M., Cruz, J., . . . Batista, N. (2005). Changes on bone mineral density after adjuvant treatment in women with non-metastatic breast cancer. *Breast Cancer Research and Treatment*, 93(1), 75–83.

Rogers, L. Q., Hopkins-Price, P., Vicari, S., Markwell, S., Pamenter, R., Courneya, K. S., . . . Verhuist, S. (2009). Physical activity and health outcomes three months after completing a physical activity behavior change intervention: Persistent and delayed effects. *Cancer Epidemiology, Biomarkers & Prevention*, 18(5), 1410–1418.

Rogers, L. Q., Hopkins-Price, P., Vicari, S., Pamenter, R., Courneya, K. S., Markwell, S., . . . Lowy, M. (2009). A randomized trial to increase physical activity in breast cancer survivors. *Medicine & Science in Sports & Exercise*, 41(4), 935–946. http://dx.doi.org/10.1249/MSS.0b013e31818e0e1b

Saad, F., Adachi, J. D., Brown, J. P., Canning, L. A., Gelmon, K. A., Josse, R. G., & Pritchard, K. I. (2008). Cancer treatment-induced bone loss in breast and prostate cancer. *Journal of Clinical Oncology*, 26(33), 5465–5476. http://dx.doi.org/10.1200/jco.2008.18.4184

Saarto, T., Blomqvist, C., Valimaki, M., Makela, P., Sarna, S., & Elomaa, I. (1997). Clodronate improves bone mineral density in post-menopausal breast cancer patients treated with adjuvant antioestrogens. *British Journal of Cancer*, 75(4), 602–605.

Saarto, T., Sievanen, H., Kellokumpu-Lehtinen, P., Nikander, R., Vehmanen, L., Huovinen, R., . . . Blomqvist, C. (2012). Effect of supervised and home exercise training on bone mineral density among breast cancer patients. A 12-month randomised controlled trial. *Osteoporosis International*, 23(5), 1601–1612. http://dx.doi.org/10.1007/s00198-011-1761-4

Saarto, T., Vehmanen, L., Elomaa, I., Valimaki, M., Makela, P., & Blomqvist, C. (2001). The effect of clodronate and antioestrogens on bone loss associated with oestrogen withdrawal in postmenopausal women with breast cancer. *British Journal of Cancer*, 84(8), 1047–1051.

Santen, R. J. (2011). Clinical review: Effect of endocrine therapies on bone in breast cancer patients. *Journal of Clinical Endocrinology & Metabolism*, 96(2), 308–319. http://dx.doi.org/10.1210/jc.2010-1679

Saquib, N., Flatt, S. W., Natarajam, L., Thomson, C. A., Bardwell, W. A., Caan, B., . . . Pierce, J. P. (2006). Weight gain and recovery of pre-cancer weight after breast cancer treatments: Evidence from the women's healthy eating and living (WHEL) study. *Breast Cancer Research and Treatment*, 96(2), 308–319. http://dx.doi.org/10.1007/s10549-006-9442-2

Schmitz, K. H., Ahmed, R. L., Hannon, P. J., & Yee, D. (2005). Safety and efficacy of weight training in recent breast cancer survivors to alter body composition, insulin, and insulin-like growth factor axis proteins. *Cancer Epidemiology, Biomarkers & Prevention*, 14(7), 1672–1680.

Schmitz, K. H., Ahmed, R. L., Troxel, A. B., Cheville, A., Lewis-Grant, L., Smith, R., . . . Chittams, J. (2009). Weight lifting for women at risk for breast cancer-related lymphedema: A randomized trial. *New England Journal of Medicine*, 304(24), 664–673.

Schmitz, K. H., Courneya, K. S., Matthews, C., Demark-Wahnefried, W., Galvao, D. A., Pinto, B. M., . . . Schwartz, A. L. (2010). American College of Sports Medicine roundtable on exercise guidelines for cancer survivors. *Medicine & Science in Sports & Exercise*, 42(7), 1409–1426.

Schmitz, K. H., Holtzman, J., Courneya, K. S., Mâsse, L. C., Duval, S., & Kane, R. (2005). Controlled physical activity trials in cancer survivors: A systematic review and meta-analysis. *Cancer Epidemiology, Biomarkers & Prevention*, 14(7), 1588–1595.

Schwartz, A. L., Winters-Stone, K., & Gallucci, B. (2007). Exercise effects on bone mineral density in women with breast cancer receiving adjuvant chemotherapy. *Oncology Nursing Forum*, 34(3), 627–633. http://dx.doi.org/10.1188/07.ONF.627-633

Segal, R., Evans, W., Johnson, D., Smith, J., Gayton, J., Woodard, S., . . . Reid, R. (2001). Structured exercise improves physical functioning in women with stages I and II breast cancer: Results of a randomized controlled trial. *Journal of Clinical Oncology*, 19(3), 657–665.

Segal, R. J., Reid, R. D., Courneya, K. S., Malone, S. C., Parliament, M. B., Scott, C. G., . . . Wells, G. A. (2003). Resistance exercise in men receiving androgen deprivation therapy for prostate cancer. *Journal of Clinical Oncology*, 21(9), 1653–1659.

Shapiro, C. L., Manola, J., & Leboff, M. (2001). Ovarian failure after adjuvant chemotherapy is associated with rapid bone loss in women with early-stage breast cancer. *Journal of Clinical Oncology*, 19(14), 3306–3311.

Sheehan, P. M., Hoskins, K., & Stolley, M. (2012). Body composition changes in females treated for breast cancer: A review of the evidence. *Breast Cancer Research and Treatment*, 135(3), 663–680.

Sherrington, C., Whitney, J. C., Lord, S. R., Herbert, R. D., Cumming, R. G., & Close, J. C. (2008). Effective exercise for the prevention of falls: A systematic review and meta-analysis. *Journal of the American Geriatrics Society*, 56(12), 2234–2243.

Speck, R. M., Courneya, K. S., Mâsse, L. C., Duval, S., & Schmitz, K. H. (2010). An update of controlled physical activity trials in cancer survivors: A systematic review and meta-analysis. *Journal of Cancer Survivorship*, 4(2), 87–100.

Stevinson, C., Lawlor, D. A., & Fox, K. R. (2004). Exercise interventions for cancer patients: Systematic review of review controlled trials. *Cancer Causes Control*, 15(10), 1035–1056. http://dx.doi.org/10.1111/j.1532-5415.2008.02014.x

Stolley, M. R., Sharp, L. K., Oh, A., & Schiffer, L. (2009). A weight loss intervention for African American breast cancer survivors, 2006. *Preventing Chronic Disease*, 6(1), A22. Retrieved from http://www.cdc.gov/pcd/2009/jan/08_0026

Svendson, O. L., Hassager, C., & Christiansen, C. (1995). Age and menopause associated variations in body composition and fat distribution in healthy women as measured by dual energy X-ray absorptiometry. *Metabolism*, 44(3), 369–373.

Sverrisdottir, A., Fornander, T., Jacobsson, H., von Schoultz, E., & Rutqvist, L. E. (2004). Bone mineral density among premenopausal women with early breast cancer in a randomized trial ofadjuvant endocrine therapy. *Journal of Clinical Oncology*, 22(18), 3694–3699.

Swenson, K. K., Henly, S. J., Shapiro, A. C., & Schroeder, L. M. (2005). Interventions to prevent loss of bone mineral density in women receiving chemotherapy for breast cancer. *Clinical Journal of Oncology Nursing*, 9(2), 177–184.

Swenson, K. K., Nissen, M. J., Anderson, E., Shapiro, A., Schousboe, J., & Leach, J. (2009). Effects of exercise vs bisphosphonates on bone mineral density in breast cancer patients receiving chemotherapy. *Journal of Supportive Oncology*, 7(3), 101–107.

Taylor, C. L., Demoor, C., Smith, M. A., Dunn, A. L., Basen-Engquist, K., Nielsen, I., . . . Gritz, E. R. (2006). Active for Life After Cancer: A randomized trial examining a lifestyle physical activity program for prostate cancer patients. *Psycho-oncology*, 15(10), 847–862.

Thivat, E., Thérondel, S., Lapirot, O., Abrial, C., Gimbergues, P., Gadéa, E., . . . Durando, X. (2010). Weight change during chemotherapy changes the prognosis in non metastatic breast cancer for the worse. *British Medical Journal*, 10, 648–656.

Twiss, J. J., Gross, G. J., Waltman, N. L., Ott, C. D., & Lindsey, A. M. (2006). Health behaviors in breast cancer survivors experiencing bone loss. *Journal of the American Academy of Nurse Practitioners*, 18(10), 471–481.

Twiss, J. J., Williams, N., Ott, C. A., Gross, G. J., Lindsey, A. M. & Moor, T. E., (2001). Bone mineral density in postmenopausal breast cancer survivors, *Journal of the American Academy of Nurse Practitioners 13*(6), 276–284.

Valachis, A., Polyzos, N. P., Georgomicronulias, V., Mavroudis, D., & Mauri, D. (2010). Lack of evidence for fracture prevention in early breast cancer bisphosphonate trials: A meta-analysis. *Gynecologic Oncology. 117*(1), 139–145. http://dx.doi.org/10.1016/j.ygyno.2009.12.001

Vehmanen, L., Elomaa, I., Blomqvist, C., & Saarto, T. (2006). Tamoxifen treatment after adjuvant chemotherapy has opposite effects on bone mineral density in premenopausal patients depending on menstrual status. *Journal of Clinical Oncology, 24*(4), 675–680. http://dx.doi.org/10.1200/jco.2005.02.3515

Vehmanen, L., Saarto, T., Elomaa, I., Makela, P., Valimaki, M., & Blomqvist, C. (2001). Long-term impact of chemotherapy-induced ovarian failure on bone mineral density (BMD) in premenopausal breast cancer patients. The effect of adjuvant clodronate treatment. *European Journal of Cancer, 37*(18), 2373–2378.

Wallace, B. A., & Cumming, R. G. (2000). Systematic review of randomized trials of the effect of exercise on bone mass in pre- and postmenopausal women. *Calcified Tissue International, 67*(1), 10–18.

Waltman, N. L., Ott, C. D., Twiss, J. J., Gross, G. J., & Lindsey, A. M. (2009). Vitamin D insufficiency and musculoskeletal symptoms in breast cancer survivors on aromatase inhibitor therapy. *Cancer Nursing, 32*(2), 143–150. http://dx.doi.org/10.1097/01.NCC.0000339262.44560.92

Waltman, N. L., Twiss, J. J., Ott, C. D., Gross, G. J., Lindsey, A. M., Moore, T. E., & Berg, K. (2003). Testing an intervention for preventing osteoporosis in postmenopausal breast cancer survivors. *Journal of Nursing Scholarship, 35*(4), 333–338.

Waltman, N. L., Twiss, J. J., Ott, C. D., Gross, G. J., Lindsey, A. M., Moore, T. E., . . . Kupzyk, K. (2010). The effect of weight training on bone mineral density and bone turnover in postmenopausal breast cancer survivors with bone loss: A 24-month randomized controlled trial. *Osteoporosis International, 21*(8), 1361–1369. http://dx.doi.org/10.1007/s00198-009-1083-y

Wampler, M. A., Topp, K. S., Miaskowski, C., Byl, N. N., Rugo, H. S., & Hamel, K. (2007). Quantitative and clinical description of postural instability in women with breast cancer treated with taxane chemotherapy. *Archives of Physical Medicine and Rehabilitation, 88*(8), 1002–1008.

Wang, Q., Hassager, C., Ravn, P., Wang, S., & Christiansen, C. (1994). Total and regional body-composition changes in early postmenopausal women: Age related or menopause related? *American Journal of Clinical Nutrition, 60*(6), 843–848.

Winters-Stone, K. M., Dobek, J., Nail, L. M., Bennett, J. A., Leo, M. C., Torgrimson-Ojerio, B., . . . Schwartz, A. (2012). Impact + resistance training improves bone health and body composition in prematurely menopausal breast cancer survivors: A randomized controlled trial. *Osteoporosis International, 24*(5), 1637–1646. http://dx.doi.org/10.1007/s00198-012-2143-2

Winters-Stone, K., Leo, M., & Schwartz, A. (2012). Exercise effects on hip bone mineral density in older, post-menopausal breast cancer survivors are age dependent. *Archives of Osteoporosis, 7*(1–2), 301–306.

Winters-Stone, K. M., Dobek, J., Nail, L., Bennett, J. A., Leo, M. C., Naik, A, . . . Schwartz, A. (2011). Strength training stops bone loss and builds muscle in postmenopausal breast cancer survivors: A randomized, controlled trial. *Breast Cancer Research and Treatment, 127*(2), 447–456.

Winters-Stone, K. M., Nail, L., Bennett, J. A., & Schwartz, A. (2009). Bone health and falls: Fracture risk in breast cancer survivors with chemotherapy-induced amenorrhea. *Oncology Nursing Forum, 36*(3), 315–325. http://dx.doi.org/10.1188/09.ONF.315–325

Winters-Stone, K. M., Torgrimson, B., Horak, F., Eisner, A., Nail, L., Leo, M. C., . . . Luoh, S. W. (2011). Identifying factors associated with falls in postmenopausal breast cancer survivors: A multi-disciplinary approach. *Archives of Physical Medicine and Rehabilitation, 92*(4), 646–652.

CHAPTER 12

ROS and RNS Signaling in Skeletal Muscle

Critical Signals and Therapeutic Targets

Luke P. Michaelson, Colleen Iler, and Christopher W. Ward

ABSTRACT

The health of skeletal muscle is promoted by optimal nutrition and activity/exercise through the activation of molecular signaling pathways. Reactive oxygen species (ROS) or reactive nitrogen species (RNS) have been shown to modulate numerous biochemical processes including glucose uptake, gene expression, calcium signaling, and contractility. In pathological conditions, ROS/RNS signaling excess or dysfunction contributes to contractile dysfunction and myopathy in skeletal muscle. Here we provide a brief review of ROS/RNS chemistry and discuss concepts of ROS/RNS signaling and its role in physiological and pathophysiological processes within striated muscle.

INTRODUCTION

Skeletal muscle is a complex organ system within the body. Although we often consider skeletal muscle contraction in support of posture, locomotion, or respiration as its main function, skeletal muscle contraction is also important for

© 2013 Springer Publishing Company
http://dx.doi.org/10.1891/0739-6686.31.367

368 ANNUAL REVIEW OF NURSING RESEARCH

guarding body cavities (i.e., muscle sphincters), for maintaining body temperature (i.e., shivering thermogenesis), for maintaining glucose control, and as a protein reserve. The health of muscle is promoted by optimal nutrition and activity/exercise that activate molecular signaling pathways to promote an increase in the functional and metabolic capacity of the muscle. Conversely, muscle health is negatively impacted by inactivity as well as disease (i.e., diabetes, muscular dystrophies, amyotrophic lateral sclerosis, sarcopenia, critical illness myopathy) often through a dysregulation through similar molecular pathways.

Reactive oxygen species (ROS) or reactive nitrogen species (RNS) have been shown to modulate numerous biochemical processes through the targeted modification of specific protein residues. In striated muscle, contractile activity and/or stretch increases ROS/RNS signaling to modulate a host of biochemical processes including glucose uptake (Chambers, Moylan, Smith, Goodyear, & Reid, 2009), gene expression, calcium signaling, and contractility (Chambers, Moylan, & Reid, 2009). In pathological conditions, ROS/RNS signaling excess or dysfunction contributes to contractile dysfunction and myopathy in skeletal muscle.

It is clear that ROS and RNS generated from numerous tissues and paracrine signaling to skeletal muscle are important in health and disease. In fact, several excellent reviews have been published that consider these pathways (Donoso, Sanchez, Bull, & Hidalgo, 2011; Ferreira & Reid, 2008; Kuster, Hauselmann, Rosc-Schluter, Lorenz, & Pfister, 2010; Lamb & Westerblad, 2011; Powers, Talbert, & Adhihetty, 2011). Emerging research is now revealing pathways by which ROS/RNS are generated within the myocyte at rest and during contraction (i.e., exercise; Jackson & McArdle, 2011; Powers, Smuder, & Judge, 2012), and novel mechanistic insights into mechanoactivation of ROS signaling have recently been reported (Khairallah et al., 2012; Prosser, Khairallah, Ziman, Ward, & Lederer, 2012). These pathways are being revealed with both in vivo and single cell studies enabled by new methods and reagents. These findings are providing unique insights into both the positive adaptations seen with exercise and the dysfunction seen with inactivity and disease. Here we provide a brief review of ROS/RNS chemistry and discuss concepts of ROS/RNS signaling and its role in physiological and pathophysiological processes within striated muscle.

MOLECULAR SIGNALING IN THE CONTEXT OF CLASSICAL NURSING THEORY

The nurse theorist Myra Estrin Levine developed a Conservation Model emphasizing the practical understanding of physiological mechanisms identified in four key principles: conservation of energy, conservation of structural integrity, conservation of personal integrity, and conservation of social integrity (Meleis, 2012). In general, these concepts identify attributes that require the nurse to help the client return to a homeostatic balance with respect to each concept. The Conservation Model indicates the nurse acts as an intermediary, helping the client to "adapt" to the life experiences involved with pathophysiological events (Levine, 1996). One of Levine's assessments evaluating the biological and physical systems responsible for disease processes included the "body movement and positioning" of the client. Understanding the client's activity with respect to their operational environment (Meleis, 2012) allows nurses to integrate a treatment plan to therapeutically "adapt" an ill client to his/her current condition. Levine's model forms a guide for the nurse to help the "ill" client reacquire a new homeostatic balance within their social, personal, and biological milieu. Then as a corollary, one may suggest this model substantiates the need for the modern nurse to consider molecular pathways, such as ROS and RNS, and their homeostatic role in physiological signaling and their contribution to disease when the signaling is out of balance.

REACTIVE OXYGEN SIGNALING AND THE ROS PARADOX

ROS are reactive molecules that contain oxygen. ROS are formed as natural byproducts of oxygen metabolism and by enzymatic activity. In both cases, ROS production is highly localized and spatially restricted, which makes it an efficient system for cell signaling processes such as glucose transport (Chambers, Moylan, Smith, et al., 2009), eicosanoid (Spiteller, 2010) and cytokine production (Sigala et al., 2011), and mitochondrial biogenesis (Austin, Klimcakova, & St-Pierre, 2011; Kang & Li Ji, 2012). However, during times of environmental stress (e.g., UV radiation or hyperthermia), metabolic stress (e.g., hyperglycemia), or in disease states (e.g., muscular dystrophy, unloaded diaphragm during mechanical ventilation), ROS levels can increase dramatically resulting in aberrant signaling (D. G. Allen, Gervasio, Yeung, & Whitehead, 2010; Davidovich et al., 2013; Faist, Konig, Hoger, & Elmadfa, 2001; Kavazis et al., 2009).

In skeletal muscle, the functional consequences of this biphasic response are well described in experiments where small increases in ROS, as seen with mild exercise, increase muscle force generation. Yet, with excessive fatiguing exercise or with an experimental increase in exogenous ROS, muscle function decreases (Andrade, Reid, & Westerblad, 2001; Ferreira et al., 2012). This biphasic effect of ROS on cell function (Andrade et al., 2001; Reid, 2001) forms the basis for the ROS "paradox," which acknowledges ROS as necessary for proper signaling pathways yet detrimental to function when in excess (see Figure 12.1).

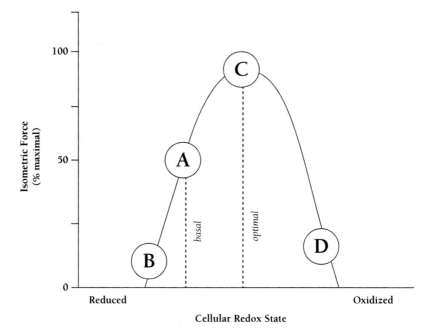

FIGURE 12.1 Model depicting the effects of the cellular oxidation state on muscle force production. A: basal state from unfatigued muscle. B: unfatigued muscle exposed to reducing agent or antioxidant. C: unfatigued muscle exposed to low level of ROS. D: muscle exposed to excess ROS as seen in fatiguing exercise or disease. The dashed vertical lines denote basal redox state (without an additional ROS stimulus) and the optimal redox state (i.e., maximal force). Used with permission from Reid, M. B. (2001). Invited Review: Redox modulation of skeletal muscle contraction: What we know and what we don't. *Journal of Applied Physiology*, *90*(2), 724–731.

Reactive Oxygen Species

ROS is a general term encompassing oxygen "free radicals"; oxygen containing molecules that contain one or more unpaired electrons (Halliwell & Gutteridge, 2007). It is important to note that not all ROS need to be a radical species. As indicated in Formulas 1 and 2 in the following text, hydrogen peroxide (H_2O_2) is a type of ROS but is not a free radical because it does not contain unpaired electrons.

Superoxide (O_2^-) is a common ROS molecule within skeletal muscle (Reid, 2001), has limited intrinsic reactivity, and its negative charge limits its membrane permeability. However, O_2^- has been shown to move through anion channels or aquaporin (Fisher, 2009; Ren, Raucci, Browe, & Baumgarten, 2008). O_2^-'s spontaneous dismutation or enzyme catalyzed dismutation (Formula 1) into the membrane permeable H_2O_2 (Cadenas & Packer, 2002) yields a potent and reactive signaling molecule.

Reactive Oxygen Species Reactions

Formula 1 $O_2^- + O_2^- + 2H^+ \rightarrow H_2O_2 + O_2$

Formula 2 $Fe^{2+} + H_2O_2 \rightarrow HO^- + OH\cdot + Fe^{3+}$

The formation of H_2O_2 can initiate key reduction/oxidation (redox) reactions. H_2O_2 forms the substrate for the production of the extremely reactive hydroxyl radical (OH·) via a Fenton Reaction with divalent metal cations, but mainly with ferrous iron (Fe^{2+}; Formula 2). The sulfhydryl group (-SH) associated with a protein may initially be oxidized to a sulfenic acid (protein-SOH). The OH· can then form irreversibly oxidized protein -SH, indicative of protein "damage" (Formulas 3 and 4; Cadenas & Packer, 2002; Thomas & Mallis, 2001).

Irreversible Protein Oxidation

Formula 3   protein-SOH + $(O_x) \rightarrow$ protein SO_2H sulfinic acid

Formula 4   protein-SO_2H + $(O_x) \rightarrow$ protein SO_3H sulfonic acid

Reactive Nitrogen Species

It is important to note other radical and nonradical species have been detected in skeletal muscle, which influences the overall redox homeostasis within the skeletal myocyte. The nitric oxide (NO·) molecule forms the parent molecule for reactive nitrogen species. In the presence of O_2^-, NO· forms the highly reactive nitrogen-intermediate peroxynitrite by the reaction in Formula 5.

Peroxynitrite Formation

Formula 5   NO·   + O_2^- $\rightarrow$ $ONOO^-$

          nitric oxide   superoxide   peroxynitrite

ROS and RNS can refer to multiple radical and nonradical types of each species. This review primarily focuses on those species indicated in Table 12.1.

ROS/RNS Formation

As outlined earlier, skeletal muscle generates O_2^- and NO· as the primary ROS/RNS species. Once generated, each lead to the formation of secondary ROS or RNS species with specific signaling roles (see Figure 12.2). They derive from several sources and the amount of each type is increased with contractile activity.

Nitric Oxide Synthase

In skeletal muscle cells, NO· is generated by neuronal nitric oxide synthase 1 (nNOS; Ferreira & Reid, 2008) from the precursor L-arginine. nNOS contains

TABLE 12.1

Reactive Oxygen Species/Reactive Nitrogen Species

ROS	
Species	Effector
O_2^-	JNK, base radical for H_2O_2, OH·, ONOO−
H_2O_2	NF-κβ, c-Src, Iκβ, TGf-β, RyR1, PKC-α
OH·	JNK

RNS	
NO·	RyR1, guanylate cyclase, albumin, hemoglobin
ONOO−	mitochondrial enzymes (aconitase), RyR1, COX

Note. COX = cyclooxygenase; JNK = c-Jun N-terminal kinase; H_2O_2 = hydrogen peroxide; NF-κβ = nuclear factor κβ; NO· = nitric oxide; OH· = hydroxyl radical; ONOO− = peroxynitrite; O_2^- = superoxide; PKC-α = protein kinase C α; RyR1 = ryanodine receptor 1; TGf-β = transforming growth factor beta.

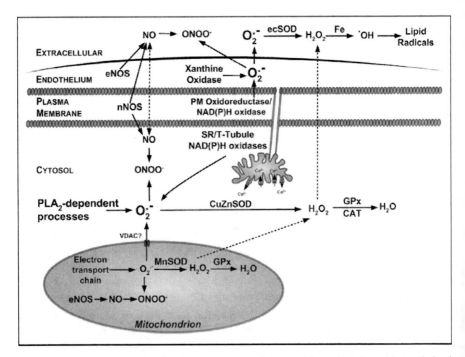

FIGURE 12.2 Potential sites for the production of superoxide and nitric oxide in skeletal muscle. Used with permission from Powers, S. K., & Jackson, M. J. (2008). Exercise-induced oxidative stress: Cellular mechanisms and impact on muscle force production. *Physiological Reviews, 88*(4), 1243–1276. http://dx.doi.org/10.1152/physrev.00031.2007

a calmodulin (CaM) binding domain making it Ca^{2+} sensitive and therefore responsive to contractile activity (Supinski & Callahan, 2007). Although NO· is a potent signaling molecule, it readily reacts with O_2^- to form peroxynitrite, which in turn reacts potently with thiol groups on protein targets. The formation of peroxynitrite also decreases the bioavailability of NO· and O_2^-, thus modifying the redox balance in the myocytes (Judge, Kass, Thompson, & Wagner, 2011; Kass, Takimoto, Nagayama, & Champion, 2007).

Xanthine Oxidase

In skeletal muscle, xanthine oxidase (XO) exists in two forms, whose primary purpose is to catabolize purines into uric acid (Corte & Stirpe, 1972; Harrison, 2002). Under basal activity conditions, XO primarily exists as the enzyme xanthine dehydrogenase (XDH). Increased oxidative stress can oxidize key cysteine amino acids, inducing reversible changes of the XDH to XO. Proteolytic enzymes may also cleave the XDH irreversibly to form XO (McNally, Saxena, Cai, Dikalov, & Harrison, 2005). Both enzymes catabolize hypoxanthine to xanthine, and then from xanthine to uric acid (Halliwell & Gutteridge, 2007; Harrison, 2002). The primary difference between the two enzymes is that the XDH uses aldehyde dehydrogenase (NAD+) as the electron acceptor as opposed to XO that uses O_2. Therefore, generally, XO forms the free radical O_2^- while XDH does not. XO primarily resides on the surface of the endothelial cells lining the skeletal muscle. However, intracellular expression of this enzyme has also been detected (Gomez-Cabrera, Domenech, & Viña, 2008; Gomez-Cabrera et al., 2005; Gómez-Cabrera, Pallardó, Sastre, Viña, & García-del-Moral, 2003; Harrison, 2002; Houston et al., 1999). It is important to note that XO can also form the free radical NO· under specific hypoxic conditions (Halliwell & Gutteridge, 2007; Harrison, 2002).

Phospholipase A2

Another source for ROS generation in skeletal muscle is from the phospholipase A_2 (PLA_2) enzyme family. These enzymes catalyze the hydrolysis reactions of membrane glycerophospholipids to form arachidonic acid (AA; Murakami & Kudo, 2002). The enzymatic pathways for cyclooxygenase (COX1, COX2) and the lipoxygenase family then catalyze AA to form eicosanoid inflammatory mediator products such as prostaglandins, leukotrienes, and thromboxanes (Harris, 2007). In skeletal muscle, the Ca^{2+} dependent $cPLA_2$ was detected along the sarcolemma and within the mitochondria, whereas the Ca^{2+}-independent $cPLA_2$ and constitutively active Ca^{2+}-independent phospholipase A2 ($iPLA_2$) isoform was detected within the cytosol.

Nethery, Stofan, Callahan, DiMarco, and Supinski (1999) used excised rat hemidiaphragm preparations to evaluate $cPLA_2$-dependent ROS generation in contracting and noncontracting muscle. The $cPLA_2$-specific inhibitor manoalide significantly decreased the ROS generation during contractile conditions when compared to the untreated control samples (Nethery et al., 1999). Furthermore, isolated mitochondrial preparations from the diaphragm muscle also suggested that AA interacted with the electron transport chain (ETC) most likely at Complex I to form ROS, as measured by a H_2O_2 assay (Nethery et al., 2000).

Mitochondria

The mitochondria are a source of free radical generation in muscle. In the process of oxidative phosphorylation, Complexes I–IV and the F_1F_0 adenosine triphosphate (ATP) synthase protein form the primary quaternary structures to oxidize reducing equivalents. The stepwise reduction transfers electrons to O_2 forming water (H_2O) while establishing hydrogen atom (H+) ion gradient between the inner and outer mitochondrial membranes. ROS are generated along the electron transport chain (ETC), particularly $O_2{}^-$, which spontaneously dismutes to H_2O_2 or the enzyme manganese $O_2{}^-$ dismutase ($Mn^{2+}SOD$) catalyzes the reduction of $O_2{}^-$ to H_2O_2 and O_2, Formula 6. The antioxidant $Mn^{2+}SOD$ is localized to the mitochondria, whereas CuZn-superoxide dismutase (CuZnSOD) is located within the cytosol.

$O_2{}^-$ Dismutation Reaction

Formula 6 $Mn(III) + O_2{}^- \leftrightarrow [Mn(III) - O_2{}^-] \rightarrow Mn^{2+} + O_2$

$Mn^{2+} + O_2{}^- \leftrightarrow [Mn^{2+} - O_2{}^-] + 2H^+ \rightarrow Mn(III) + H_2O_2$

Net reaction $O_2{}^- + O_2{}^- + 2H^+ \rightarrow O_2 + H_2O_2$

This reaction is important because the SOD enzymes remove the O_2- from the overall oxidant pool. Initial research estimated approximately 2% of the total oxygen within mitochondrial samples of rat liver, rat heart, and pigeon heart-generated H_2O_2 (Chance, Sies, & Boveris, 1979). Further insight into mitochondrial oxygen metabolism suggested less ROS are generated from the electron transport during oxidative phosphorylation. Using specific complex inhibitors, St-Pierre and colleagues (St-Pierre, Buckingham, Roebuck, & Brand, 2002) estimated that only 0.1%–0.2% of the oxygen is consumed for ROS formation. The amount and rate of ROS generation are important. The $O_2{}^-$ is membrane impermeable, but the dismutation product H_2O_2 can form OH·, which acts as a significant oxidant.

NADPH Oxidase

Nicotinamide adenine dinucleotide phosphate oxidase (NADPH oxidase or Nox) is a family of multiprotein enzymes first described in phagocytic cells (Hohn & Lehrer, 1975). In phagocytic cells, the Nox enzymes are responsible for generating a large amount of the free radical $O_2{}^-$ as a microbicidal mechanism. The active oxidase structure localized to the membrane includes the two membrane proteins gp91phox and p22phox forming the b_{558} reductase complex (Chowdhury et al., 2005). Three cytosolic proteins—p40phox, p47phox, p67phox—and the small, guanosine triphosphate (GTP)-binding protein Rac form the remaining structure of the Nox enzyme. Upon stimulation, the cytosolic proteins translocate to the membrane to form a complex with the two membrane proteins, which results in enzymatic activation and production of O_2^-. The variants of the catalytic subunit, gp91phox, form the different isoforms: Nox 1–5 and the dual oxidase (DUOX) Nox2 homologues DUOX 1 and 2 (Bedard & Krause, 2007; Brown & Griendling, 2009). Continued research of this enzyme family revealed these multiple isoforms are differentially expressed in tissues and do not only perform microbicidal functions. The ROS generated from Nox are key signaling intermediates within inflammatory, angiogenic (Vokurkova, Xu, & Touyz, 2007; Xu & Touyz, 2006), apoptotic, cell proliferation (Sauer, Klimm, Hescheler, & Wartenberg, 2001), and tumorigenic pathways (Arbiser et al., 2002).

The Nox2 and Nox4 isoforms are the predominant Nox enzymes expressed in skeletal muscle. Both have been detected within the transverse tubule system and at the plasma membrane (Hidalgo, Sanchez, Barrientos, & Aracena-Parks, 2006; Javesghani, Magder, Barreiro, Quinn, & Hussain, 2002). It is believed that Nox4 is active at rest whereas Nox2 may be activated through several mechanisms. For example, Nox2 enzymes have been implicated in ROS formation with depolarization (Espinosa et al., 2006), osmotic stress (Martins, Shkryl, Nowycky, & Shirokova, 2008), as well as the exercise pressor reflex (H. J. Wang, Pan, Wang, Zucker, & Wang, 2009). In addition, H_2O_2 has been shown to activate the tyrosine kinase Src, in mouse skeletal muscle (Gervasio, Whitehead, Yeung, Phillips, & Allen, 2008). Activation of Src is important because this kinase phosphorylates the cytosolic subunit p47phox. Phosphorylated p47phox translocates to the plasma membrane and complexes with the membrane bound b_{558} subunits. The subunit p67phox binds to the phosphorylated p47phox and is transported concurrently to the plasma membrane. The p40phox and Rac1 subunits then also bind to form a complete Nox2 enzyme. Osmotic stress has been shown to generate ROS, but the physiological importance of this type of mechanical stretch is debatable.

Recent work by our group and others has implicated the Nox pathway as the major source of O_2^- ROS in the skeletal muscle cell during repetitive contractions (Michaelson, Shi, Ward, & Rodney, 2010; Sakellariou et al., 2012). ROS production with contraction has been shown to arise from the sarcolemma and T-tubules by activation of transmembrane Nox2 (Espinosa et al., 2006; Khairallah et al., 2012; Prosser, Ward, & Lederer, 2011; Sakellariou et al., 2012). It was further suggested that Nox2 generated O_2^- then promoted Nox4 activation within the mitochondria to generate ROS that was released into the cytosol

(Whitehead, Streamer, Lusambili, Sachs, & Allen, 2006; Whitehead, Yeung, & Allen, 2006). However, experiments to directly address this hypothesis have not supported that idea (Sakellariou et al., 2012).

Mechanotransduction Activated NOX2-Dependent ROS Production

Recent investigation into the mechanisms by which exercise or activity regulates ROS/RNS production in the muscle has focused on how the mechanical stress of contraction is converted to a signal that activates ROS (i.e., the mechanotransduction-dependent activation of ROS). Experiments and methods used to mechanically manipulate single, enzymatically isolated muscle cells were pioneered by several groups (Calaghan, Belus, & White, 2003; Gannier, White, Lacampagne, Garnier, & Le Guennec, 1994; Le Guennec, White, Gannier, Argibay, & Garnier, 1991). These approaches have recently been coupled with high-speed fluorescence microscopy and have begun to reveal new mechanistic insight into the mechanoactivation of ROS signaling in skeletal muscle.

The concept of cellular "tensegrity" proposes that the microtubule (MT) filament network resists mechanical perturbations in cells and in doing so acts as a mechanotransducer (Ingber, 2008; Stamenovic, Mijailovich, Tolic-Norrelykke, Chen, & Wang, 2002; N. Wang, Butler, & Ingber, 1993; N. Wang et al., 2001). The initial hypothesis that the MT network was a mechanosignaling element in heart arose from elegant work in the literature (Calaghan et al., 2003; Calaghan, Le Guennec, & White, 2004; Iribe et al., 2009). Working with the knowledge that Nox2 is activated by either contraction (i.e., contraction/compression followed by relaxation/stretch), osmotic stress (stretch or compression; Isaeva, Shkryl, & Shirokova, 2005; Martins et al., 2008; Shkryl et al., 2009; Ullrich, Fanchaouy, Gusev, Shirokova, & Niggli, 2009), or stretch (Murdoch, Zhang, Cave, & Shah, 2006), our group focused attention on a hypothesis whereby an MT-dependent mechanotransduction pathway could translate a mechanical signal to Nox2 to activate ROS. To address this question, we developed new tools and methods (Khairallah et al., 2012; Prosser et al., 2011) enabling us to establish a model of stretch-activated mechanotransduction in striated muscle. This novel individual muscle fiber device removed the potential confounders of contraction, membrane-damaging force (eccentric injury), or nonphysiologic experimental stress such as osmotic shock.

Using these new methods coupled with high-speed confocal fluorescence imaging approaches, we revealed that in muscle cells loaded with the ROS indicator dichlorofluorescein (DCF), a brief, acute physiologic stretch elicits a burst of ROS production. Because DCF is a nonspecific ROS indicator, we used selective inhibitors and genetic approaches to reveal that the MT network acted as a mechanotransducer to activate NoX2-dependent *ROS* generation, a pathway termed *X-ROS* signaling (Khairallah et al., 2012; Prosser et al., 2011). In heart cells, others reported that X-ROS directly or indirectly lead to posttranslational modification of the ryanodine receptors (RyR2s), increasing the sensitivity of RyR2s to $[Ca^{2+}]i$ and thus promoting the fidelity of excitation-contraction (EC) coupling. We confirmed many of the features of X-ROS signaling in heart and also in skeletal muscle (Khairallah et al., 2012; Palomero, Pye, Kabayo, & Jackson, 2012); however, we demonstrated that the signaling involves a stretch-activated sarcolemmal channel whose opening is enhanced by Nox2-derived ROS. Our ongoing experiments are defining the role of X-ROS in modulating signaling during the contraction cycle. However, we have firmly established that X-ROS is an important pathological component in Duchenne muscular dystrophy, where an increase in MT network density and Nox2 expression leads to a detrimental enhancement of X-ROS signaling (Khairallah et al., 2012).

Targets of ROS/RNS in Skeletal Muscle

ROS/RNS have been shown to modulate multiple processes in skeletal muscle, such as transcription factor activity, ion transport, apoptosis, metabolism including numerous proteins critical for muscle cell function (R. G. Allen & Tresini, 2000; Barbieri & Sestili, 2012). Within proteins, -SH are susceptible to either oxidation or the formation of disulfide bonds. Physiological reduction and oxidation of sulfhydryl moieties take part in the modulation of protein function (Thomas & Mallis, 2001). For example, oxidation, S-nitrosylation (Foster, McMahon, & Stamler, 2003; Sun, Xin, Eu, Stamler, & Meissner, 2001), or S-glutathionylation of key cysteine in the ryanodine receptor 1 (RyR1) calcium release channel of skeletal muscle can significantly alter the mean open time and the permeability of the channel (Aracena-Parks et al., 2006; Hamilton & Reid, 2000; Hidalgo et al., 2006). In addition to the RyR1, the sarcoplastic/endoplasmic reticulum calcium ATPase pump (i.e., SERCA pump; Lehotsky, Kaplan, Murin, & Raeymaekers, 2002; Squier, 2001; Trebak, Ginnan, Singer, & Jourd'heuil, 2010), membrane lipids (Spiteller, 2010), or DNA (Ragu et al., 2007), CaM Kinase (Franklin, Rodriguez–Mora, LaHair, & McCubrey, 2006; Pinto, de Sousa, & Sorenson, 2011), and contractile proteins (Ferreira et al., 2012; Stasko, Hardin, Smith, Moylan, & Reid, 2013) have all been shown to be modified by ROS/RNS.

ROS has also been shown to act as a second messenger in the stretch-dependent activation of the nuclear factor $\kappa\beta$ (NF-$\kappa\beta$) pathway (Kumar & Boriek, 2003). This pathway, when in excess, promotes degeneration and atrophy of skeletal muscle (Reid & Li, 2001) across multiple disease states (Ferreira et al., 2012). In addition, several inflammatory disorders/conditions (i.e., rheumatoid arthritis, heart failure, systemic lupus erythematosus) affect skeletal muscle function, and new evidence supports cytokine receptor-dependent activation and subsequent intracellular second messenger ROS signaling as a contributor in the functional deficits (see Figure 12.3).

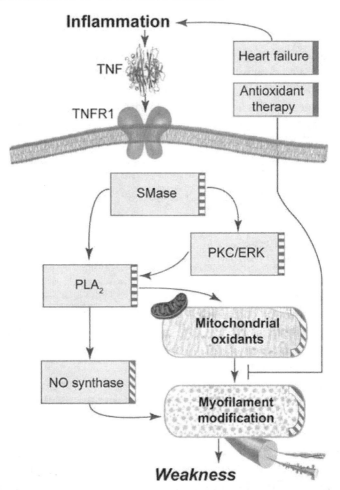

FIGURE 12.3 Model of signaling events that mediate inflammation-induced skeletal muscle weakness in heart failure. Model shows hypothetical mechanism by which chronic heart failure could depress specific force of skeletal muscle. Boxes below the sarcolemma (horizontal band) depict intracellular events that regulate TNFR1/oxidant signaling (right edge, red dashed bar) and oxidative inhibition of myofilament function (green hatched bar). Boxes above sarcolemma represent extracellular events that modulate the process (blue bar). TNF = tumor necrosis factor; TNFR1 = TNF receptor subtype 1; SMase = sphingomyelinase; PKC = phosphokinase C; ERK = extracellular regulatory kinase; PLA$_2$ = phospholipase A2; NO = nitric oxide. Reproduced with permission from Reid, M. B., & Moylan, J. S. (2011). Beyond atrophy: Redox mechanisms of muscle dysfunction in chronic inflammatory disease. *Journal of Physiology, 589*(Pt. 9), 2171–2179. http://dx.doi.org/10.1113/jphysiol.2010.203356

Finally, ROS has been shown to be a critical modulator in several transcriptional pathways that respond to activity/exercise in muscle. Peroxisome proliferator-activated receptor-γ coactivator-1α (PGC1-α) is a transcriptional coactivator shown to activate mitochondria biogenesis (Spiegelman, 2007). As mitochondrial deficits contribute to numerous skeletal muscle diseases (diabetes, amyotrophic lateral sclerosis, Duchene muscular dystrophy), this pathway is thought to represent a novel, therapeutic target (Guevel et al., 2011; Hsieh et al., 2011; Santos, Tewari, Goldberg, & Kowluru, 2011). The regulation of the PGC1-α pathway is in fact redox sensitive, which suggests that ROS plays a role in its regulation (Chen et al., 2011; Spiegelman, 2007).

The transcriptional regulators histone deacetylase 4 and 5 (HDAC4, HDAC5) are important in regulating muscle plasticity and metabolism with activity. Recently, Nox2-dependent ROS has been shown to regulate the nuclear effluxes of the HDAC4 and HDAC5 after intense muscle activity (Liu, Hernandez-Ochoa, Randall, & Schneider, 2012). Finally, nuclear factor (erythroid-derived 2)-like 2 (Nrf2) is a transcription factor that regulates the transcription of more than 200 genes responsible for antioxidant defenses in cell and antioxidant enzymes. Nrf2 is kept in the cytoplasm by a cluster of proteins that degrade it quickly. Under oxidative stress, Nrf2 is released from the protein cluster and travels to the nucleus where it initiates transcription of the antioxidative genes and their proteins (Guerrero-Beltran, Calderon-Oliver, Pedraza-Chaverri, & Chirino, 2012; Mann et al., 2007).

CONCLUSION

Until recently, ROS/RNS have been considered toxic species resulting in cellular oxidative stress and leading to pathogenesis and premature aging (Amicarelli et al., 1999; Bejma & Ji, 1999; Fielding & Meydani, 1997; Lawler, Cline, Hu, & Coast, 1997; Pansarasa, Bertorelli, Vecchiet, Felzani, & Marzatico, 1999; Reid & Durham, 2002; Vasilaki et al., 2006). We now, however, understand that ROS/RNS are also important signaling molecules that regulate physiological processes (Barbieri & Sestili, 2012). This apparent dichotomy in the role of ROS/RNS in skeletal muscle is a focus of much investigation.

It is reasonable to assume that the concentration of ROS/RNS distinguishes between physiological and pathological signaling (Barbieri & Sestili, 2012). In support, generalized ROS scavenging has been shown to be deleterious to acute exercise adaptation in healthy muscle (Petersen et al., 2012; Strobel et al., 2011) showing that a basal level of ROS signaling is important for positive adaptation. These global ROS reduction strategies have been overall therapeutically ineffective. Instead, evidence from prior and current research suggest the source and types of ROS are likely disease specific and will require targeted therapy (i.e., idebenone [Buyse et al., 2011], coenzyme Q 10 [Spurney et al., 2011], tocopherol [Arthur, Austin, & Roberts, 1988]).

Our understanding of ROS/RNS signaling is moving rapidly. This brief review of ROS/RNS chemistry and concepts of ROS/RNS signaling will hopefully spur the reader to explore this topic further in the reviews and primary literature cited here. We expect that this knowledge will rapidly make its way into clinical practice as novel treatments are developed to target diseases and disorders by ROS/RNS-dependent mechanisms.

REFERENCES

Allen, D. G., Gervasio, O. L., Yeung, E. W., & Whitehead, N. P. (2010). Calcium and the damage pathways in muscular dystrophy. *Canadian Journal of Physiology and Pharmacology, 88*(2), 83–91. http://dx.doi.org/10.1139/Y09-058

Allen, R. G., & Tresini, M. (2000). Oxidative stress and gene regulation. *Free Radical Biology & Medicine, 28*(3), 463–499. http://dx.doi.org/10.1016/S0891-5849(99)00242-7

Amicarelli, F., Ragnelli, A. M., Aimola, P., Bonfigli, A., Colafarina, S., Di Ilio, C., . . . Miranda, M. (1999). Age-dependent ultrastructural alterations and biochemical response of rat skeletal muscle after hypoxic or hyperoxic treatments. *Biochimica et Biophysica Acta, 1453*(1), 105–114.

Andrade, F. H., Reid, M. B., & Westerblad, H. (2001). Contractile response of skeletal muscle to low peroxide concentrations: myofibrillar calcium sensitivity as a likely target for redox-modulation. *FASEB Journal, 15*(2), 309–311. http://dx.doi.org/10.1096/fj.00-0507fje00-0507fje

Aracena-Parks, P., Goonasekera, S. A., Gilman, C. P., Dirksen, R. T., Hidalgo, C., & Hamilton, S. L. (2006). Identification of cysteines involved in S-nitrosylation, S-glutathionylation, and oxidation to disulfides in ryanodine receptor type 1. *The Journal of Biological Chemistry, 281*(52), 40354–40368. http://dx.doi.org/10.1074/jbc.M600876200

Arbiser, J. L., Petros, J., Klafter, R., Govindajaran, B., McLaughlin, E. R., Brown, L. F., . . . Lambeth, J. D. (2002). Reactive oxygen generated by Nox1 triggers the angiogenic switch. *Proceedings of the National Academy of Sciences, 99*(2),715–720.

Arthur, H., Austin, L., & Roberts, L. J. (1988). A pilot trial of plasma infusions in Duchenne muscular dystrophy. *Australian Paediatric Journal, 24*(Suppl. 1), 24–30.

Austin, S., Klimcakova, E., & St-Pierre, J. (2011). Impact of PGC-1α on the topology and rate of superoxide production by the mitochondrial electron transport chain. *Free Radical Biology and Medicine, 51*(12), 2243–2248. http://dx.doi.org/10.1016/j.freeradbiomed.2011.08.036

Barbieri, E., & Sestili, P. (2012). Reactive oxygen species in skeletal muscle signaling. *Journal of Signal Transduction, 2012,* 982794. http://dx.doi.org/10.1155/2012/982794

Bedard, K., & Krause, K. H. (2007). The NOX family of ROS-generating NADPH oxidases: Physiology and pathophysiology. *Physiological Reviews, 87*(1), 245–313. http://dx.doi.org/10.1152/physrev.00044.2005

Bejma, J., & Ji, L. L. (1999). Aging and acute exercise enhance free radical generation in rat skeletal muscle. *Journal of Applied Physiology, 87*(1), 465–470.

Brown, D. I., & Griendling, K. K. (2009). Nox proteins in signal transduction. *Free Radical Biology & Medicine, 47*(9), 1239–1253. http://dx.doi.org/10.1016/j.freeradbiomed.2009.07.023

Buyse, G. M., Goemans, N., van den Hauwe, M., Thijs, D., de Groot, I. J., Schara, U., . . . Mertens, L. (2011). Idebenone as a novel, therapeutic approach for Duchenne muscular dystrophy:

Results from a 12 month, double-blind, randomized placebo-controlled trial. *Neuromuscular Disorders*, 21(6), 396–405. http://dx.doi.org/10.1016/j.nmd.2011.02.016

Cadenas, E., & Packer, L. (2002). *Handbook of Antioxidants (Oxidative Stress and Disease)* (2nd ed.). New York, NY: Marcel Dekker, Inc.

Calaghan, S. C., Belus, A., & White, E. (2003). Do stretch-induced changes in intracellular calcium modify the electrical activity of cardiac muscle? *Progress in Biophysics and Molecular Biology*, 82(1–3), 81–95. http://dx.doi.org/10.1016/S0079-6107(03)00007-5

Calaghan, S. C., Le Guennec, J. Y., & White, E. (2004). Cytoskeletal modulation of electrical and mechanical activity in cardiac myocytes. *Progress in Biophysics and Molecular Biology*, 84(1), 29–59. http://dx.doi.org/S0079610703000579

Chambers, M. A., Moylan, J. S., & Reid, M. B. (2009). Physical inactivity and muscle weakness in the critically ill. *Critical Care Medicine*, 37(10 Suppl.), S337–S346. http://dx.doi.org/10.1097/CCM.0b013e3181b6e974

Chambers, M. A., Moylan, J. S., Smith, J. D., Goodyear, L. J., & Reid, M. B. (2009). Stretch-stimulated glucose uptake in skeletal muscle is mediated by reactive oxygen species and p38 MAP-kinase. *Journal of Physiology*, 587(Pt 13), 3363–3373. http://dx.doi.org/10.1113/jphysiol.2008.165639

Chance, B., Sies, H., & Boveris, A. (1979). Hydroperoxide metabolism in mammalian organs. *Physiological Reviews*, 59(3), 527–605.

Chen, S. D., Yang, D. I., Lin, T. K., Shaw, F. Z., Liou, C. W., & Chuang, Y. C. (2011). Roles of Oxidative Stress, Apoptosis, PGC-1alpha and Mitochondrial Biogenesis in Cerebral Ischemia. *International Journal of Molecular Sciences*, 12(10), 7199–7215. http://dx.doi.org10.3390/ijms12107199

Chowdhury, A. K., Watkins, T., Parinandi, N. L., Saatian, B., Kleinberg, M. E., Usatyuk, P. V., . . . Natarajan, V. (2005). Src-mediated tyrosine phosphorylation of p47phox in hyperoxia-induced activation of NADPH oxidase and generation of reactive oxygen species in lung endothelial cells. *The Journal of Biological Chemistry*, 280(21), 20700–20711. http://dx.doi.org/10.1074/jbc.M411722200

Corte, E. D., & Stirpe, F. (1972). The regulation of rat liver xanthine oxidase. Involvement of thiol groups in the conversion of the enzyme activity from dehydrogenase (type D) into oxidase (type O) and purification of the enzyme. *Biochemical Journal*, 126(3), 739–745.

Davidovich, N., Dipaolo, B. C., Lawrence, G. G., Chhour, P., Yehya, N., & Margulies, S. S. (2013). Cyclic stretch-induced oxidative stress increases pulmonary alveolar epithelial permeability. *American Journal of Respiratory Cell and Molecular Biology*. 49(1),156–164. http://dx.doi.org/10.1165/rcmb.2012-0252OC

Donoso, P., Sanchez, G., Bull, R., & Hidalgo, C. (2011). Modulation of cardiac ryanodine receptor activity by ROS and RNS. *Frontiers in Bioscience*, 16, 553–567.

Espinosa, A., Leiva, A., Pena, M., Muller, M., Debandi, A., Hidalgo, C., . . . Jaimovich, E. (2006). Myotube depolarization generates reactive oxygen species through NAD(P)H oxidase; ROS-elicited $Ca2+$ stimulates ERK, CREB, early genes. *Journal of Cellular Physiology*, 209(2), 379–388.

Faist, V., Konig, J., Hoger, H., & Elmadfa, I. (2001). Decreased mitochondrial oxygen consumption and antioxidant enzyme activities in skeletal muscle of dystrophic mice after low-intensity exercise. *Annals of Nutrition and Metabolism*, 45(2), 58–66.

Ferreira, L. F., Moylan, J. S., Stasko, S., Smith, J. D., Campbell, K. S., & Reid, M. B. (2012). Sphingomyelinase depresses force and calcium sensitivity of the contractile apparatus in mouse diaphragm muscle fibers. *Journal of Applied Physiology*, 112(9), 1538–1545. http://dx.doi.org/10.1152/japplphysiol.01269.2011

Ferreira, L. F., & Reid, M. B. (2008). Muscle-derived ROS and thiol regulation in muscle fatigue. *Journal of Applied Physiology*, 104(3), 853–860. http://dx.doi.org/10.1152/japplphysiol.00953.2007

Fielding, R. A., & Meydani, M. (1997). Exercise, free radical generation, and aging. *Aging (Milano)*, 9(1–2), 12–18.

Fisher, A. B. (2009). Redox signaling across cell membranes. *Antioxidants & Redox Signaling*, 11(6), 1349–1356. http://dx.doi.org/10.1089/ARS.2008.2378

Foster, M. W., McMahon, T. J., & Stamler, J. S. (2003). S-nitrosylation in health and disease. *Trends in Molecular Medicine*, 9(4), 160–168. http://dx.doi.org/10.1016/S1471-4914(03)00028-5

Franklin, R. A., Rodriguez–Mora, O. G., LaHair, M. M., & McCubrey, J. A. (2006). Activation of the calcium/calmodulin-dependent protein kinases as a consequence of oxidative stress. *Antioxidants & Redox Signaling*, 8(9–10), 1807–1817. http://dx.doi.org/10.1089/ars.2006.8.1807

Gannier, F., White, E., Lacampagne, A., Garnier, D., & Le Guennec, J. Y. (1994). Streptomycin reverses a large stretch induced increases in [Ca2+]i in isolated guinea pig ventricular myocytes. *Cardiovascular Research*, 28(8), 1193–1198.

Gervasio, O. L., Whitehead, N. P., Yeung, E. W., Phillips, W. D., & Allen, D. G. (2008). TRPC1 binds to caveolin-3 and is regulated by Src kinase—Role in Duchenne muscular dystrophy. *Journal of Cell Science*, 121(Pt 13), 2246–2255. http://dx.doi.org/10.1242/jcs.032003

Gomez-Cabrera, M. C., Borrás, C., Pallardo, F. V., Sastre, J., Ji, L. L., & Viña, J. (2005). Decreasing xanthine oxidase-mediated oxidative stress prevents useful cellular adaptations to exercise in rats. *Journal of Physiology*, 567(Pt. 1), 113–120. http://dx.doi.org/10.1113/jphysiol.2004.080564

Gomez-Cabrera, M. C., Domenech, E., & Viña, J. (2008). Moderate exercise is an antioxidant: Upregulation of antioxidant genes by training. *Free Radical Biology and Medicine*, 44(2), 126–131. http://dx.doi.org/10.1016/j.freeradbiomed.2007.02.001

Gómez-Cabrera, M. C., Pallardó, F. V., Sastre, J., Viña, J., & García-del-Moral, L. (2003). Allopurinol and markers of muscle damage among participants in the Tour de France. *Journal of the American Medical Association*, 289(19), 2503–2504. http://dx.doi.org/10.1001/jama.289.19.2503-b

Guerrero-Beltran, C. E., Calderon-Oliver, M., Pedraza-Chaverri, J., & Chirino, Y. I. (2012). Protective effect of sulforaphane against oxidative stress: Recent advances. *Experimental and Toxicologic Pathology*, 64(5), 503–508. http://dx.doi.org/10.1016/j.etp.2010.11.005

Guevel, L., Lavoie, J. R., Perez-Iratxeta, C., Rouger, K., Dubreil, L., Feron, M., . . . Megeney, L. A. (2011). Quantitative proteomic analysis of dystrophic dog muscle. *Journal of Proteome Research*, 10(5), 2465–2478. http://dx.doi.org/10.1021/pr2001385

Halliwell, B., & Gutteridge, J. M. C. (2007). *Free radicals in biology and medicine* (4th ed.). New York, NY: Oxford University Press.

Hamilton, S. L., & Reid, M. B. (2000). RyR1 modulation by oxidation and calmodulin. *Antioxidants & Redox Signaling*, 2(1), 41–45.

Harris, R. E. (Ed.). (2007). *Inflammation in the pathogenesis of chronic diseases* (Vol. 42). New York, NY: Springer.

Harrison, R. (2002). Structure and function of xanthine oxidoreductase: Where are we now? *Free Radical Biology and Medicine*, 33(6), 774–797. http://dx.doi.org/10.1016/S0891-5849(02)00956-5

Hidalgo, C., Sanchez, G., Barrientos, G., & Aracena-Parks, P. (2006). A transverse tubule NADPH oxidase activity stimulates calcium release from isolated triads via ryanodine receptor type 1 S-glutathionylation. *Journal of Biological Chemistry*, 281(36), 26473–26482.

Hohn, D. C., & Lehrer, R. I. (1975). NADPH oxidase deficiency in X-linked chronic granulomatous disease. *The Journal of Clinical Investigation*, 55(4), 707–713. http://dx.doi.org/10.1172/JCI107980

Houston, M., Estevez, A., Chumley, P., Aslan, M., Marklund, S., Parks, D. A., . . . Freeman, B. A. (1999). Binding of xanthine oxidase to vascular endothelium. Kinetic characterization and oxidative impairment of nitric oxide-dependent signaling. *Journal of Biological Chemistry*, 274(8), 4985–4994.

Hsieh, C. J., Weng, S. W., Liou, C. W., Lin, T. K., Chen, J. B., Tiao, M. M., . . . Wang, P. W. (2011). Tissue-specific differences in mitochondrial DNA content in type 2 diabetes. *Diabetes Research and Clinical Practice*, 92(1), 106–110. http://dx.doi.org/10.1016/j.diabres.2011.01.010

Ingber, D. E. (2008). Tensegrity and mechanotransduction. *Journal of Bodywork and Movement Therapies*, 12(3), 198–200. http://dx.doi.org/10.1016/j.jbmt.2008.04.038

Iribe, G., Ward, C. W., Camelliti, P., Bollensdorff, C., Mason, F., Burton, R. A., . . . Kohl, P. (2009). Axial stretch of rat single ventricular cardiomyocytes causes an acute and transient increase in Ca2+ spark rate. *Circulation Research*, 104(6), 787–795. http://dx.doi.org/10.1161/CIRCRESAHA.108.193334

Isaeva, E. V., Shkryl, V. M., & Shirokova, N. (2005). Mitochondrial redox state and Ca2+ sparks in permeabilized mammalian skeletal muscle. *Journal of Physiology*, 565(Pt. 3), 855–872.

Jackson, M. J., & McArdle, A. (2011). Age-related changes in skeletal muscle reactive oxygen species generation and adaptive responses to reactive oxygen species. *Journal of Physiology*, 589(Pt. 9), 2139–2145. http://dx.doi.org/10.1113/jphysiol.2011.206623

Javesghani, D., Magder, S. A., Barreiro, E., Quinn, M. T., & Hussain, S. N. (2002). Molecular characterization of a superoxide-generating NAD(P)H oxidase in the ventilatory muscles. *American Journal of Respiratory and Critical Care Medicine*, 165(3), 412–418.

Judge, D. P., Kass, D. A., Thompson, W. R., & Wagner, K. R. (2011). Pathophysiology and therapy of cardiac dysfunction in duchenne muscular dystrophy. *American Journal of Cardiovascular Drugs*, 11(5), 287–294. http://dx.doi.org/10.2165/11594070-000000000-00000

Kang, C., & Li Ji, L. (2012). Role of PGC-1α signaling in skeletal muscle health and disease. *Annals of the New York Academy of Sciences*, 1271(1), 110–117. http://dx.doi.org/10.1111/j.1749-6632.2012.06738.x

Kass, D. A., Takimoto, E., Nagayama, T., & Champion, H. C. (2007). Phosphodiesterase regulation of nitric oxide signaling. *Cardiovascular Research*, 75(2), 303–314. http://dx.doi.org/10.1016/j.cardiores.2007.02.031

Kavazis, A. N., Talbert, E. E., Smuder, A. J., Hudson, M. B., Nelson, W. B., & Powers, S. K. (2009). Mechanical ventilation induces diaphragmatic mitochondrial dysfunction and increased oxidant production. [Research Support, N.I.H., Extramural]. *Free Radical Biology & Medicine*, 46(6), 842–850. http://dx.doi.org/10.1016/j.freeradbiomed.2009.01.002

Khairallah, R. J., Shi, G., Sbrana, F., Prosser, B. L., Borroto, C., & Mazaitis, M. J. (2012). Microtubules underlie dysfunction in duchenne muscular dystrophy. *Science Signaling*, 5(236), ra56. http://dx.doi.org/10.1126/scisignal.2002829

Kumar, A., & Boriek, A. M. (2003). Mechanical stress activates the nuclear factor-kappaB pathway in skeletal muscle fibers: A possible role in Duchenne muscular dystrophy. *FASEB Journal*, 17(3), 386–396. http://dx.doi.org/10.1096/fj.02-0542com

Kuster, G. M., Hauselmann, S. P., Rosc-Schluter, B. I., Lorenz, V., & Pfister, O. (2010). Reactive oxygen/nitrogen species and the myocardial cell homeostasis: An ambiguous relationship. *Antioxidants & Redox Signaling*, 13(12), 1899–1910. http://dx.doi.org/10.1089/ars.2010.3464

Lamb, G. D., & Westerblad, H. (2011). Acute effects of reactive oxygen and nitrogen species on the contractile function of skeletal muscle. *Journal of Physiology*, 589(Pt. 9), 2119–2127. http://dx.doi.org/10.1113/jphysiol.2010.199059

Lawler, J. M., Cline, C. C., Hu, Z., & Coast, J. R. (1997). Effect of oxidant challenge on contractile function of the aging rat diaphragm. *American Journal of Physiology*, 272(2, Pt. 1), E201–E207.

Le Guennec, J. Y., White, E., Gannier, F., Argibay, J. A., & Garnier, D. (1991). Stretch-induced increase of resting intracellular calcium concentration in single guinea-pig ventricular myocytes. *Experimental Physiology, 76*(6), 975–978.

Lehotsky, J., Kaplan, P., Murin, R., & Raeymaekers, L. (2002). The role of plasma membrane Ca2+ pumps (PMCAs) in pathologies of mammalian cells. *Frontiers in Bioscience, 7,* d53–d84.

Levine, M. E. (1996). The conservation principles: A retrospective. *Nursing Science Quarterly, 9*(1), 38–41. http://dx.doi.org/10.1177/089431849600900110

Liu, Y., Hernandez-Ochoa, E. O., Randall, W. R., & Schneider, M. F. (2012). NOX2-dependent ROS is required for HDAC5 nuclear efflux and contributes to HDAC4 nuclear efflux during intense repetitive activity of fast skeletal muscle fibers. *American Journal of Physiology, 303*(3), C334–C347. http://dx.doi.org/10.1152/ajpcell.00152.2012

Mann, G. E., Niehueser-Saran, J., Watson, A., Gao, L., Ishii, T., de Winter, P., . . . Siow, R. C. (2007). Nrf2/ARE regulated antioxidant gene expression in endothelial and smooth muscle cells in oxidative stress: Implications for atherosclerosis and preeclampsia. *Sheng Li Xue Bao, 59*(2), 117–127.

Martins, A. S., Shkryl, V. M., Nowycky, M. C., & Shirokova, N. (2008). Reactive oxygen species contribute to Ca2+ signals produced by osmotic stress in mouse skeletal muscle fibres. *Journal of Physiology, 586*(1), 197–210.

McNally, J. S., Saxena, A., Cai, H., Dikalov, S., & Harrison, D. G. (2005). Regulation of xanthine oxidoreductase protein expression by hydrogen peroxide and calcium. *Arteriosclerosis, Thrombosis, and Vascular Biology, 25*(8), 1623–1628. http://dx.doi.org/10.1161/01.ATV.0000170827.16296.6e

Meleis, A. I. (2012). *Theoretical nursing: Development & progress* (5th ed.). Philadelphia, PA: Wolters Kluwer/Lippincott Williams & Wilkins.

Michaelson, L. P., Shi, G., Ward, C. W., & Rodney, G. G. (2010). Mitochondrial redox potential during contraction in single intact muscle fibers. *Muscle Nerve, 42*(4), 522–529. http://dx.doi.org/10.1002/mus.21724

Murakami, M., & Kudo, I. (2002). Phospholipase A2. *Journal of Biochemistry, 131*(3), 285–292.

Murdoch, C. E., Zhang, M., Cave, A. C., & Shah, A. M. (2006). NADPH oxidase-dependent redox signalling in cardiac hypertrophy, remodelling and failure. *Cardiovascular Research, 71*(2), 208–215. http://dx.doi.org/10.1016/j.cardiores.2006.03.016

Nethery, D., Callahan, L. A., Stofan, D., Mattera, R., DiMarco, A., & Supinski, G. (2000). PLA2 dependence of diaphragm mitochondrial formation of reactive oxygen species. *Journal of Applied Physiology, 89*(1), 72–80.

Nethery, D., Stofan, D., Callahan, L., DiMarco, A., & Supinski, G. (1999). Formation of reactive oxygen species by the contracting diaphragm is PLA(2) dependent. *Journal of Applied Physiology, 87*(2), 792–800.

Palomero, J., Pye, D., Kabayo, T., & Jackson, M. J. (2012). Effect of passive stretch on intracellular nitric oxide and superoxide activities in single skeletal muscle fibres: Influence of ageing. *Free Radical Research, 46*(1), 30–40. http://dx.doi.org/10.3109/10715762.2011.637203

Pansarasa, O., Bertorelli, L., Vecchiet, J., Felzani, G., & Marzatico, F. (1999). Age-dependent changes of antioxidant activities and markers of free radical damage in human skeletal muscle. *Free Radical Biology & Medicine, 27*(5–6), 617–622.

Petersen, A. C., McKenna, M. J., Medved, I., Murphy, K. T., Brown, M. J., Della Gatta, P., . . . Cameron-Smith, D. (2012). Infusion with the antioxidant N-acetylcysteine attenuates early adaptive responses to exercise in human skeletal muscle. *Acta Physiologica (Oxf), 204*(3), 382–392. http://dx.doi.org/10.1111/j.1748-1716.2011.02344.x

St-Pierre, J., Buckingham, J. A., Roebuck, S. J., & Brand, M. D. (2002). Topology of superoxide production from different sites in the mitochondrial electron transport chain. *Journal of Biological Chemistry, 277*(47), 44784-44790. http://dx.doi.org/10.1074/jbc.M207217200

Pinto, J. R., de Sousa, V. P., & Sorenson, M. M. (2011). Redox state of troponin C cysteine in the D/E helix alters the C-domain affinity for the thin filament of vertebrate striated muscle. *Biochimica et Biophysica Acta (BBA)/General Subjects, 1810*(4), 391–397. http://dx.doi.org/10.1016/j.bbagen.2010.11.008

Powers, S. K., & Jackson, M. J. (2008). Exercise-induced oxidative stress: Cellular mechanisms and impact on muscle force production. *Physiological Reviews, 88*(4), 1243–1276. http://dx.doi.org/10.1152/physrev.00031.2007

Powers, S. K., Smuder, A. J., & Judge, A. R. (2012). Oxidative stress and disuse muscle atrophy: Cause or consequence? *Current Opinion in Clinical Nutrition & Metabolic Care, 15*(3), 240–245. http://dx.doi.org/10.1097/MCO.0b013e328352b4c2

Powers, S. K., Talbert, E. E., & Adhihetty, P. J. (2011). Reactive oxygen and nitrogen species as intracellular signals in skeletal muscle. *Journal of Physiology, 589*(Pt. 9), 2129–2138. http://dx.doi.org/10.1113/jphysiol.2010.201327

Prosser, B. L., Khairallah, R. J., Ziman, A. P., Ward, C. W., & Lederer, W. J. (2012). X-ROS signaling in the heart and skeletal muscle: Stretch-dependent local ROS regulates [Ca$^2+$] i. *Journal of Molecular and Cellular Cardiology, 58,* 172–181. http://dx.doi.org/10.1016/j.yjmcc.2012.11.011

Prosser, B. L., Ward, C. W., & Lederer, W. J. (2011). X-ROS signaling: Rapid mechano-chemo transduction in heart. *Science, 333*(6048), 1440–1445. http://dx.doi.org/10.1126/science.1202768

Ragu, S., Faye, G., Iraqui, I., Masurel-Heneman, A., Kolodner, R. D., & Huang, M. E. (2007). Oxygen metabolism and reactive oxygen species cause chromosomal rearrangements and cell death. *Proceedings of the National Academy of Sciences of the United States of America, 104*(23), 9747–9752. http://dx.doi.org/10.1073/pnas.0703192104

Reid, M. B. (2001). Invited Review: Redox modulation of skeletal muscle contraction: What we know and what we don't. *Journal of Applied Physiology, 90*(2), 724–731.

Reid, M. B., & Durham, W. J. (2002). Generation of reactive oxygen and nitrogen species in contracting skeletal muscle: Potential impact on aging. *Annals of the New York Academy of Sciences, 959,* 108–116.

Reid, M. B., & Li, Y. P. (2001). Tumor necrosis factor-alpha and muscle wasting: A cellular perspective. *Respiratory Research, 2*(5), 269–272.

Reid, M. B., & Moylan, J. S. (2011). Beyond atrophy: Redox mechanisms of muscle dysfunction in chronic inflammatory disease. *Journal of Physiology, 589*(Pt. 9), 2171–2179. http://dx.doi.org/10.1113/jphysiol.2010.203356

Ren, Z., Raucci, F. J., Jr., Browe, D. M., & Baumgarten, C. M. (2008). Regulation of swelling-activated Cl(-) current by angiotensin II signalling and NADPH oxidase in rabbit ventricle. *Cardiovascular Research, 77*(1), 73–80. http://dx.doi.org/10.1093/cvr/cvm031

Sakellariou, G. A., Vasilaki, A., Palomero, J., Kayani, A., Zibrik, L., Jackson, M. J., . . . McArdle, A. (2012). Studies of mitochondrial and nonmitochondrial sources implicate nicotinamide adenine dinucleotide phosphate oxidase(s) in the increased skeletal muscle superoxide generation that occurs during contractile activity. *Antioxidants & Redox Signaling, 18*(6), 603–621. http://dx.doi.org/10.1089/ars.2012.4623

Santos, J. M., Tewari, S., Goldberg, A. F., & Kowluru, R. A. (2011). Mitochondrial biogenesis and the development of diabetic retinopathy. *Free Radical Biology & Medicine, 51*(10), 1849–1860. http://dx.doi.org/10.1016/j.freeradbiomed.2011.08.017

Sauer, H., Klimm, B., Hescheler, J., & Wartenberg, M. (2001). Activation of p90RSK and growth stimulation of multicellular tumor spheroids are dependent on reactive oxygen species generated after purinergic receptor stimulation by ATP. *FASEB Journal, 15*(13), 2539–2541. http://dx.doi.org/10.1096/fj.01-0360fje

Shkryl, V. M., Martins, A. S., Ullrich, N. D., Nowycky, M. C., Niggli, E., & Shirokova, N. (2009). Reciprocal amplification of ROS and Ca(2+) signals in stressed mdx dystrophic skeletal muscle fibers. *Pflügers Archiv: European Journal of Physiology, 458*(5), 915–928. http://dx.doi. org/10.1007/s00424-009-0670-2

Sigala, I., Zacharatos, P., Toumpanakis, D., Michailidou, T., Noussia, O., Theocharis, S., . . . Vassilakopoulos, T. (2011). MAPKs and NF-κB differentially regulate cytokine expression in the diaphragm in response to resistive breathing: The role of oxidative stress. *American Journal of Physiology. Regulatory, Integrative and Comparative Physiology, 300*(5), R1152–R1162. http://dx.doi.org/10.1152/ajpregu.00376.2010

Spiegelman, B. M. (2007). Transcriptional control of mitochondrial energy metabolism through the PGC1 coactivators. *Novartis Foundation Symposia, 287*, 60–63; discussion 63–69.

Spiteller, G. (2010). Is lipid peroxidation of polyunsaturated acids the only source of free radicals that induce aging and age-related diseases? *Rejuvenation Research, 13*(1), 91–103. http:// dx.doi.org/10.1089/rej.2009.0934

Spurney, C. F., Rocha, C. T., Henricson, E., Florence, J., Mayhew, J., Gorni, K., . . . Escolar, D. M. (2011). CINRG pilot trial of coenzyme Q10 in steroid-treated Duchenne muscular dystrophy. *Muscle Nerve, 44*(2), 174–178. http://dx.doi.org/10.1002/mus.22047

Squier, T. C. (2001). Oxidative stress and protein aggregation during biological aging. *Experimental Gerontology, 36*(9), 1539–1550. http://dx.doi.org/10.1016/S0531-5565(01)00139-5

Stamenovic, D., Mijailovich, S. M., Tolic-Norrelykke, I. M., Chen, J., & Wang, N. (2002). Cell prestress. II. Contribution of microtubules. *American Journal of Physiology, 282*(3), C617–C624. http://dx.doi.org/10.1152/ajpcell.00271.2001

Stasko, S. A., Hardin, B. J., Smith, J. D., Moylan, J. S., & Reid, M. B. (2013). TNF signals via neuronal-type nitric oxide synthase and reactive oxygen species to depress specific force of skeletal muscle. *Journal of Applied Physiology, 114*(11), 1629–1636. http://dx.doi.org/10.1152/japplphysiol.00871.2012

Strobel, N. A., Peake, J. M., Matsumoto, A., Marsh, S. A., Coombes, J. S., & Wadley, G. D. (2011). Antioxidant supplementation reduces skeletal muscle mitochondrial biogenesis. *Medicinen & Science in Sports & Exercise, 43*(6), 1017–1024. http://dx.doi.org/10.1249/MSS.0b013e318203afa3

Sun, J., Xin, C., Eu, J. P., Stamler, J. S., & Meissner, G. (2001). Cysteine-3635 is responsible for skeletal muscle ryanodine receptor modulation by NO. *Proceedings of the National Academy of Sciences, 98*(20), 11158–11162. http://dx.doi.org/10.1073/pnas.201289098201289098

Supinski, G. S., & Callahan, L. A. (2007). Free radical-mediated skeletal muscle dysfunction in inflammatory conditions. *Journal of Applied Physiology, 102*(5), 2056–2063. http://dx.doi. org/10.1152/japplphysiol.01138.2006

Thomas, J. A., & Mallis, R. J. (2001). Aging and oxidation of reactive protein sulfhydryls. *Experimental Gerontology, 36*(9), 1519–1526. http://dx.doi.org/10.1016/S0531-5565(01)00137-1

Trebak, M., Ginnan, R., Singer, H. A., & Jourd'heuil, D. (2010). Interplay between calcium and reactive oxygen/nitrogen species: An essential paradigm for vascular smooth muscle signaling. *Antioxidants & Redox Signaling, 12*(5), 657–674. http://dx.doi.org/10.1089/ars.2009.284

Ullrich, N. D., Fanchaouy, M., Gusev, K., Shirokova, N., & Niggli, E. (2009). Hypersensitivity of excitation-contraction coupling in dystrophic cardiomyocytes. *Heart and Circulatory Physiology: American Journal of Physiology, 297*(6), H1992–H2003. http://dx.doi.org/10.1152/ajpheart.00602.2009

Vasilaki, A., Mansouri, A., Remmen, H., van der Meulen, J. H., Larkin, L., Richardson, A. G., . . . Jackson, M. J. (2006). Free radical generation by skeletal muscle of adult and old mice: Effect of contractile activity. *Aging Cell, 5*(2), 109–117. http://dx.doi. org/10.1111/j.1474-9726.2006.00198.x

Vokurkova, M., Xu, S., & Touyz, R. M. (2007). Reactive oxygen species, cell growth, cell cycle progression and vascular remodeling in hypertension. *Future Cardiology*, 3(1), 53–63. http://dx.doi.org/10.2217/14796678.3.1.53

Wang, H. J., Pan, Y. X., Wang, W. Z., Zucker, I. H., & Wang, W. (2009). NADPH oxidase-derived reactive oxygen species in skeletal muscle modulates the exercise pressor reflex. *Journal of Applied Physiology*, 107(2), 450–459. http://dx.doi.org/10.1152/japplphysiol.00262.2009

Wang, N., Butler, J. P., & Ingber, D. E. (1993). Mechanotransduction across the cell surface and through the cytoskeleton. *Science*, 260(5111), 1124–1127.

Wang, N., Naruse, K., Stamenovic, D., Fredberg, J. J., Mijailovich, S. M., Tolic-Norrelykke, I. M., . . . Ingber, D. E. (2001). Mechanical behavior in living cells consistent with the tensegrity model. *Proceedings of the National Academy of Sciences*, 98(14), 7765–7770. http://dx.doi.org/10.1073/pnas.141199598

Whitehead, N. P., Streamer, M., Lusambili, L. I., Sachs, F., & Allen, D. G. (2006). Streptomycin reduces stretch-induced membrane permeability in muscles from mdx mice. *Neuromuscular Disorders*, 16(12), 845–854.

Whitehead, N. P., Yeung, E. W., & Allen, D. G. (2006). Muscle damage in mdx (dystrophic) mice: Role of calcium and reactive oxygen species. *Clinical and Experimental Pharmacology and Physiology*, 33(7), 657–662.

Xu, S., & Touyz, R. M. (2006). Reactive oxygen species and vascular remodelling in hypertension: Still alive. *Canadian Journal of Cardiology*, 22(11), 947–951.

Index

NOTE: Page references followed by *f* and *t* denoted figures and tables, respectively.

Acculturation, physical activity in Latinas and, 217
Acute phase changes, cytokine-induced, 28–31
Adjuvant endocrine therapy, bone health and, 345–346
Aerobic exercise
  Latinas, 222
  recommendations for HIV patients, 282
Animal models
  exercise and obesity, 1–17
  exercise in nursing research, 9
  human disease and, 11–12
Atrophy, study of, 6–7

Behavioral only interventions, PA for people with COPD, 300, 305–308t, 316–317t
Blood-brain barrier, cytokines and, 29–30
Body composition (BC), physical activity and, healthy women, 71–142
Bone health
  adjuvant endocrine therapy and, 345–346
  architecture, 346–347

in cancer survivors, 337–353
  chemotherapy effects, 338–339, 345
  exercise effects, 339–344t
  exercise for, 347–352
  measurement of, 346
  turnover, 347
Bone mineral density, 346
Breast cancer
  body composition and exercise in, 329–332
  body weight effects, 331
  lean mass and adipose tissue, 331–332
  posttreatment exercise interventions, 332–333, 333–336t

Cancer. *see also* specific type
  exercise and, 327–365
    future research directions, 353
Cancer survivors, bone health, fractures, and interventions, 337–353
Cardiac measure, HIV patients, 284
Cardiac outcomes, exercise in HIV patients, 286–287
Cardiorespiratory fitness
  exercise therapy after kidney transplant, 257–265
  exercise therapy in CKD, 250–252

Cardiovascular disease (CVD)
   after kidney transplant, residual kidney
      function effects, 266–268
   CKD and, 235–237
   impact of exercise conditioning,
      37–38
   people living with HIV, 279–285
   residual kidney function effects,
      253–255
Chemotherapy, effects on bone health,
   338–339, 345
Chronic kidney disease (CKD)
   CVD risk and, 236–237
   exercise as potential intervention,
      240
   exercise therapy, 235–275
      cardiorespiratory and muscular
         fitness, 250–252
      functional limitations and disability,
         252–253
      residual kidney function and CV risk,
         253–255
      stages 2-4, 243–244, 245–249t
      physical function and related outcomes,
         237–240
Chronic obstructive pulmonary disease
   (COPD), interventions for
      increased PA, 297–326, 300f
Committee on Rat Nomenclature, 1992, 3
Community-based interventions, Latinas,
   222–223
Conditioning
   impact on cardiovascular disease,
      37–38
   from long-term exercise, 34–37
Core temperature, fever effects, 33–39
Corticotropin-releasing factor (CRF)
   endogenous, fever and, 31–32
   IL-1 and, 25

Cryogens, 31–32
Cultural tradition, barrier to PA in Latinas,
   219–221
Cytokines, 19–46
   see also specific Cytokine
   acute phase changes induced by,
      28–31
   mediators of fever, 22–28, 23t

Diabetes. see also Gestational diabetes
      mellitus (GDM); Type 1 diabetes;
      Type 2 diabetes
   HIV-positive patients, 282–283
Diabetes Control and Complications Trial
   (DCCT), 48
Diet and nutrition, diabetes in youth and,
   53
Diet-induced obesity (DIO), 10
Disability
   exercise therapy after kidney transplant,
      265–266
   exercise therapy in CKD, 252–253

Education, physical activity in Latinas
   and, 215
Effector mechanisms, cytokines and,
   31
Endogenous antipyretics, 31–32
Environmental factors
   physical activity in Latinas and,
      217
   physical activity interventions for
      Latinas, 223
Exercise. see also Aerobic exercise;
      Resistance exercise
   acute, core temperature set-point and,
      33–39

animal models, 1–17
cancer and, 327–365
  future research directions, 353
cancer survivors, bone health and
  fractures, 337–353
controlling weight gain in pregnancy,
  158–166, 163t, 165t
guidelines for pregnancy, 146–147
PA for people with COPD, 300,
  301–304t, 311–315t
people living with HIV, 277–296
  cardiac outcomes, 286–287
  heart rate, 287
  metabolic outcomes, 287–288
  risks, 285
  strength outcomes, 288
posttreatment for breast cancer,
  332–333, 333–336t
during pregnancy, 143–173
  future research, 166
prevention of pregnancy-specific
  diseases, 147–158
prostate cancer survivors, 329
protocols using rats and mice, 5–6
Exercise performance, origins of research
  in, 5
Exercise recovery
  nursing research in, 9t
  study of, 6–7
Exercise therapy
  after kidney transplantation, 256–269,
    258–262t
  chronic kidney disease, 235–275
  patients in renal replacement therapy,
    240–243

Faith-based interventions, PA for Latinas,
  223

Family-focused interventions, PA for
  Latinas, 224
Fatigue, barrier to PA in Latinas,
  218–219
Fever, 19–46
  adaptive value of, 33
  cytokines and, 29
  cytokines as endogenous mediators,
    22–28
  endogenous CRF and, 31–32
  historical perspective, 20–21
  induction and downregulation,
    22f
Fractures
  in cancer survivors, 337–353
  nonskeletal approaches to prevention,
    352–353
  risk, measuring bone health, 346
Function-focused care
  definition, 177
  dissemination and implementation of,
    193–195, 196–199t
  20-site study, 202–204
  environment and policies/procedures,
    181–184, 182–183t
  evidence of effectiveness,
    190–191
  examples of activities, 178t
  family help, 185t
  implementation of, 181–190
  moderate to severe cognitive
    impairment and, 192–193
  physical activity among older adults,
    175–208
  physical capability scale,
    186–189f
  social-ecological model, 179f
  theoretical model to guide integration,
    179–181

Gestational diabetes mellitus (GDM),
    exercise and, 150–151,
    155–157t
Granulocytic pyrogen (GP), 20

Harlan Laboratory, 3
Heart rate, exercise in HIV patients,
    287
Highly active anti-retroviral therapy
    (HAART)
    CVD prior to introduction of,
        280–281
    HIV and metabolic function with,
        281–282
Hispanic women. see also Latinas
    inclusion criteria, 211
    physical activity, 209–234
        limitations, 225–226
        older women, 224
    physical activity interventions,
        221–225
    search heuristics, 211–212
HIV
    cardiac measure, 284
    cardiovascular disease and,
        279–285
    diabetes effects, 282–283
    exercise effects, 277–296
    metabolic function, use of HAART and,
        281–282
    metabolic measures, 284
    obesity effects, 282
    recommendations for aerobic exercise,
        283
    recommendations for resistance
        exercise, 283–284
    resistance measure, 284
    risk of exercise, 285

Home-based interventions, PA for Latinas,
    223–224
Hypothalamus, cytokines and, 31

Immobilization models, 7–8
Inactivity models, 7–8
Inflammation, 377, 378f
Interferon, 27
Interleukin-1 (IL-1), 23–24
    CRF and, 25
    PGE$_2$ and, 24–25
Interleukin-1β (IL-1β), psychological
    stress and, 24
Interleukin-6 (IL-6), 27–28
Irreversible protein oxidation, 371

Jackson Labs, 3

Kidney transplantation
    exercise therapy, residual kidney
        function and CV risk, 266–268
    exercise therapy after, 256–269,
        258–262t
    cardiorespiratory and muscular
        fitness, 257–265
    functional limitations and disability,
        265–266

Laboratory rat, origins, 2–3
Latinas. see also Hispanic women
    physical activity
        acculturation and, 217
        barriers to, 218–221
        education, 215
        environmental factors, 217
        facilitators and barriers to, 214

limitations, 225–226
self-efficacy, 214–215
social support, 216
in the U. S., 212–213
Lifestyle factors
diabetes in youth and, 51–53
pregnancy and weight gain,
159–160
Link Animal Models to Human Disease
(LAMHDI), 4

Mechanotransduction, NOX2-dependent
ROS production, 376
Metabolic function, HIV, use of HAART
and, 281–282
Metabolic measures, HIV patients,
284–284
Metabolic outcomes, exercise in HIV
patients, 287–288
Mitochondria, 374
Molecular signaling, 368–369
Mouse Genome Informatics (MGI), 4
Muscular fitness
exercise therapy after kidney transplant,
257–265
exercise therapy in CKD, 250–252

NADPH oxidase, 374–376
National Bio Resource Project (NBRP), 4
Negative health behavior, 280
Nitric oxide synthase (NOS), 371–372,
372f

O$_2$– dismutation reaction, 374
Obesity
animal models, 1–17
human disease and, 11–12

HIV-positive patients, 282
physical activity intervention studies,
72–73
prevention strategies, 133
youth with type 1 diabetes, 47–69,
56–59t
Older adults, physical activity,
175–208
Overweight, youth with type 1 diabetes,
47–69, 56–59t

Peroxynitrite formation, 371
Phospholipase A2, 373–374
Physical activity (PA)
body composition in healthy women,
71–142
diabetes in youth and, 51–53
with diet, 124, 126, 128t, 129
as a health behavior, 73–74
Hispanic women, 209–234
definitions, 213
statistics, 213–214
interventions, 130–132
for Hispanic women, 221–225
for people with COPD, 297–326,
300f
measurement, 132
older adults, 175–208
during pregnancy, 145146
public health implications,
132–133
recommendations, 74
self-report and objective measures of,
74–82
systematic review of interventions, 75,
76–80t, 83f, 84–88t, 90–123t
theoretical approaches, 132
without diet, 123, 125, 127, 128t

Physical capability scale, for function-focused care, 186–189*f*
Preeclampsia, exercise and, 147–149, 149*f*, 152–153*t*
Pregnancy, 143–173
    behavioral interventions for physical activity, 160–162
    future research on physical activity, 146–147, 166
    guidelines for exercise, 146–147
    lifestyle and weight gain, 159–160
    social meaning of, 143–145
Pregnancy-specific diseases, exercise in prevention of, 147–158
Prostaglandin E$_2$ (PGE$_2$), 24
    IL-1 and, 24–25
    pathway, cytokines and, 30
Prostate cancer, body composition and exercise in, 329, 330*t*
Protocols, exercise, using rats and mice, 5–6
Pulmonary rehabilitation, PA for people with COPD, 300, 301–304*t*, 311–315*t*
Pyrexin, 20

Rat Genome Database, 3–4
Reactive nitrogen species (RNS)
    definition, 371
    formation, 371–372, 372*t*
    signaling in skeletal muscle, 367–387
    targets in skeletal muscle, 377, 378*f*
Reactive oxygen species (ROS)
    definition, 370
    formation, 371–372, 372*t*
    mechanotransduction activated NOX2-dependent production, 376

reactions, 370–371
    =signaling in skeletal muscle, 367–387
    ROS paradox, 369–379, 370*f*
    targets in skeletal muscle, 377, 378*f*
Renal replacement therapy, exercise therapy in, 240–243
Research, exercise performance, 5
Research Book for the Design of Animal Exercise Protocols (APS), 4
Resistance exercise, recommendations for HIV patients, 282–283
Resistance measure, HIV patients, 284
Restorative care. *see* Function-focused care
Rodent models
    comprehensive databases, 3–4
    exercise and obesity, 4–5
    obesity, 11*t*
    thermoregulation, 10
ROS paradox, ROS signaling and, 369–379, 370*f*

SEARCH for Diabetes in Youth Study Group, 49
Sedentary behaviors, diabetes in youth and, 52
Self-efficacy, predictor for PA, 214–215
Skeletal muscle, ROS and RNS signaling, 367–387
Sleep, diabetes in youth and, 52
Social support, physical activity in Latinas and, 216
Sprague-Dawley rat, 5
Strength outcomes, exercise in HIV patients, 288
Superoxide, 370, 372*f*

Thermoregulation, 19–46
    exercise-induced rodent model, 10
Tumor necrosis factor (TNF), 25–27
Type 1 diabetes (T1D)
    future research and practice,
        62–63
    overweight and obese youth, 47–69,
        56–59t
        epidemiology, 49–51

Type 2 diabetes (T2D)
    overweight and obese youth, 48–69
        epidemiology, 49–51

Wistar rat, 4–5

Xanthine oxidase (XO), 373